Lyman Abbott

An illustrated commentary on the Gospels according to Mark and Luke For family use and reference

Lyman Abbott

An illustrated commentary on the Gospels according to Mark and Luke For family use and reference

ISBN/EAN: 9783337283438

Printed in Europe, USA, Canada, Australia, Japan

Cover: Foto ©Thomas Meinert / pixelio.de

More available books at **www.hansebooks.com**

AN

ILLUSTRATED COMMENTARY

ON

THE GOSPELS ACCORDING TO

MARK AND LUKE.

FOR FAMILY USE AND REFERENCE, AND FOR THE GREAT BODY
OF CHRISTIAN WORKERS OF ALL DENOMINATIONS.

By REV. LYMAN ABBOTT,
AUTHOR OF "LIFE OF CHRIST," "DICTIONARY OF RELIGIOUS KNOWLEDGE," ETC.

VOLUME II.

A. S. BARNES & COMPANY,
NEW YORK, CHICAGO, AND NEW ORLEANS.
1878.

PREFACE

TO ALL THE VOLUMES OF THIS SERIES OF COMMENTARIES.

THE object of this Commentary is to aid in their Christian work those who are endeavoring to promote the knowledge of the principles which Jesus Christ came to propound and establish—clergymen, Christian parents, Sunday-School teachers, Bible-women, lay-preachers. Intended for Christian workers, it aims to give the results rather than the processes of scholarship, the conclusions rather than the controversies of scholars; intended for laymen as well as for clergymen, it accompanies the English version of the New Testament, in all references to the original Greek gives the English equivalent, and translates all quotations from the French, German, Latin and Greek authors.

The introduction to Volume I contains a statement of those principles of interpretation which appear to me to be essential to the correct understanding of the Word of God. This Commentary is the result of a conscientious endeavor to apply those principles to the elucidation of the New Testament.

It is founded on a careful examination of the latest and best text; such variations as are of practical or doctrinal importance are indicated in the notes. It is founded on the original Greek; wherever that is inadequately rendered in our English version, a new translation is afforded by the notes. The general purpose of the writer or speaker, and the general scope of the incident or teaching, is indicated in a Preliminary Note to the passage, or in an analysis, a paraphrase, or a general summary at the close. Special topics are treated in preliminary or supplementary notes. The results of recent researches in Biblical archæology have been embodied, so as to make the Commentary serve in part the purpose of a Bible Dictionary. A free use is made of illustrations, from antiques, photographs, original drawings, and other trustworthy sources. They are never employed for mere ornament, but always to aid in depicting the life of Palestine, which remains in many respects substantially unchanged by the lapse of time. Since the Commentary is prepared, not for devotional reading, but for practical workers, little space has been devoted to hortatory remarks or practical or spiritual reflections. But I have uniformly sought to interpret the letter by the spirit, and to suggest rather than to supply moral and spiritual reflections, a paragraph of hints is affixed to each section or topic, embodying what appears to me to be the essential religious lessons of the incident or the teaching; sometimes a note is appended elucidating them more fully. The best thoughts of the best thinkers, both exegetical and homiletical, are freely quoted, especially such as are not likely to be accessible to most American readers; in all such cases the thought is credited to the author. Parallel and contrasted passages of Scripture are brought together in the notes; in addition, full Scripture references are appended to the text. These are taken substantially from Bagster's large edition of the English version of the Polyglot Bible, but they have been carefully examined and verified in preparing for the press, and some modifications have been made. For the convenience of that large class of Christian workers who are limited in their means, I have endeavored to make this Commentary, as far as practicable, a complete apparatus for the study of the New Testament. Maps and a Gazetteer give a condensed account of all the principal places in Palestine, mentioned in our Lord's life; and an introduction traces the history of the New Testament from the days of Christ to the present, giving some account of the evidence and nature of inspiration, the growth of the canon, the character and history of the manuscripts, the English version, the nature of the Gospels and their relation to each other, a brief life of Christ, and a complete tabular harmony of the four Gospels.

The want of all who use the Bible in Christian work is the same. The *wish* is often for a demonstration that the Scripture sustains the reader's peculiar theological tenets, but the *want* is always for a clearer and better knowledge of Scripture teaching, whether it sanctions or overturns previous opinions. I am not conscious that this work is written in the interest of any theological or ecclesiastical system. In those cases in which the best scholars are disagreed in their interpretation, the different views and the reasons which lead me to my own conclusions have been given, I trust, in no controversial spirit. For the sole object of this work is to ascertain and make clear the meaning of the Word of God, irrespective of systems, whether ecclesiastical or doctrinal.

No work is more delightful than that which throws us into fellowship with great minds; of all work the most delightful is that which brings us into association with the mind of God. This is the fellowship to which the student of the Bible aspires. I can have for those who use this work no higher hope than that they may find in its employment some of the happiness which I have found in its preparation, and that it may serve them as it has served me, as a guide to the Word of God, and through that Word to a better acquaintance with God himself.

CORNWALL-ON-HUDSON,   LYMAN ABBOTT.

TABLE OF CONTENTS.

THE GOSPEL OF MARK.

	PAGE
INTRODUCTION TO THE GOSPEL OF MARK	3
SUPPLEMENTARY NOTES IN MARK—	
CEREMONIAL WASHINGS	32
AUTHENTICITY OF MARK 16 : 9–20	65

THE GOSPEL OF LUKE.

INTRODUCTION TO THE GOSPEL OF LUKE	3
SUPPLEMENTARY NOTES—	
ON LUKE'S PREFACE	6
THE GOSPEL OF THE INFANCY	6
THE ANGEL'S MESSAGE	21
THE MINISTRY OF JOHN THE BAPTIST	29
PARABLE OF THE TWO DEBTORS	51
COMMISSION OF THE SEVENTY	60
PARABLE OF THE GOOD SAMARITAN	66
PARABLE OF THE FIG-TREE	80
PARABLES OF LOST SHEEP, COIN, AND SON	90, 94
PARABLE OF THE UNJUST STEWARD	99, 102
PARABLE OF RICH MAN AND LAZARUS	103
PARABLE OF LORD AND SERVANT	107
THE PENITENT THIEF	142

LIST OF ILLUSTRATIONS.

Most of the engravings in this volume, especially those illustrating ancient manners and customs, have been drawn and engraved expressly for this work from sketches by Mr. A. L. Rawson.

MARK.

	PAGE		PAGE
PALESTINE IN THE TIME OF CHRIST	Front	SANDALS—SHOES	28
THE LAKE OF GENNESARET	8	THE CHARGER	29
CHRIST HEALING THE PARALYTIC	9	EXECUTIONER	29
THE GRABATUS	10	MODERN HAND-WASHING	32
ANCIENT CANDLE-STICK	16	LOAVES OF BREAD	37
ANCIENT SKIFF	19	TOWER OF TIBERIAS	37
ROCK-CUT TOMB AT GADARAN	21	TREASURY BOXES	55
ANCIENT MOURNING-WOMEN	25	DIAGRAM OF JEWISH SEPULCHRE	62
TOOLS OF AN EGYPTIAN CARPENTER	26	PLAN OF TOMB DOOR OR GOLAL	63
STAFF, SCRIP, AND SKIN BOTTLE	28	TOMB DOOR	63

LUKE.

	PAGE		PAGE
PRIEST OFFERING INCENSE	8	VICINITY OF NAZARETH	34
NAZARETH	12	ORIENTAL FISHERS	36
WRITING TABLET	15	RED WHEAT OF PALESTINE	39
COIN OF CÆSAR AUGUSTUS	17	MOUNT OF BEATITUDES	40
SWADDLING CLOTHES	18	MEASURING GRAIN	43
AN EASTERN INN	19	FUNERAL PROCESSION	45
AN EASTERN MANGER	19	ALABASTERS	49
MASTER AND SERVANT	18	SALUTATIONS	61
SLAVE LOOSING SHOE-LATCHET	29	TYRE ON THE MAINLAND	62
WINNOWING THE GRAIN	29	CAPERNAUM	62
ANCIENT BOOK	32	ROAD TO JERICHO	65

LIST OF ILLUSTRATIONS.

	PAGE		PAGE
Scorpion	70	The Lost Sheep Saved	93
The Synagogue.—Showing Uppermost Seats	72	Drachma	94
		Husks	96
An Eastern Porter	73	Scribe and Writing Materials	101
The Eastern Housetop	74	Sycamine or Mulberry Branch	107
Sparrows in Marshes	75	Lord and Servant	108
Lily of Chalcedon	77	Group of Lepers	109
An Eastern Oven	78	View of the Site of Jericho	116
Fig-Tree	81	An Eastern Beggar	117
Oriental Dining-Room	86	A Sycamore Tree	118
An Indiscriminate Group gathered from Streets, etc., from Eastern City	88	The Temple Site	126
		Ancient Sieve	133
		Wailing Place of the Jews	140

MAPS AND PLANS.

Palestine in the Time of Christ	*Frontispiece*
The Holy Land under the Sons of Herod the Great	26
Triclinium	85

FULL-PAGE ILLUSTRATIONS.

Jesus Undaunted	Mark x, 32
The Temple as Jesus found it	Mark xi, 15
The Last Supper	Mark xiv, 22–26
The Child Jesus	Luke ii, 43
Jesus in the Synagogue	Luke iv, 17
Mob at Nazareth	Luke iv, 29
The Penitent and the Pharisee	Luke vii, 37
Blessing Little Children	Luke xviii, 16
Jesus Giving Sight	Luke xviii, 35
Zaccheus Invited	Luke xix, 4

The Gospel

ACCORDING TO

Mark,

WITH

NOTES AND COMMENTS.

THE GOSPEL ACCORDING TO MARK.

INTRODUCTION.

By whom written. The author of this Gospel has been universally believed to be Mark or Marcus, designated in Acts 12 : 12, 25 ; 15 : 37 as John Mark, and in chapter 13 : 5, 13, as John. For some evidences of authorship see Intro., pp. 15-19. His mother's name was Mary (Acts 12 : 12); she was a sister of Barnabas (Col. 4 : 10), and dwelt in Jerusalem (Acts 12 : 12). Mark was converted to Christianity through the instrumentality of Peter (1 Peter 5 : 13); became the minister, *i. e.*, the attendant of Paul and Barnabas in their first missionary journey (Acts 12 : 25); and was the cause of the contention between those Apostles and their separation on their second journey (Acts 15 : 39), after which Mark accompanied Barnabas (Acts 15 : 39). Subsequently the estrangement between Paul and Mark appears to have been removed ; so, at least, we may infer from Paul's cordial references to him in the Epistles—Col. 4 : 10 ; 2 Tim. 4 : 11 ; Phil. 24. The N. T. gives no further information respecting him, and subsequent tradition is untrustworthy. It represents him as the first bishop of Alexandria and as a martyr there. He has been identified with the young man, whom he alone mentions, who barely escaped capture at the time of Christ's arrest (Mark 14 : 51, 52), with one of those who turned back from following the Lord at the hard saying in John, ch. 6 : 66, and with one of the seventy mentioned in Luke 10 : 1; but these are mere hypotheses, unsupported by evidence.

Sources of information. Mark was not one of the twelve ; and there is no reason to believe that he was an eye and ear witness of the events which he has recorded ; but an almost unanimous testimony of the early fathers indicates Peter as the source of his information. The most important of these testimonies is that of Papias, who says : "He, the presbyter (John), said : Mark, being the interpreter of Peter, wrote exactly whatever he remembered ; but he did not write in order the things which were spoken or done by Christ. For he was neither a hearer nor a follower of the Lord, but, as I said, afterward followed Peter, who made his discourses to suit what was required, without the view of giving a connected digest of the discourses of our Lord. Mark, therefore, made no mistake when he wrote down circumstances as he recollected them. For he was very careful of one thing, to omit nothing of what he heard, and to say nothing false in what he related." Thus Papias writes of Mark. This testimony is confirmed by other witnesses, the most important of which are the following. *Irenæus:* "Matthew wrote a Gospel while Peter and Paul were preaching the Gospel at Rome and founding a church there. And after their decease, Mark, the disciple and interpreter of Peter, delivered to us in writing the things that had been preached by Peter." *Clement of Alexandria:* "The occasion of writing the Gospel according to Mark was this : Peter, having publicly preached the word at Rome, and having spoken the Gospel by the Spirit, many present exhorted Mark to write the things which had been spoken, since he had long accompanied Peter, and remembered what he had said ; and that when he had composed the Gospel, he delivered it to them who had asked it of him, which, when Peter knew, he neither forbade nor encouraged it." *Tertullian:* "Although that Gospel likewise which Mark published may be said to be Peter's, whose interpreter Mark was." *Origen,* as given by Eusebius : "The second Gospel is that according to Mark, who wrote it as Peter directed him ; who also calls him his son."

It is not at all certain, however, that these are independent testimonies, and how far they are to be accepted as true is a vexed question among Christian scholars. It has even been denied that the Gospel referred to by Papias is the present Gospel of Mark, which it is claimed does not correspond in character to his description. For a discussion of this question the student is referred to Alford's Greek Testament, Prolegomena, *Mark's Gospel, Sec. II*; Smith's Bible Dictionary, arts. *Mark* and *Mark, Gospel of*; Davidson's Intro. to the New Testament ; Westcott's Notes to the Study of the Gospels, etc. It must suffice here to say, (1) that there seems to me no reason whatever for doubting that Papias refers to our Gospel of Mark. I agree with Edward Cone Bissel (*Historic Origin of the Gospels*, p. 192) that "the description which he here gives of Mark's method well accords with the characteristics of the second Gospel, as being not a complete record of the life of our Lord, chronologically arranged, but a vivid and picturesque arrangement of leading facts only, having a definite moral as well as historic end ;" (2) That, while it must ever remain uncertain how far the influence of Peter extended in the composition of this Gospel, its character seems to me to confirm this testimony, and to indicate that one of the Twelve directly participated in its composition. Remembering that the early teaching of the Apostles consisted largely of a narrative of the facts in the life, sufferings, death, and resurrection of our Lord (see Intro., Pt. II, § 2, p. 32), it is reasonable to suppose that Mark derived his information from these discourses of Peter, and perhaps also from Peter's conversation, but embodied them in his own language. In other words, he was a true historian, not a mere amanuensis; but as a historian derived most of his information from Peter.

Characteristics. Mark's Gospel is occupied almost entirely with the ministry in Galilee and the events of the Passion week; it is the shortest of the four Gospels, and contains almost no incident or teaching which is not contained in one of the other two Synoptists; its report of the teaching of our Lord is much less full and systematic than that of Matthew, but *it is by far the most vivid and dramatic in its narratives, and their pictorial character indicate not only that they were derived from an eye and ear witness, but also from one who possessed the observation and the graphic artistic power of a natural orator, such as Peter emphatically was.* As the systematic but inartistic narrative of Matthew's Gospel harmonizes with the character of its reputed author—a tax-gatherer, and the spiritual and even metaphysical character of John's Gospel with such indications as are afforded of his character by the few incidents in his life and by his other writings, so the graphic but external character of Mark's Gospel harmonizes with the ardent, impulsive, oratorical, but not deep or tender character of Peter, to whose influence its composition is traditionally imputed. "It is Mark who reveals to us the comprehensive gaze of Christ (3:5, 34; 5:32; 10:23; 11:11); his loving embrace of the children brought to him (9:36; 10:16); his preceding his disciples while they follow in awe and amazement (10:32); we see him taking his seat to address his disciples (9:35); and turning around in holy anger to Peter (8:33); we hear the sighs which burst from his bosom (7:34; 8:12); and listen to his very accents (5:41; 7:34; 14:36); at one time we have an event portrayed with a freshness and pictorial power which places the whole scene before us with its minute accessories—the paralytic (9:1-12), the storm (4:39-41), the demoniac (5:1-20), Herod's feast (6:21-29), the feeding of the five thousand (6:35-45), the lunatic child (9:14-29), the young ruler (10:17-22), Bartimeus (10:46-52), etc.; at another, details are brought out by a single word (1:7; 1:10; 1:41; 4:11; 6:53; 7:21, 23; 9:26; 10:22; 14:3; 14:67) or by the substitution of a more precise and graphic word for one less distinctive (1:12; 2:12; 4:37; 5:29; 6:46; 7:9; 14:33); it is to Mark also that we are indebted for the record of minute particulars, of persons, places, times, and number, which stamp on his narratives an impress of authenticity."—*Kitto's Cyclopædia.* Further illustrations of this character of Mark's Gospel will be found on almost every page of this Commentary, and generally referred to in the notes. The references to Peter in this Gospel throw little or no light on the question of his connection with it. See them collated in *Smith's Bible Dictionary,* art. *Mark, Gospel of.*

Time and place of composition. This is uncertain. Internal evidence indicates that it was written before the destruction of Jerusalem. Otherwise the omission of all reference to so signal a fulfilment of our Lord's prophecies would be inexplicable. According to Irenæus it was composed after the death of Peter and Paul, which would place it as late as A. D. 63. The place also is unknown. The traditions are conflicting and untrustworthy.

Object and language. As it is clear from internal indications that Matthew's Gospel was written for Hebrew readers, so it is evident that Mark's Gospel was written for Gentile readers. He omits the genealogical registers given by Matthew and Luke; he rarely cites from the O. T., except in reporting discourses of our Lord; he interprets Hebrew or Aramaic expressions (3:17; 5:40; 7:11; 10:46; 14:36; 15:34); he explains Jewish names and customs (7:3,4; 12:42; 15:6); he contains no references to the law of Moses; even the word law (νόμος) does not occur; and matter that might offend or be misapprehended by Gentile readers is omitted (comp. Matt. 10:5, 6 with Mark 6:7, 8). There is every indication, both external and internal, that this Gospel was written originally in the Greek language, and no reason to doubt this, which is the almost universal opinion of scholars.

THE GOSPEL ACCORDING TO
MARK.

CHAPTER I.

THE beginning of the gospel of Jesus Christ, the [a] Son of God;

2 As it is written in the prophets,[b] Behold, I send my messenger before thy face, which shall prepare thy way before thee.

3 The [c] voice of one crying in the wilderness, Prepare ye the way of the Lord, make his paths straight.

4 John[d] did baptize in the wilderness, and preach the baptism of repentance for the remission [e] of sins.

5 And there went out unto him all the land of Judæa, and they of Jerusalem, and were all baptized of him in the river of Jordan, confessing [f] their sins.

6 And John was clothed with camel's hair, and with a girdle of a skin about his loins; and he did eat locusts[g] and wild honey;

7 And preached, saying, There [h] cometh one mightier than I after me, the latchet of whose shoes I am not worthy to stoop down and unloose.

8 I indeed have baptized you with water: but he shall baptize [i] you with the Holy Ghost.

9 And it came to pass in those days, that Jesus came from Nazareth of Galilee, and was baptized [j] of John in Jordan.

10 And straightway coming up out of the water, he saw the heavens opened, and the Spirit,[k] like a dove, descending upon him:

11 And there came a voice from heaven, *saying*, Thou art my beloved Son,[l] in whom I am well pleased.

12 And immediately the Spirit driveth him into the wilderness.

13 And[m] he was there in the wilderness forty days, tempted of Satan; and was with the wild beasts; and the angels ministered unto him.

14 Now after that John was put in prison, Jesus[n] came into Galilee, preaching the gospel [o] of the kingdom of God,

15 And saying, The time [p] is fulfilled, and the kingdom of God is at hand: repent [q] ye, and believe [r] the gospel.

16 Now [s] as he walked by the sea of Galilee, he saw Simon, and Andrew his brother, casting a net into the sea: for they were fishers.

17 And Jesus said unto them, Come ye after me, and I will make you to become fishers of men.

---

a Heb. 1 : 1, 2....b Mal. 3 : 1....c Isa. 40 : 3....d Matt. 3 : 1 ; Luke 3 : 3 ; John 3 : 23....e Acts 22 : 16....f Lev. 26 : 40-42 ; Ps. 32 : 5 ; Prov. 28 : 13 ; 1 John 1 : 8-10....g Lev. 11 : 22....h Matt. 3 : 11 ; John 1 : 27 ; Acts 13 : 25....i Joel 2 : 28 ; Acts 1 : 5 ; 2 : 4 ; 10 : 45 ; 11 : 15, 16 ; 1 Cor. 12, 13....j Matt. 3 : 13 ; Luke 3 : 21 k Isa. 42 : 1 ; John 1 : 32....l Ps. 2 : 7....m Matt. 4 : 1, etc. ; Luke 4 : 1, etc....n Matt. 4 : 23....o Luke 8 : 1....p Dan. 9 : 44 ; 9 : 25 ; Gal. 4 : 4 ; Ephes. 1 : 10....q Acts 2 : 38....r Rom. 16 : 26....s Matt. 4 : 18, etc. ; Luke 5 : 4, etc.

Ch. 1 : 1-8. JOHN THE BAPTIST AND HIS PREACHING. Matt. 3 : 1-12, notes ; Luke 3 : 1-18, notes. See for a different phase of his ministry, John 1 : 19-36, notes ; for his character, Matt. 11 : 2-19, notes ; for a brief account of his life, Matt. 14 : 1-12, notes, and Mark 6 : 17-30, notes.

1. This is a general introduction to the Gospel. Matthew and Luke alone give any account of the birth and childhood of Christ. Mark and John begin with his baptism, which precedes and inaugurates his public ministry. Tischendorf omits from this verse the words, "the Son of God." Alford retains them. Observe that the preaching of John the Baptist, the forerunner, is accounted the beginning of the glad tidings of Jesus the Messiah.

2, 3. The prophets. The better reading is *Isaiah the prophet*. There are, however, two references, the first to Mal. 3 : 1, the second to Isaiah 40 : 3. "As Matthew, in chap. 21 : 4, 5, quotes from Zachariah under the title of one prophet, and adds something from Isaiah 62 : 11 ; and as Paul also in Rom. 9 : 26, 27, mentions Isaiah by name, and has added something from Hosea 1 : 10, so Mark here refers to two prophets, and yet names only one, the prophet Isaiah."—(*Bengel*.) As to the meaning of the two references, see notes respectively on Matt. 11 : 10 and 3 : 3.—**The voice of one crying in the wilderness.** "A preacher should, if possible, be nothing but a voice, which should be always heard and never seen."—(*Quesnel*.)

4. In the wilderness. Of Judea (Matt. 3 : 1).—**For the remission of sins.** Not merely for the pardon of sin, but for the putting away of and cleansing from sin. See Matt. 26 : 28, note, and references there quoted. This John declared was necessary for all the children of Israel, not merely for the heathen (Luke 3 : 8), and was to be obtained not by sacrifices, but by abandonment of sin (Matt. 3 : 2, note).

8. With the Holy Ghost. Matthew and Luke add, "and with fire." See Matt. 3 : 11, note.

Ch. 1 : 9-11. THE BAPTISM OF JESUS. Matt. 3 : 13-17; Luke 3 : 21, 22; John 1 : 32-34. See notes on Matthew.

Ch. 1 : 12, 13. THE TEMPTATION. Matt. 4 : 1-11; Luke 4 : 1-13. It is not mentioned by John. Mark's account is briefest, but the statement that Christ "was with the wild beasts" is peculiar to him. The ministry of the angels (ver. 13) was at the close of the temptation. (Matt. 4 : 11.) See notes on Matthew.

Ch. 1 : 14-20. BEGINNING OF GALILEAN MINISTRY. Between the baptism and the commencement of Christ's public ministry in Galilee occurred the events narrated in John, chaps. 2, 3 and 4. To this ministry belongs the Sermon and consequent mob in Nazareth (Luke 4 : 16-31), which preceded the call of the four disciples here narrated. For notes on this ministry, see Matt. 4 : 12-25 ; for notes on the call of the four Apostles, Luke 5 : 1-11.

15. And believe in the Gospel. Peculiar to Mark. John had already preached faith as well as repentance (John 1 : 29, 36), though perhaps only privately to his own disciples. Christ did not as

18 And straightway they forsook their nets, and followed him.
19 And when he had gone a little farther thence, he saw James the *son* of Zebedee, and John his brother, who also were in the ship mending their nets.
20 And straightway he called them; and they left their father Zebedee in the ship with the hired servants, and went after him.
21 And they went into Capernaum; and straightway on the sabbath day he entered into the synagogue, and taught.
22 And ᵗ they were astonished at his doctrine: for he taught them as one that had authority, and not as the scribes.
23 And ᵘ there was in their synagogue a man with an unclean spirit; and he cried out,
24 Saying, Let *us* alone; what have we to do with thee, thou Jesus of Nazareth? art thou come to destroy us? I know thee who thou art, the Holy One of God.
25 And Jesus rebuked him, saying, Hold thy peace, and come out of him.

---

t Matt. 7 : 28.... u Luke 4 : 33, etc.

---

yet preach faith in himself as the Messiah, but only faith in the glad tidings that the time was fulfilled and the kingdom of God (Mark 3 : 2, note) was at hand.

Ch. 1 : 21-38. THE MINISTRY OF A DAY.—CHRIST A SAVIOUR: HE DELIVERS THE MIND; HE HEALS THE BODY; HE SAVES THE SOUL; HE CARRIES THE GOSPEL BOTH TO THE AWAKENED AND TO THE INDIFFERENT.— THE BUSIEST HAVE TIME FOR PRAYER.

Verses 21-38 give the record of a single day in Christ's life. There is no reason to suppose it an exceptional day. The account of the healing of the demoniac (verses 21-28) is peculiar to Mark and Luke (chap. 4 : 31-37). For a discussion of the phenomenon of demoniac possession, see Matt. 8 : 28-34, note, p. 123. The harmonists are not agreed as to the time and occasion of this and the other contemporaneous incidents. Alford puts them after the Sermon on the Mount, and the call and ordination of the twelve Apostles. Robinson, Ellicott, Andrews, and Townsend, with much better reason, place all the incidents in this chapter at the commencement of Christ's Galilean ministry, and prior to the ordination of the Twelve and the Sermon on the Mount. Christ had previously preached the sermon at Nazareth, which led to the mob there and his final departure from that city to take up his home in Capernaum (Luke 4 : 16-31).

21. Into Capernaum. For description of Capernaum see Matt. 4 : 13, note. It was situated upon the Sea of Galilee.—**Straightway.** That is, probably, on the sabbath immediately following the call of the four Apostles. He goes to give his disciples their first lessons in catching men (verse 17), and to inspire them with faith in him. Observe the rapidity of Christ's movement. Apparently on his first sabbath in Capernaum he preaches the Gospel. Compare the example of Paul, who preached the first sabbath after his conversion (Acts 9 : 20). Observe, too, that Christ preaches in the synagogues until he is driven out of them. Corruption in the church is not a sufficient reason for refusing to work in it.—**The synagogue.** For description of the Jewish synagogue, see Matt. 4 : 23, note.

22. Doctrine. Rather *teaching;* not so much the thing taught as the manner and spirit of the teaching astonished the people.—As one having authority. Matt. 7 : 28, 29, note.—**As the scribes.** For description of Jewish scribes, see Matt. 5 : 20, note.

23. A man in an unclean spirit. Luke's description is still more explicit: "*Having the spirit of an unclean devil,*" rather *demon.* Observe the peculiar phraseology here; not *with* but *in* an unclean spirit. As Christ dwells in his children and they in him, so the evil spirit dwells in the children of the devil. That there is here described not a case of physical and mental disease merely, but a real and actual possession of the soul by a fallen spirit, I think clear, both from the tenor of the narrative here, and from other parallel passages in the N. T. How could a lunatic know Christ to be the Holy One of God, when as yet he was unknown even to his own disciples? How should he fear that Christ would destroy him, who came to heal the sufferer but destroy the devil? How could lunacy be said to "come out of him" and to "cry with a loud voice?" See the whole question discussed on p. 123, Matt. 8 : 28-34, note.

24. Let alone. Some manuscripts omit this exclamation here. But it is found in Luke; where its authenticity is unquestionable. It is in the original an exclamation rather than a request, and answers nearly to our *away.*—**What have we to do with thee?** This is a common Jewish phrase, signifying a wish not to be troubled by the importunity or interference of another (Matt. 8 : 29, note). The customary demand of the devil is to be "let alone" (1 Kings 18 : 17; Acts 16 : 20; 17 : 5).—**Jesus the Nazarene.**. The epithet Nazarene can hardly be regarded here as other than opprobrious (Matt. 2 : 23; John 1 : 46).—**Art thou come to destroy us?** Observe, (1) an unconscious and significant testimony to the true mission of Christ, which is to destroy the devil and his works (1 John 3 : 8; Rev. 20 : 10). Comp. expression of the devil in Matt. 8 : 29. (2.) That here there is no indication that Christ literally destroyed the demon; what he destroyed was the demon's supremacy over the soul. (3.) That Christ had not directly threatened to disturb that supremacy; but his mere presence is always a disturbance and a destruction of the devil. (4.)

26 And when the unclean spirit had torn him, and cried with a loud voice, he came out of him.
27 And they were all amazed, insomuch that they questioned among themselves, saying, What thing is this? what new doctrine *is* this? for with authority commandeth he even the unclean spirits, and they do obey him.
28 And immediately his fame spread abroad throughout all the region round about Galilee.
29 And ᵛ forthwith, when they were come out of the synagogue, they entered into the house of Simon and Andrew, with James and John.
30 But Simon's wife's mother lay sick of a fever; and anon they tell him of her.
31 And he came and took her by the hand, and lifted her up; and immediately the fever left her, and she ministered unto them.
32 And at even, when the sun did set, they brought unto him all that were diseased, and them that were possessed with devils.

33 And all the city was gathered together at the door.
34 And he healed many that were sick of divers diseases, and cast out many devils; and suffered not the devils to speak, because they knew him.
35 And in the morning, rising up a great while before day, he went out, and departed into a solitary place, and there prayed.
36 And Simon, and they that were with him, followed after him.
37 And when they had found him, they said unto him, All *men* seek for thee.
38 And he said unto them, Let us go into the next towns, that I may preach there also: for therefore ʷ came I forth.
39 And he preached in their synagogues throughout all Galilee, and cast out devils.
40 And ˣ there came a leper to him, beseeching him, and kneeling down to him, and saying unto him, If thou wilt, thou canst make me clean.

ᵛ Matt. 8 : 14; Luke 4 : 38. ... ʷ Isa. 61 : 1, 2; John 17 : 8. ... ˣ Matt. 8 : 2; Luke 5 : 12.

That the demon speaks in the plural, Destroy us. "The demons make common cause."—(*Bengel*.)—**I know thee who thou art, the Holy of God.** This demon had a better creed about Christ than any one in the synagogue, but no faith in him (James 2 : 19). *The* Holy, not *a* holy. This word (ὁ ἅγιος) is employed, as here, as a noun, to designate the Temple (Heb. 9 : 1, etc.). In a sense every Christian is *a* temple of God; but Christ was *the* temple of God, in whom dwelt the fullness of the Godhead bodily (Col. 2 : 9). It was the demon's sense of the God in Christ that extorted from him this cry.

25. **Hold thy peace.** Christ seems to have habitually forbidden the demons to testify to him (verse 34; chap. 3 : 12; Luke 4 : 41; comp. Acts 16 : 16–18). Calvin suggests what may be the true explanation: "The devil dexterously acknowledges that Christ is the Holy One of God, in order to insinuate into the minds of men a suspicion that there was some secret understanding between him and Christ." And such appears to have been in part the effect. Comp. Mark 3 : 11 with Mark 3 : 22. "The devil and the world never praise but in order to seduce. It is a necessary part of prudence not to lay ourselves open to their commendations." —(*Quesnel*.)

26. **And when the unclean spirit had torn him.** Rather, *thrown him into convulsions*. Comp. Mark 9 : 26. The man was not hurt (Luke 4 : 35). The final outgoing of Satan or any of his emissaries is almost always accompanied with violence, which is the sign of his wrath (Rev. 12 : 12). But this violence can do no permanent harm.—**Cried with a loud voice.** This was not in defiance of Christ's command. For that forbade speech, and this was an inarticulate cry.—**He came out of him.** The whole language of this verse unmistakably shows that the Evangelist believed in a real possession of the soul by a personal evil spirit.

27. **They were all amazed.** That is, all in the synagogue. What surprised them was, not merely the cure of the demoniac, but that the demon obeyed the simple voice of Christ. For the Lord used no charm, or exorcism.

28. A fuller description of this widening fame of Christ is given by Matthew. See ch. 4 : 25, note.

29–34. THE HEALING OF PETER'S MOTHER-IN-LAW. See Matt. 8 : 14, 15, notes; Luke 4 : 38–40. The only differences in the accounts are verbal, Mark giving some graphic touches that are not found in the other Evangelists, such as verse 29, "with James and John;" verse 31, he "lifted her up;" verse 33, "all the city was gathered together at the door." The knowledge possessed by the devils (verse 34) is interpreted by Luke, "They knew that he was Christ (Luke 4 : 41), *i. e.*, the Messiah. The time for the full disclosure of that fact had not yet come.

35–39. CHRIST'S FIRST CIRCUIT IN GALILEE. Luke 4 : 42–44; Matt. 4 : 23, 25.

35. **Rising a great while before day.** Matt. 8 : 17 intimates a reason why he could not sleep, viz., the burden of others' sorrows which he took upon himself. Observe, (1) the rest for the restless here indicated—prayer; (2) the correction of a notion, popularly current in these days, that one can pray equally well at all times and in all places—Christ was accustomed to seek *solitude* for special occasions of prayer (Mark 5 : 46; Luke 5 : 16; 6 : 12; 22 : 41).

36. **Simon.** More generally known in the N. T. as Peter; here, as throughout his career, a leader. It is characteristic of him that he has no fear of obtruding on the retirement of his Master. On his character, see p. 147, Note on the Twelve Apostles.

38. **Towns.** Literally, *village-cities*, *i. e.*, unwalled towns. Christ had no ambition to be a metropolitan preacher. Having awakened spiritual desires in the people of Capernaum, he went elsewhere that he might awaken them in

41 And Jesus, moved with compassion, put forth *his* hand, and touched him, and saith unto him, I will; be thou clean.
42 And as soon as he had spoken, immediately *y* the leprosy departed from him, and he was cleansed.
43 And he straitly charged him, and forthwith sent him away;
44 And saith unto him, See thou say nothing to any man: but go thy way, shew thyself to the priest, and offer for thy cleansing those things *z* which Moses commanded, for a testimony *a* unto them.
45 But he went out, and began to *b* publish *it* much, and to blaze abroad the matter, insomuch that Jesus could no more openly enter into the city, but was without in desert places; and *c* they came to him from every quarter.

y Ps. 33 : 9 ; John 15 : 3, ... z Lev. 14 : 2–32, ... a Rom. 15 : 4 ; 1 Cor. 10 : 11, ... b Ps. 77 : 11, 12 ; Tit. 1 : 10 .... c ch. 2 : 13.

others also. His example does not require, but it certainly justifies an itinerant ministry.—**That I may preach.** As yet the Apostles did not preach. Apparently four only had been called—James, John, Andrew, and Simon.—**I came forth for this purpose.** Not, I came forth from the city—for his purpose in that had been retirement and prayer; but, I came forth from the Father (John 16 : 28). His mission is here indicated, viz., to herald the glad tidings of divine love to all the world, a mission which he leaves to his followers to complete (John 17 : 18).

39. Throughout all Galilee. This describes the first missionary circuit in Galilee, the same described in Matt. 4 : 23–25 (see notes there). Galilee, the northernmost province of Judea, was the scene of Christ's most abundant labors; all the Apostles except Judas Iscariot were Galileans; its inhabitants were simple-minded, and comparatively free from the control of the priestly class, which ruled in Judea, and from the bigotry and intolerance of the Judeans. (For history, see Matt. 2 : 22, note.) The immediate vicinity of the Sea of Galilee was the home of a crowded and busy population. This sea, or lake, is 13 miles long, 4 to 6 miles wide, 165 feet deep in the deepest part, and lies near 700 feet below the surface of the Mediterranean. Its climate is, and its productions were, those of an almost tropical nature. Grapes and figs ripened on its

THE LAKE OF GENNESARET, SHOWING THE MIRACLES AND JOURNEYS OF OUR LORD IN ITS NEIGHBORHOOD.

1. Peter's draught of fishes, Matt. 4 : 18–22; Mark 1 : 16–20; Luke 5 : 1–11.
2. Stilling the waves, Matt. 8 : 23–27; Mark 4 : 35–41; Luke 8 : 22–25.
3. Miracles with the Gergesenes, Matt. 8 : 28–34; Mark 5 : 1–20; Luke 8 : 26–39.
4. Return to Capernaum, Matt. 9 : 1; Mark 2 : 1.
5. Journey to the Desert, Matt. 14 : 13; Mark 6 : 31; Luke 9 : 10.
6. Feeding the 5,000, Matt. 14 : 14–21; Mark 6 : 32–41; Luke 9 : 11–17; John 6 : 1–15.
7. Christ walks on the sea, Matt. 14 : 22–34; Mark 6 : 45–56; John 6 : 16–21.
8. Feeding the 4,000, Matt. 15 : 32–38; Mark 8 : 1–9.
9. Return to the parts of Dalmanutha, Matt. 15 : 39; Mark 8 : 10.
10. Crosses to the East side, Matt. 16 : 5; Mark 8 : 13.
11. Reminds of the miraculous feeding, Matt. 16 : 6–10; Mark 8 : 14–21.
12. Heals the blind near Bethsaida, Mark 8 : 22–26.

shores ten months in the year. Its waters abounded with fish, which supplied the country for miles around. On the south-western shore some warm mineral springs constituted a favorite resort of wealthy Romans; on the north and north-western shore five cities of considerable size were crowded along thirteen miles of coast-line,—Tiberias, Magdala or Dalmanutha (see Mark 8 : 10, note), Chorazin, Capernaum, and Bethsaida. It was on the direct route between Damascus and the Mediterranean, and so was commercially important. It was thus an appropriate centre for Christ's Galilean ministry. It is now utterly desolate; there is only one boat on the

CH. II.] MARK. 9

CHAPTER II.

AND again he entered into Capernaum after *some* days; and it was noised that he was in the house.
2 And straightway many were gathered together, insomuch that there was no room to receive *them*, no, not so much as about the door; and he preached ^d the word unto them.
3 And ^e they come unto him, bringing one sick of the palsy, which was borne of four.

d Ps. 40 : 9....e Matt. 9 : 1, etc.; Luke 5 : 18, etc.

lake; and of the populous cities only the town of Tiberias and the little village of Migdel (Magdala) are left. The accompanying map and table indicate the most important miracles and journeys of our Lord in the immediate vicinity of this lake itself, the heart and centre of the province. The greater part of Mark's Gospel is devoted to an account of this Galilean ministry, and to a graphic picture of the *works* rather than a systematic account of the *teachings* of our Lord.

40-45. HEALING OF THE LEPER. Matt 8 : 2-4; Luke 5 : 12-15. See notes on Matthew. The Leper's disobedience of Christ's command (verse 45) is not stated by Matthew.

Ch. 2 : 1-12. THE HEALING OF THE PARALYTIC.— A PARABLE OF REDEMPTION; THE HELPLESSNESS AND THE HOPE OF THE SINNER.—THE NATURE AND THE EFFICACY OF FAITH.—THE POWER AND THE OFFICE OF CHRIST: THE REMISSION OF SINS.—THE TEST OF ALL PRIESTLY CLAIMS TO LIKE OFFICE AND AUTHORITY: ARE THE PRIESTHOOD ABLE TO REMIT THE PHYSICAL PENALTY OF TRANSGRESSION?

CHRIST HEALING THE PARALYTIC.

This account is also given in Matthew 9 : 2-8, where nothing is said of letting the paralytic through the roof, and in Luke 5 : 17-26, where is one important addition (ver. 17). The healing probably took place at or about the time indicated here and in Luke, that is, in the early part of Christ's Galilean ministry, before the Sermon on the Mount, and before the call of Matthew, who was not, therefore, an eye-witness. The evidence of this is the order indicated in Mark and Luke.

1. Capernaum. For description see Mat-

4 And when they could not come nigh unto him for the press, they uncovered the roof where he was: and when they had broken it up, they let down the bed wherein the sick of the palsy lay.

5 When Jesus saw their faith,[f] he said unto the sick of the palsy, Son, thy sins be forgiven thee.
6 But there were certain of the scribes sitting there, and reasoning in their hearts,

---

f Acts 14 : 9 ; Ephes. 2 : 8.

---

thew 4 : 13, note.—**It was noised that he was in a house.** Not necessarily his own house, though this may have been the case. His house, so far as he had one, was at Capernaum (Matt. 4 : 13).

2. Many were gathered together. Luke (5 : 17) says that among them were Pharisees and doctors of the law from Galilee, Judea, and Jerusalem. He also intimates that other cures were performed at this time. See note there. — **No room to receive them.** One of the incidental evidences of Christ's popularity as a preacher at this stage of his work and in Galilee; it was doubtless increased by curiosity to witness his miracles.—**And he preached the word unto them.** That is, the word of the Kingdom of God, that it was at hand, and that repentance and faith were the necessary preparations for it (Matt. 4 : 17; 13 : 19, 20). Observe how simple must have been the preaching of Christ, a house-to-house preaching; and that there is no evidence that it was accompanied with any formal order of service or worship. But for public worship other and abundant provision was made by the Temple and the synagogues.

3. One palsied. The original Greek word rendered here *palsied* signifies literally a loosening or relaxing. It is defined by Celsus, a writer on medicine of about the time of Christ, as "a weakness of the nerves, either throughout the whole body or throughout the part diseased."— (*Rob. Lex.*, art. παραλυτικός.) Mr. Barnes (note on Matt. 4 : 24) classifies the infirmities included under the general name of palsy in the N. T. as follows : 1st. The paralytic shock, affecting the whole body. 2d. The hemiplegy, affecting only one side of the body—the most frequent form of the disease. 3d. The paraplegy, affecting all the system below the neck. 4th. The catalepsy, caused by a contraction of the muscles in the whole or a part of the body, and very dangerous (Matt. 12 : 10–13). 5th. The cramp, in eastern countries a fearful malady, and by no means infrequent. It originates from chills in the night. The limbs, when seized by it, remain immovable, and the person afflicted with it resembles one undergoing a torture (Matt. 8 : 6; Luke 7 : 2). Death follows from this disease in a few days. It is evident from the narrative that the patient in this case was rendered utterly helpless by his palsy. The disease in its worst forms is generally incurable.

4. And not being able to come nigh unto him for the throng, they unroofed the roof where he was. To do this they went up on the roof (Luke 5 : 19), possibly by outside stairs, which sometimes led up from the street to the house-top, perhaps by a ladder brought for that purpose, or perhaps by the stairs in a neighboring house. As they were in a city, the houses would adjoin, and it would be easy to pass from one roof to another. What is meant by uncovering the roof is not clear. Luke says they "let him down through the tiling." The roofs of Jewish houses were often made of tile, *i. e.*, burnt clay. The larger Jewish houses were built around an open square. See picture in note on Matt. 26 : 69, etc. This was sometimes protected from the rain and sun by an awning or broad roofing, sometimes by a more permanent roof supported on columns, with an aperture in the centre, and a corresponding basin below to receive the rain-water which flowed through the opening. Into this court opened the rooms of the house. It may be that Christ stood in one of these rooms, and the crowd in the court, and that the hearers of the palsied man removed enough of the tiling, either of the parapet of the roof proper, or of the roof over the court, possibly by widening the aperture in it, to let the sick man down; or it may be that Christ was standing in the room within, and that the roof proper was broken up for the purpose of reaching him. See in Dr. Thomson's *Land and Book*, II : 7, a description of the modern roof in Palestine, and of the method of uncovering it, which he says he has often seen done. On either hypothesis, the significance of the fact remains, viz., that the sick man and his friends showed their faith by overcoming great obstacles in order to come to Christ for help. And this showed their confidence both in his willingness and his ability to help.—**They let down the bed.** Mark specifies the kind of bed by the

THE GRABATUS.

word he uses (κράββατος), *grabatus*. This was a small, low couch or bed of the commonest description, such as was used by poor people, having a mere network of cords stretched over the frame to support the mattress. The annexed

7 Why doth this *man* thus speak blasphemies? Who can forgive sins ᵍ but God only?
8 And immediately, when Jesus perceived in his spirit that they so reasoned within themselves, he said unto them, Why reason ye these things in your hearts?
9 Whether is it easier to say to the sick of the palsy, *Thy* sins be forgiven thee; or to say, Arise, and take up thy bed, and walk?
10 But that ye may know that the Son of man hath

g Isa. 43 : 25; Dan. 9 : .9

engraving is from Rich's *Dictionary*. The *grabatus* could easily be carried about.

5. And when Jesus saw their faith. As exemplified by their actions. And observe the illustration of true faith, not a strong conviction of any doctrine *about* Christ, but a strong trust and confidence *in* Christ. The term "*their* faith" includes that of the sick man, for they would scarcely have carried him to Christ against his will. The conclusion of Quesnel, therefore, though just, is hardly justified by this incident: "God willingly accepts the desires, prayers, and good works which are offered for the conversion of sinners, who are not themselves sensible of their misery." Observe, too, that, apparently, Christ answers the prayer before it is presented. They say nothing; he speaks to the silent prayer of their actions. Indeed, the four were probably still on the roof, and could not, if they would, well present a petition. The man's helplessness is his prayer.—**He said unto the sick of the palsy.** To Mark's report Matthew adds the words *Be of good cheer;* the word here and there rendered *Son* (τέκνον) is a term of endearing address nearly equivalent to "my child;" and the verb, rendered in the English in the imperative, *Thy sins be forgiven thee,* is in the perfect tense, and signifies a forgiveness already perfected. The spirit of Christ's address may, therefore, be thus rendered: *Be of good cheer, my child, thy sins have been forgiven thee.* There was, on the part of the sick man, no request for forgiveness, but the Jews regarded disease as a punishment for sin (John 9 : 2), and while specific disease is not always a punishment for specific transgression, yet there is a deeper sense in which all sickness and death is the fruit of sin, a fact which Christ here and elsewhere recognizes (John 5 : 14). Calvin's comment, therefore, is legitimate: "The only way of obtaining deliverance from all evil is to have God reconciled to us."

6, 7. Certain of the scribes. Among them were those who had come up from Judea and Jerusalem (Luke 5 : 17), where Christ never had the popularity he possessed in Galilee.—**Reasoning in their hearts.** Matthew says *within themselves.*—**Why doth this man thus speak? He blasphemes.** This is the better reading; it is adopted by both Alford and Tischendorf. By blaspheme the scribes do not mean, speaks evil of God, nor, takes God's name in vain, but, arrogates to himself the function and office of God. On the nature of blasphemy under the Jewish law see Note on Blasphemy against the Holy Ghost, p. 108 (*f*), and Matt. 26 : 57-68, Prel. Note.—**Who can forgive sins except one—God?** Christ had not as yet assumed to forgive sins; he had simply declared that the man's sins were forgiven. "Christ says nothing more than the prophets frequently say when they announce the grace of God."—(*Calvin.*) But he does now assume the power which they have denied him, and this without calling in question their principle, that only God can forgive sins.

8. And Jesus, immediately perceiving in his spirit that they so reasoned within themselves. Not, as in our English version. *when he perceived,* but *instantly perceiving.* The knowledge was supernatural, and was itself as great a testimony of his divine power as was the healing which followed (Luke 7 : 39, 40 ; John 2 : 24, 25).—**Why reason ye these things in your hearts?** Matthew's report is, *Wherefore think ye evil in your hearts?* Their reasonings therefore, it is evident, did not spring from a sincere reverence for God, nor from an honest mental perplexity, but from jealousy and ill-will. It was the beginning of their opposition to Jesus as the Messiah, and it affords an illustration of the spirit of theological cavil in all ages. Chrysostom notes the gentleness of Christ's rebuke: "He said not, O accursed and sorcerers, as ye are; O ye envious and enemies of men's salvation, but, Wherefore think ye evil in your hearts?" And he applies Christ's example to the modern teacher: "We must, you see, use gentleness to eradicate the disease; since he who has become better through the fear of man, will quickly return to wickedness again."

9. Whether is it easier to say, etc. "In our Lord's argument it must be carefully noted that he does not ask which is easiest, to forgive sins or to raise a sick man—for it could not be affirmed that that of forgiveness was easier than this of healing—but, which is easiest, to *claim,* this power or that, to *say,* Thy sins be forgiven thee, or, Arise and walk. The former is easiest; and I will prove my right to say it by saying with effect, and with an outward consequent setting the seal to my truth, the harder word, Arise and walk. By saying that which is capable of being put to the proof I will indicate my right and power to do that which in its very nature is incapable of being proved."—(*Trench.*)

power[h] on earth to forgive sins, (he saith to the sick of the palsy,)

11 I say unto thee, Arise, and take up thy bed, and go thy way into thine house.

12 And immediately he arose, took up the bed, and went forth before them all; insomuch that they were all amazed, and glorified God, saying, We[i] never saw it on this fashion.

b Acts 15 : 3. .... i John 7 : 31 ; 9 : 32.

Christ's argument here affords a fair test of all priestly claims to absolve from sin. *If the priest has power to remit the eternal punishment of sin, he should be able certainly to remit the physical and temporal punishment of sin.* This Christ did; this the priest does not and cannot do.

10. But that ye may know that the son of man, i. e., the Messiah. The term *Son of man,* when used in the Gospels, always refers to Christ, and generally, if not always, to him as the Messiah. It is his customary designation of himself. It is borrowed from Daniel (Dan. 7 : 13), where it is applied prophetically to the Messiah (see Matt. 10 : 23, note). Here, therefore, the claim is a purely personal one; it does not indicate a power vested in man, or in the Apostles, or in a hierarchy. Yet there is a significance in the fact that both judgment (John 5 : 27) and forgiveness, that is, all dealing with sin, is attributed to him who, as the *son of man,* had full experience of temptation (Heb. 2 : 18 ; 4 : 15, 16). —**Hath authority on earth to forgive sins.** Not merely, authority while on the earth to forgive sins, nor, authority to forgive sins committed on the earth, but, authority to exercise the function of forgiveness of sins upon the earth, i. e., that ye may know that this is the Messiah's earthly mission. "Christ's meaning was, that forgiveness of sins ought not to be sought at a distance ; for he exhibits it to men in his own person, and as it were in his hands."—(*Calvin.*) And here, as everywhere in the N. T., forgiveness of sins is really the remission or putting away of sin as well as its punishment. Only he who has *power* to do the one has *authority* to do the other.

11. Arise, take up thy bed. This he could easily do, the *grabatus* being light and easily carried. Observe, (1) that the evidence of the man's forgiveness did not follow *immediately* after the forgiveness was declared, nor the declaration of pardon immediately after forgiveness was secured. He was forgiven the moment that, with unfeigned penitence for his sins, he began to seek the Lord (Isaiah 55 : 7) ; forgiveness was declared by Christ to be already perfected when he came into Christ's presence (ver. 5, note); but the *evidence* of the forgiveness, in the healing, was not given until after the conflict with the Scribes. Pardon and the personal assurance of pardon are not always contemporaneous; (2) there was no *natural* ability in the paralytic to obey the divine command ; his attempt to obey was an act of faith, and with the faith that attempted obedience came the power to obey. The cure illustrates the principle of divine grace, as set forth in Phil. 2 : 12. "Let us bring what is ours ; God will supply the rest."—(*Chrysostom.*) It is not faith to do nothing and leave all to God ; it is faith to do what we can and leave all to God.

12. They were all amazed. Luke says, *Filled with fear ;* Matthew, according to the best readings, *Were afraid.* The immediate disclosure of God at first awakens in the soul the feeling of fear (Matt. 17 : 7, note ; Luke 5 : 8). —**And glorified God.** The Scribes charged Christ with blasphemy, i. e., derogating from the divine dignity by claiming a divine function. In fact, his act led the people to *glorify God.* And so, whenever Christ has been accepted as God manifest in the flesh, and as the One who forgives sins on earth, the worship and glory of God, the Father, has been increased, not lessened.—**Saying, We never saw it thus.** Luke says, *We have seen strange things to-day ;* Matthew contains an important addition, "The multitude glorified God, *which had given such power unto men.*" To them Jesus was simply a man, a rabbi, perhaps an inspired prophet; and his miraculous powers, like those possessed by certain of the O. T. prophets, were accounted among God's gifts to the human race.

Of this whole incident it may be remarked, (1) that it strikingly illustrates the difference in spiritual authority between Christ and his Apostles, none of whom assumed to forgive sins. Compare Acts 8 : 22-24, where Peter refers Simon to God for forgiveness ; (2) that it affords a test for all claims by a hierarchy to pardon sin, or even officially and authoritatively to promise absolution of sin ; if they possessed power to absolve from sin they should be able, as Christ, to relieve from the temporal consequences of sin ; (3) that it illustrates the gentleness of Christ in his language of reassurance to the sick, *Be of good cheer my child,* and in his language of rebuke to the Scribes, *Why do ye think evil?* (4) that it may be regarded as an enacted parable of sin and redemption. The paralytic typifies the sinner, by his original helplessness (Isaiah 40 : 30; John 6 : 44 ; 15 : 5) ; faith, by his earnestness to come to Christ in spite of obstacle (Psalms 25 : 15 ; 86 . 2, 7) ; a common Christian experience, by the delay he suffers between his repentance and faith, and his cure (James 5 : 7, 8) ; and the power of divine grace, in the ability to obey Christ's command, received in the very attempt to comply with it (Phil. 4 : 13).

CH. III.] MARK. 13

13 And he went forth again by the sea side; and all the multitude resorted unto him, and he taught them.

14 And¹ as he passed by, he saw Levi the *son* of Alphæus sitting at the receipt of custom, and said unto him, Follow me. And he arose and followed him.

15 And ᵏ it came to pass, that, as Jesus sat at meat in his house, many publicans¹ and sinners sat also together with Jesus and his disciples: for there were many, and they followed him.

16 And when the scribes and Pharisees saw him eat with publicans and sinners, they said unto his disciples, How is it that he eateth and drinketh with publicans and sinners?

17 When Jesus heard *it*, he saith unto them, They ᵐ that are whole have no need of the physician, but they that are sick: I came not to call the righteous, but sinners ⁿ to repentance.

18 And ᵗʰᵉ disciples of John and of the Pharisees used to fast: and they come and say unto him, Why do the disciples of John and of the Pharisees fast, but thy disciples fast not?

19 And Jesus said unto them, Can the children of the bridechamber fas¹, while the bridegroom ᵒ is with them? As long as they have the bridegroom with them, they cannot fast.

20 But the days will come when the bridegroom shall be taken away from them, and then ᵖ shall they fast in those days.

21 No man also seweth a piece of new cloth on an old garment: else the new piece that filled it up taketh away from the old, and the rent is made worse.

22 And no man putteth new wine into old bottles; else the new wine doth burst the bottles, and the wine is spilled, and the bottles will be marred: ᵠ but new wine must be put into new bottles.

23 And ʳ it came to pass, that he went through the corn fields on the ˢ sabbath day; and his disciples began, as they went, to pluck ᵗ the ears of corn.

24 And the Pharisees said unto him, Behold, why do they on the sabbath day that which is not lawful?

25 And he said unto them, Have ye never read what David did,ᵘ when he had need, and was an hungred, he, and they that were with him?

26 How he went into the house of God in the days of Abiathar the high priest, and did eat the showbread,ᵛ which is not lawful to eat but for the priests, and gave also to them which were with him?

27 And he said unto them, The sabbath was made for man,ʷ and not ˣ man for the sabbath:

28 Therefore ʸ the Son of man is Lord also of the sabbath.

CHAPTER III.

AND ᶻ he entered again into the synagogue; and there was a man there which had a withered hand.

2 And they watched ᵃ him, whether he would heal him on the sabbath day; that they might accuse him.

3 And he saith unto the man which had the withered hand, Stand forth.

4 And he saith unto them, Is it lawful to do good on the sabbath days, or to do evil? to save life,ᵇ or to kill? But they held their peace.

5 And when he had looked round about on them with anger, being grieved for the hardness of their hearts, he saith unto the man, Stretch forth thine hand. And he stretched *it* out: and his hand was restored whole as the other.

6 And the Pharisees went forth, and straightway took counsel with the ᵇ Herodians against him, how they might destroy him.

---

j Matt. 9 : 9; Luke 5 : 27....k Matt. 9 : 10, etc....l Luke 15 : 1-5.... m Matt. 9 : 12, 13; Luke 5 : 31, 32.....n Is. 1 : 18; 55 : 7; Matt. 18 : 11 Luke 19 : 10; 1 Cor. 6 : 9-11; 1 Tim. 1 : 15....o Matt. 25 : 1....p Acts 13 : 2... q Job 32 : 19; Ps. 119 : 80, 83....v Matt. 12 : 1, e c.; Luke 6 : 1, etc....s Deut. 23 : 25. ..t 1 Sam. 21 : 6....u Exod. 29 : 32, 33; Lev. 24 : 9....v Neh. 9 : 14; Isa. 58 : 13; Ezek. 20 : 12, 20....w Col. 2 : 16....x John 9 : 14; Ephs. 1 : 22; Rev. 1 : 10....y Matt. 12 : 9. etc.; Luke 14 : 1.. .a Hosea 6 : 6....b Matt. 22 : 16.

The student will observe that there is no verbal expression of either penitence or faith on the man's part, and no demand by Christ for such expression. However this may accord with our method of dealing with sinful and suffering souls, it accords with Christ's method, who customarily by his insight perceived and by his gracious helpfulness developed the first germs of repentance and faith, not always waiting till they had wakened even into consciousness (Luke 7 : 47-50; 23 : 42, 43; John 5 : 8, 9, 14; 8 : 11). It is the disclosure of divine forgiveness that leads to repentance (Rom. 2 : 4).

13-22. THE CALL OF LEVI (Matthew) AND CHRIST'S CONSEQUENT TEACHING. Matt. 9 : 9-17; Luke 5 : 27-39. See Notes on Matthew. The phrase here, *In his house* (verse 15) means the house of Levi or Matthew (Luke 5 : 29), not the house of Jesus, who had none (Matt. 8 : 20).

23-28. Ch. 3 : 1-6. THE LAW OF THE CHRISTIAN SABBATH ILLUSTRATED. Matt. 12 : 1-8; Luke 6 : 1-11. See Notes on Matthew. I treat here only one or two points, peculiar to Mark.

26. In the days of Abiathar the high-priest. The reference is to 1 Sam. 21 : 1-9. There, however, Ahimelech is represented as the high-priest, and elsewhere Abiathar is represented as his son. The most probable explanation is that Abiathar was the son of Ahimelech and ministered with his father, and perhaps personally gave the shew-bread to David, and being subsequently high-priest is here given his title, a title which did not, however, properly become his until a later period.

27. Peculiar to Mark. It implies (1) the perpetuity of a sabbath rest; it was made for *man*, not merely for the Jews, and the law requiring it is written in man's physical and spiritual nature; (2) its universality; it was made for *man*, not for any single class, for man-servant and maid-servant, and the stranger within the gates (Exod. 20 : 10); (3) its object, *for* man—*man's* day, therefore, as truly as the Lord's day; hence, whatever is for man's highest and truest welfare, whatever *generally adopted*, will tend to the physical, intellectual and spiritual development of man, *not of exceptional individuals, but of the community or the race*, is appropriate for the day which was made *for* man, and whose observance is tested by its usefulness to man.

Ch. 3 : 3. Stand forth. His object apparently, was to call attention to the cure and make it prominent in order to emphasize his teaching.

4. Is it lawful * * * to save life or to kill? "A terrible home-thrust. He was intending to do good, to relieve a disabled fellow-man—they were harboring murderous thoughts. They would fain destroy Jesus. 'Which of us,' he virtually asks, 'is breaking the sabbath, you or I?'"—(*Furness*.)

7 But Jesus withdrew himself with his disciples to the sea: and a great*multitude from Galilee followed him, and from Judæa,
8 And from Jerusalem, and from Idumæa, and *from* beyond Jordan; and they about Tyre and Sidon, a great multitude, when they had heard what great things he did, came unto him.
9 And he spake to his disciples, that a small ship should wait on him because of the multitude, lest they should throng him.
10 For he had healed many;^d insomuch that they pressed upon him for to touch him, as many as had plagues.

11 And^e unclean spirits, when they saw him, fell down before him, and cried, saying, Thou art the Son of God.
12 And he straitly charged them that they should not make him known.^f
13 And^g he goeth up into a mountain and calleth *unto him* whom he^h would: and they came unto him.
14 And he ordained twelve, that they should be with him, and that he might send them forth to preach,
15 And to have power to heal sicknesses, and to cast out devils:
16 And Simonⁱ he surnamed Peter;

c Luke 6 : 17....d Matt. 12 : 15; 14 : 14....e ch. 1 : 24; Matt. 14 : 33; Luke 4 : 41; James 2 : 19....f ch. 1 : 25, 34....g Matt. 10 : 1....
h John 15 : 16....i John 1 : 42.

---

5. With anger being grieved. Grief and indignation are not inconsistent emotions. Only that anger which grieves at sin is the Christian's anger.—**The hardness of their hearts.** Exemplified by their silence, as an evidence of their obdurate persistence in their murderous designs.
6. Pharisees. Matt. 3 : 7, note.—**Herodians.** Matt. 22 : 16, note.
7-12. CHRIST'S PERIOD OF POPULARITY IN GALILEE.—Parallel to Mark's account here, is Matt. 12 : 15-21. See notes there, especially on verses 17-21, which are peculiar to Matthew. Mark's account of the multitude which followed Christ is more detailed. He also narrates the incident of the boat kept for Jesus' disciples (ver. 9). There appears to be no chronological order observed by Mark in this chapter. The ordination of the twelve Apostles (verses 13-19) and the Sermon on the Mount, which Mark does not report, but which accompanied their ordination, preceded the teaching of Christ on the Sabbath question (ch. 2 : 23-28; 3 : 1-6) and the incidents narrated here. For other evidences of Christ's great popularity at this period of his ministry, consult Matt. 14 : 13; Mark 5 : 24; 6 : 33; Luke 8 : 45; 12 : 1.
7, 8. To the sea, *i. e.,* the Sea or Lake of Galilee. See map and description, ch. 1 : 39.—**From Galilee.** The northern province of Palestine. On its character and inhabitants, see ch. 1 : 39; Matt. 2 : 22; 4 : 14-16, notes.—**From Judea.** Compare Luke 5 : 17.—**And from Idumen.** A Greek word answering to the Hebrew Edom. It was the region inhabited by the descendants of Esau or Edom (Gen. 25 : 30), whence its name. Originally the Edomites occupied a tract of country extending from the Dead to the Red Sea, about fifteen or twenty miles broad and one hundred miles long; but after the Babylonish captivity they were permitted to settle in Southern Palestine, and subsequently, under the Maccabees, were subdued and compelled to submit to the Jewish rites and Jewish government, and were practically incorporated in the Jewish nation. Herod the Great, the last king of the Jews, was an Idumean.—**They about Tyre and Sidon.** See note on Matt. 11 : 21.
9. A small boat. Probably a row-boat, used for fishing, and perhaps also furnished with a sail. See Mark 4 : 36 for illustration. Christ's object was probably twofold, in part retirement, for by the boat he could easily escape to the eastern and comparatively solitary shores of the sea (Matt. 14 : 13), in part labor, for from the prow of the boat, he could preach to the people on the shore, without being hindered by the throng (Luke 5 : 3). We may fairly deduce Christ's fondness for both the water and the mountains, from this and analogous incidents in his ministry.
10. Pressed upon him. Literally, *threw themselves upon him.*—**As many as had plagues.** Literally, *scourges.* Disease was regarded by the Jews as a scourge from God. Not any particular kind of contagious disease is meant; all physical afflictions would be included under the general word here rendered *plagues.*
11, 12. And unclean spirits, *i. e.,* persons possessed with them. See Note on Demoniacal Possession, Matt. 8 : 28-34, p. 123. For the reason of Christ's command to silence, see notes on Matt. 8 : 4; Mark 1 : 25.
13-19. THE CALL AND ORDINATION OF THE TWELVE.—This occurred previous to the events recorded in the preceding part of this chapter. Immediately following this ordination Christ preached the Sermon on the Mount. Matthew gives the ordination of the twelve out of its order, in connection with their first commission to preach the Gospel (Matt. 10 : 1-4); Luke in its proper order (Luke 6 : 13-16). On the ordination of the twelve, see Matt. 10 : 1-4, and notes, and on their individual lives and characters, Note on the Twelve Apostles, Matt. chap. 10, p. 147.
14, 15. Mark states more definitely than either of the other Evangelists the office of the Apostles. They were to be *with* Christ that they might bear personal witness to what they had themselves seen (John 15 : 27; Acts 1 : 21, 22), and Paul rests his claim to be an Apostle on his having been an eye-witness to Christ's resurrection (1 Cor. 9 : 1; 15 : 8, 9); this was their preparation for their work.

17 And James the *son* of Zebedee, and John the brother of James; and he surnamed them Boanerges, which is, The sons of thunder: [j]
18 And Andrew, and Philip, and Bartholomew, and Matthew, and Thomas, and James the *son* of Alphæus, and Thaddæus, and Simon the Canaanite,
19 And Judas Iscariot, which also betrayed him: and they went into an house.
20 And the multitude cometh together again, so [k] that they could not so much as eat bread.
21 And when his friends heard *of it*, they went out to lay hold on him: for they said, He [l] is beside himself.
22 And the scribes which came down from Jerusalem said, He [m] hath Beelzebub, and by the prince of the devils casteth he out devils.
23 And he called them *unto him*, and said unto them in parables, How can Satan cast out Satan?
24 And if a kingdom be divided against itself, that kingdom cannot stand.
25 And if a house be divided against itself, that house cannot stand.
26 And if Satan rise up against himself, and be divided, he cannot stand, but hath an end.

27 No [n] man can enter into a strong man's house, and spoil his goods, unless he will first bind the strong man; and then he will spoil his house.
28 Verily I say unto you, All [o] sins shall be forgiven unto the sons of men, and blasphemies wherewith soever they shall blaspheme:
29 But he that shall blaspheme against the Holy Ghost [p] hath never forgiveness, but is in danger of eternal damnation;
30 Because they said, He hath an unclean spirit.
31 There [q] came then his brethren and his mother, and, standing without, sent unto him, calling him.
32 And the multitude sat about him; and they said unto him, Behold, thy mother and thy brethren without seek for thee.
33 And he answered them, saying, Who is my mother, or my brethren?
34 And he looked round about on them which sat about him, and said, Behold my mother and my brethren!
35 For whosoever shall do [r] the will of God, the same is my brother, and my sister, and mother.

j Isa. 58 : 1 ; Jer. 23 : 29.... k ch. 6 : 31....l Hosea 9 : 7 ; John 10 : 20....m Matt. 9 : 34 ; 10 : 25 ; 12 : 24 ; Luke 11 : 15 ; John 7 : 20 ; 8 : 48, 52 ....n Isa. 49 : 24, 26 ; 61 : 1 ; Matt. 12 : 29....o Matt. 12 : 31 ; Luke 12 : 10... p Heb. 10 : 29....q Matt. 12 : 46-48 ; Luke 8 : 19-21....r James 1 : 25 ; 1 John 2 : 17.

They were to *preach*, literally to *herald, i. e.,* to go before and proclaim the coming of the Messiah, in person to the Jewish nation, in spirit and in power to the whole world, and in his second advent to his church; this was their work. And they were to have *power to heal the sick and cast out devils*, a power subsequently exercised by the Apostles; this was the divine seal and evidence of their authority. In strictness of speech the Apostles can have no successors, for none after that generation can bear personal witness to Christ's life, death, and resurrection, and none can show the miraculous evidence they showed of their authority. But every true minister of the Gospel must be a successor to the Apostles, and read his commission in this verse. He must have Christ with him (Matt. 28 : 20), and testify out of his personal experience to the Christ he knows (Acts 26 : 16 ; 1 Cor. 2 : 12 ; 1 John 4 : 14, 16) ; must act as a herald of the Messiah and Saviour, preaching not himself but the Lord Jesus Christ; and he must attest his divine authority by his power in and through Christ to fulfil Christ's mission of mercy. Luke 4 : 18, 19, with John 19 : 18.

16-19. Simon he surnamed Peter, *i. e., a rock.* This he did previously (John 1 : 42), for Peter and Cephas are different words with the same meaning—the former Greek, the latter Hebrew. The reason for this title Christ explains subsequently (Matt. 16 : 18, note). — **Boanerges.** This word is composed of two Hebrew words signifying "sons of thunder." The reason of this appellation, which appears only here, is not given. It may signify the character and power of James and John as preachers, though their subsequent history does not justify this explanation. More probably it referred to their natural fiery temperament, of which we see signs in Mark 9 : 38 and Luke 9 : 54.—**Judas Iscariot.** See Note on Character, etc., of Judas Iscariot, Matt. 27 : 1-10, p. 303, 304.

19-35. ATTEMPTED INTERRUPTION OF CHRIST'S PREACHING BY BOTH FRIENDS AND FOES. Comp. Matt. 12 : 22-50 and Luke 8 : 19-21; 11 : 14-26. See notes on Matthew for a consideration of the time, p. 166, 172 ; for discussion of Blasphemy against Holy Ghost, pp. 168, 169 ; for attempt by Christ's mother to interrupt his preaching, p. 172.

19-21. And they went into a house. Not, as one might suppose from the English version here, immediately after the ordination by the twelve. The incidents and teachings recorded here took place at a later period in Christ's ministry. See Matt. 12 : 22-37, Prel. Note, p. 166.—**So that they could not so much as eat bread.** That is, Christ and his apostles had no time or opportunity for their ordinary meals.—**And when his kinsfolk heard of it.** The original (οἱ παρ᾽ αὐτοῦ) is ambiguous; it may mean either *companions* or *kinsfolk*. The latter meaning is given by both Robinson and Winer, and better suits the context. The interference here referred to is that attempted by Christ's mother and brethren (ver. 31-35), the intervening verses being parenthetical. At the same time that the Pharisees were attempting to put a stop to Christ's ministry by their accusations, his mother and brethren, thinking that he was carried beyond the bounds of prudence by his religious enthusiasm, endeavored to get him out of the crowd and away from the enmity in which he had involved himself.

23. In parables. That is, with illustrations or in figures. These are reported in verses 24, 25, 27, and another one is added in Matt. 12 : 43-45.

29. Is subject to eternal sin. The received text has here *eternal judgment* (κρίσις), but

CHAPTER IV.

AND[a] he began again to teach by the sea side; and there was gathered unto him a great multitude, so that he entered into a ship, and sat in the sea; and the whole multitude was by the sea on the land.

2 And he taught them many things by parables,[b] and said unto them in his doctrine,

3 Hearken;[c] Behold, there went out a sower to sow:

4 And it came to pass, as he sowed, some fell by the way side, and the[v] fowls of the air came and devoured it up.

5 And some fell on stony[w] ground, where it had not much earth; and immediately it sprang up, because it had no depth of earth:

6 But when the sun was up, it was scorched; and[x] because it had no root, it withered away.

7 And some fell among thorns;[y] and the thorns grew up, and choked it, and it yielded no fruit.

8 And other fell on good[z] ground, and did yield fruit[a] that sprang up and increased; and brought forth, some thirty, and some sixty, and some an hundred.

9 And he said unto them, He that hath ears to hear, let him hear.

10 And[b] when he was alone, they that were about him with the twelve asked of him the parable.

11 And he said unto them, Unto[c] you it is given to know the mystery of the kingdom of God; but unto them that are without,[d] all *these* things are done in parables:

12 That[e] seeing they may see, and not perceive; and hearing they may hear, and not understand; lest at any time they should be converted, and *their* sins should be forgiven them.

13 And he said unto them, Know ye not this parable? and how then will ye know all parables?

14 The sower[f] soweth the word.

15 And these are they by the way side, where the word is sown; but when they have heard, Satan cometh[e] immediately, and taketh away[h] the word that was sown in their hearts.

16 And these are they likewise which are sown on stony ground; who, when they have heard the word, immediately receive it with gladness;

17 And have no root[i] in themselves, and so endure but[j] for a time: afterward, when affliction or persecution ariseth for the word's sake, immediately[k] they are offended.

18 And these are they which are sown among thorns; such as hear the word,

19 And the[l] cares of this world, and the deceitfulness[m] of riches, and the[n] lusts of other things entering in, choke the word, and it becometh unfruitful.[o]

20 And these are they which are sown on good ground: such as hear the word, and receive *it*, and bring forth fruit,[p] some thirtyfold, some sixty, and some an hundred.

21 And he said unto them, Is a candle brought to be put under a bushel, or under a bed? and not to be set on a candlestick?

22 For[q] there is nothing hid, which shall not be manifested; neither was any thing kept secret, but that it should come abroad.

23 If any man have ears to hear, let him hear.

24 And he said unto them, Take heed what ye hear; with[s] what measure ye mete, it shall be measured to you; and unto you that hear shall more be given.

25 For he that hath, to him shall be given: and he that hath not, from[t] him shall be taken even that which he hath.

26 And he said, So[u] is the kingdom of God, as if a man should cast seed into the ground,

<small>k Matt. 13:1, etc... Luke 8:4, etc... t ver. 34; Ps. 78:2... u ver. 9, 23; ch. 7:16... v Gen. 15:11... w Ezek. 11:19; 36:26... x Ps. 1:4; James 1:11... y Jer. 4:3... z Heb. 6:7, 8... a Col. 1:6... b Matt. 13:10, etc... c Ephes. 1:9... d Col. 4:5; 1 Thess. 4:12; 1 Tim. 3:7... e Isa. 6:9, 10; John 12:40; Acts 28:26, 27; Rom. 11:8... f Isa. 32:20; 1 Pet. 1:25... g 1 Pet. 5:8; Rev. 12:9... h Heb. 2:1... i Job 19:28... j Job 27:10... k 2 Tim. 1:15... l Luke 14:18-20; 1 Tim. 6:9, 17; 2 Tim. 4:10... m Prov. 23:5... n 1 John 2:16, 17... o Isa. 5:2, 4... p Rom. 7:4; Col. 1:10; 2 Pet. 1:8... q Eccles. 12:14; Matt. 10:26; Luke 12:2; 1 Cor. 4:5... r 1 Pet. 2:2... s Matt. 7:2... t Luke 8:18... u Matt. 13:24.</small>

Alford and Tischendorf both have *sin* (ἁμάρτημα), and this is undoubtedly the correct reading. Interpreted by John 3:19 and Rev. 22:11, it explains the nature of the penal consequences of which Christ warns the Pharisees, viz., a character given over to hopeless and irredeemable sin.

31-35. See notes on Matt. 12:46-50, for a consideration of the lessons of this incident.

Ch. 4:1-25. PARABLE OF THE SOWER; ITS EXPLANATION; OTHER INSTRUCTIONS. The parable of the sower is found also in Matt. 13:1-23 and Luke 8:4-15. Matthew gives much the fullest report of these parables by the sea. See notes there. The phrases in verse 7, *It yielded no fruit*, and in verse 8, *That sprang up and increased*, are peculiar to Mark. On the explanation by Christ of the reason he used parables (ver 10-12), see Prel. Note to Matt., ch. 13, § 3, p. 173. The language here, "That seeing they may see, and not perceive," etc., is from Isaiah 6:9, 10, but the passage is suggested, not fully cited. The words of the prophet are: "Make the heart of this people fat, and make their ears heavy, and shut their eyes; lest they see," etc., and this language, though in form a command, is in fact simply a prophecy, equivalent to, They will certainly make their own hearts fat, etc. See Henderson on the passage.

Matthew, who repeats Christ's language more fully, gives by his citation both the true meaning of the prophecy and of our Lord's application of it. His meaning is not, These things are done in parables, lest they should be converted, but, Their eyes they have closed, etc., lest at any time they should be converted. That is, men wilfully close their hearts to the truth lest they should be led to repentance and reformation; hence Christ speaks in parables, *that he may gain entrance for the truth* into hearts unwilling to receive it.

21-25. These verses appear in the same connection in Luke 8:16-18, but in Matthew in various passages and in different connections. On verse 21 see Matt. 5:15, note; on verse 22, Matt. 10:26, note; on verse 23, Matt. 11:15, note; on verse 24, Matt. 7:2, note; on verse 25, Matt. 13:12, note. The accompanying illustration shows the candle and candlestick of the

[CH. IV.] MARK. 17

27 And should sleep and rise, night and day, and the seed should spring and grow up, he knoweth not how. 28 For the earth bringeth forth fruit of herself; ᵛ first— the blade, then the ear; after that, the full corn in the ear.

29 But when the fruit is brought forth, immediately he ˣ putteth in the sickle, because the harvest is come. 30 And he said, Whereunto shall we liken the kingdom of God? or with what comparison shall we compare it?

v Gen. 1 : 11, 12....w Eccles. 3 : 1, 11....x Rev. 14 : 15.

East; they are really a lamp and light-stand. The connection of these verses with the rest of the chapter is not very clear. I doubt whether they were spoken at this time; rather surmise that they were incorporated here by Mark and Luke on account of their parabolic character. If they really belong in the discourse by the seaside, their object may be to indicate that, though now the mystery of the Kingdom of God was hid from the people, the Apostles were not to keep it to themselves, as the priests of heathenism the sacred mysteries of their religions, but were to measure it out to others. Observe the practical teaching of verse 24: the way out of skepticism is a ready and unprejudiced hearing of such truth as is made plain; all is not disclosed at once. Observe the difference in phraseology here and in Luke 8 : 18. In Mark, Take heed *what* ye hear; in Luke, *How* ye hear. Both admonitions are important, and both apply to reading as well as hearing.

Ch. 4 : 26-29. PARABLE OF THE SEED GROWING SECRETLY.—DILIGENCE IN SOWING, PATIENCE IN WAITING, PROMPTNESS IN HARVESTING ARE THE CONDITIONS OF A SUCCESSFUL SPIRITUAL HUSBANDRY.

This parable is peculiar to Mark, but belongs with the parable of which Matthew (ch. 13) has given the fullest report. On its relations to those parables, see Prel. Note, § 4, p. 174. It does not exactly correspond to either of the parables there, though analogous in part to those of the tares and the mustard seed. Its general lesson is enforced by parallel passages, *e. g.*, Isaiah 55 : 10, 11; James 5 : 7, 8; 1 Pet. 1 : 23-25. In the kingdom of grace as in nature, we are laborers together with God, the results of our work depend on him, and for the perfection of these results he takes his own time (1 Cor. 3 : 6-9). Hence, (1) it is ours to sow the seed (the truth), his to give it growth; (2) having sown, we are to wait for time and God to perfect it; (3) this he does according to a definite order of development—first the blade, then the ear, then the full corn in the ear; (4) not until there has been time for the development and perfection of the truth are we to expect to reap. The lesson is one of trust and hope; first, for ourselves in our own personal experience; second, for all ministers, Sabbath-school teachers and parents, in working for others. Gal. 5 : 22, 23, describes the fruits of the spirit which grow thus secretly and require time for development and perfection. Ephes. 4 : 15,

and Col. 2 : 6, 7, show the source whence this growth is derived, namely, the Lord Jesus Christ. Phil. 2 : 12, and 2 Pet. 1 : 5, show that though the growth is the work of God, still diligence is required of the spiritual as of the natural husbandman.

26. As if a man should cast seed into the ground. The man of the parable is not Christ; for, (1) it cannot be said of him that "he knoweth not how" the seed springs and grows up; nor does he leave the seed to itself, and "sleep and rise night and day," but, on the contrary, is continually with his church, and by his presence and blessing germinates the truth (Matt. 28 : 18-20); (2) the very point of the parable is to teach that we may throw off the care as to results upon him, not that he throws it off and leaves it to itself. The point of the parable is the *growth*, and the *sower* must be regarded as incidental, either a mere necessary figure to give it life-likeness, or perhaps the human sower, the preacher, teacher, or friend.

27. And should sleep and rise night and day. Sleeping by night, and rising by day to go about other work, leaving the seed to the influences of nature, *i. e.*, to God. But this is no excuse for sleeping by day, *i. e.*, for sloth and carelessness.—**And the seed should spring,** *i. e.*, germinate, **and grow up,** *i. e.*, develop from the germ into the plant. Often the truth, dropped in the heart by a word in public teaching or private conversation, seems to be lost, but getting lodgment germinates in after months or years, seeming to lie meanwhile dead, yet never having lost its power. Often by our impatience to force an immediate growth, or to examine for it, we frustrate our own work.—**He knoweth not how.** Compare John 3 : 8; and observe Christ's emphatic declaration that *how* the truth in the heart produces the results on character we cannot tell. And yet by far the fiercest theological discussions have been concerning this, the unknown in theology, not concerning the practical question, How shall we best inculcate the truth and develop its results? But because we cannot force immediate results from the truth, it does not follow that we are not to watch for results, nor that we are not to foster and cultivate the seed. "We cannot do the saving; but we can do the destroying."—(*Arnot.*) And this either by our mismanagement or our neglect. Compare Matt. 13 : 22.

28. For the earth bringeth forth fruit of

31 *It* is like a grain of mustard seed, which, when it is sown in the earth, is less than all the seeds that be in the earth:
32 But when it is sown, it groweth up, and becometh greater ᶻ than all herbs, and shooteth out great branches; so that the fowls of the air may lodge under the shadow of it.
33 And with many such parables spake he the word unto them, as ᵃ they were able to hear *it*.

34 But without a parable spake he not unto them: and when they were alone, he expounded all things to his disciples.
35 And the same day, when the even was come, he saith unto them, Let us pass over unto the other side.
36 And when they had sent away the multitude, they took him even as he was in the ship: and there were also with him other little ships.

y Matt. 13 : 31, 32; Luke 13 : 18, 19. . . . z Prov. 4 : 18; Isa. 11 : 9; Dan. 2 : 44; Mal. 1 : 11. . . . a John 16 : 12.

---

herself. Literally, *the spontaneous earth bringeth forth fruit.* But the earth is not to be likened to the heart and the conclusion drawn that the latter has a natural power to receive and germinate the truth. For "by nature," *i. e.*, natural growth "we are the children of wrath" (Ephes. 2 : 3). But, as in nature divine forces begin to operate straightway on the seed, so in grace, divine influences begin straightway to fructify the truth. It is ours to study seeds and soils, *i. e.*, to adapt our teaching to the hearts of those before us, and leave the rest to God.—**First the blade,** etc. There is not only a divine development but a definite order of development. Some growths are quicker than others, but *in all there is growth.* And we have no right to look for the end at the beginning, the ripened Christian experience in the young convert, the full corn in the first appearance of the blade. Observe, too, that we can know that there is a growth by its results, though we know not the *how,* and that each stage of the growth is more apparent than the preceding stage. The germ is unseen; the blade of corn is not easily distinguished from that of an unfruitful grass; the ear is more apparent; there is no mistaking the full corn in the ear. "The growing is a secret thing; but the grown ripened grain is visible."—(*Arnot.*)
29. The harvest is come. Not here, as in Matt. 13 : 39, the end of the world; for (1) "*he*" *i. e.*, the sower, not Christ, puts in the sickle; and (2) the language of the verse implies that the appearance of the fruit is the evidence that the harvest has come, and a warrant to the sower to reap (comp. John 4 : 35). I understand, then, that this verse teaches that *whenever* fruit is brought forth (literally, *presents itself*) then is the harvest-time, *i. e.*, whenever the results of religious teaching show themselves in character and conduct, then are the individuals to be gathered into the church, the granary. We are not to wait for a definite time as in nature, before we gather in, but "when the fruit presents itself *immediately*" we are to put in the sickle. Comp. John 4 : 35, 36; Matt. 9 : 37, 38, and Psalm 126 : 6.
30-31. PARABLE OF THE MUSTARD SEED. Comp. Matt. 13 : 31-35, and notes, and Luke 13 : 18, 19. For illustration of Christ's exposition of parables, see Matt. 13 : 36-43, 49, 50; 15 : 15-20.

Ch. 4 : 35-41. STILLING OF THE TEMPEST.—CHRIST THE LORD OVER NATURE. "FAITH IS COURAGEOUS; INCREDULITY IS FEARFUL."
Compare Matt. 8 : 23-27, and Luke 8 : 22-25. The narrative is most graphic here. Matthew indicates for the incident a different point in Christ's ministry. But Mark alone gives a definite note of time, and the best harmonists follow him in placing it immediately after the parables by the sea.
35. On that same day. Immediately preceding occurred the offer of certain persons to follow Christ, and Christ's rejoinder (Matt. 8 : 18-22; Luke 9 : 57-62, notes).—**When the even was come.** The Hebrews reckoned two evenings (Exod. 12 : 6, marg. reading); the first, according to Pharisaic reckoning, began with the declining sun, hence the hour of evening sacrifice was 3 P. M. ; the second, with the setting sun. A like distinction was made by the Greeks between the former and the latter evening. Here, probably, the early evening, *i. e.*, late in the afternoon, is intended, for, notwithstanding the delay occasioned by the storm, Christ found the swineherds watching their swine on the other side of the sea ; probably, therefore, it was then still daylight.—**Let us pass over unto the other side.** That is of the Sea of Galilee. Probably (see Mark 8 : 18) his object was to escape from the multitude and obtain rest. How wearied he was with his labors is indicated by his sleeping through the storm.
36. They took him even as he was. That is, without preparation. Under the mild skies of Palestine it was no hardship to sleep out of doors wrapped in the cloak answering to the modern burnoose (Matt. 5 : 40, note).—**In the ship.** Rather *boat.* In Mark 3 : 9 we are told that one had been provided for Christ and his disciples by Christ's direction, and it is there described more definitely as a *small boat* (πλοιάριον). That it was propelled by oars is evident from John 6 : 19. Josephus designates the fishermen's boats on the sea of Galilee as *skiffs,* a name descriptive of a vessel answering to our modern pinnace, or perhaps launch. Our illustration of the ancient skiff is from a Pompeian painting. Observe the form of the stern, which afforded a convenient rest for the head of the sleeper. Doubtless the skiff in which Christ and his disciples embarked was larger than the one here

MARK.

37 And ^b there arose a great storm of wind, and the waves beat into the ship, so that it was now full.
38 And he was in the hinder part of the ship, asleep on a pillow: and they awake him, and say unto him, Master,^c carest thou not that we perish?
39 And he arose, and rebuked the wind, and said unto the sea, Peace, be still. And ^d the wind ceased, and there was a great calm.
40 And he said unto them, Why are ye so fearful? ^e how is it that ye have no faith?
41 And they feared ^f exceedingly, and said one to another, What manner of man is this, that even the wind and the sea ^g obey him?

b Matt. 8 : 24; Luke 8 : 23....c Ps. 10 : 1; Isa. 40 : 27; Lam. 3 : 8....d Ps. 89 : 9; Lam. 3 : 31, 32....e Ps. 46 : 1, 2; Isa. 43 : 2....
f Jonah 1 : 10, 16 ...g Job 38 : 11.

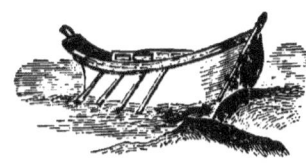

ANCIENT SKIFF.

represented; but the general character was probably the same.—**And there were also with him other boats.** Probably containing some of his audience who embarked to follow him. Compare for a similar following of Christ, Mark 6 : 33. Perhaps in these boats were some of those who had just offered to join the band of Apostles (Matt. 8 : 18-22).

37. And there arose a great storm of wind. The Sea of Galilee lies six hundred feet below the level of the Mediterranean. The snowy peaks of Lebanon are directly to the north. The heated tropical air of the valley is a constant invitation to the cold and heavy winds from the north, which sweep down with great fury and in sudden storms through the ravines of the hills, which converge to the head of the lake, and act like gigantic funnels. See Thomson's *Land and Book*, II : 33. Luke's language, "*There came down a storm of wind*," exactly corresponds to the phenomena of these sudden storms as described by modern travellers. Matthew describes it as a "*great tempest*" or tornado (σεισμός), literally a *shaking* or *concussion*. — **And the waves beat upon the ship,** *i. e.,* beat over it. —**So that it was now filling.** Not full. In Matthew the rendering should be, *was getting covered by the waves*, and in Luke, *was getting filled*. The process of filling was going on. Luke adds that they were *in jeopardy*.

38. And he was in the stern of the boat, asleep on a pillow. Rather a cushion; one such as are used for passengers in our modern row-boats. Bengel's statement that a part of the boat is intended appears to be without any adequate authority. Trench contrasts the sleep of Jesus with that of Jonah (Jonah 1 : 5). "We behold in him exactly the reverse of Jonah; the fugitive prophet asleep in the midst of danger out of a dead conscience, the Saviour out of a pure conscience; Jonah by his presence making the danger, Jesus yielding the pledge and the assurance of deliverance from the danger."—**And they awake him and say unto him.** It is curious and significant that while each of the three Evangelists reports the words with which Christ was awakened, they do not agree. Matthew's report is, *Lord, save us, we perish;* Mark, *Teacher, carest thou not that we perish?* Luke, *Master, Master, we perish.* The difference is not merely verbal; there is also a difference of tone in the three appeals. The first is the language of appeal, the second that of reproach, the third that of importunity aroused by imminent danger. It seems to me impossible to reconcile such variations with the doctrine of verbal inspiration. But they are just what we might expect from honest and independent eye-witnesses. Probably all three feelings were commingled in the disciples, and perhaps all three had expression. Is it asked, Which Evangelist gives the correct account? The answer may be that each gives, in dramatic form, that phase of feeling which was most prominent to his own mind, but neither of them the exact words.

39. And he arose. More literally, *and being awakened.* Note the sudden change from the deep sleep to the scene of confusion and terror. "It is such cases as these—cases of sudden, unexpected terror, met without a moment of preparation—which test a man, what spirit he is of, which show not only his nerve, but the grandeur and purity of his whole nature."—(*Trench.*) —**And rebuked the wind and said unto the sea, Peace, be still.** Literally, *Be muzzled.* I cannot see, with Trench, in this language "a tracing of all the discords and disharmonies in the outward world to their source in a person," *viz.,* Satan; rather a rebuke of that notion, and a distinct implication that the winds and waves are the servants of God, and do his bidding. Mark alone gives the words of command, *Peace, be still.*—**And the wind ceased, and there was a great calm.** The command was addressed to both wind and wave, and *both obeyed.* The stopping of the wind might have been thought an accidental coincidence, for these sudden storms cease as suddenly as they arise. But it always requires time for the sea to subside; here the calm was instant.

40. And he said unto them. There is an-

CHAPTER V.

1 AND[b] they came over unto the other side of the sea, into the country of the Gadarenes.
2 And when he was come out of the ship, immediately there met him out of the tombs a man with an unclean spirit,
3 Who had *his* dwelling[i] among the tombs: and no man could bind him, no, not with chains:
4 Because that he had been often bound with fetters and chains, and the chains had been plucked asunder by him, and the fetters broken in pieces: neither could any *man* tame him.
5 And always, night and day, he was in the mountains, and in the tombs, crying, and cutting himself with stones.
6 But when he saw Jesus afar off, he ran and worshipped[j] him,
7 And cried with a loud voice, and said, What have I to do with thee, Jesus, *thou* Son of the most high God? I adjure thee by God, that thou torment me not.
8 For he said unto him, Come[k] out of the man, *thou* unclean spirit.
9 And he asked him, What *is* thy name? And he answered, saying, My name *is* Legion;[l] for we are many.

b Matt. 8 : 28, etc. ; Luke 8 : 26, etc.... i Isa. 65 : 4.... j Ps. 72 : 9.... k Acts 16 : 18; Heb. 2 : 14; 1 John 3 : 8.... l Matt. 12 : 45.

other instructive difference in the three reports of the Evangelists here. According to Matthew, Christ first rebuked the disciples; according to Mark and Luke, first the sea, then the disciples. According to Matthew he characterizes them as of "*little faith;*" according to Mark he asked, *How have ye no faith?* according to Luke, *Where is your faith?* The spirit of the rebuke is the same in all the accounts; very probably neither has preserved Christ's exact words. That he first stilled the tempest and then addressed his admonition to the disciples seems to me most probable; for during the howling of the storm his admonition could have had but little effect. Observe that it is Matthew, whose representation of the appeal of the disciples is, *Lord save, we perish,* who reports his reply as "Ye of *little* faith." There may have been a glimmering hope in their call, that he who had wrought other miracles could save them from this peril. That they did not *expect* it is evident from the next verse. Trench expresses well their mental state. "They had it (faith) as the weapon which a soldier has, but cannot lay hold of at the moment when he needs it the most. Their sin lay, not in seeking help of him; for this indeed became them well; but in the *excess* of their terror." It must not, however, be forgotten that the peril was, in seeming, imminent. Nothing less would have terrified these fishermen, accustomed to the perils of the sea.

41. And they feared exceedingly. Matthew says, *The men feared,* which Alford interprets as "the men who were in the ship, besides our Lord and his disciples." But there is no indication that there were any other men. See ver. 36. That his disciples should be astonished at the miracle accords with what is said of them on other occasions (Matt. 16 : 6, 7 ; Mark 6 : 52 ; John 6 : 5-9 ; 20 : 25).

The direct lesson of this incident appears to me to be that Christ is the Lord of nature, that we may trust him in times of peril from wind, or lightning, or wave, or earthquake. He does not always deliver; but always the winds and the sea obey him. Compare the O. T. teaching of Psalms 89 : 8, 9 ; 93 : 4. Contrast with his command to nature Elijah's prayer to the God of nature (James 5 : 17, 18). The commentators have delighted to treat this incident allegorically. Thus Augustine : "We are sailing in this life as through a sea, and the wind rises, and storms of temptation are not wanting. Whence is this, save because Jesus is sleeping in thee. If he were not sleeping in thee, thou wouldest live calm within. But what means this, that Jesus is sleeping in thee, save that thy faith, that which is from Jesus, is slumbering in thine heart? What shalt thou do to be delivered? Arouse him, and say, Master, we perish. He will awaken; that is, thy faith will return to thee, and abide with thee always. When Christ is awakened, though the tempest beat into, yet it will not fill thy ship; thy faith will now command the winds and the waves, and the danger will be over." So again Quesnel: "The ship in the midst of the sea is an emblem of the church in the midst of the world. We ought to expect to meet with tempests in the church, and to see it covered with waves." "The waves of heresy toss it from without; but the corruption of manners within, like the water which beat into this ship, puts it in much greater danger of perishing." Carrying out this allegory, we may observe, (1) Christ's presence does not prevent our ship of life from being endangered; but if he is with us it cannot be wrecked. (2.) Our unuttered but often heart-felt reproaches of a seemingly indifferent Christ, "Carest thou not that we perish?" are always unjust. (3.) To timid disciples, who imagine, because of sudden and serious storms, that all is lost for themselves, their children, the nation, or the church, Christ still says, Why are ye fearful? How is it that ye have no faith? (4.) He does not always bring the help he might, nor as soon as he might (comp. Mark 6 : 48 ; John 11 : 6). But he asks us to trust him alike when he comes and when he tarries, when he seems to be watching and when he seems to be sleeping.

Ch. 5 : 1-21. CURE OF THE GADARENE DEMONIAC. Matt. 8 : 28-35 ; Luke 8 : 26-39. See notes on Matthew, where I have discussed, briefly,

CH. V.]   MARK.   21

10 And he besought him much, that he would not send them away out of the country.
11 Now there was there, nigh unto the mountains, a great herd of swine [m] feeding.
12 And all the devils besought [n] him, saying, Send us into the swine, that we may enter into them.
13 And forthwith Jesus gave [o] them leave. And the unclean spirits went out, and entered into the swine: and the herd ran violently down a steep place into the sea, (they were about two thousand,) and were choked in the sea.
14 And they that fed the swine fled, and told it in the city, and in the country. And they went out to see what it was that was done.
15 And they come to Jesus, and see him that was possessed with the devil, and [p] had the legion, sitting, and clothed, and in his right mind: and they were afraid.[q]

16 And they that saw it, told them how it befell to him that was possessed with the devil, and also concerning the swine.
17 And they began to pray him to depart [r] out of their coasts.
18 And when he was come into the ship, he that had been possessed with the devil prayed him that he might be with him.
19 Howbeit, Jesus suffered him not, but saith unto him, Go home to thy friends, and [s] tell them how great things the Lord hath done for thee, and hath had compassion on thee.
20 And he departed, and began to publish in Decapolis how great things Jesus had done for him: and all men did marvel.
21 And when Jesus was passed over again by ship unto the other side, much people gathered unto him: and he was nigh unto the sea.

m Lev. 11 : 7, 8; Deut. 14 : 8....n Job 1 : 10, 12; 2 : 5, 6....o Rev. 13 : 7; 1 Pet. 3 : 22; Job 6 : 26....p Isa. 49 : 25; Col. 1 : 13....
q Job 13 : 11; Ps. 14 : 5; 2 Tim. 1 : 7....r Job 21 : 14; Luke 5 : 8; Acts 16 : 39....s Ps. 66 : 16; Isa. 38 : 19.

the phenomena of demoniacal possession, p. 12 '. Matthew mentions two possessed of devils, Mark and Luke but one. On this discrepancy see notes on Luke.

3–6. This description of the possessed is more detailed, definite, and graphic than is afforded by either of the other Evangelists. Matthew attempts no description ; Luke's is briefer. The great muscular strength, and the habit of self-wounding here referred to, are not uncommon in certain cases of modern lunacy. Luke adds that "he wore no clothes;" and the propensity to go entirely naked is also characteristic of certain forms of mental disease. The tombs are not infrequently used in Palestine by certain of the poorer classes as dwelling-places. Their character (caves cut in the rock) makes them a perfect shelter. Tombs are found in the immediate vicinity of Gersa, the scene of this miracle. The annexed cut of such a tomb is from *The New Testament Illustrated*.

10. That he would not send them out of the country. Equivalent to, "That he would not command them to go out into the deep," that is, back into their prison-house. See Luke 8 : 31, note.

18–20. On this request and Christ's reply, see note on Luke 8 : 38, 39. It is not mentioned by Matthew.—**Decapolis.** See note on Matt. 4 : 25.

Ch. 5 : 22–43. CURE OF THE WOMAN WITH AN ISSUE OF BLOOD.—RAISING OF JAIRUS' DAUGHTER.—CHRIST'S CURE OF SUPERSTITION.—CHRIST'S INTERPRETATION OF DEATH.

Compare Matt. 9 : 18–26, and Luke 8 : 41–56.

ROCK CUT TOMB AT GADARA.

Matthew gives a definite note of time, from which it appears that these miracles immediately followed the feast made by Matthew or Levi to Christ (Matt. 9 : 18). But when that feast was given is not

22 And, behold, there cometh one of the rulers of the synagogue, Jairus by name; and when he saw him, he fell at his feet,
23 And besought him greatly, saying, My little daughter lieth at the point ⁿ of death: *I pray thee*, come and lay thy hands on her, that she may be healed; and she shall live.
24 And *Jesus* went with him; and much people followed him, and thronged him.
25 And a certain woman, which had an issue ᵛ of blood twelve years,
26 And had suffered many things of many physicians, and had spent all that she had, and was nothing ʷ bettered, but rather grew worse,
27 When she had heard of Jesus, came in the press behind, and touched ˣ his garment:
28 For she said, If I may touch but his clothes, I shall be whole.
29 And straightway the fountain of her blood was dried up: and she felt in *her* body that she was healed of that plague.
30 And Jesus, immediately knowing in himself that virtue ʸ had gone out of him, turned him about in the press, and said, Who touched my clothes?

t Matt. 9 : 18, etc.; Luke 8 : 41, etc.....u Ps. 107 : 18....v Lev. 15 : 19, etc....w Job 13 : 4; Ps. 106 : 12; Jer. 30 : 12, 13....x 2 Kings 13 : 21; Matt. 14 : 36; Acts 5 : 15; 19 : 12....y Luke 6 : 19.

so clear (see Matt. 9 : 9-13, Prel. Note, p. 127). There is some difference in the accounts of the three Evangelists, those of Mark and Luke being much fuller than that of Matthew. The comparison of these three accounts is instructive, and indicates the independence of the narrators, while their substantial accord sustains their trustworthiness. The more important differences are noted below.

22. One of the rulers of the synagogue. That is, one of the board of presbyters or elders who managed the affairs of the synagogue; probably the chief or president of the board. See Matt. 4 : 23, note.—**He fell at his feet.** Matthew's language, *worshipped him*, is interpreted by the language here and in Luke. See Matt. 8 : 2, note.

23, 24. My little daughter. She was an only daughter, twelve years old (Luke 8 : 42).—**Lieth at the point of death.** Matthew reports Jairus as saying, "My daughter is even now dead." But Matthew makes no mention of the delegation described here in verse 35, which reported her death. He probably embodied the two appeals in one, giving a summary of the events which Mark and Luke more fully describe. Luke's language is, "She lay a dying."—**And she shall live.** He speaks with an assurance of faith.—**And much people followed him.** Perhaps drawn by curiosity to see whether he could heal the maiden. This would furnish an additional reason for Christ's exclusion of all from the room (ver. 40).

25-29. An issue of blood. A hemorrhage, either from the bowels or the womb, probably the latter. A private note from Dr. William H. Thomson, of New York, to me, in reply to a question on this subject, states the reasons for this opinion to be, (1) that the latter disease is much more common with females than the former; (2) that certain peculiar conditions produce prolonged attacks of uterine hemorrhage, which are still unmanageable by the most proficient members of the profession, and that Lev., ch. 15, contains severe regulations concerning the latter, but says nothing concerning the former disease. He adds the noteworthy suggestion:
"I think the circumstances of the N. T. narrative render the inference almost certain that this account was meant for the consolation of those multitudes of stricken women, in all ages, who seem to be afflicted with sorrows in very unequal measure, compared with the stronger, and so generally also the more depraved, sex."—**And had suffered many things of many physicians.** Medicine was not in that age a science; disease was exorcised by charms; the physicians resembled in knowledge and practice the medicine-man of the North American Indians. See Abbott's *Jesus of Nazareth*, pp. 157, 158. Lightfoot gives an account of some of the prescriptions contained in the Rabbinical books for this disease. One will suffice to illustrate the sort of things she had suffered from the physicians: "Let them dig seven ditches, in which let them burn some cuttings of such vines as are not circumcised (*i. e.*, are not yet four years old); let her take in her hand a cup of wine; let them lead her away from this ditch, and make her sit down over that; let them remove her from that, and make her sit down over another. In every removal you must say to her, 'Arise for thy flux.'"—**But rather grew worse.** Observe her sorrowful condition, sick, impoverished, helpless.—**Touched his garment.** Matthew and Luke say, "The hem of his garment." This was a peculiar fringe, required by the law (Numb. 15 : 37-40; Deut. 22 : 12). The Jews paid to it a superstitious reverence (Matt. 23 : 5, note and illus.). Sharing this superstition, and imagining that Christ healed by a sort of magic, this woman touched it in hope of cure. An ordinary teacher would have rebuked her superstition; Christ used it to teach her better. Observe that Christ complied with Jewish law and Jewish usage in his attire.—**For she said.** "Within herself" (Matt. 9 : 21).—**She was hea'ed.** Compare Mark 6 : 56; Luke 6 : 19, for similar cases of healing, in all of which, however, says Olshausen, "the cures plainly appear to be actions of his (Christ's) will." See, also, Acts 5 : 15; 19 : 12.

30. Jesus immediately knowing that power had gone out of him. According to Luke, he said, "I perceive that power is gone

31 And his disciples said unto him, Thou seest the multitude thronging thee, and sayest thou, Who touched me?
32 And he looked round about to see her that had done this thing.
33 But the woman, fearing and trembling, knowing what was done in her, came and fell down before him, and told [a] him all the truth.
34 And he said unto her, Daughter, thy faith [a] hath made thee whole: go [b] in peace, and be whole of thy plague.

[a] Ps. 30 : 2... a ch. 10 : 52; Acts 14 : 9... b 1 Sam. 1 : 17; 20 : 42; 2 Kings 5 : 19.

out of me." He consciously put forth the power for her healing. The idea that the woman was healed by the garment and without the conscious will of Christ, repeats the superstition of the woman, which this incident is recorded to correct. Christ, not his garment, healed. See below, *Lessons of this incident*.—**And said, Who touched my clothes?** Not because he was ignorant, for his searching glance showed to the woman that she was not hid from him (Luke 8 : 47), but to draw out her confession of her faith. For illustration of similar questions, see Gen. 3 : 9; 4 : 9; 2 Kings 5 : 25; Luke 24 : 19. Olshausen and Trench compare the question to that of "a father coming among his children, and demanding, Who committed this fault? himself conscious, even while he asks, but at the same time willing to bring the culprit to a free confession, and so to put him in a pardonable state."

31. His disciples said unto him. Peter was the spokesman (Luke 9 : 45). The commentators have noted the difference between *thronging* Christ and *touching* him. "Many throng Christ; his is name; near to him outwardly; in actual contact with the sacraments and ordinances of his church; yet not touching him, because not drawing nigh in faith, not looking for, and therefore not obtaining, life and healing from Him." —(*Trench*.) The contrasted notes of Wordsworth and Alford on this verse are so suggestive that I transcribe them both. "A solemn warning to all who crowd on Christ; who use his name lightly and profanely; who make familiar addresses to him in so-called religious hymns; who treat with carelessness and irreverence his day, his house, his sacraments, his ministers; or who read his holy Scriptures in a carping spirit, handling them as a common book. Although such as these may crowd upon Christ in his word, with a pressure of earthly labor and learning, they never *touch* him."—(*Wordsworth*.) "It is difficult to imagine how the miracle should be, as Dr. Wordsworth, 'a solemn warning to all who crowd on Christ;' or how such a forbidding to come to him could be reconciled with 'Come unto me, all ye that labor.' Rather should we say, seeing it was one of those that thus crowded on him who obtained grace from him, that it is a blessed encouragement to us not only to crowd on him, but even to touch him; so to crowd on him as never to be content until we have grasped, if it be but his garment, for ourselves; not to despise or discourage any of the least of those who make familiar addresses to him in so-called religious hymns, seeing that thus some of them may touch him to the healing of their souls. I much fear that if my excellent friend had been keeping order among the multitude on the way to the house of Jairus, this poor woman would never have been allowed to get near to Jesus. But I hope and trust that he and I shall rejoice together one day in his presence, amidst a greater crowd, whom no man can number, of all nations and kindreds and peoples and tongues."—(*Alford*.)

32. To see her who had done this thing. Observe, not to see *who* had done it, *i. e.*, inquiringly, but to see *her who had done it*. The implication is that she was already known to him.

33, 34. The woman fearing and trembling. If the hemorrhage was from the womb, the woman would be ceremonially unclean, and whoever touched her would be unclean until even (Lev. 15 : 25, 27). Perhaps the woman feared Christ's anger, and his rebuke for polluting him by her touch, or possibly, the indignation of others in the crowd, in which she had joined, without in any way indicating her uncleanness. It thus showed a very considerable confidence in him, to throw herself upon his compassion and tell all, as she did.—**Knowing what was done in her.** And that "she was not hid" (Luke 8 : 47). —**Thy faith hath made thee whole.**—Because by faith she had laid hold on Christ who had made her whole. Compare Ephes. 2 : 8. "More than once a person first learned that he had faith when the Saviour told him of it."— (*Bengel*.)—**Go in peace.** So the healing was to mind as well as to body. Go, not fearing and trembling, nor in uneasiness lest the trouble return.—**Be whole of thy plague,** *i. e.*, permanently whole. These words are Christ's assurance that the relief is not temporary but final.

Lesson of this incident. To suppose that virtue resided in Jesus' garment, not in his will, is to wholly miss the meaning of this incident. The woman superstitiously reverenced the sacred fringe and pressed forward to touch it, hoping so to be healed. Christ knowing her approach cured her, not by touch, or even word, but by a mere act of will. Then, when she was healed, he turned him about, fixed his eye upon her, then made manifest to her that she was not hid and by his question called forth a public

35 While he yet spake, there came from the ruler of the synagogue's *house, certain* which said, Thy daughter is dead:[c] why troublest thou the Master any further?
36 As soon as Jesus heard the word that was spoken, he saith unto the ruler of the synagogue, Be not afraid, only [d] believe.

37 And he suffered no man to follow him, save [e] Peter, and James, and John the brother of James.
38 And he cometh to the house of the ruler of the synagogue, and seeth the tumult, and them that wept and wailed greatly.
39 And when he was come in, he saith unto them, Why make ye this ado, and weep? the damsel is not dead, but sleepeth.[f]

c John 5 : 25 ; 11 : 25....d 2 Chron. 20 : 20 ; Job 11 : 40....e ch. 9 : 2 ; 14 : 33....f John 11 : 11-13.

---

confession from her who, before the healing, lacked the courage to make it. So interpreted I find in it these lessons : (1.) It is not merely *intelligent* faith which saves, but *faith*, even when mated to and marred by superstition. The superstitious reverence which regards the hem of Christ's garment is better than the supercilious wisdom which rejects Christ himself. "This is a most encouraging miracle for us to recollect when we are disposed to think despondingly of the ignorance or superstition of much of the Christian world; that he who accepted this woman for her faith, even in error and weakness, may also accept them."—(*Alford*.) (2.) The proper method of dealing with and curing honest superstition, viz., not by attacking the superstition, but by encouraging the faith which underlies it, and directing that faith from the material object to the living Christ. Compare Paul's course in Athens, Acts 17 : 22, 23, note, and apply to our dealings with honest Romanists whose faith in the hem of Christ's garment is sometimes a rebuke to our doubt of Christ himself. (3.) Christ's tenderness with the weak and the ignorant. "A bruised reed will he not break." Ignorance and error need never keep the soul from him. "It would have been too hard to have required her, before her cure, to speak openly in the presence of the people. Our gracious Lord, therefore, softened the difficulty by making this demand subsequent to the cure, and thus helped her along the narrow way."—(*Olshausen*.) (4.) But he required an open confession, a very striking illustration of the truth that "Christ will have himself openly confessed, and not only secretly sought; that our Christian life is not, as it is sometimes called, merely a thing between ourselves and God; but a good confession to be witnessed 'before all the people' (Luke 8 : 47)."—(*Alford*.) Comp. Matt. 10 : 32; 1 Tim. 6 : 12.

35, 36. There came * * * certain. According to Luke, a single messenger; Mark's language indicates more than one. Probably others, volunteers, accompanied the messenger.—**Thy daughter is dead.** It is clear, then, that the immediate friends did not believe in the modern theory that this was a case of syncope.—**Why troublest thou the Master?** This might be the language of those who truly recog-

nize in Jesus a Master. I should rather regard it as an indication that only the ruler had faith in Christ, and that his friends, who could not dissuade him from appealing to our Lord while his daughter lived, hoped to do so by the report of her death. The language of verse 40 confirms this opinion.—**As soon as Jesus had overheard.** The original in the best MSS. indicate that the message was not intended for Jesus, but was overheard by him. Tischendorf renders it, *Having casually heard the word*; Alford, *Having straightway overheard*. It is noted that Christ anticipates the ruler and speaks words of cheer, before the latter can give expression to doubt and fear.—**Be not afraid; only believe.** Luke adds, "And she shall be made whole."

37. The whole multitude, doubtless, followed Jesus to the house. It was after the exclusion of the mourners (verse 40) that he suffered only the three disciples and the parents to go with him into the room where the dead lay. This is the first time, but not the last, that peculiar honor was conferred upon these three. Comp. Mark 9 : 2; 14 : 33. Why this choice among the chosen twelve? We can no more answer, than we can tell why, in this day, Christ discriminates in his gifts to his church. We can only say, It is his will.

38. Them that wept and wailed greatly. Including professional mourners, in Matthew designated as "minstrels." "In the Orient, yet more than with us, mourning customs are conventional. Fashion dictates them. The friends of the dead beat their breasts, make the house resound with their lamentations, cover their heads, cut their flesh, put on the habiliments of grief, and rend their garments. There are with them, as with us, various shades of grief nicely expressed in external symbol. The length of the rent in the garments is accurately determined by the relation of the deceased. Professional women, skilful in the simulation of grief, are hired to swell the songs of lamentation on these occasions (Jer. 9 : 17, 18; Amos 5 : 16). Acquainting themselves with the private sorrows of their auditors, and interweaving in their chants the story of their woes, they evoke their tears, and thus add amateur to professional weeping. Such was the scene which Christ found enacted in the house of the prelate when he arrived."—(*Abbott's Jesus of Nazareth*.) Playing of dirges on flutes

40 And they laughed him to scorn. But when he had put them all out, he taketh the father and the mother of the damsel, and them that were with him, and entereth in where the damsel was lying.
41 And he took the damsel by the hand, and said unto her, Talitha cumi: which is, being interpreted, Damsel, I say unto thee, arise.⁵

42 And straightway the damsel arose, and walked; for she was *of the age* of twelve years. And they were astonished with a great astonishment.
43 And he charged ʰ them straitly that no man should know it; and commanded that something should be given her to eat.

g Acts 9 : 40....h ch. 3 : 12 ; Matt. 9 : 4 ; 12 : 16-19 ; Luke 5 : 14.

or other instruments accompanied this professional mourning. Similar customs prevailed in Greece and Rome, and to the present day exist in Ireland. In France and Italy professional mourners are also employed in the funerals of the wealthy. The annexed cut, from an ancient sarcophagus, represents three professional mourners in the attitudes and actions of grief. Christ's act in excluding these mourners from the house, is a protest against conventional and hypocritical grief.

ANCIENT MOURNING-WOMEN.

39. **Not dead but sleepeth.** Even so evangelical a writer as Olshausen has taken this literally, and supposed the case of the maiden to be one of syncope. But, according to Lightfoot, it was a common thing among the rabbis to express the idea of death by the metaphor of sleep. Christ's language here is not more explicit than in John 11 : 11. Comp. Deut. 31 : 16 ; 1 Thess. 4 : 13. The whole account of this incident is inconsistent with the idea that the maiden was simply raised from slumber or a fainting fit. She is reported dead by the messenger (ver 35); is known to be dead to the bystanders (Luke 8 : 53); on Christ's taking her by the hand her spirit returns to her again (Luke 8 : 55 ; comp. 1 Kings 17 : 21, 22), though this does not of itself necessarily imply her death (comp. Judges 15 : 19); and the account of the cure (ver. 42, note) implies, not a natural awakening from sleep, but a miraculous resurrection from the dead. It seems to me unquestionable that the historian believed in the death, and the miraculous resurrection from the dead, of this maiden.

40. **And they laughed him to scorn.** Because they knew that she was dead (Luke 8 : 53). Chrysostom suggests that it was Christ's object to impress upon the minds of the people the death of the maiden, that he might anticipate the objection of subsequent unbelievers that she was not dead; and he quotes as parallel the cases of Moses and his rod (Exod. 4 : 2), and of Lazarus (John 11 : 34, 39).—**When he had put them all out.** From a comparison of the three accounts, it would appear that the minstrels were in an outer room ; Christ stops the mourning, orders the mourners to leave, and then enters the inner room where the damsel is, accompanied only by the parents and the three disciples. The reason of this exclusion, and of the prohibition of verse 43, is, he will not have the faith of the people rest on his miracle. Meyer observes that Christ never forbids that men should know his teaching. He has no mysteries in his doctrines which he hides from the public. Observe the incidental evidence of the father's faith ; though the maiden is dead, he allows the mourning to be stopped and the mourners to be sent away. Christ is truly "master" in this house.

41. **Talitha cumi.** This is Aramaic, the language generally spoken by the common people in Palestine at the time of Christ. Its presence here, and in Mark 7 : 34 and 15 : 34, is an indication that Christ used this language in his ordinary intercourse with the Jews. But sometimes, as in his conference with Pilate, he must probably have used the Greek. The indication of verbal fidelity in this report is considered an evidence that Mark derived his report from Peter, who was an ear-witness.—**Damsel awake.** "I say unto thee" is properly put in parenthesis ; it is not in the original Aramaic phrase, but is added as an interpretation by the Evangelist. The word which I have rendered *awake* is different from that translated *arise* in the following verse.

42, 43. **And straightway;** not after a time, as if arousing from a trance, or as in the case of the boy raised by the prayer of Elisha (2 Kings 4 : 34, 35).—**The damsel arose;** the verb is the same used in the N. T. in describing undoubted resurrection from the dead (Luke 16 : 31 ; John 6 : 54 ; 11 : 23, 24 ; 20 : 9) ; **and walked;** an evidence of the completeness of her restoration. One who had been at the point of death (ver. 23), and was simply aroused from syncope, could not have walked, except by the miraculous imparta-

CHAPTER VI.

AND he went out from thence, and came into his own country; and his disciples follow him.

2 And[1] when the sabbath day was come, he began to teach in the synagogue: and many, hearing *him*, were astonished, saying, From[j] whence hath this *man* these things? and what wisdom *is* this which is given unto him, that even such mighty works are wrought by his hands?

3 Is not this the carpenter, the son of Mary, the brother of James,[k] and Joses, and of Juda, and Simon? and are not his sisters here with us? And they were offended[l] at him.

---

l Matt. 13 : 54, etc.; Luke 4 : 16, etc. . . . j John 6 : 42, . . . k Gal. 1 ; 19, . . . l Matt. 11 ; 6.

---

tion of strength. The command to give her something to eat evidenced the reality of the resurrection; it was a tangible proof to the parents that it was no apparition they saw. Comp. Luke 24 : 30; John 20 : 27; 21 : 13. Perhaps it was given in part to prevent too great revulsion of feeling in the parents, by giving them something to do. Comp. John 11 : 44.—**They were astonished.** Luke says, "Her parents."— **That no man should know it.** Matthew, who describes this event from the position of one without, and gives less details, says that the fame of the miracle went abroad.

There are three specific cases of resurrection from the dead wrought by Christ—this, that of the son of the widow of Nain (Luke 7 : 11–18), and that of Lazarus (John, ch. 11). In the first the miracle is performed immediately after death; in the second, at least twenty-four hours after death, and during the passage of the funeral procession to the grave; in the third, four days after burial, and after corruption would naturally have commenced; in the first case privately, in the second before the people, in the third before embittered enemies; in each case by a word, with no effort, with no appeal to God, though in the case of Lazarus with a public acknowledgment to God. Thus Christ shows his power to destroy the last enemy, which is death. "Let no man, therefore, beat himself any more, nor wail, neither disparage Christ's achievement. For indeed he overcame death. Why then dost thou wail for nought? The thing is become a sleep. Why lament and weep?"—(*Chrysostom*.)

Ch. 6 : 1–6. CHRIST REJECTED AGAIN AT NAZARETH. Matt. 13 : 53–58. See notes there. He had been rejected by the Nazarenes once before (Luke 4 : 14–29, and notes).

2, 3. Whence hath this man these things? This question of the Nazarenes uttered in contempt, we may repeat in seriousness, to the unbelief of to-day, which accounts Jesus of Nazareth only a carpenter's son.— **The carpenter.** The implication is, that he actually worked with his father at the trade; and it is confirmed by the fact that every father was required by Jewish custom, to teach his son a trade, that he might be able by his industry to earn an independent livelihood. The fact is itself a rebuke of the unchristian pride which despises mechanical employments. The Jews derived their civilization largely from Egypt; therefore the annexed cut, representing the tools of an Egyptian carpenter, the originals of which are now in the British Museum (see *Wilkinson's Egypt*, II, 112), probably gives a just idea of the general

EGYPTIAN CARPENTER'S TOOLS.

1, 2, 3, 4. Chisels and drills.
5. Part of drill.
6. Nut of wood belonging to drill.
7, 8. Saws.
9. Horn of oil.
10. Mallet.
11. Bag for nails.
12. Basket which held the tools.

4 But Jesus said unto them,ᵐ A prophet is not without honour, but in his own country, and among his own kin, and in his own house.
5 Andⁿ he could there do no mighty work, save that he laid his hands upon a few sick folk, and healed *them*.
6 And he marvelledᵒ because of their unbelief. Andᵖ he went round about the villages, teaching.
7 Andᵍ he called *unto him* the twelve, and began to send them forth by two and two, and gave them power over unclean spirits;
8 And commanded them that they should take nothing for *their* journey, save a staff only; no scrip, no bread, no money in *their* purse:

9 But *be* shodʳ with sandals;ˢ and not put on two coats.
10 And he said unto them, In what place soever ye enter into an house, there abide till ye depart from that place.
11 And whosoever shall not receive you, nor hear you, when ye depart thence, shakeᵗ off the dust under your feet for a testimony against them. Verily I say unto you, It shall be more tolerable for Sodom and Gomorrah in the day of judgment, than for that city.
12 And they went out, and preached that men should repent.ᵘ
13 And they cast out manyᵛ devils, and anointed with oilʷ many that were sick, and healed *them*.

m Matt. 13 : 57; John 4 : 44 ...n ch. 9 : 23; Gen. 19 : 22....o Isa. 59 : 16; Jer. 2 : 12....p Matt. 9 : 35; Luke 13 : 22; Acts 10 : 38....q ch. 3 : 13, etc.; Matt. 10 : 1, etc.; Luke 9 : 1, etc.; 10 : 3, etc....r Ephes. 6 : 15....s Acts 12 : 8....t Neh. 5 : 13; Acts 13 : 51....u Luke 24 : 47; Acts 2 : 38; 3 : 19....v Luke 10 : 17....w James 5 : 14.

nature of the tools used in Joseph's carpenter's shop in Nazareth.

4. Not without honor but in his own country. A superficial knowledge of Jesus may prevent a truer and more spiritual acquaintance with him.

5. And he could there do no mighty work. Matthew states definitely the reason, "because of their unbelief" (Matt. 13 : 58). Alford says, "The want of ability here spoken of is not *absolute* but *relative*. The same voice which could still the tempest, could anywhere and under any circumstances have commanded diseases to obey; but in most cases of human infirmity, it was our Lord's practice to require faith in the recipient of aid, and that being wanting, the help could not be given." Similarly Theophylact, "Not that he was weak, but that they were faithless." But is this all? May we not say that among the conditions to which Christ subjected himself on earth was this, that he put forth his powers of healing only as a means of spiritual development, and only, therefore, to those in whom at least a germ of faith was awakened; and that this being wanting, he could not heal, without violating the fundamental principle of his life? Nay, may we not go further and think it at least probable, since Christ always called for the exercise of faith in the patient, that his miraculous cures were not wrought merely by the exercise of a physical power on the body, but in a considerable measure through the connection of mind and body, the healing power of Christ having, by the very constitution of human nature, to act on the mental or spiritual nature, before it could prove effectual on the body, and hence it could not prove effectual except as the sufferer exercised faith? And may we not say further, that this essential principle still holds good, that, by its very nature, his salvation can be made available only to such as are willing in humble trust to accept it, and that where that trust is wanting, it is still true that Christ cannot do the mighty work of salvation? The language employed here does not *necessarily* imply a literal want of power, as is evident from the analogous expression in Gen. 32 : 25. That the divine remedy is in fact efficacious only where there is faith to receive it, is illustrated and enforced by many passages of Scripture. See, for examples, Isaiah 59 : 1, 2; Mark 9 : 23; Hebrews 4 : 2.

6. He marveled. Their unbelief was a real wonder to him. Compare Matt. 8 : 10, note.— **He went round about the villages.** See Matt. 9 : 35, note.

7-13. CHRIST'S COMMISSION OF THE TWELVE. Matt. 10 : 1-42; Luke 9 : 1-6. The account is much the fullest in Matthew. See notes there. According to Matthew they were not to provide a *staff*; here one is permitted. The true explanation is, that they were to go as they were, without providing a staff for the journey, but using one if they already possessed it. The *scrip* was a bag used for carrying food, answering to the modern haversack. For *bread*, they were to depend on the hospitality of the villages (Matt. 10 : 11-14). The "*money*" here is, literally, *brass* or *copper*; even the smallest money was not to be provided by them. In Matthew they are directed not to wear *shoes*; here, to be shod with sandals. The shoe of the ancients resembled the modern shoe; the sandal was simply a sole of leather, felt, cloth, or wood bound upon the feet by thongs, the shoe-latchet of Mark 1 : 7. The former was for more delicate use. See Matt. 10 : 10, note. Our illustrations show the staff and the scrip of the East, and the ancient shoes and sandals. With the staff and scrip is also represented a leather or skin bottle, such as travelers often used for carrying liquids on journeys where water was likely to be inaccessible. The reference to anointing with oil (ver. 13) is peculiar to Mark. Oil was in the O. T. a symbol of divine grace, and anointing with oil a symbol of the gift of the Spirit. See Matt. 25 : 1-13, Prel. Note. Anointing with oil appears here to have been used as a means of teaching the lesson that the healing was wrought by the disciples, not as necromancers—with whom they might otherwise have been confounded, but as Apostles

14 And ᵏ king Herod heard *of him;* (for his name was spread abroad ;) and he said, That John the Baptist was risen from the dead, and therefore mighty works do shew forth themselves in him.
15 Others ʸ said, That it is Elias. And others said, That it is a prophet, or as one of the prophets.

16 But when Herod heard *thereof,* he said, It is John, whom I beheaded; he is risen from the dead.
17 For Herod himself had sent forth and laid hold upon John, and bound him in prison, for Herodias' sake, his brother Philip's wife: for he had married her.

g Matt. 14 : 1, etc.; Luke 9 : 7, etc. . . . y ch. 8 : 28; Matt. 16 : 14.

of the Lord, and through the gift of his grace. It is evident from the general tenor of the instructions that the oil was not taken by them, but was such as they found at the houses. The practice of using oil in this way was practiced long after (James 5 : 14). There is nothing in this passage to justify the extreme unction of the Romish Church, for that is administered in the

SHOES.

STAFF, SCRIP, AND SKIN BOTTLE.

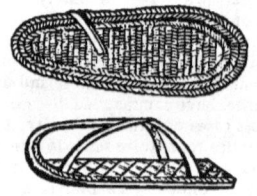

SANDALS.

hour of death, to prepare the soul spiritually for the last great change; this in case of sickness, as a symbol of the miraculous gift of restoration of the body to health.

11-29. The Death of John the Baptist. Matt. 14 : 1-12; Luke 9 : 7-9. See notes on Matthew. Luke refers to, but does not describe the death of John the Baptist. Mark gives some particulars not given in Matthew. From his account we learn that it was Herodias who instigated the imprisonment of John (ver. 17), that Herod was kept back from earlier putting John to death, not only by a fear of the people (Matt. 14 : 5), but also by a real regard for the prophet (ver. 20), that the snare for the king was laid by the mother (ver. 21, and), that the maiden went and asked counsel of her mother before preferring her request for the head of the prophet, and that he was beheaded by one of the Tetrarch's body-guard (ver. 27, note). On the true chronology, see Matt. 11 : 1.

14. And king Herod heard of him. In strictness of speech he was *Tetrarch*, not king. Matt. 14 : 1.—**His name was spread abroad.** Increasingly so by the mission of the twelve.

15. A prophet, like one of the prophets. The conjunction *or* is not in the original. Alford gives the meaning well: "He is not the Prophet for whom all are waiting, but only some prophet like those who have gone before."

17. Bound him in prison. This prison, as we learn from Josephus, was in the fortified citadel of Machærus. See Matt. 11 : 2, note. Recent investigations have brought to light the ruins of this fortress, and even the dungeons connected with it. Mr. Tristram (*Land of Moab,* p. 272) thus describes the citadel and dungeons annexed to it: "The citadel was placed on the summit of the cone, which is the apex of a long flat ridge, running for more than a mile from west to east. The whole of this ridge appears to have been one extensive fortress, the key of which was kept on the top of the cone, an isolated and almost impregnable work, but very small, being circular and exactly one hundred yards in diameter. The wall of circumvallation can be clearly traced, its foundations all standing out for a yard or two above the surface; but the interior remains are few. One well of great depth, a very large and deep, oblong, cemented cistern, with the vaulting of the roof still remaining, and—most interesting of all—two dungeons, one of them

MARK.

18 For John had said unto Herod, It is not lawful [z] for thee to have thy brother's wife.

19 Therefore Herodias had a quarrel against him, and would have killed him; but she could not.

20 For Herod feared [a] John, knowing that he was a just man and an holy, and observed him; and when he heard him, he did many things, and heard him gladly.

21 And when a convenient day was come, that Herod on his [b] birthday made a supper to his lords, high captains, and chief *estates* of Galilee;

22 And when the daughter of the said Herodias came in, and danced,[c] and pleased Herod and them that sat with him, the king said unto the damsel, Ask of me whatsoever thou wilt, and I will give *it* thee.

23 And he sware unto her, Whatsoever [d] thou shalt ask of me, I will give *it* thee, unto the half of my kingdom.

24 And she went forth, and said unto her mother, What shall I ask? And she said, The head of John the Baptist.

25 And she came in straightway with haste unto the king, and asked, saying, I will that thou give me by and by, in a charger, the head [e] of John the Baptist.

26 And the king was exceeding sorry: *yet* for his oath's sake, and for their sakes which sat with him, he would not reject her.

27 And immediately the king sent an executioner, and commanded his head to be brought: and he went, and beheaded him in the prison,

28 And brought his head in a charger, and gave it to the damsel: and the damsel gave it to her mother.

29 And when his disciples heard *of it*, they [f] came and took up his corpse, and laid it in a tomb.

30 And [g] the apostles gathered themselves together

z Lev. 18 : 16....a Exod. 11 : 13; Ezek. 2 : 5–7....b Gen. 40 : 20....e Isa. 3 : 16....d Esther 5 : 3, 6; 7 : 2....e Ps. 37 : 12, 14....
f Acts 8 : 2....g Luke 9 : 10.

deep and its sides scarcely broken in, were the only remains clearly to be defined. That these were dungeons, and not cisterns, is evident from there being no traces of cement, which never perishes from the walls of ancient reservoirs, and from the small holes still visible in the masonry, where staples of wood and iron had once been fixed. One of these must surely have been the prison-house of John the Baptist." But apparently he was not, throughout his imprisonment, kept in such close confinement as this would indicate, since his disciples had access to him.

18. It is not lawful. See Matt. 14 : 4, note, and Prel. Note to that chapter.

19. Therefore Herodias was angry with him. More literally, *held herself against him*. "Had a quarrel " indicates a personal controversy between them, whereas there is nothing to show that the two ever met.—**She could not.** On account of her husband's opposition to her, described in the next verse.

20. For Herod feared John. Matthew says, "he feared the multitude." The two accounts are not inconsistent. His conscience and his fears supported each other.—**And preserved him.** Not *observed* him, as in our English version. The Greek verb (συντηρέω) is elsewhere rendered *preserved* (Matt. 9 : 17; Luke 5 : 38), and *kept* (Luke 2 : 19). He guarded John from his wife's malice, and at the same time kept him in prison, and so silenced his public rebuke.

21. A convenient day. Rather, *a seasonable day*, *i. e.*, for the execution of Herodias' plans. The implication is that Herodias watched her opportunity to obtain by device from her husband the death of her enemy, and seized this as a favorable occasion.—**Lords, high captains, and first men of Galilee.** The first were princes, civilians but men of official rank, the second military officers, the third, perhaps, simply leading men, influential but without special rank or office.

22-25. Compare notes on Matt. 14 : 6–9. The word here rendered *by and by* (ver. 25) should rather be rendered *immediately*. The *charger* or platter (Luke 11 : 39) was a flat dish answering somewhat to the modern waiter. Our illustra-

THE CHARGER.

tion represents this dish and its use, as seen at the present day in Palestine.

26. For his oath's sake and for their sakes that sat with him. His conscience, which regarded his oath more than his higher duty, and his fear of public reproach, operated now to drive him on to the murder, as before they had kept him from it.

27. An executioner. Rather, one of his body-guard. The Latin version renders it "*spiculator*." " Under the empire, this name was given to a select body of men retained for the service of the prince's person, as a sort of detective force and body-guard. They were armed with a lance, and are frequently represented on the columns of Trajan and Antoninus,

EXECUTIONER—
Spiculator.

unto Jesus, and told him all things, both what they had done, and what they had taught.
31 And he said unto them, Come ye yourselves apart into a desert place, and rest a while: for there were many coming and going, and they had no leisure so much as to eat.
32 And they departed into a desert place by ship privately.
33 And the people saw them departing, and many knew him, and ran afoot thither out of all cities, and outwent them, and came together unto him.
34 And Jesus, when he came out, saw much people, and was moved with compassion toward them, because ᵇ they were as sheep not having a shepherd ; and he began to teach them many things.
35 And ⁱ when the day was now far spent, his disciples came unto him, and said, This is a desert place, and now the time *is* far passed :
36 Send them away, that they may go into the country round about, and into the villages, and buy themselves bread : for they have nothing to eat.
37 He answered and said unto them, Give ye them to eat. And they say unto him, Shall we ʲ go and buy two hundred pennyworth of bread, and give them to eat?
38 He saith unto them, How many loaves have ye? go and see. And when they knew, they say, Five, and two fishes.
39 And he ᵏ commanded them to make all sit down by companies upon the green grass.
40 And they sat down in ranks by hundreds, and by fifties.
41 And when he had taken the five loaves and the two fishes, he looked up to heaven, and blessed,ˡ and brake the loaves, and gave *them* to his disciples to set before them ; and the two fishes divided he among them all.
42 And they ᵐ did all eat, and were filled.

43 And they took up twelve baskets full of the fragments, and of the fishes.
44 And they that did eat of the loaves were about five thousand men.
45 And straightway ⁿ he constrained his disciples to get into the ship, and to go to the other side before unto Bethsaida, while he sent away the people.
46 And when he had sent them away, he º departed into a mountain to pray.
47 And when even was come, the ship was in the midst of the sea, and he alone on the land.
48 And he saw them toiling ᵖ in rowing ; for the wind was contrary unto them : and about the fourth watch of the night he cometh unto them, walking upon the sea, and would have passed ᵩ by them.
49 But when they saw him walking ʳ upon the sea, they ˢ supposed it had been a spirit, and cried out :
50 For they all saw him, and were troubled. And immediately he talked with them, and saith unto them, Be of good cheer : ᵗ it is I ; be not afraid.
51 And he went up unto them into the ship ; and the ᵘ wind ceased ; and they were sore amazed in themselves beyond measure, and wondered.
52 For they considered not *the miracle* of the loaves : for their heart ᵛ was hardened.
53 And ʷ when they had passed over, they came into the land of Gennesaret, and drew to the shore.
54 And when they were come out of the ship, straightway they knew him,
55 And ran ˣ through that whole region round about, and began to carry about in beds those that were sick, where they heard he was.
56 And whithersoever he entered, into villages, or cities, or country, they laid the sick in the streets, and besought him that they might touch,ʸ if it were but the border ᶻ of his garment : and as many as touched him were made whole.

ᵇ 1 Kings 22 : 17   ⁱ Matt. 14 : 15, etc. ; Luke 9 : 12, etc. ; John 6 : 5, etc....ʲ Numb. 11 : 13, 22 ; 2 Kings 4 : 43....ᵏ ch. 8 : 6 ; Matt. 15 : 35....
1 Sam. 9 : 13 ; Matt. 26 : 26 ; Luke 24 : 30....ᵐ Deut. 8 : 3....ⁿ Matt. 14 : 22, etc. ; John 6 : 17, etc....º ch. 1 : 35 ; Matt. 6 : 6 ; Luke
6 : 12....ᵖ Jonah 1 : 13....ᵩ Luke 24 : 28....ʳ J b 9 : 8....ˢ Luke 24 : 37....ᵗ Isa. 43 : 2....ᵘ Ps. 93 : 3, 4....ᵛ Isa. 63 : 17....ʷ Matt. 14 : 34.
....ˣ ch. 2 : 1-3 ; Matt. 4 : 24....ʸ ch. 5 : 27, 28 ; Matt. 9 : 20 ; Acts 19 : 12....ᶻ Numb. 15 : 38, 39.

---

in attendance upon the emperor, or keeping guard before his tent, in the manner shown by the example annexed."—(*Rich's Dictionary.*)

30–56. THE FEEDING OF FIVE THOUSAND.— WALKING ON THE SEA. Of these incidents, the first is narrated by all four of the Evangelists— Matt. 14 : 13–21 ; Luke 9 : 10–17 ; John 6 . 1–14 ; the latter is omitted by Luke, but narrated by the other three. John's narrative is fullest. Comp. especially John 6 : 5–8. But Matthew alone narrates Peter's attempt to walk on the sea (Matt. 14 : 2–32). Immediately after the return of Christ and his Apostles to Capernaum followed the sermon in the synagogue, which John alone reports. On the chronological order, see note on Matthew ; on the incidents themselves and the subsequent sermon, see notes on John, ch. 6.

30, 31. These verses are peculiar to Mark. By a *desert place* is meant merely an uninhabited region of country, not necessarily a barren district. Luke (9 : 10) identifies the spot as "a desert plain belonging to the city called Bethsaida," a city on the northern coast of the sea, at the point where the river Jordan enters it. Observe Christ's recognition of the need of seasons as well as days or hours of rest.

45. To go before unto the other side (εἰς τὸ πέραν) **in the direction of Bethsaida** (πρὸς βηθσαϊδάν). According to Luke, the miracle of the feeding took place in the vicinity of Bethsaida (Luke 9 : 10), and according to John (6 : 1), on the opposite shore of the sea from Capernaum. Hence it has been conjectured that there were two cities called Bethsaida, one the well-known place of that name, on the northern shore of the sea, to which Luke refers, the other a place now extinct, which is supposed to have been situated somewhere on the western coast. This theory was originated by Reland, and has nothing whatever to sustain it but a laudable desire to reconcile the accounts of the Evangelists, which, however, require no such hypothetical second city. If the reader will look at the map of the Sea of Galilee, which accompanies this work (page 342), he will see the site of the true Bethsaida at the point where the River Jordan enters the Sea of Galilee. East of this, on the edge of the sea, is a grassy plain, shut in by the mountains to the east and south, which is admirably adapted to such a miracle as that of the feeding of the five thousand, and answers to the description of ver. 39 and John 6 : 10. The ship which Jesus took in the morning, with the twelve, at Capernaum, is properly described as

CHAPTER VII.

THEN came ᵃ together unto him the Pharisees, and certain of the scribes, which came from Jerusalem. 2 And when they saw some of his disciples eat bread with defiled, that is to say, with unwashen, hands, they found fault. 3 For the Pharisees, and all the Jews, except they wash *their* hands oft, eat not, holding the tradition ᵇ of the elders. 4 And *when they come* from the market, except they wash,ᶜ they eat not. And many other things there be, which they have received to hold, *as* the washing of cups, and pots, brazen vessels, and of tables. 5 Then the Pharisees and scribes asked him, Why walk not thy disciples according to the tradition of the elders, but eat bread with unwashen hands?

a Matt. 15 : 1, etc.... b Gal. 1 : 14; Col. 2 : 8, 22, 23 .... c Job 9 : 30, 31.

---

going over the Sea of Galilee (John 6 : 1) to "a desert place belonging to the city called Bethsaida" (Luke 9 : 10), or even, in general terms, as going "to Bethsaida," as Alford's reading gives it. On the various readings see note on Luke 9 : 10. When the meal was ended, and the multitude were dismissed, Christ directs his disciples to take boat and "go away *to* the other (*i. e.*, the western) side" (*viz:* representing the final end of their journey), in the direction of Bethsaida (πρὸς representing not the end, but the direction), which would lie in their course; where, after the multitude had departed, Christ purposed to rejoin them. And it is while the disciples are rowing against the wind, which prevailingly sweeps down upon the sea, from the Lebanon range on the north through the valley of the Jordan, that Christ comes on the waves to meet them.

55, 56. Comp. Matt. 14 : 34–36, note. Observe that the people "besought him that they might touch" his garment, an incidental evidence that the healing was afforded, not by any magic in the garment itself, but by the will of Christ, and was so recognized by the people. Comp. notes on Mark 5 : 25–34.

Ch. 7 : 1–23. OF EATING WITH UNWASHEN HANDS. —CHRIST'S TEACHING CONCERNING THE RELIGION OF RITUALISM : ITS WORSHIP IS VAIN (vers. 6, 7), ITS ORIGIN IS HUMAN (ver. 8), ITS EFFECT IS THE DISPLACEMENT OF THE DIVINE LAW BY HUMAN CEREMONIES (vers. 9–13). — CHRIST'S TEACHING CONCERNING PURITY : IT IS INTERNAL, NOT EXTERNAL (vers. 14–16).

This discourse is recorded only by Mark and Matthew (15 : 1-20). The former's report is fullest ; but the timid remonstrance of the disciples, and Christ's reply, are peculiar to Matthew (ch. 15 : 12-14, and notes). The time is not certain ; probably the summer of A. D. 29 (*Andrews*), immediately after the sermon at Capernaum (John, ch. 6), and during the missionary circuit briefly described in Mark 6 : 55, 56 ; Matt. 14 : 34–36. If so, it was near the close of Christ's Galilean ministry.

1. Coming from Jerusalem. Probably sent there, formally or informally, by the Sanhedrim, to investigate the character and mission of Christ, as a previous delegation had been sent to attend the ministry of John the Baptist. See John 1 : 19.

2-5. And when they saw some of his disciples. Not necessarily here any of the twelve, but probably that is the meaning.—**Eat with defiled hands.** The word here rendered defiled, is rendered *common* in Acts 10 : 14, 28, and *unclean* in Rom. 14 : 14.—**That is, with unwashen hands.** Not with dirty hands, but with hands which had not been subjected to the ceremonial process described below.—**They found fault.** "The Pharisee takes more pleasure in blaming another than in amending himself."—(*Quesnel.*)—**For the Pharisees and all the Jews,** *i. e.*, the Judeans, the inhabitants of Judea, the southern province of the Holy Land, where the influence of the ecclesiastics was very considerably greater than in Galilee.—**Except they wash their hands oft.** There is some uncertainty as to the meaning of the word rendered *oft*. Some critics give the rendering of our English version, others, as Alford, render it "sedulously." It is, literally, *with the fist*, and that appears to me to be the better rendering. It is, then, a reference to the Rabbinical rules, which are said to have required the rubbing of the open palm with the closed fist.—**Eat not, holding fast.** Not merely *holding* but *holding firmly*. See for analogous use of the same word, Col. 2 : 19; 2 Thess. 2 : 15; Heb. 4 : 14; Rev. 2 : 13; 3 : 11. And observe, by examining these references, what the Christian should hold fast.—**The tradition of the elders.** Alford, following Meyer, renders this *of the ancients*, and Hebrews 11 : 1 is an evidence that the Greek is capable of this meaning. But the original (πρεσβυτέρος), generally signifies, in the N. T., a certain class of officials, partly ecclesiastical, partly political. See Matt. 16 : 21, note. That it is used in this ecclesiastical sense here, is indicated by Lightfoot's quotations from the Rabbinical writings: "The words of the elders are weightier than the words of the prophets." In fact, their "words" were traditions derived from their ancestors, and exalted above Scripture, as at a later day the traditions of the church were exalted above Scripture by the church of Rome.—**And coming from the market except they plunge;** literally *baptize*. The Greek word here is not the same as that rendered *wash* in the previous verse. Apparently, in the ritual of the Pharisees,

6 He answered and said unto them, Well hath Esaias prophesied ^d of you hypocrites, as it is written, This people honoureth me with *their* lips, but their heart is far from me.

7 Howbeit, in vain do they worship me, teaching *for* doctrines the commandments of men.

8 For laying ^e aside the commandment of God, ye hold the tradition of men, *as* the washing of pots and cups: and many other such like things ye do.

9 And he said unto them, Full well ye reject the commandment of God, that ye may keep your own tradition.

d Isa. 29 : 13. . . . e Isa. 1 : 12.

washing by the pouring on of water sufficed for those who remained at home, while the immersion of the hands in water was required for those who had gone abroad. It was the hands, not the whole body, nor the article brought from market, that was required to be washed.—**And many other things there be which they have received to hold, as the washing** (literally, *baptizing*) **of cups and pots** (or *measures*) **and brazen vessels,** wooden ones were to be broken if unclean (Lev. 15 : 12), **and couches;** not *tables*, but the couches on which the guests reclined at the meal. (See Matt. 26 : 20, note and illustration.) It is hardly credible that these lounges were immersed; we have, therefore, here an evidence that the Greek word rendered in the N. T. baptism or baptize, does not in the N. T. usage *always* signify immersion. The ceremonial cleansing of the furniture in the room was probably done by sprinkling; while that of the person appears to have been done by immersion.—**Why walk not thy disciples according to the traditions of the elders?**—The common question of ecclesiasticism in all ages, which makes the traditions of the church, not the law of God, the standard of life.

The law of Moses required ceremonial wash-

MODERN HAND-WASHING.

ings: (1) of certain sacred persons, as the priests at their consecration (Exod. 40 : 12; Lev. 8 : 6; comp. Num.

8 : 5-7, 21), and habitually before sacrificing (Exod. 30 : 18-21; 40 : 30-32; Lev. 16 : 4, 21); (2) of all the people on certain special occasions, as the leper on being pronounced clean of his leprosy (Lev. 14 : 8, 9), the man with an issue, etc. (Lev. 15 : 5, 6, etc.); (3) as a testimony to innocence (Deut. 21 : 1-9). Analogous to the first of these is the modern practice by the priests in the Romish and Greek churches of washing the hands immediately before celebrating mass; analogous to the second is the use of holy water by all the worshippers. The Mohammedan still washes five times a day that he may approach God acceptably in prayer. Our illustration, which is taken from actual life, shows the practice as it is scrupulously observed to the present day in Palestine. It is evident that the Jewish requirements were partly sanitary; this is clearly the case with certain of the requirements in Lev. ch. 15; but they were partly ceremonial. The Pharisees converted the Mosaic ablutions into an elaborate and burdensome ritual. They never entered their houses without washing, lest they should have unknowingly contracted defilement in the streets; and as the hands were held to communicate uncleanness to the food, they never ate without a previous ceremonial washing of the hands. This was required to be done in a prescribed manner, by plunging them three times up to the wrists, in running water, which was fresh, and had done no work. Whether water was ceremonially fresh which had been kept so by the intermixture of vinegar or lemon-juice, whether it had done no work if in it fish had been bred or eggs boiled,—these were serious theological problems. Such a ceremonialism was not regarded by the common people, who were content simply to wash their hands for the purpose of actual cleanliness, before meals. The scribes condemned the disciples, not for eating literally with unwashen hands, but with hands which had not been *ceremonially* washed, and this only as a means of condemning Christ, who, as a religious teacher, was expected to require the ritualism of his day from his immediate followers. "Their wonder was that Jesus had not inculcated this observance on his followers, and not, as some have fancied, that he had enjoined them to neglect what had been their previous practice."—(*Kitto*.)

6. **Esaias.** Isaiah 29 : 13. Observe the rest

CH. VII.]   MARK.   33

10 For Moses said, Honour ᶠ thy father and thy mother; and, Whoso curseth ᵍ father or mother, let him die the death.
11 But ye say, If a man shall say to his father or mother, *It is* Corban,ʰ that is to say, a gift, by whatsoever thou mightest be profited by me; *he shall be free.*
12 And ye suffer him no more to do ought for his father or his mother;
13 Making the word of God of none effect through your tradition, which ye have delivered: and many such like things do ye.
14 And when he had called all the people *unto him*, he said unto them, Hearken unto me, every one *of you*, and understand:ⁱ
15 There is nothing from without a man that, entering into him, can defile him: but the things which come out of him, those are they that defile the man.
16 If any ʲ man have ears to hear, let him hear.

f Exod. 20 : 12; Deut. 5 : 16....g Exod. 21 : 17; Lev. 20 : 9; Prov. 20 : 20....h Matt. 15 : 5; 23 : 18....i Prov. 8 : 5; Isa. 6 : 9; Acts 8 : 30....j Matt. 11 : 15.

of the prophet's description of the formalists: "Their fear toward me is taught by the precept of men."
7-9. In vain do they worship me. Comp. Isaiah 1 : 10-15.—Teaching as doctrines the commandments of men. Not *for, i. e.*, in lieu of doctrines, but teaching doctrines which are of human origin.—For laying aside the commandment of God; this the rigorous ceremonialist generally does; ye hold fast the traditions of men, literally, *the things given by men.* That is, a tradition of men which is handed down from father to son, is traceable only to a human author, yet is cited by the ecclesiastic as an authority, as though it came from God.—Excellently well. The language is that of bitter sarcasm.—Ye displace the commandment of God, that ye may observe the traditions of men. Literally, *keep close watch over;* comp. Matt. 19 : 17, note, latter clause. On the whole passage, comp. Matt. 23 : 16-19; and Col. 2 : 18-23, and observe here, (1) the nature of that which Christ reprobates, the employment *as an authority in religion* of systems of doctrine, ethics or ritual, which are of human origin, a radical vice, whether the system be a Protestant creed, a Romish ritual, or a Jewish ceremonial; (2) the folly of all religion founded on such human authority; "*In vain* do they worship me," because it substitutes allegiance to man for allegiance to God; (3) the effect of it, the displacement of the divine laws which concern the heart-life, by human rules, which require only external conduct. An unconscious desire to be rid of God's spiritual law is the true secret of all additions to the simple religion of the Bible. What follows is an illustration taken from Jewish casuistry, of the nature and effect of this substitution of human for divine authority.

10-12. For Moses said. In Matthew (15:4), it is, "For God commanded." "A remarkable testimony from our Lord to the divine origin of the Mosaic law; not merely of the Decalogue as such, for the second commandment quoted is not in the Decalogue."—(*Alford.*)—Honor thy father and mother. See Exod. 20 : 12; Deut. 5 : 16.—And whoso curseth father or mother let him die the death, *i. e.*, let him be put to death, literally, *Let him end in death.* The quotation is from Exod. 21 : 17; Lev. 20 : 9.—But ye say. The quotation which follows is from the Rabbinical rules. There are two difficulties in its interpretation: (1) Its grammatical construction; (2) the uncertainty respecting the law to which it refers. As to its grammatical construction, our translators have undoubtedly given the sense correctly, but the addition of the words *he shall be free* is not grammatically necessary, though sanctioned by some of the critics. The true meaning of the passage may be thus rendered, *If a man shall say to his father or mother, That by which thou mightest be profited by me is corban* (that is, a *gift*, consecrated to God), *ye suffer him no more to do aught for his father or mother.* So in the parallel passage in Matt. 15 : 5, 6, the verb *honor not his father or his mother* is, according to the best readings, in the future, and the passage reads, "*Whosoever shall say to his father or his mother, That by which thou mightest have been profited by me is a gift, he shall not honor his father or his mother.*" For different grammatical readings, see Schaff's Note on Matt. 15 : 5, 6, in *Lange on Matthew.* As to the Rabbinical law to which it refers, the facts appear to have been as follows. The Mosaic law laid down rules for vows both affirmative and negative. By the former, persons, animals, and property might be devoted to God; by the latter, persons interdicted themselves, or were interdicted by their parents, from the use of certain things, either temporarily or permanently (Lev. ch. 27; Num. ch. 30; Judges 13 : 7; Acts 18 : 18; 21 : 23, 24). On these rules the rabbis enlarged, and laid down that a man might not only interdict himself from using for himself, but also *from giving to another* anything. The thing thus interdicted was considered as corban, that is, as consecrated to God, yet the person making the vow might use it for himself; his vow only bound him not to give it to the other. So far was this doctrine carried, that the contemptuous or angry use of the language of a vow was held to exempt the person making it from his obligations of assistance, so that a child, on being applied to for aid by his parents, might even contemptuously reply, Let it be corban whatever of mine might profit you, and this simple expression freed him from the filial obligation of supporting his par-

17 And when ᵏ he was entered into the house from the people, his disciples asked him concerning the parable.
18 And he saith unto them, Are ye so without understanding also? Do ye not perceive, that whatsoever thing from without entereth into the man, it cannot defile him;
19 Because it entereth not into his heart, but¹ into the belly, and goeth out into the draught, purging all meats?
20 And he said, That which cometh out of the man, that defileth the man.
21 For from ᵐ within, out of the heart of men, proceed evil thoughts, adulteries, fornications, murders,
22 Thefts, covetousness, wickedness, deceit, lasciviousness, an evil eye, blasphemy, pride, foolishness:
23 All these evil things come from within, and defile the man.
24 And from ⁿ thence he arose, and went into the borders of Tyre and Sidon, and entered into an house, and would have no man know it: but he ᵒ could not be hid.

25 For a *certain* woman, whose young daughter had an unclean spirit, heard of him, and came and fell at his feet:
26 The woman was a Greek, a Syrophenician by nation; and she besought him that he would cast forth the devil out of her daughter.
27 But Jesus said unto her, Let the children first be filled; for ᵖ it is not meet to take the children's bread, and to cast it unto the dogs.
28 And she answered and said unto him, Yes, Lord: yet the ᵠ dogs under the table eat of the children's crumbs.
29 And he said unto her, For ʳ this saying go thy way; the devil is gone out of thy daughter.
30 And when she was come to her house, she found the devil gone ˢ out, and her daughter laid upon the bed.
31 And again,ᵗ departing from the coasts of Tyre and Sidon, he came unto the sea of Galilee, through the midst of the coasts of Decapolis.
32 And they bring unto him one that was deaf, and had an impediment in his speech; and they beseech him to put his hand upon him.

k Matt. 15 : 15, etc....l 1 Cor. 6 : 13....m Gen. 6 : 5; Ps. 14 : 1, 3; 53 : 1, 3; Jer. 17 : 9....n Matt. 15 : 21, etc....o ch. 2 : 1....
p Matt. 7 : 6; 10 : 5, 6....q Rom. 15 : 8, 9; Ephes. 2 : 12-14....r Isa. 66 : 2....s 1 John 3 : 8....t Matt. 15 : 29, etc.

---

ents. Such casuistry would be incredible were not its parallel to be found in the Jesuitical casuistry of the seventeenth century.

13. Making the word of God of none effect through your traditions. The conference began by an accusation of illegal teaching, brought by the scribes against Christ; it ends with an accusation of illegal teaching, brought by Christ against the scribes.

14, 15. And when he had called all the people. The previous conference was with the scribes who had come up from Jerusalem for the purpose of confounding Christ (ver. 1; Matt. 15 : 1). The teaching that follows was public.—**There is nothing from without a man that entering in can defile him; but, etc.** This verse is to be interpreted by the subject-matter and by verses 18 and 19. Nothing that is and remains external to man, and enters only into his body, not into his heart to become a part of his character, can defile. The Pharisees feared defilement from their food; it is of this defilement our Lord speaks. Comp. Matt. 15 : 11. "Not that which goeth *into the mouth.*" But underlying this is the deeper truth, that nothing which is external to character can defile the soul, so long as it remains external, does not become incorporated in the character. Evidently this verse is only a brief epitome of a considerable discourse.

16. See Matt. 11 : 15, note.

17-19. His disciples asked him. By disciples is here meant, probably, the twelve. According to Matthew, Peter was the spokesman.—**Without understanding,** *i. e.,* without spiritual appreciation of the truth.—**Because it entereth not into his heart.** That which is from without and *does enter the heart* can defile a man.—**Goeth out into the draught, cleansing all the food.** Whatever food the body needs it assimilates, and whatever it needs is unclean nor defiling. Whatever it does not need, it, by a natural process, rejects from the system. Thus nature provides for its own purification, and the laws of health are the only laws of cleanness and uncleanness which the Christian need recognize. In this declaration is the germ of the doctrine which Paul subsequently expounded more fully (Rom. 14 : 2, 3, 14; 1 Cor. ch. 8).

20-23. Observe in these verses, (1) that the defilement which Christ recognizes is one of the soul, and consists, therefore, of something *in* the heart, not foreign to it; (2) that all the vices here catalogued and described as *evil thoughts,* the evil even of adultery, murder and theft, lie primarily and chiefly *in the thought,* only secondarily in the outward act and its visible effects; (3) that Christ refutes the idea, sometimes expressed, that if there is evil in a man he had better let it out in expression rather than keep it in; our Lord declares that the *coming out* itself defiles. The "evil eye" is not merely, as Lange, an "envious eye," but an eye which is apt, in any form, to evil, the eye here standing for the desires which look through it and are inflamed by it. Comp. Prov. 28 : 22; Matt. 6 : 22, 23; 18 : 9; 20 : 15; 1 John 2 : 16.

20. To this verse Matthew makes the significant addition: "But to eat with unwashen hands," *i. e.,* with hands not subjected to a ceremonial washing, "defileth not a man."

24-30. THE SYROPHŒNICIAN WOMAN. Peculiar to Matthew (15 : 21-28) and Mark. See notes on Matthew, whose account is fullest. Observe in verse 24 here the incidental evidence of Christ's extended fame and wide popularity among the common people.

Ch. 7 : 31-37. **HEALING OF THE DEAF AND DUMB.**—CHRIST'S MISSION: TO GIVE POWER TO RECEIVE AND

CH. VII.] MARK. 35

33 And he took him aside from the multitude, and put his fingers into his ears, and he ᵘ spit, and touched his tongue;
34 And looking ᵛ up to heaven, he ʷ sighed, and saith unto him, Ephphatha, that is, Be opened.
35 And straightway ˣ his ears were opened, and the string of his tongue was loosed, and he spake plain.

36 And he charged them that they should tell no man: but the more he charged them, so much the more a great deal they published it;
37 And were beyond measure astonished, saying,ʸ He hath done all things well; he maketh ᶻ both the deaf to hear, and the dumb to speak.

u ch. 8 : 23; John 9 : 6....v ch. 6 : 41; John 11 : 41; 17 : 1... w John 11 : 33, 38... x Matt. 8 : 3, 15....y Ps. 139 : 14; Acts 14 : 11....
z Exod. 4 : 10, 11.

POWER TO PROCLAIM THE TRUTH.—AN ILLUSTRATION OF HIS METHOD OF AWAKENING FAITH IN THOSE BEYOND THE REACH OF HIS SPOKEN WORD.

Peculiar to Mark. It is one of the miracles described in general terms by Matt. 15 : 30, 31. The chronological order is the same in both Gospels; the miracle belongs to Christ's period of retirement, subsequent to the close of his public ministry in Galilee, and before his going up to Jerusalem, i. e., between John, chaps. 6 and 7. **31. Tyre and Sidon.** See Matt. 11 : 21, note.—**He came through the midst of the territory of Decapolis.** Matt. 4 : 25, note. Probably Christ made a detour round the northern shore of the Lake of Galilee (see map, p. 340), coming thus into the region of the sea, but still keeping in retirement by remaining in heathen territory. That the word here rendered *coast* is equivalent to *territory* see Matt. 2 : 16; 4 : 13; 8 : 34, etc.—**They bring unto him,** *i. e.*, the people bring; **one that was deaf and had an impediment in his speech.** Literally, a *dumb stammerer*. That he could speak, but not plainly, is indicated by the effect of his cure, "he could speak plain" (ver. 35). **33, 34. He took him aside.** As he did subsequently the blind man (ch. 8 : 23), because he was seeking retirement with his disciples, and wished to avoid publicity. The indications that his public ministry in Galilee was at an end, and that he sought retirement with his apostles for rest and private instruction, are repeated continually in this portion of his life. See ver. 24, ch. 8 : 27 and Matt. 15 : 29-39, note, p. 195, and ref. there. But Trench's remark on our Lord's course here is suggestive. "The Lord does now oftentimes lead a soul apart, sets it in the solitude of a sick-chamber, or in loneliness of spirit, or takes away from it earthly companions and friends, when he would speak with it and heal it."—**And put his fingers into his ears, and having spit,** *i. e.*, probably, touched his finger with spittle, he **touched his tongue,** *i. e.*, the dumb man's tongue. I can only understand this by supposing it was a chosen means of communicating with the dumb man, and by sympathy through the touch awakening his faith. For all other media of communication were closed except that of touch, unless we suppose the man able to read writing and Christ provided with implements of writing, neither of which is prob-

able. It was an appeal to the man's trust, like that made in other cases by a word, and required of the man at least a tacit obedience, as a requisite to the cure.—**And sighed.** Possibly this expresses the idea of an inarticulate prayer, as Robinson interprets it (*Rob. Lex.*, ἀγενάζω); more probably it is an expression of Christ's deep-felt sympathy with the suffering of sin-stricken humanity, as in the parallel case at the resurrection of Lazarus (John 11 : 33-35).—**And said unto him, Ephphatha.** An Aramaic expression. See note on Mark 5 : 41. **35. And straightway.** Immediately.—His hearing, not his ears; the word is different from that rendered ears in verse 33 (it is ἀκοή, not οὖς), and the language implies a deep-seated difficulty.—**Was opened; and the string of his tongue,** the hinderance, whatever it was, which before prevented his speaking plainly.—**Was loosed.** Evidently the imperfection in utterance was not merely a consequence of loss of hearing, but there was a physical difficulty with the organs of speech.—**And he spake plain.** Impliedly, both here and in verse 32, he could speak before, but not so as to be easily understood. **36. Comp. Matt. 8 : 4, note.** Here there was special reason for the prohibition in that Christ was seeking to avoid the public and to secure quiet conference with his apostles. See verse 33, note. **37. He hath done all things well.** Comp. Gen. 1 : 31. "This work was properly and worthily compared with that first one of creation—it was the same Beneficence which prompted and the same Power that wrought it."—(*Alford*.)—**He maketh both the deaf to hear and the dumb to speak.** Spiritually this characterizes Christ's ministry, for still he opens the ears of those deaf to spiritual truth, so that hearing they hear and do understand, and unstops the tongue of silent disciples, and teaches them to speak his praise. Comp. Isaiah 35 : 5; Matt. 13 : 16. See also 1 Cor. 2 : 10, 14-16. **Ch. 8 : 1-10.** THE FEEDING OF THE FOUR THOUSAND. This miracle is recounted only here and in Matt. 15 : 32-38. It is not to be confounded with the feeding of the five thousand, described by all four Evangelists (Matt. 14 : 13-21; Mark 6 : 32-44; Luke 9 : 10-17; John 6 : 1-14). "Every circumstance which can vary, does vary, in the two accounts.

CHAPTER VIII.

IN those *days the multitude being very great, and having nothing to eat, Jesus called his disciples *unto him*, and saith unto them,

2 I have compassion *b* on the multitude, because they have now been with me three days, and have nothing to eat:

3 And if I send them away fasting to their own houses, they will faint by the way: for divers of them came from far.

4 And his disciples answered him, From whence *c* can a man satisfy these *men* with bread here in the wilderness?

5 And he asked them, How many loaves have ye? And they said, Seven.

---

a Matt. 15 : 32, etc. ... b Ps. 145 : 8, 15 ; Heb. 5 : 2. ... c ch. 6 : 36, 37, etc.

The situation in the wilderness, the kind of food at hand, the blessing and breaking and distributing by means of the disciples, these are common to the two accounts, and were likely to be so; but *here* the matter is introduced by the Lord himself, with an expression of pity for the multitude who had continued with him three days; here, also, the provision is greater, the numbers are less than on the former occasion."—(*Alford*.) What is conclusive on this question, however, is our Lord's reference to both miracles (Matt. 16 : 9, 10), which, as Alford justly says, "must have been forged if the two are identical;" and his discrimination there between the traveling baskets employed on the one occasion, and the grain baskets on the other,—a discrimination which tallies exactly with the language of the two narratives. In all four accounts of the first miracle the baskets used in gathering up the fragments are designated in the original by the word *cophinus* (κόφινος), "traveling basket," while in both the Evangelists the baskets used on the occasion of the feeding of the four thousand are designated by the word *sporta* (σπυρίς), *grain basket*. This distinction is recognized by Christ in his subsequent recall of the two miracles. See Matt. 16 : 9, 10, note, where illustrations of the two kinds of baskets are given. Unfortunately, there is nothing in our English version to indicate this difference. The only reason for imagining the two miracles to be identical, is the seemingly singular fact that the disciples, after witnessing the feeding of the five thousand, should be perplexed what to do for the provision of the four thousand. But, (1) the disciples did not on this occasion, as on the other, propose to send the people away (Matt. 14 : 15), though now three and then but one day had passed ; they waited for Christ to do as he would ; (2) their question here (ver. 4) hardly indicates a doubt; it is elicited by Christ's previous question, and is such as they might readily have proposed, if they wished merely to leave all to Christ without suggesting, as they never did throughout all his ministry, the performance of a miracle ; (3) even if the facts showed a failure to believe and trust in divine power, similar instances are common in Scripture history, and, unhappily, not rare in the Christian experience of the disciples of to-day. Comp. Exod. 16 : 13 with Numb. 11 : 21, 22, and Exod. 17 : 1–7, following the passage of Israel through the middle of the Red Sea. With the account of this miracle should be carefully compared that of the feeding of the five thousand. The spiritual significance of the two is the same ; and for that the reader is referred to the notes on John, ch. 6, especially verses 1–14.

1, 2. In those days. The time is apparently during Christ's period of retirement, after his withdrawal from Galilee as indicated by Matt. 15 : 21; the place, the high table-land east of the Sea of Galilee (Matt. 15 : 29 with Mark 7 : 31), in the territory of Decapolis, which was occupied largely by a Roman population. This ministry of feeding does not then belong properly to Christ's Galilean ministry. The former feeding was on the northern coast of the Sea of Galilee, among the Jews; this one was among the heathen. — **Nothing to eat.** Not to be taken literally ; for this would imply, either a three-days' fast, or a singularly improvident consumption of their provisions. They had with them no *adequate supply* for their wants. In the East, meat is used much less than with us. Milk, fruits, and various preparations of bread are staple articles of diet. Three days' sojourn in the wilderness would not, therefore, require with them so great preparation as with us. And the wilderness (ver. 4) was not a true desert, but a country district, remote from towns, and consequently from habitations, since, on account of wild beasts and robbers, the people lived almost wholly in towns and villages.

3–5. From afar. Comp Matt. 4 : 25, note. —**Bread—Loaves.** The bread of the East is baked in thin round cakes or sheets, like our crackers in form. They were often baked by spreading the dough, when prepared, on stones previously heated, or throwing it on to the heated embers itself, or placing it between layers of dung, which burns slowly, and is therefore especially adapted to the purpose. Dr. Robinson (*Biblical Researches*, II, 406) describes such a baking : "They had brought along some flour, or rather meal, of wheat and barley filled with chaff, of which they now kneaded a round, flat cake of some thickness. This they threw into the ashes and coals of a fire they had kindled, and after due time brought out a loaf of bread as black on the outside as the coals themselves, and

CH. VIII.]   MARK.   37

6 And he commanded the people to sit down on the ground; and he took the seven loaves, and gave thanks, and brake, and gave to his disciples to set before them; and they did set them before the people.
7 And they had a few small fishes: and he blessed,ᵈ and commanded to set them also before them.

8 So they did eat, and were ᵉ filled: and they ᶠ took up of the broken meat that was left seven baskets.
9 And they that had eaten were about four thousand: and he sent them away.
10 And straightway ᵍ he entered into a ship with his disciples, and came into the parts of Dalmanutha.

d Matt. 14 : 19....e Ps. 107 : 5, 6; 145 : 16....f 1 Kings 17 : 14–16; 2 Kings 4 : 2–7, 42–44....g Matt. 15 : 39.

not much whiter within." Comp. note on John 6 : 9. The accompanying illustration represents some loaves as they were discovered in a baker's shop at Pompeii; they are about eight inches in diameter, and in shape and size resemble those

LOAVES OF BREAD.

then in use among the Jews. Besides the loaves the disciples had "a few small fishes" (verse 7). Fish, both fresh and salt, appear to have been a common article of food, especially about the Sea of Galilee.

6–9. Gave thanks and brake. Christ's practice of giving thanks before meal (comp. 6 : 41; 14 : 22; Luke 24 : 30) is a precedent for the modern custom of asking a blessing at meal time.—**And gave to his disciples to set before them.** A symbol of the truth that only as Christ's ministers receive the truth from Christ can they distribute the truth to the people. For Christ, by his sermon after the previous feeding (John, ch. 6), makes of the miracle an enacted parable.—**So they did eat and were filled,** i. e., satisfied. Observe the simplicity of the narrative; seven loaves and a few small fishes blessed by Christ, and four thousand people adequately fed by them—of these two facts the narrators are sure, for they were eye-witnesses; the reader is left to draw his own conclusions. —
Seven baskets. See Prel. Note above, and note on Matt. 16 : 9, 10, for illustration of baskets.

10. Into the parts of Dalmanutha. Matt.

15 : 39 says Magdala, or, according to the better reading, Magadan. The exact location is uncertain; it appears from the narrative to have been on the western coast of the sea, though it is not necessarily implied that Jesus crossed the sea. Both Matthew (15 : 39) and Mark here use indefinite language, one saying he " came into the coasts of Magdala," the other that he came " into the parts of Dalmanutha." He may therefore have landed at a point near two towns which were adjacent; and this is the ordinary view. The map, p. 342, shows the general location. Dr. Howard Crosby, however, has suggested the not improbable conjecture that the two may be identified. A private note to me thus states this conjecture : " One of the Levitical cities of Naphtali was Kartan (Josh. 21 : 32), apparently in the southern part of Naph-

TOWER OF TIBERIAS.

tali. Kartan is not mentioned in Josh. 19 : 35–38, as so prominent a Levitical city would naturally be. The other Levitical cities, Kedesh and

11 And the Pharisees came forth, and began to question with him, seeking of him a sign from heaven, tempting him.
12 And he sighed deeply in his spirit, and saith, Why doth this generation seek after a sign? verily I say unto you, There shall no sign be given unto this generation.
13 And he left them, and entering into the ship again departed to the other side.
14 Now the disciples had forgotten to take bread, neither had they in the ship with them more than one loaf.
15 And he charged them, saying, Take heed, beware of the leaven of the Pharisees, and of the leaven of Herod.
16 And they reasoned among themselves, saying, It is because we have no bread.
17 And when Jesus knew it, he saith unto them, Why reason ye, because ye have no bread? perceive ye not yet, neither understand? have ye your heart yet hardened?

18 Having eyes, see ye not? and having ears, hear ye not? and do ye not remember?
19 When I brake the five loaves among five thousand, how many baskets full of fragments took ye up? They say unto him, Twelve.
20 And when the seven among four thousand, how many baskets full of fragments took ye up? And they said, Seven.
21 And he said unto them, How is it that ye do not understand?
22 And he cometh to Bethsaida: and they bring a blind man unto him, and besought him to touch him.
23 And he took the blind man by the hand, and led him out of the town; and when he had spit on his eyes, and put his hands upon him, he asked him if he saw ought.
24 And he looked up, and said, I see men as trees, walking.
25 After that he put his hands again upon his eyes, and made him look up: and he was restored, and saw every man clearly.

b Matt. 12 : 38 ; 16 : 1, etc ; John 6 : 30....i Prov. 19 : 27 ; Luke 12 : 1....j Exod. 12 : 20 ; Lev. 2 : 11 ; 1 Cor. 5 : 6-8....k ch. 6 : 52....
l ch. 3 : 5 ; 16 : 14.....m Isa. 44 : 18.....n 2 Pet. 1 : 12....o ch. 6 : 38, 44 ; Matt. 14 : 17-21 ; Luke 9 : 12-17 ; John 6 : 5-13....p ver.
1-9 ; Matt. 15 : 34-38....q Isa. 35 : 5, 6 ; Matt. 11 : 5....r ch. 7 : 33.....s Judges 9 : 36 ; Isa. 29 : 18 ; 1 Cor. 13 : 11, 12....t Prov.
4 : 18 ; Isa. 32 : 3 ; 1 Pet. 2 : 9.

Hammath, are. Migdal-el (Josh. 19 : 28) I therefore conjecture to be Kartan. If so, it would be naturally called Migdal-Manutha (Hebrew, Migdal-Menath), 'tower of the portion,' i. e., the Levitical portion." From this compound name might easily come the two names Magdala and Dalmanutha, the former being the original name, Migdal-el ; the latter, an abbreviation of the fuller name Migdal-Manutha. It is true that the supposed site of Magdala is a little south of the supposed boundary of Naphtali ; but neither can be fixed with sufficient certainty to make this conclusive. It would appear not improbable that sites often received their name, as in the case of Magdala, from a tower in connection with them. The accompanying cut shows the ruins of an ancient tower at Tiberias. The reader is looking north ; before him is the Sea of Galilee ; Mt. Hermon is in the distance ; to the left, hidden behind the town, is the site of Magdala or Dalmanutha, which means tower.

11-13. REQUEST OF A SIGN FROM HEAVEN. See notes on Matt. 16 : 1-4. The statement here, "He sighed deeply in his spirit," is peculiar to Mark, and is a touching testimony to the pity of Christ, which embraced even such captious and cavilling spirits as these Pharisees. His departure again so soon to the eastern shore of the lake is one of the many indications that he considered his public ministry ended, and was seeking retirement. See Matt. 15 : 29-39, note.

14-21. WARNING AGAINST THE LEAVEN OF THE PHARISEES AND OF HEROD. Matt. 16 : 5-12, notes. There are some graphic touches here not in Matthew, as the statement that they had but one loaf (ver. 14), the additional reproof (ver. 18), and the reference to the two miracles of feeding, given here more at length (ver. 19-21). According to Matthew, Christ's warning was against the leaven of the Pharisees and the Sadducees.

Matthew adds the disciples' understanding of Christ's admonition (Matt. 16 : 12).

Ch. 8 : 22-26. CURE OF A BLIND MAN.—GRACE IS SOMETIMES GRADUAL.

This miracle is recorded only by Mark. It is peculiar in that it represents, more distinctly than any other miracle, a gradual cure, and its successive stages. There is no reason to doubt that the chronology is correctly indicated by Mark, i. e., that it occurred after the close of Christ's public Galilean ministry, and during his period of retirement.

22. And they came to Bethsaida. This is the better reading. Bethsaida was a town on the northern shore of the sea of Galilee, at the entrance of the river Jordan into the lake. See Mark 6 : 45, note.—**And they bring a blind man unto him.** The people, not the disciples, brought him.

23. And taking the hand of the blind man, he led him out of the town. Rather, village (κώμη). Bethsaida (house of fish) was originally a fishing village. The tetrarch Philip enlarged it, raised it to the dignity of a town, and gave it the name of Julias. This part of the town was on the eastern bank of the Jordan, the original fishing hamlet was on the western bank. The language here implies that Christ was in the fisherman's part of the town, the unwalled village. Observe that Christ personally leads the blind man, a mark of tenderness and condescension, and that the blind man entrusts himself, apparently unquestioningly, to the leading of this stranger, a mark of his confidence in Christ, and a touching illustration of that peculiar attractive power which Christ exercised over all men by his personal presence.—**And when he had spit on his eyes.** Spittle was regarded as medicinal by the ancients. Why Christ used it here is not

26 And he sent him away to his house, saying, Neither go into the town, nor tell *it* to any in the town.
27 And Jesus ⁿ went out, and his disciples, into the towns of Cæsarea Philippi: and by the way he asked his disciples, saying unto them, Whom do men say that I am?
28 And they answered, John ᵒ the Baptist: but some *say,* Elias; and others, One of the prophets.
29 And he saith unto them, But whom say ye that I am? And Peter answereth and saith unto him, Thou ʷ art the Christ.
30 And he charged them that they should tell no man of him.
31 And he began to teach them, that the Son of man must suffer many things, and be rejected of the elders, and *of* the chief priests, and scribes, and be killed, and after three days rise again.
32 And he spake that saying openly. And Peter took him, and began to rebuke him.
33 But when he had turned about and looked on his disciples, he rebuked ˣ Peter, saying, Get thee behind me, Satan: ʸ for thou savourest not the things that be of God, but the things that be of men.

34 And when he had called the people *unto him* with his disciples also, he said unto them, Whosoever ᶻ will come after me, let him deny himself, and take up his cross, and follow me.
35 For ᵃ whosoever will save his life shall lose it; but whosoever shall lose his life for my sake and the gospel's, the same shall save it.
36 For what shall it profit a man if he shall gain the whole world, and lose his own soul?
37 Or what shall a man give in exchange for his soul?
38 Whosoever ᵇ therefore shall be ashamed of me, and of my words, in this adulterous and sinful generation, of him also shall the Son of man be ashamed, when he cometh in the glory of his Father, with the holy angels.

CHAPTER IX.

AND he said unto them, Verily ᶜ I say unto you, That there be some of them that stand here, which shall not ᵈ taste of death, till they have seen the kingdom of God come with power.
2 And ᵉ after six days Jesus taketh *with him* Peter

ᵘ Matt. 16 : 13, etc.; Luke 9 : 18, etc.....v Matt. 14 : 2.....w John 1 : 41-42; 6 : 69; 11 : 27; Acts 8 : 37; 1 John 5 : 1.....x Rev. 3 : 19 .....y 1 Cor. 8 : 5.....z Matt. 16 : 28; 16 : 24; Luke 9 : 23; 14 : 27; Tim. 2 : 12.....a Esther 4 : 14; Matt. 10 : 39; 16 : 25; Luke 9 : 24; 17 : 33; John 12 : 25; 2 Tim. 2 : 11; 4 : 6, 8; Rev. 2 : 10; 7 : 14 17.....b Luke 12 : 9; 2 Tim. 1 : 8.....c Matt. 16 : 28; Luke 9 : 27.....d John 8 : 62; Heb. 2 : 9.....e Matt. 17 : 1, etc.; Luke 9 : 28, etc.

clear. Perhaps as the readiest means of strengthening the faith of the blind man (see Mark 7:33, 34, note); perhaps (this I am inclined to think the true explanation) to make as little impression with the miracle as possible, because he was now seeking retirement, and wished to avoid the throng and publicity which miracles always brought upon him.
24, 25. And he looked up. In order to make a trial of his eyes.—**And said, I see men; for** (things) **like trees I see, walking.** This is the literal rendering of the Sinaitic, Alexandrine, and Vatican MSS., and is adopted by Lachmann, Tregelles, Tischendorf, and Alford. The meaning appears to be this: I see men; for, though what I see resemble trees, they cannot be so, for they are walking about. The very vagueness of the language pictures forcibly the groping of one through an uncertain vision toward the truth. To a blind man, who knew trees only by feeling, that is, only knew the trunks, men might well seem like trees, except for their motion.—**Then again he put his hands upon his eyes; and he saw discriminatingly, and was thoroughly restored, and saw all things plainly.** There is some uncertainty as to the reading here. That which I have given is adopted by Alford, Tischendorf, and Tregelles. The meaning is that the blind man was at once able to distinguish objects, and being perfectly restored, thereafter saw all things clearly.
26. The double prohibition of this verse has given the commentators needless perplexity. How, they have asked, could he tell any man in the town if he did not go into it? The prohibition is simply emphatic. The reason is Christ's desire to preserve his retirement. His public ministry in Galilee is ended.

Those who believe, as I do, that the ministry of Christ's healing is a symbol of his redemption, will easily trace the spiritual lessons in this miracle. He who in his blindness consents to be led, *in the dark,* by Christ, is led toward the light. His sight may come to him gradually; if so he is not to be discouraged; nor are those that see clearly to be impatient at the delay. The end of Christ's ministry of grace is that the blind not only see, but see with discrimination, and clearly.
27-30. PETER'S CONFESSION. Matt. 16: 13-20; Luke 9 : 18-21. Cæsarea Philippi was in Northern Palestine, and a heathen town. It would appear as though Christ were finally driven out of Galilee in his endeavor to obtain a season of repose for the confidential instruction of his apostles. The chronology is as given here. It is the same in Matthew and Luke. Luke says this colloquy took place when Christ and his disciples were alone and he was praying. Matthew adds to the account here a blessing promised by Christ on Peter for his faith. With this exception their accounts do not differ materially from Mark's. For a full consideration of the passage see notes on Matthew.
8:31 to 9:1. FIRST ANNOUNCEMENT OF OUR LORD'S PASSION AND RESURRECTION. Matt. 16 : 21-28; Luke 9 : 22-27. This prophecy, as indicated by all three Evangelists, was uttered immediately after the confession of Peter and prior to the transfiguration. Luke omits the rebuke of Peter. Mark alone (ver. 34) indicates the presence of other than the apostles; but Luke (9 : 23, "to all,") intimates it. Ver. 38 is also peculiar to Mark in this connection; but the same utterance is repeated by Matthew in another connection, and in a slightly different form (Matt. 10 : 32, 33, note). The language there, *deny,* is nearly equivalent to the language here, *be ashamed of;*

and James, and John, and leadeth them up into an high mountain apart by themselves: and he was transfigured before them.

3 And his raiment became shining, exceeding white *f* as snow; so as no fuller on earth can white them.

4 And there appeared unto them Elias, with Moses; and they were talking with Jesus.

5 And Peter answered and said to Jesus, Master, it is good for us to be here: *g* and let us make three tabernacles: one for thee, and one for Moses, and one for Elias.

6 For he wist *h* not what to say; for they were sore afraid.

7 And there was a cloud that overshadowed them: and a voice came out of the cloud, saying, This *i* is my beloved Son; hear *j* him.

8 And suddenly, when they had looked round about, they saw no man any more, save Jesus only with themselves.

9 And as they came down from the mountain, he charged them that they should tell no man what things they had seen, till the Son of man were risen from the dead.

10 And they kept that saying with themselves, questioning one with another what the rising from the dead should mean.*k*

11 And they asked him, saying, Why say the scribes that Elias *l* must first come?

12 And he answered and told them, Elias verily cometh first, and restoreth all things; and how it is written *m* of the Son of man, that he must suffer many things, and be *n* set at nought.

13 But I say unto you, That *o* Elias is indeed come, and they have done unto him whatsoever they listed, as it is written of him.

14 And when he came to *his* disciples, he saw a great multitude about them, and the scribes questioning with them.

---

f Dan. 7:9; Matt. 28:3....*g* Ps. 63:2; 84:10....*h* Dan. 10:15; Rev. 1:17... *i* Ps. 2:7; Matt. 3:17; 2 Pet. 1:17....*j* Deut. 18:15.... *k* Acts 17:18....*l* Mal. 4:5....*m* Ps. 22:1, etc.; Isa. 53:3, etc.; Dan. 9:26; Zech. 13:7....*n* Ps. 74:22; Luke 23:11; Phil. 2:7.... *o* Matt. 11:14; Luke 1:17.

---

the one represents the external manifestation, the other the inward feeling. With this verse comp. Hebrew 2:11; 11:16. On the whole passage see notes on Matthew.

2-13. THE TRANSFIGURATION. EXPLANATION AS TO ELIAS. Matt. 17:1-13; Luke 9:28-36. See notes on Matthew and Luke, especially former.

10. "Questioning one with another what the rising from the dead should mean." This is peculiar to Mark. The Jews believed in a final resurrection (John 11:24; Acts 23:8), to be accompanied by a general judgment. How, after such a resurrection, they were to tell men of the transfiguration, they could not comprehend; nor did they understand that Christ was to be a first-fruits of them that slept, and rise, straightway, from the dead.

11, 12. Why say the scribes and Pharisees that Elias (*Elijah*) must first come? As was prophesied in Mal. 4:5.—**And he answered and said unto them, Elias verily cometh first and restoreth all things.** The prophecy respecting Elijah was fulfilled in the spirit by the coming of John the Baptist (Matt. 17:11-13).—**And why is it written of the Son of man that he must suffer many things and be set at nought?** Christ answers the question of the scribes with another. If they can interpret prophecy and make it bear testimony against the Lord's Messiahship, let them interpret the prophecies which foretell his passion and death. For the prophecies referred to, see marg. ref.

Ch. 9:14-29. **HEALING OF THE LUNATIC BOY.**—THE HOPELESSNESS OF THE SIN-STRICKEN AND THE SUFFERING WITHOUT CHRIST: ILLUSTRATED BY THE FATHER AND HIS SON.—THE WEAKNESS OF THE CHURCH WITHOUT CHRIST: ILLUSTRATED BY THE FAILURE OF THE DISCIPLES.—THE LONG-SUFFERING OF CHRIST (ver. 19).—THE CONDITION OF RECEIVING HIS HELP: FAITH (ver. 23).—THE PRAYER OF THE DOUBTING DISCIPLE: HELP MY UNBELIEF (ver. 24).—THE CONDITION OF SUCCESSFUL CHRISTIAN WORK (vers. 28, 29; Matt. 17:20, 21).

This miracle is reported also in Matt. 17:14-21 and Luke 9:37-42. The three Evangelists agree in placing it immediately after the transfiguration, and therefore during Christ's period of retirement, subsequent to his Galilean and prior to his principal Judean ministry. Its connection with the transfiguration is intimate and instructive. Mark's account is the fullest and most graphic. He paints more vividly than the others the condition and sufferings of the boy; he alone gives the conference between Jesus and the father (vers. 21-24), and his picture of the cure is the most detailed. Most evangelical commentators treat this as a case of real demoniacal possession. That evil spirits do really sometimes gain absolute control of men I believe and have argued elsewhere (see Note on Demoniacal Possession, p. 123); but that this is such a case is not so clear. The father characterizes his son as taken by a spirit (vers. 17, 18; Luke 9:39); Christ addresses the spirit (ver. 25); Mark and Luke speak of him as convulsed by the spirit (ver. 20; Luke 9:42); but in Matthew he is described as a lunatic (Matt. 17:15); his difficulty had existed from childhood (ver. 21), and therefore, presumptively, before his own wilful transgression could have given the devil control over him; the symptoms described are those of epilepsy; it is known that various diseases, especially those accompanied by convulsions, were attributed by the Jews to evil spirits; the word here used in describing this sufferer's condition is (except in Luke 9:42) *spirit* ($\pi\nu\epsilon\tilde{\nu}\mu\alpha$), not *devil* ($\delta\alpha\iota\mu\omega\nu$, $\delta\alpha\iota\mu\acute{o}\nu\iota\sigma\nu$), and while the latter word is used in the Gospels only to describe a distinct evil spirit, the former is used also to describe the spirit of man himself (Matt. 26:41; Mark 9:12; Luke 1:47). Accepting, as I do, the doctrine of demoniacal possession, I regard this as a case of that description; but *if there were no other evidence of real demoniacal possession*, this might be inter-

15 And straightway all the people, when they beheld him, were greatly amazed; and running to *him*, saluted him.
16 And he asked the scribes, What question ye with them?
17 And one of the multitude answered and said, Master, I have brought unto thee my son, which hath a dumb ᵖ spirit:

18 And wheresoever he taketh him, he teareth him; and he foameth,ᑫ and gnasheth with his teeth, and pineth away; and I spake to thy disciples, that they should cast him out; and they could not.
19 He answereth him, and saith, O faithless ʳ generation! how long shall I be with you? how long shall I suffer you? bring him unto me.
20 And they brought him unto him: and when he

p Matt. 12 : 22; Luke 11 : 14....q Jude 13....r Deut. 32 : 20; Ps. 78 : 8; Heb. 3 : 10.

---

preted as simply a case of epilepsy, accompanying or producing deafness and dumbness.

14. And when he came to his disciples. Three of them, Peter, James, and John, were with him on the Mount of Transfiguration (ver. 2). The time was the day after the transfiguration (Luke 9 : 37); the place the foot of the mount, which was probably not Mount Hermon, for the scribes would not have been in heathen territory, nor Mount Tabor, the top of which was the site of a fortified town. Observe the contrast between "the open heaven and the sons of glory on the mount, and the valley of tears with its terrible forms of misery, and pain, and unbelief."—(*Stier*, in *Alford*.) This contrast illustrates the greater change of scene between Christ in his glory with the Father and Christ in the humiliation of his earthly life (Phil. 2 : 5-8). Compare, for an analogous contrast, Moses on the mountain-top and the people in their idolatry below (Exod. 31 : 18; 32 : 1-6). Observe, too, that if Peter's request to abide in the mountain-top (ver. 5) had been granted, the father's woe would not have been relieved. It is not by abiding in ecstasy with a transfigured Christ, but by following in daily duty a healing Christ, that we show our attachment to him.—**Questioning with them.** The spirit of the scribes' questions can easily be gathered from their language to Jesus on other occasions, for example, Matt. 21 : 15, 16; Mark 2 : 6, 7; 3 : 22; Luke 5 : 30; 11 : 53, 54. Doubtless they were taunting the disciples with their failure. The conference which follows indicates a skilful, because an indirect defence of the disciples, whom afterward, but in private, Christ rebuked (vers. 28, 29; Matt. 17 : 20).

15, 16. Were greatly amazed. Possibly at his unexpected appearance upon the scene. But, remembering how Moses' countenance glistened on his descent from the mount (Exod. 34 : 29, 30; 2 Cor. 3 : 7), the hypothesis is not unreasonable that a similar glory irradiated Christ's face. The former brightness awed the people; this attracted them.—**Greeted him.** An indication of Christ's popularity.—**And he asked the scribes;** "taking the baffled and hard-pressed disciples under his own protection, and declaring that whatever question there was more, it must be with himself."—(*Trench*.) And observe that both they and the disciples are silent, the one

from fear of Christ, the other from self-humiliation. It is the father who replies.

17, 18. According to Luke the son was an only child (Luke 9 : 38); according to Matthew a lunatic (Matt. 17 : 15), literally moon-struck, it being a notion with the ancients, and even in later times, that the influence of the moon produced mental disorder (Ps. 121 : 6). The symptoms here described are those of epilepsy, and according to Dr. Robinson (Lexicon of N. T.) the original in Matthew translated *lunatic* (σεληνιάζομαι) in Greek usage indicates *to be epileptic;* but for this statement he cites but one authority. Comp. with Mark's description of the boy's condition Luke 9 : 39. The boy was *deaf and dumb* (ver. 25), and was subject to convulsions. Matthew (17 : 15) says he *suffered severely*, for this is the significance of the phrase rendered "sore vexed."—**Teareth him.** Rather throws him to the ground, as one wrestler throws another (ῥήγνυμι).—**Pineth away.** Perhaps, becomes dry or stiff, a phenomenon often accompanying or following epileptic convulsions; either translation is admissible. Luke adds, "he suddenly crieth out," *i. e.*, with an inarticulate cry, and "it," *i. e.*, the evil spirit, "hardly," *i. e.*, with difficulty, "departeth from him." In other words, the convulsions were sudden, severe, and long-continued.—**And they could not.** "The faith of the disciples wavered by the plain difficulty of the thing which seemed impossible to overcome, when so many evils were digested into one,—deafness, dumbness, phrensy, and possession of the devil; and all these from the cradle."—(*Lightfoot*.)

19. O unbelieving race, how long shall I be with you? How long shall I suffer you? Literally, *Hold up under you*. The language illustrates the sense in which Christ bears our weaknesses, our woes, and our sins—how they burden him. Comp. Matt. 8 : 17, note. The language is not, as Calvin interprets it, that of indignant invective, but of pity and soul-weariness (comp. John 14 : 9). It is true that Matthew and Luke add to the phrase *unbelieving generation* the adjective *perverse*, but this does not necessarily indicate invective or an indignant spirit, for the verb is in the perfect passive, and the literal translation would be *perverted race, i. e.*, race turned aside from the truth. Christ's indignation went out against those who had perverted the people, their reli-

saw him, straightway the spirit tare him; and he fell on the ground, and wallowed foaming.
21 And he asked his father, How long is it ago since this came unto him? And he said, Of a child:
22 And ofttimes it hath cast him into the fire, and into the waters, to destroy him: but if thou canst do anything, have compassion on us, and help us.
23 Jesus said unto him, If thou canst believe, all things *are* possible to him that believeth.
24 And straightway the father of the child cried out, and said with tears," Lord, I believe; help* thou mine unbelief.
25 When Jesus saw that the people came running to-gether, he rebuked the foul spirit, saying unto him, *Thou* dumb and deaf spirit, I charge thee, come out of him, and enter no more into him.
26 And *the spirit* cried, and rent" him sore, and came out of him: and he was as one dead; insomuch that many said, He is dead.
27 But Jesus took him by the ² hand, and lifted him up; and he arose.
28 And when he was come into the house, his disciples asked him privately, Why could not we cast him out?
29 And he said unto them, This kind can come forth by nothing but by ⁷ prayer and fasting.⁸

a Job. 5 : 7 ; Ps. 51 : 5....t eb. 11 : 23 ; 2 Chron. 20 : 20 ; Matt. 17 : 20 ; Luke 17 : 6 ; John 11 : 40 ; Heb. 11 : 6....u Ps. 126 : 5....v Heb. 12 : 2....w Rev. 12 : 12....x Isa. 41 : 13....y Ephes. 6 : 18....z 1 Cor. 9 : 27.

gious leaders; his pity embraced those who were perverted by a false education. And his language here is called forth, not by the malignance of the scribes, but by the unbelief of his disciples. It is not directed to either scribes, disciples, or people alone, but to the Jewish race, as a race, and even still to his church and to humanity. On the Greek word (γενεά), here rendered *generation*, see note on Matt. 24 : 34.— **Bring him unto me.** The language of calm assurance. The disciples could not cure him; bring him then to the Master. Often this is the direction of Christ to the sin-stricken soul. The minister has failed to give comfort; the failure is itself a call from the Lord to himself. Comp. 2 Kings 4 : 31–37, where the prophet's staff fails, but the prophet does not.

20. And when he, the boy; saw him, Christ; **straightway the spirit convulsed him.** "The kingdom of Satan in small and great is ever stirred into a fiercer activity by the coming near of the kingdom of Christ. Satan has great wrath when his time is short."—(*Trench.*)

21-24. This instructive conference with the father is given only by Mark. The question and the father's answer operates as a plea for the disciples, by showing how serious and deep-seated is the disease.—**Of a child.** Literally, *from childhood*, here probably equivalent to *from infancy*. If this was a true case of demoniacal possession, it is the only one in the N. T. in which the possession was congenital, and hence not possibly due to the victim's own wrong-doing. Can a true demoniacal possession be inherited?—**If thou canst do anything.** A very natural doubt, since the disciples had failed to cure.—**Help us.** *Come to our help.* The Greek (βοηθέω) literally signifies *to run up at a cry for help.* See Josh. 10 : 6; Acts 16 : 9; 21 : 28. Observe how the father and the child are one in their misery: help *us* is his prayer. Comp. the similar language of the Syro-Phœnici:n woman (Matt. 15 : 22, note).—**Jesus said unto him this** (saying): **if thou canst believe, all things are possible to him that believeth.** There is some uncertainty as to the proper rendering of the original. That which I have given, adopted by Alford, seems to me to accord best with the grammatical construction of the sentence. It indicates that the saying was one repeated by Christ on other occasions, as we know its substance to have been. Comp. Matt. 9 : 29, and Christ's language to his own disciples (Matt. 17 : 20), subsequent to the cure here recorded. Christ's answer implies, (1) that the difficulty of healing was not and never is in any weakness of the Lord, but in the want of faith of the supplicant; and this because, (2) the healing is to be wrought, if at all, not in answer to the challenge "if thou canst do anything," but in answer to a humble, devout trust in him who can do all things. "Hence may be learned a useful doctrine, which will equally apply to all of us, that it is not the Lord who prevents his benefits from flowing to us in large abundance, but that it must be attributed to the narrowness of our faith, that it comes to us only in drops, and that frequently we do not even feel a drop, because unbelief shuts up our heart."—(*Calvin.*)—**I believe. Come to the help of mine unbelief.** "The little spark of faith which has been kindled in his soul reveals to him the abysmal deeps of unbelief which are there."—(*Trench.*) This is always the true prayer of the doubting Christian. It is noteworthy that in this case, *where the child is incapacitated from the exercise of faith*, he is healed upon the faith of the father, or rather upon the father's aspiration after faith.

25-27. This description of the cure is much fuller and more graphic than in either Matthew or Luke. The miracle is wrought before the people have crowded round the patient, that, as far as possible, publicity may be avoided; it is permanent, being accompanied by the command, "Enter no more into him;" it is in seeming, at first, no cure, for the boy is more terribly convulsed than before, and at first taken to be dead; but the work begun by the word is finished by the touch of Christ, "Jesus took him by the hand." The commentators note in the frightfulness of the last convulsion a symbol of Satan's outgoing in the moral world, always with

30 And they departed thence, and passed through Galilee; and he would not that any man should know it. 31 For he taught his disciples, and said unto them, The Son of man is delivered into the hands of men, and they shall kill him; and after that he is killed, he shall rise the third day.

32 But they understood not that saying, and were afraid to ask ª him. 33 And ᵇ he came to Capernaum: and being in the house, he asked them, What was it that ye disputed among yourselves by the way?

a John 16 : 19.... b Matt. 18 : 1, etc. ; Luke 9 : 46, etc. ; 22 : 24, etc.

seemingly destructive violence. In the quaint words of Fuller, he is "like an outgoing tenant that cares not what mischief he does." Comp. Mark 1 : 26, note.

28, 29. Matthew's report of the private conference between Christ and his disciples is fuller than Mark's. To their question, "Why could we not cast him out?" Christ replies: "Because of your unbelief," and adds the promise to faith, subsequently repeated at the time of the withering away of the fig-tree (Matt. 17 : 20). See note on Mark 11 : 22–26. — **Prayer and fasting.** *Prayer*, because it is only in and through the divine power that the power of the devil can ever be conquered (Ephes. 6 : 10, 11?); *fasting*, because (1) this is the outward symbol of self-denial which is a condition of following Christ, and therefore of successful Christian achievement; (2) because the most intense spiritual labor, as the most intense intellectual labor, is naturally accompanied by a cessation, for a time, of the bodily wants. Comp. John 4 : 31–34. On the general subject of Christian fasting, see Matt. 9 : 15, note.

In this miracle, as in nearly if not absolutely all Christ's miracles of healing, the student may easily trace a parable of redemption. The soul is under the bondage of Satan (John 8 : 34 ; 2 Pet. 2 : 19) ; it is deaf, ignorant of the glories of the divine kingdom; dumb, unable to speak God's praise (1 Cor. 2 : 14) ; no human helper is able to ransom, no minister, no priest (Psalm 49 : 7 ; Acts 4 : 12) ; the disease is in the soul, as in the race, from its infancy (Rom. 5 : 14 ; Ephes. 2 : 3) ; a deliverance is possible through faith to every one that believeth (Rom. 3 : 22) ; even the unbelieving may have help in their unbelief (Ephes. 2 : 8) ; the first approach of Christ to the soul often seems to aggravate the evil (Exod. ch. 5) ; the command of Christ leaves the soul dead, as to the world; but the love of Christ raises it from the dead to newness of life in him (Rom. 6 : 11 ; Gal. 2 : 20). Observe, also, that faith is the essential strength of the Christian (1 John 5 : 4) ; its lack subjects us to Christ's just rebuke (ver. 19) ; it gives power not only with God, but also, if rightly exercised, power over men (Gen. 32 : 8) ; it is attainable only by prayer, *i. e.*, communion with God, and fasting, *i. e.*, abstinence from whatever impedes, permanently, or for the occasion, the highest spiritual life.

Ch. 9 : 30-32. PROPHECY OF OUR LORD'S DEATH AND RESURRECTION.—HISTORY IS THE TRUE INTERPRETER OF PROPHECY. See Luke 9 : 43–45, notes.

Matt. 17 : 22, 23; Luke 9 : 43–45. See notes on Luke, who gives some particulars not given here. Compare also previous prophecy of his Passion. Matt. 16 : 21, notes ; Mark 8 : 31, notes.

30. And he would not that any man should know. One of the numerous indications that this period was one of retirement, not of public ministry. See Matt. 15 : 29–39, note. The reason of this retirement is indicated in the following verse.

31. For he was teaching his disciples, *i. e.*, the twelve. Not as in our English version, *he taught*, but *at this time he was teaching them, i. e.*, concerning his passion and resurrection. He went through Galilee secretly, because this period of retirement was devoted to the confidential instruction of his Apostles.—**Is delivered.** The present tense with the force of the future, but expressing more impressively the nearness and the certainty of the predicted event. Comp. Matt. 26 : 2.

32. Understood not that saying.—That even the twelve apostles had no understanding of the Passion, and no correct apprehension of the spirituality and universality of Christ's mission until after Christ's resurrection, is evident from many references. See Matt. 16 : 22 ; Mark 16 : 14 ; Luke 18 : 34; 24 : 25–27, 44. That it was not intended that they should *clearly* apprehend our Lord's death or his resurrection, is indicated by Luke 9 : 45. See note there.—**Were afraid to ask him.** Perhaps simply from the awe with which they regarded him (Mark 10 : 32 ; John 16 : 18, 19) ; rather, I should think, because they dimly perceived the terrible sorrow which was in store for them, and shrank from knowing it more fully.

Ch. 9 : 33–50. DISCOURSE CONCERNING THE KINGDOM OF HEAVEN.—TRUE GREATNESS : TO FORGET SELF; TO SERVE OTHERS (33–37).—NEVER THWART WORK DONE FOR CHRIST, BECAUSE IT IS DONE IRREGULARLY (38–40). —THE CONDEMNATION OF THE TEMPTER (42–48).—SELF-SACRIFICE NECESSARY IN THE CHRISTIAN LIFE (49, 50).

Of these instructions, Matthew (ch. 18) gives a fuller, and Luke (9 : 46–50) a briefer account. They may possibly be not a single discourse, but a summary of instruction afforded by Christ during the period of retirement with the twelve, after the close of his Galilean ministry, but this is not probable. On the whole discourse, see notes on Matt. 18 ; verses 1 to 9 are parallel to verses here. I treat here only such expressions as are not found in Matthew.

34 But they held their peace: for by the way they had disputed among themselves who *should be* the greatest.

35 And he sat down, and called the twelve, and saith unto them, If ͨ any man desire to be first, *the same* shall be last of all, and servant of all.

36 And he took a child, and set him in the midst of them: and when he had taken him in his arms, he said unto them,

37 Whosoever ᵈ shall receive one of such children in my name, receiveth me: and whosoever shall receive me, receiveth not me, but him that sent me.

38 And John answered him, saying, Master, we saw ᵉ one casting out devils in thy name, and he followeth not us: and we forbad him, because he followeth not us.

39 But Jesus said, Forbid him not: for there ᶠ is no man which shall do a miracle in my name, that can lightly speak evil of me.

40 For ᵍ he that is not against us, is on our part.

41 For ʰ whosoever shall give you a cup of water to drink in my name, because you belong to Christ, verily I say unto you, he shall not lose his reward.

42 And whosoever shall offend ⁱ one of *these* little ones that believe in me, it is better for him that a millstone were hanged about his neck, and he were cast into the sea.

43 And ʲ if thy hand offend thee, cut it off: it is better for thee to enter into life maimed, than, having two hands, to go into hell, into the fire that never shall be quenched;

44 Where ᵏ their worm dieth not, and the fire is not quenched.

45 And if thy foot offend thee, cut it off: it is better for thee to enter halt into life, than, having two feet, to be cast into hell, into the fire that never shall be quenched;

46 Where their worm dieth not, and the fire is not quenched.

47 And if thine eye offend thee, pluck it out: it is better for thee to enter into the kingdom of God with one eye, than, having two eyes, to be cast into hell fire:

48 Where their worm dieth not, and the fire ˡ is not quenched.

49 For every one shall be salted with fire, and every sacrifice ᵐ shall be salted with salt.

50 Salt *is* good: but if the salt ⁿ have lost his saltness, wherewith will ye season it? Have ᵒ salt in yourselves, and have ᵖ peace one with another.

c ch. 10:43; Matt. 20:26, 27....d Luke 9:48....e Numb. 11; 26-29....f 1 Cor. 12:3....g Matt. 12:30....h Mark. 10:42; 25:40. ..i Matt. 18:6; Luke 17:1, 2....j Deut. 13:6; Matt. 5:29....k Isa. 66:24; Rev. 14:11....l ver. 44, 46; Luke 16:24.. .m Lev. 2:13; Ezek. 43:24....n Matt. 5:13; Luke 14:34....o Col. 4:6....p Ps. 34:14; 2 Cor. 13:11; Heb. 12:14.

33. In the house. Possibly of Peter who resided at Capernaum (Mark 1:29).—**What was it that ye disputed?** For seeming discrepancies in the accounts of the three Evangelists and their reconciliation, see notes on Matt. 18:1.

35. The same shall be last. Equivalent to "last among you all" in Luke, and interpreted by, "Whosoever shall humble himself as this little child" in Matthew.—**And servant of all.** Peculiar to Mark. But the same proverb is often repeated. See, on its meaning, Matt. 23:11, 12, note. It adds an element wanting in Matthew's and Luke's reports. The two conditions of greatness in Christ's kingdom are, (1) voluntary humility, a willingness to take the lowest and least place; and (2) an enthusiasm of love, showing itself in practical serving of others. Observe, "servant *of all*." The love which serves only a class, a church, a sect, or especial and congenial friends, cannot claim anything under this declaration of our Lord's. Compare Matt. 5:46-48; Luke 10:29-37; Rom. 1:14. This meaning is best interpreted by his own example. See Phil. 2:5-11.

37. Receiveth not me; i. e., not merely me. —But him that sent me. God the Father (John 17:18). Compare John 5:23, and Matt. 10:40, note.

38-40. This interruption by John, and our Lord's reply, are not reported by Matthew. The disciples had shortly before returned to Christ from their first missionary tour, in which they were empowered to cast out devils (Matt. 10:8). The man here referred to they probably met during this tour. He must have been a disciple of Christ, who was enabled by his faith, yet without a commission, to cure the possessed. It is not necessary to trace a logical connection between John's question and Christ's preceding instruction. The Lord has rebuked the pride of the disciples; and exclusiveness is always the result of pride. John feels, rather than sees, that his act was inconsistent with the spirit of Christ's teaching, and reports it for further instruction. The force of Christ's reply is somewhat impaired by our English version.—**Forbid him not:** for there is no one (not merely no *man*) who shall do a mighty work,(not merely a miracle, not αγαπιον but δυναμις) and shall be able hastily to speak evil of me. The work he has done in Christ's name, will itself prevent him from forthwith using an influence against Christ. The principle inculcated forbids discouraging any work, *by whomsoever undertaken, minister or layman, man or woman*, which is really accomplishing spiritual results (comp. Numb. 11:26-29; 1 Cor. 12:3; Phil. 1:16-18). "Let them heed this who confine spiritual gifts to a canonical succession" (*Bengel*); or, let me add, to a clerical office, forbidding either laymen or lay-women to cast out devils in Christ's name. But, though doing mighty works in Christ's name is never to be forbidden, he who does them may not be a true child of God (Matt. 7:22, 23).

40. He that is not against us is for us. The converse of this proposition is true; "he that is not with me is against me" (Matt. 12:30, note). So far from being inconsistent, the two sayings represent opposite poles of the same truth. Every one is either for Christ or against him; neutrality is impossible. Therefore (1), let him that is not consciously working for Christ, beware lest he be found working against him; (2) let no one thwart or hinder any work that is not clearly opposed to Christ, for it may prove to be work for him (comp. Acts 5 : 38, 39).

41. See Matt. 10 : 42, note. The connection here is this: Even since the *smallest* service done in and for Christ shall not be unrewarded, so great an one as casting out of devils, should not be prohibited.

42-48. The phraseology here is very nearly the same as in the parallel passage in Matt. 18 : 6-8. See notes there, and on Matt. 5 : 22. But the solemn addition of verses 44, 46, 48, "Where their worm dieth not and the fire is not quenched," is peculiar to Mark. There is some doubt about the genuineness of verses 44 and 46, but not about verse 48. There is some doubt, also, as to the genuineness of the phrase in verse 45, "into the fire that never shall be quenched." Alford doubts, and Tischendorf omits it. The phrase "where their worm dieth not, and the fire is not quenched" (verses 44, 46 and 48), is quoted from Isaiah 66 : 24. It there unquestionably indicates, not the torture, but the utter destruction of transgressors. They, *i. e.* their corpses, should be consumed with a fire like that of Gehenna, which consumed the offal of Jerusalem (Matt. 5 : 22, note), and eaten with worms, as the unburied on the battle-field; and this destruction should be open, public, continuous, a warning to others; for Isaiah adds, "they shall be an abhorring to all flesh." The symbol here, therefore, of the worm and the fire, is not of ever-during torment, but of a complete destruction from which there would and could be no deliverance, and after which no restoration. Whether the destruction of the wicked here and elsewhere foretold (Matt. 13 : 30; 2 Thess. 1 : 9) is to be literally or spiritually interpreted, is another question, to be determined, if at all, by reference to other passages of Scripture.

49, 50. These verses are confessedly difficult of interpretation. They are peculiar to Mark. In respect to the proper rendering of verse 49, I remark (1) the substitution of *in* for *with* will render the meaning somewhat clearer, and it is grammatically justifiable. (The Greek student will observe that the dative alone is sometimes in the N. T. usage equivalent to the dative coupled with *ἐν*. Compare in Greek Testament, 1 Pet. 4 : 1, first clause with last clause, and Tit. 1 : 13 with Tit. 2 : 2.) (2.) The clause, "And every sacrifice shall be salted with salt," is not in the Vatican or Sinaitic manuscript. It is omitted by Tischendorf, but retained by Alford. I incline to regard it as spurious. It is, however, true that in the O. T. ritualism the meat-offerings (Lev. 2 : 13), and later the burnt-offerings (Ezek. 43 : 24), were required to be salted. To this law the clause in question refers, whether it was uttered by our Lord, or added by a copyist. The conjunction *and* is equivalent to *even as*, and *shall be salted* is equivalent to *is required to be salted*. The future is used because the law is quoted, not because futurity is referred to. Verse 49, then, will read thus: For every one (under the N. T. dispensation) shall be salted in fire, even as every sacrifice (under the O. T. dispensation) is required to be salted with salt. The proper rendering of verse 50 presents no difficulties. In interpreting these verses, consider (1) the Scripture meaning of the symbolism here employed. *Fire* is sometimes a symbol of destruction (Isaiah 33 : 14; Obad. 18; Rev. 20 : 9; 21 : 8; verse 44 above), sometimes a symbol of purification by trial (Jer. 23 : 29, and references below), sometimes a symbol of God's presence, but always of his presence to purify, either the individual sinner by consuming his sins, or the world by consuming the irredeemable sinners (Deut. 4 : 24; Heb. 12 : 29; Mal. 3 : 2, 3; comp. Matt. 13 : 40-42, 49, 50). *Salt* is employed by Christ in a parallel passage (Matt. 5 : 13, note), as a symbol of Christians, who, *because of their spirit of willing self-sacrifice*, exert a purifying and preserving power upon a corrupt world—a power to flavor it with divine grace. (2.) Notice the connection. The conjunction *for* (ver. 49) connects these aphorisms with the previous exhortation to voluntary self-sacrifice (ver. 43-48), and the whole is connected closely with, and springs out of the previous controversy among the twelve as to which should be the greatest (ver. 33, 34). These facts interpret the meaning of the passage which may be paraphrased thus : *Cut off the right hand or the right foot, or pluck out the right eye, i. e.,* sacrifice what is dearest to you, *rather than suffer it to lead you or others into sin ; for every one* of my disciples *must be salted in the fire of trial, i. e.,* prepared to become a living sacrifice (Rom. 12 : 1) by fiery trial, *even as* under the O. T. dispensation, *every sacrifice is required to be salted with salt*. Ye are, as I have before told you, the *salt of the earth*. *But if the salt hath lost its saltness, i. e.,* the Christian the spirit of voluntary self-sacrifice, by which alone his purifying influence is exerted, *whence shall it derive its moral power. Have salt in yourselves,* have, that is, this spirit of self-sacrifice, *and you will have peace one with another,* there will be an end to unseemly strife as to which shall be the greatest. The passage as thus interpreted accords with the declaration of John the Baptist concerning the mission of Christ: He shall baptize you with the Holy Ghost and with fire (Matt. 3 : 11, note; comp. Matt. 20 : 22) with Christ's own declaration concerning his mission. "I am come to send fire on the earth" (Luke 12 : 49), and with the subsequent employment of the same symbol by the Apostles (1 Cor. 3 : 13; 1 Pet. 1 : 7; 4 : 12, 13). It accords, also, with the unsymbolic teaching of Christ, in other passages, respecting the necessity of self-sacrifice in his followers (Luke 9 : 23; 14 : 26, 27; John 12 : 25, etc.), and

CHAPTER X.

1 AND⁹ he arose from thence, and cometh into the coasts of Judæa, by the farther side of Jordan: and the people resort unto him again; and, as he was wont, he taught them again.

2 And the Pharisees came to him, and asked him, Is it lawful for a man to put away *his* wife? tempting him.

3 And he answered and said unto them, What did Moses command you?

4 And they said, Moses' suffered to write a bill of divorcement, and to put *her* away.

5 And Jesus answered and said unto them, For the hardness of your heart he wrote you this precept:

6 But from the beginning of the creation God made* them male and female.

7 For¹ this cause shall a man leave his father and mother, and cleave to his wife:

8 And they twain shall be one* flesh: so then they are no more twain, but one flesh.

9 What therefore God hath joined together, let not man put asunder.

10 And in the house his disciples asked him again of the same *matter*.

11 And he saith unto them, Whosoever shall put away his wife, and marry another, committeth adultery against her.

12 And if a woman shall put away her husband, and be married to another, she committeth adultery.

13 And" they brought young children to him, that he should touch them: and *his* disciples rebuked those that brought *them*.

14 But when Jesus saw *it*, he was much* displeased, and said unto them, Suffer the little children to come unto me, and forbid them not; for of such ʸ is the kingdom of God.

15 Verily I say unto you, Whosoever shall not receive the kingdom of God as a little child, he shall not enter therein.

16 And he took them up in his arms, put *his* hands upon them, and blessed them.

17 And* when he was gone forth into the way, there came one running, and kneeled to him, and asked him, Good Master, what shall I do that I may inherit eternal life?

18 And Jesus said unto him, Why callest thou me good? *There is* none good but one,* *that is*, God.

19 Thou knowest the ᵇ commandments, Do not commit adultery, Do not kill, Do not steal, Do not bear false witness, Defraud not, Honour thy father and mother.

20 And he answered and said unto him, Master, all ᶜ these have I observed from my youth.

21 Then Jesus beholding him, loved him, and said unto him, One ᵈ thing thou lackest: go thy way, sell whatsoever thou hast, and give to the poor, and thou shalt have treasure ᵉ in heaven: and come, take up the cross, and follow me.

22 And he was sad at that saying, and went away grieved; for he had great possessions.

23 And Jesus looked round about, and saith unto his disciples, How hardly shall they that have riches enter into the kingdom of God!

24 And the disciples were astonished at his words. But Jesus answereth again, and saith unto them, Children, how hard is it for them that trust ᶠ in riches to enter into the kingdom of God!

25 It is easier for a camel to go through the eye of a needle, than for a rich man to enter into the kingdom of God.

26 And they were astonished out of measure, saying among themselves, Who then can be saved?

27 And Jesus looking upon them saith, With men *it is* impossible, but not with God: for ᵍ with God all things are possible.

28 Then Peter began to say unto him, Lo, we have left all, and have followed thee.

29 And Jesus answered and said, Verily I say unto you, There is no man that hath left house, or brethren, or sisters, or father, or mother, or wife, or children, or lands, for my sake, and the gospel's,

30 But he shall receive an hundredfold now in this time, houses, and brethren, and sisters, and mothers, and children, and lands, with persecutions; and in the world to come eternal life.

---

q Ma t. 19 : 1, etc.; John 10 : 40....r Deut. 24 : 1; Matt. 5 : 31....s Gen. 1 : 27; 5 : 2; Mal. 2 : 15... t Gen. 2 : 24....u 1 Cor. 6 : 16; Ephes. 5 : 31...v Matt. 5 : 32; 19 : 9; Luke 16 : 18; Rom. 7 : 3; 1 Cor. 7 : 10, 11....w Matt. 19 : 13; Luke 18 : 15....x Ephes. 4 : 26....y Matt. 19 : 19; 1 Cor. 14 : 20; 1 Pet. 2 : 2; Rev. 14 : 5....z Mat. 19 : 16, etc.; Luke 18 : 18, etc....a Ps. 36 : 5; 118 : 68....b Exod. 20; Rom. 13 : 9....c Isa. 58 : 2; Ezek. 33 : 31, 32; and. 3 : 8; Rom 7 : 9; Phil. 3 : 6....d James 2 : 10....e Matt. 6 : 19, 20; Luke 12 : 33; 16 : 9....f Job 31 : 24; Ps. 62 : 7; 62 : 10; Hab. 2 : 9; 1 Tim. 6 : 17; Rev. 3 : 17....g Gen. 18 : 14; Job 42 : 2; Jer. 32 : 17; Luke 1 : 37.

---

with the actual experience of the Christian church, in which it is almost universally observable that those who have suffered in Christ's fiery trial, possess an indescribable flavor and power of character and experience, which makes them in a peculiar sense, the salt of the community or the church.

Ch. 10 : 1. THE MISSION IN PEREA. See note on parallel passage in Matt. 19 : 1, 2.

2-12. CHRIST'S LAW OF MARRIAGE AND DIVORCE. See notes on Matt. 19:3-13. Of these instructions Luke gives only a hint (Luke 16 : 18). Verse 12 here is peculiar to Mark. "It is expressed as though the woman were the active party, and put away her husband, which was allowed by Greek and Roman law (1 Cor. 7 : 13), but not by Jewish (Deut. 24 : 1; Josephus' Antiquities XV : 7, 10)."—(*Alford*.) It confirms what I have said on Matt. 19 : 9, that the principles respecting divorce here inculcated apply equally to either sex. The other variations in language between the accounts of Matthew and Mark are unimportant. For the most important see note on Matt. 19 : 4-6.

13-16. CHRIST BLESSES LITTLE CHILDREN. Matt. 19 : 13-15; Luke 18 : 15-17. See notes on Matthew. Mark adds some graphic touches not given by Matthew, viz., that "*he was much displeased*," and that "*he took them up in his arms*." Verse 15 is given by Mark and Luke, but not by Matthew. On the respects in which we must become like little children in order to enter Christ's kingdom, see notes on Matt. 18 : 3, 4.

17-22. THE RICH YOUNG RULER. Matt. 19 : 16-22; Luke 18 : 18-23. In studying this incident compare these accounts with care. On the whole incident consult notes on Matthew. The pictorial and graphic nature of Mark's writing is illustrated in his account here. It is he alone who tells us that the young man came running (a token of his earnestness), and kneeled to Jesus (a token of his reverence) in the way, *i. e.*, on the public road (a token of humility). He alone tells us (ver. 21) that "Jesus beholding him loved him"; he graphically portrays the change in the young man at our Lord's answer:

"Jesus went before them; and they were amazed; and, as they followed, they were afraid."

CH. X.] MARK. 47

31 But ʰ many *that are* first shall be last; and the last first.
32 And ⁱ they were in the way going up to Jerusalem; and Jesus went before them: and they were amazed; and as they followed, they were afraid. And he took again the twelve, and began to tell them what things should happen unto him,
33 *Saying*, Behold, we ʲ go up to Jerusalem; and the Son of man shall be delivered unto the chief priests, and unto the scribes, and they shall condemn him to death, and shall deliver him to the Gentiles;

34 And ᵏ they shall mock him, and shall scourge him, and shall spit upon him, and shall kill him; and the third day he shall rise again.
35 And James and John, the sons of Zebedee, come unto him, saying, Master, we would that thou shouldest do for us whatsoever we shall desire.
36 And he said unto them, What would ye that I should do for you?
37 They said unto him, Grant unto us that we may sit, one on thy right hand, and the other on thy left hand, in thy glory.

h Matt. 20 : 18 ; Luke 13 : 30.... I Matt. 30 : 17, etc. ; Luke 18 : 31, etc....j Acts 20 : 22....k Ps. 22 : 6, 7, 13.

"He saddened at the saying and went away grieved" (ver. 22).

23 - 31. DISCOURSE CONCERNING RICHES. Matt. 10 : 23-30 ; Luke 18 : 24-30. See notes on Matthew. Mark's report contains some important particulars not given by the others. To him we are indebted for what is the key-note to the entire discourse, and, indeed, to the whole Scripture teaching on the subject of wealth. "How hard is it for them that *trust* in riches to enter into the kingdom of God" (ver. 24); to him also for the explicitness of the language in which Christ's promise of earthly prosperity is clothed, the words "now in this time, houses, and brethren, and sisters, and mothers, and children, and lands, with persecutions," being peculiar to Mark. On the promise see note on Matthew, p. 230. After this discourse, and forming an integral part of it, follows the parable of the laborers in the vineyard, reported alone by Matthew, ch. 20 : 1-16.

Ch. 10 : 32-34. PROPHECY OF CHRIST'S PASSION AND RESURRECTION. — CHRIST'S CONSTANCY THE CHRISTIAN'S EXAMPLE (Heb. 12 : 2).

Matt. 20 : 17-19 ; Luke 18 : 31-34. The place of this prophecy is the road leading to Jerusalem (Luke 19 : 1); the time is intermediate the close of the ministry in Perea (Matt. 19 : 1, 2, note) and the Passion week, and, in the judgment of the best harmonists, after the resurrection of Lazarus (John, ch. 11).

32. This graphic description is found only in Mark.—In **the way. The public highway.— Amazed * * * afraid.** In a ministry of three months in Jerusalem the Jews sought to assassinate Jesus, twice mobbed him, and once issued an order for his arrest (John 7 : 19, 32 ; 8 : 59 ; 10 : 31, 39). Their enmity was increased by the resurrection of Lazarus (John 2 : 46-50). The disciples were *amazed* that Jesus should return to Jerusalem in the face of this hostility. They were *afraid* to follow, yet would not turn back (John 11 : 8 with 6 : 67, 68). It is in answer to their unexpressed amazement and fear that Christ, who would have all his followers count the cost (Luke 14 : 27, 28), foretells his approaching death. There may have been something in his determined gait and mien, expressed here in the words, "Jesus

went before them," which enhanced their awe. Wordsworth notes this as one of the indications in the N. T. of the peculiar effect produced on others by Christ's external appearance and deportment; I should add, by the unconscious manifestation of his moral and spiritual power. See for other illustrations of this, Matt. 21 : 12 ; Mark 9 : 15 ;. Luke 4 : 20, 30 ; John 7 : 44-46 ; 18 : 6. The spirit of Christ's going up to Jerusalem as described here by Mark illustrates and is illustrated by Heb. 12 : 2. He "endured the cross, *despising* the shame."—**Began to tell.** More fully and clearly than ever before. This was the third prophecy of his sufferings (Matt. 16 : 21 ; 17 : 22), but now for the first time he distinctly declares that he is to be crucified (Matt. 20 : 19).

33, 34. Luke adds, "All things that are written by the prophets concerning the Son of man shall be accomplished," a clear recognition of the truth that the Passion of the Messiah was a distinct subject of O. T. prophecy (Luke 18 : 31, note).— **Betrayed,** by Judas Iscariot, unto the chief priests and scribes, *i. e.*, the Sanhedrim (see Matt. 2 : 4, note).—**And they shall condemn him to death,** etc. For the literal fulfillment of these prophecies see Matt. 26 : 14-16, 47, 66 ; 27 : 2, 28-31, 35 ; 28 : 19. Luke adds that the disciples did not understand Christ's prophecy (Luke 18 : 33, note). This, too, is evident from the incident that follows.

Ch. 10 : 35-45. AMBITIOUS REQUEST OF THE SONS OF ZEBEDEE.—ILLUSTRATIONS OF UNANSWERED PRAYER: A UNITED PRAYER OF FAITH DENIED.—THE FALSE AND THE TRUE ASPIRATION FOR GLORY (ver. 37 with John 17 : 5 ; Rom. 2 : 7 ; 2 Tim. 4 : 7, 8).—THE ANSWER OF CHRIST TO THE CHRISTIAN'S PRAYER FOR GLORY (vers. 38, 39; Rom. 5 : 3-5 ; 8 : 18).—CHRIST THE ADMINISTRATOR OF THE FATHER'S WILL (ver. 40).—THE HEATHEN AND THE CHRISTIAN IDEAS OF GREATNESS CONTRASTED (vers. 42-44).—THE MISSION OF THE MESSIAH (ver. 45).

Comp. Matt. 20 : 20-28. There is no material difference in the two accounts, except that Matthew represents the request as preferred by the mother, Salome. But in Matthew Christ's reply is made to the sons. Probably the sons brought their mother with them, as the modern office-seeker seeks through the intervention of another; perhaps, too, they remembered the re-

48   MARK.   [CH. X.

38 But Jesus said unto them, Ye¹ know not what ye ask. Can ye drink of the cup that I drink of? and be baptized with the baptism ᵐ that I am baptized with?
39 And they said unto him, We can. And Jesus said unto them, Yeⁿ shall indeed drink of the cup° that I drink of: and with the baptism that I am baptized withal, shall ye be baptized:
40 But to sit on my right hand and on my left hand, is not mine to give; but *it shall be given to them* for whom it is prepared.ᵖ
41 And when the ten heard *it*, they began to be much displeased with James and John.
42 But Jesus called them *to him*, and saith unto them, Yeᵠ know that they which are accounted to rule

l James 4 : 3.... m Luke 12 : 50. .. u Matt. 10 : 25; John 17 : 14.... o ch. 14 : 36.... p Matt. 25 : 34; Heb. 11 : 16.... q Luke 22 : 25.

---

bukes previously administered to the twelve for their ambition (Mark 9 : 33-37).

36-37. James and John. On the character and lives of these apostles, see note on Matthew, ch. 10, pp. 147-150. They thought the kingdom of God would appear immediately (Luke 19 : 11), and probably expected the immediate realization of Christ's promise of kingly honor (Matt. 19 : 28). The fact that John united in this request does not tally with his traditional character, as one, *by nature*, humble and spiritually minded. See Mark 3 : 17, note. Compare this prayer with Christ's promises (Matt. 19 : 19), and observe that the denial here of a petition, in which two were agreed and which was apparently founded upon a faith in Christ as a Messiah, whose reign was not distant, constitutes a divine limitation of that promise. Comp. James 4 : 3.—**One on thy right hand and the other on thy left.** The places of special honor. In Josephus (Ant. 6 : 11, 9), Jonathan is represented as sitting at Saul's right hand and Abner at his left. In the Rabbinical books God is represented with the Messiah on his right and Abraham on his left. Comp. 1 Kings 2 : 19; 22 : 19; Heb. 1 : 13. Observe the promises of the Lord are places of *trust, power*, and *activity* (Matt. 19 : 28; 25 : 21, 23); the request here is simply for places of *honor.—***In thy glory.** Compare Christ's prayer, whose language is similar, but whose spirit how different. John 17 : 5, 24. Observe that he asks to participate in the glory of the Father *after* he has finished his work, the disciples before they have done theirs. Comp. Rom. 2 : 10; 2 Tim. 4 : 7, 8.

38. Ye know not what ye ask. An illustration this of ignorant prayer. Within a month they saw the places on his right hand and his left occupied by the two thieves in his crucifixion; and they could not have failed to realize then the solemn significance of Christ's declaration and of the question which followed.—**Are ye able to drink of the cup * * * and be baptized with the baptism? * *** The cup and the baptism are Scriptural emblems of sorrow; it is not fanciful to regard the first as a symbol of inner and spiritual bitterness, the second as a symbol of outer persecution and trial (Isa. 51 : 22; Matt. 26 : 42; 3 : 11, note). There appears to be here a latent reference to the sacraments. In that case the cup of the Lord's Sup-per must be regarded by the communicant as a pledge to share in the sorrows of him who was in travail for the sins of the world, and baptism as an admission to the kingdom whose perfected glory is the harvest of a sowing of trials and tears (Rom 6 : 5-8; 2 Tim. 2 : 12).

39. We can. The language of assurance; but assurance may be of faith or of ignorance; here it is of ignorance. They could say this because they knew not what it meant. When the Master drank the cup they shared not his sorrow, but slept; when he entered into the baptism of his Passion they forsook him and fled (Mark 14 : 33-37, 50).—**Ye shall.** "One of these brethren was the first of the apostles to drink the cup of suffering and be baptized with the baptism of blood (Acts 12 : 1, 2); the other had the longest experience among them of a life of trouble and persecution."—(*Alford*.) See Matt. 10, pp. 147-150.

40. But to sit on my right hand and on my left hand is not mine to give, but (is for those) **for whom it is prepared.** Matthew adds, *By my Father*. This declaration is not to be interpreted away by translating it (ἀλλά οἷς) except (to those) "*for whom it has been prepared*," as Owen and Alford, which is doubtful Greek (see Winer, § 53 : 10, and *Rob. Lex.*, art. ἀλλά); nor by rendering it, "*Is not mine to give on the ground of private friendship*" (*Owen*), "*in an arbitrary way*" (*James Morison*), or "*It is not mine to promise now*" (*Matthew Henry*), all of which are more than doubtful interpretations. The spirit of the original is correctly rendered by our English version. The works which Christ does are done by the power of the Father dwelling in him (John 5 : 36; 9 : 4; 10 : 25); the words which he speaks are his Father's words (John 14 : 10); his life is to do his Father's will (Luke 2 : 49; John 4 : 34); the glory he had before the foundation of the world he had with the Father (John 17 : 5); the power of the present and the glory of the future he derives from the Father (Col. 1 : 19; Phil. 2 : 9; Heb. 1 : 2, 4). So, the place which he goes to prepare for his disciples (John 14 : 2), and the crown which he will give his followers (2 Tim. 4 : 8), are given *as they have been willed by the Father*. In brief, the final adjudication of rewards and punishments, as in all else, Christ executes the Father's will.

41. They began to be much displeased.

over the Gentiles exercise lordship over them ; and their great ones exercise authority upon them.
43 But so shall it not be among you: but ʳ whosoever will be great among you, shall be your minister:
44 And whosoever of you will be the chiefest, shall be servant of all.
45 For even the Son of man came not to be ministered unto, but ˢ to minister, and to ᵗ give his life a ransom for many.
46 And ᵘ they came to Jericho: and as he went out of Jericho with his disciples and a great number of people, blind Bartimæus, the son of Timæus, sat by the highway side, begging.
47 And when he heard that it was Jesus of Nazareth,

he began to cry out, and say, Jesus, *thou* Son of David, have mercy on me.
48 And many charged him that he should hold his peace: but he cried the more ᵛ a great deal, *Thou Son* of David, have mercy ʷ on me.
49 And Jesus stood still, and commanded him to be called. And they call the blind man, saying unto him, Be of good comfort, rise : he ˣ calleth thee.
50 And he, casting ʸ away his garment, rose, and came to Jesus.
51 And Jesus answered and said unto him, What wilt thou that I should do unto thee ? The blind man said unto him, Lord, that I might receive my sight.
52 And Jesus said unto him, Go thy way ; thy ᶻ faith hath made thee whole. And immediately he received his sight, and followed Jesus in the way.

r ch. 9 : 35 ; Matt. 20 : 26, 28 ; Luke 9 : 48....s John 13 : 11 ; Phil. 2 : 7....t Isa. 53 : 11, 12 ; Dan. 9 : 26 ; 2 Cor. 5 : 21 ; Gal. 2 : 13 ; 1 Tim 2 : 6 ; Tit. 2 : 14....u Matt. 20 : 29, etc. ; Luke 18 : 35, etc....v Jer. 29 : 13....w Ps. 62 : 12....x John 11 : 28....y Phil. 3 : 7-9....z ch. 5 : 34 ; Matt. 9 : 22.

The same spirit of self-seeking which incited the request of James and John incited the displeasure and indignation (Matt. 20 : 24) of the ten. Christ rebukes both.

42-44. But Jesus called them. Their controversy had been carried on aside, and apart from Jesus.—**They which are accounted to rule over the Gentiles.** "Not equal to, *Those who rule*, which God alone does."—(*Alford.*) Moreover, the *apparent* are rarely the *real* rulers. —**Lord it over them.** The original verb, in both cases, is compounded with a preposition (κατά), which gives a peculiar tone to the language, as of lordship and authority exercised *over* and *against* the ruled. And this is the essential spirit of all despotism, whether civil or ecclesiastical. See note below.—**But whosoever will be great among you.** Primarily, in the Christian church ; secondarily, in Christian communities.—**Shall be your servant.** The word (διάκονος) properly signifies one who waits on guests at a table ; hence it is taken typically in the N. T. to signify a preacher and pastor (2 Cor. 11 : 23). Here it is not used in the ecclesiastical, but in the more general sense. Greatness is to be achieved in serving, not in compelling the service of others.—**And whosoever of you will become first, shall be the bondman of all.** The original (δοῦλος) never signifies hired servant, but always slave. The idea conveyed by the metaphor is not, however, submission to the *authority of others* (see on the contrary Matt. 23 : 1-12, note ; John 8 : 32 ; 1 Cor 7 : 23 ; Gal. 32 : 5), but *subserviency to their real interests and needs.* It is interpreted by the verse succeeding.

45. For even the Son of man. The Messiah. See Matt. 10 : 23, note.—**Came not to be ministered unto, but to minister.** This is still true, and he best serves Christ, not who offers him the best service, but who hungeringly seeks and humbly receives from him the most. For illustrative interpretation of this saying, see Luke 10 : 38-42.—**And to give his life a ransom for many.** It is hardly possible to

misunderstand the meaning of this metaphor, which clearly implies a true sacrificial offering by Christ, in order to redeem from sin the souls of those that trust in him. Isaiah 35 : 10 ; 51 : 10 ; Jer. 31 : 11 ; Hosea 13 : 14 ; 1 Cor. 6 : 20 ; Gal. 1 : 4 ; Titus 2 : 14 ; 1 Pet. 1 : 18, 19. The ransom is offered for *all*, 1 Tim. 2 : 6 ; it is efficacious for the *many* who accept it, the great multitude, which no man could number, of Rev. 7 : 9, 10.

The principles here inculcated (vers. 42 t–45) do not forbid classes in society, nor the exercise of legitimate authority, by appointed officials in church or state. But they do require that all apparent rulers shall be the real servants of the people, and shall use their place and authority as a means of serving others, not of self-aggrandizement. Quesnel's notes on the parallel passage, Matt. 20 : 25-28, should be read by those who have the opportunity. His deductions concerning the duty of the clergy, are the more noteworthy, because he is a Roman Catholic. The clergy are not to lord it over the laity, not to assume the air and deportment of secular princes ; they are to look upon their office as only a service or ministry, to be, in service though not in submission, the bondmen of the people, and to be always ready to spend and be spent for their flocks (John 10 : 11 ; 2 Cor. 12 : 15 ; 1 John 3 : 16).

46-52. HEALING OF BLIND BARTIMÆUS. Matt. 20 : 29-34 ; Luke 18 : 35-44. See notes on Luke, where the accounts are compared and the variations noted.

Ch. 11 : 1-11. THE TRIUMPHANT ENTRY INTO JERUSALEM. Of this entry we have four accounts. Comp. Matt. 21 : 1-11 ; Luke 19 : 29-44 ; John 12 : 12-19. See notes on Luke for all that is common to the four accounts and for a consideration of the probable chronology. Two or three details are peculiar to Mark.— **Straightway he will send him hither.** There is some uncertainty as to the correct reading of this phrase. According to Origen, Lachmann, Tischendorf, and Tregelles, it should

CHAPTER XI.

1 AND^a when they came nigh to Jerusalem, unto Bethphage, and Bethany, at the Mount of Olives, he sendeth forth two of his disciples,

2 And saith unto them, Go your way into the village over against you: and as soon as ye be entered into it, ye shall find a colt tied, whereon never man sat; loose him, and bring *him*.

3 And if any man say unto you, Why do ye this? say ye that the Lord hath need ^b of him; and straightway he will send him hither.

4 And they went their way, and found the colt tied by the door without, in a place where two ways met; and they loose him.

5 And certain of them that stood there said unto them, What do ye, loosing the colt?

6 And they said unto them even as Jesus had commanded: and they let them go.

7 And they brought the colt to Jesus, and cast their garments on him; and ^c he sat upon him.

8 And many spread their garments in the way; and others cut down branches off the trees, and strawed *them* in the way.

9 And they that went before, and they that followed, cried, saying, Hosanna; Blessed ^d *is* he that cometh in the name of the Lord:

10 Blessed *be* the kingdom ^e of our father David, that cometh in the name of the Lord: Hosanna in the highest.^f

11 And Jesus entered into Jerusalem, and into the temple: and ^g when he had looked round about upon all things, and now the eventide was come, he went out into Bethany with the twelve.

12 And ^h on the morrow, when they were come from Bethany, he was hungry:

13 And seeing a fig tree afar off, having leaves, he came, if haply he might find anything thereon: and when he came to it, he found nothing ⁱ but leaves; for the time of figs was not *yet*.

14 And Jesus answered and said unto it, No man eat fruit of thee hereafter for ever. And his disciples heard *it*.

<sub>a Matt. 21 : 1, etc.; Luke 19 : 29, etc.; John 12 : 14, etc....b Acts 17 : 25....c Zech. 9 : 9....d Ps. 118 : 26....e Isa. 9 : 7; Jer. 33 : 15....
f Ps. 148 : 1....g Zeph. 1 : 12; Mal. 3 : 9....h Matt. 21 : 18, etc....i Isa. 5 : 7.</sub>

read, *Straightway he, i. e.,* the Lord, *will send him back again.* That is, it is a promise to the owner of a speedy return of the ass. Alford retains our English version, which interprets the words as a prophecy to the disciples that the owner will send the animal at once on receiving the message, "The Lord hath need of him."—**Where two ways meet.** Rather, "*In the roundabout way;*" either, as Wordsworth, "in the back way which led round the house;" or, as James Morison, "a topographical note that could only be given by an eye-witness; the likelihood is that the village would be straggled along a road that deviated from the highway, but came round to it again." — **Cut down branches off the trees.** This corresponds with the parallel passages in Matthew and John. But the best reading here is, "*And others twigs, having cut them out of the fields.*" The original (*στιβάς*) indicates small twigs, such as are fit for a bed or mattress, and might include rushes or leaves."—**And strawed them in the way.** This phrase is wanting in the best manuscripts. It is borrowed probably from Matthew, and correctly describes the facts. Verse 11 is peculiar to Mark. Matthew and Luke write as though Jesus drove the cattle and dealers out of the Temple that same day, though they do not so explicitly say so. Greswell's supposition is a reasonable one, that the traders and their effects had been removed for the day, but that Christ saw the indications of their presence, and, returning the next day, drove them out as described by the three Evangelists. It would appear from this verse and Matt. 21 : 17 and Luke 21 : 37, that during the Passion week he remained in Jerusalem only by day, spending the night either at Bethany, just over the Mount of Olives, or on the mount itself. In that climate and at that season sleeping in the open air was no hardship. Probably two motives conspired to this course: safety from the machinations of the priest and a desire for quiet for devotion, and perhaps for private conferences with his disciples, which he could not secure in the now over-crowded city.

Ch. 11 : 12–26. CURSING OF THE BARREN FIG-TREE. —CASTING OUT THE TRADERS FROM THE TEMPLE.— THE PRAYER OF FAITH.—THE PUNISHMENT OF FRUITLESS PROFESSION IS DEATH.—THE CONSECRATION AND DESECRATION OF GOD'S TEMPLE: IT IS CONSECRATED TO THE USE OF ALL NATIONS; IT IS DESECRATED WHEN PERVERTED TO A MEANS OF PECUNIARY PROFIT.—THE PROMISE TO THE PRAYER OF FAITH AND ITS CONDITIONS.

Parallel with this account is Matt. 21 : 12–22 and Luke 19 : 45–48. Luke does not mention the cursing of the fig-tree.

12–14. Few passages in the N. T. have given rise to more discussion or presented more difficulties than this incident. The difficulties, and what I believe to be the true solution, may be, perhaps, best represented by embodying them in the form of question and answer. I. How can we reconcile Christ's ignorance of the fruitless condition of this tree with his divine character? (1.) It is not stated that he was ignorant of its fruitless character, or that he expected to find fruit upon it; only that he went to it as if seeking for fruit. (2.) He may, however, have been ignorant; and this is implied, though not asserted, in this narrative. For it was a part of his voluntary humiliation to subject himself to all the ordinary conditions of humanity, and he did not use his divine knowledge except for the sake of others and in the execution of his divine mission. See ch. 13 : 32, note. II. How could he, as a reasonable man, have expected fruit if "the time of figs was not yet?" This difficulty has led to various explanations; first, to proposed emendations of the text, as, "Where he was it

"My house shall be called of all nations the house of prayer; but ye have made it a den of thieves."

15 And they come to Jerusalem: and Jesus went into the temple, and began to cast out them that sold and bought in the temple, and overthrew the tables of the moneychangers,ᵏ and the seats of them that sold doves;
16 And would not suffer that any man should carry *any* vessel through the temple.
17 And he taught, saying unto them, Is it not writ-ten,ˡ My house shall be called of all nations the house of prayer? but ye have made it a den ᵐ of thieves.
18 And the scribes and chief priests heard *it*, and sought how they might destroy him: for they feared him, because all the people was astonished ⁿ at his doctrine.
19 And when even was come, he went out of the city.

j Matt. 21 : 12, etc. ;   Luke 19 : 45, etc. ;   John 2 : 14, etc. . . . k Deut. 14 : 25, 26 . . . l Isa. 56 : 7 . . . m Jer. 7 : 11 . . . n ch. 1 : 22 ;   Matt. 7 : 28 ;   Luke 4 : 32.

---

was the season of figs," or, "Was it not the time of figs?" but neither of these are admissible; and, second, to different renderings of the present text, as, "It was not a good season for figs that year," or, "It was not the harvest season for figs," that is, the time for gathering them; hence our Lord might reasonably expect to find figs there; but neither of these accords with the facts or with the text. The reader will find a compact statement of these and the other explanations in Trench's Notes on the Miracles. The facts are that figs are produced in Palestine at two or even three seasons of the year, viz., the end of June, or sometimes a little earlier, the middle of August, and the late fall; the latter figs remaining on the tree through the winter. But the early fig usually appears *before the leaf;* hence in this case (it was the beginning of April) the leaf was precocious, and justified a hope if not an expectation of finding precocious fruit, and the language here, "If haply he might find anything," indicates that it was only a bare possibility which he or his disciples had in mind. Mr. Thomson (*Land and Book*, I, 538) says that he has plucked the early figs as early as May on the Lebanon, one hundred and fifty miles north of Jerusalem; a warm and sunny spot on the slope of the Mount of Olives might have produced leaves as early as April on a specially early fig-tree. III. Why should Christ have inflicted judgment on the tree, or been angry with it for failing to furnish him with fruit? Of anger there is not the slightest trace in the narrative. This has been invented and imputed to Christ by a cavilling criticism. Judgment, in the true sense, there was none. For the tree, without moral responsibility, was neither guilty of sin nor capable of receiving punishment. But it was a natural parable of the condition of the Jewish nation, and the withering away which ensued (ver. 20) was an enacted parable of the punishment which divine providence would bring upon that nation, which was morally responsible for its condition, and morally capable of being judged and punished. The act here is thus parallel to and interpreted by the parable in Luke 13 : 6-9; comp. Matt. 3 : 8; 7 : 16; 21 : 43. "The tree, by its precocious leaves, made a pretence of fruitfulness, and thus exactly symbolized the Jewish nation, whose sin was not so much that it was without fruit, as that it boasted of so much." "It (the tree) was punished, not for being without fruit, but for proclaiming by the voice of those leaves that it had fruit; not for being barren, but for being false." —(*Trench*.) The present and personal application of this incident is to all those who make a fair show of religion, but bring not forth the fruits thereof, as Paul describes them in Gal. 5 : 22, 23.

15-19. Christ had, at the commencement of his ministry, cast the traders out of the Temple. That event, described by John (2 : 13-17) is not to be confounded with the one described here and by the other Synoptists. See Matt. 21 : 12, 13, note. For description of the Temple, and notes on the signification of the cleansing, see on John. The part of the Temple occupied by the traders was the Court of the Gentiles; they were thus practically excluded from all participation in its benefits, since they were not allowed in the inner courts. The priests winked at this desecration, and probably participated in the profits. "*He would not suffer any vessel to be carried through the Temple,*" indicates, not a prohibition to carry through these outer courts the sacred utensils of the Temple proper, but a prohibition of the use of the outer court for the purpose of a thoroughfare. The word here rendered *vessel* is translated in Matt. 12 : 29 and Mark 3 : 27 *goods*, and in Luke 17 : 31 *stuff*. The references in Christ's address which follow are to Isaiah 56 : 7 and Jer. 7 : 11. The peculiar language here, "*My house shall be called a house of prayer for all nations,*" reported only by Luke and mistranslated in our English version, indicates that this act was a rebuke, not only of the sacrilege put upon the Temple by converting it into a market-place, but also of the Jewish bigotry which, by thus using the only part of the Temple which was accessible to the Gentiles, excluded them from its benefits. The Temple was not merely for Jewish worshippers, but for *all* nations. The language, "*Ye have made it a den of thieves,*" indicates that it was a corrupt and fraudulent traffic which a corrupt and fraudulent priesthood had permitted to encroach on the worship of God. There is scarcely anywhere in the N. T. a more striking illustration of the marvellous moral power of

20 And in the morning, as they passed by, they saw the fig tree dried up from the roots.
21 And Peter, calling to remembrance, saith unto him, Master, behold, the fig tree which thou cursedst is withered away!
22 And Jesus, answering, saith unto him, Have faith in God.
23 For verily, I say unto you, That whosoever ° shall say unto this mountain, Be thou removed, and be thou cast into the sea; and shall not doubt in his heart, but shall believe that those things which he saith shall come to pass; he shall have whatsoever he saith.
24 Therefore I say unto you, What ᵖ things soever ye desire when ye pray, believe that ye receive *them*, and ye shall have *them*.
25 And when ye stand praying, forgive,ᑫ if ye have aught against any; that your Father also which is in heaven may forgive you your trespasses.
26 But ʳ if ye do not forgive, neither will your Father which is in heaven forgive your trespasses.
27 And they come again to Jerusalem: and ˢ as he was walking in the temple, there come to him the chief priests, and the scribes, and the elders,
28 And say unto him, By ᵗ what authority doest thou these things? and who gave thee this authority to do these things?
29 And Jesus answered and said unto them, I will also ask of you one question, and answer me, and I will tell you by what authority I do these things.
30 The baptism of John, was *it* from heaven, or of men? Answer me.
31 And they reasoned with themselves, saying, If we shall say, From heaven; he will say, Why then did ye not believe him?
32 But if we shall say, Of men; they feared the people: for ᵘ all *men* counted John, that he was a prophet indeed.
33 And they answered and said unto Jesus, We ᵛ cannot tell. And Jesus answering, saith unto them, Neither do I ʷ tell you by what authority I do these things.

---

o Matt. 17 : 20; Luke 17 : 6....p Matt. 7 : 7; Luke 11 : 9; 18 : 1; John 14 : 13; 15 : 7; 16 : 24; Jas. 1 : 5, 6....q Matt. 6 : 14; Col. 3 : 13....
r Matt. 18 : 35....s Matt. 21 : 23, etc.; Luke 20 : 1, etc. t Numb. 16 : 3....u ch. 6 : 20; Matt. 3 : 5, 6; 14 : 5....v Isa. 1 : 3; 29 : 14;
Jer. 8 : 7; Hos. 4 : 6....w Luke 10 : 21, 22.

Christ than this act of his in cleansing the Temple, single-handed, of a corruption so entrenched. Yet we must not forget that in it he was doubtless supported by the sympathies of the Gentiles and the more pious Jews, as well as by the consciences of the very men who were driven out; and that while the priests winked at the traffic, they would hesitate openly to sanction it.

20, 21. Observe that the effect to the fruit-tree exceeds the sentence; that simply condemns it to fruitlessness. But both in nature and in grace fruitlessness always issues in death. It is only by and through fruit-bearing that life is ever perpetuated.

22-26. Have faith in God. Comp. John 14 : 1; Heb. 11 : 6. Here evidently faith in a God who is master over nature. It is an exhortation which in this age of naturalism the church needs ever to recall.—**To this mount.** That is, the Mount of Olives, on which they were standing; the language points out a particular mountain.—**And shall not doubt in his heart.** Literally, *Shall not be at variance with himself in his heart*. The original (διακρίνω) is rendered *staggered* in Rom. 4 : 20, and *wavering* in James 1 : 6.—**But shall have faith that those things which he saith shall come to pass.** Not merely a general faith in God or even in prayer, but a faith in God as then present and hearing, and in that particular prayer as then heard and to be answered.—**He shall have whatsoever he saith.** The words *Whatsoever he saith* are omitted by Tischendorf and doubted by Alford. But the omission does not materially modify the meaning of the promise.—**For this reason I say unto you.** Because the promise of blessing is only to the prayer of faith (James 1 : 6, 7; 5 : 15), therefore we need to strengthen our faith in the time of prayer.—**And when ye stand.** "To stand is the attitude of praying with confidence; to be prostrate, of praying with deprecation."—(*Bengel.*)—**Forgive if ye have aught against any.** Comp. Matt. 5 : 23, 24. The connection appears to me to be this: Christ's faith had wrought itself out in a symbolical condemnation of an unfruitful nation. The disciples were to imbibe his faith, but not to imitate its exercise. Their prayers were to be, not for the punishment, but for the pardon of offenders. Comp. John 9 : 54-56. Only Mark contains verses 25 and 26 in this connection, and there is some doubt as to the authenticity of verse 26. Alford retains it; Tischendorf and Tregelles omit it.

There is a difficulty in these verses (22-26), which probably every reader feels, and which the commentaries do not help much to solve. No one takes the promise here literally, "He shall have whatsoever he saith," and, "Believe that ye receive them and ye shall have them." It is true that Christ sometimes taught by hyperboles, but he never employed mere exaggeration to produce an effect. I confess, therefore, that the largeness of the promise perplexes me; I can only note three facts in partial interpretation of it. (1.) The promise is only to him *who has faith that those things which he saith shall come to pass*. But this faith must rest on some foundation. It cannot be a mere baseless expectation. The promise, therefore, carries some limitations in its terms; it is made only to such prayers as are based on and accord with the revealed will of God; (2) it teaches emphatically that the benefit of prayer is not wholly a spiritual benefit to the one praying, but that it also is efficacious to change or modify, by the divine intervention, the course of natural phenomena; (3) it involved a promise of miracles in answer to prayer in the apostolic age, when miracles were needed to carry on God's work; but it involves no such

CHAPTER XII.

1 AND he began to speak unto them by parables. A ᵃ *certain* man planted a vineyard, and set an hedge about *it*, and digged *a place for* the winefat, and built a tower, and let it out to husbandmen, and went into a far country.
2 And at the season he sent to the husbandmen a servant, that he might receive from the husbandmen of the ʲ fruit of the vineyard.
3 And they caught *him*, and beat him, and sent *him* away empty.
4 And again he sent unto them another servant; and at him they cast stones, and wounded *him* in the head, and sent *him* away shamefully handled.
5 And again he sent another; and him they killed, and ᵃ many others; beating some, and killing ᵇ some.
6 Having yet therefore one son, his well-beloved, he ᶜ sent also last unto them, saying, They will reverence my son.
7 But those husbandmen said among themselves, This is the heir; come, let us kill him, and the inheritance shall be ours.
8 And they took him, and killed *him*, and cast *him* out ᵈ of the vineyard.
9 What shall therefore the lord of the vineyard do? He will come and ᵉ destroy the husbandmen, and will ᶠ give the vineyard unto others.
10 And have ye not read this scripture; The ᵍ stone which the builders rejected is become the head of the corner:
11 This was the Lord's doing, and it is marvellous in our eyes?
12 And ʰ they sought to lay hold on him, but feared the people: for they knew that he had spoken the parable against them: and they left him, and went their way.
13 And ⁱ they send unto him certain of the Pharisees and of the Herodians, to catch him in *his* words.
14 And when they were come, they say unto him, Master, we know that thou art true, and carest for no man: for thou regardest not the person of men, but teachest the way of God in truth: Is it lawful to give tribute to Cæsar, or not?
15 Shall we give, or shall we not give? But he, knowing their hypocrisy, said unto them, Why tempt ye me? Bring me a penny, that I may see *it*.
16 And they brought *it*. And he saith unto them, Whose *is* this image and superscription? And they said unto him, Cæsar's.
17 And Jesus, answering, said unto them, Render to Cæsar ʲ the things that are Cæsar's, and to God ᵏ the things that are God's. And they marvelled at him.
18 Then ˡ come unto him the Sadducees, which say ᵐ there is no resurrection; and they ask him, saying,
19 Master, Moses wrote ⁿ unto us, If a man's brother die, and leave *his* wife *behind him*, and leave no children, that his brother ᵒ should take his wife, and raise up seed unto his brother.
20 Now there were seven brethren: and the first took a wife, and dying, left no seed.
21 And the second took her, and died: neither left he any seed: and the third likewise.
22 And the seven had her, and left no seed: last of all the woman died also.
23 In the resurrection therefore, when they shall rise, whose wife shall she be of them? for the seven had her to wife.
24 And Jesus answering said unto them, Do ye not therefore err, because ye know not the scriptures, neither the power of God?
25 For when they shall rise from the dead, they neither marry nor are given in marriage; but ᵖ are as the angels which are in heaven.
26 And as touching the dead, that they rise; have ye not read in the book of Moses, how in the bush God spake unto him, saying,ᵠ I *am* the God of Abraham, and the God of Isaac, and the God of Jacob?
27 He is not the God of the dead, but the God of the living: ye ʳ therefore do greatly err.
28 And ˢ one of the scribes came, and having heard them reasoning together, and perceiving that he had answered them well, asked him, Which is the first commandment of all?
29 And Jesus answered him, The first of all the commandments *is*,ᵗ Hear, O Israel; The Lord our God is one Lord:

ᵃ Matt. 21 : 33 ; Luke 20 : 9, etc......y Cant. 8 : 11 ; Micah 7 : 1 ; Luke 12 : 48 ; John 15 : 1-8....ᵃ Heb. 11 : 37....ᵇ Neh. 9 : 30; Jer. 7 : 25, etc.
....ᵇ Matt. 23 : 37.....ᶜ Heb. 1 : 1, 2....ᵈ Heb. 13 : 12....ᵉ Prov. 1 : 24-31 ; Isa. 5 : 5-7; Dan. 9 : 26....ᶠ Jer. 17 : 3....ᵍ Ps. 118 : 22.... ʰ ch.
11 : 18 ; Joh 7 : 30....ⁱ Matt. 22 : 15; Luke 20 : 20, etc....ʲ Matt. 17 : 25-27; Rom. 13 : 7; 1 Pet. 2 : 17....ᵏ Eccl. 5 : 4, 5; Mal. 1 : 6....
ˡ Matt. 22 : 24; Luke 20 : 27, etc....ᵐ Acts 23 : 8....ⁿ Deut. 25 : 5....ᵒ Ruth 1 : 11, 13....ᵖ 1 Cor. 15 : 42-53....ᵠ Exod. 3 : 6....ʳ ver.
24....ˢ Matt. 22 : 35....ᵗ Deut. 6 : 4, 5 ; Luke 10 : 27.

---

promise now, since there is no ground on which we can base a just expectation that God will work miracles in answer to prayer, and cannot, therefore, in accordance with the laws of the human mind, believe that if we ask for them we shall have them.

27-33. CHRIST'S AUTHORITY QUESTIONED. Compare Matt. 21 : 23-27, and Luke 20 : 1-8. The accounts are almost verbally identical. See notes on Matthew.

Ch. 12 : 1-12. PARABLE OF THE WICKED HUSBANDMEN. Narrated, also, in Matt. 21 : 33-46, and Luke 20 : 9-19. There is no material variance in the reports, except that Mark gives some details here in verses 4 and 5, not given by the others, and their condemnation here expressed by Christ (ver. 9) in Matthew, he is represented as compelling his auditors to express themselves. Both may well be true. For notes, see Matthew.

13-17. CONCERNING TRIBUTE TO CÆSAR. Compare Matt. 22 : 15-22, and Luke 20 : 20-26. Luke gives the object of the inquiry of the Pharisees, "That they might take hold of his words, that so they might deliver him into the power and authority of the government," and their failure, "They could not take hold of his words." Mark puts the question more directly than the others: "Shall we give, or shall we not give?" Otherwise the accounts are substantially identical. See notes on Matthew.

18-27. THE SADDUCEES SILENCED. Compare Matt. 22 : 23-33, and Luke 20 : 27-40, and notes in both places.

28-34. THE GREAT COMMANDMENT. Peculiar to Matt. 22 : 34-40, and Mark here. See notes on Matthew. There is a seeming but not real discrepancy in their reports. According to Matthew the scribe asks the question of our Lord, "tempting him." Mark's language indicates no such hostile purpose, and the scribe's response, and Christ's commendation of him (vers. 33, 34), have been thought inconsistent with Matthew's interpretation of his motives. He *may* have been an honest inquirer whom Matthew classed with the other inquirers "without entering into careful

54 MARK. [Ch. XII.

30 And thou shalt love the Lord thy God with all thy heart, and with all thy soul, and with all thy mind, and with all thy strength. This *is* the first commandment.
31 And the second *is* like, *namely* this, Thou ᵘ shalt love thy neighbor as thyself. There is none other commandment greater than these.
32 And the scribe said unto him, Well, Master, thou hast said the truth; for there is one God; and ᵛ there is none other but he:
33 And to love him with all the heart, and with all the understanding, and with all the soul, and with all the strength, and to love *his* neighbor as himself, is more ʷ than all whole burnt offerings and sacrifices.
34 And when Jesus saw that he answered discreetly, he said unto him, Thou art not far from the kingdom of God. And no man after that durst ask him ˣ *any question.*
35 And Jesus answered and said, while he taught in the temple, How say the scribes that Christ is the son of David?
36 For David himself said by ʸ the Holy Ghost, The ᶻ Lord said to my Lord, Sit thou on my right hand, till I make thine enemies thy footstool.
37 David therefore himself calleth him Lord: and whence is he *then* his son? And the common people heard him gladly.
38 And he said unto them ᵇ in his doctrine, Beware ᶜ of the scribes, which love to go in long clothing, and *love* salutations in the market-places,
39 And ᵈ the chief seats in the synagogues, and the uppermost rooms at feasts;
40 Which devour widows' houses,ᵉ and for a pretence make long prayers: these shall receive greater damnation.
41 And ᶠ Jesus sat over against the treasury, and beheld how the people cast money into the treasury: and many that were rich cast in much.

u Lev. 19:18; Matt. 22:39; Rom. 13:9...., v Deut. 4:39; Isa. 45:5, 6, 14; 46:9....w 1 Sam. 15:22; Hosea 6:8; Micah 6:6-8....
x Matt. 22:46....y Ma't. 22:41; Luke 20:41, etc....z 2 Sam. 23:2; 2 Tim. 3:16....a Ps. 110:1....b ch. 4:2....c Matt.
23:1; Luke 20:46, etc....d Luke 11:43 ....e 2 Tim. 3:6....f Luke 21:1, etc.

and accurate discrimination" (*Alford*); but this is not a necessary hypothesis. He may have been a caviller, not a disciple, and yet not so encased in prejudice but that he could appreciate the force of Christ's simple but eloquent response, and acknowledge its truth and beauty. On ver. 34, Alford's comment is worthy of study by those who are inclined to regard *obedience*, not *faith*, as the root and foundation of a religious life. "This man had hold of that principle in which Law and Gospel are one. He stood, as it were, at the door of the kingdom of God. He only wanted (but the want was indeed a serious one) repentance and faith to be *within* it. The Lord shows us here that even outside his flock those who can answer discreetly, who have knowledge of the *spirit* of the great command of Law and Gospel, are nearer to being of his flock than the formalists; but then as Bengel adds, 'If thou art not far off, enter; otherwise it were better that thou wert far off.'" Comp. Matt. 19:16-22.

35-37. The Pharisees baffled. See notes on parallel passage in Matt. 22:41-46. Observe in verse 36, here, Christ's testimony to the inspiration of the O. T. Scripture, and in verse 37, Mark's account of the effect of Christ's teaching on the common people, they "heard him gladly;" while according to Matthew (22:46) the Pharisees and Sadducees were confounded by it. Perhaps the common people were not sorry to see their aristocratic teachers put to confusion.

38-40. Denunciation of the Scribes. Mark's language here, "And he said unto them in his teaching," indicates that these verses are only a quotation from a longer discourse. Such is the fact. The discourse occupies the whole of Matt., ch. 23. The verses here and in Luke 20:45-47 are parallel to Matt. 23:5, 6, 14. See notes there. The language here "love to go in long clothing" answers to "enlarge the borders of their garments," in Matthew. The "long clothing"(Gr. στολή, *stole*) was a long, flowing robe reaching to the feet, and worn by king and priests, and by the scribes, probably as a symbol of sanctity, and as a means of attracting attention and securing the reverence of the common people. The holy garments of Aaron, Exod. 28:2, and the white "robes" of Rev. 7:13, are both in the Greek "stoles," the same word here rendered "long clothing." Observe that here are condemned, (1) the spirit that is more scrupulous concerning the outward ceremonials than the inward spirit of religion (ver. 38); (2) that which covets the praise of men more than honor from God (ver. 38; comp. Matt. 6:1-5, 16-18); (3) social pride and vain-glory (ver. 39; comp. Luke 14:7-11); (4) the concealment of practical selfishness by a pretence of piety (ver. 40; comp. Isaiah 1:10-15).

Ch. 12:41-44. THE WIDOW'S MITES.—A rebuke to the proud rich; an inspiration to the humble poor.

This incident is recorded only by Mark and Luke (21:1-4). The report is fuller here. The time and occasion are uncertain; there is, however, no especial reason to doubt that it occurred at this time and in conjunction with the discourse against the Scribes and Pharisees.

41-42. And Jesus was sitting over against the treasury. What this treasury was, is uncertain. According to the Mishna there were in the Temple thirteen treasure chests for the reception of gifts of money, to be devoted to so many special purposes, designated by the inscriptions upon them. These chests were called "trumpets," probably from the shape of the openings into which the contributions were dropped. To such a chest there is a reference in 2 Kings 12:9, 10; comp. 22:4, 5. Possibly the reference is to these chests. It is, however, clear from John 8:20 that there was a room in the Temple called the treasury. To such a room Josephus refers in *Antiq.* 19:6, 1. That there were side-rooms of the Temple used for receiving and keeping the

CH. XIII.]   MARK.   55

42 And there came a certain poor widow and she threw in two mites, which make a farthing.
43 And he called *unto him* his disciples, and saith unto them, Verily I say unto you, That ᵍ this poor widow hath cast more in, than all they which have cast into the treasury:
44 For all *they* did cast in of their abundance; ʰ but she of her want did cast in all that she had, *even* all ⁱ her living.

CHAPTER XIII.

AND ʲ as he went out of the temple, one of his disciples saith unto him, Master, see what manner of stones and what buildings *are here!*
2 And Jesus, answering, said unto him, Seest thou these great buildings? there ᵏ shall not be left one stone upon another, that shall not be thrown down.
3 And as he sat upon the Mount of Olives, over against the temple, Peter and James and John and Andrew asked him privately,
4 Tell us, when shall these things be? and what *shall be* the sign when all these things shall be fulfilled?

5 And Jesus, answering them, began to say, Take ˡ heed less any *man* deceive you:
6 For many shall come ᵐ in my name, saying, I am *Christ;* and shall deceive many.
7 And when ye shall hear of wars and rumours of wars, be ⁿ ye not troubled; for *such things* must needs be; but the end *shall* not *be* yet.
8 For nation shall rise against nation, and kingdom against kingdom; and there shall be earthquakes in divers places, and there shall be famines and troubles: these *are* the beginnings of sorrows.
9 But take heed to yourselves; for they shall ᵒ deliver you up to councils; and in the synagogues ye shall be beaten; and ye shall be brought before rulers and kings for my sake, for a testimony against them.
10 And ᵖ the gospel must first be published among all nations.
11 But when they shall lead *you*, and deliver you up, take no thought beforehand what ye shall speak, neither do ye premeditate; but whatsoever shall be given you in that hour, that speak ye: for it is not ye that speak, but ᵠ the Holy Ghost.

g 2 Cor. 8 : 2, 12....h 1 Chron. 29 : 3, 17; 2 Chron. 24 : 10....i Deut. 24 : 6 ...j Matt. 24 : 1, etc ; Luke 21 : 5, etc....k Luke 19 : 44....l Jer. 29 : 8; Eph. 5 : 6; 2 Thess. 2 : 3; Rev. 20 : 7, 8....m Acts 5 : 36 39; 1 John 4 : 1....n Ps. 27 : 3; 46 : 1, 2; Prov. 3 : 25; John 14 : 1, 27...
o Matt. 10 : 17, etc.; Rev. 2 : 10....p Matt. 28 : 19; Rev. 14 : 6....q Acts 2 : 4; 4 : 8, 31; 6 : 10.

TREASURY BOXES.

tithes, both in money and kind, is evident from Neh. 10 : 38, 39; 1 Chron. 28 : 11, 12. I judge the reference here to be to this treasury chamber, in which, perhaps, Christ was teaching at the time, and in which possibly the treasure chests referred to in the Mishna, may have been kept. Our illustration shows the treasury boxes used in the East in the synagogues.—**Was watching how the people cast money into the treasury.** The original indicates that he was purposely observing the people, studying their action and characters; a hint to the preacher how to get both subjects for discourse, and knowledge how to treat those subjects. Christ still keeps like watch in his church. See Rev. 1 : 13.—**Two mites.** The mite was the least Jewish coin, about equivalent to two mills of our money. Observe, she had *two;* she might have retained one.

43. Calling his disciples. To direct their attention to this woman and to emphasize the lesson which he wished to inculcate.—**This poor woman hath cast more in.** Because God reckons not according to the gift, but according to the giver; not according to the value of that which is bestowed, but according to the self-sacrifice in the bestowal. Compare 2 Cor. 8 : 12.

Ch. 13. CHRIST'S DISCOURSE ON THE LAST DAYS. This discourse is reported also in Matt. ch. 24, and Luke 21 : 5-38. For the analysis of this discourse, its general lessons, and all that is common in the three accounts, see notes on Matthew. Here I call the attention of the student only to phraseologies peculiar to Mark.

1, 2. The language here is more dramatic than in Matthew, and more expressive of the admiration of the disciples for the Temple structure. Matthew brings before us most vividly the structure itself: "His disciples came for to show him all the buildings of the Temple;" Mark, the substantial materials employed in the structure: "What manner of stones and what manner of buildings;" Luke, the ornaments and offerings: "How it was adorned with goodly stones and gifts."

3. Peter etc. asked him privately. This may either mean apart from the multitude, but in the presence of the rest of the disciples (*James Morison*), or apart from the other disciples, and in a purely private conference (*Lance*). The language rather implies the latter; the fullness of Matthew's report indicates, however, that he was present.

5-8. The language here is almost verbally identical with Matt. 24 : 3-8. Luke's language (21 : 8-11) differs only in one or two respects.

9-11. These verses are not in Matthew. But

12 Now the brother shall betray the brother to death, and the father the son: and children shall rise up against *their* parents, and shall cause them to be put to death.
13 And ye shall be hated of all *men* for my name's sake: but he that shall endure unto the end, the same shall be saved.
14 But when ye shall see the abomination of desolation, spoken of by Daniel the prophet, standing where it ought not, (let him that readeth understand,) then let them that be in Judæa flee to the mountains:
15 And let him that is on the housetop not go down into the house, neither enter *therein*, to take any thing out of his house.
16 And let him that is in the field not turn back again for to take up his garment.
17 But woe to them that are with child, and to them that give suck in those days!
18 And pray ye that your flight be not in the winter.
19 For *in* those days shall be affliction, such as was not from the beginning of the creation which God created unto this time, neither shall be.
20 And except that the Lord had shortened those days, no flesh should be saved: but for the elect's sake, whom he hath chosen, he hath shortened the days.
21 And then if any man shall say to you, Lo, here *is* Christ; or, Lo, *he is* there: believe *him* not:
22 For false Christs and false prophets shall rise, and shall shew signs and wonders, to seduce, if *it were* possible, even the elect.
23 But take ye heed; behold, I have foretold you all things.
24 But in those days, after that tribulation, the sun shall be darkened, and the moon shall not give her light,
25 And the stars of heaven shall fall, and the powers that are in heaven shall be shaken.
26 And then shall they see the Son of man coming in the clouds, with great power and glory.
27 And then shall he send his angels, and shall gather together his elect from the four winds, from the uttermost part of the earth, to the uttermost part of heaven.
28 Now learn a parable of the fig tree; When her branch is yet tender, and putteth forth leaves, ye know that summer is near.
29 So ye in like manner, when ye shall see these things come to pass, know that it is nigh, *even* at the doors.
30 Verily, I say unto you, that this generation shall not pass, till all these things be done.
31 Heaven and earth shall pass away: but my words shall not pass away.
32 But of that day and *that* hour knoweth no man, no, not the angels which are in heaven, neither the Son, but the Father.

---

analogous warnings and instructions are embodied in Christ's first commission to the twelve. See Matt. 10 : 18-20, notes.—**Take heed to yourselves.** Not as a means of escaping from persecution, but as a means of preparing for it, as Christ bade Peter take heed against temptation (Matt. 26 : 41).—**They shall deliver you up to councils.** Jewish courts. There were, besides the one national council or Sanhedrim (p. 258, note), smaller councils organized in all the principal towns.—**But when they shall lead you and deliver you up, be not anxious beforehand.** The original verb here (μεριμνάω), is the same as that translated in Matt. 6 : 25; 10 : 19, "take no thought." It does not forbid forethought, but an anxious and troubled spirit. —**Neither premeditate.** A mistranslation; rather, Do not prepare your speech beforehand, (see on Luke 21 : 14).—**Ye who speak are nothing, but the Holy Spirit.** "The Greek is not susceptible of the translation in our English version. The contrast is between 'ye speaking' and 'the Holy Spirit.' The Holy Spirit is everything. Everything depends on Him, not on you."—(*Crosby*.) Observe that this direction affords no countenance whatever to preaching the truth without previous preparation. It is simply a warning against allowing the mind to be divided in time of danger, between the desire of personal safety and the desire to be faithful to the truth. Christ exemplifies his own directions in his course before Pilate and Caiaphas (Matt. 26 : 64; John 18 : 37). His direction is here enforced by promises which Luke alone records (Luke 21 : 15, 18); and it is less a caution for their personal protection, than an admonition to prevent them from proving false to the truth, through self-reliance and lack of trust in God.

12, 13. This warning is parallel to that of Matt. 24 : 9, but is more specific. It interprets Christ's repeated declaration that those who love father or mother more than him, are not worthy of him. It has been abundantly verified in the history of religious persecution; and this history illustrates the power for evil of a depraved conscience; it overcomes even natural affection.

14-23. The language here is almost verbally the same with that of Matthew (24 : 15-25). Luke is less full, but gives some directions and some details of the sufferings, during the prophesied period, not found in either Matthew or Mark.

21-31. The language of these verses is nearly parallel to that of Matt. 24 : 29-35.—In these days signifies not the days of the destruction of Jerusalem, but the days of peril and persecution, the tribulation and travail (ver. 8) which must intervene between the death and the future final coming of Christ. Of this travail the destruction of Jerusalem is only a part. See Prel. Note to Matthew, ch. 24, and note on verse 29 there.

32. How to reconcile this declaration with the ordinary theological doctrines concerning the divinity of Jesus Christ, has greatly perplexed orthodox commentators. The following are the chief interpretations offered : (1.) That it is an addition by later heretical hands (*Adam Clarke*). But there is no reason to doubt its genuineness; it is in all the manuscripts, and in the three oldest manuscripts in the parallel passage in Matt. 24 : 36. It is more probable that the copyists expunged it there. (2.) That the word *know* here is equivalent to *does not make known* (*MacKnight*,

Ch. XIV.] MARK. 57

33 Take ye heed, watch and pray: for ye know not when the time is.
34 For *the Son of man is* as a man taking a far journey, who left his house, and gave authority to his servants, and to every man his work, and commanded the porter to watch.
35 Watch ye therefore; for ye know not when the master of the house cometh, at even, or at midnight, or at the cock-crowing, or in the morning;
36 Lest coming suddenly, he find you sleeping.
37 And what I say unto you, I say unto all, Watch.

CHAPTER XIV.

AFTER two days was *the feast of* the passover, and of unleavened bread: and the chief priests and the scribes sought how they might take him by craft, and put *him* to death.
2 But they said, Not on the feast *day*, lest there be an uproar of the people.
3 And being in Bethany, in the house of Simon the leper, as he sat at meat, there came a woman having an alabaster box of ointment of spikenard, very precious; and she brake the box, and poured *it* on his head.
4 And there were some that had indignation within themselves, and said, Why was this waste of the ointment made?
5 For it might have been sold for more than three hundred pence, and have been given to the poor. And they murmured against her.
6 And Jesus said, Let her alone: why trouble ye her? she hath wrought a good work on me.
7 For ye have the poor with you always, and whensoever ye will ye may do them good: but me ye have not always.
8 She hath done what she could: she is come aforehand to anoint my body to the burying.
9 Verily I say unto you, Wheresoever this gospel shall be preached throughout the whole world, *this* also that she hath done shall be spoken of for a memorial of her.

e Matt. 24 : 42; 25 : 13 ; Luke 12 : 40; 21 : 34; Rom. 13 : 11, 12 ; 1 Thess. 5 : 6 ; Rev. 16 : 16....d Matt. 26 : 6....e vers. 33, 35...
f Matt. 26 : 6, etc. ; Luke 7 : 37 ; John 12 : 1, etc....g Deut. 15 : 11.

Wordsworth, and others), and 1 Cor. 2 : 2 is cited as an evidence that the original is capable of such a translation. But the original (*oida*) never signifies to make known, and 1 Cor. 2 : 2 does not sustain such a translation, which wrests the language of Scripture to adapt it to theology. (3.) That Christ *knew* the day, but that "the knowledge was not lodged with him for the purpose of being communicated to man" (*Kenrick*, *Chrysostom*). But this again is *not* what Christ says, and true reverence for his teaching will accept his statements in humility, not interpret them away in order to reconcile them with a supposed reverence for his person; moreover, the idea that knowledge was "lodged with him" is no more congruous with the idea of his divinity than his own declaration of ignorance. (4.) That he knew as God, but not as man. This is the most common interpretation, and is presented in different forms by Bengel, Barnes, Owen, James Morison, and others. We have, however, no authority in the Gospels for drawing a metaphysical line in Christ's nature, and saying that certain things he did as man, and certain things as God. He is always represented as *one*, and as doing all things as the *one God-man*. (5.) I understand Christ literally, as do Calvin, Meyer, Stier, Alford and Alexander. He did not know, in the same sense in which men and angels do not know. In his voluntary humiliation, in taking upon him the form of a servant (Phil. 2 : 6-8), he laid aside, not only external glory, but also knowledge and power (Matt. 20 : 23; Mark 10 : 40). This declaration of ignorance here is no more inexplicable than the declaration that he grew in wisdom (Luke 2 : 52), learned obedience (Heb. 5 : 8), marveled (Matt. 8 : 10, note), was tempted (Matt. 4 : 1-11; Prel. Note, § 6, p. 15), uttered desires in prayer (Luke 6 : 12, etc). Any theory of Christ which denies, or interprets away these and similar significant declarations of the limitations of his nature, is unscriptural. It were better frankly to concede, that in the mystery of his being, the full interpretation of them is hidden from us, than to make them clear by denying their force and meaning. The practical lesson of the verse is well put by Dr. Schaff: "His voluntarily not knowing the day of judgment during the days of His flesh, is a warning against chronological curiosity and mathematical calculations in the exposition of Scripture prophecy. It is not likely that any theologian, however learned, should know more or ought to know more on this point than Christ himself, who will judge the quick and the dead, chose to know in the state of His humiliation."

33-37. Parallel to this is Matt. 24 : 42-51. See notes there. It is a briefer report, but not a condensation. The independence of the two writers is evident from a careful comparison of them in the original. And this may be with equal truth said of the two accounts of this discourse throughout. The verbal differences are just such as would characterize two reports of the same discourse by different hearers. "*The porter* is the door-keeper (John 18 : 16, note), whose office it would be to look out for approaching travelers, answering especially to ministers of the word (Ezek. ch. 33), watchmen to God's church."—(*Alford.*) The four watches here mentioned are those into which the Jews, after the Roman supremacy, and following the Romans, divided the night. The first or evening lasted till 9 P. M., the second till midnight, the third till the early cock-crowing, or 3 P. M., the fourth till about sunrise, or 6 A. M. The language here is somewhat indefinite, but is that of the common people.

Ch. 14 : 1-9. THE ANOINTING AT BETHANY. Recorded by Matt. 26 : 6-16, and John 12 : 1-8. It is not to be confounded with the analogous incident recorded in Luke 7 : 36-50. The time of its occurrence is not certain, whether

10 And ʰ Judas Iscariot, one of the twelve, went unto the chief priests, to betray ⁱ him unto them.
11 And when they heard *it*, they were glad, and promised to give him ʲ money. And he sought how he might conveniently betray him.
12 And the first day of ᵏ unleavened bread, when they killed the passover, his disciples said unto him, Where wilt thou that we go and prepare, that thou mayest eat the passover?
13 And he sendeth forth two of his disciples, and saith unto them, Go ˡ ye into the city, and there shall meet you a man bearing a pitcher of water: follow him.
14 And wheresoever he shall go in, say ye to the goodman of the house, The Master ᵐ saith, Where is the guest-chamber, where I shall eat ⁿ the passover with my disciples?
15 And he will show you a large upper room furnished *and* prepared: there make ready for us.
16 And his disciples went forth, and came into the city, and found ᵒ as he had said unto them: and they made ready the passover.
17 And in the evening he cometh with the twelve.
18 And as they sat and did eat, Jesus said, Verily I say unto you, One of you which eateth ᵖ with me shall betray me.
19 And they began to be sorrowful, and to say unto him one by one, *Is* it I? and another *said*, *Is* it I?
20 And he answered and said unto them, *It is* one of the twelve, that dippeth with me in the dish.

21 The Son of man indeed goeth, as it is written of him: but woe to that man by whom the Son of man is betrayed! good ᵠ were it for that man if he had never been born.
22 And ʳ as they did eat, Jesus took bread, and blessed, and brake *it*, and gave to them, and said, Take,ˢ eat; this is my body.
23 And he took the cup; and when he had given thanks, he gave *it* to them: and they all drank of it.
24 And he said unto them, This ᵗ is my blood of the new testament, which is shed for many.
25 Verily I say unto you, I will drink no more of the fruit of the vine, until that day that I drink it ᵘ new in the kingdom of God.
26 And when they had sung an hymn, they went out into the Mount of Olives.
27 And Jesus saith unto them, All ye shall be offended because of me this night: for it is written,ᵛ I will smite the shepherd, and the sheep shall be scattered.
28 But ʷ after that I am risen, I will go before you into Galilee.
29 But ˣ Peter said unto him, Although all shall be offended, yet *will* not I.
30 And Jesus saith unto him, Verily I say unto thee, That this day, *even* in this night, before the cock crow twice, thou shalt deny me thrice.
31 But he spake the more vehemently. If I should die with thee, I will not deny thee in any wise. Likewise also said they all.

h Matt. 26 : 14, etc. ; Luke 22 : 3, etc....i John 13 : 2....j 1 Kings 21 : 10 ; Prov. 1 : 10-16....k Exod. 12 : 8, etc....l ch. 11 : 2, 3 ; Heb. 4 : 13. ...m John 11 : 28 ; 13 : 13...n Rev. 3 : 20....o John 16 : 4....p Ps. 41 : 9 ; 55 : 13, 14....q Matt. 18 : 6, 7....r Matt. 26 : 26, etc. ; Luke 22 : 19 ; 1 Cor. 11 : 23, etc....s John 6 : 48-58....t 1 Cor. 10 : 16 ; John 6 : 53....u Joel 3 : 18 ; Amos 9 ; 13, 14..., v Zech. 13 : 7.... w ch. 16 : 7....x Matt. 26 : 33, 34 ; Luke 22 : 33, 34 ; John 13 : 37, 38.

two days or six days before the Passover. Compare John, and note on Matthew. Bethany was a village about two miles east of Jerusalem, on the eastern slope of the Mount of Olives, and the supper was given in the house of Mary and Martha, the sisters of Lazarus. Of the Simon here mentioned nothing is known ; it is conjectured that he was the father of the two sisters, or the husband of one of them. He is not mentioned in the other accounts of the family, from which it is presumed that he was not living. The 300 pence (*denarii*) mentioned in verse 5, was a sum equal to about $54; but as one penny was a day's wages, we may regard it as equivalent to at least $300. See Matt. 20 : 2, note. On the entire incident, see notes on Matthew and John, especially the latter.

10, 11. THE TREACHERY OF JUDAS ISCARIOT. See Matt. 26 : 14-16, notes ; and on the character of Judas, Matt. 27 : 3-10, p. 305.

12-16. PREPARATION FOR THE PASSOVER. Compare Matt. 26 : 17-19, and Luke 22 : 7-13. For notes, see Luke. For chronological order of the events of this evening, see Matt. 24 : 1. The omission of the names of the two disciples sent by Christ, Peter and John, Alford regards as an indication that this Gospel was not drawn up under the superintendence of Peter. But why, any more than John's habitual omission of his own name from his Gospel indicates that he is not its author?

17-21. PROPHECY OF THE BETRAYAL. Compare Matt. 26 : 21-25; Luke 22 : 21-23; John 13 : 21-35. For notes, see Matthew and John; the latter's account is much the fullest.

22-26. INSTITUTION OF THE LORD'S SUPPER. Compare Matt. 26 : 26-29 ; Luke 22 : 19-21 ; 1 Cor. 11 : 23-25. John does not mention the Lord's Supper. See notes on Matthew. The language of ver. 23, "They *all* drank of it," does not prove that Judas participated in the supper. The *all* that were present are intended.

27-31. PROPHECY OF PETER'S DENIAL. See Matt. 26 : 31-35, and Luke 22 : 31-38, notes. The warning reported here, and in Matthew, was given immediately after the Lord's Supper, apparently on the way to the Mount of Olives; that reported in Luke and John (12 : 36-38), was given previous to the supper.

32-42. CHRIST'S AGONY IN GETHSEMANE. Recorded also in Matthew 26 : 36-46, and Luke 22 : 40-46. Matthew's account is the fullest, though Luke alone mentions the bloody sweat and the appearance of an angel from heaven strengthening Christ. See notes on Matthew. The phrase " sore amazed " (ver. 33), is peculiar to Mark, and implies that the experience of sorrow, however it is to be interpreted, came upon Christ, if not literally as a surprise, at least with new and unexpected force ; "*the hour*" (ver. 35), is equivalent to *the cup* in the next verse, and refers to the approaching Passion, with all its accumulation of physical and mental anguish ; the language of ver. 40, "*and spake the same words,*" appears to describe more accurately the third than the second prayer. Matthew notices

"One of you which eateth with me shall betray me."

32 And they came to a place which was named Gethsemane: and he saith to his disciples, Sit ye here, while I shall pray.
33 And he taketh with him Peter and James and John, and began to be sore amazed, and to be very heavy;
34 And saith unto them, My soul is exceeding sorrowful unto death: tarry ye here, and watch.
35 And he went forward a little, and fell on the ground, and prayed that, if it were possible, the hour might pass from him.
36 And he said, Abba, Father, all things *are* possible unto thee; take away this cup from me: nevertheless not what I will, but what thou wilt.
37 And he cometh, and findeth them sleeping, and saith unto Peter, Simon, sleepest thou? couldest not thou watch one hour?
38 Watch ye, and pray, lest ye enter into temptation. The spirit truly *is* ready, but the flesh *is* weak.
39 And again he went away, and prayed, and spake the same words.
40 And when he returned, he found them asleep again, (for their eyes were heavy,) neither wist they what to answer him.
41 And he cometh the third time, and saith unto them, Sleep on now, and take *your* rest: it is enough, the hour is come: behold, the Son of man is betrayed into the hands of sinners.
42 Rise up, let us go; lo, he that betrayeth me is at hand.
43 And immediately, while he yet spake, cometh Judas, one of the twelve, and with him a great multitude with swords and staves, from the chief priests and the scribes and the elders.
44 And he that betrayed him had given them a token, saying, Whomsoever I shall kiss, that same is he: take him, and lead *him* away safely.
45 And as soon as he was come, he goeth straightway to him, and saith, Master, Master: and kissed him.
46 And they laid their hands on him, and took him.
47 And one of them that stood by drew a sword, and smote a servant of the high priest, and cut off his ear.
48 And Jesus answered and said unto them, Are ye come out, as against a thief, with swords and with staves to take me?
49 I was daily with you in the temple, teaching, and ye took me not: but the scriptures must be fulfilled.
50 And they all forsook him, and fled.
51 And there followed him a certain young man, having a linen cloth cast about *his* naked *body:* and the young men laid hold on him:
52 And he left the linen cloth, and fled from them naked.
53 And they led Jesus away to the high priest: and with him were assembled all the chief priests and the elders and the scribes.
54 And Peter followed him afar off, even into the palace of the high priest; and he sat with the servants, and warmed himself at the fire.
55 And the chief priests and all the council sought for witness against Jesus to put him to death; and found none.
56 For many bare false witness against him, but their witness agreed not together.
57 And there arose certain, and bare false witness against him, saying,
58 We heard him say, I will destroy this temple that is made with hands, and within three days I will build another made without hands.
59 But neither so did their witness agree together.
60 And the high priest stood up in the midst, and asked Jesus, saying, Answerest thou nothing? What is it which these witness against thee?
61 But he held his peace, and answered nothing. Again the high priest asked him, and said unto him, Art thou the Christ, the Son of the Blessed?
62 And Jesus said, I am: and ye shall see the Son of man sitting on the right hand of power, and coming in the clouds of heaven.
63 Then the high priest rent his clothes, and saith, What need we any further witnesses?
64 Ye have heard the blasphemy: what think ye? And they all condemned him to be guilty of death.
65 And some began to spit on him, and to cover his face, and to buffet him, and to say unto him, Prophesy: and the servants did strike him with the palms of their hands.

---

y Matt. 26:36, etc.; Luke 22:39, etc.; John 18:1, etc....a Heb. 5:7.... b Rom. 8:15; Gal. 4:6....c Ps. 40:6; John 4:34; 5:30; 6:38, 39; 18:11; Phil. 2:8....d Rom. 7:18-25; Gal. 5:17....e John 7:30; 8:20; 13:1....f Matt. 26:47; Luke 22:47, etc.; John 18:3, etc....g Ps. 3:1, 2....h Ps. 2:1, 2 Sam. 20:9; Ps. 55:21; Prov. 27:6....i Luke 6:46....k Ps. 22:1, etc.; Isa. 53:3, etc.; Luke 24:44....l ver. 27; Ps. 68:8; Isa. 63:3....m ch. 13:16....n Matt. 26:57, etc.; Luke 22:54, etc.; John 18:13, etc.... o Ps. 35:11....p ch. 15:29; John 2:19....q Matt. 26:62, etc.; r Ps. 39:9; Isa. 53:7; 1 Pet. 2:23....s Dan. 7:13; Matt. 24:30; 26:64; Luke 22:69; Rev. 1:7....t Isa. 37:1....u ch. 15:19; Isa. 50:6.

---

a difference between the first and second prayers. Compare Matt. 26:39 with 42, and see note on ver. 42.

43-52. THE BETRAYAL AND ARREST OF JESUS. Compare Matt. 26:47-56; Luke 22:47-53; John 18:1-12. See notes on Matthew and John. The language of ver. 44 is rather "lead him away *securely*," and implies a fear of resistance, rescue, or flight; see Matt. 26:48, note. Mark alone mentions the young man in ver. 51. Nothing else is known concerning him. Conjectures have been busy, but are valueless. The incident appears to be introduced to show the wanton character of the motley crowd that arrested Jesus, and to set forth more strongly the remarkable escape of the disciples from arrest. The linen cloth (*sindon*, σινδών), was hardly, as Mr. Barnes, a part of the bed-clothes, rather a night-dress, answering to our own analogous night apparel.

53-65. TRIAL OF JESUS BEFORE CAIAPHAS AND THE COUNCIL. Of this, which I believe to be the formal trial of Christ before the Sanhedrim, there are two other accounts, viz., Matt. 26:57-68; Luke 22:63-71. John narrates only the preliminary hearing before Caiaphas (ch. 18:13-27). On the apparent discrepancies in these accounts, see Matt. 26:57-68, Prel. Note. Mark's account is nearly identical with Matthew's. See throughout notes there.

66-72. PETER'S DENIAL OF OUR LORD. These are narrated by all four Evangelists: Matt. 26:69-75; Luke 22:54-62; John 18:15-17, 25-27. For a comparison of these accounts, their discrepancies, and their harmony, and for the general lessons of the incident, see notes on Matt. 26:69-75.—**Beneath in the courtyard.** That is, beneath the room in which the examination of Christ was going on. This, probably, opened upon the courtyard and was raised above it.—**Warming himself.** At a fire kindled in the courtyard, probably in a brazier (John 18:18, note).—**She looked upon him.** Earnestly (Luke 22:56); studying his countenance.—**Neither understand I what thou sayest.** Not to be

MARK. [CH. XV.

66 And as Peter was beneath in the palace, there cometh one of the maids of the high priest:
67 And when she saw Peter warming himself, she looked upon him, and said, And thou also wast with Jesus of Nazareth.
68 But he denied, saying, I know not, neither understand I what thou sayest. And he went out into the porch; and the cock crew.
69 And a maid saw him again, and began to say to them that stood by, This is one of them.
70 And he denied it again. And a little after, they that stood by said again to Peter, Surely thou art one of them; for thou art a Galilæan, and thy speech agreeth *thereto*.
71 But he began to curse and to swear, *saying*, I know not this man of whom ye speak.
72 And the second time the cock crew. And Peter called to mind the word that Jesus said unto him, Before the cock crow twice, thou shalt deny me thrice. And when he thought thereon, he wept.

CHAPTER XV.

AND straightway in the morning the chief priests held a consultation with the elders and scribes and the whole council, and bound Jesus, and carried *him* away, and delivered *him* to Pilate.
2 And Pilate asked him, Art thou the King of the Jews? And he, answering, said unto him, Thou sayest *it*.
3 And the chief priests accused him of many things: but he answered nothing.
4 And Pilate asked him again, saying, Answerest thou nothing? Behold how many things they witness against thee.
5 But Jesus yet answered nothing; so that Pilate marvelled.

6 Now at *that* feast he released unto them one prisoner, whomsoever they desired.
7 And there was *one* named Barabbas, *which lay* bound with them that had made insurrection with him, who had committed murder in the insurrection.
8 And the multitude, crying aloud, began to desire *him to do* as he had ever done unto them.
9 But Pilate answered them, saying, Will ye that I release unto you the King of the Jews?
10 For he knew that the chief priests had delivered him for envy.
11 But the chief priests moved the people, that he should rather release Barabbas unto them.
12 And Pilate answered, and said again unto them, What will ye then that I shall do *unto him* whom ye call the King of the Jews?
13 And they cried out again, Crucify him.
14 Then Pilate said unto them, Why, what evil hath he done? And they cried out the more exceedingly, Crucify him.
15 And so Pilate, willing to content the people, released Barabbas unto them, and delivered Jesus, when he had scourged *him*, to be crucified.
16 And the soldiers led him away into the hall called Prætorium; and they call together the whole band.
17 And they clothed him with purple, and platted a crown of thorns, and put it about his *head;*
18 And began to salute him, Hail, King of the Jews!
19 And they smote him on the head with a reed, and did spit upon him, and bowing *their* knees, worshipped him.
20 And when they had mocked him, they took off the purple from him, and put his own clothes on him, and led him out to crucify him.

---

v Matt. 26: 69, etc.; Luke 22: 55, etc.; John 18: 16, etc.....w 2 Tim. 2: 12, 13....x Acts 2: 7....y 2 Cor. 7: 10....z Ps. 2: 2; Matt. 27: 1, etc.; Luke 23: 1, etc.; John 18: 28, etc.; Acts 3: 13; 4: 26.. .a Isa. 53: 7; John 19: 9....b Matt. 27: 15; Luke 23: 17; John 18: 39.... c Pr. 27: 4; Eccl. 4: 4; Acts 13: 45; Tit. 3: 3....d Acts 3: 14.....e Ps. 2: 6; Jer. 23: 5; Acts 5: 31... f Isa. 53: 9. ..g Matt. 27: 27; John 18: 28, 33; 19: 9....h ch. 14: 65....i ch. 10: 34; Job 13: 9; Ps. 35: 16; Matt. 20: 19; Luke 22: 63; 23: 11, 36.

---

taken literally. It answers to our colloquial expression, "I do not know what you are talking about."—**And the cock crew.** See Matt. 26: 74. Only Mark mentions this crowing of the cock.—**The maid saw him again.** Not *a* maid, as in our version. Mark's language clearly implies that the same maid followed him to the door; Matthew, that he was questioned by another maid; and Luke, by a man. Each may be true; evidently, suspicion of him was increasing and widening.—**For moreover thou art a Galilean.** The conjunction, *moreover* (και), omitted in our English version, indicates that his Galilean origin was only an additional ground for the charge against him.—**And thy speech agreeth thereto.** These words are omitted by the best manuscripts, and by Lachmann, Tischendorf, Tregelles, and Alford.—**To curse and to swear.** Matt. 26: 74, note.—**When he thought thereon.** Much difficulty has been experienced in rendering the Greek word (ἐπιβαλών), so translated. For a list of interpretations see Alford. Our English version is probably the best. "He thought thereon," is not synonymous with "he called to mind." "That was the bare momentary remembrance, the word occurred to him; this is the thinking, or, as we sometimes say, casting it over, going back step by step over the sad history."—(*Alford.*) Comp.

Psalm 119: 59; Lam. 3: 40; Hag. 1: 5.—**He wept.** The verb is in the imperfect tense, and signifies something more than a mere transient outburst of tears. He wept, and continued weeping.

Ch. 15: 1-20. THE TRIAL OF JESUS BEFORE PILATE. Comp. Matt. 27: 1, 2; 11-31; Luke 23: 1-25; John 18: 28-40; 19: 1-16. Mark's account differs but very slightly from Matthew's. See notes there, where the differences are noted. For consideration of Pilate's character, and the lessons to be drawn from his course, see notes on John.

21-41. THE CRUCIFIXION. Comp. Matt. 27: 32-56; Luke 23: 26-49; John 19: 17-30. Mark's account is almost exactly parallel to Matthew's. One notes there. The identification of Simon as the father of Alexander and Rufus is peculiar to Mark; they are, perhaps, referred to in Rom. 16: 13 and 1 Tim. 1: 20, or Acts 19: 33. The *wine mingled with myrrh*, ver. 21, is the same as *vinegar mingled with gall* (Matt. 27: 4, note). Mark alone mentions the hour of crucifixion, the third hour (ver. 25), that is, 9 A. M. For reconciliation of this statement with John 19: 14, see note there. The reference in ver. 28 to the O. T. prophecy is wanting in the best manuscripts, and is omitted by Tischendorf and Alford; the latter thinks it was borrowed from Luke

MARK.

21 And they compel one Simon a Cyrenian, who passed by, coming out of the country, the father of Alexander and Rufus, to bear his cross.
22 And they ʲ bring him unto the place Golgotha, which is, being interpreted, The place of a skull.
23 And they gave him to drink wine mingled with myrrh: but he received *it* not.
24 And when they had crucified him, they parted ᵏ his garments, casting lots upon them, what every man should take.
25 And it was the third hour; and they crucified him.
26 And the superscription of his accusation was written over, THE KING OF THE JEWS.
27 And with him they crucify two thieves; the one on his right hand, and the other on his left.
28 And the scripture ˡ was fulfilled, which saith, And he was numbered with the transgressors.
29 And they ᵐ that passed by railed on him, wagging their heads, and saying, Ah, thou ⁿ that destroyest the temple, and buildest *it* in three days,
30 Save thyself, and come down from the cross.
31 Likewise also the chief priests, mocking, said among themselves with the scribes, He saved others; himself he cannot save.
32 Let Christ the King of Israel descend now from the cross, that we may see,⁰ and believe. And they that were crucified with him reviled him.
33 And ᵖ when the sixth hour was come, there was darkness over the whole land until the ninth hour.
34 And at the ninth hour Jesus cried with a loud voice, saying, Eloi,ᑫ Eloi, lama sabachthani? which is, being interpreted, My God, my God, why hast thou forsaken me?ʳ
35 And some of them that stood by, when they heard *it*, said, Behold, he calleth Elias.

36 And one ran and filled a sponge full of vinegar, and put *it* on a reed, and gave ˢ him to drink, saying, Let alone; let us see whether Elias will come to take him down.
37 And ᵗ Jesus cried with a loud voice, and gave up the ghost.
38 And the vail of the temple was rent in twain, from the top to the bottom.
39 And when the centurion, which stood over against him, saw that he so cried out, and gave up the ghost, he said, Truly this man was the Son of God.
40 There were also women looking on afar ᵘ off; among whom was Mary Magdalene, and Mary the mother of James the less, and of Joses, and Salome;
41 (Who also, when he was in Galilee, followed him, and ministered ᵛ unto him;) and many other women which came up with him unto Jerusalem.
42 And now when the even was come, because it was the Preparation, that is, the day before the sabbath,
43 Joseph of Arimathæa, an honourable counsellor, which also waited ʷ for the kingdom of God, came, and went in boldly unto Pilate, and craved the body of Jesus.
44 And Pilate marvelled if he were already dead: and calling *unto him* the centurion, he asked him whether he had been any while dead.
45 And when he knew *it* of the centurion, he gave the body to Joseph.
46 And he bought fine linen, and took him down, and wrapped him in the linen, and laid him in a sepulchre which was hewn out of a rock, and rolled a stone ˣ unto the door of the sepulchre.
47 And Mary Magdalene and Mary *the mother* of Joses beheld where he was laid.

j Matt. 27 : 33, etc.; Luke 23 : 33, etc.; John 19 : 17, etc....k Ps. 22 : 18....l Isa. 53 : 12....m Ps. 22 : 7....n ch. 14 : 58; John 2 : 19.... o Rom. 3 : 3; 2 Tim. 2 : 13....p Matt. 27 : 45; Luke 23 : 44....q Ps. 22 : 1....r Ps. 42 : 9; 71 : 11; Lam. 1 : 12....s Ps. 69 : 21....t Matt. 27 : 50; Luke 23 : 46; John 19 : 30....u Ps. 38 : 11....v Luke 8 : 2, 3....w Luke 2 : 25, 38....x ch. 16 : 3, 4.

---

22 : 37. The reference is to Isaiah 53 : 12. The language of mockery in ver. 32, "that we may see and believe," is peculiar to Mark. Observe that this is the customary demand of infidelity, which insists that faith shall rest always on sight. Mark's account of the response to Christ's cry (vers. 35, 36), Eli, Eli, lama sabachthani, differs slightly from Matthew's. For a comparison of the four accounts, see notes on Matthew. Mark does not mention the earthquake and resurrection, described by Matthew, and attributes the awe of the centurion to the sublimity of Christ's death, not, as Matthew, to the portents which accompanied it. It was probably produced by both. The words "*He so cried out*," in ver. 39, are wanting in the Sinaitic and Vatican manuscripts, and are omitted by Tischendorf and Alford. Whether a part of the original text or not, they correctly explain it. "Salome," ver. 40, is the same as "the mother of Zebedee's children," Matt. 27 : 56. The addition of "many other women who came up with him unto Jerusalem," in ver. 41, is peculiar to Mark.

42-47. THE BURIAL OF JESUS. Compare Matt. 27 : 57-61; Luke 23 : 50-56; John 19 : 36-42. See John for notes on what is common to the four Evangelists. Nicodemus came with Joseph of Arimathea (John); the tomb belonged to Joseph (Matthew); and was in a garden near the place of crucifixion (John). Mark and Luke (23 : 53) describe the tomb. Only Mark narrates Pilate's surprise at learning of the death of Jesus (ver. 44).—**The even was come.** Here, evidently, the first of the two evenings recognized in Jewish reckoning, *i. e., before* sunset, because the Sabbath began on sunset (Lev. 23 : 32).—**The preparation, that is, the fore-Sabbath;** or, as we should say, in analogy with our Christmas-eve, Sabbath-eve. In the Syriac N. T. the word "preparation" is rendered "eve." It would appear that the close of Friday, perhaps from the ninth hour, 3 P. M., was at first called the "preparation," and that later the term extended to the whole of Friday, as in German the usual name of Saturday is Sonnabend, *i. e.,* "Sunday-eve." See John 19 : 31, note. That the bodies might not remain on the cross over the Sabbath, the Jews had asked to have death accelerated (John 19 : 31), and now Joseph asks permission to give the body honorable burial.—**Joseph of Arimathea.** On his character, see notes on John.—**An honorable counsellor,** *i. e.,* a member of the Sanhedrim and occupying some station of honor or dignity. Luke adds the information respecting him, that he was a "good man and just," and had not consented to the condemnation pronounced against Christ by the Sanhedrim.—**Which also waited for the kingdom of God.** That is, he belonged to that portion of the Pharisees (Matt. 3 : 7, note) who

CHAPTER XVI.

AND when ⁷ the sabbath was past, Mary Magdalene, and Mary the *mother* of James, and Salome, had bought sweet spices,¹ that they might come and anoint him.

2 And very early in the morning, the first *day* of the week, they came unto the sepulchre at the rising of the sun.

3 And they said among themselves, Who shall roll us away the stone from the door of the sepulchre?

4 And when they looked, they saw that the stone was rolled away: for it was very great.

y Matt. 28 : 1, etc.; Luke 24 : 1, etc.; John 20 : 1, etc. . . . z Luke 23 : 56.

---

were in expectation of the coming of a Messiah to inaugurate the kingdom of God. Comp. Luke 2 : 25.—**Went in boldly.** Of course this ended for him all position of honor in the Jewish court and nation (John 9 : 22). Moreover it identified him with a man crucified on a charge of sedition against the Roman government. Mr. Farrar notes a case in history in which such a request cost the petitioner his life. — **Pilate wondered if he were already dead.** Because crucifixion is a lingering death, and rarely proves mortal in so short a space. Christ had not been on the cross more than six hours, probably not so long. Comp. ver. 25 with 34. See note on Physical Cause of Christ's Death, John 19 : 34, 35. — **Whether he had been any while dead.** Because he would make sure of his death. Observe the incidental testimony that the resurrection of Christ was no arousal from a syncope or fainting fit, as rationalistic criticism has sometimes regarded it.—**He gave the body.** Often the privilege of burial was bought with a bribe by the friends of the deceased. Pilate, as a measure of relief to his conscience, *gave* the body to Joseph.

Ch. 16 : 1-8. THE RESURRECTION OF JESUS CHRIST. See note on Matt. 28 : 1-17. Parallel to the account here is Matt. 28 : 2-10 ; Luke 24 : 1-11 ; comp. John 20 : 1-10. For a comparison of the different evangelical narratives of the resurrection of our Lord, and for the evidence of the reality of that resurrection, see note on the Resurrection of Jesus Christ, p. 330. For notes on what is common to Matthew and Mark, see notes on Matthew. Mark here, as elsewhere, furnishes some vivid details, which we should not otherwise possess. — **When the Sabbath was past, Mary, etc., purchased aromatics.** It is not very clear when they were purchased. The verb is in the aorist tense, not, as in our English version in the pluperfect. The indication here is, certainly, that this purchase was made on the Sabbath, after sunset; the indication in Luke 23 : 55, 56, is that it was made on Friday night, after the burial. It may be, that the purchases were begun then, but not completed, the evening coming on quickly, and the shops being closed, so that the women had to postpone the completion till the Sabbath was past.—**That they might come and anoint him.** An indication that they had no expectation of his resurrection. It was customary among the Jews, as a mark of honor to the deceased, after washing the corpse, to anoint it with certain perfumes, or to enclose them in the grave-clothes in which the body was wrapped. They were sometimes also burned as an incense. The hurried burial had not permitted this anointing to be completed; it had been commenced by Nicodemus at the time of the interment (John 19 : 39, 40). Perhaps the women were ignorant of that; perhaps they wished to add their own offerings. The aromatics employed for this purpose appear from John to have been aloes and myrrh.

2-4. **They came unto the sepulchre at the rising of the sun.** Matthew says, "As it began to dawn"; John, "When it was yet dark." This discrepancy is only verbal; the language describes the same substantial time, and differs only as we should expect the language of independent writers would. At sunrise is in popular language equivalent to dawn (Judges 9 : 33; Ps. 104 : 22). John's language is the most minutely accurate, and he is the one most likely to have been accurately informed. The women came probably before the sun was fairly up.—**Who shall roll us away the stone?** The language here ex-

TOMB.

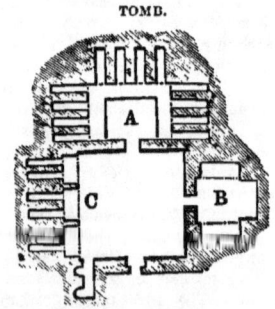

Diagram of Jewish Sepulchre.

actly corresponds with the known structure of the Jewish tomb and door, one of those incidental evidences of the authenticity of our Gospels with which they abound. The form of the ordinary Jewish tomb will be best understood by the annexed plan. It consisted of a chamber or chambers, A, B, C, cut in the rock, from which openings

Ch. XVI.] MARK.

5 And entering into the sepulchre, they saw a young man sitting on the right side, clothed in a long white garment; and they were affrighted.
6 And he saith unto them, Be not affrighted: Ye seek Jesus of Nazareth, which was crucified: he is risen; ª he is not here: behold the place where they laid him.
7 But go your way, tell his disciples and Peter that he goeth before you into Galilee: there shall ye see him, as he said unto you.
8 And they went out quickly, and fled from the sepulchre; for they trembled and were amazed: neither said they any thing to any man; for they were afraid.
9 Now when *Jesus* was risen early the first *day* of the week, he appeared first to Mary Magdalene, out of whom he had cast seven devils.

10 And she went and told them that had been with him, as they mourned and wept.
11 And they, when they had heard that he was alive, and had been seen of her, believed not.
12 After that he appeared in another form unto two ᵇ of them, as they walked, and went into the country.
13 And they went and told *it* unto the residue; neither believed they them.
14 Afterward he ᶜ appeared unto the eleven as they sat at meat, and upbraided them with their unbelief ᵈ and hardness of heart, because they believed not them which had seen him after he had risen.
15 And he said unto them, Go ᵉ ye into all the world, and preach the gospel to every creature.ᶠ

ª Ps. 71:20...ᵇ Luke 24:13...ᶜ Luke 24:36; 1 Cor. 15:5...ᵈ Luke 24. 25...ᵉ Matt. 28:19; John 20:21...ᶠ Rom. 10:18; Col. 1:23.

branched out, about two feet wide and three feet high. These, called *loculi*, held the bodies of the dead. Sometimes, but probably only at a later period, they were found as indicated in B. The interior of such a tomb is represented in a cut illustrating the resurrection of Lazarus,

PLAN OF TOMB DOOR OR GOLAL.

and accompanying John, ch. 11. Sometimes, doubtless, the tomb consisted simply of the cave or larger chamber, without the accompanying *loculi*. The door of the cave consisted, at least in some cases, of a circular stone, like a mill-stone, which could be rolled across the

DOOR OF TOMB.

doorway, closing the aperture, or rolled back into a niche, cut in the adjoining rock to receive it, so as to leave the doorway open. The accompanying plan and picture illustrates the method. The picture is from the tombs of the kings, still existing in the neighborhood of Jerusalem. The opening of such tombs is generally low, so that on entering them it is necessary to stoop (Luke 24:12; John 20:5, 11). In the case of Jesus, the anointing had not been completed, and if there were *loculi*, the body could hardly have been laid away in one of them, for Mary Magdalene, without entering the sepulchre, saw two angels sitting, one at the head, and the other at the foot, where the body of Jesus had lain (John 20:12), which they could not have done, in the *loculus*. The facts, then, would appear to be that the women, coming to the sepulchre early in the morning to complete the anointing, feared that they could not roll back into its niche the *golal* or circular stone, the groove into the niche generally inclining upwards, so that it required considerable exertion of strength to roll back the door; that when they came they found it already rolled back, and entering in they saw the young man (ver. 5), the angel of Matthew (ch. 28:2). Whether he was sitting in a partially reclining attitude on the door when they entered, and was not disclosed to them till after they entered, or whether Matthew's statement of his sitting on the stone is merely indicative of his previous posture, as a symbolic act of victory over the grave, is a matter of conjecture merely.—**And when they looked, etc.** These words are correctly placed in our English version in a parenthesis. The narrator breaks in upon his narrative to set in contrast with their anxiety the unexpected and supernatural removal of the stone. The moral has often and fairly been drawn, that when Christian love undertakes a difficult duty, God will remove the obstacles which are too great for its own strength.

5-8. **A young man.** That there were *two* is evident from John 20:12; that they were angels, appears from Matt. 28:2; see note there. —**Clothed in a long white garment.** Liter-

16 He ᵍ that believeth, and is baptized, shall be saved; but he ʰ that believeth not, shall be damned.
17 And these signs shall follow them that believe: In my ⁱ name shall they cast out devils; they shall speak ʲ with new tongues;
18 They shall take up serpents; ᵏ and if they drink any deadly thing, it shall not hurt them; they ˡ shall lay hands on the sick, and they shall recover.

19 So then ᵐ after the Lord had spoken unto them, he was received up into heaven, and sat ⁿ on the right hand of God.
20 And they went forth and preached every where, the Lord ᵒ working with *them*, and confirming the word with signs following. Amen.

g John 3 : 18, 36 ; Acts 16 : 31-33 ; Rom. 10 : 9 ; 1 Pet. 3 : 21....h John 12 : 48 ; 2 Thess. 2 : 12....i Luke 10 : 17 ; Acts 5 : 16 ; 8 : 7 ; 16 : 18 ¹ 19 : 12....j Acts 2 : 4 ; 10 : 46 ; 1 Cor 12 : 10, 28....k Luke 10 : 19 ; Acts 28 : 5....l Acts 5 : 15, 16 ; 28 : 8 ; James 5 : 14, 15....m Acts 1 : 2, 3 ; Luke 24 : 51....n Ps. 110 : 1 ; 1 Pet. 3 : 22 ; Rev. 3 : 21....o Acts 5 : 12 ; 14 : 3 ; Heb. 2 : 4.

---

ally, a *stole* (Gr. στολῇ). See ch. 12 : 38–40, note.—**Be not affrighted.** The angel's reassuring response to the women, who started back at the unexpected apparition.—**And Peter.** Observe that as Christ's first appearance is to Mary Magdalene (John 20 : 18), out of whom he had cast seven devils, so his special message is to Peter who had denied him. "Tell Peter, for it will be news more welcome to him than to any of them, for he is in sorrow for sin; and he will be afraid lest the joy of this good news do not belong to him."—(*Matthew Henry.*)—**They trembled and were afraid.** Rather, *Were in an ecstasy* or *in a maze;* a commingled feeling of fear, awe, hope, and strange expectation is indicated by the language here and in Matthew.—**Neither said they anything to any man.** That is, on their way to tell the disciples. See 'Matt. 28 : 8, note.

Ch. 16 : 9-20. APPEARANCES OF JESUS AFTER HIS RESURRECTION.—COMMISSION TO THE ELEVEN.—ASCENSION.—CHRIST'S FIRST APPEARANCE IS TO THE WOMAN TO WHOM HE HAS SHOWN THE GREATEST MERCY (9).—THE MISTAKE OF MOURNING: IT WEEPS AT THE GRAVE OF THE RISEN (10, 11).—THE REPROACH OF CHRIST'S CHURCH: ITS SLOWNESS TO BELIEVE (14).—THE COMMISSION OF CHRIST TO HIS CHURCH: ITS FIELD IS THE WORLD; ITS WORK IS TO PREACH THE GOSPEL; ITS CONGREGATION EMBRACES EVERY CREATURE; ITS OFFER IS A FREE AND FULL SALVATION; THE CONDITION OF SALVATION IS FAITH IN CHRIST AND CONFESSION OF AND CONSECRATION TO HIM: THE CONSEQUENCE OF REJECTING CHRIST'S PROFFERED SALVATION IS ETERNAL CONDEMNATION.

The question whether this passage properly belongs to Mark's Gospel or is an addition by a later hand, is one of the most difficult in Biblical criticism. I shall here state briefly the reasons for and against its authenticity, and then my own conclusion. I. *External considerations.* It is found in the Alexandrine, Ephraem and Cambridge Manuscripts (See Intro., pp. 23, 24), and in the Vulgate, Ethiopic, Curetonian Syriac, Peshito, Jerusalem Syriac, Memphitic and Gothic Versions. It is wanting in the two oldest and most valued manuscripts, the Vatican and Sinaitic. If not a part of the original Gospel, it must have been added at a very early date, probably during the first century. II. *Internal considerations.* Verse 8 ends so abruptly as to forbid the idea that this was the close of the original Gospel.

The last word in the Greek is a connective particle. "*For they were afraid*" is literally, *They were afraid for* (ἐφοβοῦντο γάρ). If Mark's Gospel really ends here, it must be either because he was suddenly interrupted, or because his original close has been lost. On the other hand, the language in the Greek of the last eleven verses is unlike the rest of Mark's Gospel. "No less than twenty-one words and expressions occur in it (and some of them several times) which are never elsewhere used by Mark, whose adherence to his own peculiar phrases is remarkable."—(*Alford.*) To which add that the summing up of verses 19, 20, is unlike Mark, who is pictorial but unsystematic, and that the language of verses 15-18, compared with Matthew's account of the same commission to the eleven (ch. 28 : 18-20), indicates a less accurate and authentic report of this legacy of our Lord to his church. See notes below. III. *Opinions of scholars.* The genuineness of this passage is affirmed by Mill, Olshausen, Eward, Lachmann, and Schaff; it is doubted or denied by Griesbach, Ewald, Meyer, Tischendorf, Tregelles, Lightfoot, and Norton. For an elaborate discussion of these and other conflicting testimonies, see James Morison's Commentary on Mark; he concludes that the passage is genuine. The weight of authority internal and external, appears to me to point to the other conclusion, viz., that Mark's Gospel either was abruptly broken off by some accident, or its close was early lost, and that verses 9-20 were appended at a very early day, probably during the first century, to give completion to the book. The question is one of secondary importance, since all that is essential in spirit and substance in this passage is to be found elsewhere in the Gospels, in accounts whose authenticity is undoubted.

9-11. The details of this appearance are given in John 20 : 11-18. See notes there. On the character of Mary Magdalene, see Matthew 27 : 56, note. Of the fact here stated, that Christ cast seven devils out of her, we have no information except the statement here and in Luke 8 : 2.

12, 13. This is a brief recapitulation of an incident recorded more fully in Luke 24 : 13-35. See notes there.

14. This appearance is more fully described in Luke 24 : 36-49, and John 20 : 19-23. See notes there.

15-18. This commission is repeated more briefly, but I believe more accurately, by Matt. 28:18–20. See notes there. At least it appears to me that they are identical, though all commentators do not so regard them. Matthew indicates that it was given in Galilee. Mark connects with it the ascension, which took place from the Mount of Olives (Acts 1:12). But neither asserts definitely the location. This can hardly be the same interview reported by Luke (24:45–49). That our Lord should have prepared the eleven for the last commission, by previous instruction, is what we might reasonably expect.—**Into all the world.** Comp. Matt. 13:38.—**Herald the glad tidings.** This was the first commission of the apostles (Matt. 10:7); they were now to be more than mere heralds of a coming Gospel—they were to be instructors of the people in the principles of a Gospel which by his death Christ had finished, which was no more *coming* but *had come* (comp. Matt. 28:19, note). It appears to me that the author of this passage has failed to recognize this change in the apostle's work, which Matthew's report clearly indicates. This variation between Mark and Matthew, is one of the indications that we have not here an authentic report of the original commission, but a summary made up by a later hand.—**To all the creation.** This is equivalent to "all nations" in Matthew. "True," as Alford says, "all creation is redeemed by Christ (Col. 1:15–23; Rom. 8:19–23); but the Gospel can be *preached* only to man.—**He that believeth and is baptized shall be saved.** *Believeth*, *i. e.*, has faith in and trusts himself to Christ as preached in the Gospel; *and is baptized*, publicly acknowledges that faith, and is consecrated to and enters upon a new life in the Father, the Son, and the Holy Ghost (John 3:5, 6; Matt. 28:19, note); *shall be saved*, from both the present dominion and the future penalty of sin (Matt. 1:21; Rom. 8:2).—**But he that believeth not shall be condemned.** Not he that is in doubt or perplexity, as the disciples in vers. 11, 13, but he that refuses to open his heart to the influence of a living and present Saviour. The declaration here is parallel to and interpreted by John 3:18, 19; comp. John 15:22; Heb. 2:3. Observe, then, that not every belief saves (James 2:19), nor does every unbelief bring into condemnation (John 20:25–27). Observe, too, that by implication baptism is not *essential* to salvation as faith is. One may be baptized and yet not believe, as Simon (Acts 8:13; 13:23), or believe and not be baptized, as the penitent thief (Luke 23:43).—**In my name shall they cast out devils.** For fulfillment of this promise, see Acts 5:16; 8:7; 16:18.—**They shall speak with new tongues.** See Acts 2:4; 1 Cor. 14:22, and notes at these places.—**They shall take up serpents.** See Acts 28:3–5.—**If they drink, etc.** Scripture affords no illustration of the fulfillment of this promise. But we may presume that of the miracles wrought after Christ's resurrection, as of those wrought by him in the body, many were not recorded (John 20:30).—**They shall lay hands on the sick, etc.** Comp. James 5:14, 15. With this whole promise compare that of Matt. 10:1–8 and Luke 10:19, from which the unknown author of this passage may have derived it. Though the miracle-working power remained in the church after the ascension of our Lord, Christianity was made less dependent on such external signs and tokens, and more and more on the moral and spiritual power of the word itself. Comp. 1 Cor. 2:4; 1 Thess. 1:5. With this promise compare the still more general one of Psalm 91. On its applicability to our own time, Alford says: "This promise is generally without limitation to the first ages of the church. *Should occasion arise for its fulfillment* there can be no doubt that it will be made good in our own or any other time. But we must remember that signs are not needed where Christianity is *professed*, nor by missionaries who are backed by the influence of the powerful Christian nations." This seems to me to be true, but only a superficial truth. Such signs as are indicated here are not needed in this age, when the divine nature of Christianity is witnessed by such historical evidences as are afforded by the moral, the religious, the social, the political, and even the commercial development which has everywhere attended on and resulted from its progress. I can hardly conceive that occasion ever can arise for the further fulfillment of this promise. Christianity is itself a greater sign than any the apostles wrought.

19, 20. Verse 19 epitomizes the fuller account afforded by Luke 24:50–53, and Acts 1:9–12. It is not necessarily implied that the ascension followed immediately after this commission. Rather, the language throughout is that of a compend or summary of events more fully recorded elsewhere, as known throughout the church by means of tradition. Ver. 20 indicates in a sentence the work wrought out in subsequent years, and detailed in part in the Book of Acts.—**Amen.** This word is not found in the best manuscripts, but is the fitting response of the church to the command and promise of its Lord. The scribe who added it, did but give voice to what should be the universal though unuttered reception accorded to it by Christ's church throughout all ages. Comp. Rev. 22:20.

The Gospel
ACCORDING TO
St. Luke,
WITH
NOTES AND COMMENTS.

THE GOSPEL ACCORDING TO LUKE.

INTRODUCTION.

By whom written. It is reasonably evident from a comparison of Luke 1 : 1-4 with Acts 1 : 1, that both books were by the same author; and the evidence that the Book of Acts was by Luke I have collated in the Introduction to Acts. To him a universal and unbroken tradition also attributes this Gospel. For some account of the chain of evidences connecting Luke and the various Gospels with the authors whose names they bear, see Vol. I of this Commentary, Intro. to the Study of the N. T., pp. 18-25.

Of Luke very little is known with any degree of certainty. The only biblical references to him, apart from such as he makes implicitly to himself, in his narrative in Acts, are Col. 4 : 14; Philem. 24; 2 Tim. 4 : 11. From these passages, coupled with those in Acts, we learn that he was probably not of Jewish extraction, since in Col. 4 : 14 he is contrasted with those referred to in ver. 11 as "of the circumcision;" that he was a physician, and therefore, presumptively, a person of some education and culture; and that he was a friend and almost constant companion of Paul in his missionary travels. See Intro. to Acts and refs. there. An ecclesiastical tradition of no great authority represents him as a painter; nothing is known as to his death. It has also been surmised that he was one of the seventy; but the only indication in support of this surmise is the fact that he is the only writer who mentions their appointment. (Luke 10:1.)

Sources of information. Luke himself expressly indicates these in the preface to his Gospel (ch. 1 : 1-4). A careful examination of this preface, which is in one or two respects incorrectly rendered in the English version,* indicates (1) that Luke's sources of information were not personal knowledge. He explicitly disavows having been himself an eye-witness of the events or an ear-witness of the teachings which he records. There is no evidence that he accompanied Christ in any of his ministry, or was a personal disciple of Christ while the latter was living, or indeed ever saw or heard him. (2.) One source was written but fragmentary narratives prepared by those who were living witnesses, and who had written down what they had seen or heard. There is abundant evidence in the *post*-apostolic writings that there were such narratives in existence in the primitive churches, which, having been absorbed in the now complete Evangelical narratives, have since

* For a consideration of the more important differences between the original Greek and the English translation, see notes on Luke 1 : 1-4.

utterly perished. (3.) In addition to these fragmentary records, Luke availed himself of personal investigation and inquiry of disciples and others who were eye-witnesses, thus at once verifying his material and adding to it.

Object. This also is indicated by his preface. Whether, as I suppose, Theophilus be regarded as an individual, or only, as some have thought, as an ideal name for every lover of God, the object of the Gospel is the same. Throughout the apostolic age the basis of religious instruction was an account of the important events in the life, death, and resurrection of our Lord. See Acts 2 : 30-33; 3 : 12-18; 5 : 28-31; 10 : 39; 1 Cor. 15 : 3-5. This instruction was imparted orally in catechetical forms to the young converts. The object of Luke was to gather up and embody in one measurably systematic book the fragments of history which were current in the church and capable of verification, and so provide a surer basis for the instruction of the catechumens of the primitive church, in the life and death of their Lord, than oral tradition afforded. In that age the life of Christ, not dogmatic theology, history not philosophy, was the basis of Christianity and the Christian Church.

Influence of Paul. An ancient tradition reports that the Gospel of Mark was written under the influence of Peter (see Intro. to Mark's Gospel); and that of Luke under the influence of Paul. No great weight is to be attached to the mere tradition; but there are some circumstances, both internal and external, which give color to this as a reasonable surmise. We know from some allusions in Paul's Epistles, and from more allusions in the Book of Acts, that Luke was Paul's constant companion; and from our knowledge of Paul's character we may well surmise that he would have put forth a powerful and effective influence on the mind of his traveling companion, and one that could hardly have failed to affect materially the tone and spirit of his writing. And when we turn to the Gospel of Luke there are not wanting indications of that influence. Of all the apostles Paul was the one who must dwell upon the universality of the Gospel of Christ, its adaptation to and its welcome for all men of all races, classes, beliefs and conditions. And of all the Gospels the Gospel of Luke is the one in which this aspect of Christ's life and teaching is the most predominant.

Its character. The character of Luke's Gospel conduces to and confirms what we have said of its authorship, object, and origin in these particulars.

(1.) A history composed not by an eye-witness but by one who gathered his material from fragmentary histories and oral traditions, would be naturally less accurate in its chronology than one prepared by a personal companion of our Lord. This is the case with Luke's Gospel. He repeats many aphorisms which are repeated by Matthew in different connections, and sometimes takes single verses out of a continuous discourse which Matthew has reported, and gives them as solitary thoughts in a quite different setting. It is true that such scholars as Alford and Godet have endeavored in these cases to show that the same thought or figure was twice used by our Lord on different occasions; and there are certainly some cases where this hypothesis is sustained by internal evidence. But there are others where only a forced and artificial connection can be maintained between the thought and the context, and where, I am persuaded, it is much more reasonable to believe that Luke has inserted, out of their original connection, epigrammatic utterances of Christ, the occasion of which he did not know and does not indicate in his narrative.

(2.) But if Luke's Gospel is less to be followed as a guide in questions of chronology and geography, it is, as might be expected, a broader and more comprehensive biography than either of the other three Gospels. Matthew and John describe chiefly what they personally saw and heard; and Mark does not purport to give a complete biography of Christ, but only detached incidents and teachings in his life. Luke, on the other hand, whose work is a compilation from all then accessible sources of information, traces the life of Christ from his birth to his ascension; and includes much that the other Evangelists did not record, probably because it did not lie within their own personal knowledge. Thus Luke alone records the vision to Zacharias and to Mary; the supernatural birth; the raising of the son of the widow of Nain; the account of the forgiveness of the woman that was a sinner; the entertainment at the house of Martha and Mary; the account of the walk to Emmaus; and the narrative of the ascension. Still more notable is the fact that it is Luke alone who gives us any full account of Christ's ministry in Perea, with its marvelous treasure of parables, including some of those that are the dearest to the Christian church, and have been so in all ages. Thus while the Gospel of Luke is less systematic in its arrangement of details, and less chronologically accurate than that of Matthew, less dramatic than that of Mark, and less tender and spiritual than that of John, it is more comprehensive than either. Luke's Gospel is like a carefully-compiled history of a campaign; Matthew's and John's Gospels are rather like the report of single officers who participated in it; Mark's Gospel is like a series of dramatic incidents selected from the story.

(3.) Partly, perhaps, because Luke's especial object was to provide a book for the instruction of converts, especially in the Greek churches founded by Paul's missionary tours, in which Luke accompanied him, but yet more, as I think, because of Paul's personal influence on Luke, his Gospel, more than any other, emphasizes the catholicity and universality of Christianity. Matthew makes predominant the fulfillment of prophecy; Mark the manifestation of power; Luke the welcome to all classes and all nations. At the beginning the angels declare the advent to be good tidings to all people. In the genealogy Christ's parentage is traced back to Adam. The ministry of Christ in Perea, a half-heathen district of the Holy Land, is narrated. The appointment of the seventy, as well as of the twelve, is given. The parables of the lost sheep, the lost coin, and the prodigal son, and the story of the forgiveness of the woman that was a sinner, are all peculiar to Luke, and they all emphasize the truth that Christ came to seek and save that which was lost, wherever the lost may be found. The parable of the marriage supper and the call of Zaccheus are also found only in his Gospel; the one directly implies the calling of the Gentiles, while the other strikingly illustrates the universality of Christ's invitation. These truths are to be found also in the other Gospels; as the power of Christ, and his fulfillment of prophecy, are to be found in Luke; but it is the catholicity of Christianity which is predominant in Luke, and this is the doctrine, or rather the spirit, which we might expect to find predominant in a book written by a companion and scribe of the Apostle Paul. The parallel between Luke's and Paul's accounts of the last supper (Luke 22 : 15-20; 1 Cor. 11 : 23-25) confirms this impression.

Time and place of writing. The Gospel of Luke was certainly written before the Book of Acts, and probably some time previous; this is implied by the language in Acts 1 : 1. The material for it must have been gathered in Palestine, and therefore presumptively during some break in the apostolic journeys in which Luke accompanied Paul. Such a break occurred during Paul's two years' imprisonment in Cæsarea (Acts 24 : 26, 27), and though we cannot certainly fix upon this as the time and place of writing, it is a reasonable surmise that it was mainly prepared, if not published, at this time. At all events, assuming that the Book of Acts was published on or before A. D. 70 (see intro. to Book of Acts), the Gospel of Luke must have been completed and published so as to have reached Theophilus, and probably to have become somewhat known to the churches before that time. The original language in which it was written was undoubtedly Greek.

THE GOSPEL ACCORDING TO
ST. LUKE.

CHAPTER I.

FORASMUCH as many have taken in hand to set forth in order a declaration of those things which are most surely believed among us,

2 Even as they delivered them unto us, which from the beginning ᵃ were eye-witnesses, and ministers of the ᵇ word ;

3 It seemed good to me also, having had perfect understanding of all things from the very first, to write unto thee in order,ᶜ most excellent Theophilus,ᵈ

4 That thou mightest know ᵉ the certainty of those things wherein thou hast been instructed.

a John 15 : 27; Heb. 2 . 3; 1 Pet. 5 : 1; 2 Pet. 1 : 16 ; 1 John 1 : 1....b Rom. 16 : 16; Ephes. 3 : 7 ; 4 ; 11, 12....c Acts 11 : 4....
d Acts 1 : 1....e John 20 : 31.

Ch. 1 : 1–4. INTRODUCTION. THE OBJECT AND THE AUTHENTICITY OF LUKE'S GOSPEL.

1. Forasmuch as many have taken in hand. Who are these *many?* Not the other Evangelists, for Matthew and John were themselves eye-witnesses and ministers of the word, and Luke in the next verse discriminates the latter from the authors with whom he ranks himself. This would leave only Mark to represent the many; and there is abundant evidence to be seen as we proceed that Luke had not Mark's Gospel before him when he wrote. The implication is that there were in the apostolic age written narratives, more or less full, of Christ's discourses and miracles, and that these narratives furnished Luke in part with the material for his history. This hypothesis is sustained by the post-apostolic writings, which are largely occupied with a simple account of Christ's life and teachings. These fragments of history being absorbed in the fuller narratives of our Evangelists were not preserved; but there are indications in the patristic literature of the existence of such narratives.—**To arrange the narrative of the events fulfilled among us.** Not *of the things most surely believed*, as Alford, following our English version, but *of the events fulfilled*, as Van Oosterzee and Godet. For (1) this latter meaning better suits the original; it is indeed capable of either translation, but the verb (πληροφορέω) when applied to persons generally signifies full persuasion, but when applied, as here, to things, generally signifies complete fulfillment (2 Tim. 4:5). (2.) It better suits the context; it is because the things are not fully known to Theophilus that Luke sets them forth, and the addition, *surely believed among us*, weakens rather than strengthens his language, and implies a question rather than certainty. I believe then with Godet, that Luke's language here implies that "these events were not simple accidents, but accomplished a precise plan." Thus Luke, no less than Matthew, represents the Gospel as a fulfillment of prophecy, though he less frequently refers to the prophets. Observe the character of these lost documents; they were *narratives* (διήγησις) not *declarations*, and they were orderly, historical narratives, though not necessarily, and not probably, complete. Presumptively, both Luke and the other Evangelists made more or less use of these fragments; hence the verbal accord frequently discerned in their accounts.

2. Even as unto us they delivered them which were from the beginning, etc. A second source of Luke's information — viz., the eye-witnesses and ministers, including the apostles, but not excluding others. *Ministers* (ὑπηρέτης) is a term applied to John Mark (Acts 13 : 5), a steward of Paul and Barnabas. It is literally *under-rower*, then under-servant of any description. Here, therefore, it signifies persons holding position in the primitive church, subordinate to that of the apostles, whose time was probably fully occupied in the work of preaching, and perhaps organizing the churches, and who left the work of reducing to writing the narrative of Christ's life and teachings to the scribes or other subordinates in the church. *From the beginning* is, as in Acts 1 : 21, 22, from the beginning of Christ's ministry, *i. e.*, his baptism. Luke, however, goes back of this beginning to the events connected with Christ's birth.

3, 4. It seemed good to me also. He cites their example as a support for his own course. The words *And to the Holy Spirit*, added in some unauthentic manuscripts, is recognized by all scholars as unquestionably spurious. They were probably added by some reverent, but not scrupulous scribe, to enforce the doctrine of inspiration.—**Having traced out accurately all things from the first.** Not, *Having had a perfect understanding, i. e.*, always known them, but, Having by personal research examined into the truth of every narrative made use of; the language implies a careful historical research by (1) a comparison of the different narratives, (2) a personal inquiry of the eye-witnesses. *From the very first* is, as in Acts 26 : 5, from his youth. It implies that this Gospel is the product of a protracted investigation and of mature thought.—**To write to thee in order.** In an orderly narrative. This does not necessarily imply, however, that Luke followed the chronological order with accuracy, or even that he always knew what it was. When he differs in chronology from Matthew, the presumption is in favor of the eye-witnesses rather than of the scribe, who derived his information from others.—**Most excellent Theophilus.** Of him nothing is known with certainty. The name is Greek, and the person was probably of Grecian extraction. The appellation *Most excellent*, implies rank as well as character. He is mentioned only here and in Acts 1:1. See note there.—**That thou mightest know the certainty of words concerning which thou hast been orally informed.** Comp. this translation, which is literal, with the English version above. The noun which I have rendered *words* (λόγος) is not to be rendered *things*, a meaning which it never rightfully bears, nor (as Alford) *histories* or *accounts*, but, literally, *words*, including both the direct teachings of Christ and those instructions which are involved in the narrative of his life and works. *Thou hast been instructed* (κατηχέω) is not *catechetically* taught (Alford, Oosterzee), for this ecclesiastical meaning belongs to a later period of church history, but *orally informed*. See on Acts 18:25. This Gospel then was written for those who knew of the life and teachings of Jesus only by tradition, and for the purpose of giving them a fuller and more accurate knowledge thereof.

In respect to this preface, it is to be observed (1) that its style is peculiar, the Greek is purer, and the diction more labored and formal—facts which "may be accounted for, partly because it is the composition of the Evangelist himself, and not translated from Hebrew sources like the rest, and partly because prefaces, especially when also dedicatory, are usually in a rounded and artificial style."—(*Alford*.) (2.) It clearly implies that Luke himself was not an eye-witness of the events which he narrates; and that the sources of his information are (*a*) the narratives of such eye-witnesses; (*b*) documentary narratives, existing in the apostolic churches, of isolated teachings and events in Christ's ministry; (*c*) personal research. (3.) His object is to impart systematic instruction and trustworthy information to those whose knowledge was imperfect and derived from oral tradition. (4.) The name Theophilus indicates that this Gospel was written for the Greek rather than for the Jew. We may thus expect from its genesis to find it less dramatic and pictorial in detail but more calm and copious in style than the other three Gospels, more orderly in its historical arrangement, but giving evidence of greater diversity in its materials, less accurate in its chronology than those of Matthew and John, but more so than that of Mark, and of all the Gospels the one most adapted to the Gentile world, the one in which the Gospel is most prominently set forth as for the whole human race. It is therefore fittingly called by Oosterzee "The Gospel of Universal Humanity," and by Godet, with less carefully guarded discrimination, "A treatise on the right of the heathen to share in the Messianic Kingdom founded by Jesus."

Ch. 1:5—25. ANNUNCIATION OF THE BIRTH OF JOHN THE BAPTIST. ANSWER TO PRAYER ILLUSTRATED.—THE GOSPEL A MESSAGE OF GOOD CHEER.—TRUE GREATNESS CONSISTS IN SELF-DENIAL, DIVINE INSPIRATION, CHRISTIAN WORK.—THE CHILD OF PRAYER AND PIETY MAY RECEIVE THE HOLY SPIRIT AT HIS BIRTH.—ZACHARIAS AND ABRAHAM COMPARED; FAITH IN ONE MAY BE UNFAITH IN ANOTHER.—THE UNBELIEVER IS DUMB.—CHILDREN ARE A GIFT FROM THE LORD.

PRELIMINARY NOTE.—The title Gospel of the Infancy is appropriately given by Godet to the first two chapters of Luke, which may be divided as follows: (1) The annunciation of the birth of the forerunner (1:5-25); (2) annunciation of the birth of Jesus (1:26-38); (3) visit of Mary to Elizabeth (1:39-56); (4) birth of the forerunner (1:57-80); (5) birth of Jesus (2:1-20); (6) circumcision and presentation of Jesus in fulfilment of the law (2:21-40); (7) development of Jesus and first definite recognition of his mission (2:41-52). This Gospel of the Infancy has become the subject of special doubt because (1) only Matthew and Luke refer to it; Mark does not, though of all writers the most minute and graphic; nor John, though made at the death of Christ the custodian of his mother (John 19:26). Nor are any of the incidents here narrated referred to in the subsequent books of the N. T., the apostolic addresses in the Acts, or the Epistles. Moreover, the accounts of Matthew and Luke, though not inconsistent, are entirely different. (2.) In both accounts angelic appearances are a pre-eminent feature, and the appearance of angels is one of the most characteristic features of legendary narrative. (3.) Neither of the accounts are given by eye-witnesses. Luke's was avowedly derived from others, either from eye witnesses or from documents already existing in the church (see above), and Matthew's must have been derived in the same way; there is no indication that he was looking for the Messiah, or had any especial interest in the promised kingdom of God before he was called by Jesus from the receipt of custom (Matt. 9:9). On the other hand, it is to be said (1) that the birth of Jesus would naturally be inquired into by his biographers, all biographers begin with the birth; Mark's narrative is the briefest, and might therefore well omit this section; John's was written subsequently to the other three, and, probably, with the three before him, he naturally

CH. I.] LUKE. 7

5 THERE was, in the days of Herod [f] the king of Judæa, a certain priest named Zacharias, of the course of Abia; [g] and his wife was of the daughters of Aaron, and her name was Elisabeth.

6 And they were both righteous [h] before God, walking in all the commandments and ordinances [i] of the Lord, blameless.

7 And they had no child, because that Elisabeth was barren, and they both were now well stricken in years.

[f Matt. 2 : 1 .... g 1 Chron. 24 : 10; Neh. 12 : 4, 17 .... h Gen. 7 : 1; 1 Kings 9 : 4; 2 Kings 20 : 3.... i 1 Cor. 11 : 2; Phil. 3 : 6.]

does not repeat what he finds in them, and, in fact, there is very little of such repetition. (2.) The particularity of Luke's narrative, the full reports of speeches, e. g., the psalms of Elizabeth and Zacharias, the song of the angels, the prophecy of Simeon, etc., all indicate that it was derived from eye-witnesses, unless it is assumed to be an absolute invention; and the artless nature of the narrative, as well as the character of the writer, forbids the hypothesis that he invented this account of the birth of his Lord. (3.) Though dissimilar, Matthew and Luke agree in the essential truth—the supernatural birth of Jesus Christ of a virgin. Their accounts, therefore, had a common origin though derived through different sources; they agree also with the spirit of the other two Gospels, which assume the supernatural character and origin of the subject of their biographies (Mark 1 : 1 ; John 1 : 14, 34 ; 3 : 13 ; 8 : 58, etc.), with that of the Epistles, which, in language more or less explicit, assume his superhuman origin (Gal. 4 : 4 ; Phil. 2 : 6, 7 ; Heb. 2 : 14), and with the distinct declaration of the O. T. prophecy (Isaiah 7 : 14). (4.) The appearance of angels, however inconsistent with modern rationalism, which approximates the ancient Sadducees in denying either resurrection or spirit (Acts 23 : 8), is entirely in accordance with the general teaching of the Scripture on this subject. This is to the effect that there are both good and evil angels (Matt. 25 : 31 ; 1 Tim. 5 : 31 ; Jude 6); that the former are clothed with the celestial body analogous to that of man (Judg. 13 : 6 ; Mark 16 : 5 ; Acts 1 : 10); that their numbers are great and that they possess great power (Psalm 88 : 17; Matt. 26 : 53); that they are holy, doing God's will (Heb. 1 : 7, 14); that they continually environ his people, though only at special times and as the result of special endowment made visible to human eyes (Psalm 68 : 17; 2 Kings 6 : 17). The appearance of angels in this narrative is in entire consonance with similar appearances in O. T. history (Gen. 18 : 2 ; 19 : 1 ; 22 : 11–18 ; vs : 12 ; 32 : 1, 24); is also in entire accordance with the general teaching of Scripture respecting the reality and mission of angels. On the assumption of the rationalist that there is neither angel nor spirit, of course this narrative must be abandoned as not historical; but on the assumption of the Christian that angels are the messengers of God, there is nothing remarkable in the fact that they are employed to announce the advent of the birth of Jesus and of his forerunner. For harmony of the two accounts of the birth of Jesus in Matthew and Luke, see on Matthew, note on the Birth of Jesus, p. 64. Luke precedes the account of the advent of the Messiah by an account of the parentage of John the Baptist and the prophecy of his birth, an account peculiar to his Gospel.

5. **In the days of King Herod.** Herod the Great. For account of the Herodian family and the character of this Herod see on Matt. 1 : 1. If we could be sure of the exact year of Christ's birth, the narrative here would fix approximately its date. For the temple was destroyed on the ninth day of the fifth month of A. D. 70, i. e., August 4th, and according to the Talmud the first priestly course was on duty then. The course of Abia was the eighteenth of the twenty-four courses in which the priesthood was divided. Calculating back, and assuming that Jesus was born four years before the date fixed by popular chronology for his birth, in other words 4 B. C. (see Matt. 1 : 18, note), the course of Abia was in this year B. C. 5, from 17th to 23d April, and from 3d to 9th Oct., and John the Baptist would be born nine months after, and Jesus probably six months still later (ver. 36), which would bring the birth of Jesus either in July or January.—**Zacharias.** Nothing is known of him but the information given of his character here. Belonging to the priesthood, he possessed none of the priestly vices, but was a man of simple and sincere faith, such as happily are sometimes to be found in the hierarchy, even in the most degenerate days of the church.—**Of the course of Abia.** Or Abijah (1 Chron. 24 : 10). The priesthood was divided under David into twenty-four courses or classes, which took turns in administering the services of the temple, their order being fixed by lot, and remaining thereafter as thus established (1 Chron. 24 : 7–18). When after the Babylonish captivity the people returned to Jerusalem, there were found but four courses out of the twenty-four, comprising about one thousand each (Ezra 2 : 36–39); but they were reorganized under the old names into twenty-four courses, and a new allotment of their services was made. The heads of these courses were the "chief priests," so often mentioned in the Bible. Each course ministered for one week, from the Sabbath to the Sabbath, beginning with the Sabbath morning service.—**And his wife was of the daughters of Aaron.** That is, of priestly extraction. Observe that the celibacy of the clergy was unknown to the ancient Jewish law, as to the primitive Christian church (1 Cor. 9 : 5).—**Elizabeth.**

8 And it came to pass, that while he executed the priest's office before God in the order of his course,
9 According to the custom of the priest's office, his lot was to burn incense when he went into the temple of the Lord.

10 And the whole multitude of the people were praying without,^k at the time of incense.
11 And there appeared unto him an angel of the Lord, standing on the right side of the altar^l of incense.

j Exod. 30 : 7, 8 .... k Lev. 16 : 17 .... l Exod. 30 : 1 ; Rev. 8 : 3, 4.

Mentioned only in the first chapter of Luke. She was a relative of Mary (ver. 36).

6, 7. And they were both righteous in the sight of God. For the meaning of this phraseology, comp. Rom. 3 : 20; 2 Cor. 7 : 12; Heb. 4 : 13; 13 : 21. It distinguished them from the priesthood generally, who were corrupt, and from the Pharisees, whose righteousness was in the sight of men only (ch. 16 : 15 ; Matt. 6 : 1, 2, 5, 16) ; and it indicated simplicity of purpose and sincerity of life.—**The commands and ordinances.** The one indicates rather the moral, the other the ceremonial laws.—**Blameless.** Relatively, not absolutely. That absolute sinlessness is not indicated is evident from the implied rebuke of Zacharias in ver. 20. Paul uses the same word in respect to himself in Phil. 3 : 6, " touching the righteousness which is in the law blameless," in describing his condition at the time when he was the "chief of sinners" (1 Tim. 1 : 12, 13, 15). Zacharias was *righteous* in the sight of God and *blameless* in the sight of the people.—**Well stricken in years.** Their age is not known. See on ver. 18.

8-10. Not only was the original assignment of the time of service of the twenty-four courses determined by lot, but the work of each priest in each course was determined in the same manner—who should kill the sacrifice, who sprinkle the blood, who burn the incense, etc. This lot was cast every week, the members of the course meeting for the purpose in a room in the temple. The lot had fallen to Zacharias to burn the incense. The altar of incense in Solomon's temple (and the structure was probably essentially the same in Herod's temple), was cedar, overlaid with gold (1 Kings 6 : 20 ; 1 Chron. 28 : 18) ; it was a cubit (about two feet) in length and breadth, and two cubits high ; it stood in the Holy Place before the vail which separated the Holy Place from the Holy of Holies. See plan of temple in notes to John, ch. 2. The incense itself was a mixture of sweet spices, described in Exod. 30 : 34-38 ; it was a symbol of prayer (Psalm 141 : 2 ; Rev. 5 : 8), and when offered by the priest a bell was rung as a signal to the people in the courts without, who all engaged in prayer in deep silence. To this feature of the Jewish ritual reference is supposed to be made in Rev. 8 : 1, 3. The whole scene is illustrated by an account in Josephus of a vision reported to have appeared to Hyrcanus, the highpriest, when he was alone offering incense, which he "openly declared before all the multitude on his coming out of the temple." The incense was burnt twice a day, at 9 A. M. and 3 P. M. (Exod. 30 : 7, 8), in a censer, probably a pan for the carriage of the coals, rather than the vase-like vessel, such as is now used in the Roman Catholic

PRIEST OFFERING INCENSE.

churches (Lev. 10 : 1 ; 16 : 12 ; 2 Chron. 26 : 19). In the accompanying illustration the altar is copied from an ancient one found at Gebal ; the staves were added to correspond to the description in Exod. 30 : 1-5. Catholics, in support of the modern practice of burning incense, cite the example of the Jewish church and the following passages, Psalm 141 : 2 ; Sol. Song 3 : 6 ; 2 Cor. 2 : 14 ; Ephes. 5 : 2 ; Rev. 5 : 8-24. By Protestant divines it is believed to have been borrowed from the heathen churches, in which burning incense was common ; and the early Christian apologists, Tertullian, Lactantius, and others, assert that Christians do not burn incense. It is asserted by some historians that it was introduced in the Christian church in the subterranean services in caverns and catacombs simply to purify the air, and that similarly candles were introduced to afford light ; but this appears to me not probable.

11-14. There appeared unto him an angel. This appearance is the first note in that "overture of angels" which introduced Christ to the world. An angel announces to Zacharias the coming of John the Baptist ; to Mary the advent of Christ himself ; then the character and superhuman origin of Christ to Joseph ; then to the shepherds that he is born ; then to Joseph

12 And when Zacharias saw *him*, he was troubled,ᵐ and fear fell upon him.
13 But the angel said unto him, Fear not, Zacharias: for thy prayer is heard; and thy wife Elisabeth shall bear thee a son, and thou shalt call his name John.ⁿ
14 And thou shalt have joy and gladness; and many shall rejoice ᵒ at his birth.
15 For he shall be great ᵖ in the sight of the Lord, and shall drink ᑫ neither wine nor strong drink; and he shall be filled with the Holy Ghost, even ʳ from his mother's womb.
16 And many of the children of Israel shall he turn to the Lord their God.
17 And he ˢ shall go before him in the spirit and power of Elias, to turn the hearts of the fathers to the children, and the disobedient to the wisdom ᵗ of the just; to make ready a people ᵘ prepared for the Lord.
18 And Zacharias said unto the angel, Whereby shall

m verse 29; Judges 13 : 22... n vers. 60, 63....o verse 68....p ch. 7 : 28....q Numb. 6 : 3....r Jer. 1 : 5....s Mal. 4 : 5, 6; Matt. 11 : 14; Mark 9 : 12, 13....t Ps. 111 : 10....u 1 Pet. 2 : 9.

Herod's design; then again to Joseph the death of Herod (ver. 26; ch. 2 : 9; Matt. 1 : 20; 2 : 13, 19). On the general Scripture teaching respecting angels and their appearances to men, see Prel. Note above.—He was troubled, agitated;—and fear fell upon him. * * * Fear not. Observe how the appearance of the heralds of Christ, both of his advent and of his resurrection, awaken fear, and how the response to the fears of man is always "fear not." Comp. ver. 30; ch. 2 : 10; Mark 16 : 6. The dispensation of awe and fear is supplanted by that of love (1 John 4 : 18).—Thy prayer is heard. *Favorably heard* (εἰσακούω). For the meaning, see Matt. 6 : 7; Acts 10 : 31; Heb. 5 : 7, where the word is the same. A prayer may be heard and yet refused. The prayer referred to was not for the advent of the Messiah, but for a son. This personal petition may have united with his prayers for the people and the nation. That this was a theme of his prayers, and the request to which the angel refers, is evident from the completion of the sentence. Nor is the surprise of Zacharias any indication of the reverse. God's generous answers are perpetually a surprise to our unbelief (Acts 12 : 14, 15).—Joy and gladness. *Joy and rejoicing;* one the inward experience, the other the outward expression. Observe how each annunciation of the advent of the Messiah and of his presence is made the occasion for an incentive to joy (ver. 32; ch. 2 : 10–14; Matt. 1 : 21). Contrast the disclosure of Jehovah in the O. T. to the people (Exod. ch. 19), and see this contrast clearly set forth in Heb. 12 : 18–24.

15. Great in the sight of the Lord. The parents, too, were righteous *in the sight of the Lord* (ver. 5), who judgeth not according to outward appearances, but by the heart (1 Sam. 16 : 7). The nature of this greatness is indicated in what follows; he should have dominion over his own appetites, the animal nature being subordinate; he should be full of the Holy Spirit, the spiritual nature being supreme; and he should be faithful in genuine Christian work, preparing the way for the coming of the Lord.— Neither wine nor strong drink. The former the juice of the grape, the latter any fermented liquor not made from grapes. Both were forbidden to priests during their service (Lev. 10 : 9), and to Nazarites altogether (Numb. 6 : 3). The special prohibition here shows the usage of the day not to be total abstinence. See Matt. 11 : 18 for the contrast between John the Baptist and Jesus Christ in this respect.—And he shall be filled with the Holy Ghost even from his mother's womb. From birth. Comp. Ephes. 5 : 18. The meaning here, as there, is that the inspiration and stimulant to the human faculties should come from above, not from below, through the spiritual, not the animal nature. Observe that here is at least one case in which the Spirit of God, and therefore, presumptively, regeneration is promised from infancy, and that in this case the condition of it is (1) godly parentage; (2) a son given in answer to prayer; (3) and by the Nazarite vow consecrated to God from infancy. Why may we not believe that the children of godly parents, given in answer to prayer, and similarly consecrated, may be habitually regenerated at birth, and from the mother's womb, true children of God ? For he that is least in the kingdom of God is greater than John the Baptist (Matt. 11 : 11). Evidently here is at least one Scripture case of "infant regeneration." See also Jer. 1 : 15.

16, 17. Shall he turn to the Lord their God. Of the success of John the Baptist's ministry among the common people we have abundant evidence in the direct testimony of Matthew, Mark, and Luke (Matt. 3 : 5, 6; Mark 1 : 5; Luke 3 : 7, 10); in the incidental testimony of John (John 1 : 14); in the allusions of Christ to the crowds that attended his ministry (Matt. 11 : 7, 12); in the fear of the Pharisees to cast any reproach upon it (Matt. 21 : 25, 26).—Go before him. That is, before the Lord their God, in the person of the Messiah, who is God manifest in the flesh (1 Tim. 3 : 16), Immanuel, God with us (Matt. 1 : 23). —In the spirit and power of Elijah. The reference is to and the quotation from Mal. 4 : 6, and the language seems to me to imply clearly that John the Baptist fulfilled that prophecy. Certain Biblical scholars, however, regard his coming as only a partial fulfillment, and look for a literal second coming of Elijah before the second coming of Christ, which appears to me to be inconsistent with the angel's language here, and with that of Christ in Matt. 11 : 14 and 17 : 11, 12. See notes there.—To turn the hearts of the fathers unto the

I know this? for I* am an old man, and my wife well stricken in years.
19 And the angel, answering, said unto him, I am Gabriel,* that stand in the presence of God; and am sent * to speak unto thee, and to shew thee these glad tidings.
20 And, behold, thou shalt be dumb,* and not able to speak, until the day that these things shall be performed, because thou believest not my words, which shall be fulfilled in their season.
21 And the people waited for Zacharias, and marvelled that he tarried so long in the temple.
22 And when he came out, he could not speak unto them: and they perceived that he had seen a vision in the temple; for he beckoned unto them, and remained speechless.

v Gen. 17 : 17.... w verse 26; Dan. 8 : 16.... x Heb. 1 : 14....y Ezek. 3 : 26.

children. Either literally, To produce domestic concord, the disruption of families being one of the most common signs of the decay of religion in the community, and the beginning of moral chaos; or figuratively, To turn the hearts of the fathers, the Israelites, to the Gentiles, the children—apostate, prodigal, outcast, but still children. This last interpretation, adopted by Lightfoot and Oosterzee, is confirmed by Isaiah 29 : 22 and 63 : 16, in which the Gentiles are treated as children, whom Israel, however, did not recognize; by the actual ministry of John the Baptist, who preached to the Roman soldiers and the publicans, as well as to the orthodox Jews (ch. 3 : 12, 14); and by the ministry of Elijah, which included prophetically the heathen (1 Kings 17 : 8-16; ch. 4 : 25, 26). This appears to me to be the best interpretation.—**And the disobedient in** (not *to*) **the wisdom of the just.** The corresponding language in Malachi is, *And the heart of the children to their fathers.* The clause is responsive to the preceding one; the meaning is, He shall bring the Gentiles to accept the wisdom of righteousness. This is their inheritance (Rom. 3 : 1, 2); in accepting it they repudiate the folly of disobedience, which is the source of heathenism. "*In* (*iv*) is joined to a verb of motion (*to turn*), to express the fact that this wisdom is a state in which men remain when once they have entered it."—(*Godet.*) Observe that righteousness is here, as elsewhere in the Bible, accounted the course of wisdom or prudence, and disobedience one of folly, and that the only true basis of peace in the church or community is the wisdom of righteousness. "Accursed be the peace and unity by which men agree among themselves apart from God."—(Calvin.) To make ready a people prepared for the Lord. This was his mission, but it was only partially successful. The common people, who heard him gladly, received with gladness the Messiah; the scribes and Pharisees, who rejected the forerunner, rejected also the King. Several of Christ's disciples seem to have been selected from those of John the Baptist (John, ch. 1); and after the latter's death his own immediate followers turned at once to Christ for sympathy (Matt. 14 : 12).

18. Whereby shall I know this? Evidently this was not the ecstacy of a visionary man, who imagined simply what he desired; for when the promise was made he doubted and questioned. His unbelief was not greater than that of Abraham (Gen. 15 : 8; 17 : 7), whose faith is eulogized by Paul (Rom. 4 : 19). But the circumstances were widely different. Abraham stood at the beginning of the history of the Church, before there had been vouchsafed any signs of God's gracious power; Zacharias at the end of a long history of gracious interposition. Abraham had just been called out of idolatry, and had yet to learn the power and nature of the true God; Zacharias was a priest, and from youth up trained in the knowledge and service of God. That which was remarkable faith in one was inadequate and culpable lack of it in the other. What, then, shall be said of our lack of faith, who stand unbelieving in this latter-day glory of a ripened Christianity?—**For I am an old man.** The Levites were superannuated at the age of fifty (Numb. 8 : 24, 25). According to Lightfoot, this was held by the rabbis not to apply to the priests. It might apply, and still the wonder of Zacharias be natural. For if he was approaching fifty and had no child, he would not hereafter expect one, and there is nothing in the narrative to imply that the birth of John the Baptist was in any sense miraculous or supernatural.

19-22. I am Gabriel. Only two angels are mentioned by name in the Scripture, Gabriel and Michael. The former is the revealer of messages of grace to man (Dan. 8 : 15-18; 9 : 21-23; Luke 1 : 26-29); the latter appears rather in the attitude of executor of the divine judgments (Dan. 12 : 1; Jude 9; Rev. 12 : 7). Thus they represent the two aspects in which God is presented to us in the Bible, as Redeemer and Judge. It has been said that without misgivings is derived from the Parsiism, but it preceded the contact of the Jews with the far East (Gen. 18 : 2, etc.; 19 : 1, etc.; 28 : 12; 32 : 24), and is more simple; and religious beliefs do not proceed from the complex and elaborate to the simple.—**Thou shalt be silent and not able to speak.** The first clause indicates a fact, *silence;* the second clause the cause of it, *inability to speak.* There is not, therefore, exactly a repetition, though the form of the sentence gives intensity to the prediction. The dumbness is a *sign* rather than a punishment, though a sign that is a punishment for unbelief.—**Because he tarried so long in the Temple.** Where

LUKE.

23 And it came to pass, that, as soon as the days of his ministration were accomplished, he departed to his own house.
24 And after those days, his wife Elisabeth conceived, and hid herself five months, saying,
25 Thus hath the Lord dealt with me, in the days wherein he looked on *me*, to take ᵃ away my reproach among men.
26 And in the sixth month the angel Gabriel was sent from God, unto a city of Galilee, named Nazareth,
27 To a virgin ᵃ espoused to a man whose name was Joseph, of the house of David; and the virgin's name was Mary.
28 And the angel came in unto her, and said, Hail, *thou that art* highly favoured,ᵇ the Lord ᶜ *is* with thee: blessed *art* thou among women.
29 And when she saw *him*, she was troubled at his saying, and cast in her mind what manner of salutation this should be.
30 And the angel said unto her, Fear not, Mary; for thou hast found favour with God.

a Gen. 30 : 23; 1 Sam. 1 : 6; Isa. 54 : 1, 4.... a Matt. 1 : 18.... b Dan. 9 : 23.... c Judges 6 : 12.

---

probably the priest ordinarily remained only long enough to burn the incense. The people without were praying at the time, and this delay made a delay in the public religious service.— **They perceived that he had seen a vision.** By some excitement in his manner or appearance in his face. Perhaps his countenance shone like that of Moses when descending from the mount, and that of Christ after the transfiguration (Exod. 34 : 29, 30; Mark 9 . 15).

23-25. The days of his ministration. The week of his appointed temple service. This indicates that he was not, as Ewald, Alford, and others suppose from ver. 62, deaf as well as dumb; if so, he could hardly have continued his ministrations. — **Hid herself five months.** Lived in retirement, a natural course of conduct. This was probably continued until the birth of John the Baptist; the five months are specified to designate the time of the annunciation to Mary (ver. 36).— **To take away my reproach among men.** To be childless was among the Jews, and still is in the Orient, a special mark of divine disfavor, and a disgrace as well as a misfortune. The course of Sarah (Gen. 16 : 1-3) and of Rachel (Gen. 30 : 1, etc.) strikingly illustrates this fact.

Ch. 1 : 26-80. THE ANNUNCIATION. THE BIRTH OF JOHN THE BAPTIST. THE CHARACTER AND THE TRUE BLESSEDNESS OF THE VIRGIN MARY (vers. 28-30; 42-45; 48, 49).—THE CHARACTER AND MISSION OF CHRIST: SAVIOUR; SON OF GOD; KING (vers. 31-33).—HIS SUPERNATURAL BIRTH (ver. 35).—THE PAST PROVIDENCE OF GOD THE FUTURE HOPE OF THE GODLY (vers. 50-55).—MAN'S OBEDIENCE FULFILLS GOD'S PROMISE (vers. 59-64).—A PSALM OF REDEMPTION—THE GOSPEL PROPHETICALLY PREACHED (vers. 67-79).

Comparing the account with that in Matthew, the course of events appears to have been as follows: First, the annunciation of the birth of John the Baptist was made to Zacharias in the temple; then, five months later, the annunciation of the birth of Jesus to Mary here described; several months subsequent, and after conception has taken place, the fact becomes known to Joseph, who supposes his betrothed to have been unfaithful, and is determined to put her away, but is prevented by the revelation made to him in a dream (Matt. 1 : 19-21); subsequent to which revelation she makes the journey to Elizabeth recorded in this chapter. For fuller chronological statement, see note on Birth of Jesus, Matt. ch. 2, Vol. I., p. 64.

26, 27. In the sixth month. After the five months referred to in ver. 24, and therefore a little more than three months before the birth of John the Baptist.—**The angel Gabriel.** See on ver. 19.—**Named Nazareth.** This village, about five miles west of Tabor, reposes in a beautiful valley, secluded by surrounding hills. Sheltered by them from the bleaker winds of the north, it luxuriates in the fragrant blossoms and ripened fruits, pomegranate, orange, fig, and olive. The modern town stands on the site of the ancient one, which has, however, been entirely destroyed. The present population is about 3,000—Greeks, Latins, Maronites, and Moslems. The neighboring hill commands a magnificent view of the surrounding country. From it the traveler may see, on the north, the snowy peaks of Hermon; on the east, over the intervening hills, a glimpse of the Sea of Galilee; closer at hand, the Mount of Beatitudes; and not far distant, Cana, where the water was made wine; Nain, where the widow's son was raised; Endor, where the witch appeared to Saul; Jezreel, the famous residence of Ahab; and Mount Carmel, the retreat of the prophet Elijah. "This valley (of Nazareth) was in Israel, just what Israel was in the midst of the earth—a place at once secluded and open; a solitary retreat, and a high post of observation, inviting meditation, and at the same time affording opportunity for far-reaching views in all directions."—(*Godet.*)—**Espoused to a man named Joseph.** Espousal was a more formal act in that age and country than with us. See Matt. 1 : 18.—**Of the house of David.** This fact is only asserted of Joseph; but that Mary was also of the lineage of David is implied by vers. 32 and 69, and by Rom. 1 : 3. Comp. Psalm 132 : 11; and see note on Matt. 1 : 1.

28, 29. And the angel came in unto her. Perhaps while she was praying. That she was a woman of piety is evident from the narrative here.—**Hail, highly favored; the Lord is with thee.** Or, *The Lord be with thee.* The

31 And, behold, thou ᵈ shalt conceive in thy womb, and bring forth a son, and shalt call his name JESUS.
32 He shall be great,ᵉ and shall be called the Son ᶠ of the Highest: and the Lord God shall give unto him the throne ᵍ of his father David:
33 And he shall reign over the house of Jacob for ever; and of ʰ his kingdom there shall be no end.
34 Then said Mary unto the angel, How shall this be, seeing I know not a man?
35 And the angel answered and said unto her, The

d Isa. 7:14; Matt. 1:21....e Matt. 12:42,...f Heb. 1:2–8....g 2 Sam. 7:11, 12; Isa. 9:6, 7....h Dan. 7:14, 27; Micah 4:7.

NAZARETH.

passage may be rendered either as a declaration or as a salutation.—**Blessed art thou among women.** Not, *Thou shalt be blessed*, i. e., honored, by women; but, *Thou art selected from among women* to be especially blessed by God. Throughout this colloquy there is no hint that Mary is other than an ordinary woman; no suggestion that she was born without sin or possessed a supernatural character; no basis for the reverence paid to her by the Romish church or for the dogma of Immaculate Conception.—**Troubled.** Rather, *agitated*, which is the true meaning of the original; here not merely put in trepidation or fear, but subjected to conflicting emotions—awe, fear, hope, perplexity.

30–33. The message of the angel consists of four parts: first, a reassurance, *Fear not*, etc. This appearance is a sign of the divine graciousness and favor, not of divine judgment. Second, a promise, *Thou shalt bring forth a son*. This promise is the same as that made to Elizabeth through Zacharias, and yet, both in the circumstances of the women and the character of the son, foretold how different! Third, a command, *Thou shalt call his name Jesus*, i. e., Saviour. This command was afterwards repeated to Joseph, and the reason for it given, "For he shall save his people from their sins" (Matt. 1:21). Fourth, a prophecy, concerning the character of the promised son. This last indicates (1) his character, *He shall be great*, i. e., as John the Baptist, "in the sight of the Lord" (ver. 15); (2) his name, *He shall be called Son of the Highest*, i. e., of God, who is in the O. T. often designated as Most High (Numb. 24:16; 2 Sam. 22:14; Psalm 7:17; 57:2, etc.); (3) the object of his birth, *that he may become King*, having a kingdom without end. Before his birth he is heralded as not only Jesus, i. e., Saviour, but as King of Israel; just before his death he declares to Pilate that it was as King he came into the world; and the last glimpse which the N. T. affords of him, in the prophetic vision of John, is as King of kings. His own language to Pilate in John 18:37, interprets the language of the angel here, and indicates the nature, both of his kingdom and of the allegiance that is due to him—the allegiance of the heart and life to absolute truth. It is possible that to Mary this prophecy meant only that her son, the long-promised Messiah, should be temporal King of the Jews, but the language itself, "Of his kingdom there shall be no end," implies much more. The case is one in

CH. I.]   LUKE.   13

Holy Ghost shall come upon thee, and the power of the Highest shall overshadow thee; therefore also that holy thing which shall be born of thee shall be called¹ the Son of God.
36 And, behold, thy cousin Elisabeth, she hath also conceived a son in her old age: and this is the sixth month with her who was called barren.
37 For ʲ with God nothing shall be impossible.
38 And Mary said, Behold the handmaid ᵏ of the Lord; be it unto me according ˡ to thy word. And the angel departed from her.
39 And Mary arose in those days, and went into the hill country with haste, into a ᵐ city of Juda;

40 And entered into the house of Zacharias, and saluted Elisabeth.
41 And it came to pass, that, when Elisabeth heard the salutation of Mary, the babe leaped in her womb; and Elisabeth was filled with the Holy Ghost:
42 And she spake out with a loud voice, and said, Blessed ⁿ *art* thou among women, and blessed *is* the fruit of thy womb.
43 And whence *is* this to me, that the mother of my Lord ᵒ should come to me?
44 For lo, as soon as the voice of thy salutation sounded in mine ears, the babe leaped in my womb for joy.

i Mark 1 : 1 ; John 1 : 34....j Matt. 19 : 26 ; Rom. 4 : 21....k Ps. 116 : 16....l Ps. 119 : 38....m Josh. 21 : 9–11....n verse 28 ; Judges 5 : 24....
o John 13 : 13.

which the historical fulfillment adds to the significance of the prophecy; this is not remarkable, since God is always better than even his word; his performance outruns his promises.

34–37. How shall it be? Not how *can*, but how *shall* it be. She does not doubt as Zacharias (ver. 18), but accepting the prophecy of the angel as to the fact, inquires of him as to the manner of its fulfillment.—**The Holy Ghost shall come upon thee, and the power of the Highest shall overshadow thee.** We are not to seek an interpretation of this metaphor either in the brooding of the bird, protecting her eggs, nor in the descent of the Sheckinah upon the mountain top, or in the tabernacle, but simply to accept it as a delicate way of expressing the fact that the conception should be supernatural and miraculous, the life being created by the direct interposition of the Spirit of God. As the new life in the individual is born of the Holy Spirit (John 3 : 5), so is He that is the Life of the world.—**Therefore, also, that holy one which shall be born of thee shall be called Son of God.** Not, Shall be, but Shall be *called*. The supernatural birth does not constitute Jesus the Son of God; it only constitutes the reason why he is recognized as such upon the earth. He existed before this supernatural birth (John 8 : 58 ; 17 : 5), and the general teaching of Scripture implies that the relationship between the Father and the Son implied by the phrase "Son of God," is not merely temporal and accidental, but eternal and inherent. Thus God is here and in other passages (Phil. 2 : 9 ; Heb. 1 : 9) represented as bestowing on the Son authority, and he is represented as returning it to the Father when his mediatorial work is ended (1 Cor. 15 : 24–28). But that he may dwell upon the earth, a physical body must be provided for his indwelling; and this was thus supernaturally begotten, because it was fitting that the Son of God should tabernacle in a body itself born of God ; and thus the supernatural birth became to men the evidence that he was God's only belovèd Son ; it did not make him so, but it afforded their justification for giving him this title. — **Thy cousin Elizabeth.** The original only indicates a blood relative, not the nature of the relationship.—**Hath conceived.** Though Mary has not asked for a sign, one is given her. The phrase *who was called barren* indicates that among her friends and relatives all hope of child-bearing for her was past. Mary accordingly accepts it as a sign from God in attestation of his word and in support of her faith.—**For with God nothing shall be impossible.** "The laws of nature are not chains which the Divine Legislator has laid upon himself; they are threads which he holds in his hand, and which he shortens and lengthens at will."—(*Oosterzee.*) In respect to the way in which his word to Mary was fulfilled, and the time of the fulfillment, Scripture is silent, and reverence for Scripture should be. We know too little of the origin of life, which is always a new manifestation of divine power and grace, to undertake an explanation of the method in which this life was imparted by the overshadowing of the Holy Spirit to the mother of Jesus.

38. Not even the Bible affords a more striking illustration of the simplicity of faith than Mary. She attests her consecration to her Lord by surrendering herself to his will and accepting the sacred trust of maternity. She does this with the knowledge that it must subject her to the suspicion of her husband, and to possible estrangement from him, to scandal among her neighbors, to the impairing of that fair fame which is dearer to the maiden than life itself. In fact, her husband did suspect her, and would have divorced her but for a divine revelation (Matt. 1 : 19–21); the later rabbinical books accuse Mary of a violation of her marriage vows; and it would appear from the innuendoes of Christ's accusers that this charge was secretly whispered in his own lifetime (John 7 : 27 ; 8 : 41).

39–41. This fact indicates that Mary was a woman of no little force of character, for to take such a journey alone was an exploit not unattended with danger.—**In those days.**—**Into the hill country.** Of Judah ; the central part, an elevated plateau from 1,500 to 2,500 feet above the level of the sea, and here employed in dis-

45 And blessed *is* she that believed: for there shall be a performance of those things which were told her from the Lord.
46 And Mary said, My ᵖ soul doth magnify the Lord,
47 And my spirit hath rejoiced ᑫ in God my Saviour.
48 For he hath regarded the low ʳ estate of his handmaiden: for, behold, from henceforth all generations shall call me ˢ blessed.
49 For he that is mighty ᵗ hath done to me great things;ᵘ and holy ᵛ *is* his name.
50 And ʷ his mercy *is* on them that fear him, from generation to generation.
51 He ˣ hath shewed strength with his arm; he hath scattered the ʸ proud in the imagination of their hearts.

52 He ᶻ hath put down the mighty from *their* seats, and exalted them of low degree.
53 He ᵃ hath filled the hungry with good things, and the rich he hath sent empty away.
54 He hath holpen his servant Israel, in ᵇ remembrance of *his* mercy;
55 As he spake ᶜ to our fathers, to Abraham, and to his seed for ever.
56 And Mary abode with her about three months, and returned to her own house.
57 Now Elisabeth's full time came, that she should be delivered; and she brought forth a son.
58 And her neighbours and her cousins heard how the Lord had shewed great mercy upon her; and they ᵈ rejoiced with her.

p 1 Sam. 2:1; Ps. 34:2, 3....q Ps. 35:9; Hab. 3:18....r Ps. 136:23....s ch. 11:27; Mal. 3:12....t Gen. 17:1....u Ps. 71:21; 126:2, 3; Ephes. 3:20....v Ps. 111:9....w Gen. 17:7; Exod. 20:6; Ps. 103:17....x Ps. 98:1; Isa. 51:9; 52:10; 63:5... y 1 Sam. 2:9; Dan. 4:37....z ch. 18:14; Job 5:11....a 1 Sam. 2:5....b Ps. 98:3....c Gen. 17:19; Ps. 132:11....d verse 14.

tinction from the plains of Judah bordering the sea and the desert. The city is unknown, probably was unknown to Luke. The language is indicative of his accuracy and truthfulness. A writer of myths would have fixed on the site of this meeting between Mary and Elizabeth. There is no ground for reading *The city of Juttah* instead of *A city of Judah*. This is purely conjectural, and without support. — **The babe leaped in her womb.** Possibly, though not necessarily, the first manifestation of life.

42-45. In this ode the language of Elizabeth is that of an inspired prophet; this is evident both from the language of the preceding verse and from the fact that she had no ordinary means of knowing the promise made to Mary. — **Blessed art thou among women.** *Among*, not *by*; see on ver. 28. — **The babe leaped in my womb for joy.** A poetical expression, not to be taken literally, as implying actual consciousness or emotion in the unborn child. — **Blessed is she that believed.** A characterization of Mary as one whose remarkable trait was her faith. — **For there shall be a performance.** This is a special prophecy respecting Mary; it is also the enunciation of the great law, She that believes is always blessed, for the ministry of grace is upon the principle, "According to your faith be it unto you" (Matt. 9:29).

46-55. This hymn of praise has the fragrance of the O. T. poetry; parts of it are probably unconsciously borrowed from Psalms, with which Mary was from her childhood familiar. Comp. the passages cited in the marg. refs., and especially the analogous song of Hannah in 1 Sam. 21:1-10. But that belongs to the O. T. and this to the N. T.; in this, therefore, there is none of that personal exultation over enemies which characterizes the song of Hannah and most of the triumphant odes of David. It is a hymn only of grace and glory. It consists of three clauses: in the first, Mary gives thanks for the divine goodness to herself (vers. 46-49); in the second, she magnifies the general power and grace of God in the whole course of divine providence (vers. 50-53); in the third, she emphasizes the redemption now afforded to Israel through her. — **God my Saviour.** Her personal Saviour, because of her faith in the Jesus promised her. To her he is already the One who saves from sin those that trust in him (Matt. 1:21). — **Shall call me blessed.** This does not justify paying any peculiar reverence to the Virgin Mary; for what she declares is simply that all generations shall recognize, not her holiness or influence in intercession, but her happiness in being selected to be the mother of the Messiah. — **He that is mighty.** He whose might has no higher manifestation in nature than the creation of man, affords the highest manifestation of that divine might in the creation of the life of the perfect man, Christ Jesus. — **And his mercy is on them that fear him.** Verses 50-53 describe God's character as illustrated by his dealings with the nations, especially Israel. Analogous are such Psalms as 103, 106, 107. "She ascribes to the providence or judgments of God what ungodly men call the game of fortune."—(*Calvin.*)—**He hath showed strength with his arm.** In all the history of Israel.—**He hath scattered the proud.** As the Midianites before Gideon, the army of Sennacherib, etc.—**He hath put down the mighty.** As Pharaoh, Nebuchadnezzar, Belshazzar. — **And exalted them of low degree.** As Joseph, Moses, David.—**He hath filled the hungry, * * * the rich he hath sent empty away.** Literally true in such contrasts as that of Ahab and the woman of Zarephath (1 Kings 17:1-14); spiritually fulfilled by Christ in such instances as those of the leper and the rich young ruler (Matt. 9:1-4; 19:16-22).—**He hath holpen his servant Israel in remembrance of his mercy.** Literally, *He hath taken hold of Israel his child to remember mercy;* i. e., his visitation to Israel is one for the purpose of mercy, not of judgment. The words *as he spake to our fathers* should be in parentheses. This merciful visitation is in fulfillment of ancient prophecy; but the mercy itself is shown to Abraham and to his seed forever. The birth

CH. I.]   LUKE.   15

59 And it came to pass, that on the eighth day they came to circumcise the child; and they called him Zacharias, after the name of his father.
60 And his mother answered and said, Not so; but he shall be called John.
61 And they said unto her, There is none of thy kindred that is called by this name.
62 And they made signs to his father, how he would have him called.
63 And he asked for a writing table, and wrote, saying, His name is ᵉ John. And they marvelled all.
64 And his mouth ᶠ was opened immediately, and his tongue *loosed*, and he spake, and praised God.
65 And fear came on all that dwelt round about them: and all these sayings were noised abroad throughout all the hill country of Judæa:
66 And all they that heard *them* laid *them* up ᵍ in their hearts, saying, What manner of child shall this be! And the hand ʰ of the Lord was with him.

e verse 13 .... f verse 20 .... g ch. 2 : 19, 51 .... h Ps. 80 : 17.

of the Messiah was in fulfillment of a promise to the patriarch (Gen. 12: 1-3; 17: 1-8), as interpreted by Paul (Gal. 3: 16).

56-58. Now Elizabeth's full time came. This would be about three months after Mary's visit to her; and this would perhaps imply that Mary remained till John was born, but the phraseology which places the account of the birth after Mary's departure, implies the reverse.—**And they rejoiced with her.** "Orientals rejoice exceedingly over the birth of sons, for he is not only to perpetuate the memory of his father, but is expected to be the support and dependence of his mother, and of the rest of the family, in a country where unprotected woman is most cruelly oppressed, and the widows and the fatherless even of the wealthiest are often reduced to penury and want."—(*Van Lennep's Bible Lands.*) For illustration, see Gen. 16 : 4-11 ; 21 : 8; 29 : 32.

59-64. They came to circumcise the child. As enjoined upon all the descendants of Abraham (Gen. 17 : 12). The name was given then, as it is with us at christening; the reason alleged is that at the institution of circumcision the names of Abram and Sara were changed to Abraham and Sarah (Gen. 17 : 5, 15). Circumcision is still practiced among the Jews on their children at the age of eight days; among the Arabs at 13 years, probably from the fact that Ishmael, their ancestor, was of that age when circumcised (Gen. 17 : 25); among other Mohammedans when they are able to repeat intelligently the Moslem profession of faith, "There is no God but God, and Mohammed is his prophet." Baptism appears to have been practiced among the Jews only on converts from heathenism and their families.—**His mother answered, No; but he shall be called John.** Meyer thinks that this fact had been supernaturally communicated to her; Alford thinks not, and supposes that she had learned it from her husband. But unless her suggestion was the result of a supernatural impulse, why should it be reported at all?—**They made signs to his father.** An indication that he was deaf as well as dumb. If not, he would have heard and understood the conference between his wife and his friends.—**He asked for a writing table.** Writing tablets among the ancients consisted of a thin piece of wood, covered on one side with wax, on which the writing was done by means of a stylus, an iron instrument resembling a pencil in size and shape, sharpened at one end to form the charac-

WRITING TABLET.

ters, and made flat and circular at the other, to obliterate what had been written when desired. The ordinary tablet consisted of two or more leaves like the modern school-slate, one side only of each leaf being covered with wax, and the wooden edge of each leaf being raised to prevent the wax sides from rubbing against each other. These tablets were used for accounts, wills and legal documents, for letters, and by pupils in school. Such tablets continued to be used down to the middle ages. Another form is still used in the East, made of wood; the students write on them with chalk or charcoal.—**And they marvelled all.** Another indication that Zacharias was deaf as well as dumb. "There would be nothing wonderful in his acceding to his wife's suggestion, if he had known it; the coincidence, apparently without this knowledge, was the matter of wonder."—(*Alford.*)—**And his mouth was opened immediately.** The angelic prophecy (ver. 13) being now fulfilled, and partly by the obedience of Zacharias himself in naming the babe John.

65, 66. The supernatural character of John's birth and the circumstances attending it, prepare the way for his ministry. The people, in consequence, were ready to believe him a prophet, and to give heed to him when he began

67 And his father Zacharias was filled with the Holy Ghost, and prophesied, saying,
68 Blessed ʲ *be* the Lord God of Israel; for he hath visited and redeemed his people,
69 And hath raised up an horn of salvation ᵏ for us, in the house of his servant David;
70 As he spake ˡ by the mouth of his holy prophets, which have been since the world began:
71 That we should be saved ʲ from our enemies, and from the hand of all that hate us;
72 To perform the mercy *promised* to our fathers, and to ᵐ remember his holy covenant;
73 The oath ⁿ which he swore to our father Abraham,
74 That he would grant unto us, that we, being delivered out of the hand of our enemies, might serve him ᵒ without fear,
75 In ᵖ holiness and righteousness before him, all ᵠ the days of our life.
76 And thou, child, shalt be called the Prophet of the Highest: for thou shalt go ʳ before the face of the Lord, to prepare his ways;
77 To give knowledge of salvation unto the people by the remission ˢ of their sins,

j Ps. 72:18....J Ps. 111:9....k Jer. 23:5, 6; Dan, 9:24....l Isa. 54:7-17; Jer. 30:10, 11....m Lev. 26:42; Ps. 105:8-10; Ezek. 16:60....n Gen. 22:16, 17....o Rom. 6:22....p Titus 2:11, 12; 1 Pet. 1:14, 15....q Rev. 2:10....r Mal. 3:1....s Acts 5:31.

preaching. Three elements are mentioned as constituting his peculiar fame: (1.) Fear, *i. e.*, awe; a recognition of the supernatural presages which accompanied his birth. This is the meaning often belonging to the word (φόβος), here rendered *fear*. (2.) A wide-extended fame. The story of his birth went throughout the hill country of Judea. God employed especial means to prepare for the Messiah the district most prejudiced by its education and the influence of its hierarchy against Him. (3.) An expectancy. The people remembered these events and waited, wondering what a child so born would become in his manhood.—**The hand of the Lord was with him.** The *hand* is a symbol of power in the Bible; here the meaning is that the fulfillment of the promise of ver. 15 was seen even in his childhood, and kept alive the wonder and expectation of the people.

67-71. **Zacharias was filled with the Holy Ghost and prophesied.** These words characterize the psalm of thanksgiving that follows. It is neither, on the one hand, the natural exultation of a father and a patriot, who rejoices because his son is to take an eminent part in what he believes to be simply a political reform and become the deliverer of an apostate and oppressed people, nor, on the other, an exposition of the Gospel, the full significance of which not even the immediate apostles of Christ comprehended till after their Lord's death. It is prophecy, in which the speaker, inspired by the Holy Ghost, uttered what he did not and could not fully comprehend, and in which the hopes of the temporal kingdom, which Zacharias shared with all the best people of his age, mingled with but became prophetic of that spiritual deliverance which his words foreshadow, and of which he must have had some conception. Like all prophecy it is clearer to us in the light of its historic fulfillment than it could have been to him who uttered it.—**Blessed be the Lord God of Israel.** The Father who sends the Son, the Horn of salvation, the Day-spring from on high, and in him visits and redeems his people.—**He hath visited.** The original (ἐπισκέπτομαι) indicates a visit for succor, as in Matt. 25:36; Acts 7:23, note; James 1:27.—**And redeem**-ed. Ransomed as from bondage; see John 8:32, 34-36.—**And hath raised up a horn of salvation for us.** For the interpretation of this favorite metaphor of power with the Hebrew poets, see Deut. 33:17; Psalm 75:10; 132:17; Jer. 48:25. The symbol is borrowed from the animal kingdom, the horn of the bull, the unicorn, the ram, being a prominent weapon both of offence and defence. (See Dan. ch. 8:3-12, 20-24). Hence to "defile the horn in the dust" (Job. 16:15) pr... nts a figure of a dying ox or stag, prostrate, with his useless horns covered with dirt. Hence, too, the horns of the altar were a refuge to those fleeing from enemies, being a symbol of divine power (1 Kings 1:50; 2:28). Jesus Christ is not only the love and grace but also the *power* of God (Rev. 5:12), but a power unto salvation (Rom. 1:16); the horn is a horn of salvation.—**Which have been since the world began.** The object of all prophecy is the same; it points forward through partial and incomplete fulfillments to the life, the sufferings, the victory, and the final coronation of Jesus as Lord of all.—**Salvation from all our enemies.** This qualifies and defines the salvation referred to in ver. 69, the intermediate clause being parenthetical. Thus the passage reads, "Hath raised up a horn of salvation * * * (as he spake by the mouth of his holy prophets * * *) salvation from our enemies," etc. To Zacharias the salvation anticipated undoubtedly included a deliverance from Roman misrule; but that, even in his thought, it included much more is evident from the language of vers. 74, 75, where it is combined with anticipations of a holy and righteous service of God.

72-75. **The oath which he swore to our father Abraham.** Gen. 24:16-18, as interpreted by Gal. 3:13-17.—**Might serve him without fear.** See 1 John 4:18. Liberty to serve God according to the individual conscience, *i. e.*, religious liberty in the largest sense, is one of Christ's gifts to the world; it does not date from the Puritan settlement of this country.—**In holiness and righteousness.** The one represents inward purity, the other outward activity; the one the inward but negative quality, the other the outward but affirmative quality; the

CH. II.] LUKE. 17

78 Through the tender mercy of our God; whereby the dayspring from on high hath visited us,
79 To 'give light to them that sit in darkness and *in* the shadow of death, to guide our feet into the way of peace.
80 And the child grew, and waxed strong in spirit, and was in the deserts till the day of his shewing unto Israel.

CHAPTER II.

AND it came to pass in those days, that there went out a decree from Cæsar Augustus, that all the world should be taxed.
2 (*And* this taxing was first made when Cyrenius was governor of Syria.)

t Isa. 9 : 2; 49 : 9.

---

one absence from stain, the other positive service.

76-80. Called the Prophet of the Highest. In contrast with ver. 32, where Jesus is called *Son* of the Highest. The one is the prince, the other only the herald. *Called*, indicates that he should not only *be* a prophet but should be recognized as one. See Matt. 14 : 5; 21 : 26.—**To prepare his ways.** As indicated in the next clause, viz., by giving a knowledge of salvation, not only a prophecy of its advent but also a description of its true nature. See ch. 3 : 1-18. Christ gives *salvation*, John only a *knowledge* of salvation. Comp. Matt. 1 : 21.—**By the remission of their sins.** The remainder of the sentence embodies the Gospel in brief. It promises (1) salvation, (2) not merely political but spiritual, a remission of and redemption from sin, (3) indicates the cause, the divine mercy (Comp. John 3 : 16; Ephes. 2 : 4-8); (4) and promises the result, light to eyes in darkness, and peace to feet straying in paths of sorrow and perplexity. *Whereby the day-spring hath visited* should rather be rendered, *in which the dawn hath visited.* Tender mercy is the atmosphere *in which* the Gospel of Christ has its birth and life, as spring has its origin in the light and warmth of a summer sun; and it is a *dawn* to those in darkness (Isaiah 9 : 2; Matt. 4 : 15, 16, notes). *Them that sit in darkness* includes the whole human race. Comp. Ephes. 2 : 3; and observe there what is implied by the promise here "to guide our feet into the way of peace."—**The child grew and waxed strong in spirit.** Comp. ch. 2 : 52, note. The one phrase refers to his physical, the other to his intellectual and spiritual growth.—**In the deserts.** The desert of Judea, a sparsely inhabited country bordering on the Dead Sea. The word indicates an uncultivated, not necessarily sterile, region. There is no ground for the surmise that John joined the Essines or received his education among or from them. Rather the reverse is implied, namely, that from early youth his education was that of studying and meditating in solitude, and his only teacher God, interpreted to him through nature, the Bible, and the direct influence of the Holy Spirit.

Ch. 2 : 1-20. **THE BIRTH OF JESUS. GOD USES ALL INSTRUMENTS TO FULFILL HIS WILL.—CÆSAR UNCONSCIOUSLY PREPARES FOR CHRIST.—THE EARTHLY HU-**

MILIATION AND THE HEAVENLY GLORY OF THE INCARNATION.—THE FIRST PREACHING OF THE GOSPEL.—ITS RECEPTION IN HEAVEN; UPON EARTH.

1, 2. Cæsar Augustus. Emperor of Rome, and immediate successor of Julius Cæsar. Judea, though not at this time a province of Rome, was tributary to her.—**That all the world should be taxed.** Rather, that a census of the population should be taken, probably as a preparation for taxation. By *all the world* is meant not merely all the land of Judea, a meaning which the Greek word (οἰκουμένη) will not bear, but the whole Roman Empire. A general survey of the Roman Empire, commenced under Julius Cæsar, had been completed B. C. 12; it was followed by Augustus with a more particular survey.

COIN OF CÆSAR AUGUSTUS.

After his death there was found written by his own hand a statistical account of the Empire, including the number of the tributary kingdoms, and embracing the number of the citizens, of the allies under arms, of the fleets, and of the tributes and taxes. The enrollment here described was one preparatory to some such census and survey of the Empire. — **And this taxing was first made when Cyrenius was governor of Syria.** Cyrenius or Quirinius was governor of Syria for a period of 5 years, from the 6th to the 11th year after Christ's birth. At that time he took a census of the Holy Land for the purpose of taxation, referred to in Acts 5 : 37, and described in Josephus's Antiq. 18 : 1. He was sent with Coponius partly for that purpose. This fact presents a chronological difficulty, which has given rise to prolonged discussions. Skeptical writers argue from it the untrustworthiness of Luke's

3 And all went to be taxed, every one into his own city.
4 And Joseph also went up from Galilee, out of the city of Nazareth, into Judæa, unto the city of David, which is called Bethlehem, (because he was of the house and lineage of David,)
5 To be taxed with Mary his espoused wife, being great with child.
6 And so it was, that, while they were there, the days were accomplished that she should be delivered.
7 And she ⁿ brought forth her firstborn son, and wrapped him in swaddling clothes, and laid him in a manger; because there was no room for them in the inn.

n Matt. 1 : 25.

narrative, on the ground that he puts the enrollment six years before it really took place. And the question of date is not unimportant, for, according to Luke, this enrollment explains how Christ, though of Galilean parentage, was born in Bethlehem, while Matthew fixes the date of the birth during the reign of King Herod, who died before the enrollment spoken of by Josephus. The principal explanations of this are as follows: (1.) For *this taxing was first made*, read *This taxing was made before that Cyrenius was governor*. The Greek is capable of this translation, and the same phraseology (πρῶτος with gen.) is used by John with this signification. The Greek student will do well to compare John 1 : 15, 30; 15 : 18; Luke 2 : 21. (2.) Some scholars read, *This taxing was first completed when*, etc., but this translation (of the verb γίνομαι) would hardly have been suggested but for the purpose of escaping the chronological difficulty. (3.) Others read, *This taxing itself was first made when*, etc.; this supposes that the account distinguishes between the enrollment at this time and the taxing afterwards under Cyrenius. (4.) Wordsworth suggests, *This enrollment became the first when*, etc., *i. e.*, after the more famous enrollment six years later; this was designed to distinguish it as the first enrollment, an improbable rendering. (5.) Dr. Woolsey (*Smith's Bib. Dict.*, art. *Cyrenius*) argues that the word rendered *governor*, is one of a more general import, and that Quirinius may have occupied some special office as commissioner, sent on for the very purpose of inaugurating this enrollment, and afterwards made governor, and completing it. This is not improbable. (6.) Zumpt has shown that there is some reason to believe that Cyrenius was twice governor. This view is maintained at length by Alford and approved by Schaff, but doubted by Godet. It is unnecessary definitely to decide between these various explanations; it is certain that Quirinius was active in an official capacity in the East at this time; there is nothing in history inconsistent with the probable supposition that the enrollment began at this time, the first enrollment ever made of the Jewish population under the Roman government; that it was suspended owing to the death of Herod and the consequent political changes; that it was again inaugurated and followed by taxation; and that this completion of it gave rise to the insurrection under Judas. Whether the preliminary enrollment here was under Cyrenius as governor or as commissioner, or not under him at all, is a matter of secondary importance.

3-5. And all went to be enrolled. The Roman method of enrolling would have taken the names, etc., at the place of residence. But Judea was still an independent, though tributary kingdom; the enrollment was therefore taken according to Jewish usage, which was adapted to the ancient division of tribes and families. The Jewish law aimed to preserve the family, tribal, and local attachments. Mary naturally accompanied him, for, under the Roman law, women were subject to a capitation tax. The fact that she accompanied him to Bethlehem indicates that she too was of the house of David.

6, 7. Wrapped him in swaddling clothes. "As soon as a babe is born it is washed in salted

SWADDLING CLOTHES.

water, clothed, and swathed in a long bandage or swaddling cloth, three or four inches wide and about ten feet long, which is firmly wound around it from the neck downward, including the arms, which are thus pinioned to its sides, so that it can neither stir hand nor foot. This is done with the idea of keeping the tender bones motionless in a proper position until they acquire sufficient strength to be allowed to move about. It is, moreover, easier for the mother to carry the little one on her arm or slung on her back."—(*Van Lennep's Bible Lands.*) The modern and ancient Oriental customs are the same. The accompanying illustration is from an original sketch by A. L. Rawson.—**And laid him in a manger, because there was no room for them in the inn.** The Eastern inn was ordinarily a caravanserai, more nearly resembling a Western wagon yard than a modern tavern. The structure, built of wood, sunburnt brick, or stone, is of one or two stories, built around an open square. There is a large gate in the middle of one of the sides, which is closed at night. Opposite the entrance is the stable, divided into small compartments. Drivers sleep here to take care of their beasts; in winter others prefer the stable, on account of the warmth produced by the presence of the animals. Feeding troughs or mangers, as shown in the accompanying illustration, are built against the wall.

AN EASTERN INN.

In the inn proper are rooms for the accommodation of guests. The yard is used for loading or unloading the beasts. In this instance, the rooms of the inn being all preoccupied, Joseph and Mary took a place in the stable with the drivers.—**In a manger.** I see no adequate reason for not accepting this literally. The child was born, and the manger was taken for his crib in lieu of a cradle. That he was exposed in the open court-yard as suggested by Sch usner (*Smith's Bib. Dict.*, art. *Manger*) is inherently incredible; the ordinary interpretation agrees with the customs of the Orient. An ancient tradition fixes on a cave as the stable in which Christ was born, and the spot is one of the "holy places" of Palestine. The Church of the Nativity marks the supposed site. There is nothing incredible in the tradition, for caves were used to house both men and beasts; but it is more probable that the stable was one of the ordinary sort connected with an Eastern inn. The identical manger in which the infant Jesus was laid is carefully preserved in the basilica of St. Maria Maggiore at Rome, and there displayed under the auspices of the pope every Christmas day! The accompanying illustration is from a sketch by A. L. Rawson of a manger at an inn on the road from Ramleh to Jerusalem. The women are carrying water and provisions into an upper chamber for the supply of the travelers, whose animals are feeding below.

8, 9. Shepherds abiding in the field, keeping watch over their flocks. The season of the year is unknown, though there are indications (see ch. 1 : 5, note) that it was either July or January. The sheep of Palestine are housed at night only in the very coldest parts of winter, not always even then. The shepherds watch them at night, sleeping on the ground or on beds made of branches of the trees, and wrapped in the heavy cloak or burnoose. The dangers to be guarded against are robbers, wolves, and sudden storms.—**An angel of the Lord.** Not *the*

AN EASTERN MANGER.

8 And there were in the same country shepherds abiding in the field, keeping watch over their flock by night.
9 And, lo, the angel of the Lord came upon them, and the glory of the Lord shone round about them, and they were sore afraid.
10 And the angel said unto them, Fear not: for, behold, I bring you good tidings of great joy, which shall be to all people.
11 For unto you ᵛ is born this day, in the city of David, a Saviour, which is Christ the Lord.
12 And this *shall be* a sign unto you: Ye shall find the babe wrapped in swaddling clothes, lying in a manger.

13 And suddenly there was with the angel ʷ a multitude of the heavenly host, praising God, and saying,
14 Glory to God in the highest, and on earth peace,ˣ good will toward men.
15 And it came to pass, as the angels were gone away from them into heaven, the shepherds said one to another, Let us now go even unto Bethlehem, and see this thing which is come to pass, which the Lord hath made known unto us.
16 And they came with haste, and found Mary, and Joseph, and the babe lying in a manger.
17 And when they had seen *it*, they made known abroad the saying which was told them concerning this child.

v Isa. 9 : 6.... w Ps. 103 : 20, 21 ; 1 Pet. 1 : 12.... x Isa. 57 : 19.

angel, which signifies a definite person, and generally, as I believe, the Lord Jesus Christ.—**Came to them.** Not necessarily nor probably in the heavens. More probably in human form, and as an earthly companion. This is the form in which most angel appearances are represented, both in the O. T. and the N. T. (Gen. 18 : 2 ; 19 : 1, 2 ; Josh. 5 : 13 ; Judges 6 · 11, etc. ; Mark 16 : 5, 6 ; Acts 27 : 23).—**And the glory of the Lord shone round about.** The shechinah, the most common manifestation of the deity to Israel. See Matt. 17 : 5, note.—**Sore afraid.** Literally, *Feared a great fear*. The universal consciousness of sin and of unfitness for the eternal world makes all mankind afraid of any unexpected disclosure of the spiritual world or revelation of the nearness of God.

10–12. Fear not. The first feeling of man at the approach of God is fear (Gen. 3 : 10) ; the message of the Gospel to him is, Fear not, alike when Christ is first revealed to the soul as a Saviour born, when he comes to him with succor in his sorrow (Matt. 14 : 26, 27), and when he seems to have departed and to have left the disciple alone in the world (Mark 16 : 6) ; alike in the hour of birth, of life-storm, and of death.—**I bring to you glad tidings of great joy.** The Greek verb (ἐυαγγελίζομαι) rendered *I bring glad tidings* is the one from which our word evangelize is derived. This angel was the first evangelist.—**Which shall be to all the people.** Notice the definite article, erroneously omitted in the English version. The people of Israel is meant ; at least the message would be so understood by the shepherds. A message to all classes rather than to all nationalities is indicated. Yet the universality of the Gospel is foreshadowed in the language of this and the preceding chapter (ver. 32 ; ch. 1 : 79, etc.).—**For unto you is born this day.** *Unto you* indicates the object of his birth. He came into the world, not to do his own will, but the will of his Father in heaven, which is that not one should perish, but that all should have eternal life (Ezek. 33 : 11 ; 2 Pet. 3 : 9).—**In the city of David.** Bethlehem.—**A Saviour, which is Christ the Lord.** A *Saviour*

because he saves his people from their sins (Matt. 1 : 21) ; *Christ*, *i. e.*, the Anointed One, because anointed by the Father to be the High-priest for the human race (Heb. 1 : 9 ; 10 : 11, 12) ; the *Lord* because creator and king (Col. 1 : 15-18). This word *Lord* (κύριος) is used continually by Luke as a designation of Jehovah (ch. 1 : 6, 8, 11, 15, 16, etc.) ; hence Alford, and following him Lange, Schaff, and Wordsworth : "I see no way of understanding this *Lord* (κύριος), but as corresponding to the Hebrew Jehovah."—**And this shall be a sign unto you.** Not only should they find the child cradled in a manger, but this would be the sign of the Messiahship. The depth of Christ's voluntary humiliation is the authentication of his divine character and mission. Comp. 1 Cor. 1 : 22–25. The sign that he is king is the fact that he is born in a stable.

13, 14. With the angel. Though not necessarily in immediate proximity to him ; the angel may have appeared on earth as a man ; the host in heaven, luminous and as angels.—**Praising God.** The incarnation is the theme of heaven's praise to the Most High. Comp. Rev., ch. 5.—**Glory to God in the highest**, *i. e.*, in the highest heavens.—**And on earth peace.** Between Jew and Gentile (Ephes. 2 : 14) ; between man and God (2 Cor. 5 : 17–21). But this is the consummation of Christ's kingdom, not the means by which it is established. See Matt. 10 : 34–36 ; James 3 : 17.—**Good will toward men**, *i. e.*, good will from God, shown to men in the Gospel (John 3 : 16). This "good will" is the cause of the peace which Christ confers on earth and the glory which he inspires in heaven. There is, however, a question whether *good will* is not in the genitive (ἐυδοκίας instead of ἐυδοκία), and governed by *men*, in which case the clause should be read, *men of good will*. This reading is adopted by Schaff (see his note in Lange for his authorities) and Godet. With this reading, the passage is interpreted by some scholars, Glory to God in the highest and on earth ; peace among men of good will ; by others, Glory to God in the highest, peace on earth among men of good will, *i. e.*, men of God's good pleasure, men chosen by him.

18 And all they that heard *it* wondered at those things which were told them by the shepherds.
19 But Mary kept all these things, and pondered *them* in her heart.
20 And the shepherds returned, glorifying and praising God for all the things that they had heard and seen, as it was told unto them.

21 And when eight days were accomplished[y] for the circumcising of the child, his name was called JESUS, which was so named of the angel[z] before he was conceived in the womb.
22 And when[a] the days of her purification, according to the law of Moses, were accomplished, they brought him to Jerusalem, to present *him* to the Lord;

y Lev. 12 : 3....z Ch. 1 : 31; Matt. 1 : 21....a Lev. 12 : 2, etc.

But in the uncertainty of textual criticism, the received reading appears to me far preferable.

15-20. Let us now go * * * and see this thing. They believe; their belief leads them to verify the message by seeking for the promised sign. To go and see is always the cure for doubt. (Ps. 34 : 8; John 1 : 46).—**They came with haste.** Observe their zeal. There is nothing to indicate how the shepherds found the manger from among all the mangers in Bethlehem. Oosterzee conjectures that it was their own stable; Olshausen that they were guided by divine influence. But the fact of a babe born in a stable would be noised abroad in Bethlehem, and it could not be difficult to find the holy family without supernatural guidance.—**They made known abroad.** Not merely to Joseph and Mary; they published it generally as they had opportunity. He that has received the Gospel and been brought to his Lord, should make known the news to others. Contrast, however, the difference in the reception by the shepherds and by Mary; the one publishes, the other meditates. Both are right; they illustrate different but not inconsistent phases of experience. Pondering and publishing are both the Christian duties.—**Kept all these words,** not *things.* Guarded them in her memory; an effort to retain the story in the *words in which it was given to her* is indicated.—**And pondered them.** Revolved them; comparing them with one another, that she might comprehend the nature of the career of the child entrusted to her keeping. May we not fairly assume that it was from Mary that the account of the angelic appearances in this and the preceding chapter, to Zacharias, to herself, and to the shepherds, was derived. "The oftener we read the 19th verse, the more assured we feel that Mary was the first and real author of the whole narrative. This pure, simple, and private history was composed by her, and preserved for a certain time in an oral form, until some one committed it to writing, whose work fell into the hands of Luke, and was reproduced by him in Greek."—(*Godet.*) This opinion is confirmed by the Aramaic or Hebrew character, which all scholars agree is born by the narrative, which bears indubitable indications of having been originally composed in Hebrew and translated into Greek.

THE ANGEL'S MESSAGE.—The angel, who is the first Evangelist, affords the first illustration of Gospel preaching. His message is (1) *Good news.* Christianity is not a mere re-enactment of the moral law, either of the O. T. or of the human conscience, but *news* of salvation to those that have broken that law and are under its penalty. (2.) *Of great joy.* Neither conviction of sin nor admonition of punishment are the Gospel, for these are not messages of great joy; they are the groundwork of preparation for the Gospel. The message of salvation to an elect few is not the Gospel, for it is the message of anguish to many and of joy to none, since none are assured that it is for them. Nothing is Gospel that is not joy-producing in those that receive it. (3.) *To all people;* all nations, all ages, all classes in society; this, though not necessarily involved in the language of the angel here, is implied in that of this and the preceding chapter. See note on ver. 10. (4.) *The cause of this joy;* the advent of one who is a Saviour, saving his people from their sins, the Highpriest of whom all previous high-priests were types, and the incarnation of the unseen Jehovah, Lord as well as Christ. (5.) *The attestation of his divinity;* the humiliation of his love, witnessed by this that he is cradled in a manger. The angel's song affords an illustration of the effect of the Gospel in heaven and on earth. An inspiration of glory in heaven; a source of peace on earth, because a testimony of God's good-will to sinners. The shepherd's course affords an illustration of how the Gospel should be received; with faith, with obedience, with an echo of the glad tidings to others who have not heard it.

Ch. 2 : 21-52. THE CONSECRATION AND CHILDHOOD OF JESUS. CHRIST IS PUBLICLY CONSECRATED TO GOD IN HIS INFANCY.—THE CHRISTIAN'S EXPECTATION OF DEATH.—CHRIST REVEALED FROM THE BEGINNING AS A SAVIOUR OF ALL MEN.—HE BRINGS A SWORD AS WELL AS PEACE.—A WOMAN HAILS THE ADVENT OF THE DELIVERER OF WOMEN.—SHE BECOMES A PREACHER OF REDEMPTION.—CHRIST A PATTERN OF CHILDHOOD; THE THEME OF HIS STUDY IS HIS FATHER'S WORK; HE IS SUBJECT TO HIS EARTHLY PARENTS; HIS THREE-FOLD GROWTH.

The incidents recorded in the rest of this chapter are peculiar to Luke, who alone gives any account of Christ's childhood. The legends in the apocryphal Gospels are wholly untrustworthy, and in striking contrast with the simplicity of the Gospel narrative.

23 (As it is written in the law of the Lord, Every ^b male that openeth the womb shall be called holy to the Lord ;)
24 And to offer a sacrifice according to that which is said in the law of the Lord, A pair of turtle doves, or two young pigeons.
25 And, behold, there was a man in Jerusalem, whose name was Simeon ; and the same man was just and ^c devout, waiting for the consolation ^d of Israel : and the Holy Ghost was upon him.
26 And it was revealed unto him by the Holy Ghost, that he should not see ^e death before he had seen the Lord's Christ.

27 And he came by the Spirit into the temple : and when the parents brought in the child Jesus, to do for him after the custom of the law,
28 Then took he him up in his arms, and blessed God, and said,
29 Lord, now ^f lettest thou thy servant depart in peace,^g according to thy word :
30 For mine eyes have seen ^h thy salvation,
31 Which thou hast prepared before the face of all people ;
32 A light to lighten the ⁱ Gentiles, and the glory of thy people Israel.

b Exod. 13 : 12 ; 22 : 29.... c verse 38 ; Mark 15 : 43.... d Isa. 40 : 1.... e Ps. 89 : 48 ; Heb. 11 : .... f Gen. 46 : 30.... g Isa. 57 : 2 ; Rev. 14 : 13.... h ch. 3 : 6 ; Isa. 52 : 10 ; Acts 4 : 12.... i Isa. 42 : 6 ; 49 : 6 ; 60 : 3 ; Acts 13 : 47, 48.

21. On the customs connected with circumcision, see ch. 1 : 59, note. That Christ submitted to circumcision affords no warrant for the perpetuation of that ordinance, nor for the substitution of another, as baptism, in its stead. For he was made subject to the law, that he might redeem those from their subjection who are by nature under the law (Gal. 4 : 5). I find no warrant in the N. T. for the supposed apostolic substitution of baptism for circumcision. But Christ's example here does seem to sanction the custom of publicly consecrating our children in infancy to God, and of receiving them publicly into covenant relations with God and the church.

22-24. And when the days of her purification * * * were accomplished. The Levitical law (Lev. ch. 12) provided that for a month after the circumcision of a child—or for a fortnight, in case the babe was a girl—the mother was to be regarded as unclean. At the end of that time she was to present an offering to the Lord ; a lamb for a burnt-offering (i. e., an offering of self-consecration), and a pigeon for a sin-offering (an atonement). If the parties were too poor to provide a lamb, a turtle-dove or pigeon might be substituted. The dove-cot was a common appendage of the dwellings of even the poor, and he who was too poor to have a dove-cot of his own might go to the rocky side of a ravine and take as many young as he pleased from the numerous nests of the wild doves in the clefts (Jer. 48 : 28). In Mary's case, a dove or pigeon appears, from the language of ver. 24, to have been substituted for the lamb ; an indication of their poverty. The "churching of women," a season of thanksgiving for the birth, which is maintained in the Roman Catholic and Episcopal churches, and is of very early origin, is probably derived from this O. T. provision.—
To present him to the Lord. The original law prescribed that the first-born male in every family should be consecrated to God, as a priest (Exod. 13 : 12 ; 22 : 29 ; Numb. 8 : 17) ; then the Levites were substituted for the first-born, but as they were less in number, provision was made for redeeming the surplus (Numb. 3 : 41-51) ; but subsequently all the first-born were required to be presented and redeemed from the priestly service by an offering of five shekels (Numb. 18 : 15, 16). It was in accordance with this law that Jesus was now presented to be redeemed in the Temple. This redemption of the first-born is done away with in Christ, since in his kingdom we are all called to be priests unto God, made so by and in Christ (1 Pet. 2 : 9 ; Rev. 5 : 10).

25-32. Whose name was Simeon. Possibly the well-known person of that name, the father of Gamaliel. But of this there is no other evidence than the name, which is a common one.—Just and devout. Just in his dealings with his fellow-men ; pious in his feelings toward God and in his observance of the ceremonial law, the two elements recognized in Micah 6 : 8, as all that the Lord requires for the perfection of character. Comp. Christ's language in Matt. 22 : 37-40.—Waiting for the consolation of Israel. The Messiah. Comp. Acts 28 : 20. The phrase is a common one in Rabbinical literature, and was used as a form of adjuration : " So let me see the consolation of Israel, if I did not see," etc. The whole nation was in a sense expecting the advent of the Messiah, but not as Simeon, in the maintenance of justice, loving-kindness, and devout trust in God. The object of John's preaching was to prepare for Christ's coming, by bringing the people to ways of justice and thoughts of piety (ch. 3 : 1-18).—And the Holy Ghost was upon him. An evidence that the Holy Ghost was not first given at Pentecost and after the death and resurrection of Jesus. See Acts 2 : 4, note.—And he came by the Spirit. Led by the Divine Spirit.—Lettest thou thy servant depart in peace. Literally, Let free thy servant. He speaks as one to whom this life is one of toil and bondage, and the other one of rest and liberty ; and he waits for the day of his emancipation—the true ideal of the aged Christian's anticipation of death.—According to the word. The promise made to him by the Spirit of God, that he should see the Messiah before his death (ver. 26).—Before the face of all peoples. The original is plural (τῶν λαῶν), not, as in our English version, singular. The con-

CH. II.] LUKE. 23

33 And Joseph and his mother marvelled at those things which were spoken of him.
34 And Simeon blessed them, and said unto Mary his mother, Behold, this *child* is set for the fall ʲ and rising again of many in Israel; and for a sign which shall be spoken ᵏ against;
35 (Yea, a sword ˡ shall pierce through thy own soul also,) that ᵐ the thoughts of many hearts may be revealed.
36 And there was one Anna, a prophetess, the daughter of Phanuel, of the tribe of Aser; she was of a great age, and had lived with an husband seven years from her virginity;
37 And she *was* a widow of about fourscore and four

j Isa. 8 : 14; Rom. 9 : 32, 33; 1 Cor. 1 : 23, 24; 2 Cor. 2 : 16; 1 Pet. 2 : 7, 8....k Acts 28 : 22....l John 19 : 25....m Judges 5 : 15, 16; l Cor. 11 : 19.

ception of the Gospel as a provision, not for the Jewish nation only, but for the whole world, is evidently not a later idea, developed by Paul. It belongs to and is seen in the germs and buds of Christian truth.—**A light to lighten the Gentiles.** See Isaiah 49 : 6; Matt. 4 : 16.— **The glory of thy people, Israel.** We ought not to forget that Christ is, according to the Scripture, the glory of Israel; that to the Jewish nation, his peculiar people, God granted the birth of the world's Saviour; and that to it we owe our Light. A superficial view covers the Jews with odium because of their crucifixion of their Lord; a profounder view recognizes in him the glory of Israel.

33-35. And Joseph and his mother. The best MSS. read, *His father and his mother;* and this is the reading sustained by Alford, Tischendorf, Tregelles, and Schaff. The latter interprets it, "The word is of course to be taken, not in the physical, but in the legal and popular sense." See note on ver. 48.—**Is set.** Appointed by God. The N. T. throughout recognizes Christ as fulfilling the Father's will, doing the Father's business, sent by the Father's appointment; a significant fact, and one not to be ignored in any attempt to settle definitely the problem of his life, character, and work. See ver. 49; John 15 : 10; 17 : 18; Heb. 1 : 9; 2 : 9, etc.—**For the fall and rising again of many in Israel.** Not for the humiliation, because of sin, and the exaltation, because of righteousness. Such humiliation before God is not a fall, but a rising. The word rendered fall (πτῶσις) is *downfall, overthrow*, as in Matt. 7 : 27. Christ brought downfall to the hopes of those who expected a temporal prince and a political millennium, and ruin to those whose desire for the kingdom of God was really a personal ambition for place and power in it, as the Pharisees, and notably Judas Iscariot among his own disciples. He brought rising again to those who were willing that God should overthrow their plans and ambitions, and accepted from him the grander gift of a universal kingdom, prepared for all peoples. Both the fall and the rising are illustrated by the experience of the disciples who, after the resurrection, met Christ on the road to Emmaus (Luke 24 : 21, 31, 35).—**For a sign which shall be spoken against.** Because disappointing all hope of political preferment and national exaltation. See John 8 : 48; 1 Cor. 1 : 22, 23. — **Yea, a sword shall pierce through thine own soul also.** Not, as Lightfoot, a prediction of Mary's martyrdom; nor as Schaff and Wordsworth, a reference to her agony on beholding the crucifixion of her son; nor as Alford, a foretelling that she also must know the agony of sorrow for sin; but, as the connection implies, a declaration that she must know, with others, a rising and falling. Her hopes for the emancipation of the nation, the reformation of the people, the immediate glorification of God through the Son given unto her, are destined to be overthrown; she will hear his unambiguous prophecy of the destruction of the temple and the holy city, will see him rejected, scorned, crucified, will see the nation given over to increasing anarchy and corruption and the wrath of God, and will rise from her desolation in the destruction of all her anticipations only when, in answer to the days of prolonged prayer (Acts 1 : 14) the Spirit is poured out upon the church, and she, with others, begins to see the length and breadth of the kingdom that knows no end.—**That the thoughts of many hearts may be revealed.** The object and result of this dispensation; that the worldliness, the selfishness, the personal ambition of the Jewish aspirations and ambitions may be discovered to themselves and to the world; and the hollowness of what passed for piety, but was not, since it only covered the spirit of trust in and consecration to self. The whole prophecy, then, may be thus paraphrased: Behold this child is appointed by God to overthrow the hopes of many, by disappointing their expectations of a temporal kingdom; and to give them resurrection again by opening before them the vision of a more glorious, a spiritual kingdom; he will be a sign not universally welcomed and accepted, but despised and rejected of men; you yourself shall know the agony of withered hopes and a bitter disappointment; and thus by their rejection of a Messiah that brings them no political preferment, the selfishness of what passes for pious thoughts and expectations will be revealed.

36-38. There was one Anna, a prophetess. Recognized among the people as speaking by the Spirit of God. Religious teaching was not confined to the male sex either under the O. T.

years, which departed not from the temple, but served God with fastings and prayers" night and day.

38 And she, coming in at that instant, gave thanks likewise unto the Lord, and spake of him to all them that ° looked for redemption in Jerusalem.

39 And when they had performed all things according to the law of the Lord, they returned into Galilee, to their own city Nazareth.

40 And the child grew, and waxed strong in spirit, filled ᵖ with wisdom ; and the grace of God was upon him.

41 Now his parents went to Jerusalem every ᑫ year at the feast of the passover.

42 And when he was twelve years old, they went up to Jerusalem, after the custom of the feast.

43 And when they had fulfilled the days, as they returned, the child Jesus tarried behind in Jerusalem ; and Joseph and his mother knew not *of it*.

44 But they, supposing him to have been in the company, went a day's journey ; and they sought him among *their* kinsfolk and acquaintance.

45 And when they found him not, they turned back again to Jerusalem, seeking him.

46 And it came to pass, that after three days they found him in the temple, sitting in the midst of the doctors, both hearing them, and asking them questions.

47 And all that heard him were astonished at his understanding ʳ and answers.

48 And when they saw him, they were amazed: and his mother said unto him, Son, why hast thou thus

n Acts 26 : 7 ; 1 Tim. 5 : 5.... o ver-e 25....p verse 52; Isa. 11 : 2, 3....q Exod. 23 : 15 ; Deut. 16 : 1....r ch. 4 : 22, 32; Ps. 119 : 99 ; Matt. 7 : 28 ; Mark 1 : 22; John 7 : 15, 46.

---

or under the N. T. dispensation, though, from the nature of woman's general occupation and duties, the cases in which she became a recognized public teacher of religious truth were rare. See 2 Kings 22 : 14; Acts 18 : 26.—**A widow of about four score and four years.** Or, *until* four score and four; this is the better reading. The implication is, not that she had been a widow eighty-eight years, which would make her a centenarian, but that eighty-eight was her present age.—**Which departed not from the temple.** Exod. 38 : 8, and 1 Sam. 2 : 22, indicates that women were employed in some cases about the temple; but whether this was of a strictly religious character or consisted in certain subordinate services, such as washing, repairing of the temple fabrics, etc., is not known. There were chambers connected with the temple, for the priests. One of these may have been assigned by them to Anna, as a special mark of honor to a recognized prophetess.—**Gave thanks to the Lord.** For the gift of the Messiah. — **And spake of him.** Not merely then. The verb is in the imperfect tense, and implies a continued habit. From this time she was accustomed to speak of him to those who were looking for the fulfillment of the divine prophecy of the redemption of Israel.

39, 40. On the growth of Jesus, see on ver. 52. Before this return to Nazareth occurred the visit of the Magi and the flight into Egypt, recorded only by Matthew. It is omitted by Luke, possibly because recorded by Matthew, possibly because he was ignorant of it. If this was the case, however, he could hardly have derived any of his information directly from Mary.

41, 42. Now his parents went every year. According to the requirements of Exod. 23 : 14–17. The letter of the law there applies only to males ; but according to the school of Hillel women were required to go once a year to the Passover.—**When he was twelve years old.** A critical age for a Jewish boy. At twelve, according to the Jewish legends, Moses left the house of Pharaoh's daughter ; Samuel heard the voice of God ; Solomon judged between the contending women ; Josiah dreamed of his great reformation. He was now required to begin learning a trade, to wear his phylacteries, to receive the title of "son of the law," and first incurred legal obligations. This was probably the first visit of Jesus to Jerusalem.

43–45. There is nothing incredible or even extraordinary in the fact that they did not miss the boy till the end of the first day's journey. The Galilean pilgrims would travel together in a caravan, including a large number. In such pilgrim bands the women and elderly men are mounted ; the younger men walk ; drums and timbrels enliven the march ; the caravan stops at every spring or well ; dates, melons, cucumbers are passed around to refresh the pilgrims ; the occasion is one of innocent mirth and festivity ; the children walk and play by the side of their parents, and wander from one group to another, often getting a ride, when wearied, on some camel or mule less heavily loaded than the rest. Thus the supposition that Jesus was in another part of the great caravan was a natural one.

46, 47. After three days. They had only come one day's journey from Jerusalem ; they must therefore have prolonged their search for some time before going to the temple. See on ver. 49.—**Of the doctors.** The rabbis of the law. The great theological schools of Jerusalem were in connection with the Temple. Such an one was that in which Saul of Tarsus was educated. (Acts 22 : 3)—**Asking them questions.** "It was the custom in the Jewish schools for the scholars to ask questions of their teachers ; and a great part of the rabbinical books consists of the answers of the rabbis to such questions."—(*Alford.*) The traditional account which represents Jesus as *teaching* the rabbis is neither consistent with the narrative nor with Jewish sentiment, which was utterly averse to all aspect of forwardness in childhood, nor with the spirit of Jesus, which was one of humility, not of arrogance or self-assertion. Yet, recalling his questioning of the doctors in the tem-

THE CHILD JESUS.
"And when he was twelve years old he went up to Jerusalem after the custom of the feast."

CH. II.] LUKE. 25

dealt with us? behold, thy father and I have sought thee sorrowing.
49 And he said unto them, How is it that ye sought me? wist ye not that I must be about ᵃ my Father's business?
50 And they understood not the saying which he spake unto them.

51 And he went down with them, and came to Nazareth, and was subject unto them: but his mother kept ᵗ all these sayings in her heart.
52 And Jesus increased ᵘ in wisdom and stature, and in favour with God and man.

ᵃ John 5 : 17 ; 9 : 4 .... ᵗ verse 19 ; Dan. 7 : 28 .... ᵘ verse 40 ; 1 Sam. 2 : 26.

---

ple years later (Matt. chs. 21, 22), and remembering that "the child is father to the man," we may well believe that the spirituality of his questions made them in fact, though not in form, a true instruction. Even at twelve, his was not a mind to be content with the literalism and superficiality of Rabbinical interpretations of Scripture. It was the depth of spiritual insight, indicated by his questions, that astonished them. It is indicative of his childhood character that the central object of interest in the Temple was not its architectural magnificence, its music, and its ritual, but its schools, where he might study more deeply than in the synagogical schools of Nazareth the truths concerning the kingdom and the word of God.

48, 49. Son, why hast thou thus dealt with us? A gentle reproach. The mother now, as later, did not comprehend her son. (Mark 3 : 21, 31 ; John 2 : 4).—**Thy father and I have sought thee sorrowing.** An indication of the historical fidelity of the narrative. A mythical writer would not have suffered Mary to speak of Joseph as the father of Jesus. Yet this would have been her language. For though not his true father, he stood in the place of one, and would naturally have assumed the title, as usually does the step-father, and not infrequently the guardian. But Christ's reply turns his mother's thoughts from the seeming to the real father. To him Joseph is not father.—**How is it that ye seek me? Wist ye not that in the affairs of my father I must needs be?** Not, *Engaged in doing my father's business;* but *Engaged concerning and interested in it.* That which, as a child, Jesus had to do with his Father's business, was to be engaged in studying it. That which surprises him—for his question indicates surprise—is not that they should have sought him, but that they should have spent three days in an anxious search along the road and in Jerusalem, and not instantly and intuitively known where to find him, namely, studying the truths concerning his Father and his Father's work. This very surprise of Jesus indicates not only that he was conscious of his supernatural birth, but also that he assumed that his mother and father knew that he was aware of it.

50, 51. They understood not that saying. Not that it was meaningless to them; but they did not fully comprehend its meaning.

Nothing but his life, and death, and resurrection could fully interpret either the spirit of self-consecration, implied in these words, or what was that business to which he must needs devote himself. Do any of us fully understand what it is to be about the Father's business? What this implied in Christ? What it implies for us?—**Was subject unto them.** Learning the carpenter's trade and working at the carpenter's bench (Mark 6 : 3). In this willing subjection of Christ, despite his real superiority to his peasant guardians, and in this cheerful abandonment of the congenial life of a student for the uncongenial work of an artisan, is a lesson to the children of our day, who find it difficult to yield, in their fancied superiority, to the wisdom of their parents. This was a part, not the least part, of his chosen humiliation (Gal. 4 : 4 ; Phil. 2 : 7).—**Kept all these sayings in her heart.** Treasured them up and pondered them; a hint of the source whence Luke derived them, if not directly, at least through other hands. See on ver. 19. Joseph is not again in the Gospels. It is generally believed, from this circumstance, that he died before Christ's public ministry began.

52. And Jesus increased in wisdom and in stature, and in favor with God and man. This declaration is not to be modified to suit any preconceived theological theories concerning the person of Christ. He experienced a fourfold growth—in stature or age, the Greek word (ἡλικία) is capable of either translation, in wisdom, in divine approval, and in popular favor. There is no difficulty in understanding the growth in stature and in popular favor; little in comprehending the growth of wisdom—for it was one of the elements in the infinite condescension of the Son of God, that he laid aside his knowledge and entered into all the conditions of mankind, including necessary growth. But how should he, who shared the divine glory with the Father before the creation of the world (John 17 : 5), grow in divine favor? On the ordinary interpretation of the doctrine of the incarnation this is inexplicable to me ; it is equally so on the Swedenborgian view, that Christ was the divine soul in a human body, and subject to human conditions. It is comprehensible on the theory that Christ was divine because wholly and entirely subject to the influence of the indwelling Spirit of God, his Son, as we are his sons, though with a perfection of allegiance and sub-

CHAPTER III.

NOW in the fifteenth year of the reign of Tiberius Cæsar, Pontius Pilate being governor of Judæa, and Herod being tetrarch of Galilee, and his brother Philip tetrarch of Ituræa, and of the region of Trachonitis, and Lysanias the tetrarch of Abilene, 2 Annas and Caiaphas being the high priests, the

v John 11 : 49, 51 ; 18 : 13 ; Acts 4 : 6.

ordination to his Father's will which we never know. But to this interpretation of his character there are grave, if not conclusive objections, in the account of his supernatural birth, and in the doctrine of his pre-existence. This much is certain, from other representations of Scripture, that he suffered real temptations; won his victories only after real conflict; and that in each new victory he received anew the approval of his Father's love. Comp. Phil. 2 : 9; Heb. 1 : 9.

Ch. 3 : 1-18. PREACHING OF JOHN THE BAPTIST. THE PREPARATION FOR THE GOSPEL IS REPENTANCE.—THE WORK OF THE CHRISTIAN CHURCH: TO PREPARE FOR THE COMING OF HER KING.—THE ELEMENTS IN THAT PREPARATION: EXALTATION; HUMILIATION; RECTIFICATION; CULTIVATION.—THE PROMISE OF THE FUTURE: A SALVATION UNIVERSALLY RECOGNIZED.—FALSE HOPE: IN THE VIRTUES OF THE DEAD.—TRUE LIFE: IN PRESENT PRACTICAL REFORM.—REPENTANCE ILLUSTRATED.—THE TWO BAPTISMS: OF MAN, OF GOD.

This account of the preaching of John the Baptist is much more fully given by Luke than by either of the other Evangelists. With the account here should, however, be compared that in Matt. 3 : 1-12, and notes, and in Mark 1 : 1-8. There is an instructive contrast between these reports and that of John 1 : 15-36; for the reason of the difference, see notes on the ministry of John the Baptist, below.

1. **In the fifteenth year of the reign of Tiberius Cæsar.** The emperor of Rome at the birth of Christ was Augustus Cæsar (ch. 2 : 1); he died August 19, 767th year of Rome, i. e., 14-15, A. D. But Tiberius had, for two years previous, shared with him his throne, and his reign here is probably dated from the time of this joint sovereignty. Christ was about twenty-nine years of age (ver. 23), assuming, as we probably may do, that the ministry of John the Baptist preceding the baptism of Jesus, lasted for six months or a year. A period, therefore, of seventeen or eighteen years intervenes between the close of the second and the beginning of the third chapter. Of Christ's life during this time nothing is known. He remained at home with his father, learned the carpenter's trade, according to an early tradition made plows and yokes, probably attended the village school which was connected with every synagogue, and where he was instructed certainly in the Scripture, and probably also in such elements of natural science as were taught in the ordinary course of education. That he did not have any professional or Rabbinical training is implied in John 7 : 15. But though the N. T. passes by in silence this part of his life, it is not one unimportant in his gracious ministry. "We are apt to forget that it was during this time that much of the great work of the second Adam was done. The growing up, through infancy, childhood, youth, manhood, from grace to grace, holiness to holiness, in subjection, self-denial, and love, without one polluting touch of sin—this it was which, consummated by the three years of active ministry, by the Passion, and by the Cross, constituted 'the obedience of one man,' by which many were made righteous."—(*Alford.*) **Pontius Pilate being governor,** etc. During the time which elapsed between Christ's childhood and his public baptism, the

THE HOLY LAND
under
THE SONS
of
HEROD THE GREAT.

LUKE.

word of God came unto John the son of Zacharias in the wilderness.
3 And ᵂ he came into all the country about Jordan, preaching the baptism of repentance ˣ for the remission of sins;
4 As it is written in the book of the words of Esaias the prophet,ʸ saying, The voice of one crying in the wilderness, Prepare ye the way of the Lord, make his paths straight.
5 Every valley shall be filled, and every mountain and hill shall be brought low; and the crooked shall be made straight, and the rough ways *shall be* made smooth;
6 And ᶻ all flesh shall see the salvation of God.

w Matt. 3 : 1; Mark 1 : 4....x ch. 1 : 77....y Isa. 40 : 3....z Ps. 98 : 2; Isa. 40 : 5; 49 : 6; 52 : 10; Rom. 10 : 12, 18.

political constitution of Palestine had undergone a radical change. On the death of Herod the Great, his kingdom had been apportioned between his three sons: Archelaus, with the title of ethnarch, received one-half of his father's dominions—Judea, Samaria, and Idumea; but after a reign of ten years was banished, in consequence of complaints by his subjects, and his dominions were added to the province of Syria. Pontius Pilate, its fifth governor, arrived there A. D. 25, 26, *i. e.*, a little prior to the commencement of John's public ministry. Herod Antipas remained tetrarch of Galilee and Perea; his reign lasted forty-two years, and therefore throughout the whole ministry of our Lord. Herod Philip retained for thirty-seven years Iturea, a country south-east of the Libanus and Trachonitis, substantially the same district as the Argob of the O. T. The precise limits of Abilene are not known. Its capital, Abila, was eighteen miles north of Daurasensand, on the eastern slope of the Antilibanus. The student will get a better idea of these political divisions from the accompanying map than from any verbal description. The *Lysanius* here mentioned is not to be confounded with the king of that name who was assassinated thirty-six years before Christ by Anthony. It is true that neither Josephus nor classic history mentions any later Lysanius, and skeptical writers have endeavored to prove that Luke is here guilty of a palpable anachronism. But recently deciphered inscriptions demonstrate that a later Lysanius—probably a descendant of the murdered king—was a tetrarch in the time of Tiberius. On the life and character of Pontius Pilate, see John 19 : 29, note; on the Herodian family, see Matt. 2 : 1, note.

2. Annas and Caiaphas being the high-priests. *High-priest* (singular) is the better reading. The Jews recognized but one high-priest, who held his office originally for life; his functions were, however, sometimes divided, one officer presiding over the Sanhedrim, the other supervising the matters of religion; and some traces of this division are found in the early history of the Jews (2 Kings 25 : 18). Annas was the father-in-law of Caiaphas, and was removed by the Roman government, and Caiaphas appointed in his place. It is probable that the Jews did not recognize this substitution, but continued to regard Annas as their real high-priest, a fact which would explain the language here and in Acts 4 : 6. On the character of both Annas and Caiaphas, see notes on John 11 : 47-52; 18 : 13, etc.—**A word of God came unto John.** That is, a special revelation of truth or a special inspiration, prompting him to commence his public ministry. See 1 Kings 12 : 22; 1 Chron. 17 : 3; Hosea 1 : 2; Jonah 1 : 1.—**In the wilderness.** Of Judea; the mountainous and broken country along the western borders of the Dead Sea.

3-6. He came into all the country about Jordan. The district on either side of the river, especially near its mouth. His was apparently an itinerant ministry.—**The baptism of repentance.** Baptism as a symbol of repentance. Certainly subsequently, probably prior to this time, heathen proselytes were baptized by immersion, as a sign that they were washed of their old errors and entered on a new life. John's preaching signified that the old must be washed away for the Jew as well as the Gentile.—**The words of Esaias the prophet.** Isaiah 40 : 3-5. On the interpretation of the quotation, see Matt. 3 : 3, note. The metaphor is derived from the Oriental practice of preparing the highway for the journey of a monarch; it is interpreted by the history of Christianity, which has lifted up the down-trodden and oppressed, brought down the proud and haughty, rectified the corrupt and crooked practices of society, and smoothed with a genuine culture its rudenesses and roughnesses, all as a preparation for the final coming of the King. When this work of preparation is completed, not before, all flesh shall see the salvation of God. Thus John the Baptist defines the duty of the church throughout all ages, a duty of preparing for the second and final coming of her King. For it is not said that John prepared the way, but that he preached that the people should prepare the way. The history of Christianity, a preparation for the coming of Christ in society, indicates also the preparation necessary in the individual heart. The depression of ignorance and superstition, the exaltation of power and pride, crooked and corrupt ways deviating from the straight lines of integrity, and rudenesses of temper born of deficient human sympathy, are all so many obstacles to the coming of the King in the soul.

7 Then said he to the multitude that came forth to be baptized of him, O ª generation of vipers! who hath warned you to flee from the wrath to come?

8 Bring forth, therefore, fruits worthy of repentance; and begin not to say within yourselves, We have Abraham to *our* father: for I say unto you, That God is able of these stones to raise up children unto Abraham.

9 And now also the axe is laid unto the root of the trees: every ᵇ tree, therefore, which bringeth not forth good fruit, is hewn down, and cast into the fire.

10 And the people asked him, saying, What shall we do then?

11 He answereth and saith unto them, He ᶜ that hath two coats, let him impart to him that hath none; and he that hath meat, let him do likewise.

12 Then came also publicans ᵈ to be baptized, and said unto him, Master, what shall we do?

13 And he said unto them, Exact ᵉ no more than that which is appointed you.

14 And the soldiers likewise demanded of him, saying, And what shall we do? And he said unto them, Do violence to no man, neither accuse *any* ᶠ falsely; and be content ᵍ with your wages.

15 And as the people were in expectation, and all men mused in their hearts of John, whether he were the Christ or not;

16 John answered, saying unto *them* all, I indeed

a Matt. 3 : 7....b ch. 13 : 7, 9; Matt. 7 : 19....c ch. 11 : 41; 2 Cor. 8 : 14; 1 John 3 : 17....d ch. 7 : 29; Matt. 21 : 32....e ch. 19 : 8; 1 Cor. 6 : 10....f Exod. 23 : 1; Lev. 19 : 11....g 1 Tim. 6 : 8.

7-9. Offspring of vipers. This was especially addressed to the Pharisees and Sadducees (Matt. 3 : 7), who came *to be baptized*, but not to repent; they were ready for a new ceremonial, but not for a new life. The phrase is perhaps interpreted by John 8 : 44, the serpent being a Jewish symbol of the devil; they are characterized as offspring of vipers in contrast with their ancestral pride as children of Abraham.—**Bring forth, therefore, fruits worthy of repentance.** Practical reformation is the only evidence which God recognizes of the genuineness of repentance (Isa. 1 : 10-20).—**The axe is laid unto the root of the trees.** A metaphor indicating that everything is ready for the execution of judgment. Comp. Isa. 52 : 10; 2 Pet. 3 : 7.

10-14. This passage is not the report of a single sermon, but a summary embodying the spirit of John's teaching at this time. After the baptism of Jesus the character of his ministry changed, and he proclaimed the Lamb of God that taketh away the sins of the world (John 1 : 29-36). Now, he was not proclaiming the Messiah, but preparing the way for the Messiah; hence the difference between his answer here and that of Jesus in John 6 : 29, and of Paul in Acts 16 : 31, to the question, What shall we do? Theirs was the answer of the N. T.; this was the answer of the last of the O. T. prophets. Observe the three virtues which John commends, generosity, honesty, justice. Comp. Micah 6 : 8; Matt. 23 : 23.—**Two coats.** Two tunics. The inner garment worn next the skin, generally with sleeves, and reaching usually to the knees, sometimes to the ankles. It answered to the modern shirt or chemise. Two tunics indicates but small wealth. Even the poor can spare something for the still poorer. The accompanying picture of a master and servant shows the master wearing a girdle over his robe, and a coat over all, illustrating the wearing of two coats—a robe and coat—at the same time. The servant has a coat, one only.—**Also publicans * * * exact no more than that which is appointed you.** The publicans or tax-gatherers

MASTER AND SERVANT.

purchased from the government the right for a fixed sum to collect the taxes in a given province or district; their profit depended on what they could extort from the people. See Matt. 9 : 9, note. Observe how the mere presence of Christ in the case of one publican (Luke 19 : 8) secured more than the preaching of John the Baptist required. John demanded only reform in the future; Zaccheus restored the ill-gotten gains of the past.—**The soldiers likewise * * * Do violence to no man, neither accuse any falsely, and be content with your wages.** Who these soldiers were is uncertain, whether armed Jewish police, soldiers in the service of King Antipas, or Roman soldiers from Judea. In an age when the army looked with contempt on the civilians, and the civil was subordinate to the military power, acts of violence were common; he whose office it was to protect became

baptize you with water; but one mightier than I cometh, the latchet of whose shoes I am not worthy to unloose: he shall baptize you with the Holy Ghost and with fire:
17 Whose fan [h] is in his hand, and he will throughly purge his floor, and will [i] gather the wheat into his garner; but the [j] chaff he will burn [k] with fire unquenchable.
18 And many other things, in his exhortation, preached he unto the people.

h Jer. 15:7....i Micah 4:12; Matt. 13:30....j Ps. 1:4....k Ps. 21:9; Mark 9:44, 48.

SLAVE LOOSING SHOE LATCHET.

an oppressor; false accusations of disaffection were made a means of extorting hush-money, and that spirit of military insubordination was already rising which ended in making the army masters of the empire. John, like Paul, counsels every man to abide in his own calling, and to work out Christian principles and the Christian disposition therein. See 1 Cor. 7: 21-24. If all war were inconsistent with divine law, John could not have given this counsel to soldiers.

15, 16. See Matt. 3: 11, note. To unloose the latchet of a sandal, the thong or strap by which it was fastened, was a menial office belonging to a slave.

17, 18. Whose fan is in his hand. The accompanying picture illustrates the Oriental method of winnowing, from which this metaphor is taken. The fan was a spade, usually of wood or iron, with which the laborer threw up the threshed grain against the wind, which carried away the lighter particles of chaff, leaving the grain to fall back upon the floor or earth. See further, Matt. 3: 12, note.

ON THE MINISTRY OF JOHN THE BAPTIST.—For an admirable study of the character and career of John the Baptist, the student is referred to a monograph by Dr. Reynolds, published by A. S. Barnes & Co. For a consideration of the nature and form of his baptism, see Matt., ch. 3, p. 72, Note on the Baptism of Jesus

WINNOWING THE GRAIN.

19 But¹ Herod the tetrarch, being reproved by him for Herodias his brother Philip's wife, and for all the evils which Herod had done,
20 Added yet this above all, that he shut up John in prison.
21 Now when all the people were baptized, it ᵐ came to pass, that Jesus also being baptized, and praying, the heaven was opened,
22 And the Holy Ghost descended in a bodily shape like a dove upon him; and a voice came from heaven, which said, Thou art my beloved Son; in thee I am well pleased.
23 And Jesus himself began to be about thirty years of age, being (as was supposed) the son ⁿ of Joseph, which was *the son* of Heli,
24 Which was *the son* of Matthat, which was *the son* of Levi, which was *the son* of Melchi, which was *the son of* Janna, which was *the son of* Joseph,
25 Which was *the son* of Mattathias, which was *the son of* Amos, which was *the son* of Naum, which was *the son* of Esli, which was *the son* of Nagge,
26 Which was *the son* of Maath, which was *the son* of Mattathias, which was *the son* of Semei, which was *the son* of Joseph, which was *the son of* Juda,
27 Which was *the son of* Joanna, which was *the son* of Rhesa, which was *the son* of Zorobabel, which was *the son* of Salathiel, which was *the son* of Neri,
28 Which was *the son* of Melchi, which was *the son* of Addi, which was *the son* of Cosam, which was *the son* of Elmodam, which was *the son* of Er,
29 Which was *the son* of Jose, which was *the son* of Eliezer, which was *the son* of Jorim, which was *the son* of Matthat, which was *the son* of Levi,
30 Which was *the son* of Simeon, which was *the son* of Juda, which was *the son* of Joseph, which was *the son* of Jonan, which was *the son* of Eliakim,
31 Which was *the son* of Melea, which was *the son* of Menan, which was *the son* of Mattatha, which was *the son* of Nathan,ᵒ which was *the son* of David,
32 Which was *the son* of Jesse,ᵖ which was *the son* of Obed, which was *the son of* Booz, which was *the son* of Salmon, which was *the son* of Naasson,

l Matt. 14:3; Mark 6:17....m Matt. 3:13, etc.; John 1:32, etc....n Matt. 13:55; John 6:42....o Zech. 12:12; 2 Sam. 5:14....p Ruth 4:18, 22.

by John. For account of his imprisonment and death, see Matt. 14:1-12, notes. Here it must suffice briefly to note the characteristics of the man and his ministry. (1.) He was inspired from his mother's womb (ch. 1:15). In the ministry here reported he is expressly described as speaking as the word of God came unto him. His ministry, therefore, was directly authorized, and, if we comprehend aright its relations to the past and the future, is instructive and authoritative. (2.) His position is expressly stated by Christ to be that of a prophet and more than a prophet (Matt. 11:9). He was more, because a forerunner who immediately preceded the King. His character and his early preaching corresponds with that of the O. T. prophets, of whom he was the last; between whom and the N. T. apostles he was a connecting link. Like them, he set the religion of a spiritual and moral life in contrast with that of sacerdotalism, which the priesthood had made the religion of the age. He was the Martin Luther of the first century. (3.) But, unlike Martin Luther, he knew nothing of the free spirit of the Gospel. He was by nature and by childhood association an ascetic. He sought reform, not by a new and divine inspiration, which he foretold, but which he could not minister to others, since it could come only through the Messiah, but by a resolute cutting off of transgressions and of occasions of transgression innocent in themselves. Hence he preached repentance, not faith; hence the Nazarite vow in his infancy; hence his anchorite life in the wilderness; hence his abstinence from all social life and enjoyment (chaps. 1:15; 3:3; Matt. 3:4; 11:18). In this respect his life was in striking contrast with that of Jesus. (4.) But he was not only the last of the O. T. prophets; he was also the first of the N. T. evangelists. The student does not rightly apprehend his ministry who does not study the contrast afforded between the reports in the Synoptists and the report in John (John 1:15-36). The Synoptists report the preaching of John before Jesus had been revealed to him as the Messiah. He is, then, a preacher of law, duty, moral obligation. He is so represented here. He preaches not the Gospel, but prepares for the Gospel. His preaching in Luke exemplifies the declaration of Paul, "By the law is the knowledge of sin." After Jesus, in the hour of his baptism, is revealed to John as the promised Messiah, the character of John's preaching changes. He becomes an evangelist; the staple of his preaching is, "Behold the Lamb of God, which taketh away the sin of the world." In Luke he is a preacher of the O. T.; in John a preacher of the N. T. (5.) The effect on the people was notable and marked, but apparently not permanent. His preaching was attended by crowds (Matt. 3:5); he was held in high honor by the people, but was rejected by the priesthood and the elders of the people (Matt. 21:25); and out of his ministry grew no permanent social or political reform. Its more enduring effect consisted in the fact that from his disciples probably a majority of Christ's apostles were chosen. Their first spiritual impulse came from John. The work which he began Christ completed. (6.) An instructive lesson is afforded by a comparison of the character and career of Elijah and John the Baptist, who in character, preaching, practices, and even external habits, so resembled each other that John's coming was foretold as the coming of Elijah (Mal. 4:5, 6; Matt. 17:10-13).

Ch. 3:19-38. THE IMPRISONMENT OF JOHN. THE BAPTISM OF JESUS. HIS GENEALOGY.

These subjects are treated in the other Evangelists, where I have considered them at length. See references below.

19, 20. See Matt. 14:1-12. Prel. note. Mark 6:14-18, notes.

LUKE.

33 Which was *the son* of Aminadab, which was *the son* of Aram, which was *the son* of Esrom, which was *the son* of Phares, which was *the son* of Juda,
34 Which was *the son* of Jacob, which was *the son* of Isaac, which was *the son* of Abraham,ᵠ which was *the son* of Thara, which was *the son* of Nachor,
35 Which was *the son* of Saruch, which was *the son* of Ragau, which was *the son* of Phalec, which was *the son* of Heber, which was *the son* of Sala,
36 Which was *the son* of Cainan, which was *the son* of Arphaxad,ʳ which was *the son* of Sem, which was *the son* of Noe, which was *the son* of Lamech,ˢ
37 Which was *the son* of Mathusala, which was *the son* of Enoch, which was *the son* of Jared, which was *the son* of Maleleel, which was *the son* of Cainan,
38 Which was *the son* of Enos, which was *the son* of Seth, which was *the son* of Adam, which was *the son* of God.ᵗ

CHAPTER IV.

AND ᵘ Jesus, being full of the Holy Ghost, returned from Jordan, and was led by the Spirit into the wilderness,
2 Being forty days tempted of the devil. And ᵛ in those days he did eat nothing: and when they were ended, he afterward hungered.
3 And the devil said unto him, If thou be the Son of God, command this stone that it be made bread.
4 And Jesus answered him, saying, It ʷ is written,

That man shall not live by bread alone, but by every word of God.
5 And the devil, taking him up into an high mountain, shewed unto him all the kingdoms of the world in a moment of time.
6 And the devil said unto him, All this power will I give thee, and the glory of them: for ˣ that is delivered unto me; and to whomsoever I will I give it.
7 If thou, therefore, wilt worship me, all shall be thine.
8 And Jesus answered and said unto him, Get thee behind me, Satan: for ʸ it is written, Thou shalt worship the Lord thy God, and him only shalt thou serve.
9 And he brought him to Jerusalem, and set him on a pinnacle of the temple, and said unto him, If thou be the Son of God, cast thyself down from hence:
10 For it is written, He ᶻ shall give his angels charge over thee, to keep thee;
11 And in *their* hands they shall bear thee up, lest at any time thou dash thy foot against a stone.
12 And Jesus, answering, said unto him, It is said, Thou ᵃ shalt not tempt the Lord thy God.
13 And when the devil had ended all the ᵇ temptation, he departed from him for a season.
14 And Jesus ᶜ returned in the power of the Spirit into Galilee: and there went out a fame of him through all the region round about.
15 And he taught in their synagogues, being glorified of all.
16 And he came to Nazareth,ᵈ where he had been

---

q Gen. 11 : 24-26....r Gen. 11 : 12....s Gen. 5 : 25....t Gen. 1 : 26; 2 : 7; Isa. 64 : 8; 1 Cor. 15 : 45, 47.... u verse 14; Matt. 4 : 1, etc.; Mark 1 : 12, etc....v Exod. 34 : 28; 1 Kings 19 : 8... w Deut. 8 : 3....x John 12 : 31; 14 : 30; Ephes. 2 : 2; Rev. 13 : 2, 7....y Deut. 6 : 13; 10 : 20....z Ps. 91 : 11... a Deut. 6 : 16....b Heb. 2 : 17, 18; 4 : 15....c John 4 : 43; A ;o : 37....d Matt. 2 : 23.

21, 22. See Matt. 3 : 13-17, notes.

23-38. This genealogical register differs widely from that given by Matthew (Matt. 1 : 1-17). On the differences and the most probable reconciliation, see notes there. Godet and Oosterzee, following Wiessler, regard Luke's genealogy as that of Mary, and render verse 23 thus: *Being, as was supposed, the son of Joseph* (in reality) *the son of Heli*. They thus supposed Heli to have been Mary's father, and put in the place of Mary, because the Jewish sentiment did not allow the mention of the mother in the genealogical register. This view is controverted by Alford, Meyer, and Lord Hervey, and is, I think, less satisfactory on the whole than the explanation suggested in the notes on Matthew, that the one register gives the regal, the other the natural descent—though both hypotheses are attended with difficulties.

Ch. 4 : 1-13. TEMPTATION OF JESUS CHRIST. —Matt. 4 : 1-11; Mark 1 : 12, 13. See notes on Matthew. *He did eat nothing*, implies the severity of the fast, and is peculiar to Luke. The order of the temptations here differs from that in Matthew, which there is little reason to doubt is the correct one.

Ch. 4 : 14-32. CHRIST'S PREACHING AND REJECTION AT NAZARETH. THE POWER OF CHRIST THE POWER OF THE SPIRIT.—CHRIST'S PRACTICE OF SABBATH OBSERVANCE.—THE OFFICE AND WORK OF CHRIST EPITOMIZED. — THE UNIVERSALITY OF CHRISTIANITY. — WORDS OF GRACE HATEFUL TO THE GRACELESS.

Alford and Olshausen regard the incident here identical with that recorded in Matt. 13 : 53-58; in this they differ from most harmonists; and though the chronology is difficult it seems to me that the reasons for supposing that Christ was twice rejected by the Nazarenes, outweigh those for identifying this rejection with that recorded by Matthew. There is nothing incredible in the supposition that Christ, once rejected, returned a second time to bless his home; that the first rejection should have been followed by a second, less vehement, because tempered by a natural pride in the increasing fame of their fellow-townsman; and that he marveled at their persistence in unbelief (Mark 6 : 6). On the other hand, variations in the two accounts are so considerable as to suggest two analogous incidents. In Luke, Jesus appears to be alone; in Mark, (Mark 6 : 1) his disciples accompany him; in Luke, he is attacked by a mob, and barely escapes threatened death; in Mark (Mark 6 : 5), he remains and heals some sick; in Luke, the incident is apparently introduced, partly to explain his change of residence from Nazareth to Capernaum, stated by Matthew, without explanation, in ch. 4 : 13; in Mark, he leaves Nazareth only to teach in the villages round about (Mark 6 : 6).

14, 15. For the events between the temptation and this Galilean ministry, see Matt. 4 : 12, note. — **In the power of the Spirit.** The power of Christ is represented in the N. T. as derived from the indwelling of the Father or the Spirit (John 14 : 9, 10; 17 : 2-22); no clear distinction between the persons of the Godhead being maintained by the N. T. writers.—**There went out**

brought up: and, as his custom was, he* went into the synagogue on the sabbath day, and stood up for to read.

17 And there was delivered unto him the book of the prophet Esaias. And when he had opened the book, he found the place where it was written,

18 The ͑ Spirit of the Lord is upon me, because he hath anointed me to preach the gospel to the poor ; he hath sent me to heal the brokenhearted,ᵉ to preach deliverance to the captives, and recovering ʰ of sight to the blind, to set at liberty them that are bruised,ⁱ

19 To preach the acceptable ʲ year of the Lord.

20 And he closed the book, and he gave it again to the minister, and sat down. And the eyes of all them that were in the synagogue were fastened on him.

21 And he began to say unto them, This day is this scripture fulfilled in your ears.

22 And all bare him witness, and wondered at the

e Matt. 13 : 54; John 18 : 20; Acts 13 : 14; 17 : 2....f Isa. 61 : 1....g 2 Chron. 34 : 27; Ps. 34 : 18; 51 : 17; 147 : 3; Isa. 57 : 15....
h Ps. 146 : 8; Isa. 29 : 18....i Isa. 42 : 3; Matt. 12 : 20....j Isa. 61 : 2; 63 : 4.

a fame of him ; the extent of it is indicated in Matt. 4 : 25 ; the cause of it in John 2 : 23.— **And he taught in their synagogues.** The subject-matter of his preaching was a continuation of John the Baptist's message: "Repent, for the kingdom of heaven is at hand" (Matt. 4 : 17). On the synagogues, their government, and order of service, see Matt. 4 : 23, note.—**Being honored by all.** At this time his ministry was simply that of a herald announcing the glad tidings of a coming kingdom ; later came the declaration of the truths that it was a spiritual kingdom, wrought out through suffering and self-sacrifice, for the whole human race—truths unpalatable to Jewish prejudice and pride.

16, 17. As his custom was. Corrupt as was the Jewish church Christ continued to worship and to preach in the synagogues till he was driven out from them.—**On the Sabbath day.** Note that Christ was accustomed to observe the Sabbath as a day for religious worship and instruction as well as for rest.—**Stood up for to read.** That is, stood up in the congregation to indicate his desire to read and comment on some passage of O. T. Scripture. It was customary to allow any Jewish rabbi or recognized prophet to take the synagogue service as an occasion for the exposition of his views of Scripture. See Acts 13 : 15, note. The fame of Christ was a sufficient reason for the permission accorded to him by the rules of the synagogue.—**Book of the prophet Esaias.** *Isaiah.* The quotation is from ch. 61 : 1-3, and agrees substantially with the septuagint version. "The meaning of this prophetic citation may be better seen when we remember that it stands in the middle of the third great division of the book of Isaiah (chaps. 49–66), that, viz., which comprises the prophecies of the person, office, sufferings, triumph, and church of the Messiah ; and thus, by implication, announces the fulfillment of all that went before, in him who then addresses them."—(*Alford.*) The book was undoubtedly a roll of parchment, comprising Isaiah, either alone or with some of the other prophetical books ; of its form the reader may get a just idea from the accompanying illustration. The O. T. is kept in this form in the Jewish synagogues to the present day. No conclusion can be drawn as to the date of the incident here recorded, from the passage selected by

ANCIENT BOOK.

Christ, because, (1) though the O. T. was divided into reading lessons, one for each Sabbath, analogous to those of the Episcopalian ritual, it is by no means certain that the present rabbinical divisions existed in the time of Christ ; (2) apparently the selection of Scripture was made by Christ for a specific purpose, not by the ruler of the synagogue.

18, 19. The language of Isaiah, here quoted, is not by accommodation applied by Christ to himself, but was originally employed by Isaiah prophetically of the Messiah. This is evident, because the mission here defined was not Isaiah's, and was Christ's. It is to be interpreted both literally and spiritually. Christianity is a gospel to the poor, whom it has elevated by stimulating industry and by diffusing wealth ; it is comfort to the broken-hearted, whom it bids not to sorrow as others who are without hope ; it is deliverance to the captives, having abolished slavery throughout Christendom ; it is the recovery of sight to the blind, also more special objects of Christ's earthly ministry of mercy ; it set at liberty the bruised, *i. e.*, the oppressed ; the religion of the N. T. having been always the precursor of civil liberty and the basis of free institutions. But it is also glad tidings to the poor in spirit (Matt. 5 : 3), healing to the contrite in heart (Isaiah 66 : 2), deliverance to those who are captives unto sin (John 8 : 34–36), spiritual sight to the spiritually blind (John 9 : 39–41) ; and freedom from bondage to the yoke of conscience and the law, by that freedom wherewith Christ makes free (Gal. 5 : 1).—**To preach the acceptable year of the Lord.** Rather *acceptable era ; i. e.,* the whole period of gracious ministry begun with

JESUS IN THE SYNAGOGUE.

"*And there was delivered unto him the book of the prophet Esaias.*"

gracious[k] words which proceeded out of his mouth. And they said, Is[l] not this Joseph's son?

23 And he said unto them, Ye will surely say unto me this proverb, Physician, heal thyself: whatsoever we have heard done in Capernaum,[m] do also here in thy country.

24 And he said, Verily I say unto you, No[n] prophet is accepted in his own country.

25 But I tell you of a truth, many[o] widows were in Israel in the days of Elias, when the heaven was shut up[p] three years and six months, when great famine was throughout all the land;

26 But unto none of them was Elias sent, save unto Sarepta, *a city* of Sidon, unto a woman *that was* a widow.

27 And[q] many lepers were in Israel in the time of Eliseus the prophet; and none of them was cleansed saving Naaman the Syrian.

[k] ch. 2:47; Ps. 45:2; Isa. 50:4; Matt. 13:54; Mark 6:2....l John 6:42....m Matt. 4:13; 11:23, etc....n Matt. 14:57; John 4:44 o 1 Kings 17:9....p James 5:17....q 2 Kings 5:14.

the advent of Christ, but not completed till his second coming and final triumph.

20-22. Gave it again to the minister. To the officer of the synagogue, who had charge of the books as well as of the building. His duties were partly of a sacred, partly of a secular character; his office corresponded with that of the modern sexton; but he was also often the teacher of the synagogical school.—**And sat down.** The Jewish rabbis taught sitting.— **And the eyes * * * were fastened on him.** An indication of that peculiar power which secures to the true orator the attention of his audience before he begins to speak. Comp. Acts 6:15.—**And he began to say to them.** The report of this sermon is not verbatim. The first part of his discourse was given to an exposition of his own ministry, as a fulfillment of this prophecy, and probably occupied some time. The narrator passes over this introduction briefly; his object is to give only so much fully as is necessary to explain the expulsion of Christ from his home in Nazareth.—**And all bare him witness.** Bore unconscious witness to the power of Christ, by their attention, and by their whispered exclamations of wonder. So later, even the soldiers sent to arrest Christ, bore witness to his power (John 7:46).—**And wondered at the words of grace.** The reference is to his grace in manner, not to his doctrine; for the universality of divine grace which he preached angered them. What they were astounded at was that the "carpenter's son" could speak with such ease and grace, having never received the rabbinical education. So the Jews were astounded at his teaching in Jerusalem, who had never learned in their preparatory schools (John 7:15).

23, 24. The meaning appears to be this. The people had heard the fame of Christ's works in Capernaum, as there they had heard of the fame of his works in Jerusalem (John 4:45). They were skeptical, because to them he was only a peasant's son; they knew him to be of obscure parentage; his father was dead, and had, perhaps, left his mother in poverty; this suspicious skepticism was aggravated by their jealousy of Capernaum. He read their thoughts and interpreted them. They would have had him first improve his own condition, and not claim to be the Prince of Israel while living on the fare and wearing the attire of the common class of laborers; and they would have had him confer fame on his own village, not go away to confer it upon other towns by working miracles, where he was little known. He answered the proverb they would have quoted to him by another, "No prophet is accepted in his own country." He then proceeded to illustrate the truth, that grace follows *faith*, not nationality, and is denied to the unbelieving Jew and granted to the believing Gentile, by two striking instances in O. T. history.

25-27. This is the first intimation of the extension of the Gospel to the heathen. Observe how skillfully Christ presents this truth, so unpalatable to the Jewish people. He does so by implication, not by assertion, and by a simple recitation of their own O. T. history, leaving them to draw their own deductions. As Elijah gave food by a miracle to the heathen widow of Sarepta, and Elisha to the heathen captain of Syria, so Christ will break to the Gentile the bread of life, which the Jew rejects, and heal the sinner who comes to him from outcast nations. And it is still true that his grace is often rejected by those who seem the nearest to it, and is accepted by those who seem the most remote.— **Three years and six months.** So in Jas. 5:17. 1 Kings 17:1, and 1 Kings 18:1, have been thought to imply that the drought lasted less than three years; but this is not a necessary implication. In the former passage Elijah prophesies to Ahab the coming drought, and in the latter, "in the third year," is sent to foretell the rain. But this phrase, "third year," may mean either the third from the prophecy, or the third of the drought; and if the former there would be no reason to believe that the drought had lasted only three years, for the expression of Elijah in giving the prophecy of the drought, is consistent with the idea that it had already lasted some time before the prophet warned Ahab of its continuance. It is evident from Christ's language here, and that of James, that the Jews generally understood from the account that the drought lasted over three years.—**Sarepta.** Same as Zarephath (1 Kings 17:9, 10), the modern Surafend. It lay between Tyre and Sidon, on the Phoenician coast. The modern village is about a mile from the ruins of the ancient one. For good description

28 And all they in the synagogue, when they heard these things, were filled with wrath,
29 And rose up, and thrust him out of the city, and led him unto the brow of the hill whereon their city was built, that they might cast him down ʳ headlong.
30 But he, passing ˢ through the midst of them, went his way;
31 And came down to Capernaum, a city of Galilee, and taught them on the sabbath days.
32 And they were astonished at his doctrine: for his word was with ᵗ power.
33 And ᵘ in the synagogue there was a man, which had a spirit of an unclean devil, and cried out with a loud voice,
34 Saying, Let *us* alone; what ᵛ have we to do with thee, *thou* Jesus of Nazareth? art thou come to destroy us? I ʷ know thee who thou art; the ˣ Holy One of God.
35 And Jesus rebuked him, saying, Hold thy peace, and come out of him. And when the devil had thrown him in the midst, he came out of him, and hurt him not.
36 And they were all amazed, and spake among themselves, saying, What a word *is* this! for with authority and power he commandeth the unclean spirits, and ʸ they come out.
37 And the fame of him went out into every place of the country round about.
38 And he arose out of the synagogue, and entered

r Ps. 37 : 14, 32, 33. ...s John 8 : 59; 10 ; 39....t Jer. 23 ; 28; Matt. 7 : 28, 29; Titus 2 : 15; Heb. 4 : 12....u Mark 1 ; 23....v James 2 : 19....w verse 41....x ch. 1 : 35; Ps. 16 : 10; Dan. 9 : 24; Acts 3 : 14....y 1 Pet. 3 : 22.

---

see Thomson's *Land and the Book*, Vol. I., 234–236.

28–30. The rage of the people was the result of their bigotry. To them it was intolerable that Israel should be rejected and the heathen ac-

VICINITY OF NAZARETH.

cepted. Analogous was the Jews' treatment of Paul when he preached a similar doctrine (Acts 22 : 22), and of Christ, when just previous to his death in Jerusalem, he declared that the stone which the builders refused would grind the nation to powder. It was this teaching (Matt. 21 : 28 to ch. 22 : 13) which turned the enthusiasm into a feeling of passionate hate, and the cry of "Hosanna" into one of "crucify him." It illustrates the declaration of John 1 : 11. The accompanying illustration shows the general character of the environs of Nazareth, and sufficiently explains the possibility of thrusting one off a precipice in its immediate vicinity. The traditional site is called the Mount of Precipitation, and is two miles away. That an infuriated mob should have undertaken to conduct the victim two miles before putting him to death is so highly improbable that the tradition would be unworthy of credence, even if it were better authenticated. It is, however, of no great antiquity. I do not believe that the escape of Christ, here or in John 8 : 59, can be regarded as properly miraculous; for there are no other instances in which Christ employed his divine power for his own preservation; the suggestion to do this was one of the temptations which he met and overcame at the beginning of his career (Matt. 4 : 2, 4 1); to have yielded to it now, would have marred the perfection of his incarnation, by which he was made under the law (Gal. 4 : 4), and in the condition of man (Phil. 2 : 7, 8). I believe with Godet, that "he passed through the group of these infuriated people with a majesty which overawed them."

31, 32. It is probable, though Alford thinks otherwise, that this mob was the occasion of Christ's change of residence from Nazareth to

MOB AT NAZARETH.
"They rose up and thrust him out of the city."

into Simon's house. And ª Simon's wife's mother was taken with a great fever; and they besought him for her.

39 And he stood over her, and rebuked the fever; and it left her: and immediately she arose, and ministered unto them.

40 Now when the sun was setting, all they that had any sick with divers diseases brought them unto him; and he laid his hands on every one of them, and healed them.

41 And devils also came out of many, crying out, and saying, Thou art Christ the Son of God. And he, rebuking *them*, suffered them not to speak: for they knew that he was Christ.

42 And when it was day, he departed, and went into a desert place: and the people sought him, and came

unto him, and stayed him, that he should not depart from them.

43 And he said unto them, I must preach the kingdom of God to other cities also; for therefore ª am I sent.

44 And he preached in the synagogues of Galilee.

CHAPTER V.

AND ᵇ it came to pass, that, as the people pressed upon him to hear the word of God, he stood by the lake of Gennesaret,

2 And saw two ships standing by the lake : but the fishermen were gone out of them, and were washing *their* nets.

---

a Matt. 8 : 14, etc.; Mark 1 : 29, etc.... a Mark 1 : 38....b Matt. 4 : 18, etc.; Mark 1 : 16, etc.

Capernaum, referred to in John 2 : 12. *Doctrine is teaching*; not *what* he taught, but the manner and spirit of the teaching. The *power* is that referred to in Matt. 7 : 29 (see note there), and illustrated in the Sermon on the Mount; the power of a direct appeal to the hearts and consciences of his hearers, of his own spiritual earnestness and consecration, and of the Spirit of God, speaking in and through him.

33-37. HEALING OF THE DEMONIAC.—Peculiar to Mark 1 : 21-27, and Luke. See notes on Mark. The phrase "hurt him not," is peculiar to Luke, whose description of diseases and their effects is characteristic of the "beloved physician" (Col. 4 : 14).

38, 39. THE HEALING OF PETER'S MOTHER-IN-LAW.—Matt. 8 : 14-17; Mark 1 : 29-34. See notes on Matthew. Luke gives the peculiar description of the fever as a *"great fever."* Fevers, in the medical language of that day, were simply divided into little and great fevers. This was one of a serious character; probably malarious. *Rebuked the fever* is also peculiar to Luke—a poetical expression, signifying that he expelled it.

40-44. FIRST CIRCUIT IN GALILEE. — Mark 1 : 35-39; Matt. 4 : 23-25. See notes on both Gospels. From Mark, it appears that Christ arose before day, and that the people who followed were led by Simon Peter. Matt. 8 : 17, which belongs chronologically with this account, gives a hint of the cause of Christ's sleeplessness, viz., his intense sympathies.

Ch. 5 : 1-11. THE CALL OF FOUR DISCIPLES. CHRIST A POPULAR PREACHER.—THE ATTRACTION AND POWER OF THE WORD OF GOD.—THE OBEDIENCE OF FAITH ILLUSTRATED.—THE PRAYER OF FEAR: DEPART FROM ME.—CHRIST'S CALL A CALL TO WORK.

Alford regards this call of the four disciples as distinct from and later than the similar incident recorded in Matt. 4 : 18-22, and Mark 1 : 16-20. In this opinion he stands almost alone. They are generally regarded as different accounts of the same event. There is small reason for regarding them as different. To suppose that Christ called these four disciples; that they forsook their fishing to follow him; left him and went back to their fishing, and were a second time called, now, with the added emphasis of a miracle, neither accords with Christ's character nor with that of the four apostles. There is no inconsistency in the three accounts. Matthew and Mark omit the preaching from the boat and the miracle, but narrate the call with greater detail than Luke. Compare with the notes here those on Matthew, and see below Alford's arguments incidentally answered.

1, 2. As the people pressed upon him to hear the word of God. Christ was a popular preacher. It was a local prejudice, stirred up by an inimical priesthood, which crucified him. The reason of his popularity is here indicated. The people heard from him the *word of God*. For the same reason he spake with authority (Matt 7 : 29). The word of God has always had power to attract as well as to convince and to convert. It was the word of God which men pressed to hear in the days of Savanarola, Huss, Luther, Wycliffe, Wesley, and which still, in our own time, they press to hear from Bible preachers, who always possess a power not their own. Contrast Christ's teaching in Nazareth (ch. 4 : 16-27) and in Capernaum. Observe his example to be unsuccessful preacher. Rejected by one city he carries his message to another. Seeming failure became to patient perseverance the precursor of abundant success.—**Lake of Gennesaret.** Otherwise called Sea of Galilee. For description see note on Matthew.—**Two ships.** Fisherman's boats. They carried sail, but were not too large to be propelled by oars (Mark 4 : 36, note).—**The fishermen. Washing their nets.** To get the full significance of this incident the reader must have some familiarity with Oriental fishing. For detailed description see Thompson's *Land and the Book*, Vol. II. p. 79. It is rarely done with the hook; generally with nets. These are of various kinds. There is the hand-net, in shape like the top of a tent, with a long cord fastened

3 And he entered into one of the ships, which was Simon's, and prayed him that he would thrust out a little from the land. And he sat down, and taught the people out of the ship.
4 Now when he had left speaking, he said unto Simon, Launch ᶜ out into the deep, and let down your nets for a draught.
5 And Simon, answering, said unto him, Master, we have toiled all the night, and have taken nothing : ᵈ nevertheless, at thy word I will let down the net.

6 And ᵉ when they had this done, they inclosed a great multitude of fishes : and their net brake.
7 And they beckoned unto *their* partners, which were in the other ship, that they should come and help ᶠ them. And they came, and filled both the ships, so that they began to sink.
8 When Simon Peter saw *it*, he fell down ᵍ at Jesus' knees, saying, Depart from me ; for I am a sinful man, O Lord.
9 For he was astonished, and all that were with him, at the draught of the fishes ʰ which they had taken :

c John 21 : 6....d Ps. 127 : 1, 2 ; Ezek. 37 : 11, 12....e Eccles. 11 : 6 ; Gal. 6 : 9....f Exod. 23 : 5 ; Prov. 19 : 24 ; Gal. 6 : 2...g Judges 13 : 22 ; 2 Sam. 6 : 9 ; 1 Kings 17 : 14 ; Isa. 6 : 5....h Ps. 8 : 6, 8.

ORIENTAL FISHERS.

to the apex ; this is tied to the fisherman's arm, and the net so folded that when it is thrown it expands to its utmost circumference ; around the bottom are beads of lead to make it sink suddenly to the bottom. The fisherman watches, sees the fish in the surf, throws the net, which encircles the victim, who is then drawn leisurely to the shore. For illustration see Matt. 4 : 18, 19, Vol. I., p. 81. There is the drag-net, worked by several fishermen together ; some row the boat, some cast out the rope, some on shore draw it in, some at the ends beat the water to frighten the fish from escaping. See Matt. 13 : 47-50, notes. There are bag nets and basket nets of various kinds, so constructed and worked as to enclose the fish in deep water. It was such a net which Dr. Thompson supposes was used here. The disciples were washing their nets to cleanse them from mud or stones, or matter accumulated from the bottom of the lake or along the shore.

3-5. It is evident that there was some previous acquaintance between Jesus and Simon, from which Alford draws the conclusion that the call of Simon, recorded in Matthew, had previously taken place. This does not follow. Peter had met Jesus some time previous at the baptism of John in the Jordan (John 1 : 40-42), and the acquaintance then founded was sufficient to account for Peter's loan of the boat and subsequent obedience to the directions of Christ. Observe that Christ preached everywhere ; that no ritualistic service, therefore, could have accompanied his service. We have no account of even a prayer or a psalm. Certainly instruction was the main element in these out-of-door services. Observe, too, the childlike trustfulness of Simon's obedience. He might not unnaturally have refused, on the point that Christ, who was a carpenter, knew nothing about fishing ; and there was no promise and no apparent expectation of a miracle.

6, 7. That a miracle is intended is unquestionable. How wrought, whether by a divine act drawing together at this time and place a shoal of fishes, or by a divine knowledge perceiving the shoal that was there, the narrator does not indicate. It is enough for us that Simon Peter, who was a fisherman, and was able to judge, accounted the event an evidence of supernatural power. It produced the desired effect on him and his co-laborers. Tristram (*Land of Israel*) says, referring to the fish of the Sea of Galilee, "The shoals were marvelous ; black masses, many hundred yards long, with their black fins projecting out of the water as thick as they could pack. No wonder any net should

CH. V.] LUKE. 37

10 And so was also James and John, the sons of Zebedee, which were partners with Simon. And Jesus said unto Simon, Fear not; from henceforth thou shalt catch men.
11 And when they had brought their ships to land, they forsook¹ all, and followed him.
12 And ʲ it came to pass, when he was in a certain city, behold, a man full of leprosy; who seeing Jesus, fell on his face, and besought him, saying, Lord, if thou wilt, thou canst make me clean.
13 And he put forth his hand, and touched him, saying, I will; be ᵏ thou clean. And immediately the leprosy departed from him.
14 And he charged him to tell no man: but go and shew thyself to the priest, and offer for thy cleansing, according as Moses commanded,ˡ for a testimony unto them.
15 But so much the more went there a fame abroad of him: and ᵐ great multitudes came together, to hear, and to be healed by him of their infirmities.
16 And ⁿ he withdrew himself into the wilderness, and prayed.
17 And it came to pass on a certain day, as he was teaching, that ᵒ there were Pharisees and doctors of the law sitting by, which were come out of every town of Galilee, and Judæa, and Jerusalem; and the power of the Lord was present to heal them.
18 And,ᵖ behold, men brought in a bed a man which was taken with a palsy: and they sought means to bring him in, and to lay him before him.

Matt. 4 : 20 ; 19 : 27 ; Phil. 3 : 7, 8....j Matt. 8 : 2, etc.; Mark 1 : 40, etc....k 2 Kings 5 : 10, 14....l Lev. 14 : 4, etc....m Matt. 4 : 25 ; Mark 3 : 7 ; John 6 : 2....n Matt. 14 : 23 ; Mark 6 : 46....o John 3 : 21....p Matt. 9 : 2, etc.; Mark 2 : 3, etc.

break which should enclose such a shoal." Peter refers to fishing all night. Night fishing is common in the East, both with the spear and the net.

8, 9. Compare Simon Peter's prayer with that of the Gadarenes in Matt. 8 : 34; the language is similar, the spirit is radically different. There they desired Christ's departure because of the injury to their property. Here, it is evident, from Simon Peter's subsequent course in leaving all to follow Christ, that he did not really desire his departure. The language was a strong expression of his own unworthiness to be in the presence of one whose divinity was even then perceived by Peter's quick intuition. Compare for an interpretation of Peter's expression, Exod. 20 : 19, 20; Judges 13 : 22; 1 Kings 17 : 18; Isa. 6 : 5; Dan. 10 : 17, " The deepest thing in man's heart under the law is this sense of God's holiness as something bringing death and destruction to the unholy creature. Below this is the utterly profane state in which there is no contradiction felt between the holy and the unholy, between God and the sinner. Above is the state of grace, in which all the contradiction is felt ; God is still a consuming fire ; yet not any more for the sinner, but only for the sin. It is still felt—felt far more strongly than ever, how profound a gulf separates between sinful man and a holy God; but felt no less that this gulf has been bridged over, that the two can meet, that in One who shares with both they have already met."—(Trench, Notes on Miracles.)

10, 11. Compare Matt. 4 : 19. Combining the two reports, it will appear that Christ said to Peter, "Fear not, for thou shalt catch men;" and afterward bid the four "follow me, and I will make you fishers of men."

In studying this incident observe, (1) That Christ employs familiar figures to illustrate the truth, and draws each soul by that which is attractive to it:—the magicians by a star (Matt. 2 : 1, 2); the hungry people by a promise of bread of life (John, ch. 6); the Samaritan woman who came to draw water, by a promise of the water of life (John 4 : 7-14); the fishermen, by the promise to make them fishers of men. (2.) His invitation. He calls us to the life of work, to follow him that so we may lead others to follow us in our following of him (1 Cor. 11 : 1). (3.) That the promised reward is success in that work. This was the hope of which the Psalmist spoke, "He shall doubtless come again with rejoicing, bringing his sheaves with him " (Ps. 126 : 6); and this was the joy which Christ had set before him, and which enabled him to endure the cross, despising the shame, since he prophetically saw of the harvest of his life and was satisfied (Isa. 53 : 11, 12 ; comp. Isa. 55 : 11). (4.) That the promise, as interpreted by this event, is a catching of many souls. It is not individual fishing, to be interpreted by the modern angling with hook or fly, but net-fishing, in which great numbers are brought into the net. It is a promise of revival scenes. Its first fulfillment was the day of Pentecost, when Peter's net drew three thousand souls into the kingdom of Christ. (5.) Peter and his co-laborers are called from a prosperous business; from a business which Christ has just made, especially and miraculously, prosperous; and the prosperity is the reason why they leave it at his call. Compare their readiness with that hesitancy and declination of those to whom no harder test was proposed (ch. 9 : 57-62; 18 : 18-23).

12-16. THE HEALING OF THE LEPER.—Comp. Mark 1 : 40-45; Matt. 8 : 2-4. I have treated it fully in Matthew; see notes there. The phrase here, "Full of leprosy," is peculiar to Luke, and is an indication of the incurable character of the disease. It had already affected the whole body.

17-26. THE HEALING OF THE PARALYTIC.—Matt. 9 : 2-8 ; Mark 2 : 1-12, notes. This miracle was wrought at Capernaum (Mark 2 : 1) at the time indicated here and in Mark. Ver. 17 here is peculiar to Luke.—**From every town of Galilee**, etc. Not to be taken literally. The people were simply from all quarters. The complaints against Christ probably came from the Judeans, who were jealous of the influence of one whom

19 And when they could not find by what way they might bring him in because of the multitude, they went upon the housetop, and let him down through the tiling, with *his* couch, into the midst before Jesus.
20 And when he saw their faith, he said unto him, Man, thy sins are forgiven thee.
21 And the scribes and the Pharisees began to reason, saying, Who is this which speaketh blasphemies? Who can forgive ⁹ sins, but God alone?
22 But when Jesus perceived their thoughts, he, answering, said unto him, What reason ye in your hearts?
23 Whether is easier, to say, Thy sins be forgiven thee ; or to say, Rise up and walk?
24 But that ye may know that the Son of man hath power upon earth to forgive sins, (he said unto the sick of the palsy,) I say unto thee, Arise, and ʳ take up thy couch, and go into thine house.
25 And immediately he rose up before them, and took up that whereon he lay, and departed to his own house, glorifying God.
26 And they were all amazed, and ⁸ they glorified God, and ᵗ were filled with fear, saying, We have seen strange things to-day.
27 And ᵘ after these things he went forth, and saw a publican, named Levi, sitting at the receipt of custom : and he said unto him, Follow me.
28 And he left all, rose up, and followed him.
29 And Levi made him a great feast in his own house : and ᵛ there was a great company of publicans and of others that sat down with them.
30 But their scribes and Pharisees murmured against his disciples, saying, Why do ye eat and drink with publicans and sinners?

31 And Jesus, answering, said unto them, They that are whole need not a physician ; " but they that are sick.
32 I came not to call the righteous, but sinners ˣ to repentance.
33 And they said unto him, Why do the disciples of John fast often, and make prayers, and likewise *the disciples* of the Pharisees ; but ʸ thine eat and drink?
34 And he said unto them, Can ye make the children of the bridechamber fast, while the bridegroom is with them?
35 But the days will come when the bridegroom shall be taken away from them, and then shall they fast ᶻ in those days.
36 And ᵃ he spake also a parable unto them : No man putteth a piece of new garment upon an old ; if otherwise, then both the new maketh a rent, and the piece that was *taken* out of the new agreeth not ᵇ with the old.
37 And no man putteth new wine into old bottles ; else the new wine will burst the bottles and be spilled, and the bottles shall perish.
38 But new wine must be put into new bottles ; and both are preserved.
39 No man also having drunk old *wine* straightway desireth new : for he saith, The old ᶜ is better.

CHAPTER VI.

AND ᵈ it came to pass on the second sabbath after the first, that he went through the corn fields ; and his disciples plucked the ears of corn, and did eat, rubbing *them* in *their* hands.

q Ps. 32 : 5 ; 103 : 3 ; 130 : 4 ; Isa. 1 : 18 ; 43 : 25.... r John 5 : 8, 12.... s Acts 4 : 21 ; Gal. 1 : 24.... t verse 8.... u Matt. 9 : 9, etc. ; Mark 2 : 13....
v ch. 15 : 1, etc.... w Jer. 8 : 22... x ch. 15 : 7, 10 ; 1 Cor. 6 : 9-11 ; 1 Tim. 1 : 15 ; 2 Pet. 3 : 9.... y ch. 7 : 34, 35... z Isa. 22 : 12.... a Matt.
9 : 16, 17 ; Mark 2 : 21, 22.... b Lev. 19 : 19 ; Deut. 22 : 11 ; 2 Cor. 6 : 16.... c Jer. 6 : 16.... d Matt. 12 : 1, etc. ; Mark 2 : 23, etc.

---

they regarded as a Galilean rabbi (John 7 : 52).— **The power of the Lord was present to heal them.** Not specifically the Pharisees and doctors, but whoever sought healing. The meaning is that at this time the power of God was manifest in and exercised by Jesus Christ in acts of healing. That his teaching was not always accompanied by acts of healing is certain (Matt. 13 : 58 ; Mark 6 : 5). Except for Luke we should not know that any other cures than that of the paralytic were wrought at this time. Ver. 19 also gives some particulars not given in Mark. For notes on the narrative, see Mark 2 : 1-12.

27-39. THE CALL OF LEVI (MATTHEW) AND CHRIST'S CONSEQUENT TEACHING. — Matt. 9 : 9-17 ; Mark 2 : 14-22. This call occurred prior to the Sermon on the Mount ; and I think the better opinion regards the call and support as contemporaneous events, though there is some doubt on that point. See notes on Matthew. Luke alone directly declares that the feast was given by Levi (Matthew), but this is fairly implied by Matthew and Mark. The expression in ver. 36 is slightly different from the analogous expression in Matthew and Mark. It should be rendered thus : " *If otherwise, then both the new he rends,*" i. e., by taking out the patch for the old, "*and the patch from the new agrees not with the old,*" and so rends that also. Comp. note on Matt. 9 : 16. The general lesson of the parable is against all attempt to patch old and effete systems with partial reformations ; here, because the attempt spoils them both. "The new loses its completeness ; the old its consistency."—(*Alford.*) The better reading of ver. 39 is, *No man also having drunk old wine desireth new ; for he saith the old is good,* omitting *straightway* and substituting *good* for better. This verse is peculiar to Luke. Its significance appears to be, The Jews, who have been accustomed to the old order of things, will not readily accept the new wine of the Gospel ; its lesson is one of patience to all Christian teachers, and to all reformers, who must expect that men habituated to one form of life, will not readily abandon it for a new and better way. "The old is good enough," is the common language of opposition to all reformers.

Ch. 6 : 1-11. THE LAW OF THE CHRISTIAN SABBATH ILLUSTRATED.

Matt. 12 : 1-14 ; Mark 2 : 23-28 ; 3 : 1-5. See notes on Matthew. For illustration, see frontispiece. I here note only some matters peculiar to Luke.

1-5. The second Sabbath after the first. (δευτεροπρώτω). There is great doubt and difference of opinion as to the meaning of the Greek word so rendered. It occurs nowhere else, and is thought by some critical scholars not to belong here, but to be a gloss which has crept into the account by a combination of two words added by different scribes in the margin. Tischendorf, after once rejecting, finally retains it ; Meyer re-

LUKE.

2 And certain of the Pharisees said unto them, Why do ye that which ᵉ is not lawful to do on the sabbath days?
3 And Jesus answering them said, Have ye not read so much as this, what ᶠ David did, when himself was an hungered, and they which were with him;
4 How he went into the house of God, and did take and eat the showbread, and gave also to them that were with him; which it is not lawful ᵍ to eat, but for the priests alone?
5 And he said unto them, That the Son of man is Lord also of the sabbath.
6 And ʰ it came to pass also on another sabbath, that he entered into the synagogue, and taught; and there was a man whose right hand was withered.

7 And the scribes and Pharisees watched him, whether he would heal on the sabbath day,ⁱ that they might find an accusation against him.
8 But he knew their thoughts,ʲ and said to the man which had the withered hand, Rise up, and stand forth in the midst. And he arose, and stood forth.
9 Then said Jesus unto them, I will ask you one thing; Is it lawful on the sabbath days ᵏ to do good, or to do evil? to save life, or to destroy *it?*
10 And looking ˡ round about upon them all, he said unto the man, Stretch forth thy hand. And he did so: and his hand was restored whole as the other.
11 And they were filled with madness; and communed ᵐ one with another what they might do to Jesus.

e Exod. 20 : 10; Isa. 58 : 13....f 1 Sam. 21 : 6.. .g Lev. 24 : 9....h chaps. 13 : 14; 14 : 3; Matt. 12 : 10, etc.; Mark 3 : 1, etc....i John 9 : 16....
j Job 42 : 2....k ch. 14 : 3; Exod. 20 : 10....l Mark 3 : 5....m Ps. 2 : 1, 2.

jects it; Alford doubts and brackets it. It seems to me more probable that it has been rejected because of the difficulty it presented, than that it has been invented and inserted. Among the various explanations, which the curious student will find at some length in Alford but still more clearly expressed in Godet, two are suggested, either of which is reasonable, but neither of which is certain. The second day of the Passover week was a Sabbath day (Lev. 23 : 6, 7), and from that day seven Sabbaths were reckoned to the Pentecost, which was the next feast, seven weeks later. It is supposed by Lightfoot, Scaliger, De Wette, Brown, and others, that here is meant the first of these seven Sabbaths, *i. e.*, the first Sabbath after the second day of the Passover. This rendering places the incident immediately after the incident and address recorded in John, ch. 5; and the feast referred to there (ver. 1) is assumed to be the Passover. The other explanation, approved by Godet and adopted by Oosterzee, is this: The Israelites recognized two years; a civil year commencing in autumn, the month of Tisru (Sept.), and the church year commencing in the spring, the month of Nisan (March). Thus there were two first Sabbaths, a first first, and a second first. The reference will then be to the second first Sabbath, *i. e.*, to the first Sabbath in the ecclesiastical year. And this explanation, like the other, brings the incident in the first Passover week. The barley harvest was in April, the wheat harvest in May. Thus the incident undoubtedly occurred about the time indicated by these two interpretations. The question is of importance only as it serves to fix a date in Christ's life, and the meaning is so doubtful that it cannot be relied upon for that purpose.—**Ears of corn.** Of grain; probably wheat or barley.— **Why do ye?** According to Matthew and Mark they address the question to the Lord, *Why do thy disciples do that which is not lawful?* It may have been addressed first to the disciples, and subsequently to the Lord.

6-11. The statement that this was *on another Sabbath*, is peculiar to Luke. It was probably on the Sabbath immediately succeeding. Matthew's report is fuller than Luke's. The question of our Lord, as there reported, if it be not lawful to save a sheep from a pit, is repeated in Luke's account

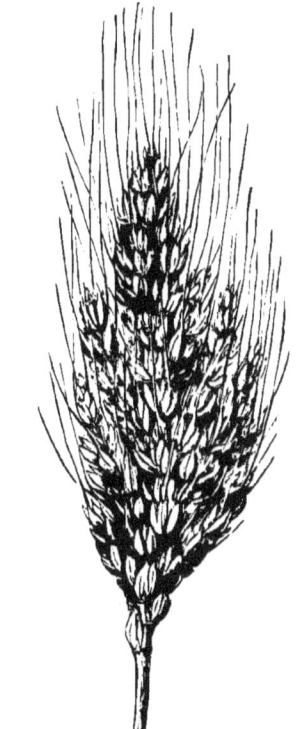

RED WHEAT OF PALESTINE.

of a similar Sabbath day healing in ch. 14 : 1-5. Hence, Alford concludes that Matthew has confounded and intermixed the two incidents. But what reason is there for believing that **Christ did** not use the same illustration on a second occasion? That he did sometimes repeat, not only the same substantial truths, but the same illustrations, and even the same forms of expression, is very certain. The synagogue where this occurred is described in Matthew as "their synagogue," *i. e.*, one in which the more rigorous of the Pharisees predominated.

12-49. Christ's Sermon on the Mount.—Of this sermon we have two reports: one in Matthew, chaps. 5, 6, 7, and one here in Luke. Several circumstances have led some critics to suppose that they are two sermons, either delivered at different periods in Christ's ministry or delivered twice on the same day; the first sermon, as reported in Matthew, being preached to the disciples; the second, as reported in Luke, being delivered immediately after, on Christ's descent from the mountain, to the multitude. The reasons for this opinion are as follows: (1.) The sermon in Matthew is expressly stated to have been delivered in the mountain (Matt. 5:1), in Luke in the plain (ver. 17). (2.) The sermon in Luke is immediately connected with the call and consecration of the twelve to an apostolic ministry. This is not the case in Matthew. (3.) The report in Matthew is much longer, yet that in Luke is not an abbreviation, for it contains some passages (vers. 24-26) not elsewhere reported in the N. T., and some others (vers. 39, 40), reported elsewhere,

MOUNT OF BEATITUDES.

but not in Matthew's account of the Sermon on the Mount, For reasons stated more fully in the notes on Matthew, I regard the two as reports of the same discourse. The only serious ground for a different opinion is the conflict in statement as to the place of delivery. And this is sufficiently explained by the topography of the Mount of Beatitudes, or Horns of Hattin. This mount or hill, for it is only sixty feet above the plain, is generally believed, partly from tradition but more from the peculiar location and character of the hill itself, to have been the place where this sermon was delivered. On the summit of this hill is a spot exactly answering to Luke's description here, which should be rendered, not *plain*, but *level place* (*vide infra*). It is capable of seating upwards of two thousand persons, and is easily accessible from the plain below. On either side of it rise the two horns, which give the hill its present name. The accompanying illustration will make this clear to the reader. Christ went up from the shore of the Sea of Galilee to spend the night in prayer with his disciples. The people, as on so many occasions, followed him up in the early morning. Descending to them from one of the horns, where he had retired for prayer, he chose from his avowed disciples the twelve to be his constant companions, and then preached to them and to all the people this memorable sermon, as an explanation of the principles of the

CH. VI.]   LUKE.   41

12 And ⁿ it came to pass in those days, that he went out into a mountain ᵒ to pray, and continued all night in prayer to God.
13 And when it was day, he called *unto him* his disciples: and of them he chose twelve,ᵖ whom also he named apostles;
14 Simon (whom ᑫ he also named Peter) and Andrew his brother, James and John, Philip and Bartholomew,
15 Matthew and Thomas, James the *son* of Alphæus, and Simon called Zelotes,
16 And Judas ʳ *the brother* of James, and Judas Iscariot, which also was the traitor.
17 And he came down with them, and stood in the plain, and the company of his disciples, and ˢ a great multitude of people out of all Judæa and Jerusalem, and from the sea coast of Tyre and Sidon, which came to hear him, and to be healed ᵗ of their diseases;
18 And they that were vexed with unclean spirits: and they were healed.
19 And the whole multitude sought to touch ᵘ him: for ᵛ there went virtue out of him, and healed *them* all.

20 And ʷ he lifted up his eyes on his disciples, and said, Blessed *be ye* ˣ poor: for yours is the kingdom of God.
21 Blessed *are ye* that hunger ʸ now: for ye shall be filled.ᶻ Blessed *are ye* that weep ᵃ now: for ye shall laugh.
22 Blessed are ye, when men shall hate ᵇ you, and when they shall separate ᶜ you *from their company*, and shall reproach *you*, and cast out your name as evil, for the Son of man's sake.
23 Rejoice ᵈ ye in that day, and leap for joy: for, behold, your reward *is* great in heaven: for in the like manner ᵉ did their fathers unto the prophets.
24 But woe unto you that are ᶠ rich! for ye have received ᵍ your consolation.
25 Woe unto you that are full! ʰ for ye shall hunger. Woe unto you that laugh ⁱ now! for ye shall mourn and weep.
26 Woe unto you when all men shall speak well ʲ of you! for so did their fathers to the false prophets.

n Matt. 14 : 23.....o Matt. 6 : 6.....p Matt. 10 : 1, etc.; Mark 3 : 13 ; 6 : 7.....q John 1 : 42.....r Jude 1.....s Matt. 4 : 25, etc.; Mark 3 : 7. etc....t Ps. 103 : 3 ; 107 : 17-20....u Numb. 21 : 8, 9 ; Matt. 14 : 36 ; John 3 : 14, 15.....v ch. 8 : 46 ; Mark 5 : 30.....w Matt. 5 : 2, etc.....x James 2 : 5....y Isa. 55 : 1....z Ps. 107 : 9....a Isa. 61 : 3 ; Rev. 21 : 4....b John 17 : 14.....c 1 Pet. 2 : 19, 20 ; 3 : 14 ; 4 : 14....d Acts 5 : 41 ; Col. 1 : 24 ; James 1 : 2.....e Acts 7 : 52 ; Heb. 11 : 32-39....f Hab. 2 : 9 ; James 5 : 1....g ch. 16 : 25....h Isa. 28 : 7 ; 65 : 13....i Prov. 11 : 13 ; Ephes. 5 : 4....j John 15 : 19 ; 1 John 4 : 5.

kingdom which he had come to establish. On the sermon and on all that is common to both reports, see notes on Matthew.

12-16. Of the twelve apostles there are four lists, viz., Matt. 10 : 2-4 ; Mark 3 : 16-19 ; Acts 1 : 13 ; and Luke 6 : 13-16. On their differences and their reconciliation, see Matt. 10 : 2, note ; on the apostles themselves and their characters see Vol. I, p. 147. Matthew gives the list, not in connection with their call and consecration, but with their subsequent commission to go out two by two to preach the Gospel. He does not indicate, however, that they were then first chosen. Nor is it necessary to suppose that Christ first exercised the choice at the time of the preaching of this sermon. We know that several of them had been heretofore called, and had attached themselves to his service. Perhaps this was true of all ; but now, for the first time, they were publicly designated and set apart to their work. Christ's example gives sanction to the custom of public ordination and to the appointment of men especially consecrated to the work of the ministry, abandoning all secular work for that purpose.

17-19. Stood in the plain. Rather, *A level place*. See above.—**They were healed.** We are not to understand that at the time of the delivery of the sermon Christ performed the miracles of healing ;here referred to. None are mentioned in Matthew as being performed at this time. The account here is parallel to the account of Christ's work in Matt. 4 : 23-25, and describes the general features of his ministry at this time. This idea is conveyed in the original by the peculiar form of the expression—the imperfect tense—which is not adequately expressed in the English. It might be rendered thus : *They also that were vexed with unclean spirits were coming ; they also were being healed ; and the whole multitude were seeking to touch him, for power was going out of him and he was healing all, i. e.,* all who came to him. That any were healed by touching Jesus without the deliberate and conscious forth-putting of power there is no evidence. In the only case narrated of such healing, it is evident, on a careful study of the narrative, that Christ deliberately healed ; the woman was not cured by the garment, but by the will of the Lord. See Mark 5 : 30-34, notes.

20-23. These beatitudes are interpreted by a fuller account of them given in Matt. 5 : 3-12. The poor are *poor in spirit, i. e.,* the humble and contrite ; the hungry, *those that hunger and thirst after righteousness*. If verses 20 and 21 stood alone, one might perhaps regard them as referring only to earthly poverty and hunger (as De Wette does), and Christ, as indicating that his disciples should be poor and hungry in this life, but should receive a compensation in wealth and abundance in the life to come ; but (1) this does not accord with Matthew's fuller report ; (2) nor with the general course of Christ's instruction ; (3) nor with the language of Luke in reporting Christ's instructions elsewhere (see ch. 12 : 21 ; 16 : 11), (4) nor with the context here (ver. 22), which speaks of suffering for the Son of man's sake ; (5) nor with the woes which follow, on which see notes. We must not however forget that the majority of Christ's hearers were poor, hungry, oppressed ; and that poverty, hunger, and suffering are blessings if we receive them aright and learn the lessons which they are meant to teach. The poor are blessed if they learn humility ; the hungry, if they obtain a higher aspiration after spiritual life ; the suffering, if they are drawn to seek refuge in God. The *kingdom of God* here is the same here as the *kingdom of Heaven* in Matthew. One Evangelist describes it by its king;

27 But I say unto you which hear, Love ᵏ your enemies, do good to them which hate you, 28 Bless them that curse you, and ˡ pray for them which despitefully use you. 29 And ᵐ unto him that smiteth thee on the *one* cheek offer also the other; and him ⁿ that taketh away thy cloke forbid not *to take thy* coat also. 30 Give ᵒ to every man that asketh of thee; and of him that taketh away thy goods ask *them* not again. 31 And ᵖ as ye would that men should do to you, do ye also to them likewise. 32 For if ye love them which love you, what thank have ye? for sinners also love those that love them. 33 And if ye do good to them which do good to you, what thank have ye? for sinners also do even the same. 34 And if ye lend *to them* of whom ye hope to receive, what thank have ye? for sinners also lend to sinners, to receive as much again. 35 But love ye your enemies,ᵠ and do good, and lend,ʳ hoping for nothing again; and your reward shall be great, and ˢ ye shall be the children of the Highest: for he is kind unto the unthankful, and *to* the evil. 36 Be ye therefore merciful, as your Father also is merciful. 37 Judge ᵗ not, and ye shall not be judged: condemn not, and ye shall not be condemned: forgive, and ye shall be forgiven. 38 Give, and it shall be given ᵘ unto you; good measure, pressed down, and shaken together, and running over, shall men give into your bosom.ᵛ For ʷ with the same measure that ye mete withal, it shall be measured to you again. 39 And he spake a parable unto them: Can ˣ the

---

k verse 35; Exod. 23:4, 5; Prov. 25:21; Matt. 5:44; Rom. 12:20....l ch. 23:34; Acts 7:60....m Matt. 5:39....n 1 Cor. 6:7..., o Deut. 15:7, 8, 10; Prov. 19:17; 21:26; Matt. 5:42, etc....p Matt. 7:12....q verse 27....r Ps. 37:26; 112:5....s Matt. 5:45...., t Matt. 7:1....u Prov. 19:17; Matt. 10:42....v Ps. 79:12....w Matt. 7:2; Mark 4:24; James 2:13....x Matt. 15:14.

---

the other by its capital. On the spiritual meaning and application of these beatitudes, see notes on Matthew.

24-26. These woes have their place in the complete sermon in Matthew, in ch. 5, between verses 12 and 13. Why they were omitted there, it is useless to conjecture. It is far more probable that a later tradition dropped them, because they were thought to be incongruous with the prevailing spirit of that discourse, than that it added them here, as Meyer has supposed. Tradition seeks to increase the blessings but to diminish the warnings of Scripture. Nor are these woes denounced against the rich and prosperous, as if the prosperity were itself a crime. The spirit is not that of the modern commune. Christ is not an agrarian. Joseph of Arimathea and Nicodemus are among his disciples. As in many other passages, if we would correctly understand the real meaning of Christ, we must give a careful study to the words themselves. The word *consolation* in ver. 24 (παράκλησις) is derived from a Greek verb, meaning, *To call to one's aid;* it is used in Luke 2:25 of the Messiah. A different form of the same word is used in John 14:16, 26; 15:26, etc., of the Holy Spirit; and throughout the N. T., of that spiritual life, which comes from calling to one's aid the Spirit of God (Acts 9:31; Rom. 15:4; 2 Cor. 1:3-5; Phil. 2:1). The woe here, too, is denounced, not merely against the rich, but against those who have made riches *their consolation, i. e.*, who have chosen it as their chief good, as their Messiah, Deliverer, Comforter, as the one thing needful. It is interpreted by Mark 10:24, and Luke 12:19, 20. Comp. 1 Tim. 6:9, 10, 17, where the warning is not against riches, but against the determination to be rich, which may be as injurious to him who fails as to him who succeeds. In ver. 25 the word *full* (ἐμπίπλημι) signifies a state of satiety, complete and entire satisfaction, wanting nothing more. To those who are filled to the full with the things of this present world, there will come a time of emptying; death will come to them as a thief (Matt. 24:43; Rev. 3:3), and then they will hunger; while those who have never been satisfied, ever hungry and thirsty after righteousness, as Paul (Phil. 3:12-14), will be filled. *They that laugh*, in verse 25, is literally, *The laughing ones* (οἱ γελῶντες), *i. e.*, those who give themselves up to a life of merriment and superficial pleasure; who will not perceive that life is serious; who are without the earnestness of purpose that makes merriment an occasional relief, not a constant aim. Parallel with this warning is that of Prov. 14:13, and Eccles. 7:6; and in no way inconsistent with it is the commendation of the merry *heart*, that doeth good like a medicine (Prov. 17:22; 15:13, 15). The fourth woe needs no interpretation. *All* men cannot and will not speak well of one who is faithful in following his own convictions of duty, and whose life is thus a rebuke to the recreant. Thus these four woes are four warnings to four different classes—those who make wealth their God; those who are satisfied with this present life, having no hungering for inward peace or future glory; those who live for present enjoyment, devoid of earnest purpose and serious thoughts; and those who sacrifice conscience to a popular adulation.

27-36. Nearly all these precepts have their parallels in Matthew's report of this sermon. The connection presented there is missed here, where the verses stand rather as separated aphorisms than as parts of one connected discourse. The variations are otherwise chiefly verbal, and not important. See notes on Matthew.

37, 38. Parallel to these verses is Matt. 7:1, 2; but the difference is such as to give color to Alford's hypothesis, that the saying as reported here, was perhaps uttered by our Lord on some other occasion; "for the connection is very strict in Matthew, and would hardly bear this expansion of what is not in that place the leading idea." Or, may it not be that Luke has amplified the idea, explaining the command,

blind lead the blind? shall they not both fall into the ditch?
40 The y disciple is not above his master: but every one that is perfect shall be as his master.
41 And why beholdest thou the mote that is in thy brother's eye, but perceivest not the beam that is in thine own eye?
42 Either how canst thou say to thy brother, Brother, let me pull out the mote that is in thine eye, when thou thyself beholdest not the beam that is in thine own eye? Thou hypocrite! cast ᶜ out first the beam out of thine own eye, and then shalt thou see clearly to pull out the mote that is in thy brother's eye.
43 For ᵃ a good tree bringeth not forth corrupt fruit; neither doth a corrupt tree bring forth good fruit.
44 For ᵇ every tree is known by his own fruit: for of thorns men do not gather figs, nor of a bramble bush gather they grapes.
45 A ᶜ good man out of the good treasure of his heart bringeth forth that which is good; and an evil man

y Matt. 10 : 24; John 13 : 16; 15 : 20 .... z Prov. 18 : 17; Rom. 2 : 1, 21, etc.... a Matt. 7 : 16, 17.... b Matt. 12 : 33.... c Matt. 12 : 35.

judge not, by the added one, *condemn not*. For (see Matt. 7 : 1, not s) the command, *judge not*, does not prohibit the formation of judgments respecting our fellow-men, but the exercise of the judicial function, in a *quasi* trial, convicting and condemning them as though we were their judges. The metaphorical language of ver. 38 is derived from the usages of the Jewish grain market of the East, as they may be seen at the present day in Jerusalem. An official, appointed by the government, measures all the grain that is bought or

MEASURING GRAIN.

sold; after he has filled the measure full to the edge, he pours on more, presses it down, shakes the measure, pours on again till no more can be heaped up, and then, by a sudden movement, with a dexterity which only long experience could give, he empties the contents of the measure into the receptacle of the waiting customer, and begins again. This receptacle is often the "bosom" of the purchaser. The long robe, skillfully gathered about the wearer, affords by its ample folds a capacious pocket, easily adjusted to the carriage of a considerable burden. A pocketful of grain carried in this way in the bosom is not an inconsiderable quantity. The accompanying cut, from an original drawing by Mr. Rawson, sketched in Jerusalem in 1874, serves to illustrate both phrases in the text. The word *men* is added by the translators; the original is shall *they* give into your bosom. Alford, following Meyer, supposes that angels are meant rather than men; angels being the ministers of the divine purpose. But a comparison of the language here with that of Matt. 7 : 2, and Mark 4 : 24, in both of which cases the same principle is enunciated, though with a different application, indicates that it is primarily of men that Christ is here speaking. As we treat them we must expect to be treated by them. See further, notes on Matt. 7 : 2.

39. On the meaning of this verse see Matt. 15 : 14, note, where the same saying is reported in a different connection. The censorious spirit of the Pharisees, begotten by their pride, makes them blind. See also John 9 : 40, 41. The connection forbids the supposition that the rest of this chapter is simply a casual collection of sayings of our Lord, thrown together by Luke; though several of them (see below) are found repeated at different times during his ministry. It is much more reasonable to suppose that Luke has given a different report of the same discourse, as that more fully, and I believe more accurately reported by Matthew, possibly interweaving some cognate sayings not uttered at this time. Alford gives the connection of the following verses well. "The parabolic saying, implying the unfitness of an uncharitable and unjustly condemning leader (the Lord was speaking *primarily to His Apostles*) to perform his office, leads to the assertion (ver. 40) that no Christian ought to assume in this respect an office of judging, which his *Master never assumed*; but rather will every well-instructed Christian strive to be humble, as his Master was. Then follows the reproof of vers. 41-43; and vers. 44, 45, and 46-49, show us, expanded in different images, what *the beam* in the eye is, to which our first efforts must be directed."—(*Alford.*)

40. Compare Matt. 10 : 24; John 13 : 16. The language here, *Every one that is perfect shall be as his Master*, is peculiar to Luke. The word ren-

out of the evil treasure of his heart bringeth forth that which is evil: for of the abundance of the heart his mouth speaketh.

46 And why call ye me,^d Lord, Lord, and do not the things which I say?

47 Whosoever cometh to me, and heareth my sayings, and doeth them, I will shew you to whom he is like:

48 He^e is like a man which built an house, and digged deep, and laid the foundation on a rock; and when the flood arose, the stream beat vehemently upon that house, and^f could not shake it; for it was founded upon a rock.^g

49 But he^h that heareth, and doeth not, is like a man that without a foundation built an house upon the earth: against which the stream did beat vehemently, and immediately it fell;ⁱ and the ruin of that house was great.

CHAPTER VII.

NOW^j when he had ended all his sayings in the audience of the people, he entered into Capernaum.

2 And a certain centurion's servant, who was dear^k unto him, was sick, and ready to die.

3 And when he heard of Jesus, he sent unto him the elders of the Jews, beseeching him that he would come and heal his servant.

4 And when they came to Jesus, they besought him instantly, saying, That he was worthy for whom he should do this:

5 For he loveth^l our nation, and he hath built us a synagogue.

6 Then Jesus went with them. And when he was now not far from the house, the centurion sent friends to him, saying unto him, Lord, trouble^m not thyself; for I am not worthy that thou shouldest enter under my roof:

7 Wherefore neither thought I myself worthy to come unto thee: but sayⁿ in a word, and my servant shall be healed.

8 For I also am a man set under authority, having under me soldiers: and I say unto one, Go, and he goeth; and to another, Come, and he cometh; and to my servant, Do this, and he doeth it.

9 When Jesus heard these things, he marvelled at him, and turned him about, and said unto the people that followed him, I say unto you, I have not found so great faith, no, not in Israel.

10 And they that were sent, returning to the house, found the servant whole that had been sick.

11 And it came to pass the day after, that he went

---

d ch. 13 : 25 ; Mal. 1 : 6 ; Matt. 7 : 21 ; 25 : 11 ; Gal. 6 : 7... e Matt. 7 : 25, 26....f 2 Pet. 1 : 10 ; Jude 24....g Ps. 46 : 1-3 ; 62 : 2....h James 1 : 24-26....i Prov. 28 : 18 ; Hosea 4 : 14....j Matt. 8 : 5, etc... k Job 31 : 15 ; Prov. 29 : 21....l 1 Kings 5 : 1 ; Gal. 5 : 6 ; 1 John 3 : 14 ; 5 : 1, 2....m ch. 8 : 49....n Ps. 107 : 20.

---

dered *perfect* (κατηρτισμένος) means primarily *mended* (see Matt. 4 : 21); *i. e.*, it is commonly used of that which has been injured and is repaired. This I believe to be the meaning here. The man that is restored by the divine grace to his true condition, shall become as the Master. Parallel to this declaration are 1 Cor. 15 : 49, and 1 John 3 : 2. It affords at once an ideal, toward which we are to strive, and a promise, by which we may be inspired.

41-45. See Matt. 7 : 3-5, 15-20 ; 12 : 33, 35, and notes there.

46-49. See Matt. 7 : 21, 24-27. The parable is carried out with greater dramatic fullness by Matthew's than by Luke's report; *digged deep*, literally, *dug and deepened*, is peculiar to Luke, a significant addition. We come to the Rock, Christ Jesus, as a life-foundation, not easily but by deep-digging, in study of the truth and in personal heart-searchings. See Prov. 2 : 4.

Ch. 7 : 1-10. HEALING OF THE CENTURION'S SERVANT.

Reported also by Matthew, ch. 8 : 5-13. The account of the miracle itself is somewhat fuller in Luke; the account of Christ's instruction to the people thereon is fuller in Matthew. See on the whole account, notes on Matthew. There is no just ground for believing that they are different events. The probable time of occurrence is that indicated here, viz., on Christ's descent from the mount, after the ordination of the twelve and the sermon thereon.

1, 2. When he had ended all his sayings in the hearing of the people. The very form of this expression indicates that Luke's report of those sayings was not a complete one. It thus confirms the opinion that Luke's and Matthew's accounts are simply different reports of the same sermon.—**Ready to die.** A more definite statement of the immediate danger than is given by Matthew. The disease was palsy, and the sufferer was "grievously tormented."

3-5. Matthew says the centurion "came beseeching him;" he says nothing of any delegation. There is no real inconsistency; what is done by another is often said to be done by the person who directs it. The *elders* are not the elders of the synagogue (ch. 13 : 14 ; Acts 13 : 15, etc.), for which a different Greek word is used (ἀρχισυνάγωγοι), but the elders of the people (πρεσβύτεροι). The intervention of these elders indicates that the centurion was a proselyte; and this is confirmed by his second message to Jesus. No heathen would have regarded himself unworthy to receive a Jewish prophet. Observe that the elders put their request on the ground that the centurion is worthy because of his attachment to the Jewish nation, while Jesus esteems him above Israel because of his faith.

6-8. In Matthew this message is reported as the centurion's reply to Christ's promise, "I will come and heal him." The promise was probably one of action, not of words. As Christ went toward the house some ran before to tell the centurion, and he sent forth this second message. To enter the Gentile house would have made Jesus ceremonially unclean. Possibly the centurion refers to this; rather, I think, to the fact which this was intended to symbolize, viz., that they who live out of covenant relations with God are not suitable or worthy companions for the children of God.

into a city called Nain; and many of his disciples went with him, and much people. 12 Now when he came nigh to the gate of the city, behold, there was a dead man carried out, the only son of his mother, and she was a widow: and much people of the city was with her.

9, 10. The additions in Matthew are important. See Matt. 8:11, 12.

Ch. 7: 11-16. RAISING OF THE WIDOW'S SON AT NAIN. THE COMPASSION OF CHRIST.—MERCY IS MORE THAN RITUAL.—THE POWER OF THE LIFE-GIVER ILLUSTRATED.—THE LEAST FAITH SUFFICES TO JUSTIFY THE GREATEST MIRACLE.

This incident is recorded alone by Luke. This casts no necessary discredit on it, since there is abundant evidence in the Gospels of numerous miracles performed by Christ of which no detailed account is given (chaps. 4:40, 41; 6:18, 19; 7:21; John 2:23, etc.). Three times Christ raised the dead: Jairus's daughter, who was just dead; this young man, who was at the time borne toward the burial; Lazarus, who had been buried four days. For a comparison of the three, see Vol. I., p. 360.

11. He went into a city called Nain. Not the place of the same name referred to by Josephus (*Wars of the Jews*, 4:9; 4). That was on the borders of Idumea; this was in Galilee. The only remains are a squalid and miserable village, containing nothing to justify its name, which means "fair;" they occupy what was once a beautiful location, on the north-west slope of the Little Hermon, about twenty-five miles from Capernaum. Almost the exact site of this miracle is determined by the locality. "No convent, no tradition marks the spot. But, under the circumstances, the name is sufficient to guarantee its authenticity. One entrance alone it could have had—that which opens on the rough hill-side in its downward slope to the plain. It must have been in this steep descent, as, according to Eastern custom, they 'carried out the dead man,' that, 'nigh to the gate' of the village, the bier was stopped, and the long procession of mourners stayed, and 'the young man delivered back to his mother.'"—(*Stanley's Sinai and Palestine.*) The time, too, may be fixed with reasonable certainty. If Christ started, as Orientals ordinarily do, in the early morning, and sailed down the Sea of Galilee to the southern end, and thence walked, he would have arrived at the city of Nain in the early afternoon.—**And many of his disciples * * * and much people.** It was the era of Christ's popularity; not yet had he made that discourse of the nature of his kingdom and its demands on his disciples, which subsequently estranged so many who were now following him, in expectation of a temporal and political redemption.

12. Nigh to the gate. The brief and simple picture of this funeral procession is illus-

FUNERAL PROCESSION.

trated by Oriental burial customs, and tallies with them in the most minute particulars. Burials were almost invariably without the city walls. Immediately upon death the friends joined in noisy, though not always sincere, demonstrations of grief. In these they were often aided by professional mourners (Mark 5:38, note). The body was dressed in the ordinary garments, or was wrapped in a long piece of cloth, answering to the modern shroud (Acts 5:5, 6, note and illustration).

13 And when the Lord saw her, he had compassion on her, and said unto her, Weep not.
14 And he came and touched the bier: and they that bare *him* stood still. And he said, Young man, I say unto thee,° Arise.
15 And he that was dead ᵖ sat up, and began to speak. And he delivered him to his mother.

o ch. 6 : 54 ; Acts 9 : 40 ; Rom. 4 : 17....p 2 Kings 4 : 32–37 ; 13 : 21 ; John 11 : 44.

The bier on which it was borne was, in the case of the poorer classes, a simple board supported on two poles. There was no coffin; the corpse was simply covered with a large cloth. Mourners accompanied the body to the grave, chanting a sorrowful refrain, broken in upon by the genuine lamentation of friends, the sympathetic expressions of bystanders and acquaintances, and the professional outcries of hired mourners. Greater respect is paid to the funeral processions in the East than with us; bystanders wait reverentially as it passes, and often swell the little cortege, following in the train as a mark of sympathy. These features are illustrated in the accompanying cut, from an original drawing by Mr. A. L. Rawson. In accordance with these usages is this narrative: The bier is met outside the city walls; it is accompanied by much people; and when Christ interferes there is no coffin to be opened, no obstacle to prevent the dead from rising up into a sitting posture at once.—**The only son of his mother, and she was a widow.** The peculiar grief of this mother has made this story sacred to many a heart. The bitterness of mourning for an only son is illustrated by several passages in the Bible (Jer. 6 : 26 ; Amos 8 : 10 ; Zech. 12 : 10). But chiefest of these is the fact that it is taken to symbolize and interpret to us the Father's love for us, in that he spared not his only begotten Son for our redemption (John 3 : 16).—**Much people.** Observe that the miracle is performed in open day, without secrecy, and before many witnesses. There is no room for deception or mistake. As in the case of Lazarus, we must believe either that the incident never occurred, *i. e.*, that it is a fictitious narrative; or that it was a deliberate fraud, in which Christ and the widow conspired to deceive the people; or that it was a divine interposition, according to Christ that power over death which is the peculiar prerogative of divinity (2 Kings 5 : 7). To suppose that the cases of resurrection recorded in the N. T. were simply restorations of suspended animation, as some rationalistic critics have suggested, involves insuperable difficulties. We must then believe that, in less than three years, three cases of suspended animation occurred within the circle of Christ's ministry, that in each criticism now discovers what was hidden from the immediate friends, and that Christ made the discovery in each case without any examination of the supposed corpse, and just at the fortunate moment when the returning life was ready to respond to his voice.

This involves a perfectly incredible doctrine of chances.

13–15. He had compassion on her. The sacred narrative assigns no other reason for this miracle than compassion for the weeping mother. It is not for us to add other reasons, *e. g.*, faith in the young man about to be raised, or a concealed purpose to restore him spiritually by raising him from the dead. To see an indication of such a purpose in the declaration of ver. 15, *He delivered him to his mother*, is to add to the Scriptural narrative, without improving upon its simplicity. We neither know that he was not before a child of God, nor that he became so afterward.—**Weep not.** This is the message of redeeming love. The end of redemption is even in this life, glorying in tribulation (Rom. 5 : 3); though our sorrow remains, it is not a hopeless sorrow (1 Thess. 4 : 13); and it is in the life to come an experience of divine comfort, in which God will wipe away all tears from our eyes (Rev. 21 : 4). There is thus a deep spiritual meaning in this incident, in which two processions meet—the one led by death, the other by the Prince of life; the one a procession of mourners, the other one of rejoicers; the one a result of the fall, the other a symbol of redemption—and in which life conquers death, joy sorrow, redemption the bitter fruit of sin.—**Touched the bier.** This was not necessary; a word would have sufficed; and the ceremonial law rendered any one unclean who touched the dead, for death was a symbol and a result of sin. But to Christ the law was made for man, not man for the law, and he never hesitated to break over the letter of the ritual in redeeming from the curse which made ceremonial law needful (Matt. 8 : 5, note).—**They that bore him stood still.** Without any other command than that of his presence or his gesture; without any other compulsion than that vague hope which his benignant divinity so often inspired in men. There is scarcely conceivable a smaller token of faith than this mere standing still to let Christ do what he would; but it was faith enough. When we can do nothing for those dear to us, we can at least stand, expectant and submissive, for Christ to do his will.—**I say unto thee, Arise.** Contrast the prayers and efforts of Elijah and Elisha (1 Kings 17 : 20–22; 2 Kings 4 : 33–35). "Elijah, it is true, raises up the dead. But he is obliged to stretch himself out upon the body of the child whom he recalls to life; and it is easily seen that he invokes a foreign power, that he withdraws from the empire of death a

16 And there came a fear on all: and they glorified God, saying, That a great prophet ᑫ is risen up among us; and, That ʳ God hath visited his people.
17 And this rumour of him went forth throughout all Judæa, and throughout all the region round about.
18 And the disciples of John shewed him of all these things.
19 And ˢ John calling *unto him* two of his disciples, sent *them* to Jesus, saying, Art thou he that should come? ᵗ or look we for another?
20 When the men were come unto him, they said, John Baptist sent us unto thee, saying, Art thou he that should come? or look we for another?
21 And in that same hour he cured many of *their* infirmities and plagues, and of evil spirits; and unto many *that were* blind he gave sight.
22 Then Jesus answering, said unto them, Go your way, and tell ᵘ John what things ye have seen and heard; how ᵛ that the blind see, the lame walk, the lepers are cleansed, the deaf hear, the dead are raised, to the poor ʷ the gospel is preached.
23 And blessed is *he*, whosoever shall not be offended ˣ in me.
24 And when the messengers of John were departed, he began to speak unto the people concerning John, What went ye out into the wilderness for to see? A reed shaken with the wind?
25 But what went ye out for to see? A man clothed in soft raiment? Behold, they which are gorgeously apparelled, and live delicately, are in kings' courts.ʸ
26 But what went ye out for to see? A prophet? ᶻ Yea, I say unto you, and much more than a prophet.
27 This is *he*, of whom it is written,ᵃ Behold, I send my messenger before thy face, which shall prepare thy way before thee.
28 For I say unto you, Among those that are born of women, there is not a greater prophet than John the Baptist: but he that is least in the kingdom of God is greater than he.
29 And all the people that heard *him*, and the publicans, justified ᵇ God, being baptized ᶜ with the baptism of John.
30 But the Pharisees and lawyers rejected the counsel ᵈ of God against themselves, being not baptized of him.
31 And the Lord said, Whereunto ᵉ then shall I liken the men of this generation? and to what are they like?
32 They are like unto children sitting in the marketplace, and calling one to another, and saying, We have piped unto you, and ye have not danced; we have mourned to you, and ye have not wept.
33 For John the Baptist came ᶠ neither eating bread nor drinking wine; and ye say, He hath a devil.
34 The ᵍ Son of man is come eating and drinking; and ye say, Behold, a gluttonous man, and a winebibber, a friend of publicans and sinners!
35 But ʰ Wisdom is justified of all her children.

q ch. 24:19....r ch. 1:68....s Matt. 11:2....t Zech. 9:9....u John 1:46....v Isa. 35:5, 6....w ch. 4:18; James 2:5....x ch. 2:34; Isa. 8:14, 15; Matt. 11:6; 13:57; John 6:66; 1 Cor. 1:21-28....y 2 Sam. 19:35; Esther 1:3, 11....z ch. 1:76....a ch. 1:16-17; Mal. 3:1....b Ps. 51:4; Rom. 3:4....c ch. 3:12; Matt. 3:5, 6....d Acts 20:27....e Matt. 11:16, etc....f ch. 1:15; Matt. 3:4; Mark 1:6....g verse 36; John 2:2; 12:2....h Prov. 8:32-36; 17:16.

soul which is not subjugated to him, and that he is not himself the master of life and death. Jesus Christ raised up the dead as easily as he performs the most common actions; he speaks as master of those who repose in an eternal sleep; and it is thoroughly felt that he is the God of the dead as of the living, never more tranquil and calm than when he is operating the grandest things."—(*Massillon's Sermons*, p. 448.) Godet draws beautifully another and a suggestive contrast, which hints not only, indeed, at the manner in which the divine voice recalls the dead from the long sleep, but at an analogy which helps our faith to accept the sublime fact. "The interruption of the connection between the soul and the body in death, as in sleep, is only relative; and as man's voice suffices to re-establish this connection between the soul and the body in any one who is wrapt in slumber, so the word of the Lord has the power to restore this interrupted connection even in the dead."—**Sat up and began to speak.** An evidence of the completeness of his restoration.—**Delivered him to his mother.** A finishing act of grace. The on-lookers were too awe-struck to act; the mother was overwhelmed by the sudden revulsion of feeling; personally helping the son from his bier, and conducting him to his mother, Christ completed his merciful interposition, and gave to the mother's feeling that opportunity for action which was necessary for her own relief. Comp. John 11:44, note.

16, 17. There came a fear on all. Not that fear which is akin to terror, but that which is akin to awe.—**A great prophet.** Only the greatest prophets had raised the dead. As yet there was no general belief, even among his own disciples, that Christ was the promised Messiah. —**And this rumor of him went forth throughout all Judea.** That is, the glory of this miracle and the consequent fame of him as a great prophet. This, extending in widening circles, was carried from Galilee even to and throughout Judea, and so came to John the Baptist, who was confined in the prison of Machaerus, on the eastern side of the Dead Sea, and led to the inquiries reported in the following verses.

18-35. MESSAGE OF JOHN THE BAPTIST, AND CHRIST'S DISCOURSE THEREON.—Reported also in Matt. 11:2-19. See notes there, where I have treated it at length. The variations in the accounts are mostly immaterial. The only ones of consequence are the following. Matthew places the incident after the commission of the twelve, Luke shortly after the Sermon on the Mount; neither definitely indicates the time. Luke's order is generally believed to be the correct one, for Herod beheaded John the Baptist while the twelve were absent fulfilling their commission (Mark 6:30; Matt. 14:13). Luke reports a little more fully John's message. Comp. vers. 19, 20, with Matt. 11:2. He alone reports the important fact in ver. 21. The language in Matthew, "Go show John again these things which ye do hear and see," implies, however, that John's messengers had personally witnessed the miracles which they were to report; but the language here indicates that these miracles were

36 And¹ one of the Pharisees desired him that he would eat with him. And he went into the Pharisee's house, and sat down to meat.
37 And, behold, a woman in the city, which was a sinner, when she knew that *Jesus* sat at meat in the Pharisee's house, brought an alabaster box of ointment,
38 And stood at his feet behind *him* weeping, and

¹ Matt. 26 : 6, etc. ; Mark 14 : 3, etc. ; John 11 : 2, etc. ... ; verse 34 ; ch. 5 : 32 ; 1 Tim. 1 : 15.

wrought at the time and for the purpose of giving a message to carry back to their Master. If so, it is, I think, the only case reported where Christ performed a miracle for the avowed purpose of demonstrating his claims. Matthew, in vers. 12-15, contains an important declaration not reported by Luke ; on the other hand, vers. 29, 30, here are peculiar to Luke. Comp. with them Matt. 21 : 25, 26. They are regarded by Alford as an addition by Luke, giving the effect of Christ's discourse on the multitude; by De Wette, Meyer, etc., as a part of Christ's discourse, in which he describes the effect of John the Baptist's preaching prior to his imprisonment. The former interpretation appears to me unquestionably the correct one. Observe the comprehensive character of Luke's classification of cures, in ver. 21, indicating, perhaps, the professional accuracy of a physician. *Infirmities* are those disorders which disable, as deafness, dumbness, paralysis, the withered hand, etc. ; *plagues*, lit., *scourges*, are the more painful forms of sickness ; the *possessed of evil spirits* are discriminated from the merely diseased.

Ch. 7 : 36-50. ANOINTING OF JESUS BY A PENITENT WOMAN. THE ATTRACTIVE POWER OF CHRIST.—THE FRIEND OF PUBLICANS AND SINNERS.—THE CHRISTIAN TREATMENT OF THE ABANDONED.—A LOVING SINNER BETTER THAN A PROUD SAINT.—WE HAVE NOTHING TO PAY.—THE SENSE OF SIN FORGIVEN IS THE INSPIRATION OF TRUE LOVE FOR CHRIST.—LOVE TO CHRIST IN THE LIFE AN EVIDENCE THAT CHRIST'S FORGIVENESS IS RECEIVED IN THE HEART.

There has been much discussion whether this anointing is not merely a different account of the same act reported by the other Evangelists (Matt. 26 : 7 ; Mark 14 : 3 ; John 12 : 3). The identity is maintained by the Latin fathers, by the later Roman Catholic expositors, and by the modern rationalistic interpreters. That they are different events is the opinion of nearly all modern evangelical scholars. The reasons for regarding them as different accounts of the same event are as follows : (1) No Evangelist mentions two anointings ; the one here described is the only one mentioned by Luke ; the one described as occurring in the Passion week is the only one mentioned by Matthew, Mark, and John. (2.) The master of the house in both cases is Simon (ver. 40 ; Matt. 26 : 6). (3.) The homage paid by the woman in the two cases is analogous. (4.) In both it is the subject of misinterpretation and conflict. Against regarding them as different accounts of the same events are the following considerations : (1) The name Simon is a common one ; nine persons of that name are mentioned in the N. T. (2.) The time, place, and circumstances are widely different ; that anointing was in Judea, just before Christ's passion, by a disciple of Christ, whom he especially loved, whose brother he had raised from the dead. The Simon there mentioned was a leper, and therefore could not well have been present. The complaint came from a disciple ; and was a complaint of extravagance. This anointing was in Galilee, in the era of Christ's great popularity, before the final conflict with the Pharisees, by a recognized harlot, whose name is unknown. It took place at the house of a well-known Pharisee, who interposed the complaint on the ground, not of extravagance, but of the woman's sinful character. (3.) The lessons are different ; that teaches that the offerings of love to Christ are never wasted ; this that penitence draws near to Christ, while pride remains afar off. I have no doubt that there were two anointings. There is no reason whatever for identifying this woman with Mary Magdalene. The exact time and place of the incident are unknown ; Meyer supposes Capernaum ; Wieseler, Nain.

36-38. And one of the Pharisees desired him that he would eat with him. As yet then the breach between Jesus and the Pharisees had not become irreparable. This single fact is sufficient evidence that the incident could not have occurred in Judea, and immediately previous to Christ's crucifixion. There is no reason to doubt that this Pharisee had heard of the fame of Jesus Christ as a prophet, and knowing little of his character, really desired to do him an honor by his invitation. The Pharisee invites Christ to come to him ; the woman seeks permission to come to Christ; the Pharisee thinks to confer honor ; the woman seeks salvation.—**Sat down to meat.** Reclined in Oriental fashion, with the feet extended behind. See Vol. I., p. 282, for illustration. Thus the woman, coming behind, easily and without observation, approached his feet. — **Behold a woman in a city which was a sinner.** Or, possibly, so some read the passage, *who was a sinner in that city, i. e.*, who had practiced her unholy calling there. She *was*, not merely *had been*, a sinner. Up to that time she had lived a life of sin. The substitution of the pluperfect for the imperfect tense by some expositors, grows out of a desire, either to explain Christ's treatment of the woman, whom they wish to

THE PENITENT AND THE PHARISEE.

"She began to wash his feet with tears, and did wipe them with the hair of her head."

CH. VII.] LUKE. 49

began to wash his feet with tears, and did wipe *them* with the hairs of her head, and kissed his feet, and anointed *them* with the ointment.

39 Now when the Pharisee which had bidden him saw *it*, he spake within himself, saying, This man, if [k] he were a prophet, would have known who and what manner of woman *this is* that toucheth him ; for she is a sinner.[l]

40 And Jesus, answering, said unto him, Simon, I have somewhat to say unto thee. And he saith, Master, say on.

41 There was a certain creditor which had two debt-

---

k John 9 : 24 .... l ch. 15 : 2.

---

represent as already reformed, or to reconcile the account here with that anointing at Bethany, reported in the other Gospels, with which they confound it. For the same reason, some have regarded the term *sinner* as a mere general one, indicating not an unchaste life, but one of vanity and worldliness. All such attempts to conform Scripture to our prepossessions are irreverent and misleading. The plain meaning of the narrative is, that this woman had been leading the life of a prostitute up to this time, and was recognized by Simon as such, either by some characteristic feature in her dress or because her character was well known. Her reform dates from this hour. That she entered the house uninvited is not strange. In the free life of the East the presence of uninvited guests, not at the table but in the room, is not uncommon. "At dinner at the consul's house at Damietta we were much interested in observing a custom of the country. In the room where we were received, besides the divan on which we sat, there were seats all round the walls. Many came in and took their places on those side seats, uninvited and yet unchallenged."—(*Narrative of a Mission to the Jews*, quoted in Trench's *Notes on the Parables*.) If, in this case, the meal was given in the guest-room, which generally lies open to the courtyard, the public would naturally have followed Christ into the court-yard. This woman followed in with them, drawn by his words of tenderness, perhaps by the invitation of Matt. 11 : 28–30, which was given at about this time in Christ's life ; her heart was drawn toward him ; the tears of an awakened sorrow, welling to her eyes, dropped upon the feet of Christ ; she saw it, knelt, and, obeying the impulse of the moment, wiped them with her long hair ; unrepelled, she softly kissed them ; and still unrepelled, took the box of ointment which had ministered to her in her unholy calling, used in adding to her seductive charms, and with it anointed his feet. The first act of reverence was an unconscious one ; each new act, in expressing her hunger, intensified her feeling.—**An alabaster box of ointment. * * * Anointed them with the ointment.** The original is simply *an alabaster*. It was probably a vase rather than a box. The accompanying illustration represents a collection of alabasters from the British Museum. Ointment was used in the East, and still is, not only in religious consecration, but also in the

ALABASTERS.

toilet. The hair and face were both anointed ; a shining skin being accounted an element of beauty (Ruth 3 : 3 ; Eccles. 9 : 8 ; Amos 6 : 6). To be without anointing was a sign of mourning (2 Sam. 14 : 2). Trench notes the fact that she wiped the Lord's feet with that which is the especial crown and glory of woman, the *hair* of her head ; kissed him with the lips that had beguiled the simple (Prov. 5 : 3 ; 7 : 13) ; and used, in holy expression of reverence toward him, the unguent once used to aid her own sinful life and gratify her vanity, thus illustrating the principle enunciated by Paul in Romans 6 : 19.

39. Spake within himself. Courtesy, or perhaps a vague feeling of awe, kept him from expressing his opinion. His conduct contrasts favorably with that of the inimical Pharisee, whom we meet elsewhere in the Gospel narratives. See, for example, Matt. 12 : 2 ; Luke 11 : 53, 54 ; 16 : 14. Nor does Christ call Simon a hypocrite ; the rebuke which he administers is one of the severity of love, not of judgment.—**This man, if he were a prophet, would have known.** The dilemma in the Pharisee's mind was this ; if Christ were an inspired man he would have read the character of this woman ; if he were a holy man he would not have suffered her homage. Of the inspiration that reads penitence in the heart, of the holiness that accepts sorrow for sin and a promise of repentance, he had no conception.

40, 41. Jesus answered. Not to any ex-

50 LUKE. [CH. VII.

ors: the one owed five hundred pence, and the other fifty:
42 And when they had nothing ᵐ to pay, he frankly forgave them both. Tell me, therefore, which of them will love him most?
43 Simon answered and said, I suppose that *he* to whom he forgave most. And he said unto him, Thou hast rightly ⁿ judged.
44 And he turned to the woman, and said unto Simon, Seest thou this woman? I entered into thine house, thou gavest me no water for my feet: but she hath washed my feet with tears, and wiped *them* with the hairs of her head.

45 Thou gavest me no kiss: but this woman, since the time that I came in, hath not ceased to kiss my feet.
46 My ᵒ head with oil thou didst not anoint: but this woman hath anointed my feet with ointment.
47 Wherefore I say unto thee, Her sins, which are many, are forgiven ; for she loved much : but to whom little is forgiven, *the same* loveth little.
48 And he said unto her, Thy sins are forgiven.
49 And they that sat at meat with him began to say within themselves, Who ᵖ is this that forgiveth sins also?
50 And he said to the woman,ᑫ Thy faith hath saved thee ; go in peace.

ᵐ Ps. 49 : 7, 8 ; Rom. 5 : 6....ⁿ Ps. 116 : 16–18 ; 1 Cor. 15 : 9 ; 2 Cor. 5 : 14 ; 1 Tim. 1 : 13–16....ᵒ Ps. 23 : 5....ᵖ Matt. 9 : 2, 3 ; Mark 2 : 7....ᑫ chaps. 8 : 48 ; 18 : 42 ; Hab. 2 : 4 ; Matt. 9 : 22 ; Mark 5 : 34 ; 10 : 52 ; Ephes. 2, 8.

---

pression by the Pharisee, though his countenance may have indicated his thoughts, but to what he had said within himself. The case is one in which Christ read the secrets of the heart. Compare Matt. 9 : 4 ; John 2 : 25.—**Master, say on.** His language is that of respect. Evidently this Pharisee is not to be confounded with those that denied and persecuted the Lord. His perplexity was an honest one ; Christ treats it with tenderness.—**Two debtors.** Compare the parable in Matt. 18 : 23–35. There, also, are two debtors ; but there, the difference between the two debts is enormous ; one owes eighteen dollars, the other a sum equivalent, at the lowest estimate, to fifteen millions. The contrast there represents the difference between our debt to God and our neighbor's debt to us. Here the difference is relatively small ; one owes fifty denarii, the other five hundred. The denarius was about equivalent to eighteen cents of our money ; the relative debts therefore were nine dollars and ninety dollars. The contrast represents simply the difference among men in their debts, *i. e.*, their unfulfilled obligations, toward God. Presumptively, this Pharisee was represented by the smaller debtor, *i. e.*, not only in his own estimation but also in reality he was a man of comparatively pure life.

42, 43. When they had nothing to pay he frankly forgave them both. They had nothing to pay, so that both were equally insolvent ; moreover, they were both conscious of this fact, so that they both accepted from the creditor a full and free remission of the debt. The contrast is not between two men, one of whom claims divine consideration because he owes but little, and the other accepts it without preferring any claim ; but between two sinners, both of whom are conscious of their utter inability to meet the requirements of the divine law, but the one of whom feels that inability more keenly than the other.—**I suppose that he to whom he forgave most.** The expression, *I suppose*, does not imply doubt or hesitation. It is rather, *As I understand the matter*. Did Simon perceive the drift of our Lord's question? Probably not fully ; and yet, it appears to me, that he could

not have been wholly oblivious of the result to which the parable tended.

44-46. It can hardly be doubted that Simon had been deficient, if not in the courtesies ordinarily paid to a guest, at least in those due to a distinguished prophet. Water for the feet (Gen. 18 : 4 ; Judges 19 : 21), the kiss of peace (Gen. 45 : 15 ; Exod. 18 : 7), and anointing the head with oil (Ps. 23 : 5), were marks of attention ordinarily paid in the East. The contrasts are very noticeable between the neglect of Simon and the homage of the woman. No water—tears, the most precious of all water ; no kiss of greeting—kisses for the feet ; no oil for the head—precious ointment for the feet. The Pharisee was decorous but cold ; the woman, under the inspiration of an ardent love, broke over the ordinary social restraints. The one omitted even the customary expressions of reverence ; the other, by her peculiar use of them, emphasized the reverence and love of her heart.

47. The difficulties which this verse has occasioned, and the discussions to which it has given rise, I have considered below. Here it must suffice to say, that Christ does not say, "Wherefore her sins, which are many, are forgiven ;" but " Wherefore *I say unto thee*, her sins are forgiven." The manifestations of the woman's love are not alleged by Christ to be the *cause of the forgiveness*, but the *occasion of his teaching*. Nor does the second clause of the sentence "*for* she loved much," imply that her love elicited the forgiveness. *For* indicates not the *cause* but the *evidence* of her pardon. "We may say, It is light, for the sun is risen ; but we may also say, The sun is risen, for it is light. So in this passage, *for* may, and according to what precedes, *must* mean : 'I say unto thee that her many sins are forgiven, *as thou must infer from this*, that she loved much.' "—(*Godet*.)

48-50. Thy sins are forgiven. The tense is the perfect, not the present, and indicates not a forgiveness, then first proffered, but already in past time perfected. His language is, *Thy sins have been forgiven*. Christ did not then forgive ; he declared a forgiveness, before extended to her. The spirit of forgiveness in Christ, which

CH. VII.] LUKE. 51

drew the publican and sinner to him, and made him their friend, attracted this woman, and elicited her penitence, purpose of reformation, and love. The consciousness that he had forgiveness for her and compassion on her, preceded and evoked her penitence. To suppose that he forgave because she previously loved, violates grammar here as well as the plain teaching of Scripture elsewhere. See below.—**Who is this that forgiveth sins also?** Comp. Mark 2 : 7; but there the language is that of open opposition; here, rather that of perplexity, not unmingled with awe.—**Thy faith hath saved thee.** As the instrument, not the cause of salvation; it had saved her, because it had led her to accept Christ in simplicity the saving grace proffered to her by the Lord. Observe, too, the illustration of faith which this incident affords; it is not an intellectual opinion, for there is no reason to suppose that the woman regarded Christ then as more than a prophet; nor an act of obedience, nor always even illustrated by one, though always involving an obedient spirit; but a trust that accepts Christ, and believes in his grace, because he proffers it.—**Go in peace.** This was the perfecting of her pardon; it is always the perfecting of Christian pardon; peace from fear, both of the past and the future (Rom. 8 : 1, 38, 39). She had felt the forgiving love of Christ before; now, first she had an assurance in his own words, that put to flight all doubts, and dried all tears but those of gratitude and love.

Two difficulties are presented by this parable, which have given rise to a voluminous discussion. I. Does it represent that our love for God is the cause of his forgiveness of our sins. That this is the teaching is maintained by many Roman Catholics, and some rationalistic divines, and by some who confound love and faith. But (1) this view is not required nor even justified by the grammatical construction of ver. 47. See note there. (2.) It does not accord with the groundwork of the parable, since the forgiveness precedes and produces the love in the story (vers. 41, 42), and neither debtor has anything to pay, whereas love is the pay that is pre-eminently due to God; (3) nor with Christ's language in the last clause of ver. 47. If our love causes God's forgiveness, Christ would have said, not, To whom little is forgiven, the same loveth little; but, Who loveth little, to the same little is forgiven. (4.) Nor with ver. 50, *Thy faith* (not thy love) *hath saved thee*. (5.) Nor with other teachings of Scripture, which uniformly represent the divine love as the *cause*, not the *effect*, of human love (John 3 : 16; Ephes. 2 : 4, 2; 1 John 4 : 10, 19). (6.) Nor with psychology, for love is itself salvation; it is that not *by* which but *unto* which we are saved. "Sin is the disease. What is the remedy? Charity? Pshaw! Charity in the large, apostolic sense of the term

is the health, the state to be obtained by use of the remedy, not the sovereign balm itself—faith of grace—faith in the God-manhood, the cross, the mediation, the perfected righteousness of Jesus, to the utter rejection and abnegation of all righteousness of our own." — (*Coleridge.*) II. If he whose sins are many and to whom much is forgiven, loves much, is sin a means of grace? Is the greatest sinner prepared to be the greatest saint? If love is the chief grace (1 Cor. ch. 13), and sin forgiven awakens it, shall we not go on to sin that grace may abound? No! for, (1.) The love is not as the sin, but as the sense of forgiveness. It depends not upon the actual guilt, but upon our consciousness of it. One of the evil effects of sin is that it dulls the moral sense, and prevents that consciousness of guilt and that appreciation of divine forgiveness which is the inspiration of love. (2.) The love of a flagrant transgressor, pardoned, may be more ardent, but not more deep; more impetuous, but not more strong; more demonstrative, but not more healthy than that of the soul which has grown up unto Christ without ever consciously wandering away from him. "It is an unquestionable fact that the *deepest penitents* are, in *one kind* of love for him who has forgiven them the most devoted; in that, namely, which consists in personal sacrifice, and proofs of earnest attachment to the blessed Saviour and his cause on earth. But it is no less an unquestionable fact, that *this love* is not the highest form of spiritual life; that such persons are, by their very course of sin, incapacitated from entering into the length, and breadth, and height, and being filled with all the fullness of Christ; that their views are generally narrow, their aims one-sided; that though love be the greatest of the Christian graces, there are various kinds of it; and though the love of the reclaimed profligate may be, and is, intense of its kind (and how touching and beautiful its manifestations are, as here !) yet *that kind* is not so high nor complete as the sacrifice of the *whole life*—the bud, blossom, and fruit—to his service, to whom in baptism we were dedicated."—(*Alford.*) (3.) But we are not to forget the deep truth of this parable, which is forgotten, I fear, in much of the ministry of the modern church, with the result of a shallow love and an imperfect consecration. Christ's love is always proportioned to the soul's sense of its own unworthiness and its consequent necessity of its divine love in redemption. Hence, to deepen Christian love and strengthen Christian consecration, it is always necessary to deepen the conviction of sin. And I believe it is true, as matter of history, that those forms of theology which have treated sin lightly, have always issued in belittling Christ's divine nature and work; and that those experiences which

CHAPTER VIII.

AND it came to pass afterward, that he went throughout every city and village, preaching and shewing the glad tidings of the kingdom of God: and the twelve *were* with him;

2 And certain women, which had been healed of evil spirits and infirmities, Mary called Magdalene, out of whom went seven devils,

3 And Joanna the wife of Chuza, Herod's steward, and Susanna, and many others, which ministered unto him of their substance.

4 And when much people were gathered together, and were come to him out of every city, he spake by a parable:

5 A sower went out to sow his seed; and as he sowed, some fell by the way side; and it was trodden down, and the fowls of the air devoured it.

6 And some fell upon a rock; and as soon as it was sprung up, it withered away, because it lacked moisture.

7 And some fell among thorns; and the thorns sprang up with it, and choked it.

8 And other fell on good ground, and sprang up, and bare fruit an hundredfold. And when he had said these things, he cried, He that hath ears to hear, let him hear.

9 And his disciples asked him, saying, What might this parable be?

10 And he said, Unto you it is given to know the mysteries of the kingdom of God; but to others in parables; that seeing they might not see, and hearing they might not understand.

11 Now the parable is this: The seed is the word of God.

12 Those by the way side are they that hear; then cometh the devil, and taketh away the word out of their hearts, lest they should believe and be saved.

13 They on the rock *are they*, which, when they hear, receive the word with joy; and these have no root, which for a while believe, and in time of temptation fall away.

14 And that which fell among thorns are they, which, when they have heard, go forth, and are choked with cares and riches and pleasures of *this* life, and bring no fruit to perfection.

15 But that on the good ground are they, which, in an honest and good heart, having heard the word, keep *it*, and bring forth fruit with patience.

16 No man, when he hath lighted a candle, cover-

---

have not led to thorough heart-searchings and penitence before God, have not led to a deep love for Christ nor a thorough consecration to his service. (4.) Nor are we to overlook another lesson, which is frequently forgotten because it lies upon the surface. This woman had as yet been subjected to none of those tests by which we are accustomed to measure the genuineness of repentance. She had not yet reformed her life, nor borne the taunts of her companions, nor the scorn of the virtuous. But Christ declared that the manifestation of her personal love for him was an adequate evidence of her forgiveness by him and its acceptance by her. A genuine, simple, outspoken love for Christ is not the cause of forgiveness, but it is always an *evidence* if not always a demonstration that Christ's forgiving love has been received and accepted, and always justifies us in receiving the penitent to our own hearts.

Ch. 8:1-3. CHRIST'S CIRCUIT OF GALILEE. THE MINISTRY OF WOMEN IN THE CHURCH.

This summary of Christ's tour of Galilee is peculiar to Luke. It embraces, in a graphic outline, the period, of which some details are given in the preceding chapters and some in the other Gospels.

1. **Throughout every city and village.** A very thorough missionary tour. Christ neither dreaded the large places nor despised the small ones.—**Heralding and showing the glad tidings of the kingdom of God.** As a herald, proclaiming the kingdom of God at hand; as an interpreter, explaining it as a kingdom of joy and gladness to man because of grace from God.

2. **And certain women.** The addition of these women made the sight still more strange. For such admixture of the sexes was in utter violation of the customs of the country. It would hardly be tolerated there even now. "Promiscuous assemblies of men and women are unknown; and even when a crowd collects to see some sight or gaze at a show, the sexes are always grouped in two distinct and separate portions. A man never walks in the street by the side of his wife or daughter, but, when he happens to be out in their company, is sure to keep several paces in advance of them. * * * In some parts of the country, and even among the Christians, a woman may not show herself unveiled before her father-in-law, and even before her own husband. She never speaks to the former except through a third person, and should he ask her a question, she must whisper her answer to some one who will repeat it aloud to him."—(*Van Lennep's Bible Lands*.) To this add, that the Jewish rabbis did not allow the law to be taught to women; that to the present day in the East women are not allowed an education; and that even in England and America the education of women has been accomplished only after much and bitter opposition, and the reader will have some conception how radical was the movement which Christ inaugurated in taking women with him as disciples. They did not teach. Whether this was because it was not Christ's will that women should ever be public teachers in the church, or because in that age and condition of society their teaching would not have been received, and the attempt would have been idle, is a question to be determined by other passages of Scripture. Little can be drawn from the mere negative fact. Subsequently, women did become recognized re-

eth it with a vessel, or putteth *it* under a bed; but setteth *it* on a candlestick, that they which enter in may see the light.

17 For¹ nothing is secret that shall not be made manifest; neither *any thing* hid that shall not be known and come abroad.

18 Take ᵐ heed therefore how ye hear; for ⁿ whosoever hath, to him shall be given; and whosoever hath not, from him shall be taken even that which he seemeth to have.

19 Then ° came to him *his* mother and his brethren, and could not come at him for the press.

20 And it was told him *by certain*, which said, Thy mother and thy brethren stand without, desiring to see thee.

21 And he answered and said unto them, My mother and my brethren are these which hear the word of God, and do it.

22 Now ᵖ it came to pass on a certain day, that he went into a ship with his disciples; and he said unto them, Let us go over unto the other side of the lake. And they launched forth.

23 But as they sailed, he fell asleep: and there came down a storm of wind on the lake; and they were filled *with water*, and were in jeopardy.

24 And they came to him, and ᵠ awoke him, saying, Master, master, we perish! Then he arose, and rebuked the wind and the raging of the water: and they ceased, and there was a calm.

25 And he said unto them, Where is your faith? And they, being afraid, wondered, saying one to another, What manner of man is this! for he commandeth even the winds and water, and they obey him.

26 And ʳ they arrived at the country of the Gadarenes, which is over against Galilee.

27 And when he went forth to land, there met him out of the city a certain man, which had devils long time, and ware no clothes, neither abode in *any* house, but in the tombs.

28 When he saw Jesus, he cried out, and fell down before him, and with a loud voice said, What have I to do with thee, Jesus, *thou* Son of God most high? I beseech thee, torment ˢ me not.

29 (For he had commanded the unclean spirit to come out of the man. For oftentimes it had caught him; and he was kept bound with chains and in fetters; and he brake the bands, and was driven of the devil into the wilderness.)

30 And Jesus asked him, saying, What is thy name? And he said, Legion: because many devils were entered into him.

31 And they besought him that he would not command them to go out into the deep.ᵗ

32 And there was there an herd of many swine feed-

---

¹ ch. 12 : 2; Eccles. 12 : 14; Matt. 10 : 26; 1 Cor. 4 : 5.....ᵐ James 1 : 21-25.....ⁿ ch. 19 : 26; Matt. 13 : 19; 25 : 29.....° Matt. 12 : 46, etc.; Mark 3 : 30, etc.....ᵖ Matt. 8 : 23, etc.; Mark 4 : 35, etc.....ᵠ Ps. 44 : 23; Isa. 61 : 9, 10.....ʳ Matt. 8 : 28, etc.; Mark 5 : 1, etc.....ˢ Isa. 27 : 1; James 2 : 19; Rev. 20 : 10.....ᵗ Rev. 20 : 3.

---

ligious teachers, though never to any considerable extent (Acts 18 : 26; 21 : 9; Phil. 4 : 3).

3. Mary, called Magdalene.—Because of Magdala. On her life and character see Matt. 27 : 56, note. Of the fact here stated, that seven devils were cast out of her, nothing else is known. She is not to be confounded with the penitent woman referred to in the preceding chapter. On demoniac possession, see Vol. I, p. 123.—**Joanna, the wife of Chuza.** Of whom nothing else is known. It has been surmised that Chuza was the court lord whose son Jesus healed, and who believed with all his house (John 4 : 46-54). It is also noted as one of the coincidences confirmatory of the truth of the N. T., that Herod, the son of one of whose courtiers was healed by Christ, and whose steward's wife was a disciple, heard much of Christ, and was perplexed by what he heard of his wonderful works (Matt. 14 : 1, 2).—**Susanna.** Not mentioned elsewhere.

4-15. PARABLE OF THE SOWER.—This parable was spoken, with others, on the shore of the sea of Galilee. The whole series constituted one discourse, and interpreted, by an allegory, the nature of the kingdom of God. They are reported more fully in Matthew (ch. 13), where I have treated the particulars and noted the variations in expression between Matthew, Mark, and Luke. See notes there.

16-18. PARABLE OF THE CANDLE.—This is given in the same connection by Mark (ch. 4 : 21-25). The same instructions are given by Matthew in various passages and in different connections. See Matt. 5 : 15; 10 : 26; 13 : 12, and notes thereon. Observe the difference between Mark and Luke in one important part. Mark says, Take heed *what*, Luke, *how* ye hear. Both are needful cautions; yet *what* we hear depends in part on *how* we hear; *i. e.*, the attention we give to the word spoken.

19-21. CHRIST'S MOTHER ATTEMPTS TO INTERRUPT HIS TEACHING.—That this was her object appears in Mark 3 : 21. The true chronological order is doubtless given by Matthew. See Matt. 12 : 46-50, notes.

22-25. CHRIST STILLS THE TEMPEST.—Comp. Matt. 8 : 23-27, and Mark 4 : 35-41. Mark is the fullest and most graphic; he alone gives a definite note of time. His language shows that it occurred on the evening following the parable by the sea-shore. See notes on Mark, where I have considered the variations in the language of the Evangelists.

26-39. THE CURE OF THE GADARENE DEMONIAC.—Matt. 8 : 28-34; Mark 5 : 1-21. See notes there, especially on Matthew, where I have considered briefly the question, what is the nature of demoniacal possession. Matthew mentions two demoniacs, Mark and Luke but one. Alford thinks that there was but one, and that Matthew's less circumstantial account is in error in this. Such a supposition is at least needless. The more violent may alone have been mentioned, or there may have been but one who expressed, after his cure, a desire to follow Jesus (ver. 38), and therefore Mark and Luke may have mentioned only him. Matthew, who refers to two demoniacs, says nothing of this request.

30. Many devils were entered into him. Luke's language is more explicit than that of Matthew or Mark. I believe it is to be taken as

ing on the mountain: and they besought him that he would suffer them to enter into them: and he suffered them.

33 Then went the devils out of the man, and entered into the swine: and the herd ran violently down a steep place into the lake, and were choked.

34 When they that fed *them* saw what was done, they fled,ᵘ and went and told *it* in the city and in the country.

35 Then they went out to see what was done; and came to Jesus, and found the man, out of whom the devils were departed, sitting at the feet of Jesus, clothed, and in his rightᵛ mind: and they were afraid.

36 They also which saw *it* told them by what means he that was possessed of the devils was healed.

37 Then the whole multitude of the country of the Gadarenes round about besought him ʷ to depart from them; for they were taken with great fear: and he went up into the ship, and returned back again.

38 Now the man out of whom the devils were departed, besought him that he might be with ˣ him: but Jesus sent him away, saying,

39 Return to thine own house,ʸ and shew how great thingsᶻ God hath done unto thee. And he went his way, and published throughout the whole city how great things Jesus had done unto him.

40 And it came to pass, that, when Jesus was returned, the people *gladly* received him: for they were all waiting for him.

41 And, behold, there ᵃ came a man named Jairus, and he was a ruler of the synagogue; and he fell down at Jesus' feet, and besought him that he would come into his house:

42 For he had one only daughter, about twelve years of age, and she lay a dying. But as he went, the people thronged him.

43 And a woman having an issue of blood twelve years, which had spent ᵇ all her living upon physicians,ᶜ neither could be healed of any,

44 Came behind *him*, and touched the border of his garment: and ᵈ immediately her issue of blood stanched.

45 And Jesus said, Who touched me? When all denied, Peter, and they that were with him, said, Master, the multitude throng thee and press *thee*, and sayest thou, Who touched me?

46 And Jesus said, Somebody hath touched me: for I perceive that virtue ᵉ is gone out of me.

47 And when the woman saw that she was not hid,ᶠ

she came trembling,ᵍ and falling down before him, she declared unto him, before all the people, for what cause she had touched him, and how she was healed immediately.

48 And he said unto her, Daughter, be of good comfort: thy faith hath made thee whole: go in peace.

49 While ʰ he yet spake, there cometh one from the ruler ⁱ of the synagogue's *house*, saying to him, Thy daughter is dead: trouble not the Master.

50 But when Jesus heard *it*, he answered him, saying, Fear not: ʲ believe only, and she shall be made whole.

51 And when he came into the house, he suffered no man to go in, save Peter, and James, and John, and the father and the mother of the maiden.

52 And all wept, and bewailed her: but he said, Weep not; she is not dead, but sleepeth.ᵏ

53 And they laughed him to scorn,ˡ knowing that she was dead.

54 And he put them all out, and took her by the hand, and called, saying, Maid,ᵐ arise.

55 And her spirit came again, and she arose straightway: and he commanded to give her meat.

56 And her parents were astonished; but he chargedⁿ them that they should tell no man what was done.

CHAPTER IX.

THEN he ᵒ called his twelve disciples together, and gave them power and authority over all devils, and to cure diseases.

2 And he sent them to preach the kingdom of God, and to heal the sick.

3 And he said unto them, Take ᵖ nothing for *your* journey, neither staves, nor scrip, neither bread, neither money; neither have two coats apiece.

4 And whatsoever house ye enter into, there abide, and thence depart.

5 And whosoever will not receive you, when ye go out of that city, shake ᑫ off the very dust from your feet, for a testimony against them.

6 And they departed, and went through the towns, preaching the gospel, and healing every where.

7 Now Herod ʳ the tetrarch heard of all that was done by him: and he was perplexed, because that it was said of some, that John was risen from the dead;

8 And of some, that Elias had appeared; and of others, that one of the old prophets was risen again.

9 And Herod said, John have I beheaded: but who

u Acts 19:16, 17....v Ps. 51:10....w Acts 16:39....x Deut. 10:20, 21; Ps. 116:12, 16....y 1 Tim. 5:8....z Ps. 126:2, 3....a Matt. 9:18, etc.; Mark 5:22, etc... b 2 Chron. 16:12; Isa. 55:2....c Job 13:4....d ch. 13:13; Matt. 8:3; 20:34....e ch. 6:19; 1 Pet 2:9.... f Ps. 38:9; Hosea 5:3....g Isa. 66:2; Hosea 13:1; Acts 16:29....h Matt. 9:23, etc.; Mark 5:35, etc....i vers. 41, 42...j John 11:25; Rom, 4:7....k John 11:11, 13....l ch. 16:14; Ps. 22:7....m ch. 7:14; John 11:43....n Matt. 8:4; 9:30; Mark 5:43....
o Matt. 10:1, etc.; Mark 3·13, etc.; 6:7, etc....p chaps. 10:4 etc.; 12:22....q Neb. 5:13; Acts 13:51; 18:6... r Matt. 14:1, etc.; Mark 6:14, etc.

---

literally true, *i. e.*, the demoniac was not under the mastery of one evil spirit, but under the anarchic control of several.

31. That he would not command them to go into the deep. Parallel to Luke's language is the expression in Mark, "That he would not send them out of the country" (Mark 5:10). The word here rendered *deep*, more properly *abyss*, does not signify the sea, but the abode of the lost. It means literally without bottom, and is generally rendered "bottomless" (Rev. 9:1, 2, 11; 11:7; 17:8; 20:1, 3). It occurs in the N. T. only here, in the passages quoted from Revelation and in Romans 10:7; in the latter passage it signifies simply the place of departed spirits.

38, 39. Now the man * * * besought, etc. The request of the man and Christ's reply are narrated by Mark, but not by Matthew. They are very significant. When Christ is rejected by

the Gadarenes, his compassion fails not, and he will not leave himself without a witness. Though he never returns to the land of the Gadarenes, he leaves a preacher there. So rejected, outcast, crucified, he bids every one from whom he has cast out sin to remain upon the earth and tell how great things God has done for him. And this is the secret of all power in Gospel preaching, which is potent only as it is made so by a conscious personal experience.

40-56. CURE OF THE WOMAN WITH AN ISSUE OF BLOOD. RAISING OF JAIRUS'S DAUGHTER.—Comp. accounts in Matt. 9:18-26 and Mark 5:22-43. For full treatment see notes in Mark, where I have also noted the few additional details given here. The time of the events is fixed by Matthew as immediately following the feast in Matthew's house, but when that was given is not certain.

CH. IX.] LUKE. 55

is this, of whom I hear such things? And he" desired to see him.
10 And the apostles, when they were returned, told him all that they had done. And he took them, and went aside privately into a desert place, belonging to the city called Bethsaida.
11 And the people, when they knew *it*, followed him: and he received ᵘ them, and spake unto them of the kingdom ᵛ of God, and healed them that had need ʷ of healing.
12 And ˣ when the day began to wear away, then came the twelve, and said unto him, Send the multitude away, that they may go into the towns and country round about, and lodge, and get victuals: for we are here in a desert ʸ place.
13 But he said unto them, Give ye them to eat. And they said, We have no more but five loaves and two fishes; except we should go and buy meat for all this people.
14 For they were about five thousand men. And he said to his disciples, Make ᶻ them sit down by fifties in a company.
15 And they did so, and made them all sit down.
16 Then he took the five loaves and the two fishes; and looking up to heaven, he blessed them, and brake, and gave to the disciples to set before the multitude.
17 And they did eat, and were all ᵃ filled: and there was taken up of fragments that remained to them, twelve baskets.
18 And it ᵇ came to pass, as he was alone praying, his disciples were with him: and he asked them, saying, Whom say the people that I am?

19 They answering, said, John ᶜ the Baptist; but some *say*, Elias; and others *say*, that one of the old prophets is risen again.
20 He said unto them, But whom say ye that I am? Peter,ᵈ answering, said, The Christ of God.
21 And he straitly charged them, and commanded *them* to tell no man that thing;
22 Saying, The Son ᵉ of man must suffer many things, and be rejected of the elders and chief priests and scribes, and be slain, and be raised the third day.
23 And he said to *them* all, If ᶠ any *man* will come after me, let him deny himself, and take up his cross daily, and follow me.
24 For whosoever will save his life, shall lose it: but whosoever will lose his life for my sake, the same shall save it.
25 For what is a man advantaged, if he gain the whole world, and lose himself, or be cast away?
26 For whosoever ᵍ shall be ashamed of me and of my words, of him shall the Son of man be ashamed, when he shall come in his own glory, and *in his* Father's, and of the holy angels.
27 But I ʰ tell you of a truth, there be some standing here, which shall not taste¹ of death, till they see the kingdom of God.
28 And ʲ it came to pass, about an eight days after these sayings, he took Peter and John and James, and went up into a mountain to pray.
29 And as he prayed, the fashion of his countenance was altered, and his raiment *was* white *and* glistering.
30 And, behold, there talked with him two men, which were Moses and Elias:

ₐ ch. 23; 8....t Rom. 10: 14, 17....u John 6: 37....v Acts 28: 31....w chaps. 1: 53; 5: 31; Heb. 4: 16....x Matt. 14: 15, etc.; Mark 6: 35, etc.; John 6: 5, etc....y Ps. 78: 19, 20; Ezek. 34: 25; Hosea 13: 5....z 1 Cor. 14: 40....a Ps. 107: 9....b Matt. 16: 13, etc.; Mark 8: 27, etc....c vers. 7, 8; Matt. 14: 2....d John 6: 69....e Matt. 16: 21; 17: 22....f ch. 14: 27; Matt. 10: 38; 16: 24; Mark 8: 34; Rom. 8: 13; Col. 3: 5....g Matt. 10: 33; Mark 8: 38; 2 Tim. 2: 12....h Matt. 16: 28; Mark 9: 1....i John 8: 52; Heb. 2: 9....j Matt. 17: 1, etc.; Mark 9: 2, etc.

Ch. 9 : 1-6. THE COMMISSION OF THE TWELVE.—Comp. Matt. 10 : 1-42; Mark 6 : 7-13. The account in Matthew is much the fullest; see notes there. Comp. with ver. 6 here Matt. 11 : 1, and observe that Christ went preaching through the cities, while the disciples carried on their mission at this time only in the villages, *i. e.*, unwalled towns.

7-9. DEATH OF JOHN THE BAPTIST.—Comp. Matt. 14 : 1-12, and Mark 6 : 14-29, who give a full account of John's death and the circumstances that led to it. See notes there.

10-17. FEEDING THE FIVE THOUSAND. — Comp. Matt. 14 : 13-27; Mark 6 : 30-44; John 6 : 1-21, notes. There is a difficulty in reconciling ver. 10 here with Mark 6 : 45. Luke reports Christ as going toward Bethsaida when departing from the west to the east shore; Mark reports Christ as going toward Bethsaida when departing, after the feeding, from the east to the west shore. Hence two Bethsaidas have been imagined, solely to satisfy the conditions of the Evangelists' narrative; for there is no geographical evidence of more than one. For the true explanation of this difficulty see Mark 6 : 45, note. The difficulty was early felt, and has probably led to the variety of manuscript readings here, some manuscripts reading, *To a city called Bethsaida*, some, *To a desert place belonging to the city called Bethsaida*, some simply, *To a desert place*. If the explanation which I have given in Mark be correct, these variations are immaterial, the fact being that the feeding took place on a grassy plain, near to and east of Bethsaida Julius.

18-21. PETER'S CONFESSION.—Matt.16 : 13-20; Mark 8 : 27-30. Matthew fixes both the time and the locality; the time, during Christ's retirement with his disciples at the close of his public Galilean ministry; the locality, near Cæsarea Philippi. The statement of ver. 18 here, that he was alone, praying with his disciples, is peculiar to Luke. Matthew alone gives the promise to Peter (Matt. 16: 17-19). See notes on Matthew.

22-27. FIRST ANNOUNCEMENT OF OUR LORD'S PASSION AND RESURRECTION.—Matt. 16 : 21-28; Mark 8 : 31; ch. 9 : 1. All three Evangelists place this prophecy immediately after the disciples' confession of Christ as the Messiah, and immediately preceding the Transfiguration. The report is fuller both in Mark and Matthew than here. The greater part of this address was delivered to, or at least in the presence of, other people. This is evident from the language of ver. 23 here, "to them all," and the language of Mark (8 : 34), "and when he had called the people," a concurrent testimony to the publicity of the latter part of this address. With ver. 25 here comp. Matt. 16 : 26 and Mark 8 : 36. The phrase here, "and lose himself or be cast away," interprets the language in Matthew and Mark, "lose his own soul." On the whole passage see notes on Matthew.

28-36. THE TRANSFIGURATION. — Compare Matt. 17 : 1-9 and Mark 9 : 1-8. I have treated the subject fully in Matthew. Luke gives some

31 Who appeared in glory, and spake of his decease which he should accomplish at Jerusalem.
32 But Peter and they that were with him were heavy ᵏ with sleep: and when they were awake, they saw his glory,ˡ and the two men that stood with him.
33 And it came to pass, as they departed from him, Peter said unto Jesus, Master, it is ᵐ good for us to be here: and let us make three tabernacles; one for thee, and one for Moses, and one for Elias: not knowing ⁿ what he said.
34 While he thus spake, there came a cloud, and overshadowed them: and they feared as they entered into the cloud.
35 And there came a voice out of the cloud, saying, This º is my beloved Son: hear ᵖ him.
36 And when the voice was past, Jesus was found alone. And they kept *it* close, and told no man in those days ᵠ any of those things which they had seen.
37 And it ʳ came to pass, that on the next day, when they were come down from the hill, much people met him.
38 And, behold, a man of the company cried out,

saying, Master, I beseech thee, look upon my son; for he is mine ˢ only child.
39 And lo, a spirit taketh him, and he suddenly crieth out; and it teareth him that he foameth again; and, bruising him, hardly departeth from him.
40 And I besought thy disciples to cast him out; and they could not.ᵗ
41 And Jesus answering, said, O faithless ᵘ and perverse ᵛ generation! how long shall I be with you, and suffer you? Bring thy son hither.
42 And as he was yet a coming, the devil threw him down, and tare *him*. And Jesus rebuked ʷ the unclean spirit, and healed the child, and delivered him again to his father.
43 And they were all amazed ˣ at the mighty power of God. But while they wondered every one at all things which Jesus did, he said unto his disciples,
44 Let these sayings sink down into your ears: for ʸ the Son of man shall be delivered into the hands of men.ᶻ
45 But ᵃ they understood not this saying, and it was hid from them, that they perceived it not: and they feared to ask him of that saying.

k Dan. 8 : 18 ; 10 : 9....I John 1 : 14.....m Ps. 27 : 4 ; 73 : 26....n Mark 10 : 38....o Matt. 3 : 17 ; 2 Pet. 1 : 17, 18....p Deut. 18 : 15 ; Acts 3 : 22....q Eccles. 3 : 1...,r Matt. 17 : 14, etc.; Mark 9 : 17, etc....s Zech. 12 : 10....t Acts 19 : 13–16....u John 20 : 27 ; Heb. 4 : 2... v Deut. 32 : 5 ; Ps. 78 : 8....w Mark 1 : 27....x Ps. 139 : 14 ; Zech. 8 : 6....y Matt. 17 : 22....z 2 Sam. 24 : 14....a chaps. 2 : 50 ; 18 : 34 ; Mark 9 : 32.

additional particulars not given by either of the other writers. He tells us the object of going up into the mountain, "to pray;" that the transfiguration of our Lord took place "as he prayed;" the nature of the transfiguration, "the fashion of his countenance was altered and his raiment was white and glistening;" the theme of conversation between Christ and the two spiritual companions, "they spake of his decease, which he should accomplish at Jerusalem;" that the vision was seen by the Apostles "when they were awake;" that Peter spoke as Moses and Elias "departed from him," and by implication to restrain their departure; that he spake "not knowing what he said;" and that the apostles obeyed the command of Christ, which Matthew alone reports, and "told no man in those days any of those things which they had seen."

29. **White and glistering.** That is, *flashing.* The idea conveyed, is of an appearance like burnished metal flashing in the sun. Comp. Ezek. 1 : 4, 7 ; Nahum 3 : 3.

31. **Spake of his decease.** More literally, "of his departure" (Greek ἔξοδος).

32. **But Peter and they that were with him had been heavy with sleep, but having kept fully awake they saw his glory.** Our English version implies that they fell asleep and were wakened to see his glory, while the original implies that though heavy with sleep they kept fully awake. "The word (keep awake διαγρηγορέω) appears to be used expressly here to show that it was not merely a vision seen in sleep."—(*Alford.*)

34. **And they,** the disciples, **feared as the others,** Christ, Moses, and Elijah, **entered into the cloud.** The original does not imply that the disciples entered into the cloud. On the contrary, in the Received Text, it distinguishes between them and the others who did enter. There is some doubt as to the reading, but the whole course of the narrative here and in the other Evangelists indicates that the cloud received the three out of the sight of the disciples.

35. **Beloved son.** The best reading here is, *My son the elect or chosen.*

36. **And they kept it close * * * in those days.** Presumptively until after Christ's resurrection, in accordance with his command. Matt. 17 : 9.

37–42. HEALING OF THE LUNATIC BOY.— Matt. 17 : 14–21 ; Mark 9 : 14–29. The description is much the fullest and most graphic in Mark. See notes there. Matthew calls this boy a lunatic; the symptoms as described here and in Mark are those of epilepsy.—**The next day.** The transfiguration was probably at night. The scene here described took place on the following morning.—**Mine only child.** Luke alone so describes him.—**Crieth out.** Peculiar to Luke. An inarticulate cry is intended ; for the boy was both deaf and dumb (Mark 9 ; 26).—**Perverse generation.** Rather, *perverted race.* The language is that of pity, not of indignation. See note on Mark 9 : 19.

Ch. 9 : 43–45. PROPHECY OF OUR LORD'S PASSION. THE MYSTERY OF PROPHECY.

Comp. Matt. 17 : 22, 23 ; Mark 9 : 30–32 ; and notes on Mark. This prophecy was uttered during Christ's retirement, after the close of his public ministry in Galilee, and before the commencement of his principal public ministry in Judea. Mark 9 : 30. See note on Matt. 15 : 29–39.

43. **But while all were wondering.** As before he gave an intimation of his passion im-

46 Then ᵇ there arose a reasoning among them, which of them should be greatest.
47 And Jesus, perceiving the thought of their heart, took a child, and set him by him,
48 And said unto them, Whosoever ᶜ shall receive this child in my name, receiveth me ; and whosoever shall receive me, receiveth him that sent me : for ᵈ he that is least among you all, the same shall be great.
49 And John answered and said, Master, we ᵉ saw one casting out devils in thy name ; and we forbad him, because he followeth not with us.

50 And Jesus said unto him, Forbid *him* not; for ᶠ he that is not against us, is for us.
51 And it came to pass, when the time was come that he should be received ᵍ up, be stedfastly set his face to go to Jerusalem,
52 And sent messengers before his face : and they went, and entered into a village of the Samaritans,ʰ to make ready for him.
53 And they did not receive him, because his face was as though he would go to Jerusalem.
54 And when his disciples James and John saw *this*,

b Matt. 18 : 1, etc.; Mark 9 : 34, etc....c Matt. 10 : 40; John 12 : 44; 13 : 20....d ch. 14 : 11 ; Matt. 23 : 11, 12....e Numb. 11 : 27-29....
f ch. 16 : 13; Matt. 12 : 30....g Mark 16 : 19; Acts 1 : 2....h John 4 : 4.

mediately after the apostles' confession of faith in his Messiahship, so now after the expression of their wonder at his miraculous power, he adapts the trial of their faith to its strength.

44. Matthew and Mark both add a prophecy of the resurrection.

45. **It was hid from them in order that** (*ινα*) **they should not perceive it.** "It was the divine purpose that they should not at present be aware of the full significance of these words."—(*Alford.*) And this is implied not only in the original, which our English version imperfectly renders, but also in the direction, "Let these sayings sink down into your ears." They were to treasure them up for future reflection and comprehension, that when the death of our Lord came, they might not be overwhelmed, and when the resurrection took place, they might be prepared to believe it. In this verse we have a hint of the office of prophecy, viz., not to make clear future events, but to give a ground of faith in the divine word, *after the fulfillment has taken place* (John 2 : 22 ; 12 : 16 ; 13 : 19 ; 14 : 29). So still the full meaning of the prophecy of Christ's second coming is, it seems to me, purposely hidden from his church.—**They feared.** See Mark 9 : 32, note.

46-50. DISCOURSE CONCERNING GREATNESS IN THE KINGDOM OF GOD.—Of this discourse much the fullest report is given by Matthew, chap. 18. Mark's briefer account contains some particulars not given by Matthew (Mark 9 : 33-50). See notes on Matthew and Mark. On the variations in the three accounts and their reconciliation, see Prel. Note in Matthew. The discussion took place openly among the disciples, on the road, and was stopped by the presence of Christ (Mark 9 : 32), but the strife and debate remained in their hearts (Luke 9 : 47). The question of John, and our Lord's reply (vers. 49, 50), is not reported by Matthew, but is by Mark ; see notes there.

Ch. 9 : 51-56. CHRIST REFUSED HOSPITALITY BY THE SAMARITANS. RELIGIOUS WRATH AND PERSECUTION PROHIBITED. — THE SPIRIT OF CHRISTIANITY ONE OF LONG-SUFFERING.

The time of this incident is entirely uncertain, except as it is fixed by ver. 51. It is not narrated by either of the other Evangelists. It occurred after the close of Christ's Galilean ministry, not on the journey to the feast of Tabernacles, as indicated in the Harmony (Vol. I, 45), for he then went up to Jerusalem, "not openly, but, as it were, in secret (John 7 : 10) ; " hardly on the journey to the feast of Dedication (John 10 : 22, etc.), as suggested by Alford, for there is nothing to indicate that between these two feasts Jesus left Judea ; he certainly did not go back to Galilee, and we have no hint of any Samaritan ministry. The chronology of all the weeks between the feast of Dedication (John 10 : 22-39) and the resurrection of Lazarus (John, ch. 11), including most of the events and instructions in Luke, chaps. 10-18, is involved in great uncertainty. See next chap., Prel. Note. This incident probably occurred at some point during this time, perhaps on Christ's way, at the close of his Perean ministry, to the resurrection of Lazarus, and probably at about the same general period as the incident in Mark 10 : 32-34.

51, 52. **And it came to pass when the time was coming.** Not come, *i. e.*, fully come, but approaching.—**His face was stedfastly set.** In full knowledge of all that he was to suffer. His steadfastness itself indicated the conflict within, over which he triumphed in thus going to Jerusalem. Compare the description in Mark 10 : 32.—**And sent messengers before his face.** It seems to me far more natural to understand by this, messengers to prepare a place for him and his disciples, than, with Alford, to suppose that they were directed "to announce the coming of Jesus as the Messiah." This he seems never to have announced, either directly or through others, in any public ministry, while he lived. His announcement to the Samaritan woman (John 4 : 26), is no exception, for that was in a private conversation. But probably he chose to be dependent, as his disciples were, on the hospitality of the people (Matt. 10 : 9-14); this would therefore involve his recognition by the people as an honored religious leader, if nothing more.

53, 54. **And they did not receive him.** The bitter hostility between Jews and Samaritans receives several illustrations in the N. T. See especially John, ch. 4, notes, and Luke 10 : 25-37, notes. The refusal to receive Christ

they said, Lord, wilt thou that we command fire to come down from heaven, and consume them, even as Elias¹ did?
55 But he turned, and rebuked them, and said, Ye know not what manner of spirit ye are of.
56 For ʲ the Son of man is not come to destroy men's lives, but to save *them*. And they went to another village.
57 And ᵏ it came to pass, that, as they went in the way, a certain *man* said unto him, Lord, I will follow thee whithersoever thou goest.
58 And Jesus said unto him, Foxes have holes, and

---

1 2 Kings 1 : 10, 12....j John 3 : 17 ; 12 : 47....k Matt. 8 : 19, etc.

---

was a distinct refusal to recognize him as a prophet, or a leader worthy of reverence; it was also a recognized indignity in the East, where hospitality is a recognized duty, and where the traveler is habitually welcomed as a guest, unless some distinct cause exists for refusing to receive him. The act is interpreted by 2 John, vers. 9 and 10; it was an emphatic repudiation of him as a heretic, a teacher of falsehood.—**Wilt thou that we command fire to come down from heaven and consume them?** There is some doubt whether the added words, *As Elias did*, is not a gloss added by a copyist, in explanation of the proposition. There is no doubt, however, that there was a reference in the disciples' minds, to 2 Kings 1 : 9-12. Their proposal indicates their spirit; they were full of zeal for their Master; believed that he was on his way to Jerusalem to enter into his kingdom, remembered the glory in which they had seen him with Moses and Elijah, on the Mount of Transfiguration, and were impatient for the disclosure of his power and authority. It was the same spirit which led Peter to rebuke the Lord for prophesying his passion, and to draw his sword to resist the arrest. It is still the same spirit which seeks to accomplish the triumphs of the Redeemer's kingdom, not by long-suffering, patience, and love, but by the exercise of authority and power.

55, 56. There is some doubt about the true reading of these verses. The phrase, "*The Son of man is not come to destroy men's lives, but to save them,*" is thought by many scholars to have been interpolated, being a customary saying of our Lord's (Matt. 18 : 11 ; Luke 19 : 10). Tischendorf also omits the other portion of the rebuke, "*Ye know not what manner of spirit ye are of,*" thus leaving the narrative simply, "*He turned and rebuked them, and they went to another village.*" But in the uncertainty of the MSS., the internal evidence may be accepted as decisive; and that is in favor of the ordinary reading. "The words have such a weight of authority against them, that they would be worthy of rejection if it were explicable how they came into the text. How easily, on the other hand, out of regard to Elijah, could an *intentional* omission take place. Moreover, the brief, simple, and pregnant word of rebuke is so unlike a copyist's interpolation, and as worthy of Jesus himself, as it is, on the other hand, hard to conceive that Luke, on an occasion so unique, limited himself to the bare, He rebuked them."—(*Meyer*.) There is also some question as to the translation of the first part of the rebuke. It may be rendered interrogatively, "*Know ye not what spirit ye are of?*" i. e., what is the spirit of Christianity, the spirit of meekness and love; or it may be rendered positively, but with the same significance, "*Ye know not what spirit ye are of,*" i. e., Ye know not, do not comprehend, the true spirit of Christianity; or, more severely, "*Ye know not your own spirit*, a spirit alien from mine." This, I doubt not, is the true interpretation, but the others are grammatically possible, and they have defenders.—**And they went to another village.** In accordance with the instructions which Christ had himself given to the twelve (Matt. 10 : 23).

This incident illustrates the Christian method of meeting insult and indignity—not by penalty but by patience, and, when possible, by avoidance. But it illustrates much more. The anger of the disciples was not aroused by a personal affront, but by one offered to their Lord; it was excited, not by self-conceit or pride, but by love and zeal for Christ. Zeal for him, when uniting with the lower passions, produces not piety but fanaticism; such zeal, so uniting, is not a Christian spirit; it may even result in a devilish spirit. Christ condemns, impliedly, all attempts to coerce respect for him, or to punish the want of it; and so, not only all religious persecution, but also all that wrath and bitterness, which is so unhappily common in religious controversies. The office of Christianity is wholly remedial, not unitive; its instruments are the forbearance and long-suffering of love, not judgment and penalty; light and warmth, not fire from heaven. We are to be patient, not merely with wrong personal to ourselves, but with the spirit of irreligion and infidelity, and with affronts offered to our Lord. We are not to hate even the enemies of Christ.

Ch. 9 : 57-62. FOLLOWING CHRIST. THREE PERSONS ALMOST PERSUADED TO BE CHRISTIANS : THE SELF-CONFIDENT AND IMPETUOUS DISCIPLE ; THE PROCRASTINATING DISCIPLE ; THE IRRESOLUTE DISCIPLE.—THE FIRST MUST COUNT THE COST ; THE SECOND MUST SUNDER THE MOST SACRED TIES ; THE THIRD MUST FORGET THOSE THINGS WHICH ARE BEHIND.—DUTIES TO THE LIVING AND DUTIES TO THE DEAD.—DANGERS OF EVEN LOOKING BACK (see note below).

This incident probably occurred immediately

birds of the air *have* nests; but the Son of man hath not where to lay *his* head.

59 And he said unto another, Follow me. But he said, Lord, suffer[1] me first to go and bury my father.

60 Jesus said unto him, Let the dead bury their dead; but go thou and preach the kingdom of God.

61 And another also said, Lord, I will follow thee; but let me first go bid them farewell which are at home at my house.

62 And Jesus said unto him, No man, having put his hand to the plough, and looking back, is fit for the kingdom of God.

---

[1] 1 Kings 19 : 20.

---

after Christ's preaching of the parables concerning the kingdom of God (Matt., ch. 13). He desired to escape from the throng, and bade his own disciples, *i. e.*, the twelve, to depart with him by boat to the other side of the Sea of Galilee. Comp. notes on Matt. 8 : 18–22, and see Mark 4 : 35, with Matt. 8 : 18.

57. A certain man. A scribe (Matt. 8 : 19, 21), and a disciple in the sense in which all were termed disciples who were learners of Jesus without having fully committed themselves to his cause. To understand his spirit we must consider both the circumstances and Christ's response; for here, as elsewhere, the *heart* of the speaker is to be read, not so much from his own words, which were perhaps contrived to hide his real feelings, as from the reply of Christ, who discerned the intents of the heart. Christ had just been proclaiming the nature of the kingdom which he had come to establish (Matt., ch. 13). He now wishes to separate himself from the throng, and seek retirement. This scribe demands to intrude himself on Christ's hours of seclusion, and bases this demand on a promise to follow him wherever he goes. Christ does not refuse his demand, but tests the value of his offer. '"What!' saith he, 'dost thou look to gather wealth by following me? Seest thou not then that I have not even a lodging, not even so much as the birds have.'"—(*Chrysostom*.) In a similar manner he tries the rich young man (Matt. 19 : 21) In neither case does he invent a peculiar and a hard condition; he simply requires that those who join his band shall share their poverty. The twelve have left all to follow him (Matt. 4 : 20, 22; 9 : 19; 19 : 27).

58. Son of man. A phrase borrowed from the prophecy of Daniel, and indicating the Messiah. See Matt. 10 : 23, note.—Hath not where to lay his head. That is, no permanent home. He was frequently the guest of disciples. Frequently he spent the night in the open air; no real hardship in Orient as in our climate. "Night by night Jesus received from the hand of his Father a resting-place, which he knew not in the morning."—(*Godet*.)

59, 60. Another. Also a disciple (Matt. 8 : 21). An ancient tradition says it was Philip; Alford suggests that the command "follow me," was occasioned by some slackness or symptoms of decadence on the part of the disciple. It appears more probable that he was a disciple only in a general sense of being a recipient of Christ's teachings, not one of the twelve.—Bury my father. "As it was the practice to bury on the day of death, it is not very likely that this disciple would have been here at all if his father had just breathed his last. * * * No doubt it was the common case of a son, having a frail and aged father not likely to live long, whose head he thinks it his duty to see under the ground ere he goes abroad."—(*Dr. Brown*.)—Let the dead bury their dead. That is, Let those that abide in the world attend to the duties and fulfill the obligations which are supposed to belong to that state. For you there is no turning; a higher duty calls you to preach the Gospel. During the midst of the battle the soldier cannot leave ranks to bury the dead or even to succor the dying. A seeming indifference to them is then his duty. It does not follow that we are to neglect what are called secular duties for those that are termed religious. Nevertheless, life presents many occasions in which duty to the living is supreme over respect to the dead; in which duty to Christ requires that we should forego works which otherwise would be sacred duties. Compare for parallel teaching, Matt. 10 : 37; for illustrative example, Mark 3 : 32–35.

61, 62. Compare Gen. 19 : 26, and 1 Kings 19 : 20, 21, where Elijah's language is satirical, and where Elisha, by his acts, though not in words, withdraws his request, leaves his cattle and his labors, and slaying two of the oxen for a feast in honor of Elijah, follows him without returning to his home.—No man having put his hand to the plough and looking back. The figure is one the agriculturist will readily appreciate. The ploughman must keep his eye on the furrow to be made, and the Christian on the life-duties to which he is called. *Looking back* spoils the furrow (comp. Phil. 3 : 13). Dr. Brown says that when Hindoos are converted and are about to be baptized, their parents often plead with them to pay them one more parting visit before taking a step that will cut them off from home altogether; and that those who yield to these parental entreaties to go home for a visit never return, or do so only after a season, in which they abandon Christianity and conform to the heathen religion again. This fact is the best possible commentary on and explanation of a passage which has seemed to some a hard requirement on Christ's part.

Dr. Brown's note on this entire passage

(though he bases it on Matt. 8 : 18-22) is admirable. The first disciple is the self-sufficient, and hence the *rash* and *precipitate* disciple. Like the Galatians, he begins with an excess of zeal; like Peter he will follow Christ everywhere (Gal. 4 : 14, 15; 5 : 7; Matt. 26 : 33, 70-74). Such need to be bidden to count the cost. The second is the *procrastinating* or *entangled* disciple. He will follow Christ, *but*—; the answer is, No duty, however sacred or solemn, is an excuse for putting off the claims of Christ to our full and unreserved service. The third is, the *irresolute* or *wavering* disciple. He halts between two opinions. To him the word of Christ is, *Now* is the accepted time. (Comp. Luke 14 : 18-20 and Matt. 13 : 20-22.)

Ch. 10 : 1-24. COMMISSION OF THE SEVENTY. THE WORK OF THE CHRISTIAN MINISTRY ILLUSTRATED. See on Matt., ch. 10.

PRELIMINARY NOTE.—The chronology of the events recorded in Luke 10 : 1 to 18 : 34, is very uncertain; the locality is also uncertain. Without entering into the unprofitable discussions of the harmonists, I give briefly what appears to me to be unquestionably the best opinion. Christ's Galilean ministry, was brought to an end by his rejection of the crown proffered to him by the people (John 6 : 15), and was followed by a brief period of retirement with his disciples, devoted to their instruction in the things concerning the kingdom of Christ (Matt. 16 : 21 to ch. 18). He then went up to Jerusalem to the feast of the Tabernacles, and in and about Jerusalem he spent about three months, from the feast of the Tabernacles to that of the Dedication. Of this Judean ministry, John alone gives any account (John, chaps. 7-10). Driven out of Jerusalem a second time by a mob, he departed into the district beyond Jordan, and taught there. Of this fact we have an intimation in Matt. 19 : 1 and Mark 10 : 1, but they give no full account of this era in his ministry. The incidents and teachings here recorded by Luke probably belong to this period. This is indeed only an hypothesis; but it is a more probable one than the supposition that after he had once gone over the cities and villages of Galilee, he returned to a second ministry there. It is borne out by a comparison of the character of the ministry with that of the land and of the people. Perea, so called from the Greek word (πέρα) *pera*, beyond, is a wild and romantic region, now but little visited by travelers to the Holy Land, who practically regard the Jordan as its eastern boundary. Even such writers as Stanley, Robinson, and Ritter, give but little information concerning it. To it belongs the Bashan and the Gilead of the O. T. It was in Christ's time a populous and prosperous district. The flourishing cities gave to its southern portion the name of Decapolis. Along the river Jordan the ruins of one hundred and twenty-seven villages have been counted. Its hill-sides were famous for pasturage, and its cattle for their size and fatness. Its population was not homogeneous. It formed a part of the Holy Land; and it was a part of Christ's mission to offer the Gospel to the entire Jewish people before turning from them to the Gentiles. But in Perea, the Israelites were intermixed with a Gentile population; the cities of Decapolis were Roman cities; the sheep of Israel, in this heathen society, were wandering sheep—to the haughty Judean, *lost* sheep. To this era of Christ's ministry naturally belong, therefore, the marvelous trio of parables—the lost sheep, the lost coin, the lost son; it is here that, in the parable of the good Samaritan, he rebukes pride of caste and race; and in the parables of the rich fool and of Dives and Lazarus, the pride of wealth. This Perean ministry extended, as I suppose, from the feast of the Dedication, in December, A. D. 29, to the time of Christ's going up for the last time to Jerusalem, March, A. D. 30, though in this time is included the resurrection of Lazarus and the brief subsequent retirement to Ephraim. The order of events is very uncertain. For a probable order, see Tabular Harmony, Vol. I, p. 45. Of this ministry, Matthew and Mark give a brief account (Matt. 19 : 1 to 20 : 16; Mark 10 : 1-31). Some few of the incidents and instructions recorded by Luke as in this era, seem, from the parallel accounts in Matthew and Mark, to belong to the Galilean ministry; of course they may have been repetitions. See for examples, Luke 13 : 18-21; 11 : 14-26; 17 : 1, 2.

To this period probably belongs the commission of the seventy. Their mission is much like that of the twelve (Matt., ch. 10); the difference is just such as the difference in circumstances would require. The seventy were to go two by two; they were endowed with the same supernatural powers; they were to depend wholly on the hospitality of the people; they were to preach the same gospel, "The kingdom of heaven is at hand." But they were seventy instead of twelve, for the territory was larger and the time shorter; they were not forbidden from entering into any Gentile city, for in Perea Gentile and Jew were associated together in the same cities; their ministry was not confined to the unwalled towns; no instructions respecting persecution were given them, for the era of bitter persecution did not come till after the death of Christ, and their appointment was purely local and temporary, while that of the twelve was for lifelong service in the church. In the main, however, the instructions given to the seventy were similar to those given to the twelve, though not covering as much ground. For the practi-

CHAPTER X.

1 AFTER^m these things the Lord appointed other seventy also, and sent them two and two before his face into every city and place, whither he himself would come.
2 Therefore said he unto them,ⁿ The harvest truly is great, but the^o labourers are few: pray ye therefore the Lord of the harvest, that he would send forth labourers into his harvest.
3 Go your ways: behold, I send you forth as lambs among wolves.
4 Carry^p neither purse, nor scrip, nor shoes: and^q salute no man by the way.
5 And into whatsoever house ye enter, first say, Peace be to this house.
6 And if the son^r of peace be there, your peace shall rest^s upon it: if not, it shall turn to you again.
7 And in the same house remain, eating and drinking such things as they give: for^t the labourer is worthy of his hire. Go not from house^u to house.
8 And into whatsoever city ye enter, and they receive you, eat^v such things as are set before you:
9 And heal the sick that are therein, and say unto them, The^w kingdom of God is come nigh unto you.
10 But into whatsoever city ye enter, and they receive you not, go your ways out into the streets of the same, and say,
11 Even^x the very dust of your city, which cleaveth on us, we do wipe off against you: notwithstanding, be ye sure of this, that the kingdom of God is come nigh unto you.
12 But I say unto you, that it shall be more tolerable in that day for Sodom, than for that city.
13 Woe^y unto thee, Chorazin! woe unto thee, Bethsaida! for^z if the mighty works which were done in Tyre

---

m Matt. 10:1, etc.; Mark 6:7, etc....n Matt. 9:37; John 4:35....o 1 Cor. 3:9; 1 Tim. 5:17....p ch. 9:3, etc....q Gen. 24:33, 56; 2 Kings 4:29; Prov. 4:25....r Isa. 9:6....s 2 Thess. 3:16; James 3:18....t 1 Cor. 9:4-14; 1 Tim. 5:18....u 1 Tim. 5:13....v 1 Cor. 10:27....w Matt. 3:2....v ch. 9:5....y Matt. 11:21, etc....z Ezek. 3:6.

---

cal and spiritual lessons, therefore, the reader is referred to the parallel and prior commission of the twelve, reported in Matthew, ch. 10. Here I note only what is peculiar to this commission.

1. **After these things.** An indefinite note of time, indicating clearly that the commission here referred to was subsequent to the events recorded in the preceding chapter. — **Others also, seventy in number.** That is, others than the twelve whose ordination is mentioned in ch. 9:1. "It is well that Luke has given us also the sending of the twelve, or we should have had some of the commentators asserting that this was the same mission."—(*Alford.*) As the twelve had a clear reference to the twelve tribes of Israel (Matt. 19:28), so the *seventy* are supposed to have reference to the seventy elders of Israel (Exod. 24:1; Numb. 11:16).—**Into every city and place whither he himself would come.** In Galilee Christ himself preached in the cities (Matt. 11:1), and the apostles in the towns and villages (ch. 9:6). In Perea, presumably, the seventy preached both in the cities and the unwalled towns, Christ following with his personal ministry chiefly in the former. It is not probable that he went into every place where his heralds went. In this respect our age is better than theirs, that Christ is always with his ministers, and that their work is always to prepare for his personal coming.

2. **The harvest truly is great.** The same metaphor is used by Christ in Matt. 9:37. See note there. There is no reason to think that Luke has misplaced it; more probably Christ in this instance, as in many others, made use of the same aphorism at different times.

3-12. These instructions are substantially the same as those given to the twelve in Matthew, ch. 10. Some matters given there are omitted here; but there is nothing here not contained there; at least the differences are little more than verbal. To the direction, *I send you forth as lambs among wolves*, Christ adds in Matthew the direc-

SALUTATIONS.

tion, *Be ye therefore wise as serpents,* etc. The direction, *Salute no man by the way,* is peculiar to Luke. The Jewish salutations, like those common in the Orient to-day, were elaborately formal, and occupied so much time as to be a serious hindrance when there was reason for haste. It is said that a complete formal salutation between two persons may consume from one to three hours. The disciples were not to stop *by the way* for these elaborate formal and insincere salutations. The immediate lesson to them was that their time was short and their business urgent. The lesson to us is that we are not to allow the formalities of life to interfere with our Gospel ministry. Verses 5 and 6 are parallel to Matt. 10:12, 13. *Peace be to this house* was a common form of Jewish salutation. *A son of peace* (the article is wanting in the original) is one who receives the salutation, *i. e.*, is ready to welcome the Gospel message of peace. Verses 7 and 8 are equivalent to Matt. 10:11. The direction simply emphasizes the instruction there given, *There abide till ye go hence.* On the one hand, the apostles were not to hesitate from a false delicacy to receive the hospitality proffered them; nor, on the other hand, discontented with it, were they to go from house to house seeking for better

and Sidon, which have been done in you, they had a great while ago repented, sitting in sackcloth and ashes.

14 But it shall be more tolerable for Tyre and Sidon at the judgment, than for you.

15 And thou, Capernaum, which^a art exalted to heaven, shalt be thrust^b down to hell.

16 He^c that heareth you, heareth me; and he^d that despiseth you, despiseth me; and^e he that despiseth me, despiseth him that sent me.

a Isa. 14 : 13-15 ; Jer. 51 : 53 ; Amos 9 : 2, 3.... b Ezek. 26 : 20 ; 31 : 18....c John 13 : 20,...d Acts 5 : 4,...e John 5 : 23.

TYRE ON THE MAINLAND.

accommodations or for social enjoyment. Verse 9 evidently imperfectly reports the authority conferred upon the seventy; from their account of the result of their mission in verse 17, it is clear that their power did not differ from that conferred on the twelve in Matt. 10 : 8. Verses 10-12 amplify the instructions contained in Matt. 10 : 14, 15. Observe that, whether accepted or rejected, the kingdom of God draws nigh, a power *in* us or a power *over* us.

13-15. The same woes against Chorazin, Bethsaida, and Capernaum are reported in Matt. 11 : 21-24. These are Galilean cities; it is quite certain that the woes against them were pronounced by our Lord in Galilee, as indicated by Matthew; but they may have been repeated by him in this connection to give solemn sanction to the admonition of the preceding verses. The accompanying illustration of the present ruins of the once prosperous and flourishing city of Capernaum shows how completely this prophecy has been fulfilled, and affords a memorable and melancholy evidence of the truth of Christ's words and the authority of his mission. For description of Capernaum and its probable site, see Matt. 4 : 13.

CAPERNAUM.

17 And the seventy returned again with joy, saying, Lord, even the devils are subject unto us through thy name.
18 And he said unto them, I beheld Satan ^f as lightning fall from heaven.
19 Behold, I give unto you power to tread on serpents ^g and scorpions, and over all the power of the enemy: and nothing shall by any means hurt you.
20 Notwithstanding, in this rejoice not, that the spirits are subject unto you; but rather rejoice, because your names are written ^h in heaven.
21 In that hour Jesus rejoiced in spirit, and said, I thank thee, O Father, Lord of heaven and earth, that thou hast hid these things from the wise and prudent, and hast revealed them unto babes: even so, Father, for so it seemed good in thy sight.
22 All things ^i are delivered to me of my Father: and no ^j man knoweth who the Son is, but the Father; and who the Father is, but the Son, and *he* to whom the Son will reveal *him*.
23 And he turned him unto *his* disciples, and said privately, Blessed *are* the eyes which see the things that ye see:
24 For I tell you, that ^k many prophets and kings

f Rev. 12:8, 9.... g Mark 16:18; Acts 28:5....h Exod. 32:32; Ps. 69:28; Isa. 4:3; Dan. 12:1; Phil. 4:3; Heb. 12:23; Rev. 13:8; 20:12; 21:27....i Matt. 28:18; John 3:35....j John 6:44, 46....k 1 Pet. 1:10.

16. Compare Matt. 10:40, note. There the Lord declares that receiving Christ's messengers is counted as receiving Him; here He adds that despising Christ's messengers, is accounted as despising Him—a solemnly suggestive declaration.

17-20. **The seventy returned again with joy.** There is nothing to indicate how long their mission lasted; very probably during most of Christ's Perean ministry, in which case this return, though reported here, did not take place until about the time of Christ's going up to Jerusalem, recorded in ch. 18:31.—**Even the devils are subject unto us through thy name.** This was in accordance with the promise made to the twelve (Matt. 10:8), and probably repeated substantially to the seventy.—**I beheld Satan as lightning fall from heaven.** Of this expression there are three interpretations: (1) the historical, *i. e.*, that Christ refers to the original fall of Satan when cast out of heaven (Isa. 14:12); (2) the mystical, *i. c.*, that Christ refers to a vision or intuition of the fall of Satan, he having realized, if not witnessed in a spiritual vision, the overthrow of Satan, while his disciples were casting the evil spirits out; (3) the prophetic, *i. e.*, that Jesus beheld the final overthrow of Satan (Rev. 12:9), of which the victories won by his disciples were prophecies. In either interpretation the overthrow of Satan includes the overthrow of all his works and of all the agencies which proceed from and co-operate with him. I prefer the historical interpretation. The disciples return exultant; Christ moderates their exultation, and at the same time deepens their assurance of final victory, by telling them that in the beginning he beheld Satan fall from heaven, and that they are but aiding to complete the work which God then began. We are co-workers with God (1 Cor. 3:9), and are battling against our already fallen foe. *As lightning* indicates both the brightness of the fallen angel and the suddenness of his fall; as lightning goes out in instantaneous and utter darkness, so the fallen angel of light.—**Power to tread on serpents and scorpions.** Comp. Ps. 91:13. The language is here symbolical; serpents and scorpions typify the poison and sting of sin, with all its dangerous and deadly effects. These, the result of the fall, are conquered in redemption, being put utterly under foot (Gen. 3:15) through him who makes us more than conquerors in all things (Rom. 8:37).—**Over all the power of the enemy.** Of Satan. The Christian has power over all evil, because by divine grace it becomes an instrument of good (Rom. 5:1-5). So is it literally true that *nothing shall by any means hurt you.* Comp. ch. 21:18; Rom. 8:28, notes.—**Rejoice not * * * but rather rejoice.** The Christian is not to rejoice in his own power, but rather in this, that he is the subject of redeeming love. Judas Iscariot was one of the twelve to whom power was given to cast out devils, but his name was not written in heaven. The most magnificent successes, the finest effects of eloquence, temples filled, conversions by thousands, are no cause of real spiritual joy to one who is not himself enrolled among the redeemed. The figure of a register in which the names of the redeemed are written is of frequent occurrence in the Scriptures (see marg. ref.). But note that the name may be blotted out (Exod. 32:33; Jer. 17:13; Rev. 22:19).

21, 22. Comp. Matt. 11:25-27. With Alford, "I am convinced that our Lord did utter on the two separate occasions these weighty words; and I find in them a most instructive instance of the way in which such central sayings were repeated by him." The immediate occasion of the utterance here, is Christ's realization of the fact, that to his unlearned disciples God has intrusted the revelation of that truth which is to overthrow finally the kingdom of Satan.

23, 24. Comp. Matt. 13:16, 17. What there he said to the disciples in Galilee he here repeats to another circle, not necessarily the seventy alone, in Perea. Of the *kings* who had desired to see and hear, David is the most striking example (See 2 Sam. 23:5; Ps. 42:2; 13:25, 26).

Ch. 10:25-37. PARABLE OF THE GOOD SAMARITAN. CHRIST'S METHOD OF DEALING WITH THE SELF-RIGHTEOUS.—THE CATHOLICITY OF CHRISTIAN CHARITY.—SPURIOUS SYMPATHY SHUNS SUFFERING; REAL SYMPATHY RELIEVES IT.—THE WORST HERESY IS THE WANT

have desired to see those things which ye see, and have not seen *them;* and to hear those things which ye hear, and have not heard *them.*
25 And, behold, a certain lawyer stood up, and tempted him, saying, Master, what¹ shall I do to inherit ᵐ eternal life?
26 He said unto him, What is written in the law? how readest thou?
27 And he answering said, Thouⁿ shalt love the Lord thy God with all thy heart, and with all thy soul, and with all thy strength, and with all thy mind; and thy º neighbor as thyself.
28 And he said unto him, Thou hast answered right: this do, and ᵖ thou shalt live.
29 But he, willing to justify ᵠ himself, said unto Jesus, And who is my ʳ neighbour?
30 And Jesus answering said, A certain *man* went down from Jerusalem to Jericho, and fell among thieves, which stripped him of his raiment, and wounded *him,* and departed, leaving *him* half dead.

l Acts 16 : 30, 31....m Gal. 3 : 18....n Deut 6 : 5....o Lev. 19 : 18....p Lev. 18 : 5 ; Neh. 9 : 29 ; Ezek. 20 : 11, 21 ; Rom. 10 : 5 ; Gal. 3 : 12...., q ch. 16 : 15 ; Job 32 : 2 ; Rom. 4 : 2 ; Gal. 3 : 11 ; James 2 : 24....r Matt. 5 : 43, 44.

OF LOVE; THE LOVING HERETIC IS BETTER THAN THE UNLOVING ORTHODOX.—THE CHARACTERISTICS OF TRUE CHARITY.—CHRIST'S WORD TO THE INQUIRER: GO AND DO.—REDEMPTION ILLUSTRATED.

Neither the time nor the place of this teaching is fixed by the narrative. It probably belongs to Christ's Perean ministry. It is peculiar to Luke.
25. A certain lawyer. One versed in the Jewish law, both the O. T. and the Rabbinical comments thereon. The term *theologian* would more nearly describe his character. — **And tempted him.** More properly *tried him.* The spirit of the inquirer appears to have been neither malicious nor docile, but self-confident. His language is respectful; he addresses Christ as Master, but his object was not to obtain guidance for himself, rather to measure the ability of the Nazarene Rabbi. Probably his conscience had been aroused by the preaching of Jesus, which Luke has not reported, but which everywhere included a demand for repentance. Fully recognizing the appropriateness of this preaching for the publicans and sinners, who were Christ's principal auditors, he did not entertain the idea that he needed repentance himself. Hence the question, What shall *I* do to inherit eternal life ? Christ answers him as he answered the rich young ruler (Matt. 19 : 16–22), in such a way as awakened in him a sense that he also needed to be justified (ver. 29) ; and Christ's method here, as there, is an example to the ministry in dealing with the self-righteous. A comparison of this lawyer's question with that of the rich young ruler (Luke 18 : 18), and that of the lawyer in Jerusalem (Matt. 22 : 34–40) shows how, in Christ's ministry as in the ministry of his disciples at the present day, the same experiences, expressed in almost identical language, were met with again and again.
26, 27. What is written in the law? Christ's principle of action in such cases is to throw the inquirer back upon his own moral sense, to require him to measure himself, not by any new standard of righteousness with which he is unfamiliar, but with that which his own conscience already recognizes. Each soul must be convicted by its own moral sense, not by that of another. So Christ refers this lawyer to his own understanding of the law. — **How readest thou?** If we read the law spiritually, recognizing its purpose (1 Tim. 1 : 5), we shall realize that whatever our outward life has been, we have not in spirit and in character conformed to its requirements. With Christ's question here compare his admonition in ch. 8 : 18.—**Thou shalt love the Lord thy God.** The lawyer quotes from Deut. 6 : 4, 5, and Lev. 19 : 18. Meyer supposes that the lawyer had before heard Christ refer to this summary of the law; and this is certainly possible, though not, it seems to me, probable. Among the Scribes and Pharisees there were some who entertained and taught spiritual views of the law of God, and this lawyer appears to have belonged to that class.
28. Thou hast answered right; this do, and thou shalt live. Christ dismisses him summarily, almost abruptly, makes no attempt to convict him of disobedience, throws him back upon his own consciousness. Is this reply unevangelical? Is it inconsistent with Rom. 3 : 20 ? No. He that does this shall live; he needs no evangel; they that be sick need a physician, not they that are whole; the Gospel is for those, and only for those, who are conscious that they have not done this, and still desire to enter into life. The preaching of the law here and everywhere in the N. T. is to produce conviction of sin and the sense of the need of a Saviour (Rom., ch. 7).
29. Willing to justify himself. The effect of Christ's teaching shows the result at which he aimed. The inquirer's own conscience became his accuser; he knew that he had not fulfilled this divine law. The question which followed was put to cover his confusion, by leading Christ away from the practical and personal question to one that was theoretical and measurably abstract. This second question Christ does not answer; he does not tell the lawyer who is the neighbor to whom kindness should be shown, but he depicts, in a dramatic form, an act which illustrates the law of love, and bids the inquirer measure his life by the law so interpreted.
30. A certain man. Presumably a Jew. The whole course of the narrative implies this, though it is not expressly stated.—**Went down from Jerusalem to Jericho.** He "*went,*" or "*was going down,*" because Jerusalem stood

31 And by chance there came down a certain priest that way ; and when he saw him, he passed by ᵃ on the other side.

32 And likewise a Levite, when he was at the place, came and looked ᵇ on him, and passed by on the other side.

ᵃ Ps. 38 : 11 ....ᵇ Ps. 109 : 25 ; Prov. 27 : 10.

considerably higher than Jericho—the latter lying nearly six hundred feet below the level of the Mediterranean sea, so that the language has its fitness in this respect—and because the going to Jerusalem, which was the metropolis, was always regarded as a going *up* (Acts 18 : 22). The distance between the two cities was about one hundred and fifty stadia—a little over eighteen miles ; the road lying through a desolate and rocky region ; "the wilderness that goeth up from Jericho" (Deut. 34 : 3 ; Josh. 16 : 1).—**And fell among thieves.** Rather *robbers*. The original indicates some of that class of brigands which was so numerous in Palestine in the time of Christ. The road is a narrow, dreary mountain pass, notoriously dangerous then, and equally dangerous still ; a considerable guard is always necessary in traversing this piece of road. In

ROAD TO JERICHO.

ancient times it was called the "Path of Blood." —**Which stripped him.** Not merely *of his raiment,* but of all that he had.

31, 32. And by chance. Certainly there is nothing in this language to justify the doctrine of chance ; but neither does the original imply the conjunction of two things, which "fell together, according to the omniscient designer's plan." The language is that of common life, and justifies our use of like language in describing those coincidences, which are a part of divine providence. Bengel well lays out the moral meaning in the phrase *by chance:* "Many good opportunities are hidden under that which may seem accidental."—**There came down a certain priest that way.** Jericho was a city of priests ; the chosen residence of many of them when not actually engaged in the performance of their priestly functions at the temple. Mercy was commanded by the law, even to a beast, and consideration to a neighbor (Exod. 23 : 4, 5 ; Deut. 22 : 1-4) ; in disregarding the claims of mercy, the

33 But a certain Samaritan,ᵘ as he journeyed, came where he was: and when he saw him, he had compassion ᵛ *on him*,
34 And went to *him*, and bound ʷ up his wounds, pouring in oil and wine, and set him on his own beast, and brought him to an inn, and took care of him.
35 And on the morrow when he departed, he took out two pence, and gave *them* to the host, and said unto him, Take care of him; and whatsoever thou spendest more, when I come again, I will repay ˣ thee.
36 Which now of these three, thinkest thou, was neighbour unto him that fell among the thieves?
37 And he said, He that shewed mercyʸ on him. Then said Jesus unto him, Go, and do thou likewise.

. u John 4:9....v Exod. 2:6....w Ps. 147:3; Isa. 1:6....x ch. 14:14; Prov. 19:17....y Prov. 14:21; Hosea 6:6; Micah 6:8; Matt. 23:23.

---

priest and Levite violated the law. Yet excuses were not wanting—there was danger in delay from the same or other robbers; it was not the priest's business; he was perhaps hastening to the temple service, or from it to reach Jericho before nightfall; he was unfamiliar with wounds and inapt in caring for them; the man was very likely too far gone to be recovered, and the priest would then have a useless burden on his hands. He was not without a certain common but spurious compassion; he *passed by on the other side*, *i. e.*, he had so much feeling that he was unwilling to look on the suffering which he thought that he was in no condition to cure.—**And likewise a Levite.** One of the inferior officers of the temple, who had charge of its subordinate ministries. The example of the preceding priest, his superior, might have served as a plea to satisfy his own conscience. Worse than the priest he "came and looked on him." Trouble awakened his curiosity, but it did not awaken his sympathy, or incite him to active help.

33-35. A certain Samaritan. On the history and character of the Samaritans, see notes on John, ch. 4. They were a mongrel race, partly Jewish, partly heathen, having the Bible, yet not holding to its precepts. Christ himself expressly implies his disapproval of their worship (John 4:22), and in his commission of the twelve, classes them with the Gentiles (Matt. 10:5). The Jewish prejudice against them, in which race and religious enmity combined, was not unreasonable, except as all prejudice is ever unreasonable. Christ contrasts the Samaritan with the priest and Levite, not to honor Samaria, nor to do despite to priests and Levites, but to teach that the most despised outcast who fulfills the law of love is better than the most honored minister of religion who disregards it.—He had compassion on him * * * bound up his wounds * * * set him on his own beast * * * took care of him * * * took out two pence and gave them to the host. Incidentally Christ teaches what are the manifestations and what the constituent elements of a genuine charity. The Samaritan has compassion, a feeling for and with the sufferer; his feeling leads him not to escape the sight of suffering, but to succor the sufferer; he does this not through another, but by a personal and a disagreeable service; at a real self-sacrifice, too, for he sets the wounded man on his own beast and walks himself; he enlists others; and he contributes money as well as service, and service as well as money. Oil and wine were usual remedies for wounds in the East. On Eastern *inns*, see ch. 2:7, note. This, however, was evidently something more than a caravanserai for the mere shelter of travelers, for there was a host, to whose care the wounded traveler he entrusted, and who was able to provide for him. *Two pence* (denarii) was two days' wages of a laboring man (Matt. 20:9, 10). It was therefore not an insignificant sum; moreover it was accompanied by a promise to give whatever further sum might be necessary for the wounded man's keeping.

36, 37. Became neighbor. Not *was neighbor*. By his spirit and his acts he that was a stranger became neighbor. "It is not place, but love, which makes neighborhood." — (*Wordsworth.*)—He that shewed mercy. The lawyer cannot bring himself to say "the Samaritan;" he answers by a circumlocution; yet, in doing so, announces a principle, instead of merely stating a fact.—**Go and do thou likewise.** There seems to me a significance in this command to *go*. The lawyer is not to stay questioning about the theory of religion; he is to go out and practice it wherever human need calls for human help. To all captious critics the direction of the Lord is to go and do.

The primary lesson of this parable is so plain that it cannot be missed. Whoever is in need is my neighbor. True love knows nothing of sectarian, or national, or race distinctions. Like the love of God, it shines on the evil and the good, the just and the unjust. Christ rebukes the spirit of pride which despises the Samaritan and cherishes only the Jew, the more effectively because indirectly. The second lesson has been oftener overlooked. The spirit of genuine philanthropy is a Christian spirit, wherever found. It is recognized by Christ in the Samaritan as well as in the Jew, in the Gentile Cornelius as well as in the orthodox Dorcas. It has often happened in the history of the church that its priest and its Levite have been over-busy with the affairs of ecclesiasticism, and have left the care of the afflicted or the oppressed to the despised and the heretical. In every such case, the church has cast Christ out of its own communion. The heretic, who exercises self-deny-

Ch. X.] LUKE. 67

38 Now it came to pass, as they went, that he entered into a certain village: and a certain woman, named Martha,ᵃ received him into her house.
39 And she had a sister called Mary, which also satᵇ at Jesus' feet, and heard his word.
40 But Martha was cumbered about much serving, and came to him and said, Lord, dost thou not care that my sister hath left me to serve alone? bid her therefore that she help me.
41 And Jesus answered and said unto her, Martha, Martha, thou artᵇ careful and troubled about many things:
42 But one thingᶜ is needful: and Mary hath chosen that good part, which shall not be taken away from her.

a John 11 : 1; 12 : 2, 3....a ch. 8 : 35; Acts 22 : 3....b ch. 21 : 34; Mark 4 ; 19; 1 Cor. 7 : 32, 35....c ch. 18 : 22; Ps. 27 : 4; 73 : 25; Eccles. 12 : 13; Mark 8 : 36; 1 Cor. 13 : 3.

ing charity, is more Christian than the ministers of the temple who refuse. The third lesson is more doubtful. I do not think that this can properly be regarded as a parable of redemption. Certainly its primary object was not to teach God's redeeming love. Yet it is not without significance that it does illustrate that love so notably. Without altogether endorsing, I copy Alford's parabolic interpretation of it: "All acts of charity and mercy done here below, are but fragments and derivatives of *that one great act of mercy* which the Saviour came on earth to perform. And as he took on him the nature of us all, being 'not ashamed to call us brethren,' counting us all his kindred,—so it is but natural that in holding up a mirror (for such is a parable) of the truth in this matter of duty, we should see in it not only the present and prominent group, but also himself and his act of mercy behind. And thus we shall not give up the interpretation of the Fathers and other divines, who see in this poor traveler, going from the heavenly to the accursed city (Josh. 6 : 26 ; 1 Kings 16 : 34),—*the race of man, the Adam who fell;*—in the robbers and murderers, *him who was a murderer from the beginning* (John 8 : 44); in the treatment of the traveler, the deep wounds and despoilment which we have inherited from the fall;—in the priest and the Levite passing by, the inefficacy of the law and sacrifice to heal and clothe us (Gal. 3 : 21):—in the good Samaritan, him of whom it was lately said, "Say we not well that *thou art a Samaritan*, and hast a devil?" (John 8 . 48)—who came to *bind up the brokenhearted*, to give them the *oil of joy for mourning* (Isa. 61 : 1–3.); who *for our sakes became poor, that we through his poverty might become rich;* who, though now gone from us, has left with us precious gifts, and charged his ministers to feed his lambs, promising them, when the chief Shepherd shall appear, a crown of glory that fadeth not away (1 Peter 5 : 2, 4)."

Ch. 10 : 38-42. JESUS AT THE HOUSE OF MARTHA AND MARY. MUCH CARE, LITTLE COMFORT. — TO RECEIVE FROM CHRIST IS THE BEST SERVICE TO CHRIST.

There can be no reasonable question that the Martha and Mary mentioned in this incident are the sisters of Lazarus, and that the village is Bethany, though Bengel supposes they are not the sisters of Lazarus, and Greswell that they had another residence in Galilee. There is nothing in the language here to determine the time of this incident; but I think it more probable that it belongs in the Judean than in the Perean ministry. Wearied with his perpetual conflicts with the priests and Pharisees in the temple, Christ found in the quiet and docile listener far sweeter rest and refreshment than in the provision for his physical wants made by the more active sister. *As they went*, *i. e.*, in their journeying, implies that this occurred at some time in Christ's itinerant ministry; but it may have been either as he was going up to Jerusalem, or as he was leaving it. For the facts known respecting this family, see notes on John, ch. 11.

38, 39. Martha received him into her house. The indication here, and in John, chaps. 11, 12 : 1-9, is that Martha was the head of the household, and therefore probably the elder sister. Simon, perhaps the father, or possibly the husband, was a leper (Matt. 26 : 6), and either dead or absent. — **Who also sat at Jesus' feet.** Both sisters were disciples of Christ; both in this incident served him—one by preparing for him a great supper, the other by listening to and receiving with gladness his instructions. Comp. John 11 : 5. This fact is important; the failure to note it has led to a frequent misinterpretation of this incident. See below.

40. But Martha was cumbered about much serving. Literally, *was drawn off*. That is, her attention was drawn off from the presence of her Lord by her very anxiety to prepare for him a worthy entertainment.—**Dost thou not care that my sister hath left me to serve alone?** To Martha, this seemed selfishness. She could not comprehend her sister's absorption in the truth and the Teacher. The active may be understood by the meditative; but the meditative are always an enigma to the active. With Martha's conduct here compare the indication of her character in John 11 : 20, and John 12 : 2.

41, 42. Martha, Martha. This repetition of the name gives solemnity to Christ's language, fixes the attention of the listener, and implies rebuke, or at least admonition.—**Thou art careful and troubled.** To be careful ($\mu\varepsilon\rho\iota\mu\nu\acute{\alpha}\omega$), is to be divided in mind between the claims of the spiritual and the earthly (see Matt. 6 : 25, note); to be *troubled*, is to be roiled, stirred up, agitated; the opposite of peaceful. The first

CHAPTER XI.

AND it came to pass, that as he was praying in a certain place, when he ceased, one of his disciples said unto him, Lord, teach us to pray, as John also taught his disciples.
2 And he said unto them, When ye pray, say, Our ᵈ Father which art in heaven, Hallowed be thy name.

d Matt. 6: 9, etc.

word, *careful*, implies the cause, the second, *troubled*, the result. A mind divided between concern respecting the inward and the outer life, is always perturbed, never knowing the perfect peace of the mind that is stayed on God. Christ does not rebuke Martha for serving, but for being careful and troubled about *much* serving; and he does not chide her till she asks him to chide her sister.—And one thing is needful. As in so many other instances, these words of Christ have a twofold meaning. Primarily, there was no need of the *much* serving; Christ did not care for bodily indulgence; simple food, a single dish, what was necessary for physical support, was all-sufficient for him. But, secondly, one thing only is essential, viz., that bread of life which Christ alone can give, and which Mary was solicitous to receive. These interpretations are not inconsistent; the one is dependent on the other. It is because spiritual good is the one thing needful, that simple provision for the body suffices, and that much serving is needless.
In studying this incident observe, (1.) Both Martha and Mary were disciples of Christ. They represent not the contrast between the follower of Christ and the follower of the world, but between different types of piety in the church. (2.) Martha's much serving was for her Lord. She desired to prepare a worthy entertainment, one worthy as an offering to him and worthy as a manifestation of her own hospitality. Love and pride combined to prompt her activity. (3.) A social lesson lies on the surface of the incident. *Much* serving is not the *best* serving. The housekeeper is not always a homekeeper. Less supper and more host, rather than less host and more supper, give the best entertainment. (4.) The religious lesson is one pre-eminently needed in our era. Not he who *works* most for Christ, but he who *receives* most from Christ, serves him best. To sit at his feet and learn, is always more acceptable than to be careful and troubled about much serving. (5.) Both types, the meditative and the active, are needed in the church; both are combined in the well-developed character. Christ did much serving, going about doing good, ministering to the body as well as to the soul; but he also sought opportunities for retirement, solitude, and communion with God.

Ch. 11: 1-36. VARIOUS TEACHINGS OF OUR LORD.—THE SPIRIT OF PRAYER ILLUSTRATED.—THE PRIVILEGE OF INTERCESSORY PRAYER.—THE DUTY OF IMPORTUNITY IN PRAYER. — THE PROMISE TO PRAYER. — THE EVIDENCE OF CHRISTIANITY IN THE MANIFEST POWER OF CHRIST.—THE FIRST INSTANCE OF MARIOLATRY AND CHRIST'S TREATMENT OF IT.—THE VALUE OF A CHEERFUL RELIGION.

1-4. As he was praying in a certain place. The time and place are wholly unknown. The greater part of this chapter contains teachings given probably at various times, and presented here out of their connection. The Lord's prayer is reported in two different forms by Matthew and Luke. It is not reported by the other Evangelists. Alford supposes that Christ had once given it to his disciples in the Sermon on the Mount; that he was subsequently asked by them to teach them to pray, and that he then repeated substantially the form of prayer previously given. The more general, and it appears to me the better opinion, is that the prayer was given in the first instance in response to a request; that it was given not as a form but as an embodiment of the spirit of all true prayer; and that Matthew inserted it in the Sermon on the Mount, because cognate to the instructions there given.

For convenience of the student, I place here, in parallel columns, the three forms of the prayer in common use. Those of Matthew, of Luke, and of the Episcopal prayer-book. That of the latter differs from the gospels in phraseology because taken not from the King James' version, but from the earlier Cranmer's Bible.

MATTHEW 6: 9-13.	LUKE 11: 2-4.	PRAYER BOOK.
Our Father which art in heaven, Hallowed be thy name. Thy kingdom come. Thy will be done in earth, as it is in heaven. Give us this day our daily bread. And forgive us our debts, as we forgive our debtors. And lead us not into temptation, but deliver us from evil: For thine is the kingdom, and the power, and the glory, for ever. Amen.	Our Father which art in heaven, Hallowed be thy name. Thy kingdom come. Thy will be done, as in heaven, so in earth. Give us day by day our daily bread. And forgive us our sins; for we also forgive every one that is indebted to us. And lead us not into temptation: but deliver us from evil.	Our Father who art in heaven, Hallowed be thy name. Thy kingdom come. Thy will be done on earth as it is in heaven. Give us this day our daily bread. And forgive us our trespasses, as we forgive those who trespass against us. And lead us not into temptation; but deliver us from evil: For thine is the kingdom, and the power, and the glory, for ever and ever. Amen.

CH. XI.] LUKE. 69

Thy kingdom come. Thy will be done, as in heaven, so in earth.
3 Give us day by day our daily bread.
4 And forgive us our sins; for ᵉ we also forgive every one that is indebted to us. And lead us not into temptation; but deliver us from evil.
5 And he said unto them, Which of you shall have a friend, and shall go unto him at midnight, and say unto him, Friend, lend me three loaves;
6 For a friend of mine in his journey is come to me, and I have nothing to set before him?
7 And he from within shall answer and say, Trouble me not: the door is now shut, and my children are with me in bed; I cannot rise and give thee.
8 I say unto you, Though he will not rise and give him because he is his friend, yet because of his importunity ᶠ he will rise and give him as many as he needeth.

9 And I say unto you, Ask,ᵍ and it shall be given you; seek, and ye shall find; knock, and it shall be opened unto you.
10 For every one that asketh receiveth; and he that seeketh findeth; and to him that knocketh it shall be opened.
11 If a son shall ask bread of any of you that is a father, will he give him a stone? or if *he ask* a fish, will he for a fish give him a serpent?
12 Or if he shall ask an egg, will he offer him a scorpion?
13 If ye then, being evil, know how to give good gifts unto your children; how much more shall *your* heavenly Father give the Holy Spirit to them that ask him?
14 And ʰ he was casting out a devil, and it was dumb. And it came to pass, when the devil was gone out, the dumb spake; and the people wondered.

e Mark 11 : 25, 26....f ch. 18 : 1-8....g Matt. 7 : 7; 21 : 22; John 15 : 7; James 1 : 5; 1 John 3 : 22....h Matt. 9 : 32; 12 : 22, etc.

For notes on the Lord's Prayer, see Matt. 6 : 9-13. *Forgive us our sins*, includes less than the phrase in Matthew, *Forgive us our debts*. The one implies only positive transgressions, the other all unfulfilled obligations. *For we also forgive every one that is indebted to us*, implies more distinctly than the language in Matthew, that prayer can be only acceptably offered to God by one who is living in allegiance to that law of love which is the law of God. The doxology in Matthew was probably added when the prayer came into liturgical use in the church, but certainly at an early date.

5-8. **Friend, lend me three loaves.** For description and illustration of the Jewish loaf see Mark 8 : 3-5, notes. Is there a hint of the largeness permitted to us in prayer? He asks one loaf for himself, one for his friend, the third for a reserve.—**I have nothing to set before him.** A suggestion of the truth, that as we have nothing wherewith to pay our debts to God (ch. 7 : 42) so nothing wherewith to supply the deeper wants of others. The bread of life, which we would impart, we must first ourselves receive (Matt. 14 : 19).—**Trouble me not * * * I cannot rise and give thee.** *Cannot* is equivalent to *will not*. The features in this picture have no allegorical significance; there is no reluctance on the part of the Heavenly Father to give to those that need (Matt. 6 : 8; Ephes. 3 : 20).—**Importunity.** Literally, *impudence*. The parable implies that the petitioner, notwithstanding the refusal, continues knocking and asking.

This parable must be read in the light of the customs of the East, where inns are exceptional, and where travelers are dependent upon hospitality. It illustrates intercessory prayer; the request being preferred by one, not for himself but for another, whose need he feels but is unable to supply. Like the parable of the unjust judge, Christ here employs the lower to illustrate the higher. If a selfish and indolent man, who will not rise from his bed for the sake of benevolence, will yield to importunity, and that the importunity which approximates impudence, much more will God, from sympathy and benevolence, yield to the importunity of his children when inspired by spiritual earnestness. There is nothing in this teaching inconsistent with Matt. 6 : 7; for repetitions that spring from intensity of feeling are not "vain repetitions" (Matt. 26 : 44). If the delay of a divine answer to prayer could be attributed to God's disapproval of our request, importunity would be impertinent; but when the delay is caused by our unreadiness to receive, importunity becomes a necessary condition of the grant. Importunity for spiritual blessings is never impertinent; as the urgency of a child for a mother's aid in learning to read; or the urgency of the child of God to receive the gift of the Holy Ghost (ver. 13). With the lesson of this parable, comp. Gen. 32 : 28; Ps. 55 : 17; 1 Thess. 3 : 10; 5 : 17; 1 Tim. 5 : 5; 2 Tim. 1 : 3.

9-13. These verses correspond with Matt. 7 : 7-11. I have shown there that they clearly belong to the Sermon on the Mount, of which they form an integral part; it seems to me irrational to suppose that Matthew borrowed and incorporated them there; and improbable that Luke borrowed and incorporated them here. More probably they were twice uttered by Christ on different occasions, and in different connections. Verse 12 is peculiar to Luke. Scorpions are a pest in Palestine, well known by every traveler, who often finds them under his pillow, inside his dress, or wakes to find them crawling over his face or hands. The natives build a ring of fire with dry grass around the scorpion, when in despair it stings itself and dies. The white body resembles an *egg*. Alford notes that the *serpent* and the *scorpion* are positively mischievous. When we ask for good, God will not give us evil; we often ask for evil, and God gives us good. In Matthew the promise is, that the Heavenly Father will give *good things;* in Luke, that he will give the *Holy Spirit, i. e.,* Himself (Ephes. 3 : 16-19). This gift of himself necessarily carries with it the gift of all good things;

15 But some of them said, He casteth out devils through Beelzebub the chief of the devils.
16 And others, tempting *him*,¹ sought of him a sign from heaven.
17 But he, knowing ʲ their thoughts, said unto them, Every ᵏ kingdom divided against itself is brought to desolation ; and a house *divided* against a house falleth.
18 If Satan also be divided against himself, how shall his kingdom stand? because ye say that I cast out devils through Beelzebub.
19 And if I by Beelzebub cast out devils, by whom do your sons cast *them* out? therefore shall they be your judges.
20 But if I with the finger ˡ of God cast out devils, no doubt the kingdom of God is come upon you.
21 When a strong man armed keepeth his palace, his goods are in peace :
22 But when a stronger ᵐ than he shall come upon him, and overcome him, he taketh from him all his armour wherein he trusted, and divideth his spoils.
23 He that is not with me is against me: and he that gathereth not with me scattereth.
24 When the unclean spirit is gone out of a man, he walketh through dry places, seeking rest ; and finding none, he saith, I will return unto my house whence I came out.
25 And when he cometh, he findeth *it* swept and garnished.
26 Then goeth he, and taketh *to him* seven other spirits more wicked than himself; and they enter in, and dwell there; and the last *state* of that man is worse ⁿ than the first.
27 And it came to pass, as he spake these things, a certain woman of the company lifted up her voice, and said unto him, Blessed º *is* the womb that bare thee, and the paps which thou hast sucked.
28 But he said, Yea, rather blessed ᵖ *are* they that hear the word of God, and keep it.
29 And when the people were gathered thick together, he began to say, This is an evil generation: they seek a sign ; and ᵠ there shall no sign be given it, but the sign of Jonas the prophet.
30 For as Jonas ʳ was a sign unto the Ninevites, so shall also the Son of man be to this generation.
31 The queen ˢ of the south shall rise up in the judgment with the men of this generation, and condemn them : for she came from the utmost parts of the earth to hear the wisdom of Solomon ; and, behold, a greater than Solomon *is* here.
32 The men of Nineve shall rise up in the judgment with this generation, and shall condemn it : for ᵗ they repented at the preaching of Jonas ; and, behold, a greater than Jonas *is* here.
33 No ᵘ man, when he hath lighted a candle, putteth *it* in a secret place, neither under a bushel, but on a candlestick, that they which come in may see the light.
34 The ᵛ light of the body is the eye : therefore when thine eye is single, thy whole body also is full of light ; but when *thine eye* is evil,ʷ thy body also *is* full of darkness.
35 Take heed, therefore, that the light which is in thee be not darkness.
36 If thy whole body therefore *be* full of light,ˣ having no part dark, the whole shall be full of light, as when the bright shining ʸ of a candle doth give thee light.

---

i Matt. 12 : 38 ; 16 : 1....j John 2 : 25....k Matt. 12 : 25 ; Mark 3 : 24.. .l Exod. 8 : 19....m Isa. 53 - 12 ; Col. 2 : 15....n John 5 : 14 ; Heb. 6 : 4 ; 10 : 26, 27 ; 2 Pet. 2 : 20, 21....o ch. 1 : 28, 48....p ch. 8 : 21 ; Ps. 119 : 1, 2 ; Matt. 7 : 21 ; James 1 : 25....q Matt. 12 : 40, etc. ; Mark 8 : 12....r Jonah 1 : 17 ; 2 : 10...s 1 Kings 10 : 1, etc....t Jonah 3 : 5, 10....u ch. 8 : 16 ; Matt. 5 : 15, etc. ; Mark 4 : 21....v Matt. 6 : 22, etc ....w Prov. 28 : 22 ; Mark 7 : 22....x Ps. 119 : 105; Prov. 6 : 23 ; Isa. 8 : 20 ; 2 Cor. 4 : 6....y Prov. 4 : 18 ; 20 : 27.

---

if we are children of God, we are also his heirs. (ch. 15 : 31 ; Rom. 8 : 17, 32 ; 1 Cor. 3 : 21-23.)

THE SCORPION.

14-26. Parallel to these verses is Matt. 12 : 22-29 ; 43-45. See notes there. The phraseology is almost identical, except in the parabolic illustration of vers. 21, 22 (comp. Matt. 12 : 29), where the difference is only verbal. According to Matthew's report, the possessed was both dumb and blind ; the people, amazed at the cure, ask, Is not this the son of David ? the complaints come from the Pharisees ; the demand for a sign from heaven (ver. 16) is made in connection with the discourse on Jonah (vers. 29-32). The *finger of God*

in ver. 20, is equivalent to the *Spirit of God* in Matt. 12 : 28. It implies the ease with which God subdues the powers of evil. I have no doubt that this discourse was given in Galilee at the time indicated by Matthew, and is reported by Luke out of its chronological order; the hypothesis of two such discourses, at different times and places, seems to me unnecessary and improbable.

27, 28. Peculiar to Luke. Analogous in its teaching is the incident in Matt. 12 : 46-50. This unspiritual and unintelligent admiration of the wonderful healer and teacher, is the first instance of that spirit of Mariolatry which crept into and corrupted the later church, and which to-day in the city of Rome, and in many Roman Catholic countries, places the Virgin Mary above the Son whom she bore. Christ's reply affords the divine corrective to this most subtle form of hero-worship. An honor is reflected upon Mary by the divine choice of her to be the Lord's mother ; but he is blessed, not because she bore and nursed him, but because she believed (ch. 1 : 45), and this blessedness belongs to all who accept and keep the word of God.

29-32. Comp. Matt. 12 : 39-42. See notes there. The discourse is in answer to the demand reported here in ver. 16. Luke alone tells us that it was delivered before the people when gathered "thick together." Jonah was a sign unto the Ninevites because the judgment and the

37 And as he spake, a certain Pharisee besought him to dine with him: and he went in, and sat down to meat.
38 And ᵃ when the Pharisee saw *it*, he marvelled that he had not first washed before dinner.
39 And the Lord said unto him, Now do ᵃ ye Pharisees make clean the outside of the cup and the platter;
but ᵇ your inward part is full of ravening and wickedness.
40 *Ye* fools, did not he that made that which is without make that which is within also?
41 But ᶜ rather give alms of such things as ye have; and, behold, all things are clean unto you.
42 But woe ᵈ unto you, Pharisees! for ye tithe the mint

a Mark 7 : 3 .... a Matt. 23 : 25, ... b Titus 1 : 15 .... c ch. 12 : 33 ; Isa. 58 : 7 .... d Matt. 23 : 23, 27.

deliverance which he had experienced was, at least, in part the theme of his preaching. 33-36. These aphorisms are repeated from the Sermon on the Mount. Comp. Matt. 5 : 15 ; 6 : 22, 23. See notes there. Ver. 36 is peculiar to Luke. Dr. Howard Crosby has suggested to me an interpretation of this passage, different from that which I have given in Matthew. It is certainly original and striking. It accords with the Greek, and is sustained by ver. 36 here. He renders the word light ($\varphi\tilde{\omega}\varsigma$) as equivalent to *radiance*, and the word darkness ($\sigma\kappa\acute{o}\tau o \varsigma$) as equivalent to *gloom*. We have then the declaration : "The eye gives radiance to the face and person—when the eye is dark the whole person is gloomy and forbidding ; so if the religion within us be one of gloom and darkness, our whole life and influence will be repellent ; but if thy whole body (nature) be full of radiance (a religion of hope and love), having no part dark, the whole (life and influence) shall be full of radiance, as when the bright shining of a candle doth give thee light."

Ch. 11 : 37-54. DISCOURSE AGAINST THE PHARISEES. See Matt., ch. 23.

The sentiments of this discourse, and in many respects the language, correspond with Christ's denunciation of the Pharisees in the temple at Jerusalem, reported in Matt., ch. 23. We must suppose either, (1) that Christ delivered no such discourse as is there reported, but that Matthew gathered up various denunciations of the Pharisees by our Lord, wove them into one discourse, and gave it a place at that period in Christ's ministry ; or, (2) that Luke was mistaken as to the time and occasion of Christ's utterance of the sentiments here reported, and borrowed them from the temple discourse, given in Matthew ; or, (3) that Christ repeated the same substantial denunciations, and in similar language, at different times and on different occasions. Either of the first two hypotheses is utterly inconsistent with the historical verity of the Gospels, for the case is not one in which either of the Evangelists leaves the occasion uncertain, and in which we may suppose that they have presented in different forms reports of the same discourse. The third hypothesis is entirely rational. It accords with the practice of other teachers, both religious and secular ; and with the practice of Christ, as indicated by the repetition of the same aphorisms at different times. In the study of this passage compare the notes on Matt., ch. 23, where I have treated the matters at length ; here I refer only to what is peculiar to Luke.

37, 38. Christ, who was the guest of publicans and sinners, did not refuse invitations from Pharisees. He went into any company willing to receive him, but made every social gathering an occasion for religious instruction. "This meal, as also that in John 21 : 12-15, was not what we now understand by *dinner*, an afternoon meal, but the first meal of the day, the breakfast or *dejeuner*, in the prime of the morning."—(*Alford*.) On the ceremonial washing practised by the Pharisees, see Mark 7 : 2-5, notes. The word *washed* here is *baptizo* ($\beta\alpha\pi\tau\acute{\iota}\zeta\omega$), an indication that that word does not always signify in N. T. usage complete submersion, for only the hands and feet were washed before meals. Still, the hands of those who had gone abroad were required to be immersed ; the pouring on of water in such case was not sufficient.

39, 40. See Matt. 23 : 25, 26, note. There Christ declares that cleansing that which is within, makes clean that which is without ; here, that if a real reverence for God induced the ceremonial scrupulousness of the Pharisees they would also be spiritually scrupulous, since the same God made both soul and body. The term *fool* is literally *thoughtless ones*. It is a different word from that used in Matt. 5 : 22, and does not imply bitterness or contempt.

41. But rather give in compassion those things which are within, and behold all things are clean unto you. This verse is peculiar to Luke. There is some difficulty about the proper interpretation, which is relieved by noting the exact significance of the original, as I have given it. Christ says not, *give alms*, the outward gift, but *give compassion* ($\check{\epsilon}\lambda\epsilon\eta\mu o\sigma\acute{\nu}\nu\eta$), the inward feeling ; he says not *of such things as ye have*, but *those things which are within* ($\tau\grave{\alpha}$ $\check{\epsilon}\nu\acute{o}\nu\tau\alpha$) ; thus he does not make mere alms-giving an atonement and reparation for sin, but he declares that works of mercy out of a sincere heart are a condition of true spiritual cleansing. Comp. Hosea 6 : 6 ; Isa. 58 : 6-8. Speaking to the Pharisees, who were covetous (ch. 16 : 14), he declares that a genuine compassion, bestowed on the needy, from within, is more cleansing to the soul in God's sight, than purification and lustration, or than

and rue and all manner of herbs, and pass over judgment and the love of God: these ought ye to have done, and not to leave the other undone.

43 Woe unto you, Pharisees! for ᵉ ye love the uppermost seats in the synagogues, and greetings in the markets.

44 Woe unto you, scribes and Pharisees, hypocrites! for ye are as ᶠ graves which appear not, and the men that walk over *them* are not aware *of them*.

45 Then answered one of the lawyers, and said unto him, Master, thus saying thou reproachest us also.

46 And he said, Woe unto you also, *ye* lawyers! for ye lade men with burdens grievous to be borne, and ye yourselves touch not the burdens ᵍ with one of your fingers.

47 Woe unto you! for ye build the sepulchres of the prophets, and your fathers killed them.

48 Truly ye bear witness that ye allow ʰ the deeds of your fathers: for they indeed killed them,ⁱ and ye build their sepulchres.

49 Therefore also said the wisdom of God, I will send them prophets and apostles, and *some* of them they shall slay and persecute:

50 That the blood of all the prophets, which was

---

e Matt. 23 : 6; Mark 12 : 38....f Ps. 5 : 9....g Isa. 58 : 6....h Ezek. 18 : 19....i Heb. 11 : 35, 37.

---

scrupulosity in giving tithes, down to the minor garden herbs. The rendering of our English version accords far better with Pharisaic than with Christian teaching, since it implies that alms-giving compensates for all vices. The ironical rendering, given by some commentators, *Ye give alms* * * * *and* (think) *all things are clean unto you,* hardly accords with the original.

42. See Matt. 23 : 23, note.

43. See Matt. 23 : 6, 7, note. The accompanying illustration, from a drawing by Mr. Rawson, shows the "uppermost seats." These are to the

THE SYNAGOGUE. SHOWING UPPERMOST SEATS.

present day hired for the Sabbath by their occupants. The price puts them beyond the reach of a poor man. The reader also pays for the privilege of holding the Roll of the Law.

44. See Matt. 23 : 27, note.

45. This interruption is peculiar to Luke, and with vers. 37, 38, indicates clearly that the discourse is one different from that reported in Matthew. The *lawyer* is not an advocate but a theologian, whose special province was the interpretation of the Mosaic law and the Rabbinical precepts.

46. See Matt. 23 : 4, note. The metaphor is taken from the custom of porterage in the East, where men often do the work done by beasts of burden with us. An Eastern porter will often carry a barrel of flour or a bale of cotton, as shown in the accompanying illustration.

CH. XI.] LUKE. 73

shed from the foundation of the world, may be required [j] of this generation;
51 From the blood of Abel [k] unto the blood of Zacharias,[l] which perished between the altar and the temple: verily I say unto you, It shall be required of this generation.[m]
52 Woe unto you, lawyers! for ye have taken away the key of knowledge: [n] ye entered not in yourselves, and them that were entering in ye hindered.
53 And as he said these things unto them, the scribes and the Pharisees began to urge *him* vehemently, and to provoke [o] him to speak of many things:
54 Laying wait for him, and [p] seeking to catch something out of his mouth, that they might accuse him.

j Exod. 20 ; 5 ; Jer. 51 : 56....k Gen. 4 : 8....l 2 Chron. 24 : 20....m Jer. 7 : 28, 29....n Mal. 2 : 7....o 1 Cor. 13 : 5....p Mark 12 : 13.

47, 48. Comp. Matt. 23 : 29, 30, notes; observe, however, that there is a marked difference between the language there and here. The fact that the present generation builds the sepulchres of the prophets, is alleged here as an evidence that it approves their murder; and the difficulty thus presented is not met by such an explanation as that of Adam Clarke, that the Jews were about to show by their persecution of Christ and

AN EASTERN PORTER.

the apostles that they were worthy sons of such fathers; for though this is true, this is not what Christ says; nor by such an explanation as that of Stier, "Instead of the penitent confession we have sinned, we and our fathers, this last and worst generation in vain protests against their participation in their fathers' guilt, which they are meanwhile developing to the utmost;" for although this is also true, this is not what Christ says. *The building of the sepulchres of the prophets* he charges upon the lawyers as a crime, and as a continuation of and participation in the murder of the prophets. I understand his meaning then to be this, Your fathers killed the prophets, you are burying them out of sight; by your interpretatious and Rabbinical additions and qualifications, making the word of God of none effect, through your traditions (Mark 7 : 13), you are building their sepulchres; so you are doing what the fathers did. They silenced the prophets by violence, you by your teachings. This interpretation accords with ver. 52, and with the actual facts; for, as in the mediæval ages, the Romish church buried the Bible beneath its legends and traditions, which they pretended to rear to its honor, so in the time of Christ the lawyers took the Bible away from the common people; the Talmud was a sepulchre reared above the buried Word of God. Wherever the teacher covers and conceals the Scripture by human tradition, creed or philosophy, he is guilty of the crime here charged by Christ upon the lawyers.

49-51. See Matt. 23 : 34, 35, notes.

52. See Matt. 23 : 13, note. The phraseology there is different, but the meaning is the same. *Knowledge* of the truth is represented as the key to the kingdom of heaven; *knowledge*, not mere emotion, but this is not the knowledge of worldly wisdom, but of spiritual apprehension, the product of humility and docility. See chaps. 10 : 21; 11 : 28; 1 Cor. 2 : 6-12. The scribes and lawyers had taught a kind of knowledge; but they had not themselves and they deprived the people of spiritual apprehension of the truth.

53, 54. Peculiar to Luke. Their spirit, and the character of their questionings, are illustrated by Christ's experiences in the temple at Jerusalem, as recorded in Matt., ch. 22, and in John, chaps. 8, 10.

Ch. 12 : 1-12. WARNING AGAINST HYPOCRISY. THE FOLLY OF AND THE REMEDY FOR HYPOCRISY.

This passage, which is intimately connected with the preceding discourse, is composed of aphorisms, nearly all of which are found verbatim in Matthew. They here form a continuous discourse, inconsistent with the hypothesis that they have been brought together by Luke from other teachings at other times. Christ had before been speaking to the scribes and Pharisees, his adversaries; he now turns and addresses his disciples—not the twelve merely, but all who

CHAPTER XII.

IN ᵍ the mean time, when there were gathered together an innumerable multitude of people, insomuch that they trode one upon another, he began to say unto his disciples first of all, Beware ye of the leaven of the Pharisees, which is hypocrisy.

2 For ʳ there is nothing covered, that shall not be revealed; neither hid, that shall not be known.

3 Therefore whatsoever ye have spoken in darkness shall be heard in the light; and that which ye have spoken in the ear in closets shall be proclaimed upon the housetops.

4 And I say unto you my ˢ friends,ᵗ Be not afraid of them that kill the body, and after that have no more that they can do.

5 But I will forewarn you whom ye shall fear: Fear him, which after he hath killed hath power to cast into hell · yea, I say unto you, Fear him.

6 Are not five sparrows sold for two farthings, and not one of them is forgotten before God?

7 But even the very hairs of your head are all numbered. Fear not therefore: ye are of more value than many sparrows.

8 Also I say unto you,ᵘ Whosoever shall confess me before men, him shall the Son of God also confess ᵛ before the angels of God:

---

q Matt. 16 : 6, etc.; Mark 8 : 15, etc.... r ch. 8 : 17; Matt. 10 : 26; Mark 4 : 22....s John 15 : 14....t Isa. 51 : 7-13; Matt. 10 : 28, etc....
u 1 Sam. 2 : 30; Ps. 119 : 46; 2 Tim. 2 : 12; Rev. 2 : 10....v Jude 24.

---

are willing to learn of him. The connection of the discourse may be indicated as follows: The Christian must make it his first care to guard against hypocrisy (ver. 1), which is always in vain (ver. 2); and against concealment of the truth (ver. 3), the cause of which, ungodly fear, is corrected by the fear of God (vers. 4, 5), and by trust in God (vers. 6, 7), whom the disciples must publicly confess (ver. 8); to deny him (ver. 9), still more to attribute his works to the evil one (ver. 10), involves divine condemnation. In making this confession trust not to prudent preparation, but to the inspiration of the Holy Ghost (vers. 11, 12).

1. **Insomuch that they trod one upon another.** One of the many indications of the popularity of Christ as a preacher. Comp. Mark 1 : 33; 2 : 2; 3 : 9; 6 : 31, etc.—**First of all.** This belongs with the following, not with the preceding clause: *Beware ye first of all of the leaven.* Hypocrisy is the greatest danger which threatens the Christian, the one most to be guarded against. On the warning, see Matt. 16 : 6.

2-5. See notes on Matt. 10 : 26-28. The flat housetop is the resort of the inmates, and the place where many household operations are carried on in Eastern cities, where the streets are narrow and private yards and gardens are but a few feet square. It is also the most con-

THE EASTERN HOUSETOP.

spicuous, and therefore a usual place for the promulgation of any news, public or private. People in the streets below and on all the neighboring housetops compose an audience. The roof is ordinarily enclosed with a low parapet of masonry or a higher one of lattice-work, as in the accompanying illustration. Vines are often trained for shade, or in their absence matting is used. Sleeping on the housetop in dry weather is a common custom. — **Fear him.** That is, God, not Satan.

6-9. See Matt. 10 : 29-33. Little birds (sparrows, white-throats, and others) are sold in the market in the Eastern cities at the present day, in bunches of five or more. When very plenty, two farthings a bunch would be an adequate price. In Matt. 10 : 29 it is said that two sparrows are sold for a farthing. Here, in accordance

CH. XII.] LUKE. 75

9 But he that denieth ʷ me before men shall be denied before the angels ˣ of God.
10 And whosoever shall speak a word against the Son of man, it shall be forgiven him; but unto him that blasphemeth against the Holy Ghost it shall not ʸ be forgiven.
11 And when they bring you unto the synagogues, and unto magistrates, and powers, take ᶻ ye no thought how or what thing ye shall answer, or what ye shall say:

12 For the Holy Ghost shall teach ᵃ you in the same hour what ye ought to say.
13 And one of the company said unto him, Master, speak to my brother, that he divide the inheritance with me.ᵇ
14 And he said unto him, Man,ᶜ who made me a judge or a divider over you?
15 And he said unto them, Take heed, and beware of covetousness: ᵈ for a man's life ᵉ consisteth not in the abundance of the things which he possesseth.

w Acts 3 : 13, 14; Rev. 3 : 8....x Matt. 25 : 31... y Matt. 12 : 31 ; 1 John 5 : 16....z ch. 21 : 14; Matt. 10 : 19 ; Mark 13 : 11....a Acts 6 : 10 Acts, ch. 26....b Ezek. 33 : 31....c John 18 : 35....d 1 Tim. 6 : 7-10....e Job v : 4 ; Matt. 6 : 25.

with the custom still universal in the East of throwing in something extra in consideration of a larger purchase, there are five for two farthings. Sparrows are caught for market mostly by chil-

SPARROWS IN MARKET.

dren, by means of little cages with a door which closes with a spring, or by twigs besmeared with bird-lime. They bring the lowest price of any game, and were the smallest living creatures offered in sacrifice under the Mosaic dispensation. It was the cleansed leper, usually reduced by his separation to great poverty, who was permitted to bring this small offering (Lev. 14 : 4). The accompanying illustration of a sparrow vendor is from an original sketch by Mr. Rawson.—**The very hairs of your head.** They have been estimated to number 140,000.
10. See Matt. 12 : 31, 32, notes.
11, 12. See Matt. 10 : 19, 20, notes.

Ch. 12 : 13-21. THE PARABLE OF THE RICH FOOL. THE OFFICE OF CHRIST AND THE CHURCH NOT TO JUDGE, BUT TO TEACH.—THE SUBTLE DANGER OF COVETOUSNESS.—TRUE AND FALSE RICHES.—THE THREE FOLLIES OF THE WEALTH-SEEKER : HE HOARDS INSTEAD OF USING ; HE ANTICIPATES LIFE, BUT NOT DEATH ; HE THINKS TO SATISFY THE SOUL WITHOUT SOUL-FOOD.

Peculiar to Luke. Time and place uncertain.

The instructions which follow (vers. 22-59) are most of them not peculiar to Luke. The connection is, however, so intimate as to justify the presumption that in this, as in many other cases, Christ repeated substantially the same instructions previously given on different occasions and in different connections.

13, 14. There has been some unprofitable discussion whether this man's claim was just or not. There is nothing to indicate that even Christ knew. Covetousness may be indicated by an inappropriate as well as by an unjust claim. The man perceives Christ's moral power over men, and proposes to use it for his own personal benefit. It is this attempt to use Christ for a personal and pecuniary benefit which he rebukes. The fault, in a different form, is common in our own day. "We cannot cast the first stone at this poor simpleton, who had no other use for the Redeemer's word than to gain by means of it a few more acres of the earth for himself; in every age some men may be found who hang on the skirts of the church for the sake of some immediate temporal benefit."—(*Arnot.*) Christ's reply is that it is not his business, and therefore impliedly not the business of the church, to undertake the settlement of personal secular disputes. The attempt to do this in the middle ages brought corruption within and oppression without. His work and that of his followers is to instil such principles and produce such a spirit among men that they will peaceably settle their own disputes. There is nothing in 1 Cor. 6 : 1-8 inconsistent with this view, for Paul there neither assumes to be judge nor advises the church to do so, but admonishes the members to settle their controversies by amicable arbitration.

15. **Take heed and beware.** This double admonition indicates the dangerously subtle character of covetousness. It is a weed which checks the best grains in the best soils (Matt. 13 : 22).—**For a man's life consisteth,** etc. This clause, which is assigned as a reason for the caution, implies that the cause of all covetousness is a deteriorated moral sense, which regards *possession* as more than *character,* *having* as more than *being.* For a comparison of the two kinds of wealth, that of property and that of charac-

16 And he spake a parable unto them, saying, The ground of a certain rich man brought forth plentifully: 17 And he thought within himself, saying, What shall I do, because I have no room where to bestow my fruits? 18 And he said, This will ᶠ I do: I will pull down my barns, and build greater; and there will I bestow all my fruits and my goods.

19 And I will say to my soul, Soul,ᵍ thou hast much goods laid up for many years; take thine ease, eat,ʰ drink, *and* be merry. 20 But God said unto him, *Thou* fool! this night thyⁱ soul shall be required of thee: then whose shall those things be, which thou hast provided?ʲ 21 So *is* he that layeth up treasure for himself,ᵏ and is not richˡ toward God.

f James 4 : 15, 16....g Ps. 49 : 19....h Eccles. 11 : 9 ; 1 Cor. 15 : 32 ; James 5 : 5....i Job 20 : 20-23 ; 27 : 8 ; Ps. 52 : 7 ; James 4 : 14....j Ps. 39 : 6 ; 49 : 16, 17 ; Jer. 17 : 11....k Hab. 2 : 9....l verse 33 ; 1 Tim. 6 : 18 ; James 2 : 5.

---

ter, see 1 Tim. 6 : 9-11. The commonness of this disease among men is indicated by the question so often asked, What is he worth? as though man's worth were measured by the value of the purse.

16-19. The ground * * * brought forth plentifully. No intimation here of any unjust or iniquitous acquisition; none of oppression of laborers, or unfair dealing, or extortion. But, on the other hand, there is a plain intimation that his wealth was evidently the gift of God, as in truth all wealth is; it was because *the ground brought forth plentifully* that he was rich.—**What shall I do?** A common perplexity of the wealthy. He did not know how to invest his surplus.—**I have no room where to bestow my fruits.** "Thou hast barns—the bosoms of the needy, the houses of the widows, the mouths of orphans and of infants."—(*Ambrose.*)—**There will I bestow all my fruits and my goods.** He would *hoard*, not *use;* the first element in the rich fool's folly. For rot, and rust, and vermin, and decay, in innumerable forms, begin their work with nimble and busy fingers on unused property. Every scholar knows that dust and mildew deteriorate books faster than careful use: many a mill-owner keeps his factory going at a loss, to save a greater loss of idleness. All mere hoarding—a form of covetousness more common in the ignorant East than in intelligent America—is folly.—**Thou hast much goods laid up for many years.** He counted on a long life; the second element in his folly. To *do* as though life is to continue, is right; to *enjoy* as though life is to continue, is wrong. We may rightly forecast; but in all our forecasting should consider the uncertainty of life as one of the contingencies to be estimated and allowed for in our plans. This man was such a fool that he did not even know that he must die.—**Take thine ease; eat, drink, and be merry.** He thought to satisfy his *soul* with granaries and their contents; the third element in his folly. He expected to satisfy that which is immortal with mortal things, that which was made in the divine image, with the food of beasts.

20, 21. But God said unto him. Not by any special revelation, but by the mortal disease which attacked him. The language is simply a dramatic form of expression, indicating the communication to him, in the ordinary way, of approaching death.—**Thou fool.** As in ch. 11 : 40, *unthinking one.* See note there. The man whom all the world praises as shrewd and sagacious, is often the one whom God calls "fool;" the man whom all the world calls rich and prosperous, is the one whom God calls poverty-stricken (Rev. 3 : 17).—**This night thy soul they shall require of thee.** *They* are God's ministering angels, whose demands the poor rich fool cannot resist.—**Then where shall these things be?** The dissipation of wealth on the death of the possessor, is one of the common experiences of life. To guard against it has been one of the great objects of men; the most successful method being by the law of primogeniture and entail. This dissipation of wealth is elsewhere in Scripture urged as an argument against setting the heart on earthly accumulation (Eccles. 2 : 18-21 ; Ps. 39 : 6 ; Jer. 17 : 11).—**So is he,** etc. That is, he is just such a fool, and is sure to come at last to a like result.—**That layeth up treasure for himself, and is not rich toward God.** Not all accumulating is condemned; Joseph accumulated; but all laying up treasure *for self, i. e.,* in selfish oblivion of others; and this is sure to be accompanied by poverty *toward God,* that is, with the absence of those qualities that tend to bring the soul into fellowship with God. It is not the desire of wealth which the Bible here or anywhere condemns, but the putting of wealth above godliness. The lesson of this parable needs no elucidation; but it needs constant application to modern life, and nowhere more than in money-getting and money-ruling America.

CH. 12 : 22-59. VARIOUS INSTRUCTIONS. TRUSTFULNESS, CHRISTIAN COURAGE, WATCHFULNESS, COMMENDED. THE REWARDS OF FIDELITY.—THE CHARGE OF INDIFFERENCE AND UNBELIEF.—THE RESPONSIBILITY OF THE PRIVILEGED.—THE CONFLICTS OF CHRISTIANITY FORETOLD.—THE DUTY OF STUDYING PROVIDENCE IN THE SIGNS OF THE TIMES.

Nearly all the teachings which follow in this chapter are found in Matthew in other connections, but with more or less difference in phraseology. There is nothing in Luke's language here, as there was in ver. 1, to indicate the time or place of these sayings of our Lord, and whether they belong to his Perean ministry, and were repetitions of what he had previously

CH. XII.] LUKE. 77

22 And he said unto his disciples, Therefore I say unto you, Take ᵐ no thought for your life, what ye shall eat; neither for the body, what ye shall put on.
23 The life is more than meat, and the body *is more* than raiment.
24 Consider the ravens: ⁿ for they neither sow nor reap; which neither have storehouse nor barn; and God feedeth them: how much more are ye better than the fowls?
25 And which of you with taking thought can add to his stature one cubit?
26 If ye then be not able to do that thing which is least, why take ye thought for the rest?
27 Consider the lilies, how they grow; they toil not, they spin not: and yet I say unto you, that Solomon in all his glory was not arrayed like one of these.
28 If then God so clothe the grass, which is to-day in the field, and to-morrow is cast into the oven, bow much more *will he clothe* you, O ye of little faith?

29 And seek not ye what ye shall eat, or what ye shall drink, neither be ye of doubtful mind?
30 For all these things do the nations of the world seek after: and your Father knoweth that ye have need of these things.
31 But ᵒ rather seek ye the kingdom of God; and all ᵖ these things shall be added unto you.
32 Fear not, little flock,ᵠ for it is your Father's good pleasure to give you the kingdom.ʳ
33 Sell ˢ that ye have, and give alms: provide yourselves bags which wax not old, a treasure ᵗ in the heavens that faileth not, where no thief approacheth, neither moth corrupteth.
34 For where your treasure is, there will your heart be also.
35 Let ᵘ your loins be girded about, and *your* lights ᵛ burning;
36 And ye yourselves like unto men that wait for their lord, when he will return from the wedding; that,

---

m Matt. 6 : 25, etc....n Job 38 : 41; Ps. 147 : 9... o Matt. 6 : 33....p Ps. 34 : 10; Isa. 33 : 16; Rom. 8 : 31, 32....q Isa. 40 : 11; John 10 : 27, 28....r Matt. 25 : 34; John 18 : 36; Heb. 12 : 28; James 2 : 5; 2 Pet. 1 : 11; Rev. 1 : 6; 22 : 5....s Matt. 19 : 21; Acts 2 : 45; 4 : 34....
t Matt. 6 : 20; 1 Tim. 6 : 19....u Ephes. 6 : 14; 1 Pet. 1 : 13....v Matt. 25 : 1, 13.

---

taught in Galilee, or whether Luke, in ignorance of or indifference to the time and place of their utterance, has put them here, is a question neither easy nor important to be determined in respect to most of them.

22-31. Almost exactly parallel is Matt. 6 : 24-34. See notes there.—**Consider the ravens.** In Matthew, *Behold the fowls of the air.* The ravens are often spoken of in Scripture as objects of the divine care. See Job 38 : 41; Ps. 147 : 9. The term raven includes the crow, rook, jackdaw, and the like. There is special significance in these references, since "every raven after his kind" was unclean (Lev. 11 : 15).—**The lilies of the field.** Probably a general term

LILY OF CHALCEDON.

for the wild flowers. The accompanying illustration of the lily of Chalcedon gives, as well as can be done without color, an idea of this, which is the most brilliant scarlet lily of all Palestine.—**The grass which is to-day in the field and to-morrow is cast into the oven.** The an-

cient oven was of various kinds, sometimes made of brick, sometimes of clay, sometimes simply a hole in the ground, clay-plastered. The accompanying illustration represents one of the most common forms of Eastern ovens. Dried grass was a customary fuel in Palestine, where there was little wood, and where coal, other than charcoal, was unknown.—**Neither be ye of doubtful mind.** Literally, *raised in the air* (μετεωρίζω). The same metaphor is common in the English; the phrase might well be rendered, *Be not in suspense.* Religious indecision Christ condemns.

32-34. Ver. 32 is peculiar to Luke. *A little flock* is a striking symbol of helplessness. The power of the church is not in itself, but in the Giver who bestows the kingdom upon it. Parallel in spirit is Matt. 10 : 16-19, 23. Parallel to vers. 33, 34 is Matt. 6 : 19-21. See notes there. *The bag* is the same as the scrip in Matt. 10 : 10 and Mark 6 : 8. See notes in both places for illustration.

35-48. This discourse on watchfulness contains the same admonitions, the same metaphors, and to some extent the same language employed by Christ in the discourse delivered in Jerusalem in the last days; but the variations are such that it is not probable that this is simply a different report of that address. Compare Matt. 24 : 42-51, where I have treated fully all that is common to the two discourses.

35-38. The metaphor of the wedding feast here suggested is elaborated by Christ in Matt. 25 : 1-13, which see for account of marriage ceremonies in the East, and for spiritual application.—**Let your loins be girded about.** The long Oriental robe requires to be taken up and the skirt fastened under the girdle to allow freedom in walking. The lesson is that he is best prepared for death who is always ready for Christian work.—**And the lights burning.** As interpreted by Matt. 25 : 3-8, the lesson is that only he is prepared for either death or work

when he cometh and knocketh, they may open unto him immediately.

37 Blessed *are* those servants, whom the lord, when he cometh, shall find watching : verily I say unto you, that he shall gird himself, and make them to sit down to meat, and will come forth and serve them.

38 And if he shall come in the second watch, or come in the third watch, and find *them* so, blessed are those servants.

39 And this know, that if the goodman of the house had known what hour the thief ˣ would come, he would have watched, and not have suffered his house to be broken through.

40 Be ye therefore ready ʸ also : for the Son of man cometh at an hour when ye think not.

41 Then Peter said unto him, Lord, speakest thou this parable unto us, or even to all ?

42 And the Lord said, Who then is that faithful and wise steward,ᶻ whom *his* lord shall make ruler over his household, to give *them their* portion of meat in due season ?

43 Blessedᵃ *is* that servant, whom his lord, when he cometh, shall find so doing.

44 Of a truth I say unto you, that he will make him ruler over all that he hath.

45 But and if that servant say in his heart, My lord delayeth his coming ; and shall begin to beat ᵇ the menservants and maidens, and to eat and drink, and to be drunken ;

46 The lord of that servant will come in a day when he looketh not for *him*, and at an hour when he is not aware, and will cut him in sunder,ᶜ and will appoint him his portion with the unbelievers.

47 And that servant which ᵈ knew his lord's will, and prepared not *himself*, neither did according to his will, shall be beaten ᵉ with many *stripes*.

48 But he ᶠ that knew not, and did commit things worthy of stripes, shall be beaten with few *stripes*. For ᵍ unto whomsoever much is given, of him shall be much required : and to whom men have ʰ committed much, of him they will ask the more.

w Matt. 24 : 46, etc....x 1 Thess. 5 : 2 ; 2 Pet. 3 : 10 ; Rev. 3 : 3 ; 16 : 15....y ch. 21 : 34, 36....z 1 Cor. 4 : 2...a verse 37....b Matt. 22 : 6....
c Ps. 37 : 9 ; 94 : 14....q James 4 : 17....e Deut. 25 : 2....f Acts 17 : 30....g Lev. 5 : 17 ; John 15 : 22 ; 1 Tim. 1 : 13....h 1 Tim. 6 : 20.

AN EASTERN OVEN.

who is supplied with the oil of divine grace.—**May open unto him immediately.** The Christian must be ready for the summons whenever it comes ; he must need no special preparation for death.—**He shall gird himself and make them sit down to meat.** Comp. Rev. 3 : 20, 21 ; contrast ch. 17 : 8, where see note for illustration of Oriental lord and servant. In the earthly wedding the lord expects to find the table prepared for him by his servants ; in the heavenly, he prepares the feast for his servants. —**Second watch * * * third watch.** The Greeks and Romans divided the night into four equal watches, terminating respectively at 9 P. M., midnight, 3 A. M., and 6 A. M. The first watch is not named, because the marriage itself occurs at that time ; nor the fourth watch, because that would postpone the return beyond the usual time.

39, 40. Christ changes the metaphor. He compares his coming to that of a thief in the night. See Matt. 24 : 43, 44, notes.

41-46. Peter's question is reported only by Luke, but our Lord's answer to it here is repeated almost verbatim in his discourse in Matthew. See Matt. 24 : 45-51, notes.

47, 48. The last clause of ver. 48 affords the key to the interpretation of this confessedly difficult passage. The principle which Christ here annunciates as that on which God will act in the day of judgment is that which men recognize as just, and upon which they act in their dealings with one another. This principle is that guilt is according to the knowledge of the criminal. The language of the whole passage is relative. No one perfectly comprehends his Lord's will ; no one is without some knowledge of it ; absolute ignorance would be a perfect palliation, but ignorance never is absolute. *That servant which*

49 I am come to send fire on the earth; and what will I if it be already kindled?
50 But I have a baptism to be baptized with; and how am I straitened till it be accomplished!
51 Suppose ye that I am come to give peace on earth? I tell you, Nay; but rather division:
52 For from henceforth there shall be five in one house divided, three against two, and two against three.
53 The father shall be divided against the son, and the son against the father; the mother against the daughter, and the daughter against the mother; the mother in law against her daughter in law, and the daughter in law against her mother in law.
54 And he said also to the people, When ye see a cloud rise out of the west, straightway ye say, There cometh a shower; and so it is.
55 And when ye see the south wind blow, ye say, There will be heat: and it cometh to pass.
56 Ye hypocrites! ye can discern the face of the sky, and of the earth: but how is it that ye do not discern this time?

57 Yea, and why even of yourselves judge ye not what is right?
58 When thou goest with thine adversary to the magistrate, as thou art in the way, give diligence that thou mayest be delivered from him; lest he hale thee to the judge, and the judge deliver thee to the officer, and the officer cast thee into prison.
59 I tell thee, thou shalt not depart thence, till thou hast paid the very last mite.

CHAPTER XIII.

THERE were present at that season some that told him of the Galilæans, whose blood Pilate had mingled with their sacrifices.
2 And Jesus answering said unto them, Suppose ye that these Galilæans were sinners above all the Galilæans, because they suffered such things?
3 I tell you, Nay; but except ye repent, ye shall all likewise perish.

l Matt. 10 : 34....j Micah 7 : 6....k Matt. 16 : 2, etc....l 1 Cor. 11 : 14....m Matt. 5 : 25....n Isa. 55 : 6....o Acts 5 : 37....p Lam. 2 : 20....q Acts 3 : 19; Rev. 2 : 21, 22.

knew his Lord's will is, primarily, he that lives in the light of revelation; *he that knew not*, the heathen; but there are degrees of knowledge in Christendom, and he that knows is the educated, he that knows not, he that has been brought up in an atmosphere of ignorance, superstition, and crime. The whole passage is interpreted by Rom. 2 : 6-23. The passage certainly teaches that there are degrees of punishment in the future life; and it seems to me, therefore, necessarily to imply that all who are punished in the future are not eternally punished.

49-53. In spirit this prophecy compares with Matt. 10 : 34-37. See notes there. Vers. 49 and 50 are peculiar to Luke, and there is some difficulty both in construction and interpretation.—**I am come to send fire.** I think it clear that *fire* here symbolizes, not, as Alford, following the older commentators, the gift of the Holy Ghost, but conflict and persecution. This is indicated (1) by the connection; Christ is speaking here, not of the coming of the Holy Ghost, but of the divisions which were not merely an incident, but one of the objects of his ministry, the fan by which he is ever separating the wheat from the chaff, and which is one of the "all things" that work together for the good of them that love God; (2) by the peculiar force of the language, which is not *I am come to send fire*, but *I am come to cast* (βαλειν) *fire*, or, as Godet, *to throw a firebrand;* (3) by the very passages to which Alford refers in support of the other interpretation. In Matt. 3 : 16, John the Baptist speaks of the Holy Ghost *and* fire, a clear indication that the fire was not, as used by him, a symbol for the Holy Ghost, but for the persecution and the trial which would consume the dross and purify the gold.—**And what will I if it be already kindled?** The utterance is broken in the original, and betokens a conflict of soul, like that in John 12 : 27, 28. In the opposition by the Pharisees (ch. 11 : 53, 54) Christ perceives the beginning of this fire; conflicting emotions, of sorrow in the present and prospective conflicts, and joy in their final result, find an utterance in this language of perplexity. *What will I, i. e.*, what more would I, *since it is already kindled?* This interpretation is confirmed by the language of the next verse.—**I have a baptism to be baptized with.** The same baptism of fire which he was to minister to his church through the ages that waited for his coming.—**And how am I straitened till it be accomplished.** Either *urged on* or *distressed*, *perplexed.* The original (συνέχομαι) will bear either translation. The latter seems to me to be preferable. Every glimpse into the future, every view of that load of sin and sorrow which was laid on him for us all, produced in a measure that inexplicable experience of anguish which was consummated in Gethsemane, and in the cry upon the cross, "My God, my God, why' hast thou forsaken me?" We must never forget that he bore our sins and sufferings, not in his body only or chiefly, but in his heart.

54-56. Comp. Matt. 16 : 2, 3, notes. On the cloud in the west, see 1 Kings 18 : 44; on the effect of the south wind, see Psalm 103 : 16.

57. Peculiar to Luke. Alford connects it with the request made to Christ to act as judge (ver. 13); but this seems to me far-fetched. The connection appears to me to be as follows: If you were wise you would see the signs of destructive storm gathering to overwhelm this nation, and would avoid the impending doom. But why, apart from these considerations, do you not of yourselves judge and do what is right?

58, 59. See Matt. 5 : 25, 26, notes. But the phraseology, and I think the application, is different in the two passages. Here the *adversary* is the Roman government; it brings the Jewish nation really to the *bar of God*, who is the mag-

4 Or those eighteen, upon whom the tower in Siloam fell, and slew them, think ye that they were sinners above all men that dwelt in Jerusalem?
5 I tell you, Nay : but except ye repent, ye shall all likewise perish.
6 He spake also this parable: A ᵗ certain *man* had a fig-tree planted in his vineyard; and he came and sought fruitᵘ thereon, and found none.
7 Then said he unto the dresser of his vineyard, Behold, these three years I come seeking fruit on this fig tree, and find none: cut it down ;ᵗ why cumbereth it the ground?
8 And he answering said unto him, Lord, let it aloneᵘ this year also, till I shall dig about it, and dung *it;*
9 And if it bear fruit, *well:* and if not, *then* after that thou ᵛ shalt cut it down.

ᵗ Isa. 5 : 1, etc.; Matt. 21 : 19....ᵘ John 15 : 16; Gal. 5 : 22; Phil. 4 : 17....ᵗ Exod. 32 : 10....u Ps. 106 : 23; 2 Pet. 3 : 9....ᵛ John 15 : 2; Heb. 6 : 8.

istrate; wisdom would dictate that the Jews should seek diligently to be delivered from him, in this case not, as in Matthew, by agreeing with the adversary (Matt. 5 : 25), but by securing the approving judgment of the Divine magistrate, by of their selves judging and doing what is right. If this interpretation be correct, the passage points out the true way of national safety in all times of national danger.

Ch. 13 : 1-9. TEACHING ON INCIDENTS OF THE DAY. PARABLE OF THE BARREN FIG-TREE. THE GREAT TEACHER TAKES TEXTS FROM LIFE.—MISINTERPRETING PROVIDENCE.—THE DOOM OF THE UNREPENTANT.—THE LONG-SUFFERING OF GOD.—FRUITFULNESS THE TEST OF CHARACTER.

The time and occasion of this teaching are unknown. The language of ver. 1, *at that season,* indicates only that it belongs in the Perean ministry.

1-3. The incident of the slaughter of the Galileans is not mentioned in secular history. But disturbances in Jerusalem, precursors of the final outbreak, were common. The slaughter of a few Galileans would not be deemed an event of sufficient importance to justify the attention of the historian. The mingling of their blood with their sacrifices is mentioned partly as a graphic method of telling their fate, partly as an expression of added horror, partly, perhaps, as an indication of their peculiar guilt. It was the Jewish theory of special providence, and it has survived Judaism, that special misfortunes or disasters were indications of the divine displeasure. This both Christ (Matt. 5 : 4, 10, 11; John 9 : 3) and his apostles (Rev. 2 : 10; 1 Cor. 11 : 32; Heb. 12 : 6) declare to be false. The language of the narrators here, or their manner, implied that they so interpreted this tragedy. Christ rebukes this mis-reading of Providence, while he makes it an occasion to re-enforce the doctrine and duty of repentance. The prophecy, *Ye shall all likewise perish,* was notably fulfilled in the case of the Jewish nation, who perished forty years later in Jerusalem, largely in the temple itself, by the sword of Titus. Christ's custom of taking the events of the day for his text is an example to his followers in the ministry.

4, 5. Jesus transfers the minds of his hearers from the massacre of the Galileans to the fall of the tower of Siloam, probably because Judeans, not despised Galileans, perished by the latter catastrophe. The fact that the good, as well as the wicked, perish by disasters, is conclusive against the theory which interprets the special disaster as a special judgment. The lesson of warning is, as before, a prophecy fulfilled in the experience of the nation ; the admonition to repentance is the same. . In both instances, Christ elucidates the truth that temporal death is a symbol of spiritual death, and that every great disaster is a warning, not of special judgment, but of impending doom on all who do not escape it by repentance.. Nothing is known of this tower of Siloam or of its fall, here mentioned. For description of Siloam and its pool and aqueduct, see John 9 : 7, note.

6-9. This parable is closely connected with what precedes ; its object is to teach the same lesson, viz., the necessity of repentance, and the alternative, utter destruction.—A certain man had a fig-tree planted in his vineyard. *His* fig-tree, because in *his* vineyard, planted by himself, and dependent for its existence on food gathered from *his* soil. In all this, it is an appropriate and significant type of man, who, by every consideration, *belongs to God.* The planting of trees in the vineyard, which is not common in Europe, is so in Palestine.—Unto the dresser of his vineyard. The gardener. There has been some unprofitable discussion whether the owner represents Christ and the dresser the Holy Spirit, or the owner the Father and the dresser Christ. Unprofitable I call it, because all such attempts to press a literal interpretation of each feature of the parable is usually unprofitable, and generally distracts from the central lesson. The N. T. nowhere recognizes any such clearly drawn lines of distinction between the Father, the Son, and the Holy Ghost, as were evolved in the later scholastic theology. Under the guise of a discussion between the owner and the dresser, is dramatically and forcefully represented the problem presented to divine love by human obduracy.—These three years I come seeking fruit. It is unquestionably a significant fact, that three years was probably the duration of Christ's ministry among the Jews. During this three years, he came seeking fruit and finding none ; his second coming will be to destroy the unfruitful and to gather the fruitful into his

10 And he was teaching in one of the synagogues on the sabbath.
11 And, behold, there was a woman which had a spirit of infirmity *w* eighteen years, and was bowed together, and could in no wise lift up *herself*.
12 And when Jesus saw her, he called *her to him*, and said unto her, Woman, thou *x* art loosed from thine infirmity.
13 And he *y* laid *his* hands on her: and immediately she was made straight, and glorified God.

w Ps. 6 : 2.... x Joel 3 : 10.... y Mark 16 : 18 ; Acts 9 : 17.

garner. — **Why cumbereth it the ground?** "*Why, besides bearing no fruit, is it impoverishing the soil.*"—(*Alford.*) No man is merely useless. Like the unfruitful tree, he is a despoiler if he be not a fruit-bearer.—**Till I shall dig about it, and dung it.** That is, "hollow out the earth from about the stem, filling up the space with manure, as one may now see done to the orange trees in the south of Italy."—(*Trench.*) A symbol of the special means of grace, provided always for the same purpose, to make fruitful that which is unfruitful (2 Pet. 3 : 9). The object of all this gracious work is "good works, which God hath before ordained that we should walk in them" (Ephes. 2 : 10).— **After that, thou shalt cut it down.** The period of grace is also one of probation; if the divine grace proves inefficacious, the unfruitful shall be destroyed. It seems to me impossible to reconcile Christ's language in the preceding instruction and in this parable, with the idea of a universal restoration.

The attempt to answer specifically the question, what is the fig-tree, what the vineyard, who the owner, who the dresser of the vineyard, etc., is worse than in vain. The beauty of the allegory is destroyed by this attempt to press to a literal interpretation all its details. But the following hints are clear: (1.) The imagery is borrowed from the parable, familiar to Christ's auditors, in Isaiah 5 : 1-7, and from other uses in the O. T. of the same figure, likening God's people to a tree in a vineyard. (2.) The fig-tree in a vineyard points rather to an individual in a favored community, enjoying the means of grace and spiritual culture, than to a nation (the Jewish) in the world. (3.) It is therefore primarily an admonition to the individual Jew, who was planted in the midst of God's special people, prided himself on that fact, and yet brought forth no fruit; but, secondarily, and with equal force, it applies to the individual of our own day, in the midst of a Christian community, enjoying Christian advantages, but bringing forth in life and character no Christian fruit to God's glory or man's benefit. (4.) It emphasizes the truth, so often

FIG-TREE.

inculcated by Christ, that the test, *and the only test* of character, is fruit-bearing; and though Christ does not here indicate what are Christian fruits, they are abundantly and clearly indicated elsewhere. See especially Gal. 5 : 22, 23. (5.) It illustrates the patience and long-suffering of God toward us—his waiting to be gracious, and it emphasizes this truth by its solemn close: *If not, then after that, thou shalt cut it down.* For the divine grace is not ignorance, indifference, or unconcern, as is shown by the certainty of divine judgment on the finally unfruitful.

Ch. 13 : 10-17. CURE OF THE INFIRM WOMAN. THE USE AND ABUSE OF THE SABBATH.

The account of this miracle is peculiar to Luke. The object of the healing appears to me to have been to afford an occasion for a rebuke of the Pharisaic abuse of the sabbath; in that respect the spiritual teaching is analogous to that of Matt. 12 : 10-13 ; Mark 3 : 1-5. The time and place of the incident are unknown.

82　　　　　　　　　　　　　LUKE.　　　　　　　　　　　　　[CH. XIII.

14 And the ruler of the synagogue answered with indignation, because that Jesus had healed ᵃ on the sabbath day, and said unto the people, There ᵃ are six days in which men ought to work: in them therefore come and be healed, and not on the sabbath day.
15 The Lord then answered him, and said, *Thou hypocrite!* ᵇ doth not each one of you on the sabbath loose ᶜ his ox or *his* ass from the stall, and lead *him* away to watering?
16 And ought not this woman, being a daughter ᵈ of Abraham, whom Satan hath bound, lo, these eighteen years, be loosed from this bond on the sabbath day?
17 And when he had said these things, all his adversaries were ashamed; ᵉ and all the people rejoiced for all the glorious ᶠ things that were done by him.

18 Then said he, Unto ᵍ what is the kingdom of God like? and whereunto shall I resemble it?
19 It is like a grain of mustard seed, which a man took and cast into his garden; and it grew, and waxed a great tree; and the fowls of the air lodged in the branches of it.
20 And again he said, Whereunto shall I liken the kingdom of God?
21 It is like leaven, which a woman took and hid in three measures of meal, till the whole was leavened.
22 And he went through the cities and villages, teaching, and journeying toward Jerusalem.
23 Then said one unto him, Lord, are there few that be saved? And he said unto them,
24 Strive ʰ to enter in at the strait gate: for many,¹

a chaps. 6:7; 11:3; Matt. 12:10; Mark 3:2; John 5:16....a Exod. 20:9....b ch. 19:1; Prov. 11:9; Matt. 7:5; 23:13, 28....c ch. 14:5....d ch. 19:9....e Isa. 45:24; 1 Pet. 3:16... f Exod. 15:11; Ps. 111:3; Isa. 4:2....g Matt. 13:31; Mark 4:30, etc....h Matt. 7:13....i John 7:34; 8:24; Rom. 9:31.

10, 11. He was teaching in one of the synagogues on the sabbath. One of the many indications that Christ was accustomed to employ the sabbath, the Jewish sabbath not our Sunday, for purposes of religious worship and instruction. For account of the synagogues, see Matt. 4:23, note.—**A woman which had a spirit of infirmity.** Apparently the case was one of paralysis.

12, 13. He called to her, and said to her. This miracle is peculiar, in that there is no evidence of any act of faith on the part of the woman. It can hardly be inferred, from ver. 14, that she came for the purpose of being healed.

14-16. The ruler of the synagogue. The president of the college of elders, who answered in some respects to the pastor of a modern church, but was more an executive officer and less a teacher.—**Answered with indignation.** We need not suppose, because Christ called him a hypocrite, that this indignation was feigned. The Rabbinical laws forbade works of healing, though the Mosaic law did not. See Matt. 12:10, note; and his indignation was that of an ecclesiastic, whose church regulations had been openly set at defiance.—**There are six days,** etc. His argument is this: This healing is not a work of necessity, since the woman might have been healed on the week day. If, as some have contended, only necessary works of mercy can be done on the sabbath-day, there would be no answer to his argument. He addresses it to the people, because too much awed by the miracle to address Jesus directly.—**Hypocrite.** Literally, *stage-player.* See Matt. 6:2, note. "The Lord saw the real thoughts of his heart; that they were false, and inconsistent with his pretended zeal. A man hardly could give forth a doctrine so at variance with common-sense and common practice, without some by-end, with which he covered his violation of truth. That by-end here was enmity to and jealousy of Jesus."—(*Alford.*)—**Loose his ox or his ass.** That motives of self-interest should be more powerful than motives of humanity,

arouses the indignation of our Lord. He implies the manifold contrast between the dumb beast and the daughter of Abraham; the one bound to the stall, the other bound by disease; the one for safe-keeping, the other by Satan; the one for a few hours, the other for eighteen years.—**Whom Satan hath bound.** It was a popular belief that disease was inflicted by evil spirits. Christ employs the language of the people in characterizing this woman's affliction. I see no reason for thinking that it was a case of demoniacal possession, though this view is entertained by some commentators. Beneath his words, however, there is a deeper meaning; disease, as well as death, is a part of the wages of sin—one of the consequences of the bondage of Satan; to release from it, is always legitimate sabbath work.

17. All his adversaries were ashamed. Rather, *brought to shame, i. e.,* shamed before the people.—**All the people rejoiced.** In this controversy between Christ and the ecclesiastics, as in the later one between Luther and the church of Rome, the people were on the side of the reformer.

18-21. PARABLES OF MUSTARD SEED AND LEAVEN.—See Matt. 13:31-33, notes. Whether the parables were repeated by Christ in this connection, as Alford supposes, or whether they are reported by Luke without reference to their connection, is not certain; neither is it important.

Ch. 13:22-35. VARIOUS INSTRUCTIONS OF OUR LORD. CONDITIONS OF SALVATION.—DEGREES IN SALVATION— AN ILLUSTRATION OF THE CHRISTIAN USE OF SATIRE.

22-25. And he was going through the cities and villages. The location and limits of this journey are not definitely fixed, but it is generally believed to have been through Perea, and to have been concluded when, in answer to the summons from Bethany, Christ reached the house of Lazarus (John 11:3-7).—**Are there few that be saved?** The Jewish doctrine of Last Days, included a belief in the destruction of all who were not admitted to the Messianic kingdom. To a devout Jew then, as to many Chris-

CH. XIII.]   LUKE.   83

I say unto you, will seek to enter in, and shall not be able.
25 When once ᶦ the master of the house is risen up, and hath shut ᵏ to the door, and ye begin to stand without, and to knock at the door, saying, Lord,ˡ Lord, open unto us; and he shall answer and say unto you, I know you not whence ye are:
26 Then shall ye begin to say, We have eaten and drunk in thy presence, and thou hast taught in our streets.
27 But he ᵐ shall say, I tell you, I know you not whence ye are; depart from me all *ye* workers ⁿ of iniquity.
28 There ᵒ shall be weeping and gnashing of teeth, when ye shall see Abraham, and Isaac, and Jacob, and all the prophets, in the kingdom of God, and you *yourselves* thrust out.
29 And they ᵖ shall come from the east, and *from* the west, and from the north, and *from* the south, and shall sit down in the kingdom of God.
30 And, behold, there ᑫ are last which shall be first, and there are first which shall be last.
31 The same day there came certain of the Pharisees, saying unto him, Get thee out, and depart hence: for Herod will kill thee.
32 And he said unto them, Go ye, and tell that fox,ʳ Behold, I cast out devils, and I do cures to-day and to-morrow, and the third *day* I shall be perfected.ˢ

ʲ Ps. 32:6; Isa. 55:6....k Matt. 25:10....l ch. 6:46....m Matt. 7:22, 23; 25:12, 41....n Ps. 6:8; 101:8....o Matt. 8:12; 13:42; 24:51....p Rev. 7:9, 10....q Matt. 19:30....r Zeph. 3:3....s Heb. 2:10.

---

tians now, it seemed as though there were very few who had complied with the conditions of salvation. The question was analogous to one often asked in our day, respecting the salvation of the heathen. Christ never answers questions in theoretical theology. To the questioner he replies, in effect, Never mind; do you strive to enter in to the heavenly kingdom. Similar in spirit is his answer to the question of the lawyer in ch. 10 : 29, to that of Peter in ch. 12 : 41, and to that of Judas (not Iscariot), in John 14 : 22.— **Strive to enter in.** The word rendered *strive* (ἀγωνίζομαι, *agonizomai*) is the one from which comes our word *agonize*, and is employed in describing the combats in the public games (1 Cor. 9 : 25). The striving to enter in must be in accord with the mighty working of God in us (Col. 1 : 29); it must be fervent and with prayer (Col. 4 : 12); it is characterized by Paul as the *good fight* or *strife*, in contrast with the strife after secular rewards (1 Tim. 6 : 12; 2 Tim. 4 : 7); to oppose us in this strife are the world, the flesh, and the devil (2 Cor. 4 : 4; Gal. 5 : 17; Eph. 6 : 12); to conquer in it we must put on the whole armor of God (Eph. 6 : 13). The lesson which Christ inculcates, is that though always a *simple*, it is not always an *easy* thing, to enter into Christ's kingdom.— **The strait gate.** That is, *narrow gate.* The spirit of real hearty allegiance to Jesus Christ, by which we enter in to him. Matt. 7 : 13, 14, note.—**Many will seek to enter in, and shall not be able when once the Master of the house is risen up,** etc. If this passage be read, not with a period at the close of ver. 24, but with a comma, much of the difficulty which has been felt in the interpretation of the passage vanishes. There is a triple contrast, (1) between striving and mere seeking, many who desire never becoming Christians, because they are not willing to take up their cross to follow Christ (ch. 14 : 33); (2) between entering in at the strait gate and attempting to climb up some other way; (3) between striving to enter *now* and waiting until the Master of the house has risen up and shut to the door. This door is shut either when there is no more space for repentance (Matt. 19 : 32; Heb. 6 : 4-6), or when death calls the soul to judgment. Thus Christ teaches in this passage the threefold conditions of salvation : an earnest spirit, the way of self-sacrifice, the present time.—**Ye begin to stand without and to knock at the door.** The figure is drawn from the customs of the wedding feast, and is elaborated in Matt. 25 : 1-13 ; see notes there.—**I know you not. Whence are ye?** This punctuation appears to me preferable to the one ordinarily adopted. Ver. 26 is an answer to this question.

26, 27. **We have eaten and drunk in thy presence, and thou hast taught in our streets.** Compare Matt. 7 : 22. There, religious work for the Lord, here the enjoyment of Christian privileges and the receipt of Christian instruction on earth, are made the ground of a claim for admission to Christ's eternal kingdom. Both are disallowed : neither enjoying religion, receiving religious instruction, or engaging in so-called religious work, is an entering into the strait gate. All these may coexist with practical injustice in the daily life. See further, notes on Matt. 7 : 21-23, and comp. Eph. 5 : 6.

28, 29. See Matt. 8 : 11, 12, notes. The connection here is, There are many that shall be saved ; beware lest *you* are cast out.

30. See Matt. 20 : 16, note. The meaning here is primarily, Many now last, *i. e.,* Gentiles, shall be first then, and many now first, *i. e.,* Jews, shall be last then ; but, secondarily, as in Matthew, Of those entering in to the kingdom, many who hold the highest place now, will begin with shame to take a lower seat, and many occupying the lower places will be bidden to go up higher (ch. 14 : 9, 10). As in the kingdom of darkness (ch. 12 : 47, 48) so in the kingdom of light, there are degrees and ranks ; in reward as in punishment.

31-33. There came certain of the Pharisees. Their object was to induce Christ to depart from their territory ; probably the Perean district, of which, as well as of Galilee, Herod was ruler. It is very possible that they were moved to this message by intimations directly received from Herod ; a little later we know that the Pharisees and the Herodians combined under

84   LUKE.   [Ch. XIV.

33 Nevertheless, I must walk to-day, and to-morrow, and the *day* following: for it cannot be that a prophet perish out of Jerusalem.
34 O Jerusalem,¹ Jerusalem, which killest the prophets, and stonest them that are sent unto thee; how often would I have gathered thy children together, as a hen *doth gather* her brood under *her* wings, and ye would not!
35 Behold, your ⁿ house is left unto you desolate: and verily I say unto you, Ye shall not see me, until *the time* come when ye shall say, Blessed ⱽ *is* he that cometh in the name of the Lord.

CHAPTER XIV.

AND it came to pass, as he went into the house of one of the chief Pharisees, to eat bread on the sabbath day, that they watched ʷ him.

---

t Matt. 23 : 37....u Lev. 26 : 31, 32; Ps. 69 : 25; Isa. 1 : 7; 5 : 5, 6; Dan. 9 : 27; Micah 3 : 12....v ch. 19 : 38; John 12 : 13....w Ps. 37 : 32; Isa. 29 : 20, 21; Jer. 20 : 10, 11.

---

the influence of a common enmity to Christ (Matt. 22 : 15, 16). The Herod here mentioned is the one who had imprisoned and killed John the Baptist (Matt. 14 : 1-12, note), whose assassination took place in Macherus, a fortress in Perea. Neither Herod nor the Pharisees were willing to take measures to assassinate Jesus, for his popularity was too great (chaps. 12 : 1; 13 : 17; 15 : 1). They therefore resorted to this subterfuge to get rid of him.—**Tell that fox.** An appropriate characterization of Herod, whose history is one of intrigue and cunning. It is almost the only case in which Christ applies an opprobious epithet to an individual. The fact is no less significant than this one remarkable exception to the general principle of his life. In this case, by a single word, he indicated to the people, the Pharisees and Herod, that he understood the design; and the word was one sure to be remembered and repeated. By his undisguised contempt he defeated the attempt to overawe the people by this unholy combination between an apostate church and a wicked king.—**I do cures to-day and to-morrow, and the third day I shall be perfected.** The language is enigmatical; there is difficulty in its interpretation. I believe, however, (1) that the word *days* is to be taken in its literal signification. The attempt to interpret the *first day* as equivalent to Christ's present working, *to-morrow* as the time intermediate the present and his passion, and the *third day* as the passion week, seems to me forced and unnatural; (2) *I shall be perfected*, clearly refers to the finishing of Christ's career by his passion and death. The same Greek word is used in this sense in John 4 : 34; 5 : 36; 17 : 4, comp. Acts 20 : 24. I believe then that we are to understand Christ's reply to the Pharisees to be, that he will remain but two days longer in that district, and that then will begin that passion at Jerusalem, which was the perfecting of his ministry. May these two days be those referred to in John 11 : 6? It is true Christ tarried, after the resurrection of Lazarus, in Ephraim (John 11 : 54); but this was only with his disciples. His public ministry, except as it was perfected in the Passion week, came to an end when he left Perea to go to Bethany.—**It cannot be that a prophet perish out of Jerusalem.** Not literally true; John the Baptist was himself an exception.

34, 35. See Matt. 23 : 27-39, notes. The discourse in which it there appears, is not reported by Luke, who gives barely a brief suggestion of it. It seems to me more probable that Luke has here inserted this apostrophe to Jerusalem out of its place, than that Christ repeated it on this occasion; because, (1) an appeal to Jerusalem, in Perea, seems not probable, though it might have been suggested by the close of the previous sentence; (2) it is not true that Jerusalem did not see Christ until his second coming, and to suppose that the close of ver. 35 refers to the greetings given him on his triumphal entry into Jerusalem (Matt. 21 : 9) deprives it of its significance, and gives to the same words here and in Matt. 23 : 39, a radically different meaning.

Ch. 14 : 1-14. VARIOUS INSTRUCTIONS AT THE HOUSE OF A PHARISEE. LAWFUL TO DO GOOD ON THE SABBATH DAY.—THE CHRISTIAN ROAD TO PREFERMENT.—THE LAW OF CHRISTIAN HOSPITALITY.

The time and place of the incident and teachings here recorded are unknown. They are all peculiar to Luke. The parable of the Great Supper (vers. 15, 24) follows immediately after, and is directly connected with the semi-social instructions contained in the first part of the chapter.

1. **To eat bread on the sabbath day.** The Pharisaic sabbath was a festival. "The day was one of festal rejoicing. Social entertainments were part of its religious observance. Every week the pious Jew repeated that Thanksgiving day which New England enjoys but once a year. Walking, social visiting, even games and dancing, were a part of the Pharisaic observance of the sabbath day. * * * 'Meet the sabbath with a lively hunger; let thy table be covered with fish, flesh, and generous wine.' 'Let the seats be soft, and adorned with beautiful cushions, and let elegance smile in the furniture of the table.' 'Assume all thy sprightliness.' 'Utter nothing but what is provocative of mirth and good humor.' 'Walk leisurely, for the law requires it, as it does also longer sleep in the morning.' 'Be resolute and merry, though ruined in debt.' Such are some of the Rabbinical precepts concerning the sabbath. Whatever else may be said of them, they certainly do not sustain the popular conception of the Jewish sabbath as a day of rigorous asceticism. On the

CH. XIV.] LUKE. 85

2 And, behold, there was a certain man before him, which had the dropsy.
3 And Jesus, answering, spake unto the lawyers and Pharisees, saying, Is ˣ it lawful to heal on the sabbath day?
4 And they held their peace. And he took *him*, and healed him, and let him go;
5 And answered them, saying,ʸ Which of you shall have an ass or an ox fallen into a pit, and will not straightway pull him out on the sabbath day?
6 And they could not answer him again to these things.
7 And he put forth a parable to those which were bidden, when he marked how they chose out the chief rooms; saying unto them,

8 When thouᶻ art bidden of any *man* to a wedding, sit not down in the highest room; lest a more honourable man than thou be bidden of him;
9 And he that bade thee and him come and say to thee, Give this man place; and thou begin with shame to take the lowest room.
10 But when thou art bidden, go and sit down in the lowest room; that when he that bade thee cometh, he may say unto thee, Friend, go up higher: then shalt thou have worship in the presence of them that sit at meat with thee.
11 For whosoeverᵃ exalteth himself shall be abased; and he that humbleth himself shall be exalted.
12 Then said he also to him that bade him, When thou makest a dinner or a supper, call not thy friends,

---

x ch. 13 : 14....y ch. 13 : 15....z Prov. 25 : 6, 7....a ch. 18 : 14; 1 Sam. 15 : 17; Job 22 : 29; Ps. 18 : 27; Prov. 15 : 33; 29 : 23; Matt. 23 : 12; James 4 : 6; 1 Pet. 5 : 5.

---

contrary, if we may believe the not altogether impartial testimony of the early Christians, it was too often wasted in idleness, and degraded by sensuality and drunkenness."—(*Abbott's Jesus of Nazareth.*) It is noteworthy that Christ, who rebukes the legalism and asceticism with which the Pharisees hedged about the sabbath, and the spirit of inhumanity which they concealed under a pretence of sabbath observance, utters no word of condemnation of the social freedom which characterized the day. Observe, too, that while he accepts all invitations, he makes every social gathering an occasion of direct religious instruction. — **They were watching him.** What sort of hospitality was this which invited him to a feast of suspicion?

2, 3. There was a certain man before him. In the free social life of the East, strangers often entered into the court-yard of the house where such an entertainment was given. See chap. 7 : 37, note. This dropsical man may have been a guest; more probably he was a stranger. It is reasonable to surmise that he came to seek healing.—**Is it lawful?** The Pharisees were watching Christ; Christ tries the Pharisees. According to Rabbinical law it was unlawful. On several occasions Christ condemned and repudiated this traditional addition to the Sabbath laws of the O. T. (chaps. 13 : 11–17, notes; Matt. 12 : 9–14, notes).

4–6. Some manuscripts, and these the better ones, for *ass* read *son* (for ὄνος, υἱός). The verse will then read, *Which of you shall have a son, or even an ox, fallen into a pit?* The argument here is precisely the same as in Matt. 12 : 11.

7–10. The language, *He put forth a parable*, implies that we are to look in this teaching for a spiritual meaning beneath the social instruction which lies on the surface. See below. The word *room* is used in the original sense of the word, as equivalent to *space* or *place*. In the East, in the time of Christ, tables were ordinarily arranged around an open square, in the manner indicated in the annexed diagram; see also Matt. 26 : 20, note, for illustration. The middle place on each couch of the triclinium was considered the place of honor, here designated as the *chief room*, (πρωτοκλισία). In our democratic society we cannot well appreciate the bitterness of the contention which often took place among guests for these places of honor. It was probably such a strife that Luke refers to in ch. 22 : 24. A strife for ecclesiastical pre-eminence, not in real power, but only in title and dignity, between the Archbishops of Canterbury and York, agitated all England for a long time, and was finally settled by making the one Primate of England and the other Primate of all England. In the interpretation of this parable observe, (1) Christ does not condemn social ranks and grades; he does not demand even the abolition of first and second places at the table. (2.) He addresses himself to the motive of approbativeness. The Bible, both in the O. T. and in the N. T., repeatedly does so. It is not an evil motive; it is evil only when made the master motive. It is not unchristian to seek honor among men; but it is Christian to obtain it by deserving and receiving, not by demanding it. (3.) The superficial lesson of the parable is not to be forgotten; in our earthly relations in social, business, and political life, as well as in Christian work, we are to be content, as was our Master, with the lowest place, and obtain exaltation, as did he, through humiliation (Eph. 2 : 8, 9). (4.) The spiritual lesson is not inconsistent with the social; but simply carries it out in a larger and higher sphere. He that is willing to take the lowest place in work for God, is the one whom God most delights to honor. Of this truth, Paul affords a notable example (1 Cor. 4 : 12, 13; Phil. 1 : 12, 13).

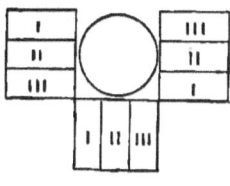

TRICLINIUM.

11. Whosoever exalteth himself, etc. This is the enunciation of a general law of abso-

nor thy brethren, neither thy kinsmen, nor *thy* rich [b] neighbours; lest they also bid thee again, and a recompence be made thee.

13 But when thou makest a feast, call the poor,[c] the maimed, the lame, the blind:
14 And thou shalt be blessed; for they cannot rec-

b Prov. 22 : 16 .... c Neh. 8 : 10, 12.

lutely universal application; but the final abasement or exaltation may not come until the future life. In addition to marg. ref., see Isaiah 5 : 12–15, etc.

12. When thou makest a dinner or a supper. The people of the East take ordinarily two regular meals a day; the first, a hearty breakfast; the second, a late dinner, usually alluded to in the O. T. under the name of *supper*. The lunch in the middle of the day, is generally an informal meal, and by working people is taken in the fields. The late dinner, here designated *supper*, is the principal meal of the day, and that to which guests are usually invited.—**Call not thy friends * * * nor thy rich neighbors.** Social entertainments in the East are often occasions, as with us, of great display. Each course consists of a single dish; sometimes as many as forty or fifty courses are given. The drawing-room is ordinarily one that opens directly upon the court-yard. The flowers and fountain in the yard, where there is often music,

ORIENTAL DINING ROOM.

and sometimes dancing, add to the attractions of the scene. In the richer mansions, the room itself is often elaborately decorated. The practice of reclining at meals is no longer in vogue. The accompanying picture represents a modern Eastern dinner-party. The intimation here certainly is, that this sabbath entertainment was one at which there were many distinguished guests. We are not to consider Christ's language here as an absolute prohibition of the interchange of hospitalities and courtesies; but, (1) there is nothing characteristically Christian in such hospitality; there is no special merit in a feast from which the host expects any personal return to himself in enjoyment, social consideration, or the like; (2) to give these only is characteristically unchristian; for (3) the disciple of Christ is to use his social advantages, not for mere personal enjoyment or benefit, but to elevate and to bless those beneath him.

13, 14. Thou shalt be recompensed at the resurrection of the just. For interpretation of this declaration, see Matt. 25 : 31–40; Luke 16 : 9.

Ch. 14 : 15–24. PARABLE OF THE GREAT SUPPER. A SERMON TO THE PROCRASTINATING.—MANY EXCUSES; ONE CAUSE—THREE GREAT HINDRANCES TO RELIGION: PROPERTY, BUSINESS, DOMESTIC TIES.—HOW TO FILL EMPTY CHURCHES.—THE CHRISTIAN MINISTRY IS A MISSIONARY MINISTRY.—HE THAT REJECTS CHRIST IS REJECTED BY CHRIST.

This parable is not to be confounded with the somewhat analogous one in Matt. 22 : 1–14. Both

LUKE.

ompense thee: for thou shalt be recompensed at the resurrection of the just.

15 And when one of them that sat at meat with him heard these things, he said unto him, Blessed *is* he that shall eat bread in the kingdom of God.

16 Then said he unto him, A certain man made a great supper, and bade many:

17 And sent his servant at supper time to say to them that were bidden, Come; for all things are now ready.

18 And they all with one *consent* began to make excuse. The first said unto him, I have bought a piece of ground, and I must needs go and see it: I pray thee have me excused.

19 And another said, I have bought five yoke of oxen, and I go to prove them: I pray thee have me excused.

20 And another said, I have married a wife, and therefore I cannot come.

21 So that servant came, and shewed his lord these things. Then the master of the house, being angry, said to his servant, Go out quickly into the streets and lanes of the city, and bring in hither the poor, and the maimed, and the halt, and the blind.

22 And the servant said, Lord, it is done as thou hast commanded, and yet there is room.

23 And the lord said unto the servant, Go out into the highways and hedges, and compel them to come in, that my house may be filled.

---

are alike in representing the kingdom of heaven by a feast, to which many are invited, and from which many turn away; but there the parallelism ends. In Matthew, the feast is given by a king; the invitations are scornfully rejected; the act is one of rebellion, and is consummated by the murder of the servants; it is punished by the death of the rebels; the good and bad are gathered into the feast; and finally one of the guests is cast out because, though he had accepted the invitation, he had not provided himself with or accepted the king's provision of a wedding garment. Here the feast is given by a private citizen; the invitations are declined with some show of respect; the declination is an indication of indifference rather than of open antagonism; the punishment is the utter exclusion of those first invited; there is no intimation that both good and bad are brought in; no incident analogous to that of the guest without a wedding garment occurs, and the foundation is not even laid for it.

15. Blessed is he that shall eat bread in the kingdom of God. The utterance of a devout Jew, who was anticipating the coming and perfection of the kingdom of God, and who looked forward to it as a time of blessedness to all permitted to see and share in it. Corresponding to it is the universal feeling of even irreligious men, that it will be a blessed thing to be a child of God in the future heavenly state. Christ's parable is responsive to this sentiment of imaginative piety. He shows that men do not really regard it as blessed to be a guest of God, but reject the invitation when it is given to them. The practical lesson of the parable is rather to the procrastinating than to the indifferent or the rebellious.

16, 17. The sending a second invitation to guests when the feast was ready was, and still is, usual in the East (Esther 5:8; 6:14). The invitation of the O. T. bade the whole Jewish nation to God's kingdom; John the Baptist and Jesus, with the message, The kingdom of God is at hand, brought the second invitation. "Come, for all things are now ready," was the burden of their ministry (Gal. 4:4). But it is also the Gospel message to-day. On God's part all is ready; the guest has simply to accept the invitation and come.

18-20. And they all with one (mind) began to make excuse. The translators supply the word *consent*, but this implies combined action, and that is not indicated by the original. The spiritual lesson is that all excuses for neglect of religion and rejection of Christ have one common cause, a disrelish of spiritual things.—**The first said unto him,** etc. The first pleads property, the second business, the third domestic duties; the first necessity, the second his plans, the third simply his will; the first is in language respectful, the second less so, the third is abrupt and almost insulting. Neither of them is kept away by anything intrinsically sinful. Neither of them proffers a good excuse; for the farm and the oxen could have waited, and the wife could have come with her husband; the claims of this life and the other are not inconsistent. Comp. 1 Cor. 7:29 for the Christian spirit respecting property, business, and domestic ties.

21-23. The master of the house being angry. Such an intimation, dropped incidentally in the teaching of Christ, is very significant. The references elsewhere in the Bible to the "wrath of God" are not human misinterpretations of the divine character.—**Go out quickly into the streets and lanes of the city.** Those in the streets and lanes are interpreted by many of the commentators to mean the Jews; those in the highways and hedges, the Gentiles. —**The poor, the maimed, the halt, and the blind.** The picture is one impossible for us to realize in our land. In the East, rich in beggars, opulent in misery, without poor-houses or hospitals, or other organized means of caring for and lessening misery, and with laws and social organism multiplying it, such a throng as is here described may be often seen in the city streets or squares, and sometimes gathered together by the rich and generous to receive in fitful gifts that charity which in Christendom is bestowed in a colder, but more systematic and

AN INDISCRIMINATE GROUP GATHERED FROM STREETS, ETC., OF EASTERN CITY.

CH. XIV.]   LUKE.   89

24 For I say unto you, That none^p of those men which were bidden shall taste of my supper.
25 And there went great multitudes with him: and he turned, and said unto them,
26 If any *man* come to me, and hate^q not his father, and mother, and wife, and children, and brethren, and sisters, yea, and his own life^r also, he cannot be my disciple.

27 And whosoever^s doth not bear his cross, and come after me, cannot be my disciple.
28 For which of you, intending^t to build a tower, sitteth not down first, and counteth the cost, whether he have *sufficient* to finish it?
29 Lest haply, after he hath laid the foundation, and is not able to finish *it*, all that behold *it* begin to mock him,

p Prov. 1 : 24; Matt. 21 : 43; Heb. 12 : 25....q Deut. 33 : 9; Matt. 10 : 37....r Acts 20 : 24; Rev. 12 : 11....s ch. 9 : 23; Matt. 16 : 24; Mark 8 : 34; 2 Tim. 3 : 12....t Prov. 24 : 27.

more helpful way. The accompanying illustration, from the pencil of Mr. Rawson, portrays an actual, not an ideal scene. The spiritual lesson to the Christian is twofold: (1) that it is the spiritually poor, maimed, halt, and blind that are worthy, since need is worth in love's eyes; (2) that when the Gospel is rejected by the rich and prosperous, guests for Christ's kingdom may always be found among the poor and unfortunate. This truth was amply illustrated by the ministry of Wesley and Whitefield, and is again in our own day by that of Mr. Moody. Directly opposed to Christ's method is that of soliciting those that refuse, by luxurious churches, fine choirs, and proffers of social consideration. The Gospel, as Christ preached it, never goes begging.—**Yet there is room.** "Neither nature nor grace suffers a vacuum."—(*Bengel*.)—**Compel them to come in.** A curious illustration of what a comment should not be is Alford's remark here: "Is there not here an allusion to infant baptism?" Hardly more reasonable is the deduction of some Roman Catholic commentators that this justifies religious persecution. For (1) there is no power in a single servant of a private citizen to drive a crowd of unwilling guests from the country; (2) the reluctance to be overcome is that of the poor to enter the rich man's dwelling and share his feast, and it is to be conquered by persuasion, not violence. The compelling is that of love. When pride declines the Gospel the Master is angry, and no further invitation is sent; when humility hesitates, love compels.

24. I say unto you. *You* is in the plural, not the singular. This is not, then, the address of the lord to his servant, but rather of Christ to his audience. So Stier and Alford understand it. "Our Lord speaks here with his usual 'For I say unto you,' to the company present; and half continuing the parable, half expounding it, substitutes himself for the master of the feast, leaving it hardly doubtful who 'these men that were bidden' are." Whichever way interpreted, the passage equally implies the impossibility of future restoration of those who have received and refused the Gospel invitation in this life.

Ch. 14 : 25-35. DISCOURSE TO THE MULTITUDES. WHAT IT COSTS TO BE A CHRISTIAN.—THE NECESSITY OF COUNTING THE COST.—CHRIST'S INSTRUCTIONS TO THOUGHTLESS ENTHUSIASTS.

There is no reason to suppose that this discourse is connected with the preceding. On the contrary, the language of ver. 25, *There were going with him*, implies that it was given during one of Christ's journeys, and was addressed to the throng which so customarily accompanied him. The contrast between the *many* who flock to hear the Gospel, especially in a time of religious excitement, as under the ministry of a Whitefield or a Moody, and the *few* who count the cost and deliberately follow Christ, is as applicable to our day as to the time of Christ.

25-27. And hate not his father and mother, * * * and his own life also. Comp. Matt. 10 : 37, 38, notes. In the interpretation of this enigmatical language, (1) we must not take *hate father*, etc., as equivalent to love father less than Christ; Christ uses language not always literally, but always accurately. (2.) The word rendered *hate* ($\mu\iota\sigma\epsilon\omega$) is never used in the N. T., unless this passage and Matt. 6 : 24 be regarded as exceptions, to mean merely a diminution of love; it always signifies a positive aversion. (3.) To *hate* is not unchristian; on the contrary, hate is predicated of God, and required of his children (Isa. 61 : 8; Jer. 44 : 4; Amos 5 : 21; Rom. 12 : 9; Rev. 2 : 6). I believe, then, that the meaning is this, that in order to follow Christ acceptably, or indeed at all, the soul must have such an enthusiasm for him, and for that purity, beauty, and truth which he embodies and sets before his followers as their possible attainment (Ephes. 5 : 1), that whatever and whoever becomes an obstacle to this attainment is, *in so far*, to be abhorred as an evil thing, an enmity to the soul and to God, and to be abhorred just in the measure in which the natural affection makes the obstacle great and the temptation severe. So Christ abhorred Peter when Peter became a tempter to him; because he loved the disciple, the disciple as a tempter was to him as Satan (Matt. 16 : 22, 23). This hate of the world and the things that are in the world (1 John 2 : 15) may be dormant in the Christian experience, but it must be there, to spring into activity, as protection against temptation, whenever even the most sacred earthly relations become instruments of temptation.—**Bear his cross.** Take it up; a willing *assump-*

30 Saying, This man began to build, and was not able to finish.ᵘ
31 Or what king, going to make war against another king, sitteth not down first, and consulteth ᵛ whether he be able with ten thousand to meet him that cometh against him with twenty thousand?
32 Or else, while the other is yet a great way off, he sendeth an ambassage, and desireth conditions of peace.

33 So likewise, whosoever he be of you that forsaketh not all ʷ that he hath, he cannot be my disciple.
34 Salt ˣ *is* good: but if the salt have lost his savour, wherewith shall it be seasoned?
35 It is neither fit for the land, nor yet for the dunghill; *but* men ʸ cast it out. He that hath ears to hear, let him hear.

u Heb. 6 : 11 .... v Prov. 20 : 18 .... w Phil. 3 : 7, 8 .... x Matt. 5 : 13; Mark 9 : 50 .... y John 15 : 6.

tion, not a patient *submission*, is implied. See Matt. 10 : 38, note.

28-30. To interpret aright this and the succeeding parable, it is necessary to bear in mind the circumstances under which and the audience to which they are addressed. Christ speaks it to a crowd who are following him, drawn by curiosity and interest, not unmingled with personal enthusiasm. His example is to be pondered and followed by all religious teachers in times of religious revival, when many are liable to mistake their enthusiastic admiration for Christ and his precepts, born of a holiday's enjoyment, for a deliberate and well-considered purpose to be Christ's, and to follow him in the double work of self-building and of warring against the world without and against wickedness within one's own nature. Building is in the N. T. a common metaphor to express the process by which character is formed, little by little, until the whole soul becomes a temple of God, for the indwelling of his Spirit. See Matt. 7 : 24; 1 Cor. 3 : 11-16; 8 : 1, where *edifieth* is equivalent to *buildeth*; and 1 Pet. 2 : 5. In framing the resolution to begin a Christian life, it is necessary to consider what it will cost, of self-renunciation, to maintain a consistent Christian character. The result of this counting the cost is always the discovery, I have not sufficient to finish; then comes either the abandonment of the plan, before it is fairly undertaken, or a going unto Christ, who is our only and our complete sufficiency in and for all things (2 Cor. 3 : 5).

31, 32. There are two interpretations of this parable. One is that of Alford: "The *two kings* here are,—the *man desirous to become a disciple*, to work out his salvation, and God, with whose just and holy law he is *naturally at variance;* these two are going to engage in war; and the question for each man to sit down and ask himself is, 'Can I, with my ten thousand, stand the charge of him who cometh against me with twenty thousand.'" The other interpretation is that of Godet: "The Christian is a king, but a king engaged in a struggle, and a struggle with an enemy materially stronger than himself. Therefore, before defying him with a declaration of war by the open profession of the Gospel, a man must have taken counsel with himself, and become assured that he is willing to accept the extreme consequences of this position, even to the giving up of his life if demanded." The lesson is therefore "a warning, which Jesus gives to those who profess discipleship, but who have not decided to risk everything, to make their submission as early as possible to the world and its prince. Better avoid celebrating a Palm-day than end after such a demonstration with a Good Friday. Rather remain an honorable unknown, religiously, than what is sadder in the world, an inconsistent Christian." The latter seems to me the better interpretation. Christ enforces the alternative of Matt. 6 : 24. As Joshua, in Josh. 24 : 15, and Elijah, in 1 Kings 18 : 21, Christ compels a choice. In effect he bids those who are not willing to take up their cross in order to follow him, to abandon all thought of becoming his disciples, and go back to their allegiance to the world. Underlying this, as the other parable, is the deep truth of the soul's need of God; no man can enter upon the life-campaign against the world, the flesh, and the devil, without alliance with and reinforcements from an Almighty Saviour.

33. Forsaketh not all that he hath. Literally, *Doth not separate himself from all.* How this is to be done Paul interprets in 1 Cor. 7 : 29-31.

34, 35. Comp. Matt. 5 : 13, note; Mark 9 : 50, note. The Christian is the salt of the earth; the *savor* is the spirit of self-sacrifice, by which Christ's disciples are to purify and save the world; if this spirit of self-sacrifice be wanting, they are utterly worthless.

Ch. 15 : 1-32. THE PARABLES OF THE LOST SHEEP, THE LOST COIN, THE LOST SON. THE SPIRIT OF CHRIST: BY SELF-SACRIFICE HE SEEKS THE LOST; ACCOUNTS THEM HIS OWN; REJOICES FREELY AND FULLY WELCOMES THEIR RETURN; CONFERS ON THEM FREE GIFTS OF GRACE, HONOR, AUTHORITY, FREEDOM, ABUNDANT SPIRITUAL FOOD.—THE SPIRIT OF THE CHRISTIAN: HE SHOULD SEEK, SEARCH FOR, LOVE, WELCOME THE WANDERER.—THE SPIRIT OF THE PHARISEE: PROUD, PASSIONATE, JEALOUS, LEGAL.—THE EXPERIENCE OF SIN: ESTRANGEMENT FROM GOD; WASTEFUL LIVING; SPIRITUAL WANT; SPURIOUS REFORM.—THE EXPERIENCE OF REPENTANCE: THOUGHTFULNESS, CONSCIOUSNESS OF SIN, SORROW FOR IT, ABANDONMENT OF IT, RETURN TO GOD.—THE EXPERIENCE OF REDEMPTION: DIVINE COMPASSION, WELCOME, PARDON, RESTORATION.—THE SORROWFULNESS OF SIN; THE JOYFULNESS OF RELIGION.

PRELIMINARY NOTE.—These three parables,

CHAPTER XV.

THEN drew ˣ near unto him all the publicans and sinners for to hear him.

2 And the Pharisees and scribes murmured, saying, This man receiveth sinners, and eateth ᵃ with them.
3 And he spake this parable unto them, saying,
4 What man ᵇ of you, having an hundred sheep, if

x Matt. 9 : 10, etc.... a Acts 11 : 3 ; 1 Cor. 5 : 9–11 ; Gal. 2 : 12.... b Matt. 18 : 12.

like the seven of the thirteenth chapter of Matthew, form one discourse; they were delivered at one time and with one object. The time and place are wholly uncertain; but their position in the evangelical narrative indicates that they belong to the Perean ministry; they are peculiar to Luke, and Luke alone gives any extended account of that ministry. The direct object, indicated by the introductory verses (1, 2), and by the culmination of the three parables in the father's declaration to the elder son (ver. 32), is to point out the spirit which the saved should manifest toward the lost, a spirit seeking to reclaim them, and toward the repentant, a spirit ready to welcome them. To accomplish this object, Christ portrays the spirit in which divine love seeks the lost and receives the repentant. This, which may be called incidental, has so far absorbed the attention of the church, that it has too generally forgotten the direct and immediate lesson of the chapter. This forgetfulness is indicated by the fact, that in the innumerable sermons on the parable of the Prodigal Son, the elder brother is either lost sight of altogether or treated as an incidental figure, and his sullenness an episode, employed to set off in more striking contrast the love of the father. Of these three parables, looked at as a representation of redeeming love, the first two may be called Calvinistic, the third Arminian; the first two represent regeneration, the third conversion; the first two God seeking the sinner, the third the sinner seeking God. The three must be taken together in order to understand the change wrought in the human soul in redemption. The prodigal son never, in fact, returns to his father's house unless the father comes after him; the lost sheep and the lost coin are never recovered without voluntarily returning to the shepherd and owner. Looked at as a representative of human duty, the first two parables represent the duty of the church to seek and to save the lost, the third the duty to welcome the repentant to a full, free, and unreproachful pardon. All represent the joyfulness of religion, both as an earthly experience and in the heavenly state. Continuing the comparison we may note the progression and climax in the series; in the first, the shepherd of a hundred sheep misses the one out of the hundred; in the second, the woman, owning but ten pieces of money, loses a tenth of her property, and searches for it with greater concern; in the third, the father of two sons loses one, who becomes to him by sin and separation as dead, and in whose death is the keenest conceivable loss the heart can suffer. "Thus we find ourselves moving in ever narrower, and so intenser, circles of hope, and fear, and love, drawing, in each successive parable, nearer to the innermost centre and heart of the truth."—(*Trench*.) We may also perhaps with Trench see a climax in sin as well as in grace—in the first, sin is represented by a silly, wandering sheep, error rather than willfulness; in the second, by a piece of money, utterly lost to its owner, and useless in itself, because castaway; in the third, by a son, knowing the love of a father and the sweetness of his home, and yet despising and forsaking both. Thus we may perhaps say that the first represents erring, the second vice, the third crime; the first sins of ignorance, the second of self-abasement, the third of willful disobedience and rebellion; and, finally, the first two, sins of original estrangement and separation from God, the third of backsliding. But these contrasts must not be pressed too closely. We must not forget that all sin is folly, vice, and crime, a blunder, a self-abasement, and a rebellion; and that all sin is a backsliding, the original state of nature being also a state of grace, and depravity being in very truth, not natural, but unnatural, depravity.

1, 2. *And there were drawing near to him all the publicans and sinners for to hear him.* The original implies, not that at this particular moment they drew near, but that at this period in Christ's ministry they were drawing near. The verb is in the imperfect tense, and implies habitual action. Christ was, in the best sense of the term, an attractive preacher. He drew. For other illustrations of his drawing power, see Mark 1 : 33–36; 2 : 1, 2; 3 : 8, 9. Nor can it be said that the people were merely attracted by curiosity to see him and his miracles; for the language is explicit, that they drew near "*to hear him.*" This was the beginning of that power to draw all men unto him, which ever since his death he has increasingly manifested as the years have rolled on. *The publicans* are the tax-gatherers of Palestine, a necessarily corrupt and a universally detested class. For some account of their character and occupation, see Matt. 9 : 10, 11, note. *The sinners* are persons notoriously criminal and outcast in consequence, not merely such as disregarded the ceremonial regulations of the stricter sect of the Pharisees. That this is the meaning is evident from the use of the term (ἁμαρτωλός) elsewhere in the Gospels. See, for example, Matt. 11 : 19; Luke 7 : 37;

he lose one of them, doth not leave the ninety and nine in the wilderness, and go after that which is lost, until he find it?

5 And when he hath found *it*, he layeth *it* on his shoulders, rejoicing.
6 And when he cometh home, he calleth together his

18 : 13, etc. — **And the Pharisees and Scribes.** The *Pharisees* were the orthodox Jews; see Matt. 3 : 7, note, for account of their history and character; the *Scribes* were primarily writers of any kind, then copyists of the Scripture, then writers of glosses and commentaries thereon. See Matt. 5 : 20, note.—**This man receiveth sinners and eateth with them.** The substance of their charge was not that he *taught* sinners, but that he *ate* with them, that is, mingled with them on terms of social equality. The modern Christian, who mingles socially and freely with modern sinners, is always liable to the same criticism from modern Pharisees. The pride of propriety never understands the liberty of love. Observe how in this sentence, as in a similar accusation at another time, the Pharisees unconsciously told a sublime truth. It is the glory of Christ that he "receiveth sinners and eateth with them." Rev. 3 : 20.

3-6. And he spake this parable. In reading and interpreting it bear in mind its double application. (1.) It is a parable of redeeming love. As such, it is borrowed from and to be interpreted by the O. T. (Ezek. 34 : 12, 13; Isaiah 40 : 11; Psalm 23). Christ comes to seek and to save that which was lost (Matt. 18 : 11) perseveres until he finds it, patiently bears it back himself through the weary way to the fold again, rejoices in the labor and weariness, because recompensed by his own love, and seeks to have the church on earth and in heaven rejoice with him. (2.) It parabolically illustrates what the spirit of Christ's church should be; it should go out after the lost (Matt. 28 : 19), should persevere despite failure and rebuff (Gal. 4 : 16-20), should bear patiently with the weakness and failures of the recovered, bearing them and forbearing with them (Gal. 6 : 2), and should do this work of redeeming love with joy, transfiguring all sorrow and making jubilant all fatigue.— **Which man of you.** The parable is an *argumentum ad hominem*, as in Matt. 12 : 11, 12. If men will take such pains for a lost sheep, how much more should the disciples of Christ for a lost soul.—**If he lose one of them.** A natural and apt type of the sinner is a lost sheep, without wisdom to return to the protection of the shepherd, and without any means of protection in himself from the dangers of the wilderness.—**Doth not leave the ninety and nine in the wilderness.** The term *wilderness* signifies not necessarily a desert place, but simply wildness, *i. e.*, an uninhabited place, and therefore presumptively good pasture land. The same word (ἔρημος) is applied by Matthew (Matt. 14 : 15)

to a place in which John (John 6 : 10) tells us there was much grass. No conclusion as to the relative number of the holy that need no salvation and the sinners, can be drawn from the numbers here mentioned, for in the next parable the proportion is one to ten, and in the third one of two. The argument of this verse, however, furnishes a conclusive answer to what is called the astronomical objection to the doctrine of redemption —the objection that God would not have chosen so insignificant a planet for the manifestation of his greatest love. To love, there is nothing strange in his leaving the innumerable host who have never sinned, and who may dwell in other worlds, to seek on this those that have sinned and need his saving grace. The duty of the church is clearly indicated. How often, instead of obeying the lesson here inculcated, it leaves the ninety and nine to stray away, while it coddles and cares for the one who is left in the fold. Its missionary work should be not its incidental but its great work.—**Go after that which is lost.** The Good Shepherd goes himself; he does not send another—man, angel, or archangel. It is by personal work, not by proxy, we are to seek and to save that which is lost.—**Until he find it.** A hint of what is the patience and perseverance of Christ, and what should be the patience and perseverance of the Christian. It is one of the passages from which the Restorationists claim a hope that *all* at last will be found. It is true that Christ always *finds* his sheep; but he does not always *recover* them. The possibility of the lost refusing to accept the proffered succor does not enter into this parable; the fact that it always is proffered, always brought to the consciousness of the soul, I believe is implied here and elsewhere in the N. T.—**He layeth it on his own shoulders.** A type of Christ's method of dealing with the reclaimed sinner after he is reclaimed. All the after-life, all the providential care and guidance, the "all things that work together for good," are Christ's labor of love in bringing the found back to the fold. He bears our burdens and our sorrows as well as our sins; we are ourselves his burden, carried, not on his shoulders, but in his heart. It is a type too of what should be the spirit in which the church should deal with those whom it has found and is seeking to reclaim; no blows, no reproaches, no driving back, no entrusting, even to an underling. The figure is true to Oriental shepherd life. The accompanying illustration, from the pencil of Mr. A. L. Rawson, is from nature, and represents a scene often witnessed at the present day in Palestine, where the pas-

friends and neighbours, saying unto them, Rejoice with me; for I have found my sheep ᶜ which was lost.

7 I say unto you, that likewise joy shall be in heaven over one sinner that repenteth, more than over ninety and nine just persons, which need ᵈ no repentance.

8 Either what woman having ten pieces of silver, if she lose one piece, doth not light a candle, and sweep the house, and seek diligently till she find *it?*

9 And when she hath found *it,* she calleth *her* friends and *her* neighbours together, saying, Rejoice with me; for I have found the piece which I had lost.

10 Likewise, I say unto you, there ᵉ is joy in the pres-

c Ps. 119 : 176 ; 1 Pet. 2 : 25 .... d ch. 5 : 32 .... e Ezek. 18 : 23, 32 ; 33 : 11 ; Acts 11 : 18 ; Philemon 15, 16.

THE LOST SHEEP SAVED.

tures are frequently wild, rocky regions, in which the sheep are often lost, or caught in some narrow cleft, where the rocks form a trap, from which a goat would escape, but where the less agile sheep, cumbered with its fleece, is hopelessly lost unless succored by the shepherd.—**Rejoicing.** See Heb. 12 : 2. In this spirit the Christian should carry those that are entrusted to his keeping, the pastor his flock, the teacher his class, the parent his children.—**He calleth together his friends and neighbors.** The great harvesting will be a great rejoicing (Psalm 126 : 6; Rev. 5 : 9-14). So every harvesting in the earthly church should be a time of thanksgiving. Praise should be as plentiful as prayer.

7. I say unto you. Christ applies the parable. There is a significance in this dignified, and even majestic, utterance. "I, who know; I who, when I tell you of heavenly things, tell you of mine own (John 1 : 51), announce to you this."— (*Trench.*)—**Over one sinner that repenteth more than over ninety and nine just persons which need no repentance.** This utterance has given some perplexity, needless, as it seems to me, to the commentators. (1.) The just persons, which need no repentance, are not "the majority which has remained outwardly faithful to the law" in contrast with publicans and sinners; the just, "Levitically and ecclesiastically speaking."—(*Godet.*) This kind of external and legal righteousness is nowhere recognized in either the O. T. or the N. T. as a true righteousness; on the contrary, the need of repentance is urged upon such by the O. T. prophets (Isaiah 1 : 10-17), by John the Baptist (Matt. 3 : 7, 8), and by Jesus (Matt. 5 : 20). Nor are they "the worlds that have not fallen" (*Alford*); for though the language would apply to them, yet they are not directly referred to throughout the parable. Christ here, as in many other instances, takes the Pharisees at their own estimate. Assuming, he says in effect, that you are what you think yourselves to be, just persons that need no repentance, there would be more joy in heaven over these repentant publicans and sinners than over you. The case is analogous to and illustrated by that of Luke 7 : 36-47. (2.) Those who are engaged in Gospel work will have no difficulty in understanding Christ's declaration when so interpreted. The joy of the pastor is greatest in the young converts of his ministry; and among these, greatest in those who have been reclaimed from the lowest depths. This experience of joy in saving the lost is the highest joy of which the soul is capable, as the redeeming work is the highest exercise of love; and it is a reflection of the divine joy, as the Christian's love for sinners is a spark caught from Christ's love.

8-10. Either what woman having ten drachmæ, etc. As an illustration of what interpretation should not be, I may refer to a fanciful allegorizing borrowed from the old writers, and

ence of the angels of God over one sinner that repenteth.
11 And he said, A certain man had two sons:

12 And the younger of them said to *his* father, Father, give me the portion of goods that falleth *to me.* And he divided unto them *his* living.ᶠ

ᶠ Mark 12: 44.

transferred to the pages of such sober and thoughtful commentators as Trench and Alford. According to this method of interpretation the *money,* coined with the image of the king upon it, represents man, on whom is impressed the image of his Creator; the *woman* is the Spirit of God in the church; the *house* is the church; the *candle* is the word of God; the *sweeping of the house* is that cleansing and purifying process, always disturbing at the time, by which the Spirit seeks for backsliders in the visible external church. This interpretation is sometimes varied; Trench, for example, making the *woman* the church, and her expression, "the piece which *I* had lost," an acknowledgment of her fault in not keeping that which had been entrusted to her. All such attempts to literalize the figure seem to me to destroy its beauty. An illustration of its unnaturalness is afforded by the fact that the coin to which Christ refers, "a piece of silver," or drachma (ὀραχμή), did not have any royal image upon it, but some device as of an owl, a tortoise, or the head of Minerva. Christ's teaching abounds in illustrations. In the first parable he employs a figure which addresses itself to the minds of the *men* in the audience, Palestine, and especially Perea, being a pastoral country; then he uses one which addresses itself to the women; finally, one which addresses itself to the universal heart. The lesson of the first two parables is the same, except that the former brings out more clearly the self-sacrifice of the Saviour, a sacrifice involved in all successful labor for the salvation of souls; this one brings out more clearly, by the lighting of the candle and the sweeping, the thoroughness of the search made by Christ and to be made by us. The former again implies the Saviour's pity for the wandering and perishing, the latter God's personal ownership in the soul and his sense of personal loss in its loss, a phase of truth which interprets the woman's language, "I have found the piece *which I had lost.*" The piece of money, or drachma, was worth about eight pence, and was equivalent to a day's wages.

DRACHMA.

11-32. THE PARABLE OF THE PRODIGAL SON.—So universally called, though the term prodigal son does not appear in the narrative. The story is peculiar to Luke. Those who object to all use of fiction must explain as best they may this story, for such it is. There is not even an application attached to it; the reader is left to make that for himself. As a representation of redeeming love, it has been well called the Gospel in the Gospel (*evangelium in evangelio*); in comparison with others, "the crown and pearl of all his (Christ's) parables." Merely in an artistic view, this is true, every detail being at once true to the external life and true to the spiritual experience which our Lord would portray. As a disclosure of divine love, we can hardly realize how truly it was a *revelation.* Contrast with it that conception of God which prevailed in the nominally Christian church in the days of the Inquisition. As a representation of human duty, we still do not realize its meaning. Contrast with it the ordinary feeling in a so-called Christian community toward the erring and the fallen. It may be regarded as consisting of five facts: vers. 11-13, sin; vers. 14-16, its results; vers. 17-20, repentance; vers. 20-24, the divine forgiveness; vers. 25-32, the Pharisaic reception of the repentant. It has been maintained, on the one hand, that this parable is inconsistent with the doctrine of mediation or atonement, since it indicates a free forgiveness, not a purchased redemption; on the other, the attempt has been made to find some analogy for Christ's sacrifice, *e. g.,* in the killing of the fatted calf (*Melancthon*), or the coming out of the father to meet his son (*Von Gerlach*). The parable certainly is inconsistent with that view of mediation which represents God as loving and forgiving the human race because Christ died for it; but this view is at variance (1) with direct Scripture teaching, which declares that God so loved the world that he gave his only begotten Son; (2) with the general representations of the divine love as inherent, uncaused, unpurchased, and unpurchasable; (3) with the analogies of human experience, implied in the fatherhood of God, forgiveness, in its highest forms, being always and by its very nature free. But this parable is not inconsistent with that view of mediation which regards the incarnation and atonement as a disclosure of the divine love, a proffer of divine forgiveness, and the method in which God comes to seek and to save that which is lost. All truth is not illustrated by one teaching; and we must not forget that this parable is only part of a discourse; the divine work in redemption, the suffering, and the toil are abundantly illustrated in the going out of the shepherd for the lost sheep, and the searching by the woman for

13 And not many days after, the younger son gathered all together, and took his journey into a far country, and there wasted his substance with riotous living.
14 And when he had spent all, there arose a mighty famine ⁿ in that land; and he began to be in want.
15 And he went and joined himself to a citizen of that country; and he sent him into his fields to feed swine.
16 And he would fain have filled his belly with the husks ʰ that the swine ⁱ did eat: and no man gave unto him.

g Amos 8 : 11, 12....b Isa. 44 : 20; Hosea 12 : 1....i Ps. 73 : 22.

the lost coin. In commenting on this parable, I do not think it necessary or advantageous to refer to fanciful interpretations simply to condemn them, or to homiletical additions to and exhortations derived from the parable. I simply endeavor to offer such suggestions as may aid the English reader in a devout study of the sacred text. The commentary is simply to be a key to the picture, not a disquisition upon it.

11, 12. A certain man had two sons. The two sons represent, not angels and men, for the spirit of the elder is anything but angelic; nor Jews and Gentiles, for the question of the admission of Gentiles was not at this period of Christ's ministry publicly raised; that belongs to a later era in the history of the church. Primarily, the elder son represents the Pharisees, the younger son the publicans and sinners (vers. 1, 2); secondarily, the elder son the self-righteous and proud, the younger son the self-abased and penitent. See further on vers. 25-32.—**Father, give me the portion of goods that falleth to me.** A demand, not a request. There is no evidence that under Jewish law the son had a right to make this demand. It was as illegal as it was unfilial. It represents the first step in sin, the demand of the soul for independence of God, the claim to own, in contradistinction to the spirit which accepts all things from God as steward and trustee. The sinner's demand is, Give me my portion of goods; the Christian's prayer is, Give me day by day my daily bread. So Adam and Eve treated the fruits of the garden as their own, to be used by them for themselves, irrespective of the divine commands.—**And he divided unto them his living.** Giving the younger son one-half of that which fell to the elder (Deut. 21 : 17), the control and use of which he reserves to himself during his lifetime (ver. 31). This division illustrates the permission of free-will to man. Its spiritual significance is illustrated by Rom. 1 : 21-28, and itself illustrates that passage. It is a striking rebuke of all attempt at religious compulsion, and is even a hint to parents that legal restraints, attempted in the case of sons that have reached a relatively mature age, is not according to God's method, "who does not compel the inclinations of a depraved heart, which can only be cured by experiencing the bitter results of sin."

13. And not many days after. But not immediately. There is a hint of the development of sin. Independence of God comes first; departure from God follows. So Adam, after disobedience, desired to hide from God.—**And took his journey into a far country.** "The far country is forgetfulness of God."—(*Augustine.*) We are always far from God when we are living without respect to, or trust in, or obedience under him; though he is never far from us. In this respect the imagery of the parable, being taken from human experience, is necessarily imperfect. The heavenly Father never loses sight of or ceases to care for, watch over, and protect his prodigal son. Even the famine and the hunger are Gospel messengers sent from him.—**And there wasted his substance with riotous living.** This ordinary English translation pictorially illustrates his course, which was clearly one of dissipation. But the Greek is literally, *Scattered what he had, living unsavingly,* and this more literal translation embodies the spiritual truth represented in the picture. For the worldly life is always a wasteful life; he that gathers not with Christ scattereth abroad (Matt. 12 : 30), and he that gathers not for eternity lives unsavingly, and dies a pauper (ch. 12 : 16-21).

14, 15. And when he had spent all, there arose a mighty famine in that land. There is always a mighty famine in the "far country;" but the soul rarely feels or knows it until all that is spent which for the time gave pleasure, though never real satisfaction. It is "a famine of truth and love, and of all whereby the spirit of man indeed lives."—(*Trench.*) But more than this, there is often a famine of the very things that gave pleasure; power is taken away, fame blasted, friends depart, in old age pleasures of the senses fail; and in this experience of famine the soul always begins to feel its own want of a something which the far country cannot supply. —**He himself began to be in want.** The experiences of Solomon in Biblical history and of Byron in secular history illustrate what is this want in time of famine. Even more strikingly is it illustrated by the autobiography of John Stuart Mill. This sense of want is itself the voice of God calling the prodigal home. Soul-weariness is Christ's invitation, "Come unto me, all ye that labor and are heavy laden, and I will give you rest."—**And he went and joined himself to a citizen of that country, and he sent him into his fields to feed swine.** The occupation of the swineherd was the very lowest imaginable to Jewish thought. No deeper degradation than this was possible. Never-

17 And when he came to himself, he said, How many hired servants of my father's have bread enough and to spare, and I perish with hunger!
18 I will arise and go to my father, and will say unto him, Father, I have sinned against heaven, and before thee,
19 And am no more worthy to be called thy son: make me as one of thy hired servants.

Ps. 32 : 5.

theless, it is not true that he "sinks lower and lower" (*Alford*), though this is the almost universal interpretation of this change. On the contrary, to fast with swine is better than to feast with harlots. The prodigal attempts to make a step upward, and fails. In spiritual experience, this attempt has its parallel in the endeavor of the sinner to retrieve himself while still far from God. He is ashamed to return to God just as he is, and desires first to better himself somewhat, to make himself presentable, at least to attest the genuineness of his repentance by his moral reform; or more generally he expects to remain in the "far country," but as a reformed man, sober, industrious, respectable.

HUSKS.

16. **And he would fain have filled his belly with the husks that the swine did eat; and no man gave unto him.** These *husks* (κερατίων) are the fruit of the carob tree; called sometimes St. John's bread-tree, from the tradition that John the Baptist fed on its fruit; it is common in southern Italy, Spain, northern Africa, and the Levant; the fruit resembles a bean-pot, though somewhat larger, and curved more in the form of a sickle; they have a hard, dark cuticle, and a dull, sweet taste; and they are used both for foddering cattle and for food by the very poor. The Greek implies, not that the prodigal would have eaten of these husks, and no man gave him, but that he did eat them, no one giving to him anything better. In the phrase, *fain have filled his belly*, is an indication that the food of the "far country," though it may fill a void, can never truly satisfy the hunger of the soul; in the characterization of the husks, as the food *that the swine did eat*, is a suggestion that it offers to man only that which at best can supply his physical and animal wants, nothing for his immortal nature; in this declaration, *no man gave unto him*, is a hint of "man's inhumanity to man," the famine of sympathy and love in the country far from God.

17. In this and the succeeding verses, every element in the experience of a true repentance is clearly traced, consciousness of sin, resolution of repentance, abandonment of sin, return to God, confession to Him without palliation or excuse, consecration to his service. Compare throughout David's repentance and action after his sin in the matter of Bathsheba (Psalm 51).—**And when he came to himself.** Sin is a craze; depravity is unnatural; in conversion the soul comes to itself as well as to its God. Christ looks on the publican and sinner with a compassion illustrated by that which we feel for the insane. Comp. Luke 23 : 34. In the same spirit is Solomon's prayer (1 Kings 8 : 47), and Isaiah's exhortation (Isaiah 46 : 8).—**How many hired servants of my father.** The prodigal, too, is a hired servant; his first thought is to change his service from that of the citizen of the far country to that of his father. We shall see how this idea changes under the influence of the father's love. The contrast between the service of the world and the service of God is implied.—**And I perish with hunger.** Literally, *Am destroying myself* (ἀπόλλυμαι, *middle*). He really destroys himself who remains in want away from the abundance of his Father's table. Observe that the very lowest possible motive suffices for a starting-point in Christian experience. The prodigal is moved by hunger in the first instance; the sense of sin and the resolution of repentance and confession came subsequently. Any motive that actually

20 And he arose, and came to his father. But when he was yet a great way [k] off, his father saw him, and had compassion, and ran, and fell on his neck, and kissed him.

21 And the son said unto him, Father, I have sinned against heaven,[l] and in thy sight, and am no more worthy to be called thy son.

22 But the father said to his servants, Bring [m] forth

k Acts 2 : 39 ; Ephes. 2 : 13, 17 .... l Ps. 51 : 4.... m Zech. 3 : 3–5.

leads the soul to repentance, suffices, no matter what it is.

18, 19. I will arise and go to my father. As departure from God is the essence of all sin, so returning to God is the essence of all repentance. Without this return repentance is spurious and reform transitory. Observe, too, that the remedy for all dissipation and riotious living is, not a resolution of total abstinence in the far country, but an abandonment of it, and a return to God.—**Father, I have sinned unto heaven.** Not *against heaven*, a meaning which the preposition ($\epsilon \iota \varsigma$) will not bear. The true signification of the phrase is interpreted by Shakespeare : "My offence is rank ; it smells to heaven." Comp. Rev. 18 : 5 (where, however, the Greek preposition is different, $\alpha \chi \rho \iota$), and Jer. 51 : 9.—**And before thee.** Comp. Psalm 51 : 4. "Against thee, thee only have I sinned," albeit David had sinned against himself, Bathsheba, Uriah, and the laws and order of his own kingdom. The sense of sin *against God* swallows up all other and lesser thoughts of sin.—**And am no more worthy to be called thy son.** Not his wastefulness or licentiousness, but that he has fallen away from his sonship, chiefly oppresses him. Whatever in us makes us unworthy to be called sons of God, should bring us to him with like confession, be the form of that sin what it may.—**Make me as one of thy hired servants.** Consecration always accompanies true confession.

20. And he arose and came toward his father. *Toward*, not *to* ($\pi \rho o \varsigma$). He did not come *to* his father, his father came out *to* him. This actual setting out on the homeward journey is the turning-point in the prodigal's life. The sinner may have conviction of sin and resolution of reform in the future, and remain unsaved in the far country ; it is actually arising and going that saves. To this God makes the promise of Isaiah 55 : 7. Whatever sense of sin suffices to lead to this return is sufficient ; no need to wait for deeper convictions ; whatever trust in God suffices to inspire to this is sufficient ; no need to wait for greater faith. Note two suggestive facts in the prodigal's experience : (1) the joy and peace, the father's kiss, ring, robe, etc., are not instantly conferred ; there is a way to be traveled first ; often in actual experience it is a long and weary one ; (2) though the prodigal brings nothing good with him, neither does he bring anything evil. He forsakes all in turning his back on

the far country. "In the act of fleeing to his father, the prodigal leaves his associates, and his habits, and his tastes behind."—(*Arnot*.) But **when he was yet a great way off.** Rather, *While he yet held himself a great way off*, as though his courage failed when he drew near, and he dared not venture into the house and the presence of the father against whom he had so sinned. This interpretation the original will bear, though it does not require it ; and this interpretation answers to that mistaken feeling of fear which is the last obstacle between a repentant soul and the heavenly Father.—**His father saw him.** An intimation that he hoped and was looking for the prodigal's return (James 4 : 8).— **And had compassion.** Literally, *his bowels*, or, as we should say, his heart *was moved*. That strange thrill is indicated, which love sends through the whole frame when powerfully excited ; a suggestive revelation of the warmth and the personality of the divine love.—**And ran and fell on his neck and kissed him.** Comp. Gen. 46 : 29. Observe the father's kiss precedes the son's confession. Comp. Ezek. 36 : 31 ; Ephes. 2 : 4 ; 1 John 4 : 10. While in this parable the story of repentance and return is predominant, yet even here we have, in the going forth of the father, and the kiss preceding confession, an intimation of that germinating and inspiring love of God which awakens love and repentance, and leads to confession and return in human experience, a truth more clearly brought out in the preceding parables. We are not to conclude that because the son arose and went to his father, that the soul goes to God before the divine influence touches and draws it. See John 6 : 44.

21. And the son said unto him. Father * * * I am no more worthy to be called thy son. But he did not add, Make me as one of thy hired servants (ver. 19). Why ? Because sonship is more than service ; and he that came expecting to be a servant, in the kiss and embrace received the spirit of adoption, whereby he cried Abba Father. See Rom. 8 : 14, 15 ; Gal. 4 : 6, 7 ; John 15 : 15. The father's love prevented the request for a servant's place. To return to God requires faith ; to receive God requires greater faith. There are many in the church who come with the prayer, Make me as one of thy hired servants, and never realize that God's answer is, This, *my son*, was dead, and is alive again, was lost, and is found. Arnot, fol-

the best robe, and put *it* on him ; and put a ring on his hand, and shoes on *his* feet :

23 And bring hither the fatted calf, and kill *it ;* and let us eat, and be merry :

24 For ⁿ this my son was dead,° and is alive ᵖ again ; he was ᵠ lost, and is found. And they began to be merry.

25 Now his elder son was in the field : and as he

---

n verse 32....o Ephes. 2 : 1 ; 5 : 14 ; Rev. 3 : 1....p Rom. 6 : 11, 13....q ch. 19 : 10 ; Ezek. 34 : 4, 16.

---

lowing and amplifying the suggestion of Bengel, well represents both the pictorial scene and its spiritual significance · "The son, lying on the father's bosom, with the father's tears falling warm on the upturned face, is some degrees further advanced in the spirit of adoption, than when he first planned repentance beside the swine in his master's field. Then and there the legal spirit of fear, because of guilt, still lingered lu his heart ; he ventured to hope for exemption from punishment, but not for restoration to the place of a beloved son. Now the spirit of bondage has been conclusively cast out by the experience of his father's love ; the fragments of stone that had hitherto remained, even in a broken heart, are utterly melted at last, as if by fire from heaven. He could not now complete the speech which he had prepared ; its later words faltered and fell inarticulate. He could not now ask for the place of a servant, for he was already in the place of a son."

22, 23. But the father said * * * and let us eat and be merry. The divine forgiveness is not merely release from punishment. It receives back the lost son to home and love, and gives to him the place and the gifts which he had thrown away. "When he ascended up on high he * * * gave gifts unto men" (Ephes. 4 : 8). And each gift in the list in the parable is at least suggestive spiritually. Without indulging in fanciful interpretations we may properly note the spiritual parallel and meaning in each. *The best robe* is not, as some commentators render it, the *former robe*, for this is not the most natural rendering of the original, and redemption does not merely reclothe us in our cast-off garments, but in a new attire. The *robe* or *stole* (στολή) was a long, flowing garment, worn as a mark of special honor (Mark 12 : 38; Luke 20 : 46), and was conferred by rich hosts on specially favored guests (Gen. 41 : 42) ; for its spiritual significance, see Isaiah 61 : 10 ; Zech. 3 : 3, 4 ; Matt. 22 : 11, note ; Col. 3 : 12 ; Rev. 6 : 11 ; 7 : 9, 13, 14. The *ring*, having on it a seal, was a symbol of authority conferred by a king on a subordinate (Gen. 41 : 42 ; Esther 3 : 10, 11 ; 8 : 2, 8). It represents in Scripture emblems, less the betrothal of the soul to Christ (Hosea 2 : 19, 20), than the dignity and power conferred upon the sons of God, whom he makes kings, giving them authority in the kingdom of God on earth (Matt. 16 : 19, note), and preparing them to reign with him hereafter (Matt. 19 : 28 ; Rev. 1 : 6 ; 5 : 10). The *shoes* were a symbol of freedom ; they were taken off, as the hat with us, in the presence of a superior, and the slave went barefoot. The son is free from the bondage of the law (Rom. 7 : 4, 6, etc.), being no more a slave but a son, heir of God and joint heir with Christ (Rom. 8 : 17 ; comp. Ephes. 6 ; 15 ; Sol. Song 7 : 1). In the East, where life is much more simple than with us, it is not unusual to kill the calf as a preparation for a meal after the guest has arrived (Gen. 18 : 6-8). Killing the *fatted calf* here is simply a symbol of the welcome accorded to the returning prodigal, and of the provision made for his wants in his father's home. There is no justification for the idea that it symbolizes the sacrifice of Christ, a notion which deserves mention only that it may be condemned. See vers. 27-30, note. The features in this scene are the more suggestive by the contrast ; the sympathy of the father with the indifference of the citizen of the far country, the best robe with the rags of the prodigal (Isaiah 64 : 6), the ring and the shoes with his former servile condition, the fatted calf with the husks that the swine did eat.

24. For this my son was dead, and is alive again. How dead, and how made alive again, is spiritually interpreted by Ephes 2 : 1-6, which is indeed a wonderful comment and interpretation on this whole parable.—**And they began to be merry.** Christ often represents religion by the metaphor of a feast ; never by that of a funeral. His portrayal of it is in strong contrast with the asceticism of all heathen religion, often borrowed by and engrafted on the Christian church. The rejoicing of the father and his household, illustrates the spirit with which the church should welcome returning prodigals.

25, 26. Now his elder son was in the field. This *elder son* represents primarily the Pharisees, secondarily all who are possessed of the Pharisaic spirit of pride and self-satisfaction in their own righteousness. It is no answer to this self-evident view to say, that it is not true of such that they have never transgressed the heavenly Father's commandment (ver. 29). This was and is their estimate of themselves (Phil. 3 : 5, 6), and Christ in this parable takes them at their own estimate. Assuming, he says in effect, that you are all that you claim to be, see what is your demeanor toward these repentant and returning publicans and sinners ; and what it ought to be. The elder brother thus answers to the nine pieces of money and the ninety-nine sheep, in the preceding parable. In fact, the elder brother now becomes a lost son, a wanderer, dead, by his mental and moral estrangement from his

LUKE.

came and drew nigh to the house, he heard music and dancing.*

26 And he called one of the servants, and asked what these things meant.

27 And he said unto him, Thy brother is come; and thy father hath killed the fatted calf, because he hath received him safe and sound.

28 And he was angry,ᵘ and would not go in; therefore came his father out, and entreated him.

29 And he, answering, said to *his* father, Lo, these many years do I ᵗ serve thee, neither transgressed ᵘ I at any time thy commandment; and yet thou never gavest me a kid, that I might make merry with my friends:

30 But as soon as this thy son was come, which hath devoured thy living with harlots, thou hast killed for him the fatted calf.

31 And he said unto him, Son, thou art ever ʷ with me, and all that I have is thine.

32 It was meet ˣ that we should make merry, and be glad: ˣ for ʸ this thy brother was dead, and is alive again; and was lost, and is found.

r Ps. 30 : 11 ; 126 : 1, 2....s Jonah 4 : 1-3 ; Rom. 10 : 19... t ch. 18 : 11 ; Isa. 65 : 5....u Phil. 3 : 6....v Rom. 9 : 4 ; 11 : 1....w Jonah 4 : 10, 11....x Pr. 51 : 8 ; Isa. 35 : 10....y verse 24.

father. See this fact illustrated below.—**He heard music and dancing.** "This is one of those by-glances into the lesser occupations and recreations of human life, by which the Lord so often stamps his tacit approval on the joys and unbendings of men. Would these festal employments have been here mentioned by Him on so blessed and solemn an occasion, if they were really among those works of the devil which He came into the world to destroy?"—(*Alford.*) Comp. Matt. 11 : 16-19, notes.—**What these things meant.** Not only to the world, but also to many in the church, the *joy* of salvation is inexplicable.

27-30. Because he hath received him safe and sound, *i. e.,* in health; to the servant, the physical restoration of the prodigal is prominent; in the Christian experience the sinner becomes spiritually safe and sound by his return. The Father is also the Great Physician. Observe that the killing of the fatted calf is *because* of the prodigal's return. This alone should have sufficed to prevent the idea that it represents Christ's atonement. The death of Christ is the *ground* of the sinner's pardon, not the *result* of it.—**And he was angry.** So the Pharisees were angry with Christ for receiving publicans and sinners (ver 2 ; ch. 19 : 7 ; Matt. 9 : 11), and the Jews were angry because Gentiles were received (ch. 4 : 28; Acts 23 : 21). — **Therefore his father came out and entreated him.** It was a part of the ministry of Christ to break down the middle wall of partition between Pharisee and publican, Jew and Gentile, the high and the low, not only by rescuing the latter from their degradation, but also by saving the former from their pride.—**Neither transgressed I at any time thy commandment.** The spirit of Pharisaism, embodied in an utterance copied, almost verbatim, from the utterance of at least one Pharisee (ch. 18 : 21).—**With my friends.** The *me* and *my*, show that this son is as really separated from his father, though being under his roof and obedient to his *commands*, as the other son, who had wandered from his father. Contrast the further language in ver. 31.—**Hath devoured thy living with harlots.**—Very probably true; nevertheless it is only the surmise of jealous suspicion. The Pharisee always aggravates every one's sins but his own. His spirit illustrates, by contrast, the charity that thinketh no evil.

31, 32. With a soft answer the father seeks to turn away wrath.—**Thou art ever with me.** The elder son by his language has made himself as one of the hired servants, *These many years do I serve thee*, and he querulously asks for his reward. The father gently reminds him that he is a son, and that to be *with him* and to be *his heir*, is his reward.—**All that I have is thine.** For the younger son had spent his portion; what remained belonged to the elder at the father's death. If we are sons of God, all that he has is also ours (1 Cor. 3 : 1-23).—**It was meet that we should make merry and be glad.** A reassertion of the spirit of thanksgiving and joyfulness with which the church should ever greet the repentance and return of the sinner. The full lesson of the contrast between the elder brother and the father, is lost if we fail to observe this radical difference; the elder brother is oblivious of the present, and thinks only of the past of the sinner; "thy son * * which hath devoured thy living with harlots;" the father forgets the past (Isaiah 44 : 27 ; Jer. 31 : 34), and thinks only of the present, or rather recalls the first only to enhance the joy of the present. "Thy brother was dead, and *is* alive again; was lost, and *is* found." Nothing is said as to whether the elder brother suffered himself to be entreated or not. Our Lord leaves each Pharisee to answer to his own conscience the question, whether he will be entreated or no.

Ch. 16 : 1-18. THE PARABLE OF THE UNJUST STEWARD, AND INSTRUCTIONS CONNECTED THEREWITH. COVETOUSNESS IS FOLLY (ch. 12 : 20); LIBERALITY IS SHREWDNESS.

This parable, and the one which follows, on the rich man and Lazarus (vers. 19-31), are peculiar to Luke. They belong to the Perean ministry of our Lord, and are closely connected, both logically and grammatically, with the parables of the preceding chapter. The opening phrase, "*And he said also,*" indicates that the teachings of this chapter followed immediately upon those of the

CHAPTER XVI.

AND he said also unto his disciples, There was a certain rich man, which had a steward; and the same was accused unto him that he had wasted his goods.

2 And he called him, and said unto him, How is it that I hear this of thee? give an account of thy stewardship; ª for thou mayest be no longer steward.

3 Then the steward said within himself, What shall I do? for my lord taketh away from me the stewardship: I cannot dig; to beg I am ashamed.

4 I am resolved what to do, that, when I am put out of the stewardship, they may receive me into their houses.

5 So he called every one of his lord's debtors *unto him*, and said unto the first, How much owest thou unto my lord?

z ch. 12 : 42; 1 Cor. 4 : 2 ; 1 Tim. 4 : 14 ; 1 Pet. 4 : 10.

---

chapter preceding. The parables of the lost sheep, the lost coin, and the lost son, are a rebuke of the pride of the Pharisees; the parables of this chapter are a rebuke of their covetousness (see ver. 14). This fact affords the key-note to what has been regarded the most difficult of our Lord's parables. The difficulties are real; but they seem to me to have been greatly exaggerated by the older commentators. The variety of interpretations which have been suggested will be sufficiently indicated to the reader by the fact that the steward has been variously taken to represent the publicans, the Pharisees, Judas Iscariot, and Pontius Pilate; and the lord of the steward to represent God, Mammon, the Romans, and the devil. Julian the apostate charged that in this parable Christ commended dishonesty; and, on the other hand, an ingenious German writer, Schultz, quoted in Trench, has undertaken to show, that there was nothing dishonest in the course of the steward. Without entering into any of these disputes, I give first, briefly, what seems to me the true explanation of particular points in the parable, and then, in a note at the close, a statement of its significance as a whole. The best modern commentators are generally substantially agreed in its interpretation—Trench, Alford, Arnot, Godet, etc.

1, 2. Unto his disciples. Not merely to the twelve; not especially to the publicans; not at all to the Pharisees, though in their hearing (ver. 14); but to such as were willing to be learners of him. The parable is a warning against Pharisaism, but it is addressed to his own pupils, to the children of light, not to those of this world (ver. 8). **There was a certain rich man, who had a steward.** Other parallel teachings of Scripture, especially of Christ (see below, and Ilag. 2 : 8 ; Psalm 50 : 10-12), represent God as master, man as steward, and property as something intrusted to his stewardship; and these should have guarded against the artificial interpretations to which I have referred above. The *steward* is a bailiff, intrusted with the entire management of the master's estate. Such stewardships, relatively unknown in this country, are common in Ireland, Italy, the East, and wherever property is owned in large estates, and the owners are not men of business, or are habitually or frequently absent from their estates. Such a steward or bailiff is necessarily intrusted with almost absolute power over his owner's property. For Scriptural illustrations of such stewardship, see the cases of Elijah and Joseph (Gen. 24 : 2-12 ; 39 : 4).—**And the same was accused unto him, that he was wasting his goods.** Not *had wasted*. The imperfect tense is used in the original, and it indicates a habit of wasting, still carried on. Here is the same sin as that of the prodigal, and represented by the same Greek word (ch. 15 : 13). All sin is a wasting of that which belongs to God; and it is always accompanied by a forgetfulness of God, so that his coming and his demand for an accounting is a surprise. Comp. Matt. 24 : 48-51.—**Give an account of thy stewardship: for thou mayest be steward no longer.** There is no trial, but sentence of condemnation. We are condemned already, and the day of judgment is a day, not of trial, but of disclosure and of reckoning. Death is thus God's call to us for an accounting of all things with which he has intrusted us. "The great truth lies in the background, that that dismissal, death itself, is the consequence of this wasting of his goods—the wages of sin is death." —(*Alford*.)

3, 4. What shall I do? * * * I cannot dig; to beg I am ashamed. A graphic picture of the perplexity and dismay of the man of the world when summoned by death to give an account of his stewardship. He has laid up for himself no treasure above; he is conscious that he has developed no powers for service in the eternal kingdom; he is ashamed to cast himself as a beggar, even before his God, and enter the kingdom simply as a suppliant.—**I am resolved what to do.** Reflection brings him, as it brought the prodigal, to himself. The conclusion here is the result of cogitation. "All at once, after long reflection, he exclaims, as if striking his forehead : I have it."—(*Godet*.) The conclusion is the one to which many a rich man is brought who, by the benefactions of his will, endeavors to compensate for the niggardliness of his life.—**That they** (*i. e.,* his lord's debtors) **may receive me.**

5-7. So he called every one of his lord's debtors. These would be either merchants or other purchasers, who had received their stores and not yet paid for them (*Alford*), or tenants,

6 And he said, An hundred measures of oil. And he said unto him, Take thy bill, and sit down quickly, and write fifty.
7 Then said he to another, And how much owest thou? And he said, An hundred measures of wheat. And he said unto him, Take thy bill, and write fourscore.

8 And the lord commended the unjust steward, because he had done wisely: for the children of this world are in their generation wiser than the [a] children of light.
9 And I say unto you, Make [b] to yourselves friends of the mammon of unrighteousness; that, when ye fail, they may receive you into everlasting habitations.

a John 12 : 36 ; Ephes. 5 : 8 .... b Eccles. 11 : 1 ; 1 Tim. 6 : 18, 19.

who paid their rent, as it is almost invariably paid in the East, and very generally in European estates, in produce. The *oil* is olive oil ; the *wheat* the most common grain of Palestine ; both are productions of the soil. The *measure of oil* (*βάτος*), contains about sixty pints ; fifty measures would be worth several hundreds of dollars : the *measure of wheat* (*χόρος*) contains a little over eleven bushels ; the twenty measures remitted would amount to over a hundred dollars in value. The steward knows his men, and calculates the degree of liberality which he must show to each in order to secure their hospitality. —**Take thy bill.** Either the receipt which the debtor had given for the goods, or the lease which he had signed for the rent. The word rendered bill is simply *writing*. This the tenant is himself to alter, perhaps that, having a direct share in the fraud, he may be precluded from informing of it, subsequently.—**Sit down quickly.** Simply a graphic touch, indicating the haste of the whole transaction.—**And write fifty.** The accompanying illustration shows the writing materials of the East and the method of writing. The ink is India ink, fine lamp-black and gum perfumed ; the pen is reed, cut aslant at the point ; the writing is usually done by public scribes, who hold the paper in the left hand in writing. Few, except the members of the learned professions, are trained to read and write.

8, 9. And the lord commended the unjust steward. That is, *his* lord commended him. It is not said by Luke that Christ praised the unjust steward, but by Christ, as part of the parable, that the master commended his servant. Of course it is implied that he discovered the trick. — **Because he had done wisely.** *Shrewdly.* He commended, not the morality but the shrewdness of his course.—**For** (what follows is Christ's comment on the whole transaction, the action of the steward and the commendation of his lord) **the children of this world are toward their generation,** not *in* (*εν*), but *unto* (*εις*), **wiser** (*shrewder*) **than the children of light.** The meaning is, not that the worldly-minded men are shrewder than spiritually-minded men in their management of earthly affairs ; nor merely that they are wiser in dealing with earthly affairs than spiritually-minded men with spiritual affairs ; but that in their dealings with one another, men of the world get more worldly profit out of the intercourse, than spiritually-minded get of spiritual profit out of their mutual intercourse. It must not be forgotten that all the characters in this parable are children of this world ; the steward contrives the fraud ; the debtors participate in it ; and the lord commends it.—**And I say unto you.** What follows is Christ's application of the parable. If that be understood, the difficulties in the parable itself are easily cleared away.—**Make to yourselves friends** (by means) **of the mammon of unrighteousness,** *i. e., the unrighteous mammon.* Not, Make this unrighteous mammon your friend, but, Use this unrighteous mammon to make friends. Mammon stands for money (see Matt. 6 : 24, note) ; *the mammon of unrighteousness* is not money made unrighteously, nor does the phrase imply that Christ regards all property-

SCRIBE AND WRITING MATERIALS.

10 He° that is faithful in that which is least, is faithful also in much: and he that is unjust in the least, is unjust also in much.
11 If therefore ye have not been faithful in the unrighteous mammon, who will commit to your trust the true *riches?*
12 And if ye have not been faithful in that which is another man's, who shall give you that which is your own?
13 No^d servant can serve two masters: for either he will hate the one, and love the other: or else he will hold to the one, and despise the other. Ye cannot serve God and mammon.
14 And the Pharisees also, who° were covetous, heard all these things: and they derided him.
15 And he said unto them, Ye are they which justify yourselves^f before men; but God^g knoweth your hearts: for that which is highly esteemed^h among men, is abomination in the sight of God.
16 Theⁱ law and the prophets *were* until John: since

---

c Matt. 25: 21, 23....d Josh. 24: 15; Matt. 6: 24....e Matt. 23: 14....f ch. 10: 29....g Ps. 7: 9; Jer. 17: 10....h Prov. 16: 5; Mal. 3: 15....i Matt. 11: 12, 13.

---

holding as a form of selfishness. Godet explains the meaning well. "The ear of Jesus must have been constantly offended with that sort of reckless language in which men indulge without scruple: *my* fortune, *my* land, *my* house. He also felt to the quick man's dependence on God, saw that there was a usurpation in this idea of ownership, a forgetfulness of the true proprietor; on hearing such language he seemed to see the former playing the landlord. It is this sin, of which the natural man is profoundly unconscious, which He lays bare in this whole parable, and which He especially designates by this expression, 'the mammon of unrighteousness.'"—**That when ye fail.** Better, *When it fails* (ἐκλίπῃ, not ἐκλίπητε, is the preferable reading).—**They may receive you into everlasting habitations.** This is not ironical, as some would have us believe; nor are they that receive the angels, an interpretation invented for theological reasons, and quite inconsistent with the structure of the parable, for those to whom the steward has given, receive him; nor can we say with Godet, "to *receive* is not to *introduce*," and that the language here assumes some other ground of claim for admission to the everlasting habitations, for the only ground in the parable for the admission of the steward to the houses of the tenants is the service which he has dishonestly rendered them. The interpretation of this declaration is to be found, firstly, in such passages as 2 Pet. 1: 11, "So an entrance shall be ministered unto you abundantly, into the everlasting kingdom of our Lord and Saviour Jesus Christ," since they have an abundant entrance into the kingdom of glory, who are welcomed to it by the many whom they have served on earth; and secondly, in such passages as Matt. 25: 31-46, the condition of admission to the kingdom of heaven being not merely faith, but that kind of faith which works by love.

NOTE ON THE PARABLE OF THE UNJUST STEWARD.—Four facts, carefully considered, relieve this parable of most, if not of all, of its difficulty. (1.) Its object is indicated by its effect; it is directed against covetousness (ver. 14); (2) Christ does not commend the unjust steward; the lord of the parable recommends him, but only for his shrewdness (ver. 8, note); (3) Christ does not advise his disciples to make the mammon of unrighteousness their friend, but to use the mammon of unrighteousness so as to make friends (ver. 9, note); (4) he elsewhere illustrates truth by contrasts, showing how, since the lowest motives conduce to certain beneficial results, higher motives certainly should do so. As in Luke 11: 6-8, he says, since a selfish friend will yield to importunity, and in Luke 18: 1-7, since even an unprincipled and an unjust judge will heed the cry of the wronged, much more will God, who is just, loving, sympathetic, answer the importunate prayers of his children; so here, he says, since even a fraudulent and unjust steward, without philanthropy, or a sense of his duty to his lord, will yet, from mere motives of policy, use the authority intrusted to him to make friends of his tenants, much more should a servant of God, who has been intrusted with property, that he may benefit humanity, so distribute it that the needy shall testify to the fidelity of his stewardship and the liberality of his love. In this parable then the rich man represents God, the steward man, especially the man of wealth, the stewardship his property, which is not his own, but is intrusted to him, the tenants the poor, the summons to account, death, which is a call to judgment. The parable may even be carried further; and it may be said that the scheme of the steward has its parallel in the tendency of men of wealth to compensate by their bequests at death for their lack of liberality in their lifetime. And the lesson is not weakened, but strengthened, by the fact that the analogy is not perfect, that the worldly steward is appointed to gather from the tenants for his lord, while the Christian steward is appointed to use his Lord's wealth for the benefit of his Lord's poor.

10-12. These aphorisms are directly connected with the preceding parable. Ver. 10 is interpreted by Matt. 25: 21. This life is a probation; fidelity here in the trust reposed in us by God leads to a larger trust in the future. Comp. ch. 19: 17. Vers. 11 and 12 simply carry out and enforce this truth. If one be unfaithful in the use of that wealth which moth and rust doth corrupt, how can he expect the eternal riches? If he is selfish and dishonest toward God in the use of what belongs to God, and is but *intrusted*

that time the kingdom of God is preached, and every man presseth into it.
17 And ¹ it is easier for heaven and earth to pass, than one tittle of the law to fail.

18 Whosoever ᵏ putteth away his wife and marrieth another, committeth adultery: and whosoever marrieth her that is put away from *her* husband, committeth adultery.

j Ps. 102:26; Isa. 40:8; 51:6.... k Matt. 5:32; 1 Cor. 7:10, 11.

to him, how can he expect that God will *give* him that which shall be his own?

13. Comp. Matt. 6:24, note. Whether this saying was repeated by Christ here, or is transferred by Luke from the Sermon on the Mount, because closely connected with the topic, is uncertain and unimportant.

14, 15. Peculiar to Luke. Ver. 14 indicates that the Pharisees understood the parable of the unjust steward as a rebuke of covetousness, and thus affords the key to its interpretation. Ver. 15 may almost be regarded as a text of which the following parable of the rich man and Lazarus is an illustration and an amplification. The latter clause of this verse, *that which is highly esteemed among men is abomination in the sight of God*, is to be interpreted by the preceding clause, *God knoweth your hearts.* Comp. 1 Sam. 16:7. Not everything honored by men is abominated by God; nor are there two such different standards of judgment that what really commends itself to man's moral sense is condemned by God. But what often *appears* admirable to man, because he sees only the outward and deceitful appearance, is known to God to be abominable, because he sees the motive out of which it springs. This declaration gives partial interpretation to Matt. 7:1, *Judge not;* it indicates that we are to be cautious in commendatory as well as in condemnatory judgments.

16-18. These aphorisms appear in Matthew in different connections. Alford and Godet endeavor, it seems to me not very successfully, to point out a logical connection here, to the following effect: The kingdom you preach has been one in which the members are justified before men; since John a kingdom has been proclaimed into which publicans and sinners are pressing; his kingdom does not destroy, but fulfills, the Mosaic law; of this fulfillment the Christian law against adultery affords an example. I prefer to regard the introduction of these aphorisms in this place as due to Luke, who puts them here because they are a part of Christ's general teaching respecting the religion of Phariseeism. I am not able to see that they have any very immediate connection with either the preceding or the succeeding parable. On ver. 16, see Matt. 11:12, note; on ver. 17, Matt. 5:18; on ver. 18, Matt. 5:31, 32, note.

Ch. 16:19-31. PARABLE OF THE RICH MAN AND LAZARUS. THE CONTRASTS OF TIME AND THE CONTRASTS OF ETERNITY.—THE REALITY OF PUNISHMENT.—THE SEPARATION IN THE FUTURE LIFE.—CHRIST'S CONDEMNATION OF THE CLAIMS OF SPIRITISM.—THE CAUSES AND THE CURE OF SKEPTICISM. See Prel. Note.

PRELIMINARY NOTE.—This parable is intimately connected with the preceding parable; like that, it is aimed at the covetousness of the Pharisees. It is no answer to this to say that the Pharisees were not characteristically prodigal and luxurious. That many of them were austere, and even ascetic (Luke 18:12), is undoubtedly true; but there is abundant indication in Christ's denunciation of the Pharisees elsewhere (see especially Matt., ch. 23; Luke 14:7-14), that the covetousness of that day, as well as of our own, sometimes accompanied the vice of hoarding, and sometimes that of a prodigal but purely selfish expenditure. The root of the vice is in either case the same unbelief; and this root is clearly brought to view at the close of this parable, where worldliness is shown to be always and of necessity accompanied with that kind of unbelief which refuses credence to moral and spiritual truths. This parable is not an allegory, and the attempt to give it an allegorical interpretation is unworthy of the conscientious commentator. It belongs to the class of the good Samaritan, not to that of the sower. It is, in truth, a chapter out of real life, the contrasts both in the present and in the future here depicted being common in all ages. This parable "is not like a type, which a man cannot read until it is turned, but like a manuscript, which delivers its sense directly and at first hand."—(*Arnot.*) As the materials for the parable are borrowed from actual life, so "the colors are almost all borrowed from the palette of the rabbis."—(*Godet.*) The references to *hades* (hell) and to *Abraham's bosom* are to be interpreted by the common philosophy of that age. Speaking to the Pharisees, Christ employs the language if he does not assume the truth of their theology. But, while we may not press literally the figures which Christ has thus borrowed, neither can we think that he has employed them to endorse and enforce false views of the future life. In substance, the truths embodied here must be accepted by those who accept Christ as a divine teacher; though it may not be easy to discriminate between the truths intended to be illustrated and the poetic figures employed simply for the purpose of illustration. This much is to me very clear: (1.) There is no ground for the opinion of Renan and some of the German commentators that this parable is aimed against riches as

19 There was a certain rich man, which was clothed in purple and fine linen, and fared sumptuously every day:
20 And there was a certain beggar named Lazarus, which was laid at his gate, full of sores,
21 And desiring to be fed with the crumbs which fell

such, the rich man being condemned for his wealth, and Lazarus saved for his poverty. "It would be hard to understand how, if wealth, *as such*, were the rich man's sin, the celestial banquet could be presided over by Abraham, the richest of the rich in Israel."—(*Godet.*) (2.) The interpretation which finds in this parable an allegory of the calling of the Gentiles, though it is supported by many of the ancient and some of the modern commentators, is an afterthought, and was neither in the mind of Christ nor in the minds of his hearers. According to this interpretation, Dives represents the Jewish nation; Lazarus represents the Gentiles; the death of Lazarus and his reception into Abraham's bosom prefigures the reception of the Gentiles into the church of God; and Dives in torments answers to the anguish and despair of the Jewish nation cast out. (3.) We may say in general with John Service (*Salvation Here and Hereafter*), that "this parable is meant to take us, as it were by storm, and once for all, out of this (the customary and earthly) way of regarding life. * * * The purpose is greater and wider than to teach us any religious lesson. It is to awaken us once for all to serious, to religious thought." And this it does by its dramatic representation of the real worthlessness of that in external condition which we are most wont to value. In this respect it is like the parable of the rich fool (ch. 12 : 16-21). But (4.) it does also teach some religious lessons, as the reality of punishment, the certain, and apparently the eternal, separation of men in the future state, impliedly the immortality of both the saved and the lost, and the futility of any revelations from the spirit world. Further than that, it seems to me that it is not safe to go in the interpretation of details, as, for example, by concluding that the lost and the saved hold converse with one another, that the lost are in literal physical torments, or that they have a sincere desire for the salvation of others upon earth.

19-21. In these verses Christ simply describes pictorially the condition of the two men as they would appear to the sight. It is as if we were walking with him through the streets of Jerusalem, and he pointed us to the mansion of the rich man, known only for and by his wealth, his sumptuous attire, and his great entertainments, and to the poor man, who lies at the gate of the mansion, feeding on such crumbs as may be supplied him by the compassion of the servants, and getting such relief as is afforded by the dogs licking his sores. We note the contrast; then Christ draws aside the veil, and we see the contrast in the other life; and the two pictures, the earthly and the heavenly, are left by the Master to produce their own impression upon our minds. That impression would be weakened, not deepened, by any analysis of the two characters of the story. We are left to draw our own conclusions respecting those characters from the course of the story itself. To conclude that Lazarus was pious, merely because his name signifies "help in God," is only less absurd than to conclude that he was carried to heaven only because he was poor upon the earth.—**There was a certain rich man.** It is a curious illustration of the untrustworthiness of priestly traditions, that the houses of the rich man and Lazarus are pointed out by the priests in Jerusalem.—**Which was clothed in purple and fine linen.** "The *purple and fine linen* are named often together (Esth. 1 : 6 ; Rev. 18 : 12), both being in highest esteem, and the combination of colors which they offered, blue and white, greatly prized. The extreme costliness of the true sea-purple of antiquity is well known. It was the royal hue; and the purple garment then, as now, a royal gift (Esth. 8 : 15); with it too the heathen idols were clothed (Jer. 10 : 9); there was as much therefore of pride as of luxury in its use. The byssus, or *fine linen*, was hardly in less price or esteem. All then of costliest and rarest be bestowed upon himself. Nor was it on some high days only that he so arrayed himself and so feasted. The '*purple and fine linen*' were his ordinary apparel, the sumptuous fare his every-day entertainment."—(*Trench.*)—**Fared sumptuously every day.** *Feasted sumptuously.* The implication is, of one devoting himself to selfish and sensual enjoyment.—**There was a certain beggar named Lazarus.** Beggary, such as is here depicted, is much more common in the East than with us, and in the absence of any more systematic provision, almsgiving to the poor was insisted upon by the O. T. (Job 29 : 13; Prov. 14 : 21; 19 : 17; 1 cor. 9 : 7.) In neglecting Lazarus, this rich man was therefore palpably disregarding the spirit of the O. T. requirements. That he knew Lazarus and his condition is clearly implied by vers. 23, 24. That the poor man's name is given and the rich man's is not, has been noted by all commentators as a significant fact. Augustine suggests that Christ found the name of Lazarus in the Book of Life; Cajetan, that Christ thus indicates that the spiritual order of things is contrary to the worldly, that here the names of the rich are widely known, hereafter their wealth does not keep their name from oblivion. The name *Dives* often given to the rich man, is taken from the Latin word *divis*, meaning rich.

from the rich man's table: moreover the dogs came and licked his sores.

22 And it came to pass, that the beggar died, and was carried by the angels into Abraham's bosom:[1] the[m] rich man also died, and was buried;

23 And[n] in hell he lift up his eyes, being in torments, and seeth Abraham afar off, and Lazarus in his bosom.

24 And he cried and said, Father Abraham, have mercy on me, and send Lazarus, that he may dip the tip of his finger in water, and cool my tongue;[o] for I am tormented in this flame.[p]

25 But Abraham said, Son, remember that thou in thy lifetime[q] receivedst thy good things, and likewise Lazarus evil things: but now he is comforted, and thou art tormented.

[1] Matt. 8:11... m Prov. 14.32....n Rev. 14:10, 11....o Zech. 14:12....p Isa. 66:24; Mark 9:44, etc....q ch. 6:24; Job 21:13; Ps. 73:12-19

—**Desiring to be fed.** It was for this purpose he was laid here by friends; whether or how far his desire was satisfied, is not indicated. But that he expected nothing but the *crumbs* which fell from the table of the rich man, is clear.— **The dogs came and licked his sores.** This touch not only adds to the dramatic force of the picture, by indicating his nakedness and forsaken condition; it also brings out the inhumanity of man by depicting the sympathy of the brutes. The contrast between the rich man and Lazarus is well epitomized by Trench: "Dives is covered with purple and fine linen, Lazarus covered only with sores. One fares sumptuously, the other desires to be fed with crumbs. One has hosts of attendants to wait on his every caprice; though this circumstance is left to our imagination to supply; only the dogs tend the sores of the other."

22. The beggar died and was carried by the angels to Abraham's bosom. Of his burial nothing is said; not, as Meyer suggests, because of the Rabbinical notion that the pious were transferred body and soul to Paradise; but because the burial of the beggar was not worthy of note. He was here to-day; to-morrow he was gone; no one knew what had become of him.— **The rich man also died and was buried.** The last service his wealth could render him was a magnificent funeral. For him life was all extinguished in the grave.

23. And in hades. In the English version of the N. T., the word *hell* is unfortunately used indiscriminately in rendering two very different Greek words (*ᾅδης* hades, and *γέεννα* Gehenna); the first, which is used here, never signifies the special place of punishment, but simply the abode of the departed. This, according to the ancient Hebraic opinion, was a deep and dark abode, generally located in the centre of the earth, where were assembled both good and evil spirits, but classed according to their spiritual character. It was thus divided into a place of punishment and one of reward, a paradise and a hell, but both temporary. At the general judgment, it was believed that all would come forth from this abode, but while the righteous would be permanently delivered from it, the wicked would be thrust back into it again.—**Seeing Abraham afar off and Lazarus in his bosom.** The language is borrowed from the custom, common in the East, of reclining on couches at meals, in such a way that each guest rested partially upon the bosom of his nearest neighbor. See Vol. I, p. 282, for illustration. This position, with respect to the master of the house, was one of especial honor, and only occupied by dear friends. Hence to lie in Abraham's bosom became among the Jews a common metaphorical expression of the highest condition and felicity. As such it is used by Christ here.

24, 25. Father Abraham. Even now the rich man bases his life on the fact that he is a son of Abraham. Abraham, in his reply, *Son, remember,* recognizes the fact, but does not recognize in it any claim whatever. It was a Rabbinical proverb, "All the circumcised are safe." This proverb Christ here impliedly, as John the Baptist directly, in ch. 3:8, repudiates. Future condition depends not on ceremonial nor on inheritance, but on personal character (John 1:13).— **Dip the tip of his finger in water.** Lazarus desired *crumbs* of bread from the rich man on earth; the rich man desires *drops* of water from Lazarus in hades.—**I am tormented in this flame.** The language is metaphorical. It is as absurd to deduce from this language a doctrine of physical torment in an actual flame, as it would be to conclude that the separation between the lost and the saved, is one interposed by a mere physical gulf, across which conversation can be carried on, and which could be easily bridged by the resources of modern engineering. But the metaphor means something. What? It is certain that our Lord, who knew whereof he spoke, would not have used such a symbol, if it were not an apt one to designate the mental and spiritual suffering of the condemned. "Hardened sinners have died crying, 'Fire!' Did the fire leave them when they left their bodies?"—(*Alford.*)—**Son, remember.** This is itself a hint of the torment; the self-reproach of a condemning memory, that will never forget.—**Thou in thy life-time receivedst thy good things.** But he does not say, Lazarus *his* evil things. They were the rich man's good things, because they were the things which he made his chief good while he lived. Comp. ch. 6:24, note, and 1 Tim. 6:9, 10. This explains the conclusion of the verse. —**He is comforted, and thou art torment-

26 And beside all this, between us and you there is a great gulf fixed: so that they which would pass from hence to you cannot; neither ʳ can they pass to us, that *would come* from thence.
27 Then he said, I pray thee therefore, father, that thou wouldest send him to my father's house:
28 For I have five brethren; that he may testify unto them, lest they also come into this place of torment.
29 Abraham saith unto him, They ˢ have Moses and the prophets; let them hear them.
30 And he said, Nay, father Abraham: but if one went unto them from the dead, they will repent.
31 And he said unto him, If ᵗ they hear not Moses and the prophets, neither will ᵘ they be persuaded, though one rose from the dead.

CHAPTER XVII.

THEN said he unto the disciples, It ᵛ is impossible but that offences will come: but woe *unto him* through whom they come!
2 It were better for him that a millstone were hanged about his neck, and he cast into the sea, than that he should offend one of these little ones.
3 Take heed to yourselves: If thy brother trespass against thee, rebuke ʷ him; and if he repent, forgive him.
4 And if he trespass against thee seven times in a day, and seven times in a day turn again to thee, saying, I repent; thou ˣ shalt forgive him.

r Ezek. 28: 24....s Isa. 34: 16; John 5: 39....t 2 Cor. 4: 3....u John 12: 10, 11....v Matt. 18: 6, 7; Mark 9: 42....w Lev. 19: 17....x Matt. 6: 12, 14; Col. 3: 13.

ed.—Not *because* the one suffered evil, and the other enjoyed luxury: Abraham does not say this; and there is not here, nor I think anywhere else in Scripture, the doctrine that "the cause of an unbroken prosperity is ever a sign and augury of ultimate reprobation." Abraham recalls the contrast between the present condition and the past condition of the two; the ground of the present condition is sufficiently indicated by the phrase, *thy* good things.

26. In the preceding verse, Abraham has maintained the justice of the condition of the rich man. In this verse he declares that condition to be unalterably fixed. The language is of course metaphorical, but the metaphor cannot be misunderstood. *The great gulf* is one which neither mercy from heaven nor repentance from hell, can bridge. Observe, however, that there is no evidence of real repentance on the part of the rich man. Compare with Christ's parabolic teaching here, that of ch. 13: 24-27; Matt. 25: 10-12, 46.

27, 28. It is not necessary, on the one hand, to attribute the petition of the rich man to a selfish aim, nor to see in it, on the other, an evidence of his partial reformation, as though the fires in which he was tormented had already accomplished a partial purification. It is not even necessary to suppose, that such a request could or would be preferred by the condemned in another life. It is here supposed by Christ simply to give occasion to the religious teaching embodied in Abraham's reply.

29-31. In this dialogue, the rich man represents the spirit of Pharisaism, which was accustomed to demand from Jesus signs from heaven as an evidence of his divine mission and authority; the spirit of modern skepticism, which demands new intellectual evidences for the truth of Christianity, and places its unbelief avowedly on the insufficiency of the evidences already forthcoming; and the spirit of modern superstition, manifested in spiritism and ecclesiasticism, which, endeavoring to meet this same demand for signs and wonders in less intellectual classes of society, provides miracles and supernatural manifestations. The answer of Abraham represents the spirit of Christianity which recognizes the secret of all skepticism to be *in the moral nature;* which recognizes in the word of God itself its own sufficient evidence; and which declares that no proof whatever of a purely intellectual character will suffice to convince those who are living worldly lives, and whose unbelief is rooted in worldliness of any form. Christ's language implies not only the adequacy of revelation, but also the futility, and therefore the improbability, of supernatural appearances of the dead, such as are maintained by modern spiritism. The truth of the declaration put here by Christ into Abraham's mouth, was strikingly verified by the effect upon the Pharisees of the resurrection of another Lazarus (John 11: 47-50), and of our Lord's resurrection (Matt. 28: 12-14). It is noted by the commentators, that the rich man hopes that his brothers will be led to repent, *i. e.*, to change their course of life; Abraham replies, they will not even be persuaded. They must change their life that they may be persuaded, not by new evidence he persuaded that they may change their life.

Ch. 17: 1-10. VARIOUS SAYINGS OF CHRIST. OFFENDERS AND OFFENCES.—THE DUTY OF FORGIVENESS.—THE POWER OF FAITH.—PHARISAISM CONDEMNED BY ITS OWN PRINCIPLES.

Of these sayings, some are reported in other connections by the other evangelists; others are peculiar to Luke; see below. Whether this is to be regarded as one discourse, including aphorisms, given elsewhere, or as a collection of Christ's sayings, made by Luke, is not very important. The connection between them is clear, and indicates that they constitute one discourse. Christ warns his disciples of offences (vers. 1, 2), and commands them to forgive (vers. 3, 4); this command leads to their request for greater faith (ver. 5), and to the consequent promise of ver. 6; which is accompanied by the parable of the servants (vers. 7-10), which is a warning against the spiritual pride, which the possession and ex-

LUKE.

5 And the apostles said unto the Lord, Increase⁷ our faith.
6 And the Lord said, If ᶻ ye had faith as a grain of mustard seed, ye might say unto this sycamine tree, Be thou plucked up by the root, and be thou planted in the sea ; and it should obey you.
7 But which of you, having a servant plowing, or feeding cattle, will say unto him by and by, when he is come from the field, Go, and sit down to meat ?
8 And will not rather say unto him, Make ready

wherewith I may sup, and gird thyself, and serve me, till I have eaten and drunken ; and afterward thou shalt eat and drink ?
9 Doth he thank that servant because he did the things that were commanded him ? I trow not.
10 So likewise ye, when ye shall have done all those things which are commanded you, say, We are ᵃ unprofitable servants : we have done that which was our duty to do.
11 And it came to pass, as he went to Jerusalem,

y Heb. 12 : 2....z Matt. 17 : 20 ; 21 : 21 ; Mark 9 : 23 ; 11 : 23....a Job 22 : 3 ; 35 : 7 ; Ps. 16 : 2, 3 ; Isa. 64 : 6 ; Rom. 11 ; 35 ; 1 Cor. 19 : 16, 17.

ercise of remarkable powers would be likely to stimulate.

1, 2. Then said he unto his disciples. *Then (δέ)* is not an adverb of time ; there is nothing in the original to indicate that this discourse was connected with the preceding parable. This warning is reported in Matt. 18 : 6, 7 ; see notes there.

3, 4. Comp. Matt. 18 : 15, 21, 22, where see notes. Observe that the duty of rebuke as well as of forgiveness, is taught by Christ. In what spirit and for what purpose this rebuke is to be given is indicated in Gal. 6 : 1, 2. Observe, also, that forgiveness is conditioned on repentance, because the Gospel idea of forgiveness includes a putting away of, a relieving from the transgression, not merely a remission of penalty, and this never can be done for another, except in concurrence with his own repentance.

5, 6. Add to our faith. Not, *Add faith to our other gifts*, for faith is the foundation (2 Pet. 1 : 5), but add to the stock of faith which we already possess. Christ, so far from rebuking this request, as though the disciple should for himself exercise faith, by his reply intimates that they should have asked not an increase but a gift of the very seed and germ of faith.—**As a grain of mustard seed.** Which is selected not, as Adam Clarke, because it increases and thrives re-

SYCAMINE OR MULBERRY BRANCH.

markably, but because it is the least of seeds (Matt. 13 : 32, note).—**Ye might say unto this sycamine tree.** Not the same as the sycamore (ch. 19 : 4). That is the Egyptian fig, this is the mulberry tree, not very common in Palestine, but sometimes found there.—**It should obey you.** Comp. Mark 11 : 22-26, notes. If we here take faith, as defined in Heb. 11 : 1, as the evidence of the unseen, Christ's language is hardly hyperbolical, for it is by the developed power to see unseen verities that man has attained all his mastery over nature.

7-10. In interpreting this parable, a slight modification must be made in the language of verse 7, which should read, not *Will say unto him by and by, when he is come from the field, Go and sit down to meat*, but *Will say unto him when he is come from the field, Go immediately and sit down to meat*. The picture is drawn in accordance with Oriental usages. The same one who serves in the field also frequently serves at the table. His clothes are girded about his loins to keep them out of his way while handing the dishes. The custom requires constant attendance at the table, to change each dish as soon as the master has done with it for a new one ; sometimes ten or twenty, or even fifty dishes, succeed on the tables of those who fare sumptuously.

In the spiritual interpretation of this parable there is a difficulty, because (1) throughout Christ assumes the relation between the disciple and his Lord to be that between a slave and his master, while elsewhere he explicitly declares that his disciples are not servants, but friends (John 15 : 15 ; comp. Gal. 4 : 7) ; (2) he elsewhere declares that when he comes he will gird himself and make his faithful servants sit down to meat, and will serve them (Luke 12 : 37) ; in his parable of the Judgment he represents himself as thanking them for the fidelity of their service (Matt. 25 : 21) ; and Paul, waiting to finish his course, declares his expectation of a crown of righteousness, which the righteous Judge shall give to all who love his appearing (2 Tim. 4 : 8). The explanation of this apparent inconsistency is to be found in the fact that Christ was habitually accustomed to descend to the moral plane of his auditors, to convict them, not by proving their principles to be wrong, but by apparently accepting and using

108 LUKE. [CH. XVII.

that he passed through the midst of Samaria [b] and Galilee.

12 And as he entered into a certain village, there met him ten men that were lepers, which stood afar [c] off:

13 And they lifted up *their* voices, and said, Jesus, Master, have mercy on us.

14 And when he saw *them*, he said unto them, Go shew [d] yourselves unto the priests. And it came to pass, that, as [e] they went, they were cleansed.

[b] ch. 9 : 51, 52 ; John 4 : 4.....[c] Lev. 13 : 45... [d] ch. 5 : 14 ; Lev. 13 : 2 ; 14 : 3 ; Matt. 8 : 4....[e] 2 Kings 5 : 14 ; Isa. 65 : 24.

LORD AND SERVANT.

tled to a seat at the table of the King? Yes. Do you treat your servants thus? When they come in from the field do you make haste to welcome them? to serve them? to thank them? I trow not. But if you are a *servant*, you must be content with a *servant's recompense.*" The moral of the parable, then, is not that the Christian is to say, "We are unprofitable servants." It is rather that he is not a servant at all, but a son. He who assumes to demand as a right a recompense for his service has no claim. But he who comes as a son, receives the inheritance from his father's love; for love gives what the law does not award. The reward is reckoned of grace, not of debt (Rom. 11 : 6); death is the *wages* of sin, but eternal life is the *gift* of God (Rom. 6 : 23); and he who as a friend and a son, in the spirit of love and for love's sake, serves his Lord, receives the gift of his Lord's love, a reward denied to him who was but a servant, who serves for wages, and who *claims* the reward as a debt. It is hardly necessary to say that the language of ver. 9 does not indicate Christ's approval of begrudging a hired servant grateful appreciation of faithful work. The servant in the parable is a slave, and the picture is taken from the actual treatment accorded to a slave by the ordinary master. Moreover, while gratitude will be given to fidelity of service, it cannot be demanded as a right.

Ch. 17 : 11-19. THE HEALING OF TEN LEPERS. LOVE IS THE HIGHEST LAW.

their own principles. Thus, when the rich young ruler (Matt. 19 : 16-22) comes to him asking, What good thing shall I do to inherit eternal life? Christ does not preach to him the doctrine of justification by faith, but replies by referring him only to the moral law, and leaving him to convict himself by the inquiry, What lack I yet? So when the lawyer asks him the same question (Luke 10 : 25-29), Christ refers him to his own interpretation of the law, and compels the lawyer to seek self-justification by the inquiry, Who is my neighbor? In this parable, as in those of the entire series in which it stands, Christ addresses himself to the Pharisees, or to the spirit of Phariseism in his own disciples. The essence of this spirit was, and is ever, a *claim* to be received and rewarded by God for work's sake. Christ in this parable says in effect to the Pharisee, "You claim to be the servant of God? Yes. A faithful servant? Yes. On that ground enti-

The time of this incident appears to me to be wholly uncertain. It is only said that it occurred as Jesus was going to Jerusalem. There is nothing to indicate that Luke himself knew definitely the date. As to the place, see on ver. 1. For a full account of leprosy, the laws of Moses respecting it, and its symbolical significance, see Matt. 8 : 2, note.

11, 12. As he was going to Jerusalem. On one of his journeys, but on which one is not indicated.—**He passed along the borders of Samaria and Galilee.** That is, from west to east toward the Jordan. One of the customary routes from Galilee to Jerusalem, taken to avoid passing through Samaria, was along the northern border of Samaria to the Jordan, across the Jordan at Scythopolis, southward through Perea to the vicinity of Galilee, where the river was recrossed, and the road pursued to Jerusalem. The language here (διὰ μέσον Σ. καὶ Γ.) may

15 And one of them, when he saw that he was healed, turned back, and with a loud voice glorified^f God,
16 And fell down on *his* face at his feet, giving him thanks: and he was a ^g Samaritan.
17 And Jesus answering said, Were there not ten cleansed? but where *are* the nine?
18 There are not ^h found that returned to give glory to God, save this stranger.
19 And he said unto him, Arise, go thy way: thy ^i faith hath made thee whole.

f Ps. 30 : 1, 2 .... g John 4 : 39–42 ... h Ps. 106 : 13 .... i Matt. 9 : 22

mean, as in our English version, *through the midst of Samaria and Galilee*, but the other rendering is the more probable one. Otherwise the reading would have been, Through the midst of Galilee and Samaria, since Samaria lay between Galilee and Judea.—**There met him ten men that were lepers.** Their misery made them companions. The lepers, being excluded from all other society, are accustomed to form groups and communities of their own. The accompanying illustration, from the pencil of Mr. A. L. Rawson, illustrates this fact. Respecting it he says, in a private note to me: "I sketched this scene outside the Jaffa Gate at Jerusalem, where it was a morning and evening spectacle during the entire summer of 1874. The beggars formerly sat outside the Zion Gate, but lately have been permitted to beg here, where the greater number of travelers pass. Many, if not all, of them are lepers. Of the chief of them I made a portrait. They gather by the roadside before sunrise, and leave at sunset. In the hottest days they disappear for three or four hours, rather than roast."—**Which stood afar off.** As required by the Mosaic law (Lev. 13 : 46). The space was fixed by rabbinical regulations, but variously by different authorities, from four to a hundred cubits. Contrast their course with that of the leper in Matt. 8 : 2; Mark 1 : 40, who broke over this law to come to the feet of Jesus to seek healing.

13, 14. They lifted up their voices. A common cause, a common cry.—**Go show yourselves unto the priests.** When a leper was cured, before he could be restored to society, he was required to show himself to the priest, to make an offering, and to be officially pronounced clean. See Lev., ch. 14; Matt. 8 : 4, note. Christ's command thus implied a promise of cure. They were to act as if they were cleansed, and trust to Christ that the cleansing would come in his own time and way. Every miracle is a parable; in this is a hint to those who wait before entering on practical Christian duty, until they have received some personal sense of divine pardon. To such the command of Christ is, Go, assume that I will and can cleanse you; and begin the life of one who has been cleansed.—**As they were going they were cleansed.** Obedience is the road to forgiveness.

15, 16. And one of them, when he saw that he was healed, turned back, with a loud voice glorifying God. The form of the sentence should have prevented the error of those who imagine that he went on to the temple, presented himself to the priest, etc., and then came back and hunted up Jesus. As soon

GROUP OF LEPERS.

as he saw that he was cleansed he immediately hurried back. The contrast between him and the others, is that between the love which disregards the letter in order to manifest gratitude, and the formal obedience which adheres to the ritual but disregards the obligations of love and gratitude. The Jews adhered to the law and forgot the Saviour; the Samaritan returned to thank his Saviour, and for the time forgot the law.—**Giving him thanks.** He gave *glory* to God, *thanks* to Christ; all along his journey he resounded God's praises; he gave thanks to Christ when he came to him.

17, 18. The lesson to us is one that needs

20 And when he was demanded of the Pharisees, when the kingdom of God should come, he answered them and said, The kingdom of God cometh not with observation:

21 Neither shall they say, Lo here! or, lo there! for, behold, the^j kingdom of God is within you.
22 And he said unto the disciples, The^k days will come, when ye shall desire to see one of the days of the Son of man, and ye shall not see it.

j Rom. 14 : 17.... k Matt. 9 : 15.

constant reiteration. How often are meetings in the church convened to pray for conversion; how rarely are they called to give thanks for conversions already wrought. How relatively earnest are the petitions of Christians; how cold and infrequent their thanksgivings.

19. **Thy faith hath saved thee.** Not *made thee whole.* The word *saved* ($\sigma\omega\zeta\omega$) is used sometimes of physical as well as of spiritual healing; but this man was already made whole; Christ now gives him assurance of something more, a cleansing of the inward sin, of which the outward leprosy was but a type. All had faith enough to obey Christ's command, and go show themselves to the priest, while as yet there was no sign of cure; but only the one had the faith which is perfected in love. They all had faith and hope; but only one had the greatest of the graces, that love which is the consummation of salvation (1 Cor. 13 : 13).

Ch. 17 : 20-37. INSTRUCTIONS RESPECTING THE KINGDOM OF GOD. IT HAS ALREADY COME.—ITS NATURE: IN THE SOUL. — ITS FUTURE: HOPE LONG DELAYED IN THE CHURCH; SUFFERING IN THE KING; EARTHINESS AND UNBELIEF IN THE WORLD; AT LENGTH A SUDDEN REVELATION; A FINAL AND A CLOSE DISCRIMINATION.

The rest of this chapter clearly consists of two discourses, or parts of discourses. The first (vers. 20, 21), is addressed to the Pharisees; the second (vers. 22-37) to the disciples; and since Christ was not accustomed to give prophecies of the future, except in parabolic form, to the multitude, the second discourse must be presumed to have been given only to a select few, though not necessarily exclusively to the twelve. Between the second discourse (vers. 22-37) and that of chap. 24 of Matthew, there is a striking similarity. There are some additions here not found there; but in the main, the course of the argument, and to some extent, the language is the same. Some commentators regard this as a different discourse, in which Christ gave his disciples a part of the same admonitions and prophetic warnings, subsequently repeated in the Passion Week at Jerusalem. Others regard it as an imperfect and fragmentary report by Luke of a part of that discourse, which he has placed in this connection, because intimately connected with the question of the Pharisees, When the kingdom of God should come (ver. 20), and his answer thereto. The latter view, though not the one taken by most orthodox commentators,

seems to me preferable. If this instruction had been given now to the twelve in Perea, they would hardly have requested its repetition a few months later in Jerusalem (Matt. 24 : 3); and if I have interpreted Matthew, chap. 24, aright, the counsel of ver. 31 here (vers. 16-18, in Matt.), refers to the impending destruction of Jerusalem, while the connection here would apparently make it refer to Christ's final coming, and its significance in that connection is not clear. See note below. I think then that it is probable that, as in several other places, Matthew, who was an eye and ear witness, gave the discourse in its time, location, and connection, while Luke, a second-hand reporter, has given the same discourse, without any knowledge of or note concerning the time, place, or circumstances of the delivery, and placed it here because it was cognate to Christ's reply to the question of the Pharisees. I consider that the whole of the second of the two discourses (vers. 22-37), except vers. 31, 32, refers not to the destruction of Jerusalem, but to the second coming of our Lord. For the reasons of this belief, see Matt., ch. 24, Prel. Note.

20, 21. **When he was demanded of the Pharisees when the kingdom of God should come.** This demand may not have been made with an evil intent. The universal belief of the age was of a temporal kingdom, with Jerusalem as mistress of the world, a second and superior Rome: the Pharisees naturally asked of one, whose followers claimed for him that he was a great prophet, and some of them that he was the Messiah, when and how this kingdom would be established. On the phrase, *kingdom of God*, see Matt. 3 : 2, note.—**The kingdom of God cometh not with observation.** That is, in such a way as to be observed.—**Neither shall they say, Look here or Look there.** That is, when it comes, there shall be nothing to compel this sort of surprise and superficial admiration.—**For Look.** Christ puts his *look!* in contrast with that of the world. The world looks without; he bids to look within. It is the same word which is rendered "lo" and "behold."—**The kingdom of God is within you.** Most modern commentators render this, *The kingdom of God is among you*, and interpret it as parallel to Luke 11 : 20. The reason for this rendering, which is grammatically possible, though less natural, is given by Alford. The words "are addressed to the Pharisees, in whose hearts it (the kingdom) certainly was not." I agree with

LUKE.

23 And¹ they shall say to you, See here; or, see there: go not after *them*, nor follow *them*.
24 For as the lightning, that lighteneth out of the one *part* under heaven, shineth unto the other *part* under heaven; so shall also the Son of man be in his day.
25 But ᵐ first must he suffer many things, and be rejected of this generation.
26 And as it was ⁿ in the days of Noe, so shall it be also in the days of the Son of man.
27 They did eat, they drank, they married wives, they were given in marriage, until the day that Noe entered into the ark, and the flood came, and destroyed them all.

28 Likewise also as it was in the days of Lot; they did eat, they drank, they bought, they sold, they planted, they builded;
29 But the same day that Lot went out º of Sodom, it rained fire and brimstone from heaven, and destroyed *them* all.
30 Even thus shall it be in the day when the Son of man is revealed.ᵖ
31 In that day, he which shall be upon the housetop, and his stuff in the house, let him not come down to take it away: and he that is in the field, let him likewise not return back.
32 Remember Lot's ᑫ wife.

l ch. 21 : 8; Matt. 24 : 23, etc.; ᵐ Mark 13 : 21....m ch. 9 : 22; Mark 9 : 31....n Gen. 7 : 11, 23.....o Gen. 19 : 23, 24....p 2 Thess. 1 : 7.... q Gen. 19 : 26.

Godet in thinking the reading of our English version to be preferable. It is more natural; it better agrees with the context. The declaration is not historical, but philosophical; the assertion not of a *fact* but of a *law*. Christ does not say that the kingdom of God is already established among the Pharisees, which was not indeed true in any sense, but that the nature of that kingdom is such that it is to be found within the heart.

There is no passage so brief in Scripture which contains so much valuable and significant truth respecting the kingdom of God, or the kingdom of heaven, as these two verses. That kingdom is not to be established by Christ's second coming; he then comes not to found but to take possession of his kingdom. Great public events, whether military, political, or religious, as the Crusades, the Reformation, and so-called revival meetings, are not the coming of his kingdom, though they may help to prepare the way for it. That kingdom is righteousness, and peace, and joy, in the Holy Ghost (Rom. 14 : 17); it is in the disposition and character of the individual, and in the development of a society, nurtured in the spirit and in accord with the precepts and principles of Jesus Christ; and therefore it comes of necessity by gradual processes and in ways which attract no observation, except in their results. The earthquake may prepare the heart of the jailer for the kingdom; but the kingdom does not come in the earthquake.

22, 21. And he said unto the disciples. Whether this is a fragmentary report of the discourse in the Passion week, more fully reported by Matthew, and partially by Luke in ch. 21, or not, it clearly was not given to the Pharisees, nor in immediate connection with the preceding verses.—**Ye shall desire to see one of the days of the Son of Man.** He refers to the universal desire throughout the church, in the absence of its Lord, for his promised reappearance.—**See here! or, See there!** A caution against the danger of deceit, whether by false prophets or misled interpreters. "A warning to all so-called expositors, and followers of expositors, of prophecy, who cry, See here! or, See there! every time that war breaks out or revolutions occur."—(*Alford*.)—**For as the lightning**, etc. The second coming of Christ will be sudden and public; no misapprehension will be possible. Comp. Rev. 6 : 12-17. See note on Matt. 24 : 26, 27.

25-30. But first he must suffer. Comp. Matt. 16 : 21; Luke 24 : 26; Acts 3 : 18.—**And be rejected.** The original implies *trial* as well as rejection, *i. e.*, rejection after trial. The suffering and rejection laid the foundation for the kingdom and the glory.—**As it was in the days of Noah.** Comp. Matt. 24 : 37-39, notes; 2 Pet. 3 : 3, 4.—**Likewise also as it was in the days of Lot.** The example of the days of Lot is peculiar to Luke.—**Even thus.** Literally, *According to these* (κατὰ ταυτά); as though these were expressly intended by God as types and symbols of the great destruction, to involve the whole world and all mankind.—**When the Son of man is revealed.** "The word revealed (ἀποκαλύπτεται, *uncovered*) supposes that Jesus is present, but that a veil conceals his person from the view of the world. All at once the veil is lifted, and the glorified Lord is visible to all."—(*Godet*.) Comp. Col. 3 : 3, 4; 2 Thess. 1 : 7; 1 Pet. 1 : 7.

31, 32. See Matt. 24 : 16-18, notes. Clearly this command, as reported by Matthew, is a practical and prudential direction to the disciples as to their course when they see the destruction of Jerusalem impending, the evidence of which is to be afforded them by the "abomination of desolation." They are then to flee instantly and without delay out of the city. Here, in my judgment, Luke has placed the counsel out of its appropriate order, and in immediate connection with a prophecy of the second coming of Christ, to which it is wholly inapplicable. From that coming the disciples will not desire to flee, and none else can. Godet, indeed, endeavors to apply it to the Last Days, with what success the reader may judge for himself. "There is no mention of *fleeing* from one part of the earth to another, but of rising from the earth to the Lord, as he passes and disappears: 'Let him not come down from

112　　　　　　　　　　　　　LUKE.　　　　　　　　　　　[CH. XVIII.

33 Whosoever^r shall seek to save his life shall lose it; and whosoever shall lose his life shall preserve it.
34 I tell you, in that night there^s shall be two *men* in one bed; the one shall be taken, and the other shall be left.
35 Two *women* shall be grinding together; the one shall be taken, and the other left.
36 Two *men* shall be in the field; the one shall be taken, and the other left.
37 And they answered and said unto him, Where, Lord? And he said unto them, Wheresoever the body is,^t thither will the eagles be gathered together.

CHAPTER XVIII.

AND he spake a parable unto them *to this end*, that men ought^u always to pray, and not to faint;
2 Saying, There was in a city a judge, which feared not God, neither regarded man;
3 And there was a widow in that city; and she came unto him, saying, Avenge me of mine adversary.
4 And he would not for a while; but afterward he said within himself, Though I fear not God, nor regard man;
5 Yet because this widow troubleth me, I will avenge her, lest by her continual coming she weary me.

r ch. 9 : 24; Matt. 16 : 25; Mark 8 : 35; John 12 : 25....s Matt. 24 : 40, 41.. t Job 39 : 30; Matt. 24 : 28,...u ch. 11 : 8; 21 : 36; Ps. 65 : 2; 102 : 17; Rom. 12 : 12; Ephes. 6 : 18; Phil. 4 : 6.

---

the roof; but forgetting all that is in the house, let him be ready to follow the Lord. So he who is in the fields is not to attempt to return home to carry upward with him some object of value. The Lord is there; if any one belongs to Him, let him leave everything at once to accompany Him." I am, however, unable to conceive how in the supreme moment of the Lord's reappearing, and on the eve of the destruction of the world and all that it contains, when even the godless are seeking only self-destruction (Rev. 6 : 16), any disciple should have any inclination to go back to his house for a coat, or down into it for household furniture. But, except for this warning, Christians in Jerusalem might well have thus delayed when the Roman armies began to encompass the city.

33. See Matt. 10 : 39. *Shall preserve* (ζωογονήσει) is, literally, *shall bring forth life*. "That day shall come as pains of labor on a woman in travail (see Matt. 24 : 8, note); but to the saints of God it shall be the birth of the soul and body to life and glory everlasting."—(*Wordsworth*.) He who is always busy saving his own soul is not the one assured of salvation; for salvation is by self-sacrifice.

34-36. See Matt. 24 : 40, 41. The reference here is clearly to the second coming of Christ, and this is quite apparent from the connection, as the discourse is reported by Matthew. "At this time, a selection will take place, a selection which will instantaneously break all earthly relations, even the most intimate, and from which there will arise a new grouping of humanity in two new families or societies, the *taken* and the *left*." —(*Godet*.) Ver. 36 is regarded as spurious by the best scholars. It has been transferred from Matthew, where its genuineness is unquestioned.

37. The disciple's curiosity our Lord refuses to gratify; he even elsewhere declares that he could not if he would (Mark 13 : 32; comp. Acts 1 : 7). His reply is a general one, that wherever there is corruption, there the ministers of God's judgments will be assembled; each new judgment being, like the destruction of Jerusalem, a type of the final judgment. See further, Matt. 24 : 28, note.

Ch. 18 : 1-14. PARABLES CONCERNING PRAYER. IMPORTUNITY IN PRAYER.—HUMILITY IN PRAYER.

Compare with the teaching here that of ch. 11 : 1-13; see notes there. As in the parable there, and in that of the Unjust Steward (ch. 16 : 1-8), Christ here in the parable of the Unjust Judge illustrates, by contrast. The argument is, If an unjust judge can be moved to do right by importunity, shall not the Judge of all the earth be much more moved by the petitions of his afflicted children? Having thus illustrated the duty of patient, persistent prayer in the first parable, in the second he illustrates the spirit which should pervade and inspire prayer. The attempt to trace a detailed parallelism, to make the widow represent the church, the adversary Satan, and the unjust judge God, appears to me to be artificial. The parable is employed to illustrate the single point, indicated in ver. 1. To press it in detail is to impair, not enhance, its full meaning. For an O. T. illustration of right and wrong kind of importunity, compare 1 Kings 18 : 26-28, with 1 Kings 18 : 43, 44.

1. **Men ought always to pray, and not to faint.** Here, as in Ephes. 6 : 18, is a suggestive hint of the truth, that persistence in prayer requires courage. Prayer is sometimes a restful communion, sometimes a soul-wrestling. *Always* is here equivalent to *at all times*. It may be true that "the earnest desire of the heart is prayer" (*Alford*), though I doubt whether this is true in any, except a poetical sense; it is true, that the heart should always maintain such relations with God, that every act and thought should be consecrated by the sense of his presence, and this may be what is meant by the exhortation to "pray without ceasing" (1 Thess. 5 : 17). But neither is the real point of the parable here, which is given to teach us, not the duty of an earnest or devout heart, but the duty of not suffering discouragement in prayer, because times are adverse, and no answer appears to be vouchsafed.

2, 3. **A judge which feared not God nor regarded man.** No lower moral state can well be imagined than is described in these two phrases. He was indifferent to the condemna-

6 And the Lord said, Hear what the unjust judge saith.
7 And shall not God avenge[v] his own elect, which cry day and night unto him, though he bear long with them?
8 I tell you that he will avenge them speedily.[w] Nevertheless, when the Son of man cometh, shall[x] he find faith on the earth?
9 And he spake this parable unto certain which[y] trusted in themselves that they were righteous, and despised others:
10 Two men went up into the temple to pray; the one was a Pharisee, and the other a publican.

v Rev. 6 : 10 .... w Ps. 46 : 5; Heb. 10 : 37; 2 Pet. 3 : 8, 9 .... x Matt. 24 : 12 .... y ch. 10 : 29.

tion pronounced by God against perversion of justice (Exod. 23 : 6-9; Lev. 19 : 15; Deut 1 : 16, 17, 2 Chron. 19 : 5-7); he was shamelessly indifferent to his own reputation among men; and he was conscious of his own audacity and gloried in his shame (ver. 4). The judges in the East are generally irresponsible and corrupt; take bribes from either or both parties; from their decisions there is in most cases no appeal; and the proceedings in execution of their decrees are summary.—**And there was a widow in that city.** In the East the position of a widow is one of absolute helplessness. In India she is regarded as suffering a special visitation of divine wrath, for her own or her ancestors' sins, is excluded from all society, and is made a common drudge and the subject of unlimited petty despotism, especially by her husband's family. The O. T. denounces this treatment of widows, and declares them to be under God's special keeping (Exod. 22 : 22-24; Deut. 10 : 18; Deut. 24 : 17; Psalm 68 : 5; 146 : 9; Jer. 7 : 6; 22 : 3; 49 : 11; Mal. 3 : 5).—**Avenge me of mine adversary.** Either Punish his wrong-doing, or Protect from his wrong-doing; the latter is probably the better meaning. The justice of her case is throughout pre-supposed.

4, 5. He would not for awhile. The reason why the unjust judge would not heed the widow's complaints, is implied to be his selfish indifference. The reason why God often appears for awhile not to heed the complaints of his people is not given. That reason lies in his own counsel, and beyond our full comprehension. There is, however, a hint of it in ver. 7, below.—**Lest by her continual coming she weary me.** Literally, *Beat me* (ὑπωπιάζω). The verb is a pugilistic one, the same used by Paul in 1 Cor. 9 : 27, and there translated, "*I keep under* my body." The hyperbole indicates the impatience and unreasonableness of the unjust judge. The language of all nations abounds with like instances of this spirit of exaggeration in the impatient. Thus, to be "pestered," is literally to be afflicted with the pest; to be "worried," is to be strangled, etc.

6-8. And the Lord said. What follows is the application of the parable, and, with the language of ver. 1, gives the key to the correct interpretation of the whole.—**Though he bear long with them.** There are two renderings of this phrase possible. It may mean, *Though he bears long with the oppressors;* it may mean, *When also he is patient toward his own elect.* The latter interpretation appears to me preferable, both from grammatical and from spiritual considerations. It then completes the contrast between the unjust judge and the loving All-Father, who is never vexed and impatient at the importunity of his chosen ones. But whichever interpretation be adopted, *forbearance*, not *indifference*, is indicated as the reason why God delays to answer the prayers of his children. He cannot deliver them without bringing judgment on the oppressors, and he waits, that his long-suffering may become the means of their salvation (Rom. 2 : 4; 2 Pet. 3 : 9, 15).—**He will avenge them speedily.** Not He will speedily come to avenge them, but When he comes he will make a speedy end (1 Sam. 3 : 12).—**Shall he find faith on the earth?** One of those mournful utterances which show how hard a burden to the heart of Christ is the unbelief of his own disciples. Comp. Matt. 17 : 17.

9. He spake this parable unto certain which trusted in themselves because they were righteous. There has been some discussion respecting the question to whom this parable was primarily addressed, whether (1) to the Pharisees, (2) to Christ's own disciples, or (3) to followers who were inclined partially to accept his teachings, but in whom the leaven of Pharisaism still remained. Clearly it was not addressed to the Pharisees, because then it could not be called a *parable;* the Pharisee was used to illustrate a spirit which Christ perceived in others. Probably it was addressed to his followers, being evoked by observing a tendency to spiritual pride among them. More important is it to note, that it is still addressed to all those in the Christian community who trust to themselves because their own character and conduct appears to them meritorious. In contrast, Christ holds up the picture of one who trusts wholly to the mercy of a forgiving God. Thus he parabolically teaches that doctrine of justification by faith alone, which was so predominant in the teachings of Paul. See, for example, Rom. 3 : 20-28; Ephes. 2 : 1-10; Phil. 3 : 4-10. Paul himself was before his conversion the Pharisee, but afterward the publican.—**And despised others.** As humility and charity are twins (1 Cor. 13 : 4), so pride and contempt.

11 The Pharisee stood and prayed thus with himself: God, I thank thee that I am not ᶻ as other men *are*, extortioners, unjust, adulterers, or even as this publican.

12 I fast twice in the week, I give tithes of all that I possess.

13 And the publican, standing afar off, would not lift up so much as *his* eyes unto heaven, but smote ᵃ upon his breast, saying, God be merciful to me a sinner.

14 I tell you, this man went down to his house justified *rather* than the other: for ᵇ every one that exalteth himself shall be abased; and he that humbleth himself shall be exalted.

15 And ᶜ they brought unto him also infants, that he

z Isa. 65 : 5; Rev. 3 : 17.... a Jer. 31 : 19.... b Job 22 : 29; Matt. 23 : 12.... c Matt. 19 : 13; Mark 10 : 13, etc.

---

10. The one a Pharisee, and the other a publican. The former a type of orthodox belief and a vigorous but legal morality; the other a type of the justly condemned and the outcast. "A Brahmin and a Pariah, as one might say, if preaching from this Gospel in India."—(*Trench*.) On the character of the Pharisees, see Matt. 3 : 7, note; on the character of the publicans, Matt. 9 : 9, note.

11, 12. The Pharisee stationed himself. The publican *stood* (ἑστώς, active); the Pharisee *stationed himself* (σταφείς, passive, with middle signification). There is no significance in the mere fact that the Pharisee *stood*, for standing was a common attitude of prayer among the Jews (1 Kings 8 : 22; 2 Chron. 6 : 12; Mark 11 : 25); but there is a significance, not recognized in our English version, in the phraseology employed to indicate the attitude of the Pharisee and the publican. The Pharisee "took his stand, planted and put himself in a prominent attitude of prayer; so that all eyes might light on him, all might take note that he was engaged in his devotions."—(*Trench*.)—**And prayed thus with himself.** Even in the prayer of the Pharisee, self is the centre of his thoughts. Though in form a prayer, his address was really a self-gratulatory soliloquy.—**God, I thank thee that I am not as the rest of men.** Not merely as some other men, but as the rest of mankind, mankind in general. Observe that humility thanks God that I am what I am (1 Cor. 15 : 9, 10); pride thanks God that I am not like other men (comp. 2 Cor. 10 : 12). In the Episcopal Prayer Book, this truth is recognized by making this parable and 1 Cor. 15 : 1-11, the Gospel and Epistle for the same Sunday, the eleventh Sunday after Trinity. Observe, too, that this Pharisee believes in the doctrine of total depravity; he rates other men very low. This doctrine may be, as here, one of pride, or, as in Paul's experience, one of humility (1 Tim. 1 : 15, 16).—**Extortioners, unjust, adulterers.** A comprehensive catalogue, including all flagrant transgressions, both against others and against self; but there is no recognition of that spirituality of the law expounded by Christ in the Sermon on the Mount (Matt. 5 : 20-48; comp. 1 Tim. 1 : 5), and of which all Pharisaism is a perpetual violation.—**I fast twice in the week, I give tithes of all that I possess.** His boast covers the two points of religious service and of benevolence. In both he claims to do more than the law requires. The Mosaic law provided for only one fast in the year, the great Day of Atonement (Lev. 16 : 29; Numb. 29 : 7). The Jews added a number of annual fasts and two weekly fasts, viz., on the fifth day, because Moses on that day went up Sinai, and the second, because on that day he came down. The Christian sects in the East still maintain a fast twice a week throughout the whole year, but content themselves with abstinence from meat and the products of the dairy. Tithes of all produce, including flocks and cattle, were required by the law to be given to the Levite (Lev. 27 : 30); this Pharisee said that he gave tithes of all that came into his possession, whether agricultural products or not. The modern equivalent of this boast would be the claim to be regular in attendance on Christian ordinances and a liberal contributor to the recognized Christian charities. But the ancient, like the modern Pharisee, claims only a legal righteousness, *i. e.*, that he has done all that is *required* of him, and even more. Of that love, without which so-called acts of charity and religion are vain (1 Cor. 13 : 1-3), he is entirely oblivious. Contrast the "boasting" of Paul, 1 Cor. 4 : 11-16; 9 : 27; 15 : 9, 10; 2 Cor. 11 : 9-17; Gal. 2 : 20.

13. And the publican standing afar off. Not merely far from the Pharisee, but remote from the other worshippers, partly from a sense of his own unworthiness and partly from a desire to be apart from the crowd and alone with God. **Would not lift up so much as his eyes unto heaven.** In contrast with the Pharisee whose gestures doubtless testified to the people his devotions (Matt. 6 : 5). **But smote upon his breast.** Various emblematic meanings have been attributed to this action, as that he thus indicated the death-stroke which sin merits from God (*Godet*), the pain experienced in his own conscience (*Bengel*), the punishment which he would himself inflict on sin in his own heart (*Augustine*). The true significance of the action is indicated by the fact, that smiting upon the breast was a common gesture for the expression of great grief and shame (Luke 23 : 48).—**God be merciful to me the sinner.** There is a significance in the definite article, which is lost in our English version. Comp. 1 Tim. 1 : 15. It does not indicate a comparison with others, and

BLESSING LITTLE CHILDREN.

"*Suffer little children to come unto me, and forbid them not.*"

would touch them: but when *his* disciples saw *it*, they rebuked them.
16 But Jesus called them *unto him*, and said, Suffer little children to come unto me, and forbid them not: for of such is the kingdom of God.
17 Verily I say unto you, Whosoever shall not receive the kingdom of God as a little child,ᵈ shall in no wise enter therein.
18 And ᵉ a certain ruler asked him, saying, Good Master, what shall I do to inherit eternal life?
19 And Jesus said unto him, Why callest thou me good? none *is* good save one, *that is*, God.
20 Thou knowest the ᶠ commandments, Do not commit adultery, Do not kill, Do not steal, Do not bear false witness, Honour thy father and thy mother.
21 And he said, All these have I kept from my youth up.
22 Now when Jesus heard these things, he said unto him, Yet lackest thou one thing: sell all that thou hast, and distribute unto the poor, and thou shalt have treasure ᵍ in heaven: and come, follow me.
23 And when he heard this, he was very sorrowful: for he was very rich.
24 And when Jesus saw that he was very sorrowful, he said, How ʰ hardly shall they that have riches enter into the kingdom of God!
25 For it is easier for a camel to go through a needle's eye, than for a rich man to enter into the kingdom of God.
26 And they that heard *it* said, Who then can be saved?
27 And he said, The ⁱ things which are impossible with men, are possible with God.
28 Then Peter said, Lo, we have left all, and followed thee.
29 And he said unto them, Verily I say unto you, There is no man that hath ʲ left house, or parents, or brethren, or wife, or children, for the kingdom of God's sake,
30 Who shall not receive manifold more in this present time, and in the world to come life ᵏ everlasting.
31 Then he took *unto him* the twelve, and said unto them, Behold, we go up to Jerusalem, and ˡ all things that are written by the prophets concerning the Son of man shall be accomplished.
32 For he shall be delivered ᵐ unto the Gentiles, and shall be mocked, and spitefully entreated, and spitted on:
33 And they shall scourge *him*, and put him to death: and the third day he shall rise again.
34 And ⁿ they understood none of these things: and this saying was hid from them, neither knew they the things which were spoken.
35 And it ᵒ came to pass, that as he was come nigh

d Ps. 131:2; Mark 10:15; 1 Pet. 1:14 ...e Matt. 19:16, etc.; Mark 10:17, etc....f Exod. 20:12-16; Deut. 5:16-20; Rom. 13:9.... g Matt. 6:19, 20; 1 Tim. 6:19....h Prov. 11:28; 1 Tim. 6:9....i ch. 1:37; Jer. 32:17; Zech. 8:6....j Deut. 33:9....k Rev. 2:10.... l Ps. 22:1; Isa. 53....m ch. 23:1; Matt. 27:2; John 18:28; Acts 3:13....n Mark 9:32; John 12:16....o Matt. 20:29, etc.; Mark 10:46, etc.

a thought of himself as the sinner above all others, but, rather, that "he is thinking of none but himself."—(*Bengel.*)

14. This man went down to his house justified rather than the other. It is evident, that *justified* here does not mean *made just*, but *absolved from sin*. No change in the character of the publican is indicated, only a change in his relations to God. Thus this parable throws no small light on the theological controversy between Romanism and Protestantism; the one makes a new character the ground of divine favor; the other makes the divine favor the ground of a new character. Pharisee and publican had each received his reward (Matt. 6:1, 2); one the praise of men and the gratulations of his own pride, the other pardon from his Father in heaven, and the peace which pardon brings.— **Every one that exalteth himself shall be abased,** etc. Christ, in this parable, affords a spiritual interpretation to the parable in ch. 14:7-11.

15-17. CHRIST BLESSES LITTLE CHILDREN.— Comp. Matt. 19:13-15; Mark 10:13-16. See notes on Matthew. The words of our Lord are *verbatim*, as in Mark. From this point the narrative again harmonizes with those of Matthew and Mark, after a divergence from ch. 9:51. The word *infants* (βρέφος), peculiar to Luke, shows clearly that children are referred to, who were too young to receive instruction and to be brought into the kingdom by an intelligent comprehension of the truth. Comp. Luke 2:12, 16; Acts 7:19; 2 Tim. 3:15; 1 Pet. 2:2; in all of which cases the Greek word is the same.

18-30. THE RICH YOUNG RULER.—Comp. Matt. 19:16-30; Mark 10:17-31. See notes on Matthew. Luke alone describes this young man as a "ruler," *i. e.*, probably a ruler of a synagogue. For description of this officer, see note on Matt. 4:23.

31-34. PROPHECY OF CHRIST'S PASSION AND RESURRECTION.—Matt. 20:17-19; Mark 10:32-34. See notes on Mark. The declaration here, *All things that are written by the prophets concerning the Son of man* (*i. e.*, the Messiah, see Matt. 10:23, note) *shall be accomplished*, is peculiar to Luke. The following are among the prophecies referred to: Psalm 16:10; 22:7, 8, 16, 18; 49:15; Isaiah 53:1-9; Dan. 9:26. The declaration of ver. 34 is also peculiar to Luke. How far the disciples were from understanding the Passion, clearly as it was foretold, is evident from the ambitious request of James and John, which immediately followed the prophecy (Mark 10:35-45). The reason why they did not understand is indicated: "The saying was hid from them," a declaration interpreted in part by John 14:29, in part by 1 Cor. 2:7, 10. The object of prophecy is not to reveal to the present age future events; this the plainest prophecies never have done; but to afford a testimony to the truth of divine revelation, after their fulfillment. See Mark 9:30-32, notes.

Ch. 18:35-43. THE HEALING OF A BLIND MAN. A PARABLE OF REDEMPTION.

The account of this miracle is given by the three Evangelists, Matthew, Mark, and Luke, but with some notable variations. Those which are merely verbal, are given below. Two other variations are of considerable importance. Matthew and Mark represent it as per-

unto Jericho, a certain blind man sat by the way side, begging:

36 And hearing the multitude pass by, he asked what it meant.

37 And they told him, that Jesus of Nazareth passeth by.

38 And he cried, saying, Jesus, *thou* son of David, have mercy ᵖ on me.

p Ps. 62 : 12.

formed on Christ's *departure from*, Luke on Christ's *approach to* Jericho. Matthew says that there were *two* blind men; Mark and Luke represent but *one*. Various attempts have been made to reconcile these differences, as by supposing that Christ healed two blind men, one on his approach, the other on his departure, and that Matthew has combined the two acts in one account. The variation however presents no difficulty except to those who maintain a doctrine of verbal inspiration, for which the Scripture itself gives no warrant. They are just such as are of the most common occurrence in history, and confirm, instead of throwing doubt over the substantial truth of the narrative. As Matthew was probably an eye-witness, since the apostles apparently accompanied their Lord on this journey, and Mark and Luke derived their information from others, it is probable that there were two blind men, and that the cure was performed on the exit from, not on the entrance into, Jericho.

35-37. He was come nigh unto Jericho. In order to harmonize Luke's account with those of Matthew and Mark, it has been proposed to read this, *He was near Jericho;* but this is certainly a forced, even if it be a possible construction of the original, and comparing this verse with ch. 19 : 1, it is evident that the writer supposed that the miracle was wrought by Jesus on approaching the city. Jericho was situated in the valley of the Jordan, opposite the point where Joshua crossed that river on entering the Holy Land. It was about fifteen miles northeast of Jerusalem and about seven from the river. The environs were well watered and rich, and the city was famous for its palm trees and its balsam. Its position made it strategically the key to the entrance of the Holy Land. After its destruction by Joshua (Josh., ch. 6) its rebuilding was prohibited, under a curse (Josh. 6 : 26), which was incurred in the days of King Ahab, by Hiel the Bethelite (1 Kings 16 : 34), who refortified it, but apparently did not literally rebuild it, since it had been an inhabited city prior to his time (Judg. 3-13; 2 Sam. 10 : 5). It subsequently became the site of a school of the prophets, presided over by Elisha (2 Kings 2 : 1-22), who sweetened the waters of the before unpalatable spring in the immediate vicinity. On its plains Zedekiah fell into the hands of the Chaldeans (Jer. 39 : 5 ; 52 : 8); three hundred and forty-five of its inhabitants are mentioned in the return from Babylon under Zerubbabel (Ezra 2 : 34; Neh. 3 : 2; 7 : 36). Its revenues were given by Anthony to Cleopatra, and were redeemed by Herod the Great, who rebuilt and ornamented it, and even founded a new town higher up on the plain than the old site. It was plundered and the palace destroyed by a slave of Herod, but was rebuilt again by Archelaus, who again planted the plains with palm trees. It was naturally on Christ's route in passing from Perea

VIEW OF THE SITE OF JERICHO.

JESUS GIVING SIGHT.

"*As Jesus passed by he saw a man which was blind from his birth.*"

Ch. XVIII.] LUKE. 117

39 And they which went before rebuked him, that he should hold his peace: but he cried q so much the more, *Thou* son of David, have mercy on me.
40 And Jesus stood, and commanded him to be brought unto him: and when he was come near, he asked him,

41 Saying, What wilt thou that I shall do unto thee? And he said, Lord, that I may receive my sight.
42 And Jesus said unto him, Receive thy sight: thy r faith hath saved thee.
43 And immediately he received s his sight, and followed him, glorifying t God: and all the people, when they saw it, gave praise unto God.

q Ps. 141 : 1....r ch. 17 ; 19....s Ps. 30 : 2....t ch. 5 : 26 ; Acts 4 : 21 ; 11 : 18 ; Gal. 1 : 24.

to Jerusalem. Its proximity to Jerusalem made it a favorite residence of the priests when released from the services of the temple; and its commercial importance made it a headquarters of the publicans or tax-gatherers. The site of the Jericho of the N. T. is believed to have been nearer the mountain called Quarantana than the one now occupied by the modern village. The accompanying illustration is from a sketch by Mr. A. L. Rawson.—**A certain blind man sat by the wayside begging.** Both beggary and blindness are much more common in the East than with us; the former, owing to unjust taxation, uneven distribution of wealth, and the total absence of public and systematized charities; the latter, owing to lack of cleanliness, and to exposure to an almost tropical sun, and to burning sands. The duty of charity to the blind was especially enjoined by the Mosaic law (Lev. 19 : 14 ; Deut. 27 : 18). There is nothing in either Evangelist to indicate the nature of the blindness in this case. The beggar's name is given by Mark, *Bartimaeus*. The accompanying illustration of an Eastern beggar, is from an original sketch by Mr. A. L. Rawson, drawn from life.—

AN EASTERN BEGGAR.

Jesus the Nazarene is coming by. Evidently the fame of the Nazarene had reached Judea; the name and epithet were sufficient to characterize him, even to this blind beggar.

38, 39. Jesus, Son of David, have mercy on me. This appeal involves a recognition of Christ's Messianic character. The phrase, "Son of David," was a common Judaic appellation of the expected Messiah (Matt. 22 : 42). It was a Jewish belief that one of the evidences of the Messiah would be his power to open the eyes of the blind; it was claimed, perhaps from such passages as Isaiah 29 : 18; 42 : 7, and was certainly confirmed by the cures of the blind which Christ had already wrought, both in Galilee and in Judea (Matt. 9 : 27–31 ; Mark 8 : 22–26 ; John 9 : 1–39).—**They which went before.** Accompanying and preceding Christ.—**Rebuked him.** Not because he called Jesus the Son of David, but because he presumed to intrude a private grief upon the King of Israel, when, as they supposed, he was going in triumph to Jerusalem, to assume his throne and deliver the nation (ch. 19 : 11). The spirit of this rebuke was precisely the same as that of Matt. 19 : 13.—**He so much the more.** From the ministers and would-be representatives of Christ, the blind man appeals directly to Christ himself.

40, 41. Commanded him to be led to him. Mark says commanded him *to be called*. He adds, also, as a significant indication of the change in popular feeling wrought by Christ's simple direction, that those who had before rebuked the blind man, now said to him, *Cheer up, rise, he calls thee* (θάρσει, ἔγειρε, φωνεῖ σε). The call of Christ is always full of cheer; always, too, a call to *do* something as a token of trust in him. Obedience is the only recognized confession of faith. —**And when he was come near.** He cast off his *garment, i. e.,* his outer mantle or shawl, not stopping to wrap it about him; an indication of his eagerness and haste.

42, 43. Receive thy sight. According to Matthew, Christ touched the eyes of both blind men.—**Thy faith hath saved thee.** In the way in which faith always saves, by making him that exercises it a willing recipient of salvation from the Saviour.

The commentators in all ages have seen in this a remarkable enacted parable of redemption. The blind man represents the sinner, who, without faith, is without the evidence of things unseen (Heb. 11 : 1); yet in his darkness he can at least dimly discern the evidences of the approach of One who gives life and light; he calls,

CHAPTER XIX.

AND *Jesus* entered and passed through Jericho.[u] ² And, behold, *there was* a man named Zacchæus, which was the chief among the publicans, and he was rich. ³ And he sought to see Jesus, who he was; and could not for the press, because he was little of stature. ⁴ And he ran before, and climbed up into a sycamore tree to see him: for he was to pass that *way*. ⁵ And when Jesus came to the place, he looked up, and saw[v] him, and said unto him, Zacchæus, make

u Josh. 6 : 26 ; 1 Kings 16 : 34. . . . v Ps. 139 : 1–3.

appealing for mercy to Jesus, *i. e.*, Saviour, and the Son of David, that is, the Great King; his cry, though not always at first answered, is heard, and he is called in turn, and receives his sight, without fee, reward, or condition of any kind, as the unpurchased and unpurchasable gift of God's love. The incident affords also a kind of parabolic illustration of the reconciliation of free-will and free-grace ; the blind man both calls and is called, elects and is elected. It also illustrates the peculiar grace of Jesus Christ, who thinks it not unworthy nor inappropriate to turn aside from the march to his triumphant passion and death, in order to hear the cry and heal the infirmity of a blind beggar.

Ch. 19 : 1–10. THE CALL AND CONVERSION OF ZACCHEUS. GENUINE REPENTANCE ILLUSTRATED : IT INVOLVES CONFESSION, REPARATION, AND A NEW LIFE.

To get the full meaning of this incident the reader must remember the twofold character of Jericho. It was a city of both priests and publicans. About fifteen miles northeast of Jerusalem, it was a favorite retreat of the priests when not actually engaged in the temple services. Its palm and balsam were thought by Anthony a present worthy of being conferred on his royal mistress, Cleopatra ; it was the site of one of the palaces of King Herod ; and being the centre of the Judean valley, whose fertility the frosts of winter never checked, it was a headquarters of the tax-gatherers. Thus religion and commerce met here without mingling ; and Christ in choosing the house of Zaccheus for his resting-place, passed by the houses of the rabbis and priests of Judaism ; and this on a journey to the capital where, as all his followers believed, he was about to establish the theocracy (see 11). It is not strange that "they all murmured." Of the language of Zaccheus there are two constructions ; either is grammatically tenable. Godet regards it as the language of self-justification ; supposes that Zaccheus tells Christ what he is accustomed to do, in answer to the charge that he is a sinner. The other view regards it as the language of confession and promised reformation. This view is more generally adopted by the commentators, and is, I have no doubt, the correct one. See notes below.

1, 2. And passed through Jericho. For history and description of Jericho, see ch. 18 : 35.
—**A man named Zaccheus.** The word means *pure;* its etymology indicates that he was of Jewish extraction ; it appears among the lists of the families who came with Zerubbabel from Babylon at the time of the Restoration (Neh. 7 : 14).
—**Was a chief among the publicans** (ἀρχιτελώνης). Probably a provincial agent, who had the general supervision of the publicans of the province.—**And he was rich.** It almost necessarily follows that he must have been extortionate and a defrauder. For account of publicans, see note on Matt. 9 : 10, 11.

3, 4. He sought to see Jesus, who he was. What sort of a person. Zaccheus had heard the fame of Jesus, and was impelled by curiosity to see what sort of a man he might be.
—**And he ran before.** He first went out and mingled with the crowd ; but such crowds are rarely reverential to great men ; they even especially delight in elbowing away the mere man of wealth, whose riches are accompanied by unpopularity. Unable to get a sight of Jesus in the crowd, Zacchens runs before it and climbs a tree, in order to accomplish his purpose. This resoluteness indicates that there was dormant much desire mingled with his curiosity.—**A sycamore tree.** Not the sycamore tree of this

A SYCAMORE TREE.

country, which is a maple, but the Egyptian fig. It flourishes in the plains and valleys, has low,

ZACCHEUS INVITED.

"*Zaccheus, make haste and come down; for to-day I must abide at thy house.*"

haste, and come down; for to-day I must abide ʷ at thy house.
6 And he made haste, and came down, and received him joyfully.
7 And when they saw it, they all murmured, saying, That ˣ he was gone to be guest with a man that is a sinner.
8 And Zacchæus stood, and said unto the Lord, Behold, Lord, the half of my goods I give to the poor; ʸ and if I have taken any thing from any man by ᶻ false accusation, I restore ᵃ him fourfold.
9 And Jesus said unto him, This day is salvation come to this house, forsomuch as he also is a son ᵇ of Abraham.
10 For ᶜ the Son of man is come to seek and to save that which was lost.ᵈ

w John 14 : 23; Rev. 3 : 20....x ch. 5 : 30, Matt. 9 : 11....y Ps. 41 : 1....z ch. 3 : 14; Exod. 20 · 16....a Exod. 22 : 1; 2 Sam. 12 : 6....b ch. 13 : 16....c Matt. 15 : 11 ...d Ezek. 34 : 16; Rom. 5 : 6.

wide-spreading horizontal branches, and so is easy of ascent.
5-7. And said unto him, Zaccheus. Jesus may have caught the name from the remarks and the jeers of the crowd; but there is nothing incredible in the belief that he who could read the heart of Zaccheus knew his name.—**Make haste and come down; for to-day I must abide at thy house.** The *must* indicates, not that this was especially ordained for him, but that it was his impelling and compelling desire to seek and to save that which is lost. He passes by the socially congenial to be the guest of the one whom he can redeem. To *abide* indicates a purpose to make the house of Zaccheus his resting-place while in Jericho, and therefore probably for that night. Observe that the Saviour invites himself to be the guest of the sinner; the story of Zaccheus illustrates the invitation of Rev. 3 : 20.—**They all murmured.** A loose expression, indicating a general expression of surprise and discontent. Probably neither the twelve nor the other publicans joined in this murmuring. It was a common complaint against Jesus (ch. 5 : 30; 15 : 2), and it is not strange that it should have been so. "'A man's a man for a' that,' the lesson that Jesus taught the Jews in Jericho, the world has not yet learned, despite the lapse of ages. To eat with social sinners is scarcely less pardonable in the 'best society' of Christendom in the nineteenth century than it was in that of Judaism in the first. Social democracy is the last, as it is the ripest, form of democracy."—(*Abbott's Jesus of Nazareth*.)
8-10. And Zaccheus standing said. Godet sees in this standing "a firm and dignified attitude, such as suits a man whose honor is attacked;" Alford, an indication of "some effort and resolve." The latter conception seems to me preferable; especially if we suppose that this took place in the house of Zaccheus while Christ was seated, possibly at table and in presence of others.—**Behold, Lord, the half of my goods I will give to the poor.** The tense is present ($\delta i\delta\omega\mu\iota$), but has a future signification. The present is used for the future in Greek, "when an action, still future, is to be designated as good as already present, either because it is already firmly resolved upon, or because it follows according to some unalterable law."—(*Winer*.) The Greek student will find illustrations of this fact in Matt. 26 : 2; Luke 12 : 54; John 14 : 3; Col. 3 : 6. It is evident that Zaccheus cannot be stating here what is his habit, for no man can habitually give away half his goods; accordingly Godet, who interprets the language of Zaccheus as that of self-justification, understands by half of his goods, "the half of his yearly income." The difficulty about this rendering is that it does not interpret what Zaccheus said, but puts into his mouth something different. The word here rendered goods ($\dot{\upsilon}\pi\dot{\alpha}\rho\chi o\nu\tau\alpha$) is never used in the N. T. as equivalent to *income*, but always for *possessions*.—**And whatsoever I have taken from any man by false accusation I will restore him fourfold.** This rendering more nearly accords with the spirit of the original than our English version; the Greek for *if I have taken*, does not necessarily indicate uncertainty. "If (ϵi), with the indicative, implies that the condition being true, that which results from it is to be regarded as real and certain."—(*Robinson*.) See Matt. 4 : 3, note; 19 : 10. It is impossible to suppose that in this sentence, if at all literally rendered, Zaccheus expresses a habit of action. A singular evidence of virtue would it be that he was accustomed to rob by false accusation, and then restore fourfold. Godet accordingly supposes that the robbing was done by his subordinates, and that perhaps the restitution was compelled from the detected thief. False accusation was a method of extorting money commonly practiced by the tax-gatherers of the East. In truth, the system of Oriental tax-gathering was and is such that an honest collector could not make a living, much less amass a fortune. See Vol. I, p. 126. The Mosaic law, Num. 5 : 6, 7, requires, when restitution was voluntary, that a fifth more than the sum unjustly taken should be restored. The promise of Zaccheus includes much more. When he had given half his property to the poor, and had restored fourfold of his unjust exactions, we may fairly assume that he would no longer be rich. The evidence of his repentance was unmistakable.—**This day is salvation come to this house.** This declaration is responsive to that of Zaccheus, and implies that it had come in and through his repentance.—**Forasmuch as he also is a son of Abraham.**

11 And as they heard these things, he added and spake a parable, because he was nigh to Jerusalem, and because ⁿ they thought that the kingdom of God should immediately appear.

12 He said therefore, A certain ᶠ nobleman went into a far country, to receive for himself a kingdom, and to return.

13 And he called his ten servants, and delivered them ten pounds, and said unto them, Occupy till I come.

14 But ᵍ his citizens hated him, and sent a message

e Acts 1 : 6.... f Matt. 25 : 14, etc.; Mark 13 : 34....g John 1 : 11; 15 : 18.

Not because he is a Jew, for Christ no less than John the Baptist, emphatically repudiated the notion that salvation belonged to the Jewish race or descended by generation ; but because he was a Jew inwardly (Rom. 2 : 28, 29; Gal. 3 : 7).—**For the Son of man is come to seek and save the lost.** See ch. 15 : 3-10. Another indication that Zaccheus was not before Christ's coming the just and generous man which ver. 8 would indicate if rendered as in our English version. To the complaint that Christ was gone to be the guest of a sinner, Christ replies that his mission is to seek and to save the sinner ; how he does this the conversion of Zaccheus illustrates.

Ch. 19 : 11-27.—PARABLE OF THE TEN POUNDS. THE KINGDOM OF GOD DOES NOT IMMEDIATELY APPEAR.—DILIGENCE IN EARTHLY DUTY A CONDITION OF ADMISSION TO HEAVENLY GLORY.—NEW TRUSTS THE DIVINE REWARD FOR FIDELITY.—USING THE LITTLE ARIGHT THE WAY TO SECURE MORE.—THE JUDGMENT OF THE CHURCH; THE JUDGMENT OF THE WORLD.—THE END OF THE REBELLIOUS : DEATH.

Analogous to this parable is that of the Ten Talents in Matt. 25 : 14-30; Mark 13 : 34-36. The analogy is so marked, that some scholars (Calvin, Olshausen, Meyer) have regarded them as identical. But the differences appear to me very marked. (1.) The time and place of each parable are fixed by the narrative ; that of Matthew being in Jerusalem during the Passion week ; that of Luke being as clearly in Jericho, at the house of Zaccheus. (2.) The structure of the two parables, though analogous, is different. In Matthew, a rich man distributed to his servants all his goods, the sum total amounting, at the lowest estimate, to many thousand dollars ; in Luke, a prince going to secure the title to his throne from the central government, leaves in the hands of a few of his servants a small sum, at the largest estimate not exceeding three hundred dollars, simply as a means of testing their fidelity. In Matthew, the talents are distributed to each man according to his several ability ; in Luke, each servant receives the same, one pound. In Matthew, only the servants are introduced ; in Luke, public enemies also. (3.) The object of the two parables, though analogous, is not identical. The primary object of the parable in Matthew, which is addressed solely to Christ's disciples, is to teach the necessity of fidelity in the church ; incidentally it indicates that a long time must elapse before the reckoning. The primary object of the parable in Luke, which is addressed to all the people, is to teach that the kingdom of God will not immediately appear ; incidentally it teaches how by diligent fidelity the servants of God are to prepare for his appearing, and what is to be the nature of the reckoning, both with them and with those who reject his rule. Godet, Trench, Alford, Lange, Oosterzee, agree in regarding the two parables as different.

11, 12. As they heard these things. The time and place of the parable are fixed as in the house of Zaccheus, and in immediate connection with the preceding instructions.—**He was nigh to Jerusalem.** About 15 miles.—**Because they thought that the kingdom of God should immediately appear.** There was a general expectancy, shared by the disciples, strengthened by such events as the cure of the blind man and the resurrection of Lazarus, that Christ was now on his way to Jerusalem to inaugurate the kingdom of God, by making the Jewish nation the master of the world and Jerusalem its capital. We must not forget that the career of Alexander and of Julius Cæsar gave a color of probability to this expectation of universal dominion. Despite this parable, the disciples continued to believe that the kingdom would immediately appear ; at least, they had no conception of the length of the intervening delay. This anticipation was strikingly manifested in the triumphal entry into Jerusalem (vers. 35-38).—**A certain nobleman.** One of noble birth ; a fitting type of One who was the Son of David, the Son of Abraham, and the eternal Son of God.—**Went into a far country to receive for himself a kingdom, and to return.** In the Roman empire it was a customary thing for those who had any claim to the throne of a tributary kingdom to go up to Rome to secure by personal solicitation and influence the ratification of their claim. Herod the Great thus secured the title and office of king ; on his death Archelaus, who later had a palace in Jericho, went similarly to the capital to obtain from Augustus a ratification of his father's will, and was followed by an embassy from Judea appointed by the citizens, who, wearied of the Herodian rule, desired of Augustus that their country might be converted into a Roman province. It is probable that this historical fact suggested the groundwork of this parable to Jesus. The *far country* represents heaven, as in Matt. 21 : 33 ; 25 : 14 ; Mark 12 : 1 ; the figure represents the fact that Christ goes

after him, saying, We will not have this *man* to reign over us.

15 And it came to pass, that when he was returned, having received the kingdom, then he commanded these servants to be called unto him, to whom he had given the money, that he might know how much every man had gained by trading.

16 Then came the first, saying, Lord, thy pound hath gained ten pounds.

17 And he said unto him, Well, thou good servant: because thou hast been faithful ʰ in a very little, have thou authority over ten cities.

18 And the second came, saying, Lord, thy pound hath gained five pounds.

19 And he said likewise to him, Be thou also over five cities.

20 And another came, saying, Lord, behold, *here is* thy pound, which I have kept laid up in a napkin:

21 For I feared thee, because thou art an austere man: thou takest up that thou layedst not down, and reapest that thou didst not sow.

22 And he saith unto him, Out ⁱ of thine own mouth will I judge thee, *thou* wicked servant. Thou knewest that I was an austere man, taking up that I laid not down, and reaping that I did not sow:

23 Wherefore ʲ then gavest not thou my money into the bank, that at my coming I might have required mine own with usury?

24 And he said unto them that stood by, Take from him the pound, and give *it* to him that hath ten pounds.

25 (And they said unto him, Lord, he hath ten pounds.)

26 For I say unto you, That ᵏ unto every one which hath shall be given; and from him that hath not, even that he hath shall be taken away from him.

27 But those mine enemies,ˡ which would not that I

h ch. 16 : 10....1 2 Sam. 1 : 16; Job 15 : 6; Matt. 12 : 37; 22 : 12; Rom. 3 : 19... J Rom. 2 : 4, 5....k ch. 8 : 18; Matt. 13 : 12; 25 : 29; Mark 4 : 25....l Ps. 2 : 4, 5, 9; 21 : 8, 9; Isa. 66 : 6, 14; Nahum 1 : 2, 8; Heb. 10 : 13.

---

away to await the consummation of that kingdom which he receives from his Father, and to return again to enter into possession of it and become King of kings and Lord of lords (Rev. 17 : 14; 19 : 16).

13, 14. And he called his ten servants. Rather, *ten of his servants*. "Besides that the original requires this, it would be absurd to suppose that, with the immense households of antiquity, which, as Seneca says, were *nations* rather than *families*, this nobleman, of consequence enough to be raised to a royal dignity, had but ten servants belonging to him."—(*Trench.*)—**Ten pounds.** The pound, or *mina*, is variously estimated as equivalent to from $15 to $60.—**Occupy till I come.** Rather, *Trade till I come.* The Greek word rendered *occupy* (πραγματεύομαι) signifies literally *to be busy;* it is the same word which, with an added preposition, is rendered in ver. 15 *gained by trading*. In the same sense the word *occupy* is used in Ezek. 27 : 9.—**But his citizens hated him.** These citizens represent those who reject the claims of Christ to be their King; primarily, the Jews (John 19 : 15, 21; Acts 4 : 25-27); secondarily, all those who league themselves in direct hostility to Christ (2 Thess. 2 : 3, 4; Rev. 13 : 1-8).

15-19. Compare Matt. 25 : 19-23, and notes there. (1.) Observe here that it is God's pound that has made the ten pounds; the fruitfulness of our work is the gift of divine grace. (2.) In God's government promotion depends on fidelity. This is in a measure true here and now; fulfillment of duty in a lower and lesser station is rewarded by the providence which bids to go up higher. (3.) Present duties are but trials of character; God gives the pound that he may test and see who is worthy of a city. (4.) The grace given here below, by our use of which we are to show ourselves capable of receiving the crown above, Jesus calls *a very little.* "What an idea of future glory is given to us by this saying!"—(*Godet.*)

20-23. Compare Matt. 25 : 24-27, notes. *The bank* here answers to the *money-changers* there. It is the broker's table or counter at which he sat in the market or public place, and upon which he set out the sums of money required for transacting his daily business. From the fact that this was transacted upon a *bench* comes our word banker; if he could not meet his liabilities his bench was broken to pieces, and he was prohibited from continuing his business; hence the term "broken bank" (Italian, *banco rotto*) and "bankrupt." Alford regards the bank here as a type of religious societies, by the aid of which the most timid may employ their Lord's money.

24-26. Them that stood by. Comp. Matt. 25 : 28-30. Perhaps, as Trench supposes, a type of the angels who are represented as taking a part in the final judgment (Dan. 7 : 10; Matt. 13 : 41; 18 : 27; 24 : 31; 2 Thess. 1 : 7; Jude 14).—**Give it to him that hath ten pounds.** "The holy works which he might have wrought here below, along with the powers by which he might have accomplished them, are committed to that servant who has shown himself the most active. This or that pagan population, for example, which might have been evangelized by the young Christian who remained on the earth the slave of selfish ease, shall be committed in the future dispensation to the devoted missionary who has used his powers in the service of Jesus."—(*Godet.*)—**Lord, he hath ten pounds.** The language of remonstrance; he has ten pounds already, why give him more?—**Unto every one which hath shall be given**, etc. Every attainment of honor, wealth, knowledge, or spiritual grace helps to render further attainment more easy and more assured; while it is spiritually as well as materially true that "the destruction of the poor is their poverty" (Prov. 10 : 15). In ch. 8 : 18 Christ says "that which he *seemeth* to have" shall be taken away. The gift, whether of knowledge, money, or grace, which

should reign over them, bring hither, and slay *them* before me.

28 And when he had thus spoken, he went before, ascending up to Jerusalem.

29 And ᵐ it came to pass, when he was come nigh to Bethphage and Bethany, at the mount called *the mount* of Olives, he sent two of his disciples,

30 Saying, Go ye into the village over against *you;* in the which, at your entering, ye shall find a colt tied, whereon yet never man sat: loose him, and bring *him hither.*

31 And if any man ask you, Why do ye loose *him?*

thus shall ye say unto him, Because the Lord hath need ⁿ of him.

32 And they that were sent went their way, and found even as he had said unto them.

33 And as they were loosing the colt, the owners thereof said unto them, Why loose ye the colt?

34 And they said, The Lord hath need of him.

35 And they brought him to Jesus: and they cast their ᵒ garments upon the colt, and they set ᵖ Jesus thereon.

36 And as he went, they spread their clothes in the way.

---

m Matt. 21 : 1, etc.; Mark 11 : 1, etc.....n Ps. 50 : 10....o 2 Kings 9 : 13....p John 12 : 14.

---

a man does not *use,* he does not really *have.* Unused possession is only a seeming possession. In ch. 25 : 30 the unprofitable servant is cast out into outer darkness; here, in being deprived of all that he hath, which includes the light of divine grace, the same sentence is really implied.

27. But those mine enemies * * * bring hither and slay them before me. In this parable the trial of the church precedes the trial of the world. Comp. 1 Pet. 4 : 18. There is in this, perhaps, a hint of the first and second resurrections (Rev. 20 : 5, 6). But in the marriage of the king's son (Matt. 22 : 7-13) the punishment of the open enemies precedes that of the guest without a wedding garment. The slaying of the enemies in the presence of the king is in accordance with the custom of the Eastern courts (1 Sam. 11 : 12; 15 : 32, 33; Jer. 52 : 10). Found in the teachings of Christ, it possesses a peculiarly solemn significance, and seems to import the terrible punishment and perhaps the literal destruction of the enemies of God (Matt. 13 : 49, 50; 21 : 44; 25 : 30, 46; 2 Thess. 1 : 6-10).

Ch. 19 : 28-48. TRIUMPHAL ENTRY INTO JERUSALEM. CHRIST A KING.—RELIGIOUS ENTHUSIASM APPROVED.—THE SYMPATHY OF CHRIST FOR SINNERS.—THE REJECTION OF CHRIST THE GREAT SIN.—THE PUNISHMENT THEREOF: DESTRUCTION.

The account of this public and triumphal entry into Jerusalem is given by all four Evangelists, but by John only briefly. The account is, on the whole, fullest and most graphic here. There are, however, particulars mentioned by the other Evangelists, which are omitted by Luke. John refers to some that came forth from Jerusalem to meet Jesus (John 12 : 18); Matthew to the children of the temple who joined in the acclamations (Matt. 21 : 15, 16). On the other hand, Luke alone records the interposition of the Pharisees, Christ's reply (vers. 39, 40), and Christ's lament over the city and prophecy of its destruction (vers. 41-44). The cleansing of the temple mentioned here and in Matthew as though it occurred on the first day of Christ's entrance into Jerusalem is distinctly stated by Mark to have occurred on the following day. I believe the order in Mark, who is more explicit than either of the other Evangelists, to be the correct one. See Mark 11 : 11, note. The significance of this entry into Jerusalem has been too little considered. It was Christ's nature to shun crowds; his custom to avoid them. He forbade his disciples from disclosing to others that he was the Messiah, and this prohibition was repeatedly given (Matt. 16 : 20; 17 : 9; Mark 3 : 12; 5 : 43; 6 : 36, etc.). This exceptional assumption of dignity and acceptance of homage is for this reason the more remarkable and significant. I believe it to be an emphasis of the truth that he was a King, and came as King; that it throws forth into prominence a truth respecting him often forgotten, namely, that he is Lord and Master as well as Saviour, crowned with authority as well as with humility and love. This triumphal entry took place at this time in Jerusalem, not in Galilee, because he would have a public testimony to the fact that it was their King the Jews crucified. It is not merely the Messiah that saves, nor the crucified One that saves, but the Messiah crucified (1 Cor. 1 : 23). The fact that this incident is attested by all of the Evangelists is important. For those who give any historical credence to these narratives cannot, in the light of this event, believe that the Messianic character was invented and imputed to Jesus by a later reverential imagination. It was claimed by himself.

28-30. Ascending up to Jerusalem. *Ascending* because Jericho was over 3,000 feet lower than Jerusalem. See ch. 10 : 30, note.—**Bethphage and Bethany.** The language is the same in Mark. *Bethany* was a suburb of Jerusalem, about two miles from that city, on the eastern slope of the Mount of Olives, near the place where the road to Jericho descends steeply to the Jordan valley. It was the home of Mary and Martha. See John 11 : 1, note. But where was *Bethphage?* No such village is mentioned elsewhere in the Bible; tradition is silent; the references in the Talmud indicate only a locality near Jerusalem. It is generally assumed to have been a village near Bethany; but Godet, following Lightfoot, supposes it to have been a district, in which Bethany was situated. The meaning of the word is *house of figs.*—**Two of his disciples.** Their names are not given. An

37 And when he was come nigh, even now at the descent of the mount of Olives, the whole multitude of the disciples began to rejoice and praise God with a loud voice, for all the mighty works that they had seen;
38 Saying, Blessed ᵠ *be* the King that cometh in the name of the Lord; ʳ peace in heaven, and glory in the highest.
39 And some of the Pharisees from among the multitude said unto him, Master, rebuke thy disciples.
40 And he answered and said unto them, I tell you, that, if these should hold their peace, the ˢ stones would immediately cry out.

41 And when he was come near, he beheld the city, and wept ᵗ over it,
42 Saying, If thou hadst known, even thou, at least in this thy day,ᵘ the things *which belong* unto thy peace! but now they are hid from thine eyes.
43 For the days shall come upon thee, that thine enemies shall cast ᵛ a trench about thee, and compass thee round, and keep thee in on every side,
44 And ʷ shall lay thee even with the ground, and thy children within thee; and they ˣ shall not leave in thee one stone upon another; becauseʸ thou knewest not the time of thy visitation.

q ch. 13 : 35; Ps. 118 : 26....r ch. 2 : 14; Rom. 5 : 1; Ephes. 2 : 14...s Hab. 2 : 11; Matt. 3 : 9....t Ps. 119 : 136; Jer. 9 : 1; 13 : 17; 17 : 16; John 11 : 35....u Ps. 95 : 7, 8; Heb. 3 : 7, 13, 15....v Isa. 29 : 2, 3; Jer. 6 : 6, 6....w ch. 13 : 34, 35; 1 Kings 9 : 7, 8; Micah 3 : 12; Matt. 23 : 37, 38....x Matt. 24 : 2; Mark 13 : 2....y Lam. 1 : 8; 1 Pet. 2 : 12.

analogous commission, to prepare the passover, was given to Peter and John (ch. 22 : 8).—**The village over against you.** Either Bethany or Bethphage. The direction was given just before reaching the village.—**Ye shall find a colt tied.** The colt of an ass; the ass was with the colt (Matt. 21 : 2). According to Matthew it was the ass that was tied.—**Whereon yet never man sat.** Beasts that had not been worked were used for sacred purposes (Numb. 19 : 2; Deut. 21 : 3; 1 Sam. 6 : 7). Hence the significance of this command to bring such a colt for Christ's entry into the holy city.

31-34. The Lord hath need of him. The Lord here may be either equivalent to Jehovah, or to Jesus Christ, the recognized Lord of all his disciples. In the former case, the language is equivalent to, He is needed for the service of God; we shall then understand that the owner was simply a godly man, and that, acting under a divine impulse, he allowed these strangers to take his animal for a service of God, the nature of which he did not understand. If we give the latter interpretation, we must assume that the owner of the ass and colt was a disciple of Jesus Christ, and that he recognized in this reply a message from his Lord, and yielded to it. This seems to me the more probable hypothesis. In either case the moral lesson is the same; whoever brings the message, The Lord hath need, we are to respond, if satisfied that it comes from him.—**And found even as he had said unto them.** Mark gives some particulars as to the place. See Mark 11 : 4, note.

35, 36. Combining the four accounts we get the following features: Some took off their outer garment, the burnoose, and bound it on the colt as a kind of saddle; others cast their garments in the way, a mark of honor to a king (2 Kings 9 : 13); others climbed the trees, cut down the branches, and strewed them in the way (Matt. 21 : 8); others gathered leaves, and twigs, and rushes (Mark 11 : 8, note). This procession was made up largely of Galileans, but the reputation of Christ, increased by the resurrection of Lazarus, had preceded him, and many came out from the city to swell the acclamations and increase the enthusiasm (John 12 : 12). Matthew adds that all this was in fulfillment of prophecy (Matt. 21 : 4, 5; comp. Zech. 9 : 9).

37, 38. At the descent of the Mount of Olives. That is, at the apex of the hill, and as they began to descend on the western slope, looking toward Jerusalem. "From this elevated point, three hundred feet above the terrace of the temple, which was itself raised about one hundred and forty feet above the level of the valley of the Cedron, an extensive view was had of the city, and the whole plain which it commands, especially of the temple, which rose opposite, immediately above the valley. All these hearts recall at this moment the miracles which have distinguished the career of this extraordinary man; they are aware that at the point to which things have come his entry into Jerusalem cannot fail to issue in a decisive revolution, although they form an utterly false idea of that catastrophe."—(*Godet.*)—**Saying, Blessed be the King.** They quote from Psalm 118 : 25, 26, a part of the great Hallel which was chanted at the Paschal feast.—**That cometh in the name of the Lord.** That is, as the representative of Jehovah.—**Peace in heaven.** The Divine King comes to proclaim peace in heaven toward those that are on earth, reconciling all things unto God by himself (2 Cor. 5 : 20; Col. 1 : 20).

39, 40. Master, rebuke thy disciples. The natural representatives of these Pharisees in the present are to be found among those who rebuke all religious enthusiasm. Observe, too, that the contrast is here clearly drawn between those who render homage to Christ as the *representative of God on the earth*, and those who condemn it as unseemly, and that Christ not only receives the homage, but rebukes the refusal to give it.—**The stones would immediately cry out.** "The prophet Habakkuk had six hundred and fifty years before, foretold the day when the stones should cry out of the wall, and the beam out of the timber should answer it (Hab. 2 : 11). Possibly Jesus referred to this prophecy, and to the hour of its fulfillment, when, because Jerusalem had no songs of welcome for its Lord, the stones of its falling towers, and walls, and temple

45 And ª he went into the temple, and began to cast out them that sold therein, and them that bought;
46 Saying unto them, It is ᵇ written, My house is the house of prayer: but ye have made it a den ᵇ of thieves.
47 And he taught ᶜ daily in the temple. But the chief priests and the scribes and the chief of the people sought to destroy him,
48 And could not find what they might do: for all the people were very attentive to hear him.

CHAPTER XX.

AND ᵈ it came to pass, *that* on one of those days, as he taught the people in the temple, and preached the gospel, the chief priests and the scribes came upon *him*, with the elders,
2 And spake unto him, saying, Tell us, by ᵉ what authority doest thou these things? or who is he that gave thee this authority?
3 And he answered and said unto them, I will also ask you one thing; and answer me:
4 The baptism of John, was it from heaven, or of men?
5 And they reasoned with themselves, saying, If we shall say, From heaven; he will say, Why then believed ye him not?
6 But and if we say, Of men; all the people will stone us: for ᶠ they be persuaded that John was a prophet.
7 And they answered, that they could not tell whence *it was*.
8 And Jesus said unto them, Neither tell I you by what authority I do these things.
9 Then began he to speak to the people this parable: A ᵍ certain man planted a vineyard,ʰ and let it forth to husbandmen, and went into a far country for a long time.
10 And at the season, he sent a servant to the hus-

ᶻ Matt. 21 : 12, 13....a Isa. 56 : 7....b Jer. 7 : 11....c John 18 : 20....d Matt. 21, 23, etc.; Mark 11 : 27, etc....e Acts 4 : 7-10; 7 : 27....f Matt. 14 : 5 ...g Matt. 21 : 33, etc.; Mark 12 : 1, etc....h Can. 5 : 11, 12; Isa. 5 : 1-7.

---

courts, cried out in wrathful tones the judgments of God against her."—(*Abbott's Jesus of Nazareth*.)

41-44. This lament over Jerusalem is reported alone by Luke. The present hour of triumph affords Jesus no personal exultation. He thinks only, with infinite compassion, of the impending destruction of Jerusalem, and the sorrow that will overwhelm those who rejected and crucified him. The prophecy of that destruction is so minute and exact, that some skeptical writers have insisted that the language must have been written subsequent to the event.—**He wept over it.** The original (κλαίω) implies not merely the shedding of tears, but other external expressions of grief; a deep sorrow, expressed by sobbings rather than silent tears, is indicated. Twice Jesus is said to have wept; once at the grave of Lazarus (John 11 : 35), once at the thought of Jerusalem's tragic end; both times they were tears of sympathy for others' woes. Unselfish tears are not unmanly.—**If thou hadst known.** Christ repeated his warning of the impending doom in his instructions during the succeeding days in the temple (Matt. 21 : 42-44; 23 : 33-39), but the city would not hear.—**Even thou, yea even in this thy day.** Thy day of mercy. It was not yet too late for Jerusalem to repent and to seek in righteousness what would make for peace. The lament is like that of Christ over every soul which is willfully indifferent to the cravings of divine love, and will not know the things that make for its peace.—**The things which** (*tend*) **unto thy peace.** *Tend* rather than *belong*; that is, the course of conduct which would secure peace. There may be a reference here to the name of the city which signifies, *Foundation of peace*.—**That thy enemies shall cast a trench about thee.** Rather, *a mound*. The original (χάραξ) signifies a military rampart around a camp or a besieged city, formed of the earth thrown out of a trench, and stuck with sharp stakes or palisades. Titus, in the siege of Jerusalem, pro-

ceeded by regular approaches, throwing up earthworks. A rampart, such as is here described, was constructed, destroyed in a sally, and replaced by a wall.—**And compass thee round.** He entirely encircled the city, making escape, after his lines were once complete, impossible.—**Shall not leave in thee one stone upon another.** For illustration of the completeness of the destruction, see ch. 21 : 6, note and illustration. For description of the siege and its horrors, see Matt., ch. 24, Prel. Note.—**Because thou knewest not the time of thy visitation.** The city was destroyed because it rejected Christ, who would have redeemed it from destruction (Matt. 21 : 33-43; 22 : 7). The student will lose the true meaning and value of this lament for himself, if he does not recognize in the destruction of Jerusalem a type of the end of the world and of the judgment that awaits each individual soul, that knows not the time of its merciful visitation, and rejects the Lord, who would bring to it peace.

45, 46. This casting out of the traders is not to be confounded with that recorded by John (John 2 : 13-16). See Mark 11 : 15-19, notes. It was an act of kingly authority.

47, 48. Compare Mark 11 : 18, 19. *The chief of the people*, probably denote the chiefs of the synagogues, who combined with the chief priests, *i. e.*, with the heads of the priestly classes and the scribes, *i. e.*, the theological teachers. *All the people were very attentive*, indicates that Christ was popular among the common people in Jerusalem, who had perhaps caught their enthusiasm from the Galileans and other strangers. Apparently he spent every night out of the city (Mark 11 : 19; Luke 21 : 38).

Ch. 20: 1-8. THE AUTHORITY OF CHRIST QUESTIONED.—Comp. Matt. 21 : 23-27; Mark 11 : 27-33. See notes on Matthew. The variations in phraseology are very slight, and are none of them very material.

bandmen, that they should give him of the fruit¹ of the vineyard; but the husbandmen beat him, and sent *him* away empty.

11 And again he sent another servant: and they beat him also, and entreated *him* shamefully, and sent *him* away empty.

12 And again he sent a third: and they wounded him also, and cast *him* out.

13 Then said the lord of the vineyard, What shall I do? I will send my beloved son: it may be they will reverence *him*, when they see him.

14 But when the husbandmen saw him, they reasoned among themselves, saying, This is the heir:ʲ come, letᵏ us kill him, that the inheritance may be our's.

15 So they cast him out of the vineyard, and killed *him*. What therefore shall the lord of the vineyard do unto them?

16 He shall come and destroy these husbandmen, and shall give the vineyard to others.ˡ And when they heard *it*, they said, God forbid.

17 And he beheld them, and said, What is this then that is written, Theᵐ stone which the builders rejected, the same is become the head of the corner?

18 Whosoever shall fall upon that stone shall be broken; butⁿ on whomsoever it shall fall, it will grind him to powder.

19 And the chief priests and the scribes the same hour sought to lay hands on him; and they feared the people: for they perceived that he had spoken this parable against them.

20 And they watched *him*, and sent forth spies, which should feign themselves just men, thatᵒ they might take hold of his words, that so they might deliver him unto the power and authority of the governor.

21 And they asked him, saying, Master, we know that thou sayest and teachest rightly, neither acceptest thou the person *of any*, but teachest the way of God truly:

22 Is it lawful for us to give tribute unto Cæsar, or no?

23 But he perceived their craftiness, and said unto them, Why tempt ye me?

24 Shew me a penny. Whose image and superscription hath it? They answered and said, Cæsar's.

25 And he said unto them, Renderᵖ therefore unto Cæsar the things which be Cæsar's, and unto God the things which be God's.

26 And they could not take hold of his words before the people: and they marvelled at his answer, and heldᑫ their peace.

27 Thenʳ came to *him* certain of the Sadducees,ˢ which deny that there is any resurrection; and they asked him,

28 Saying, Master, Moses wroteᵗ unto us, If any man's brother die, having a wife, and he die without children, that his brother should take his wife, and raise up seed unto his brother.

29 There were therefore seven brethren: and the first took a wife, and died without children.

30 And the second took her to wife, and he died childless.

31 And the third took her; and in like manner the seven also: and they left no children, and died.

32 Last of all the woman died also.

33 Therefore in the resurrection whose wife of them is she? for seven had her to wife.

34 And Jesus answering said unto them, The children of this world marry, and are given in marriage:

35 But they which shall be accounted worthyᵘ to obtain that world, and the resurrection from the dead, neither marry, nor are given in marriage:

36 Neitherᵛ can they die any more; for they are equal unto the angels;ʷ and are the ˣ children of God, being the children of the resurrection.

37 Now that the dead are raised, even Moses shewedʸ at the bush, when he calleth the Lord the God of Abraham, and the God of Isaac, and the God of Jacob.

38 For he is not a God of the dead, but of the living: forᶻ all live unto him.

39 Then certain of the scribes answering said, Master, thou hast well said.

40 And after that they durst not ask him any *question at all*.

41 Andᵃ he said unto them, How say they that Christ is David's son?

---

¹ John 15:16; Rom. 7:4....j Ps. 2:8; Rom. 8:17; Heb. 1:2....k Matt. 27:21-25; Acts 2:23; 3:15....l Neh. 9:36, 37....m Ps. 118:22....n Dan. 2:34, 35....o Matt. 22:15, etc.; Mark 12:13....p Rom. 13:7....q Titus 1:10, 11....r Matt. 22:23, etc.; Mark 12:18, etc.. s Acts 23:6, 8....t Deut. 25:5-8....u ch. 21:36; Rev. 3:4....v Rev. 21:4....w 1 Cor. 15:49, 52; 1 John 3:2....x Rom. 8:17....y Exod. 3:2-6....z Rom. 14:8, 9....a Matt. 22:42; Mark 12:35, etc.

9-19. Parable of the Wicked Husbandmen.—Comp. Matt. 21:33-46; Mark 12:1-12. See notes on Matthew. The variations in phraseology are considerable. Luke alone tells us that the parable was spoken to the people. *The season* (ver. 10) is equivalent to *the time of the fruit* (Matt. 21:34), *i. e.*, the harvest period, when the rent in produce would naturally be payable. *What shall I do?* (ver. 13), a graphic representation of the Heavenly Father's grief over the rebellion of his children, is peculiar to Luke. The prophetic declaration of punishment, *he shall come and destroy these husbandmen*, appears from a comparison with Matthew to have been elicited from the people by Christ's question, and to have elicited in turn the involuntary response from the Pharisees, *God forbid*.

20-26. Concerning Tribute to Cæsar.—Comp. Matt. 22:15-22; Mark 12:13-17. Verse 20 is peculiar to Luke, but accords with and perhaps is implied by the language of Matt. 22:15, 16.

27-40. The Sadducees Silenced.—Comp. Matt. 22:23-33; Mark 12:18-27. See notes on Matthew. Vers. 34-36 are peculiar to Luke, and give much more fully than Matthew or Mark Christ's reply. But this reply is preceded by a severe rebuke of the Sadducees reported by the other evangelists, but not by Luke. Marriage being ordained to preserve the human species, to which otherwise death would soon put an end, ceases with death. Those who are accounted worthy to obtain eternal life and *the resurrection of the dead, i. e.*, the first resurrection (Rev. 20:5, 6), or the resurrection of life (John 5:29), become, not angels, but *equal with the angels*, in the two respects that they do not know death and do not marry. The last clause of ver. 36, *are the children of God, being the children of the resurrection*, implies that it is their resurrection which gives them a right to be regarded as the children of God. It is this resurrection into the divine likeness, for which the Psalmist aspired (Ps. 17:15); for which Paul strove (Phil. 3:11); for which John hoped (1 John 3:2). The last clause of ver. 38, *for all live unto him*, is also peculiar to Luke. The meaning appears to be that only to men do the departed seem dead; in the sight of God all are

42 And David himself saith[b] in the book of Psalms, The LORD said unto my Lord, Sit thou on my right hand,
43 Till I make thine enemies thy footstool.
44 David therefore calleth him Lord, how is he then his son?
45 Then in the audience of[c] all the people he said unto his disciples,
46 Beware[d] of the scribes, which desire to walk in long robes, and love greetings[e] in the markets, and the highest seats in the synagogues, and the chief rooms at feasts;
47 Which[f] devour widows' houses, and for a show[g] make long prayers: the same shall receive greater[h] damnation.

CHAPTER XXI.

AND he looked up, and[i] saw the rich men casting their gifts into the treasury.
2 And he saw also a certain poor widow casting in thither two mites.
3 And he said, Of a truth I say unto you, that this poor widow hath cast in more[j] than they all.
4 For all these have of their abundance cast in unto the offerings of God; but she of her penury hath cast in all the living that she had.
5 And[k] as some spake of the temple, how it was adorned with goodly stones and gifts, he said,
6 As for these things which ye behold, the days will come, in the which[l] there shall not be left one stone upon another, that shall not be thrown down.

b Ps. 110:1; Acts 2:34....c 1 Tim. 5:20....d Mark 12:38, etc....e ch. 11:43....f Isa. 10:2; Matt. 23:14; 2 Tim. 3:6....g 1 Thess. 2:5....h ch. 10:12, 14; James 3:1....i Mark 12:41....j 2 Cor. 8:12....k Matt. 24:1, etc.; Mark 13:1, etc....l ch. 19:44, etc.

living. The declaration of vers. 39, 40, is implied in Matt. 22:34; comp. Matt. 22:46.

41-44. THE PHARISEES BAFFLED. Comp. Matt. 22:41-46; Mark 12:35-37. See notes on Matthew. This question followed the question addressed to Christ by the lawyer, concerning the great commandment in the law.

45-47. DENUNCIATION OF THE SCRIBES. — These verses embody a bare suggestion of a discourse reported in full by Matthew (ch. 23). Some of the same thoughts and almost identical expressions reported there in Matthew are given by Luke in other connections (Luke 11:42-54; 13:33-35). On the verses here, see Matt. 23:5, 6, 14, and Mark 12:38-40. For illustration of *highest seats in the synagogues*, see Luke 11:43.

Ch. 21:1-4. THE WIDOW'S MITES.—Comp. Mark 12:41-44, notes.

Ch. 21:5-36. DISCOURSE ON THE LAST DAYS.—See Matt., ch. 24. This discourse was delivered apart to the disciples, perhaps only to Peter, James, John, and Andrew, and on the Mount of Olives over against Jerusalem (Mark 13:3). The fullest and most systematic report is afforded by Matt., ch. 24. For analysis of discourse, a brief statement of the different interpretations, and notes on what is common to the three accounts, see Matthew. Matthew and Mark are very nearly identical; though the verbal differences are such as to indicate that they are from independent sources. Luke's language is quite different, and though his report is least full of the three, and gives indications of not being by an eye and ear witness, it contains some matters not afforded by either of the other accounts. In the notes here I confine myself to these peculiar features.

5-6. This was said by the disciples as they, with Jesus, were leaving the temple. Comp. Mark 13:1, 2, notes.

7-11. They asked him. His disciples, privately (Mark 13:3, note). For analysis of their question, which affords a key to the discourse, see in Matt. 24:3.—**The time draweth near.** That

THE TEMPLE SITE.

LUKE. [CH. XXI.

7 And they asked him, saying, Master, but when shall these things be? and what sign *will there be* when these things shall come to pass?

8 And he said, Take ᵐ heed that ye be not deceived: for many shall come in my name, saying, I am *Christ;* and ⁿ the time draweth near: go ye not therefore after them.

9 But when ye shall hear of wars and commotions, be ᵒ not terrified: for these things must first come to pass; but the end *is* not by and by.

10 Then said he unto them,ᵖ Nation shall rise against nation, and kingdom against kingdom:

11 And great earthquakes shall be in divers places, and famines, and pestilences; and fearful sights and great signs shall there be from heaven.

12 But before all these, they shall lay their hands on you, and persecute *you,* delivering *you* up to the synagogues, and into prisons,ᑫ being brought before kings ʳ and rulers for my name's sake.

13 And ˢ it shall turn to you for a testimony.

14 Settle *it* therefore in your hearts, not to ᵗ meditate before what ye shall answer:

15 For I will give you a mouth and wisdom, which all your adversaries shall not be able to gainsay ᵘ nor resist.

16 And ᵛ ye shall be betrayed both by parents, and brethren, and kinsfolks, and friends; and ʷ *some* of you shall they cause to be put to death.

17 And ye shall be hated ˣ of all *men* for my name's sake.

18 But ʸ there shall not an hair of your head perish.

19 In your patience ᶻ possess ye your souls.

m 2 Thess. 2 : 3, 9, 10; 1 John 4 : 1; 2 John 7....n Rev. 1 : 3.....o Prov. 3 : 25, 26....p Haggai 2 : 22....q Acts 4 : 3; 5 : 18; 12 : 4; 16 : 24; Rev. 2 : 10....r Acts 25 : 23....s Phil. 1 : 28; 2 Thess. 1 : 5....t ch. 12 : 11; Matt. 10 : 19....u Acts 6 : 10.. v Micah 7 : 5, 6....w Acts 7 : 59; 12 : 2; 26 : 10; Rev. 2 : 13; 6 : 9; 12 : 11....x John 17 : 14....y Matt. 10 : 30....z Rom. 5 : 3, Heb. 10 : 36; James 1 : 4.

---

is, the time of the second coming of the Messiah and the manifestation of his kingdom. These are the words with which the false prophets would endeavor to deceive the church.—**There shall not be one stone left upon another that shall not be thrown down.** The accompanying illustration shows how completely this prediction has been realized. It is a view of the temple site as it now is, standing near and west of the present Mosque of Omar. The Temple of Herod has entirely disappeared, and its materials have been carried away and used in other buildings.—**The end is not immediately.** The Greek word (εὐθέως), here rendered *by and by,* is never so translated in the N. T. except here and in Luke 17 : 7. In both cases, the word *immediately* would better convey the meaning. The use of the phrase, "*by and by,*" as equivalent to *immediately,* has become obsolete. The meaning is, that the end of the world will not immediately follow the troublous times predicted in the preceding part of this sentence.—**Fearful sights and great signs shall there be from heaven.** These words are not found in Matthew or Mark. Josephus gives an account of prodigies accompanying the destruction of Jerusalem, which may be a fulfillment of this prophecy. See Matthew, ch. 24, Prel. Note. These are not to be confounded with the signs mentioned in ver. 25. See on Matt. 24 : 29-31.

12-19. Compare Mark 13 : 9-11, and notes. Matthew's report is not so full, and contains neither the directions nor the promises here given; but parallel to them is Matt. 10 : 17-22; see notes there.—**But before all these.** That is, before the perfected fulfillment of this prophecy. The language here confirms the view maintained in the notes on Matthew, that Christ's prophecy in this chapter was not fulfilled by the destruction of Jerusalem and the dispersion of the Jewish nation. It still awaits its perfect fulfillment.—**It shall result to you for a testimony.** That is, the malice of Christ's foes shall be made by God a means of testifying to the faithfulness of Christ's disciples to him, and his faithfulness to his disciples. Thus the blood of the martyrs becomes the seed of the church.—**Settle it in your hearts.** The dangers, therefore, were to be a subject of premeditation, and for them they were to make preparation; but for such dangers the Christian's preparation is that of the heart rather than that of the head, trust in God rather than shrewdness and self-trust.—**Not to practice beforehand your defence.** The original (προμελετάω) is used in classic Greek of the practice of a professional rhetorician of his declamation (see Sophocles, and authorities there cited); and I see no authority in the N. T. for our English version, though it is sanctioned by Robinson's Lexicon. The Lord does not prohibit *premeditation;* but he directs his disciples to rest their defence not on the artifices of the rhetorician, but on trust in God and the truth.—**But I will give you both a mouth and wisdom;** *i. e.,* both wisdom to guide, and power of utterance.—**Shall not be able to gainsay or withstand;** *i. e.,* to *speak against,* for the disciples' arguments should be unanswerable; or to counteract; for the effect of their trial and defence should be only to promote the cause their enemies sought to overthrow. In fact, some of the most eloquent and effective defences of Christianity have been the unpremeditated responses of persecuted Christians in the hour of peril. For Scripture illustrations, see Acts 4 : 19, 20; 5 : 29-32; 7 : 26.—**But there shall not a hair of your head perish.** Comp. Matt. 10 : 30. "Not *literally* but *really* true; not corporeally, but in that real and only life which the disciple of Christ possesses."—(*Alford.*) But we may say more than this. It is *literally* though not *corporeally* true, that not a hair of their head should perish, since not a single suffering of any description, borne for Christ's sake, has perished; the disciple, as the Master, shall see of the travail of his soul and be satisfied (Isaiah 53 : 11).—**In your endurance ye shall acquire your life.** This is not a mere direction, as our

20 And when ye shall see Jerusalem compassed with armies, then know that the desolation thereof is nigh.
21 Then let them which are in Judæa flee to the mountains; and let them which are in the midst of it depart out; and let not them that are in the countries enter thereinto.
22 For these be the days of vengeance, that all ᵃ things which are written may be fulfilled.
23 But woe unto them ᵇ that are with child, and to them that give suck, in those days! for there shall be great distress in the land, and wrath upon this people.
24 And they shall fall by the edge of the sword, and shall be led away captive into all nations: and Jerusalem ᶜ shall be trodden down of the Gentiles, until the times ᵈ of the Gentiles be fulfilled.
25 And there shall be signs in the sun, and in the

---

a Deut. 28 : 25, 48; Dan. 9 : 26, 27; Zech. 11 : 6; 14 : 1, 2....b Lam. 4 : 10....c Dan. 12 : 7; Rev. 11 : 2....d Rom. 11 : 25.

English version renders it, to keep the soul patient in trouble, but a declaration that the Christian obtains his true life by patient endurance of tribulation. The original Greek word rendered patience (ὑπομονή) is literally *remaining under;* hence the significance of the promise, applicable to all ages of the church, that true life is obtained, not by ingenious contrivances to escape from life's ills, but by patiently remaining under whatever burden Christ bids us carry for his sake. It therefore interprets such declarations as Isaiah 53 : 4, and is interpreted by such passages as Matt. 10 : 39; see note there.

20-21. And when ye shall see Jerusalem encompassed with armies. This sign of the approaching desolation is generally regarded as identical with Matt. 24 : 15. "When ye therefore shall see the abomination of desolation spoken of by Daniel the prophet, stand in the holy place." This seems to me improbable. See note there. I should rather agree with Alford, that Matthew and Mark give the inner or domestic sign of the approaching calamity to be seen in Jerusalem and possibly in the temple itself, designated by the phrase Holy Place, while Luke gives the outward and contemporaneous state of things. An opportunity to flee was afforded by the course of history. Cestius Gallus, the Roman prefect, made an attack on Jerusalem in the fall of A. D. 66, but was beaten off and retreated. It was not till the beginning of A. D. 70, that Titus made his appearance before the walls of the city to inaugurate the final and successful siege. Thus time and warning were afforded to those that believed Christ's prophecy of the approaching desolation of the city; and the early Christian writers tell us that the Christians availed themselves of it and fled from the city, so that not one is known to have perished in the siege.—**Let not them that are in the country districts enter into it,** *i. e.,* into Jerusalem. Those that dwelt in the country might naturally, on the approach of the Roman legions, enter Jerusalem, either as a protection or to reenforce it. This Christ's disciples are forbidden to do, for the reason stated in the next verse.—**These be the days of vengeance,** *i. e.,* of divine vengeance. To resist the Roman army would therefore be fighting a vain battle against God himself. "We may call to mind the expression even of a Titus: 'That God was so angry with this people, that even he feared His wrath, if he should suffer grace to be shown to the Jews,' and how he refused every mark of honor on account of the victory obtained, with the attestation that he had been only an instrument in God's hands to punish this stiff-necked nation."—(*Lange.*) **All things that are written.** The reference cannot be to Christ's previous intimations of the destruction of Jerusalem (John 2 : 19 ; Matt. 21 : 41 ; 23 : 38), for these were not as yet written. The language refers to O. T. prophecies, such as Lev. 26 : 14-23 ; Deut. 28 : 15, etc. ; 29 : 19-28 ; Dan. 9 : 26, 27 ; Zech., ch. 11 ; 14 : 42.—**Distress in the land,** *i. e.,* of Palestine; **and wrath** (of God) **upon his people,** the Jews. Let them who wish to eliminate the conception of divine wrath from theology, consider whether they can eliminate such scenes as the destruction of Jerusalem from history.—**They shall fall by the mouth of the sword,** etc. For description of fulfillment of this prophecy, see Matt. 24 : 21, note, and Prel. Note to that chapter. Over a million of Jews are said by Josephus to have been slain, and ninety-seven thousand to have been taken captive.—**Shall be trodden down of the nations** (comp. Rev. 11 : 2), **until the time of the nations shall be fulfilled.** There is no reason philologically for regarding the word *Gentiles* (ἔθνος) here as equivalent to Romans; the ordinary significance in N. T. usage, is *heathen nations.* The language describes aptly the present and past condition of Jerusalem, which since the dispersion of the Jews has been under the feet of successive Gentile nations, is so now, and is to remain so *until the time of the Gentiles shall be fulfilled,* i. e., not till they have fulfilled their mission as executors of divine punishment (so Oosterzee and Bengel), but till their time of trial and redemption is past, as the time of trial and redemption of the Jewish nation *as a nation,* was ended with the destruction of the holy city. So, substantially, Alford. The times of the Gentiles are the Gentile dispensation, just as the time of Jerusalem is the Jewish dispensation; the great rejection of the Lord by the Gentile world, answers to its type, his rejection by the Jews. This being finished, the end of all things shall come, the time of which the destruction of Jerusalem was a type. So we have in Rev. 11 : 18. "The time of the dead," which is interpreted

Ch. XXI.] LUKE. 129

moon, and in the stars; and upon the earth distress [e] of nations, with perplexity; the sea and the waves roaring;
26 Men's hearts failing them for fear, and for looking after those things which are coming on the earth: for the [f] powers of heaven shall be shaken.
27 And then shall they see the Son of man coming [g] in a cloud with power and great glory.
28 And when these things begin to come to pass, then look up, and lift up your heads; for your redemption [h] draweth nigh.

29 And [i] he spake to them a parable; Behold the fig tree, and all the trees;
30 When they now shoot forth, ye see and know of your own selves that summer is now nigh at hand.
31 So likewise ye, when ye see these things come to pass, know ye that the kingdom of God is nigh at hand.
32 Verily I say unto you, This generation shall not pass away till all be fulfilled.
33 Heaven [j] and earth shall pass away: but my words shall not pass away.

e Dan. 12 : 1....f 2 Pet. 3 : 10-12....g Rev. 1 : 7; 14 : 14....h Rom. 8 : 23....i Matt. 24 : 32; Mark 13 : 28....j Isa. 40 : 8; 51 : 6.

there as the time "that they should be judged."

25-28. I believe the language here to be parallel to, perhaps only a different report of, that in Matt. 24 : 27-31, and to be descriptive, not of signs which shall accompany the destruction of Jerusalem, but of those to accompany the final coming of Christ, after a long period of tribulation. See Matt., ch. 24, Prel. Note. The direction of verse 28 must be regarded as addressed through the then hearers to the universal church, as indeed the whole prophecy is. Nor must we forget in interpreting it, that it was not the divine design that the disciples should know how long was to be the period of tribulation, that it was meant that the church in every age should live in expectancy of it, and that even Christ himself did not know the day and the hour (Matt. 13 : 32, note).—**And there shall be signs in the sun, and in the moon, and in the stars.** Compare the more definite language of Matt. 24 : 29.—**And upon the earth distress of nations.** Literally, *a shutting up*, as of men in a besieged city. The world will be beleaguered, and from it there will be no escape. Observe that in the original, the word here rendered *nations*, is that in verse 41 rendered *Gentiles*. In the destruction of Jerusalem the distress fell upon the Jews, and was inflicted by the Gentiles; in the time now spoken of (the time of the Gentile nations) the distress will fall upon them; they will be the beleagured and the anxious.—**With perplexity.** They will doubt what the portents may mean, and their fear will be interspersed by the feeling that they know not what a day or an hour may bring forth.—**The sea and the waves roaring.** Natural signs on the earth will accompany those in the heavens. The picture is partially interpreted by what occurs during an earthquake on the seacoast.—**Men's hearts fainting** (as in a swoon) **for fear** (of what they already see) **and for expectation of those things coming upon the habitable globe.** Not upon Judea or Palestine; the original Greek word is never used with that limited sense in the N. T. See Matt. 24 : 13, 14, note. Clearly something more than any of the events, terrible as those were, which accompanied the destruction of Jerusalem, is indicated by the language here.—**Then shall they see.** Not merely the Jews but *the nations*, *i. e.* the Gentile nations, shall see. It is not true that either Jew or Gentile recognized in the destruction of Jerusalem a sign of the truth that Jesus was the Christ. See Matt. 29-31, note; and on the phrase "Son of man," Matt. 10 : 23, note. Comp. with the language here, Matt. 25 : 31; 26 : 64; Mark 14 : 62, where Christ uses analogous language, and where he indubitably refers to his final coming to judge the world.—**And when these things begin to come to pass,** *i. e.*, the first appearance of the promised signs of Christ's final coming.—**Look up and lift up your heads.** The metaphor is of one sitting down in grief, with bowed head, who on the coming of succor lifts up the head, both to receive the word and let it awaken hope.—**Because your redemption draweth nigh.** That coming of Christ which will fill the unbelievers with terror, will fill his own children with joy (Psalm 90 : 11-13, with Rev. 1 : 7).

For reasons partly indicated in the notes here, and more fully in the notes on Matt., ch. 24, it seems to me impossible to regard these verses (25-28) as merely a prophecy of the destruction of Jerusalem and the dispersion of the Jews. This, though a common orthodox interpretation, requires us to give to such language as that of verses 25 and 27 a meaning which belittles, if it does not positively falsify, Christ's words; to attribute to the words *nation* ($\xi\vartheta\nu o\varsigma$) and *earth* ($\tau\tilde{\eta}\varsigma\ \gamma\tilde{\eta}\varsigma$) a meaning which they nowhere else bear in the N. T.; to ignore the teaching of parallel passages of Scripture, and partly of Christ's own words elsewhere employed in describing his Second Coming; and to ignore his explicit declaration in Mark 13 : 32, that he does not know when that Second Coming will take place. The language here and in Matthew should be compared with that of Rev. 6 : 12-17, and the remarkable parallel between Christ's prophecy and John's vision noticed. In both the sun and moon are darkened and the stars fall from heaven; in one, the heavens are shaken, in the other, rolled together as a scroll; in both, the powers of nature are shaken upon the earth; here, the sea and waves roaring; there, mountains and islands moved out of their

34 And take heed* to yourselves, lest at any time your hearts be overcharged with surfeiting,¹ and drunkenness, and cares of this life, and so that day come upon you unawares.

35 For™ as a snare shall it come on all them that dwell on the face of the whole earth.

36 Watch° ye therefore, and pray always, that ye may be accounted° worthy to escape all these things that shall come to pass, and to ᵖ stand before⁴ the Son of man.

37 And in the day time he was teaching in the temple; and at night he went out, and abode in the mount ᵣ that is called *the mount* of Olives.

38 And all the people came early in the morning to him in the temple, for to hear him.

k Rom. 13 : 12, 13; 1 Thess 5 : 6–8 ; 1 Pet. 4 : 7.... l Isa. 28 : 1–3 ; 1 Cor. 6 : 10...., m 1 Thess, 5 , 2 ; 2 Pet. 3 : 10; Rev. 16 : 15....
n Matt. 25 : 13 ...o ch. 20 : 35.....p Ps. 1 : 5....q Jude 24....r John 8 : 1, 2.

places; in both, the nations are represented as in fear and perplexity and faintheartedness, and endeavoring to escape from the besieged earth. I know not how any one can read the two accounts together and not be satisfied that John's vision was of that event which his Lord had previously described.

29–33. See notes on Matt. 24 : 32–35.—**My words shall not pass away.** Nothing apparently is so fugitive as words, and the words of Christ were spoken, not reduced to writing by him, or in his lifetime ; yet history has demonstrated the truth of this declaration, and his words have proved more enduring than monuments, temples, cities, or even civilizations, and shall in their influence outlast the world itself. Observe in the structure of this promise an additional indication, that the prophecy here relates to the end of the world, not merely to the end of the Jewish dispensation. On the meaning of the word *generation* (γενεά) which would be better, rendered *race*, see on Matt 24 : 34.

34–36. These verses are peculiar to Luke. Parallel to them is Matt. 24 : 38–51, and Mark 13 : 33–37. In all these reports the practical lesson is the same, the duty of prayer and watchfulness. The language interprets the more general direction in Matthew and Mark, "Watch ye, therefore;" this watching is not in order to give the disciple a better and earlier apprehension of the approach of the last day, but to guard against insidious dangers which threaten to make even the disciple of the Lord unprepared for it and for Him (Matt. 24 : 42, note).—**Lest your hearts grow heavy.** This expression is equivalent to *was gross* in Matt. 13 : 15; see note there. **With surfeiting and drunkenness and cares of this life.** Two very incongruous vices are here mentioned, equally inconsistent with the spirit of true piety ; the one the vice of self-indulgence, the other that of worldly anxiety ; the one the vice of the spendthrift, the other that of a mere worldly thrift. Comp. Matt. 13 : 22, note.—**And that day come upon you unforeseen.** Not merely suddenly—it will come so to all—but *unlooked for* ; or, as in our English version, *unawares, i. e.*, upon us while unwatchful, unguarded, and so unprepared for its coming.— **For as a snare shall it come.** If the Bible afforded the material for foretelling, even approximately, the time of its coming, this would not be true.—**On all them that dwell on the face of the whole earth.** Clearly here our Lord is speaking, not of the destruction of Jerusalem, but of the last great day. And this is usually the meaning in the N. T. of the phrase *that day*, when used absolutely, as here (Matt 22 : 42, note).—**Watch ye, therefore, in every season** (ἐν παντὶ καιρῷ). In prosperity, against the enticements of self-indulgence ; in adversity, against the encroachments of earthly cares.— **Praying that ye may be accounted worthy.** Observe, not *be* worthy, but *reckoned* worthy. Here is the germ of that doctrine of justification by grace through faith, of which we find the elaboration in Paul's epistles (Rom. 4 : 2–6). —**To be made to stand before the Son of man.** Not *to stand*, as in our English version ; the verb (σταθῆναι) is in the passive, not the active voice. We are not, and cannot be worthy, to stand before the Messiah ; but we may be *accounted* as worthy *to be made to stand* before him, by his grace. It is through Christ we have access by faith into the divine peace, in which we stand here against the wiles and assaults of the devil (Ephes. 6 : 13, 14), and by that grace we are to be made to stand before him in the last great day (Jude 24), the evidence of our faith being our obedience, manifested in a life of watching and prayer. Comp. James 2 : 18. On the meaning of the phrase, "to stand before the Son of man," see Psalm 1 : 5 ; Mal. 3 : 2 ; John 2 : 28. On this whole admonition against forgetfulness of the Lord, and consequent self-indulgence and sin, compare Rom. 13 : 11–14 ; Ephes. 5 : 3–6 ; Col. 3 : 1–6.

37, 38. He was by day in the temple teaching ; at night going out he bivouacked on the mount called of Olives. In that climate and at that season there was no hardship in sleeping in the open air, wrapped in his burnoose or cloak. Some nights he seems to have spent at Bethany (Matt. 21 : 17), probably at the house of Martha and Mary. Bethany was on the other side of the Mount of Olives.—**And all the people came early in the morning to him in the temple.** This does not necessarily indicate anything more than curiosity on their part, and is not inconsistent with the subsequent demand for his crucifixion. Such inflections of popular feeling are common, and in a city

CHAPTER XXII.

NOW* the feast of unleavened bread drew nigh, which is called the Passover.

2 And¹ the chief priests and scribes sought how they might kill him; for they feared the people.

3 Then" entered Satan into Judas surnamed Iscariot, being of the number of the twelve.

4 And he went his way, and communed with the chief priests and captains, how he might betray him unto them.

5 And they were glad, and covenanted ᵛ to give him money.

6 And he promised, and sought opportunity to betray him unto them in the absence of the multitude.

7 Then came the day ʷ of unleavened bread, when the passover must be killed.

8 And he sent Peter and John, saying, Go and prepare us the passover, that we may eat.

9 And they said unto him, Where wilt thou that we prepare?

10 And he said unto them, Behold, when ye are entered into the city, there shall a man meet you, bearing a pitcher of water; follow him into the house where he entereth in.

11 And ye shall say unto the goodman of the house, The Master saith unto thee, Where is the guestchamber, where I shall eat the passover with my disciples?

12 And he shall shew you a large upper room furnished: there make ready.

13 And they went, and found as he had said unto them: and they made ready the passover.

14 And ˣ when the hour was come, he sat down, and the twelve apostles with him.

ᵗ Matt. 26 : 2; Mark 14 : 1, etc ... t Ps. 2 : 2. Acts 4 : 27 ..., u Matt. 26 14. Mark 14 10, etc., John 13 : 2, 27... v Zech. 11 : 12.... w Exod., ch. 12. ..x Matt. 26 20. Mark 14 17.

---

thronged as Jerusalem was on Passover week, there may well have been two parties, one who admired and another who hated him. It was the nature of his teaching to awaken both love and hostility. These two verses are peculiar to Luke. They do not necessarily imply that Christ taught in the temple after this time; and a comparison of the four Gospels shows that his invective against the Pharisees (Matt., ch. 23) was the last discourse delivered in the temple. See verse 39 there. Here Luke simply states in general terms what was Christ's habit during his brief ministry in Jerusalem. This was to teach in the temple by day, but to escape from the multitude and seek repose in the country by night.

Ch. 22 : 1-13. PREPARATION FOR THE LAST SUPPER.—Parallel to Luke's account of the Last Supper is Matt. 26 : 1–35; Mark 14 : 1–31. See notes throughout on Matthew. John gives no account of the institution of the Last Supper, though he refers to it (John 13 · 2), and gives more fully than either of the other Evangelists a report of Christ's instructions to his disciples at that time (John, chaps. 14–16). Luke gives more fully than the other Evangelists Christ's directions to Peter and John for the preparation of the Passover (vers. 7-13), and alone gives the account of the strife between the disciples which should be greatest (vers. 24-30). The instructions of vers. 35–38 are also peculiar to Luke.

1, 2. See Matt. 26 : 1–5. Observe the indication here and in ver. 6, that Christ was popular with the multitude, even in Jerusalem. The mob was one stirred up against him by the sedulous endeavors of the priests (Matt. 27 : 18, 20).

3-6. See Matt. 26 : 14–16, notes. The connection in Matthew indicates the immediate occasion of the treachery of Judas, namely, his anger at our Lord's rebuke. On the character of Judas, see Matt. 27 : 3–10, notes. With the expression here, *Then entered Satan into Judas,* compare John 13 : 2, 27. No demoniacal possession is indicated, nor any such Satanic control as violated the liberty of Judas, but just that influence proceeding from the evil spirit against which Paul cautions us in Ephes. 6 : 12.

7, 8. Then came the day of unleavened bread, etc. The language is explicit that the Lord observed the Passover *on the day on which it was observed by other Jews,* the 14th day of Nisan, when the lambs were slain in the temple to be eaten in the Paschal feast of that evening. I have no doubt that the chronology of the Synoptics is in this respect to be accepted; that the Lord's Supper was a true Passover supper, not a special preparatory or prophetic feast, nor one celebrated out of the appropriate time; and that the references to John, which are quoted in support of the opposite view, are not, when thoroughly considered, inconsistent with this one. See Note on Lord's Supper, Vol. I, p. 286.—**Go and prepare us the Passover.** On the nature of the preparation required, see Matt. 26 : 17, note.

9-13. There shall a man meet you bearing a pitcher of water. Doubtless a servant, the drawing of water being in the East a service usually performed by the servants or the women of the household.—**Ye shall say unto the good man of the house.** The master or owner of the house (οἰκοδεσπότης). During the Passover week hospitality was recognized as a universal duty in Jerusalem; pilgrims and strangers were received, and rooms were allotted to them for the celebration of the feast. But it is not probable that a room would have been given to entire strangers without previous arrangement, and the language which the disciples are instructed to use, *The Master saith unto them,* seems to me clearly to indicate that the good man of the house recognized Jesus as Master; in other words, was in some sense at least a disciple. Whether Christ had previously arranged with him for the use of a room, or whether the instruction to Peter and John was founded wholly on supernatural knowledge of the wel-

15 And he said unto them, With desire I have desired to eat this passover with you before I suffer:
16 For I say unto you, I will not any more eat thereof, until⁷ it be fulfilled in the kingdom of God.
17 And he took the cup, and gave thanks, and said, Take this, and divide *it* among yourselves:
18 For I say unto you, I will not drink of the fruit of the vine, until the kingdom of God shall come.
19 And ᶻ he took bread, and gave thanks, and brake *it*, and gave unto them, saying, This is my body, which is given for you: this do in remembrance of me.
20 Likewise also the cup after supper, saying, This cup *is* the new testament in my blood, which is shed for you.
21 But, behold, the hand of him that betrayeth me *is* with me ᵃ on the table.
22 And truly the Son of man goeth, as it was determined: ᵇ but woe unto that man by whom he is betrayed!
23 And they began to inquire among themselves, which of them it was that should do this thing.
24 And ᶜ there was also a strife among them, which of them should be accounted the greatest.
25 And he said unto them, The ᵈ kings of the Gen-

y ch. 14 : 15 ; 1 Cor. 5 : 7, 8 ; Rev. 19 : 9,....z 1 Cor. 10 : 16 ; 11 : 24, etc.....a Ps. 41 . 9 ; John 13 : 26,... b ch. 24 : 46 ; Acts 2 : 23 ; 4 :28 ; 1 Cor 15 : 3....c ch. 9 : 46 ; Mark 9 : 34.....d Matt. 20 : 25 ; Mark 10 : 42.

come which would be accorded to him, we have no means of knowing. Jesus knew the projected treachery of Judas; by confiding in this manner to Peter and John the preparation of the room, he prevented the possible interruption of the feast, since not even one of the disciples knew the place selected for their meeting.—**The Master saith unto thee.** The full message was, *My time is at hand; I will keep the Passover at thy house with my disciples* (Matt. 26 : 18); *where is the guest-chamber*, etc. The disciples alone ate with Jesus; the host probably observed the Passover in another room with his own household.—**A large upper room furnished.** This upper chamber was a sort of guest-chamber, not in common use, where the ancients received company and held feasts, and which was usually, though not always, in the upper story, and sometimes on or connected with the roof. This room was *furnished, i. e.*, provided with a supper-table and couches. For illustration of table, and method of reclining, see Matt. 26 : 20, note.

14-23. The Lord's Supper. Prophecy of Christ's Betrayal.—See Matt. 26 : 26-30; Mark 14 : 22-25; 1 Cor. 11 : 23-25. In comparing these accounts, it must be remembered that Luke and Mark were not of the twelve, and therefore were not present. This may account in part for the diversity in chronology. For notes on the Lord's Supper, see Matthew, where the chronology is given. For notes on the prophecy of betrayal, see John 13 : 21-30.

15. Peculiar to Luke. The intensity of Christ's desire to eat this last Passover with his disciples, like his desire for their sympathy and prayers in his agony in Gethsemane (Matt. 26 : 37, 39, 40), hints at the character of his love, as one which yearned for *human sympathy and love*. May we not say that he still earnestly desires to eat this supper with his disciples, and that every cold and formal celebration of this memorial service is, as it were, a personal disappointment and sorrow to him?

16. Until it be fulfilled. The Passover was a prophecy of the Lord's Supper; that, in turn, is prophetic of the Marriage Supper of the Lamb (Matt. 26 : 29, note).

17. He took the cup. Not the one mentioned in verse 20. This cup preceded, that followed the supper. See account of Passover ceremonial, Matt. 26 : 26-30, Prel. Note.

18, 19. I will not drink of the fruit of the vine. In Matthew this expression is reported at the close of the meal; here at the commencement. Perhaps Christ repeated it. As the verse stands here, it implies that Christ did not partake of the bread and wine; but in Matthew the language is different, "I will not drink henceforth;" and this is probably the meaning here. Verse 15 appears to me to imply that he partook as well as his disciples. For discussion of this question, see Matt. 26 : 26, note.

20. After supper. Not *a* cup of wine after the paschal supper was ended, but *the* cup of wine which, according to the Jewish ceremonial, closed the supper. See Matt. 26 : 26-30, Prel. Note, and Supplemental Note, § 2.

21-23. This occurred prior to the institution of the Lord's Supper, though during the beginning of the paschal meal (Matt. 26 : 21). The language here, "The hand of him that betrayed me is with me on the table," is not, therefore, conclusive upon the difficult question whether Judas was at the Lord's Supper. On the whole, the balance of evidence is that he had left the room; but, as only John mentions his departure, and John says nothing of the institution of the Lord's Supper, the question cannot be determined with certainty. For notes on Christ's prophecy of his betrayal, see John 13 : 21-35, and Matt. 26 : 21-25.

Ch. 22 : 24-30. Christ rebukes his disciples' strife. True greatness is greatness of service.

The reader must remember that Luke was not one of the twelve. He was not, therefore, present, and he gives no distinct note of time; he merely indicates that a strife occurred at about this time, whether before or after the supper he did not perhaps know. The seats at the Oriental table were arranged in regular order, the seat nearest the master of the feast being the seat of honor. Contentions for the highest place were common. See ch. 14 : 7-11, note. I believe that

tiles exercise lordship over them; and they that exercise authority upon them are called benefactors.

26 But ⁿ ye *shall* not *be* so: but he that is greatest among you, let him be as the younger; and he that is chief, as he that doth serve.

27 For whether *is* greater, he that sitteth at meat, or he that serveth? *is* not he that sitteth at meat? but ᶠ I am among you as he that serveth.

28 Ye are they which have continued with me in my temptations.ᵍ

29 And I appoint unto you a ʰ kingdom, as my Father hath appointed unto me;

30 Thatⁱ ye may eat and drink at my table in my kingdom, and sit on thrones, judgingʲ the twelve tribes of Israel.

31 And the Lord said, Simon, Simon, behold, Satan hath desiredᵏ *to have* you, that he may siftˡ *you* as wheat:

32 But I ᵐ have prayed for thee, that thy faith fail not: and when thou art converted, strengthenⁿ thy brethren.

33 And he said unto him, Lord, I am ready to go with thee, both into prison, and to death.

34 And he said, I tell thee, Peter, the cock shall not

---

e 1 Pet. 5 : 3 ; 3 John 9, 10....f John 13 : 13, 14; Phil. 2 : 7....g Heb. 4 : 15....h ch. 12 : 32; Matt. 25 : 34; 1 Cor. 9 : 25 ; 1 Pet. 5 : 4 ...i Rev. 19 : 9....j Matt. 19 : 28; 1 Cor. 6. 2 ; Rev. 3 : 21....k 1 Pet. 5 : 8....l Amos 9 : 9....m John 17 : 9, 15 ; Heb. 7 : 25 ; 1 John 2 : 1.... n Ps. 51 : 13; John 21 : 15-17.

---

this contention which should be regarded as greatest, took place as the twelve were taking their seats; that Christ interrupted it by the feet-washing, recorded only by John (John 13 : 3-5); and that he then followed the feet-washing with the instructions given here. This makes clear and significant the language of ver. 27. Similar contentions had occurred before among the twelve. Comp. Matt. 18 : 1-4, notes; Mark 10 : 42-45, notes. The language in the latter passage is very analogous to that employed here.

21-27. Should be accounted the greatest. It is not a generous emulation for true greatness, but a selfish strife for *appearance* of greatness, which Christ rebukes.—**Are called benefactors.** Examples of this title, assumed by ancient monarchs, are given in Ptolemy, Josephus, and other ancient writers. See *Rob. Dict.*, art. εὐεργέτης.—**I am among you as he that serveth.** True of Christ's whole life, which was one of the service of others; but peculiar significance was lent to it by the service just rendered them in the washing of their feet, which was the work of a menial.

28-30. Ye are they which have continued with me in my trials. In this sentence he appeals both to their past history and to their future glory, as well as to his own example, in rebuking their unseemly strife. When others had turned back, because to follow him involved poverty, humiliation, and self-sacrifice, they had still adhered to him (John 6 : 65-69).—**And I appoint unto you a kingdom, as my Father hath appointed me.** That is, the same kind of kingdom; one to be conquered and governed by love and truth, not by ambition and guile; a kingdom not of this world, yet over this world (John 18 : 36, 37). Every follower of Christ is, or should be, a prince, as their Leader is King. "The truth and life which Jesus preached shall come to dwell in them, and thereby they shall reign over all, as he himself has reigned over them. Are not Peter, John, and Paul at the present day the rulers of the world?"—(*Godet.*) But there is also in this and the succeeding verse an unmistakable reference to the time when Christ will come in power and glory to take full possession of his kingdom, and when his disciples shall share his glory and his authority with him (Matt. 19 : 28, note ; 1 Cor. 6 : 1-1).—**Ye may eat and drink at my table.** How ignoble the strifes for earthly precedence of those who are the children and princes of God; whose houses, thrones, dominions, are eternal and divine!

Ch. 22 : 31-38. PROPHECY OF PETER'S DENIAL. THE DANGER, THE DUTY, AND THE REFUGE OF THE DISCIPLE.—THE NECESSITY OF BEING FOREWARNED AND FOREARMED.

Christ appears to have twice warned Peter of his danger, once before the Lord's Supper (Luke; John 13 : 36-38), once after the supper, and perhaps on the way to the Mount of Olives (Matt. 26 : 31-35; Mark 14 : 27-31). At least, this is the more probable hypothesis, though Dr. Robinson regards the four accounts as different versions of the same warning, and some harmonists suppose that the warning was thrice repeated. The immediate occasion of the one here reported is indicated by John. It was Peter's question, "Why cannot I follow thee now?" and perhaps also his participation in the strife for the first places at the table, recorded only by Luke.

31. Simon. This was Peter's original name; Peter was a new name given him by the Lord (John 1 : 42; Matt. 16 : 18). It is Simon not Peter, the old man not the new man in Christ, whom Satan hopes to obtain.—**Satan hath demanded you.** As he demanded Job (Job 1 : 9-12; 2 : 4-6).—**That he may sift you as wheat.** In the agricultural and domestic life of Palestine, the wheat and the flour from the wheat were shaken in a sieve, to separate the good from the refuse and dirt. This sieve was made of parchment perforated with holes, of horse-hair, thread, papyrus, or rushes interwoven. The Egyptian, and probably the Jewish, sieves were made of papyrus and rushes. The accompanying illustration is taken from a bas-relief on the Column of Trajan. Christ's figure illustrates both the

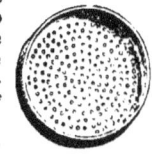

ANCIENT SIEVE.

crow this day, before that thou shalt thrice deny that thou knowest me.

35 And he said unto them, When ⁿ I sent you without purse, and scrip, and shoes, lacked ye any thing? And they said, Nothing.

36 Then said he unto them, But now, he that hath a purse, let him take it, and likewise his scrip; and he that hath no sword, let him sell his garment, and buy one.

37 For I say unto you, that this that is written ᵖ must yet be accomplished in me, And he was reckoned among the transgressors: for the things concerning me have an end.

38 And they said, Lord, behold, here are two swords. And he said unto them, It is enough.

39 And ᵠ he came out, and went, as he was wont, to the mount of Olives; and his disciples also followed him.

o ch. 9 : 3....p Isa. 53 : 12....q Matt. 26 : 36; Mark 14 : 32, etc.; John 18 : 1, etc.

process and the results of temptation. By it, both in the individual and the church, temporary confusion and disorder is produced, but the good and the evil are separated. Thus, in Peter's case, both the weakness (of self-confidence) and the strength (of penitence, faith, and love) are clearly disclosed, to himself as well as to others, only by his temptation and temporary fall.

32. But I have prayed for thee. Against the *demand* of Satan is the *prayer* of Christ.— **That thy faith fail not.** The object of Christ's intercessory prayer, the armament that gives the Christian his victory, is faith (1 John 5 : 4, 5). Peter's faith failed now, for he did not believe Christ's warning; therefore he failed in the hour of temptation.—**When thou art converted.** Was he not, then, at this time converted? The answer is that it is only as the Christian is *continually converted*, *i. e.*, turned away, by the Spirit of God, from self-confidence and self-seeking, that he can strengthen others in the spirit of faith and humility. Compare Matt. 18 : 3, note.—**Strengthen thy brethren.** Christian grace in ourselves must precede Christian work upon others. Compare Ps. 51 : 10-13; John 21 : 15-17.

33. Lord, I am prepared to go with thee. That is, already prepared, and hence do not need to be converted. Peter thus resents both Christ's warning and the imputation of weakness which it involves. Compare similar spirit in Hazael (2 Kings 8 : 10-13). Observe that Christ did not account even himself "ready" for his trial hour, until by prayer in Gethsemane he had acquired strength from above.

34. And he said, I tell thee, Peter, *i. e.*, *Thou rock*. This is the only place in the Gospels where our Lord addresses Peter by this name. There appears to me to be in its use here a kindly sarcasm. He is a "rock," not by his native strength of character, but only by his faith; and will belie his name when his faith fails.—**Shall not crow.** The cock-crowing here referred to is the second crowing at dawn. See Matt. 26 : 34, note.

The effect on Peter of this warning and the experience of temptation and sin which ensued, is very apparent in Peter's Epistles. None of the apostles dwell more earnestly on the truth that all strength is from God, and that watchfulness and humility are necessary preparations for temptation. Observe particularly 1 Pet. 1 : 5, 7, 13; 4 : 12; 5 : 6-9; 2 Pet. 1 : 5; 2 : 9.

35-38. To interpret these directions literally is to fall into the error of the disciples, which Christ rebukes. To symbolize them, as by regarding the sword as the sword of the Spirit, is to miss the true significance of the passage, by imputing to it a meaning which certainly Christ did not convey to his auditors. The language is figurative; he contrasts their past with their future experiences; reminds them of the time when, in Galilee, they travelled as representatives of their Lord, without purse or provisions, depending, like the ancient prophets, on the hospitality of the people; warns them that in the future they can do this no more; there will be no hospitality; they will be the followers of the Crucified, one who has been numbered among evil-doers; and they must depend on their own foresight for provision and protection. —**When I sent you without purse,** etc. See Matt. 10 : 9-15, notes; Mark 6 : 8, 9, notes.— **And he that hath none, let him sell his garment and buy a sword.** Not that hath no sword, but that hath no purse. This is the more natural rendering of the Greek; and he who had a *purse* would have no occasion to sell his garment to buy a sword.—**This must yet be accomplished in me.** The prophecy referred to is in Isaiah 53 : 12, and plainly relates to the promised Messiah.—**For the things concerning me have an end.** Rather, *an accomplishment*. The meaning is that all the sacred prophecies, including those of his sufferings and death, must be accomplished, and that the time of their fulfillment was already at hand. —**Here are two swords.** Probably provided as a protection from the dangers of the way. "The road from Jericho to Jerusalem (ch. 10 : 30) was much infested with robbers; and it was the custom of the priests, and even of the quiet and ascetic Essenes, to carry weapons when travelling."—(*Alford*.) Peter had one of these swords (John 18 : 10).—**It is well.** This is not a commendation of their foresight; nor does it mean, These are enough. It is simply a dismissal of the subject. To interpret Christ's language here, as some Roman Catholic commentators

40 And when he was at the place, he said unto them, Pray that ye enter not into temptation.
41 And he was withdrawn from them about a stone's cast, and kneeled down, and prayed,
42 Saying, Father, if thou be willing, remove this cup from me: nevertheless, not my will, but thine, be done.
43 And there appeared an angel [r] unto him from heaven, strengthening him.
44 And [s] being in an agony, he prayed more earnestly: and his sweat was as it were great drops of blood falling down to the ground.
45 And when he rose up from prayer, and was come to his disciples, he found them sleeping for sorrow,

r Matt. 4 : 11 .... s Lam. 1 : 12 ; John 12 : 27 ; Heb. 5 : 7.

---

have done, as a warrant for the use of the sword in defending and extending the kingdom of God, is to repudiate Christ's direct and explicit instructions. See Matt. 26 : 52–54; John 18 : 36. The language here, however, taken with that of Matt. 10 : 9–15, shows clearly that the instructions there given were local and temporary, and they give abundant warrant for foresight and provision in carrying on the work of the kingdom, as, for example, by a regularly paid ministry.

39-46. CHRIST'S AGONY IN GETHSEMANE.—Recorded also by Matthew (26 : 36-46) and Mark (14 : 32-42). See notes on Matthew, whose account is fullest. There are some features, however, peculiar to Luke, which I treat here.

40. At the place. John (18 : 1) locates it as "over the brook Cedron," and describes it as "a garden," i. e., probably an orchard; Matthew and Mark designate it by name as "Gethsemane."—**Pray that ye enter not into temptation.** This direction may have been given to all the disciples, though, if so, it is not mentioned by the other Evangelists. I should rather regard this as a condensed account of the fuller report given in the other Gospels of the request to the three disciples, Peter, James, and John, to watch with their Lord.

41, 42. About a stone's cast. Peculiar to Luke. Matthew and Mark have only "a little further." The distance described is not that from the body of the disciples, but from the three whom our Lord took to watch with him, but whose opportunity and neglect Luke does not describe.—**Kneeled down.** Matthew and Mark are more precise: "Fell on his face" (Matthew), "on the ground" (Mark).—**If thou be willing.** For comparison of the three accounts of the prayer see Matt. 26 : 39, note.

43. There is some uncertainty respecting the genuineness of this verse. Alford and Tischendorf both retain it, and the explanation of its omission given by Epiphanius is generally accepted, viz., that it was expunged by the orthodox, who imagined it inconsistent with the divine nature of our Lord. Alford asserts that both the appearance and the strengthening were *physical;* Olshausen that they were *inward and spiritual;* but neither assigns any reason for his view. The fact that Christ was divinely strengthened to drink the cup, which it was not possible should pass from him, is clear. How that strength was imparted we are not told, and conjectures are worthless. Spiritually, the experience is paralleled by the two experiences of Paul recorded in Acts 27 : 23, 24 and 2 Cor. 12 : 8, 9. In one case there was evidently a visible appearance of the angelic messenger; in the other not. Divine aid was similarly afforded to Christ in the temptation (Mark 1 : 13).

44. And being in an agony. Literally, *a conflict.* This word ($\dot{a}\gamma\omega\nu\iota a$) occurs in the N. T. only here; but a different form of the same word ($\dot{a}\gamma\omega\nu$) occurs six times, and is rendered "conflict," "contention," "fight," and "race" (1 till. 1 : 30; Col. 2 : 1; 1 Thess. 2 ; 2 ; 1 Tim. 6 : 12; 2 Tim. 4 : 7; Heb. 12 : 1). These references indicate its meaning here, a true mental conflict between the wish to avoid the suffering of the Passion and the supreme purpose to fulfill, at whatever personal cost, the will of the Father. On its nature, see notes on Matthew. For evidence of its reality and bitterness, see Heb. 2 : 18; 4 : 15; 5 : 7.—**He prayed more earnestly.** Now, however, not that the cup might pass from him, but that he might be able to fulfill the divine will in completing his sacrifice (Matt. 26 : 42, note).—**And his sweat was as it were great drops of blood falling down to the ground.** I can see no reason to doubt that this description is to be taken literally; that our Lord's mental agony so acted upon his physical frame as to produce, not only a perspiration, but one which was discolored by the exudation of blood. It was thus not drops of blood, nor mere drops of perspiration, but drops of a bloody perspiration. Mr. Stroud (*Physical Cause of Christ's Death*) has shown that in certain cases of great mental conflict the palpitation of the heart is so greatly increased, and the circulation of the blood so accelerated, that the pressure becomes very great on the blood-vessels, and results, sometimes in a hemorrhage, and sometimes in an exuding of the blood, which mingles with and discolors the perspiration. There are only a few such cases on record; but they are enough to show that the bloody sweat experienced in the garden of Gethsemane was not an impossible, nor even a miraculous phenomenon, and to throw light upon it as an indication of the degree of the agony experienced. They also connect this hour of agony with the death upon the cross. Alone it would have been sufficient to cause Christ's death, had he not been supernaturally strengthened to sustain it

46 And said unto them, Why sleep ye? rise and pray, lest ye enter into temptation.
47 And while he yet spake, behold ᵘ a multitude, and he that was called Judas, one of the twelve, went before them, and drew near unto Jesus, to kiss him.
48 But Jesus said unto him, Judas, betrayest thou the Son of man with a kiss?
49 When they which were about him saw what would follow, they said unto him, Lord, shall we smite with the sword?
50 And one of them smote the servant of the high priest, and cut off his right ear.
51 And Jesus answered and said, Suffer ye thus far. And he touched his ear, and healed him.
52 Then Jesus said unto the chief priests, and captains of the temple, and the elders, which were come to him, Be ye come out as against a thief, with swords and staves?
53 When I was daily with you in the temple, ye stretched forth no hands against me: but this is your hour, and the power of darkness.
54 Then took they him, and led *him*, and brought him into the high priest's house. And Peter followed afar off.

55 And when they had kindled a fire in the midst of the hall, and were set down together, Peter sat down among them.
56 But ʷ a certain maid beheld him as he sat by the fire, and earnestly looked upon him, and said, This man was also with him.
57 And he denied him, saying, Woman, I know him not.
58 And after a little while ˣ another saw him, and said, Thou art also of them. And Peter said, Man, I am not.
59 And about the space of one hour after, another ʸ confidently affirmed, saying, Of a truth this *fellow* was with him: for he is a Galilæan.
60 And Peter said, Man, I know not what thou sayest. And immediately, while he yet spake, the cock crew.
61 And the Lord turned, and looked upon Peter. And ᶻ Peter remembered the word of the Lord, how he had said unto him, Before ᵃ the cock crow, thou shalt deny me thrice.
62 And ᵇ Peter went out, and wept bitterly.
63 And ᶜ the men that held Jesus mocked him, and smote *him*.

t verse 40.. u Matt. 26 : 47, etc.; Mark 14 : 43, etc.: John 18 : 3, etc....v Job 20 : 5; John 19 : 27....w Matt. 26 : 69; Mark 14 : 66, 69; John 18 : 17....x Mat. 26 : 71; Mark 14 : 69; John 18 : 25.....y Matt. 26 : 73; Mark 14 : 70; John 18 : 26....z Matt. 26 : 75; Mark 14 : 72,... a verse 34....b Ps. 130 : 1–4; 143 : 1–4; Jer. 31 : 18; Ezek. 7 : 16; 1 Cor. 10 : 12; 2 Cor. 7 : 10, 11....c Matt. 26 : 67, 68; Mark 14 : 65.

(Matt. 26 : 35, note); and when it was followed by the withdrawal of God's countenance, and a new sense of the burden of sin laid upon him in the hour of the crucifixion, it may well have resulted in a rupture of his weakened heart, which I believe to have been, physically, the cause of his death. See John 19 : 34, note.

45, 46. Sleeping for sorrow. Observe the two ways of meeting sorrow; the disciples try to forget it in sleep, Christ conquers it by prayer.—**Rise and pray lest ye enter into temptation.** This appears to have been said previously. See the fuller reports of Matthew and Mark.

47–53. The Betrayal and Arrest of Jesus.—Matt. 26 : 47–56; Mark 14 : 43–52; John 18 : 1–12. See notes on Matthew and John. There are some features in the account of the arrest peculiar to Luke. He alone reports the question addressed by our Lord to the traitor (ver. 48), *Judas, betrayest thou the Son of man with a kiss?* In this question Christ reasserts himself to be the Messiah (Matt. 10 : 23 and note)"; thus dissipates any doubts which Judas might have entertained, and makes a final appeal to his conscience. These are Christ's last words to him, and I think follow the kiss. Luke alone mentions the healing of the servant's (Malchus) ear (ver. 51) The fact that our Lord *touched his ear* indicates that it was not entirely severed. Moreover, there is no case in the Bible of the creation of a new member by a miracle. The words *Suffer ye thus far* appear to have been addressed by Jesus to the guard, who had already seized him. They are a request for sufficient liberty to effect the healing. Verse 52 alone indicates that any of the priests or elders personally accompanied the band. *This is your hour and the power of darkness* (ver. 53) is also peculiar to Luke. It is our

Lord's answer to his own question, an explanation of the reason why the Pharisees had not arrested Christ before, viz., because the night was a proper hour for such a deed of darkness. I doubt the exegesis which interprets the word "darkness" as equivalent to the evil one. I should rather understand, with De Wette, The darkness gives you courage to seize me. Compare John 3 : 20.

54–62. Denials of our Lord by Peter.—These are reported by the four Evangelists. Matt. 26 : 69–75; Mark 14 : 66–72; John 18 : 15–27. See notes on Matthew and John, especially Matthew, for harmony of the accounts. I believe that the denials took place during a preliminary examination before Caiaphas (not Annas), reported only by John, and prior to the formal trial by the Sanhedrim reported by the three Synoptists. For plan and cut of Jewish house, see notes on Matthew; for illustrations of the kind of fire used, see notes on John. Luke alone mentions the fact that the Lord turned and looked upon Peter (ver. 61). This may indicate that the examination proceeded in a room opening upon the courtyard where Peter was standing, or that the look was given as Christ was led out from the palace to the council-chamber for trial. The latter supposition is more probable, since the last denial appears to have taken place not in the courtyard, but in the porch or entrance.

63–71. Trial of Jesus before Caiaphas and the Council.—Most scholars are agreed that Luke here reports the formal trial and conviction of Christ. Some, however, identify it with the meeting of the council referred to in Matt. 27 : 1, and distinguish it from that reported in Matt. 26 : 57–68; Mark 14 : 55–65, which they regard as a preliminary

64 And when they had blindfolded him, they struck him on the face, and asked him, saying, Prophesy, who is it that smote thee?
65 And many other things blasphemously spake they against him.
66 And ᵈ as soon as it was day, the elders of the people and the chief priests and the scribes came together, and led him into their council, saying,
67 Art ᵉ thou the Christ? tell us. And he said unto them, If I tell you, ye will not believe:
68 And if I also ask *you*, ye will not answer me, nor let *me* go.
69 Hereafter shall the Son of man sit on the right hand ᶠ of the power of God.
70 Then said they all, Art thou then the Son of God? And he said unto them, Ye say that I am.
71 And they said, What need we any further witness? for we ourselves have heard of his own mouth.

CHAPTER XXIII.

AND ᵍ the whole multitude of them arose, and led him unto Pilate.
2 And they began to accuse ʰ him, saying, We found this *fellow* ⁱ perverting the nation, and forbidding to give tribute ʲ to Cæsar, saying that he ᵏ himself is Christ a King.
3 And Pilate asked him, saying, Art thou the King of the Jews? And ˡ he answered him, and said, Thou sayest *it*.
4 Then said Pilate to the chief priests and *to* the people, I find no ᵐ fault in this man.

d Matt. 27 : 1; Acts 4 : 26-28.....e Matt. 26 : 63, etc.; Mark 14 : 61, etc....f Heb. 1 : 3; 8 : 1; Rev. 3 : 21....g Matt. 27 : 2, 11, etc.; Mark 15 : 1, etc.; John 18 : 28, etc....h Zech. 11 : 8....i verse 5; Acts 16 : 20, 21; 17 : 6, 7....j Matt. 17 : 27; 22 : 21; Mark 12 : 17....k John 18 : 36; 19 : 12....l 1 Tim. 6 : 13....m John 18 : 38; 19 : 4; Heb. 7 : 26; 1 Pet. 2 : 22.

examination. The similarity of the proceedings appears to me to forbid this hypothesis, and to render far more reasonable the opinion that the three Evangelists narrate the same event, and that this event is not a preliminary and informal examination, but the final trial of Jesus before the Sanhedrim. It must be remembered that in the Orient, judicial proceedings were then and are now characterized by no such regularity and formality as habitually characterize such proceedings with us. The Oriental courts are often scenes of popular turbulence; the sympathies of the people are generally against the accused; the presumptions of the court are practically adverse to him; and popular indignities are showered upon him without interference from the authorities. For a general consideration of the apparent discrepancies in the Evangelical narratives of this trial, and for its moral and doctrinal lessons, see notes on Matt. 26 : 57-68.

63-65. These indignities are placed by Matthew and Mark subsequent to the trial. They were inflicted by the servants (Mark 14 : 65), possibly both before and after Christ's final condemnation. Verse 65 here is peculiar to Luke.

66. As soon as it was day. A Jewish trial could not take place at night. Daybreak was about four o'clock in the morning. Probably the parallelism in expression between this verse and Matt. 27 : 1, has led to the supposition that the two meetings were identical.—**The elders of the people and the chief priests and the scribes came together.** That is, the Sanhedrim, or Jewish Council, assembled. See Prel. Note, Matt. 26 : 57-68.—**And led him into their council.** The original signifies either the council or the council-chamber. The context here seems to indicate that the Sanhedrim assembled in the temple. This is confirmed by the incident recorded in Matt. 27 : 5; see note there. The council-chamber was a large circular room of stone, connected with the temple, approached through a vestibule and spacious hall, and lighted from the roof.

67, 68. Saying, Art thou the Christ? First an attempt was made to convict Jesus of blasphemy by false witnesses. This failed. Then the oath was administered to him by the high priest, and he was called on, in violation of the Jewish law, which forbade the condemnation of an accused on his own confession, to testify concerning his own claims and character. To this he returns a solemn and dignified protest. If I tell you, ye will not believe; if I question you (to prove my own innocence by your testimony), ye will not answer me nor release me. After uttering this protest, he bears the testimony concerning himself recorded by the three synoptic Evangelists.

69-71. See notes on Matt. 26 : 64-66. That Christ should a second time have been asked to testify against himself, and should a second time have given the testimony called for, seems to me far less probable than to suppose that we have in the different narratives accounts of the same event, with those unimportant variations which are elsewhere common, both in sacred and secular history.

Ch. 23 : 1-25. TRIAL BEFORE PILATE.—Described in Matt. 27 : 11-31; Mark 15 : 1-23; John 18 : 28 to 19 : 16. John's account is the fullest. See notes there, especially for estimate of Pilate's character and lessons from his course. See on Matthew, Prel. Note, for harmony of the four narratives.

1, 2. Led him unto Pilate. Prior to this there was a private conference, at which the course to be pursued before Pilate was determined on, and at which Judas appeared and returned the blood-money (Matt. 27 : 1-10).—**Began to accuse him.** Luke alone reports the accusation. They first endeavor to secure from Pilate a ratification of the death sentence without a trial, and failed (John 18 : 29-31).—**Perverting the nation, and forbidding to give tribute to Cæsar, saying that he himself, the Messiah, is a king.** The first statement

5 And they were the more fierce," saying, He stirreth up the people, teaching, throughout all Jewry, beginning from Galilee to this place.
6 When Pilate heard of Galilee, he asked whether the man were a Galilæan.
7 And as soon as he knew that he belonged unto Herod's ° jurisdiction, he sent him to Herod, who himself also was at Jerusalem at that time.
8 And when Herod saw Jesus, he was exceeding glad: for ᵖ he was desirous to see him of a long *season*, because ᵠ he had heard many things of him; and ʳ he hoped to have seen some miracle done by him.

9 Then he questioned with him in many words; but ˢ he answered him nothing.
10 And the chief priests and scribes stood and vehemently accused him.
11 And Herod with his men of war set him at nought,ᵗ and mocked *him*, and arrayed him in a gorgeous ᵘ robe, and sent him again to Pilate.
12 And the same day Pilate and ᵛ Herod were made friends together: for before they were at enmity between themselves.
13 And Pilate, when he had called together the chief priests and the rulers and the people,

n Ps. 57:4....o ch. 3:1....p ch. 9:9....q Matt. 14:1; Mark 6:14....r 2 Kings 5:11....s Ps. 38:13,14; 39:1,9; Isa. 53:7....
t Isa. 49:7; 53:3....u John 19:5....v Acts 4:27.

was so far true that Christ had certainly turned away the hearts of the people from their then religious leaders (Matt., ch. 24), which they would regard as a perversion; the second was absolutely false (Matt. 22:15-22); the third was true, but not in the sense in which they intended (John 18:37). See for grounds of this accusation, John 18:33, note. Observe that their charge differs entirely from that on which Christ had been condemned before the Sanhedrim (Matt. 27:65, note).

3, 4. This conference is reported much more fully in John 18:33-38. It took place within Pilate's judgment-hall and apart from the crowd. Were it not for John's report of Christ's explanation of the nature of his kingdom, Pilate's acquittal of him would be utterly inexplicable; an illustration how in other instances a fuller knowledge would explain difficulties which, in our comparative ignorance, are inexplicable.

5-7. Luke alone reports this incident of the sending of Jesus to Herod.—**He stirreth up the people, teaching throughout all Jewry;** *i. e.*, throughout all Judea. This is an unconsciously true characterization of Christ's ministry, which always excites the people and instructs them. Comp. Acts 16:20, 21; 17:6. The instruction and excitement of the people is always odious to despotic governments; the accusation preferred by the priests was therefore well adapted to stimulate Pilate's prejudices.—**Herod's jurisdiction.** For character and life of this Herod, see Matt. 14:1-12, notes. Palestine was divided into different provinces under different governors; Herod was tetrarch of Galilee. See Luke 3:1, note. Under the Roman law, the prisoner might be tried before the governor of the province or district where he belonged, or of that where the offence was committed. Pilate seems to have sent Christ to Herod, partly as an act of royal courtesy, partly to relieve himself of responsibility. Herod's palace was situated in the upper city or Mount Sion. The trial of Jesus before Pilate, took place, probably, at the tower of Antonia on Mount Moriah (John 18:28, note). A bridge, the remains of which are still standing, spanned the ravine which separated these two hills. The relation of the temple, the tower, and the palace of Herod, with the bridge over which Christ was probably led, are shown in the map, Vol. I, p. 278. It is surmised that Herod was at Jerusalem for the purpose of attending the paschal feast.

8-11. The fame of Jesus had reached the ears of Herod long before (Matt. 14:1; Luke 13:31). Observe (1) Herod's desire: to see Christ; (2) its cause: curiosity; (3) his position: an inquirer; (4) his treatment: Christ answered him nothing. Is there not in this an explanation of the reason why Christ often treats with silence those who seem to be earnestly seeking to see and learn of him; and a lesson for those who, in the church or out of it, manifest a desire for the presence of Christ, not because they want his spiritual inspiration, but because they are curious to see or ambitious to share in the manifestation of his mighty works. No words could have so utterly rebuked the murderer of John the Baptist as did silence. Contrast Christ's treatment of Pilate in his honest perplexity (John 18:33-37). The result here—"Herod set him at naught and mocked him"—shows how little in earnest he was in his seeking. This mockery is not mentioned by the other Evangelists, nor is the mockery before Pilate mentioned by Luke. The *gorgeous robe* is not to be confounded with the scarlet robe afterward put upon him by Pilate's soldiers (Matt. 27:28). The original ($\lambda\alpha\mu\pi\varrho\delta\varsigma$) indicates a *white* dress; the same word is translated *bright* in Acts 10:30, *white* in Rev. 15:6; 19:8, and *clear* in Rev. 22:1. Calvin, on the mockery by Herod's retinue, suggests that "the honor which is due to God is seldom rendered to him in the character of king."

12. Were made friends together; for before they were at enmity. The cause of this enmity is unknown. It probably concerned some question of jurisdiction between them, which was conceded by Pilate in sending Jesus to Herod, and waived by Herod in sending him back again. Some of the commentators notice that Christ by his death thus brought together Jew (Herod) and Gentile (Pilate), a prophecy of that breaking down of the partition wall between them, which he has accomplished (Ephes. 2:14). More observable is the fact, that hostility to Christ, as well as love for him,

14 Said unto them, Ye have brought this man unto me, as one that perverteth the people; and, behold, I,[w] having examined *him* before you, have found no fault in this man, touching those things whereof ye accuse him:
15 No, nor yet Herod: for I sent you to him; and, lo, nothing worthy of death is done unto him.
16 I will therefore chastise [x] him, and release *him*.
17 (For of necessity he must release one unto them at the feast.)
18 And they cried out all at once, saying, Away with this *man*, and release unto us Barabbas;
19 (Who for a certain sedition made in the city, and for murder,[y] was cast into prison.)
20 Pilate therefore, willing to release Jesus, spake again to them.
21 But they cried, saying, Crucify *him*, crucify him.
22 And he said unto them the third time, Why, what evil hath he done? I have found no cause of death in him: I will therefore chastise him, and let *him* go.
23 And they were instant [z] with loud voices, requiring that he might be crucified. And the voices of them and of the chief priests prevailed.
24 And Pilate gave sentence that it should be as they [a] required.
25 And he released unto them [b] him that for sedition and murder was cast into prison, whom they had desired; but he delivered Jesus to their will.
26 And [c] as they led him away, they laid hold upon one Simon, a Cyrenian, coming out of the country, and on him they laid the cross, that he might bear *it* after Jesus.
27 And there followed him a great company of people, and of women, which also bewailed and lamented him.

---

w verse 4....x Isa. 53 : 5....y Acts 3 : 14....z verse 5; Ps. 22 : 12....a Exod. 23 : 2....b Acts 3 : 14....c Matt. 27 : 32, etc.; Mark 15 : 21, etc.; John 19 : 17.

---

unites those who are naturally opposed to one another. United, "as Samson's foxes, to do mischief to others rather than to do good to themselves." To this Alford objects, that the present feeling of Pilate was anything but hostile to the person of Christ; and Herod, by his treatment of him, shows that he thought him beneath his judicial notice; but the enmity of Pilate and Herod are typical of that which prevails against Christ. This is generally either the opposition of self-interest, which crucifies Christ rather than suffer with him, or that of pride, which makes naught of and mocks him.

13-15. This declaration of Christ's innocence appears to be distinct from that reported by the other Evangelists. Pilate's language indicates that Herod sent an unreported message of acquittal. *Done unto him* is a mistranslation for done *by him*.

16. Chastise him. The original ($\pi\alpha\iota\delta\epsilon\dot{\upsilon}\omega$) signifies literally, to educate or instruct, and is sometimes so rendered in the N. T. Here it may mean, I will instruct him, that is, correct his fanatical notions respecting a kingdom, and release him; but this view, adopted in my *Jesus of Nazareth*, on consideration, appears to me less tenable than that of our English version. Pilate proposes to save the pride of the priests, by convicting the accused and punishing him, and to save his own conscience, by not inflicting the death penalty.

17-25. Of necessity. This is partially explained by Matt. 27 : 15, note; John 18 : 39.—**Release one of them.** The demand of this popular privilege first came from the people (Mark 15 : 8).—**They cried out all at once.** Not *immediately;* some little time intervened, during which the chief priests and elders were busy stirring up the people (Matt. 27 : 20); but *all together, i. e.,* with clamorous and combined voices.—**Barabbas.** See Matt. 27 : 17, note.— **The voices of them and of the chief priests.** The latter mixed with the crowd and swelled the tumult with their own voices.—**He delivered Jesus to their will.** An indication that he suffered them to choose the form of execution, namely, crucifixion. Before this took place, Christ was scourged and mocked by the soldiers (Mark 27 : 26-30), and two more efforts were made by Pilate for his release (John 19 : 4, 5; 14, 15).

Ch. 23 : 26-49. THE CRUCIFIXION. THE CRUCIFIED IS NOT AN OBJECT OF PITY (27-31).—THE DIVINE COMPASSION EXEMPLIFIED IN THE INTERCESSION OF THE CROSS, "FATHER, FORGIVE THEM" (34).—THE GOSPEL EXEMPLIFIED IN THE PENITENCE, THE FAITH, AND THE PARDON OF THE DYING BRIGAND.—CHRIST'S DEATH A PATTERN FOR THE DYING CHRISTIAN (46).

Comp. Matt. 27 : 32-56; Mark 15 : 21-41; John 19 : 17-30. Matthew and Mark are almost exactly parallel. Peculiar to Luke are the incidents of the weeping women (vers. 27-31), Christ's prayer for the forgiveness of his enemies (34), the penitence of one of the thieves (39-43), and Christ's final prayer commending his spirit into his Father's hands (46). For comparison of the four accounts, and notes on what is common to them, see Matthew; 26. See Matt. 27 : 32, notes.

27. A great company of people and of women. Not his disciples, but such a crowd as curiosity would gather in a great city to witness such a procession. That the women were not those subsequently described as standing before the cross (ver. 49) is evident, because they were Galileans, while these are described as "daughters of Jerusalem." It appears from Rabbinical writings that an association of women was formed at Jerusalem to alleviate the sufferings of those condemned to die; they accompanied the accused to the place of execution, and administered a drink of acid wine mixed with myrrh, which acted as an anodyne. This fact probably explains the incident mentioned in Matt. 27 : 34; and these may have been the women there referred to. It is, at all events, a reasonable surmise that, seeing the inscription

140 LUKE. [Ch. XXIII.

28 But Jesus turning unto them, said, Daughters of Jerusalem, weep not for me, but weep for yourselves, and for your children.
29 For, behold, the days ᵈ are coming, in which they shall say, Blessed *are* the barren, and the wombs that never bare, and the paps which never gave suck.
30 Then ᵉ shall they begin to say to the mountains, Fall on us; and to the hills, Cover us.

d ch. 21 : 23 ; Matt. 24 : 19.....e Isa. 2 : 19 ; Hosea 10 : 8 ; Rev. 6 : 16 ; 9 : 6.

borne before the cross, "Jesus of Nazareth, King of the Jews," and knowing little or nothing of the trial before the Sanhedrim, which had taken place secretly about daybreak, they lamented what they regarded as a new indignity inflicted upon their nation. The original indicates that their lamenting was of a vehement sort, according to the Jewish fashion, including beating upon their breasts and loud wailing (*αί καί έκόπτοντο καί έθρήνουν αὐτόι*). For description of Jewish wailing, see Mark 5 : 38, note.

Ostentatious and vehement mourning appears to have been always displeasing to Jesus. Comp. Mark 5 : 39.

28-31. Jesus turning unto them. This was evidently after he had been relieved of the cross; perhaps he avails himself of the moment of delay occasioned by the impressment of Simon. Notice the indication of accuracy in this description of a subordinate detail.—**Weep for yourselves and for your children.** In the valley just outside the walls of Jerusalem is a

WAILING PLACE OF JEWS.

point known as the "wailing place of the Jews," where they gather every day to read the law and prophets, and to chant a mournful refrain. With trembling lips and tearful eyes, they sing, "Be not wroth very sore, O Lord, neither remember iniquity forever; behold, see, we beseech thee, for we are all thy people. Thy holy cities are a wilderness; Zion is a wilderness; Jerusalem a desolation" (Isa. 64 : 9, etc.). Thus to the present day the daughters of Jerusalem weep for themselves and their children.—**The days are coming.** The primary reference is to the destruction of Jerusalem. Some of those who now bewail him probably perished in that siege, and doubtless many of their children did so. For a description of its horrors, see Matthew, ch. 24, Prel. Note.—**Blessed are the barren.** Children were considered by the Jews as a special divine blessing, and their absence a divine punishment (Gen. 30 : 1; Deut. 7 : 14; Ps. 127 : 3; Hosea 9 : 14). The language here, therefore, was to these mothers a graphic suggestion of the terrible days which Christ foretold.—**Then shall they begin to say.** This is cited from Hosea 10 : 8, and was partially fulfilled in the destruction of Jerusalem, when, toward the end of the siege, multitudes of the Jews sought to escape death by hiding in the subterranean passages and sewers under the city. Those who recognize the truth that history is itself prophetic, and that the judgment of God against the Jewish nation in the destruction of Jerusalem is itself a prophecy of the final judgment of all nations, will recognize in these words here, as elsewhere in Scripture (Isa. 2 : 10; 19 : 21; Rev. 6 : 16), a reference to the last judgment.—**If they do these things in the green tree, what shall be done in the dry?** That is, if the Jewish rulers and the

31 For if they do these things in a green tree, what shall be done in the dry?
32 And there were also two other, malefactors, led with him to be put to death.
33 And when they were come to the place, which is called Calvary, there they crucified him, and the malefactors, one on the right hand, and the other on the left.
34 Then said Jesus, Father, forgive them; for they know not what they do. And they parted his raiment, and cast lots.
35 And the people stood beholding. And the rulers also with them derided him, saying, He saved others; let him save himself, if he be Christ, the chosen of God.
36 And the soldiers also mocked him, coming to him, and offering him vinegar,
37 And saying, If thou be the king of the Jews, save thyself.

f Prov. 11 : 31; Jer. 25 : 29; Ezek. 20 : 47; 21 : 4; 1 Pet. 4 : 17....g Isa. 53 : 12....h Matt. 5 : 44; Acts 7 : 60; 1 Cor. 4 : 12....1 Ps. 22 : 7.

Roman government, conspiring together, crucify the Messiah of the nation and of the world, as the beginning of their work, what will they bring upon the nation in its consummation? If this is the leaf and blossom of the springtime of their malice, what will be the autumn end? This appears to me better than the ordinary interpretation of what is a confessedly difficult proverb. That interpretation represents the green tree as Christ, and the dry tree as the Jewish nation, and thus renders the contrast equivalent to that of 1 Pet. 4 : 18, "If the righteous scarcely be saved, where shall the ungodly and sinner appear?" So Alford, Lange, Farrar, Schenckel, Meyer, Lightfoot, Barnes, etc. But the contrast here is not between what is done *to* the green tree and *to* the dry tree, but what is done *in* the tree when green, that is, in the beginning, and when dry, that is, at the end. And observe, it was the spirit of intolerance for the Gentiles in the Jews, which was the secret of their hate for a Messiah who promised redemption to all nations (ch. 4 : 28, 29; comp. Acts 22 : 21, 22), and the spirit of contempt for the Jews in the Romans, which manifested itself in the scourging and mockery, and the spirit of inhumanity and cruelty in both, which manifested itself in the crucifixion of Christ; and it was these qualities in Jew and Gentile which brought on the war between Roman and Jew, and the scenes of carnage which accompanied the destruction of Jerusalem. The spirit exhibited in the conflict between Pilate and priests was exactly the same as that exhibited in the long conflict between Titus and the besieged Jews in Jerusalem.

The practical lesson of this incident is plain, though often forgotten. He who endures the cross, despising the shame, is not an object of pity (Heb. 12 : 2). There is nothing pitiable in the sight of one dying, even a cruel death, and in the very prime of life, if he dies in the fulfillment of duty, for the sake of others, a death in whose fruits others shall rejoice. "He could have been an object of pity only had he, from fear of the horrors of death, preferred a broken life to death."—(*Schenckel.*) We are to weep, not over Christ's suffering, but at the remembrance of our sins, which crucified him, and in reflecting upon the judgments which these sins entail. For his death, wrought out by sin in the green tree, is itself a prophecy of the woes which sin will bring upon the persistent sinner when sin has finished its course. This passage impliedly forbids all attempts to excite tears of commiseration by dramatic oratorical portraitures of Christ's sufferings, and its spirit is violated by much in so-called "sacred art."

32, 33. The word *malefactors* is emphatic, and distinguishes them from Jesus. See below, on vers. 39–43. *Calvary* is not a correct rendering of the original. It is an anglicized form of the Latin translation, *calvaria*, correctly rendered in the parallel passages (Matt. 27 : 33; Mark 15 : 22; John 19 : 17) *a skull.* The proper translation here would be, *When they were come to the place which is called a skull.* The Hebrew name was Golgotha. As to its supposed site, see Matt. 27 : 33, note.

34. Father, forgive them, for they know not what they do. This prayer is reported only by Luke. "The living and divine beauty of this prayer is disclosed, when we understand it as having burst from his lips when they were nailing him to the cross, and as immediately referring to his brutal and ignorant executioners."—(*Furness.*) This is true; yet it is also true that we may regard it as including all who directly participated in the crucifixion, of all of whom it may be truly said that they knew not what they did. Compare Peter's language in his address to the people of Jerusalem (Acts 2 : 28, 39; 3 : 17); the latter passage expressly includes both people and rulers in this prayer of intercession: "I wot that through ignorance ye did it, as did also your rulers." Thus it may be regarded as the beginning of Christ's intercession for sinners, though preceded by the prayer of intercession for his church (John, ch. 17), and as a true interpretation of the language of his cross, for all the world and for all time. It is noted by Alford as a fulfillment of the prophecy of Isaiah 53 : 12, "He made intercession for the transgressors." It was only by coming to a knowledge of what they had done that the crucifiers could be brought to a sense of sin, repentance, confession, and so to divine forgiveness; hence the first apostolic preaching is directed to bringing home to the mind of Jew and Gentile the enormity of this sin of crucifying the "Prince of Life." Observe in this prayer a wonderful

38 And a superscription also was written over him, in letters of Greek, and Latin, and Hebrew, THIS IS THE KING OF THE JEWS.
39 And one ʲ of the malefactors which were hanged railed on him, saying, If thou be Christ, save thyself and us.
40 But the other answering, rebuked him, saying, Dost not thou fear ᵏ God, seeing thou art in the same condemnation?
41 And we indeed justly; for we receive the due reward of our deeds: but this man hath done nothing ᵐ amiss.
42 And he said unto Jesus, Lord, remember ⁿ me when thou comest into thy kingdom.
43 And Jesus said unto him, Verily ᵒ I say unto thee, To-day shalt thou be with me in paradise.ᵖ
44 And it was about the sixth hour, and there was a darkness over all the earth until the ninth hour.

j ch. 17 : 34–36....k Ps. 36 : 1....l Jer. 5 : 3....m 1 Pet. 1 : 19....n Ps. 106 : 4, 5; Rom. 10 : 9, 10; 1 Cor. 6 : 10, 11....o Rom. 5 : 20, 21....p 2 Cor. 12 : 4; Rev. 2 : 7.

exemplification of our Lord's instruction to his followers, "Pray for them which despitefully use you."—**They parted his raiment,** etc. See John 18 : 23, 24, notes.

35-37. Comp. Matt. 27 : 30-44, notes. The statement that the soldiers mocked him, is peculiar to Luke. On the offering of the vinegar in mockery, see Matt. 27 : 47-49, notes. Alford regards this as distinct from the incidents there narrated. "It was about the time of the midday meal of the soldiers, and they in mockery offered him their pasca or sour wine, to drink with them." But I see no reason for this supposition, nor even how such an offering to the thirsty sufferer can be regarded as a mockery, except in some such connection as is indicated in the accounts of the other Evangelists.

38. On the variation in the four reports of this inscription, and on Pilate's refusal to modify it, see John 19 : 19-22, notes.

39-43. This incident of the penitent thief is recorded only by Luke. Matthew and Mark represent both malefactors as reviling Christ. On the reconciliation of this discrepancy, see Matt. 27 : 44, note.—**If thou be the Messiah.** The language of the brigands (Matt. 27 : 38, note) here and in verse 42, indicates that both were Jews. They were probably Galilean zealots, who believed in a coming Judean kingdom, made their patriotism a cover for robbery and murder, and had finally been arrested and condemned. It is a reasonable hypothesis that they belonged to the band of which Barabbas was the leader. On the character of this band, see Mark 15 : 7. In that case, the outbreak for which they were condemned, had taken place in Jerusalem, and had been accompanied by murder (ch. 23 : 19). —**Dost thou not then fear God because we are in the same condemnation?** The brigands and Jesus were condemned to death on the same charge, viz., sedition against the Roman government (ch. 23 : 2). The one brigand, because Christ was subject to the same condemnation and punishment, makes that fact an occasion of reviling his claim to be Messiah; the other declares that it is known to them both that Christ's condemnation was unjust, that he had no share in their violence or their seditious designs.— **This man hath done nothing amiss.** This was more true than he thought. Comp. John 8 : 46; 1 Pet. 2 : 22. Observe in the language here an important testimony, if one were needed, to the injustice of the sentence pronounced against Jesus by the Roman governor.—**When thou comest in thy kingdom.** Not *into thy kingdom* (εἰς), but *in thy* kingdom (ἐν). Parallel to this expression is Christ's own language respecting himself (Matt. 25 : 31), "When the Son of man shall come *in his glory.*" Comp. Col. 3 : 4. The dying brigand refers to a future and glorious coming of Christ, as a revealed and recognized Messiah, of which coming the ancient prophets had spoken, and to which Christ in both public and private instructions, had explicitly and repeatedly referred. It is hardly possible that the petitioner would have used this language if he had not been a Jew and known something of Jesus prior to this time, by reputation if not personally.—**To-day shalt thou be with me in paradise.** Observe how the promise of grace transcends the prayer of penitence. The repentant brigand only asks a remembrance in some far future day in Christ's second coming; Christ promises a remembrance to-day. The construction which joins "to-day," with, "I say unto thee," rendering the declaration, "I, to-day, say unto thee that thou shalt be (*i. e.,* at some future time) with me in paradise," only deserves mention as a curious illustration of the extent to which perversion of Scripture has been carried, for the purpose of avoiding its real or supposed inconsistency with preconceived systems of theology.

We must look, not to the literature of later patristic theology, nor to that of Jewish scholasticism, but to the usage of the common people in Palestine, for an interpretation of this word *paradise,* and so for the meaning of this promise; for only thus shall we understand it as the thief would have understood it. The word is of Persian origin, and signifies *beautiful land.* It is said (*Kitto*) to have first appeared in Greek literature about 400 B. C., and is employed in the Septuagint as a term to designate the first abode of man, the Garden of Eden. Hence it came to be employed as a designation of the future home into which the holy will be admitted by the grace of God, and thence, in Jewish popular belief, as the name of that portion of Hades, or the abode of the dead, in which the patriarchs and

45 And the sun was darkened, and the veil of the temple was rent in the midst.
46 And when Jesus had cried with a loud voice, he said, Father, into ⁹ thy hands I commend my spirit: and ʳ having said thus, he gave up the ghost.
47 Now when the centurion saw what was done, he glorified God, saying, Certainly this was a righteous man.
48 And all the people that came together to that sight, beholding the things which were done, smote their breasts, and returned.

49 And all his acquaintance, and the women that followed him from Galilee, stood afar ⁸ off, beholding these things.
50 And, behold, *there was* a man named Joseph, a counsellor; *and he was* a good man, and a just:
51 (The same had not consented to the counsel and deed of them ;) *he was* of Arimathea, a city of the Jews: who ᵗ also himself waited for the kingdom of God.
52 This *man* went unto Pilate, and begged the body of Jesus.
53 And he took it down, and wrapped it in linen, and

q Ps. 31 : 5 ; 1 Pet. 2 : 23....r Matt. 27 : 50, etc. ; Mark 15 : 37, etc.; John 19 : 30....s Ps. 38 : 11; 142 : 4....t ch. 2 : 25, 38; Mark 15 : 43.

---

prophets dwelt, and into which the saints were believed to enter to await the final judgment and consequent admission to their everlasting home. Hence to repose in Abraham's bosom (Luke 16 : 23), was to have a high place of honor in this abode of the blessed. This brigand would then have understood Christ's promise as one of immediate entrance into a state of conscious peace and joy. The promise throws little light on the question of an intermediate state, for there was no time to correct erroneous or even superstitious ideas concerning the future. But it is certainly inconsistent with (1) the Roman Catholic doctrine of purgatory; for if ever one needed the fire of discipline to purge away the evil of his nature and atone for that of his life, this tardily repentant brigand did ; (2) the doctrine of an unconscious state between death and the judgment; for this promise was to be fulfilled, not in the future, but *to-day*; (3) the idea of a mere gradual development going on in the next life from the stage of progress reached by habit of life and education in this; for then this brigand would have entered on that development at almost the lowest point in the scale. This promise can be reconciled with the facts subsequently stated of Christ's resurrection and appearance to his disciples, only by the reasonable supposition, apparently confirmed by other passages of Scripture (1 Pet. 3 : 18, 19 ; 4 : 6), that Christ entered immediately after death into paradise, and remained with the dead, during the time when, to sight, he appeared to be reposing in the grave. This, too, accords with his declaration that to those that believe in him, and much more therefore to himself, there is no such thing as death (John 11 : 26). In respect to the spiritual lessons of this incident, observe, (1) That the penitent thief illustrates true repentance and faith ; repentance in the confession, "We receive the due reward of our deeds ;" faith in the appeal, "Lord, remember me when thou comest in thy kingdom." At a time when even the disciples despair of that kingdom, and lose faith in the king, this man hopes for the one and trusts in the other ; (2) that Jesus Christ illustrates this nature of divine mercy. Though one's whole life has been wasted and misspent, there is divine forgiveness and redemption to the penitent and believing soul, who has nothing to carry to Christ but his need ; (3) that the lesson is often misread. There is no evidence that this brigand had ever known personally of Jesus Christ before, and therefore in this acceptance of his tardy repentance there is no encouragement for those to whom Christ is presented in life and health, and who deliberately reject him, with an expectation of accepting his redemption at the last. "He who pardons the sinner that repents, will grant no repentance to the sinner that presumes."—(*Augustine.*) Comp. note on Parable of the Laborers, Matt. 20 : 1-16. (4.) That the Gospel is both a savor of life and of death (2 Cor. 2 : 16). To both malefactors Christ crucified is presented ; one is hardened, and blasphemes; the other is softened, and prays.

41-46. On the discrepancy in time between the statement here and in John 19 : 14, see note there. On the nature and significance of the supernatural darkness and the rending of the veil here mentioned, see on Matt. 27 : 45, 51-53. The rending of the veil took place, according to Matthew's more precise account, not at noon, but at 3 P. M.; the darkness lasted from noon till 3 P. M., and was followed by an earthquake. The cry "with a loud voice" was that reported by Matthew and Mark, "Eli, Eli, lama Sabachthani ;" this was followed by the words, reported only by John, "It is finished ;" the words here reported, "Father, into thy hands I commit my spirit," were Christ's last words. They do not seem to me to justify the inference of Alford, that his death was "a determinate delivering up of his spirit to the Father," if I understand aright his meaning, viz., that Christ's death was a voluntary act of his own divine will, and not a succumbing of the power of nature to grief and exhaustion. The language is appropriate for any child of God, whose death, if it be in consciousness, should always be a calm and trustful committal of the soul to the Heavenly Father. The language is borrowed from Ps. 31 : 5 ; comp. Acts 7 : 59. On the physical cause of Christ's death, see John 19 : 34, note.

47-49. See notes on Matt. 27 : 54-56. Ver. 48 is peculiar to Luke, and shows that the centurion was not the only one affected by the darkness and the earthquake.

laid it in a ª sepulchre that was hewn in stone, wherein never man before was laid.

54 And that day was the ᵛ preparation, and the sabbath drew on.

55 And the women ʷ also, which came with him from Galilee, followed after, and beheld the sepulchre, and how his body was laid.

56 And they returned, and ˣ prepared spices and ointments; and rested the sabbath day, according ʸ to the commandment.

CHAPTER XXIV.

NOW ᶻ upon the first *day* of the week, very early in the morning, they came unto the sepulchre, bringing the spices which they had prepared, and certain *others* with them.

2 And they found the stone rolled away from the sepulchre.

3 And they entered in, and found not the body of the Lord Jesus.

4 And it came to pass, as they were much perplexed thereabout, behold,ᵃ two men stood by them in shining garments:

5 And as they were afraid, and bowed down *their* faces to the earth, they said unto them, Why seek ye the living among the dead?

6 He is not here, but is risen: remember how he spake ᵇ unto you when he was yet in Galilee,

7 Saying, The Son of man must be delivered into the

---

u Isa. 53 : 9....v Matt. 27 : 62....w verse 49; ch. 8 : 2....x Mark 16 : 1...y Exod. 20 : 8-10... z Matt. 28 : 1, etc.; Mark 16 : 2, etc.; John 20 : 1, etc....a John 20 : 12; Acts 1 : 10....b ch. 9 : 22; Matt. 16 : 21; 17 : 22, 23; Mark 8 : 31; 9 : 31; John 2 : 22.

50-56. THE BURIAL OF JESUS.—Comp. Matt. 27 : 57-61; Mark 15 : 42-47; John 19 : 36-42. See John for notes on what is common to the four Evangelists.—**A counsellor.** A member of the Jewish Sanhedrim.—**A good man and just.** Peculiar to Luke. Mark only describes his *position;* Luke his *character.*—**The same had not consented to the counsel and deed of them.** That is, of the Sanhedrim. The report of the trial indicates that the condemnation of Christ was unanimous (Mark 16 : 64); the implication, therefore, is that Joseph was not present.—**The sabbath was approaching.** The Sabbath began at sunset (Lev. 23 : 32). It was then not quite sunset. The Greek (ἐπιφώσκω), to *dawn,* is here used metaphorically for, to *approach.*

Ch. 24 : 1-53. THE RESURRECTION AND ASCENSION. HE THAT HONORS CHRIST CRUCIFIED FINDS CHRIST RISEN.—SEEK NOT THE LIVING CHRIST IN THE TOMB OF THE DEAD PAST.—SEEK NOT LIVING FRIENDS IN THE HABITATIONS OF THE DEAD.—COMMUNING ABOUT CHRIST LEADS TO COMMUNION WITH CHRIST.—FAITH IN CHRIST AS AN INSPIRED PROPHET AND FAITH IN CHRIST AS A DIVINE REDEEMER CONTRASTED.—CHRIST'S FAMILIARITY WITH THE OLD TESTAMENT.—HIS INTERPRETATION OF THE OLD TESTAMENT.—CHRIST COMES TO THOSE THAT INVITE HIM; HE PASSES BY THOSE THAT DO NOT.—CHRIST REVEALS HIMSELF IN THE BREAKING OF BREAD.—CHRIST'S RESURRECTION BODY CHARACTERIZED.—THE MISSION OF CHRIST'S CHURCH DEFINED BY ITS LORD.

PRELIMINARY NOTE.—The four Gospels give four very different, though not inconsistent, accounts of the events connected with and subsequent to the resurrection. For a tabular statement showing these differences, and a probable harmony of the three accounts, see Vol. I, p. 310. Godet suggests an ingenious explanation of the difference. "As friends, who for a time have traveled together, disperse at the end of the journey, to take each the way which brings him to his own home, so in this last part the peculiar object of each Evangelist exercises an influence on his narrative yet more marked than before." Thus he supposes that Luke prepares for the account of the growth of the Christian work which he intends to give in Acts; Matthew closes his demonstration of the Messiahship of Jesus by an account of the great commission; Mark shows the glory and activity of Christ co-operating from heaven with his disciples; John perfects his history of the development of faith by his account of the victory of faith over unbelief, as in the case of Thomas. This view, however, seems to me more ingenious than sound; it attributes a definite dogmatic purpose to each of the Evangelists which is foreign to the artless and simple character of their narratives. I should rather believe that each historian has recorded those events of which he was personally cognizant, or which he heard from eye-witnesses, and only those, without any attempt to make a complete or a connected narrative of the events subsequent to the crucifixion.

1-3. Compare Matt. 28 : 1-8, note.—**Very early in the morning.** Literally, *in the deep dawn, i. e.,* just at the beginning of the dawn. Comp. Mark 16 : 2 with John 20 : 1, and see Matt. 28 : 1, note.—**They came unto the sepulchre.** These were Mary Magdalene and Mary the mother of Joses (Matt. 28 : 1), Salome the mother of James and John (Mark 16 : 1), and Joanna the wife of Chuza, Herod's steward (ver. 10; comp. ch. 8 : 3).—**Bringing the spices.** To complete the anointing of the body, which had been interrupted by the sabbath. See Mark 16 : 1, note. The Christian disciples were still Jews, and not even their reverence for their Lord seemed to them to justify breaking over the rigorous rules of Rabbinical sabbath observance. —**They found the stone rolled away.** This stone was a circular door closing the entrance to the tomb. See Mark 16 : 2-4, note and illustration.

4-7. They were much perplexed. To know what had become of the body.—**Two men.** Described in Mark and Luke as *men,* according to their appearance; in Matthew and John as *angels,* according to the reality.—**Bowed**

hands of sinful men, and be crucified, and the third day rise again.

8 And they remembered his words,
9 And returned from the sepulchre, and told all these things unto the eleven, and to all the rest.
10 It was Mary Magdalene, and ᶜ Joanna, and Mary *the mother* of James, and other *women that were* with them, which told these things unto the apostles.
11 And their words seemed to them as idle tales,ᵈ and they believed them not.
12 Then ᵉ arose Peter, and ran unto the sepulchre: and stooping down, he beheld the linen clothes laid by themselves, and departed, wondering in himself at that which was come to pass.
13 And behold, two ᶠ of them went that same day to a village called Emmaus, which was from Jerusalem *about* threescore furlongs.
14 And they talked together of all these things which had happened.
15 And it came to pass, that, while they communed ᵍ *together* and reasoned, Jesus himself drew near, and went with them.
16 But their eyes were holden,ʰ that they should not know him.
17 And he said unto them, What manner of communications *are* these that ye have one to another, as ye walk, and are sad?
18 And the one of them, whose name was Cleopas,ⁱ answering said unto him, Art thou only a stranger in Jerusalem, and hast not known the things which are come to pass there in these days?

---

c ch. 8 : 3....d Gen. 19 : 14 ; 2 Kings 7 : 2 ; Job 9 : 16 ; Ps. 126 : 1 ; Acts 12 : 9. 15....e John 20 : 3, 6....f Mark 16 : 12....g verse 36 ; Mal. 3 : 16 ; Matt. 18 : 20....h John 20 : 14, 15 ; 21 : 4....i John 19 : 25.

---

down their faces to the earth. A form of salutation used among the Orientals before a superior.—**Why seek ye the living among the dead?** Christ is the Living One. It is still a mistaken and a misleading love, which goes into the past and seeks him only there; which stops at the cross and at the tomb, forgetting that the Lord is risen (Rom. 5 : 10; 2 Cor. 5 : 16). The angels' question addresses itself also to every Christian mourner whose heart goes with the body to the grave and seeks among the dead those who are among the living.—**When he was yet in Galilee.** The women were from Galilee; this language, therefore, brings to their recollection Christ's prophecies of his Passion and his resurrection in that most joyous period of his ministry. For those prophecies, see marg. refs.

8-11. They remembered his words. These had never been fully comprehended (Mark 9 : 10; Luke 18 : 34), and had therefore passed, not indeed wholly from the disciples' memory, yet from their thoughts. The meaning of these prophecies was interpreted by events, and so they were recalled.—**Told all these things.** This is not inconsistent with Mark 16 : 8, "Neither said they anything to any man." On their way to tell the disciples they said nothing to any whom they met upon the road.—**Mary Magdalene,** etc. See on ver. 24.—**Seemed to them as idle tales.** One of the many evidences that the disciples were not anticipating the resurrection of their Lord, and quite conclusive against Renan's theory that they were easily imposed upon by their own imaginations. On the contrary, they were skeptical and despairing (Mark 16 : 10-14; John 20 : 9, 11-13, 24, 25).

12. Compare John 20 : 1-10. Luke gives from the accounts of others a brief and imperfect reference to an event reported much more fully by John, who was an eye-witness.

13, 14. The account of the appearance of Christ to the two disciples on their walk to Emmaus is referred to by Mark (ch. 16 : 12), but is otherwise peculiar to Luke. The narrative is apparently derived from an eye and ear-witness; the graphic and pictorial details indicate this. Alford supposes Luke's informant to have been Cleophas, the other disciple not being named, perhaps because not known to Luke. The theory that the other disciple was Luke himself, though defended by Godet, seems to me inconsistent with Luke's introduction (ch. 1 : 1-4).—**A village called Emmaus.** There were three places in Palestine bearing this name, one on the Sea of Galilee, another on the Philistine plain, and this village, six or eight miles from Jerusalem, and referred to by Josephus (*Wars of the Jews,* 7 : 6, 6). This Emmaus is the only one mentioned in the Bible. Scholars are disagreed in respect to the location of this village. It is variously placed at Kubeibeh, about nine miles north-west of Jerusalem, at Kolonieh, about four miles east-south-east from Jerusalem, and at Kuriet-el-Enab, north-west of Jerusalem. The furlong was equivalent to 600 feet, making the distance as indicated by Luke about seven miles.

15-17. While they communed together and reasoned. Rather, *talked and inquired.* The Passion and reported resurrection of Christ were the themes of their conversation, and their spirit was that of seekers after the truth.—**Their eyes were holden.** This was their own subsequent explanation to themselves of their failure to recognize their Lord. It would be idle to attempt any other interpretation of the fact than Christ's will; he did not choose to be recognized. According to Mark he appeared to them "in another form" (Mark 16 : 12). So Mary thought him to be the gardener until he spoke her name (John 20 : 15, 16).—**That they should not know him.** The original implies result rather than purpose, and may be rendered, *So that they did not know him.*—**And are sad.** Their sadness showed itself in their countenances. For the nature of their feeling, see ver. 21, note.

18-24. Cleophas. According to John 19 : 25, the mother of James and Joses was the wife of Cleophas; according to Matt. 10 : 3, the father of James was Alphœus. The two words are

19 And he said unto them, What things? And they said unto him, Concerning Jesus of Nazareth, which was a ʲ prophet mighty ᵏ in deed and word before God and all the people:
20 And ˡ how the chief priests and our rulers delivered him to be condemned to death, and have crucified him.
21 But we trusted that it had been ᵐ he which should have redeemed Israel; and beside all this, to-day is the third day since these things were done.
22 Yea, and certain women ⁿ also of our company made us astonished, which were early at the sepulchre;
23 And when they found not his body, they came, saying, that they had also seen a vision of angels, which said that he was alive.

24 And certain ᵒ of them which were with us went to the sepulchre, and found *it* even so as the women had said: but him they saw not.
25 Then he said unto them,ᵖ O fools, and slow of heart to believe all that the prophets have spoken!
26 Ought ᵠ not Christ to have suffered these things, and to enter ʳ into his glory?
27 And beginning at Moses,ˢ and all the prophets,ᵗ he expounded unto them in all the scriptures the things concerning himself.
28 And they drew nigh unto the village whither they went: and he ᵘ made as ᵛthough he would have gone further.
29 But they constrained him, saying, Abide with us: for it is toward evening, and the day is far spent. And he went in to tarry with them.

j ch. 7 : 16 ; John 3 : 2 ; Acts 2 : 22....k Acts 7 : 22....l ch. 23 : 1 ; Acts 13 : 27, 28.....m ch. 1 : 68 ; Acts 1 : 6....n vers. 9, 10....o verse 12.....
p Heb. 5 : 11, 12....q verse 46 ; Acts 17 : 3 ; Heb. 9 : 22, 23....r 1 Pet. 1 : 3, 11....s verse 44 ; Acts 3 : 22....t Acts 10 : 43 ; 26 : 22....
u Gen. 32 : 26 ; Mark 6 : 48.

only different forms of the same Hebrew word. Hence the supposition that Cleophas and Alphæus are the same. But it is not certain that the disciple here named is to be identified with the father of James and Joses. Nothing else is known of him.—**Art thou only a stranger in Jerusalem?** The language of Cleophas incidentally confirms the report in Matthew of the great darkness and the earthquake which accompanied the crucifixion; for there was nothing remarkable in the simple execution of a Jew in Jerusalem. Had the crucifixion not been accompanied by extraordinary portents, the seeming ignorance of the unknown would not have surprised Cleophas.—**What things?** Christ does not ask in order to know their thoughts; but in answering him they reveal to themselves the limits of their faith and the bitterness of their disappointment, and prepare the way for him to instruct them in the Scriptures.—**Which was a prophet * * * but we hoped that it had been he,** etc. First they declare their unshaken conviction in the prophetic and inspired character of their Master; then they describe the hope which they had entertained that he was the promised Messiah—a hope utterly overthrown by his crucifixion. It was this ruin of the very foundations of their religious faith which filled the souls of the disciples with unutterable anguish. They could not distrust the Jesus whom they knew and loved; but they *knew* that he was dead, and his life and the hopes which they had built upon it were of the past; they could not conceive that a crucified prophet was the Redeemer and King of Israel.—**Certain women also * * * came, saying that they had also seen a vision of angels, which said that he was alive.** "Hearsay of a hearsay. This form shows how little faith they put in those reports."—(*Godet.*)—Compare ver. 11, note and refs. there.—**And certain of them which were with us went to the sepulchre.** The language of ver. 12 would lead to the impression that Peter went alone;

the language here recognizes the fact that he had a companion, as reported in John 20 : 1-10.

25-29. O unthinking, and slow of heart to believe all that the prophets have spoken. Christ points out the two fruitful causes of religious error, (1) lack of personal, individual, independent thought, the habit of taking without consideration the traditional views and interpretations of the church; (2) reluctance to receive truth which is opposed to pride and prejudice; in other words, intellectual sloth and spiritual torpor. The disciples did believe much that the prophets had spoken, but they did not believe *all*, partly because they had not made an independent study of those prophecies, partly because they were not willing to receive the doctrine that true victory is achieved only by self-sacrificing love.—**Ought not the Messiah to have suffered these things?** That is, Were not these sufferings necessary to the fulfillment of O. T. prophecy? See Isaiah, ch. 53.—**And to enter into his glory?** That is, through self-sacrifice; for the glory of love is the glory of self-sacrifice. See Phil. 2 : 9-11; Heb. 2 : 10, 18. —**And beginning at Moses * * * he expounded unto them in all the Scriptures the things concerning himself.** As he could not have had a complete copy of the O. T. Scriptures with him, since the manuscript copy would have been too bulky for that purpose, this passage indicates a very thorough, perhaps even a verbal, knowledge of the Bible. His treatment of the O. T. here also indicates both his recognition of its inspired character and divine authority, and its essential prophetic character as a book of preparation for the clearer revelations of divine love and law in the life and teachings of Christ himself. What he expounded was the things concerning *himself*. "The whole Scriptures are a testimony to Him; the whole history of the chosen people, with its types, and its laws, and its prophecies, is a showing forth of Him; and it was here the whole that He laid out before them. This general leading into the

30 And it came to pass, as he sat at meat with them, he ᵛ took bread, and blessed *it*, and brake, and gave to them.
31 And their eyes were opened, and they knew him; and he vanished out of their sight.
32 And they said one to another, Did not our heart burn ʷ within us, while he talked with us by the way, and while he opened to us the scriptures?
33 And they rose up the same hour, and returned to Jerusalem, and found the eleven gathered together, and them that were with them,
34 Saying, The Lord is risen indeed, and hath ˣ appeared to Simon.
35 And they told what things *were done* in the way, and how he was known of them in breaking of bread.
36 And ʸ as they thus spake, Jesus himself stood in the midst of them, and saith unto them, Peace *be* unto you.

37 But they were terrified and affrighted, and supposed ᶻ that they had seen a spirit.
38 And he said unto them, Why are ye troubled? and why do thoughts arise in your hearts?
39 Behold my hands and my feet, that it is I myself: handle me, and see; for a spirit hath not flesh and bones, as ye see me have.
40 And when he had thus spoken, he shewed them *his* hands and *his* feet.
41 And while they yet believed ᵃ not for joy, and wondered, he said unto them, Have ᵇ ye here any meat?
42 And they gave him a piece of a broiled fish, and of an honeycomb.
43 And he took *it*, and did eat ᶜ before them.
44 And he said unto them, These ᵈ *are* the words which I spake unto you, while I was yet with you,

v Matt. 14 : 19....w Ps. 39 : 3; Jer. 20 : 9; 23 : 29....x 1 Cor. 15 : 5....y Mark 16 : 14, etc.; John 20 : 19, etc... z Mark 6 : 49....a Gen. 45 : 26....b John 21 : 5, etc....c Acts 10 : 41....d Matt. 16 : 21.

meaning of the whole, as a whole, fulfilled in Him, would be much more opportune to the place and time occupied than a direct exposition of selected passages."—(*Alford*.)—**He made as though he would have gone further.** Not a deception; he would have gone further had they not constrained him. The delicacy of Christ's love forbids his intrusion of himself uninvited. Had the disciples been satisfied with the disclosures of truth already made to them, they would not have received the fuller disclosure of Christ himself. "Every gift of God is an invitation to claim a greater. Grace for grace (John 1 : 16). But most men stop very quickly on this way, and thus they never reach the full blessing (2 Kings 13 : 14-19)."—(*Godet*.)—**Abide with us,** *i. e.*, for the night.—**To tarry with them.** As if to do so.

30-32. He took bread and blessed it. Taking position as the householder, not as a guest. So, when we invite him to come in and sup with us, he becomes our host (Rev. 3 : 20).—**And their eyes were opened.** In this familiar act there was that which brought him to their minds. It was thus the natural means to make him known to them, which was especially chosen by him for that purpose. There is no reason whatever to regard this bread-breaking as a celebration of the Last Supper, though the Romanists so regard it, and cite it in defence of the doctrine that only one kind is to be distributed to the laity.—**Did not our heart burn within us.** A graphic suggestion of the warmth enkindled by his words.—**While he opened to us the Scriptures.** Which had been to them before as a closed book.

33-35. And they rose up the same hour. Eager to tell the news.—**Found the eleven gathered together, and them that were with them.** This appears to have been an evening service in which the apostles, or some of them, had gathered the other disciples to communicate to them the story of the resurrection. This meeting is probably the same as that described in John 20 : 19-23. Both were held the first day of the week, in the evening; in both assemblages Christ suddenly appeared; and in both he overcame their fear and skepticism by showing them the wounds in his hands and feet.

36-40. Jesus himself stood in the midst. Though the doors were shut for fear of the Jews (John 20 : 19).—**Peace be unto you.** A common Jewish salutation.—**But they were terrified and affrighted.** The two words are used simply to emphasize the fact of their fear.—**Why are ye agitated? and why do questionings arise in your hearts?** He first seeks to pacify them, then to instruct them. Their terror and their questionings show how little they were prepared for his appearance, and how small was their faith in, or at least their realization of his resurrection.—**Behold my hands and my feet. * * * handle me and see; for a spirit hath not flesh and bones, as ye see me have.** He showed them the print of the nails in his hands, and the sword-thrust in his side. This throws some light on the subsequent language of Thomas (John 20 : 25); he desired the same evidence which had been vouchsafed to his co-disciples. Christ's language here shows clearly that his body after the resurrection was his natural earthly body. I believe that he retained it until the ascension, when it was changed "in a moment, in the twinkling of an eye," and the corruptible put on incorruption and the mortal put on immortality. His entrance into a room through a closed door, with a natural body, is no more inexplicable than his walking upon the water; it was simply a miracle. If this opinion be correct, then in his ascension, as in his resurrection, Christ was the "first-fruit," illustrating both the resurrection of the dead and the mysterious change which Paul tells us will take place in the bodies of the living at the last day (1 Cor. 15 : 51-52).

41-43. And while they yet believed not for joy. First fear, then joy, produced skepticism; they were too excited calmly to consider

that all ͤ things must be fulfilled, which were written in the law of Moses, and *in* the ͨ prophets, and *in* the psalms,ᵍ concerning me.

45 Then opened he their understanding, that they might understand the scriptures.

46 And said unto them, Thus it is written, and thus it behoved Christ ʰ to suffer, and to rise ⁱ from the dead the third day:

47 And that repentance and ʲ remission of sins should be preached in his name among all nations, beginning at Jerusalem.

48 And ye are witnesses ᵏ of these things.

49 And, behold, I send the promise of my Father upon you: but tarry ye in the city of Jerusalem, until ye be endued with power ˡ from on high.

50 And he led them out as far as to Bethany, and he lifted up his hands, and blessed them.

51 And it came to pass, while he blessed them, he was parted from them, and carried ᵐ up into heaven.

52 And ⁿ they worshipped him, and returned to Jerusalem with great joy:

53 And were continually in the temple, praising ᵒ and blessing God. Amen.

e ch. 21 : 22 ; Acts 3 : 18 ; 13 : 27, 33....f verse 27....g Ps. 22, 90, etc....h Isa. 53 : 3, 5 ; Acts 4 : 12....i 1 Pet. 1 : 3....j Acts 5 : 31 ; 13 : 38....
k Acts 1 : 8....l Isa. 44 : 3 ; Joel 2 : 28, etc. ; Acts 1 : 8 ; 2 : 1-21....m Acts 1 : 9 ; Heb. 4 : 14 ...n Matt. 28 : 9, 17....o A... 2 : 46, 47 ; 5 : 42.

and intelligently to understand and receive the truth that their Lord, though crucified, had conquered death, and thus had proved himself a greater King and a mightier Messiah than they had ever dreamed of.—**And he took it and did eat before them.** Another evidence of his bodily resurrection. If his were a spiritual body this eating would have been but a pretence.

44-49. In these words Luke gives a summary of the events and teachings prior to the ascension. This is a much more reasonable interpretation than the hypothesis that he believed that the ascension took place immediately after the resurrection, and at the close of this interview with the disciples, on the very evening of the day on which Christ rose from the dead. For in Acts 1 : 3 Luke distinctly avers that Christ for forty days after his resurrection was seen by his disciples, and taught them. If, as is maintained by the rationalistic commentators, Luke's Gospel contained an earlier tradition and the Book of Acts a later one, he would certainly have corrected the error of the former treatise, to which he explicitly refers in the subsequent one. In studying the Lord's commission given to the Christian church, the student should compare the accounts in Matt. 28 : 18-20 and in John 20 : 22, 23, with vers. 47-49 here. Christ here defines the preacher's subject, field, mission, and power. The subject of preaching is *repentance* on the part of man, and *release from sin*, both its present power and its future penalty, by the act of God and in the name of Christ ; the field of the preacher is the world (Matt. 13 : 38) ; he is to go out carrying his message *among all nations;* his work begins at home, but does not end there ; his mission is that of witness—he is to testify to the truth of a Gospel the power of which he has first personally experienced ; and his power is in the possession of the Spirit of God, promised by the Father through Jesus Christ (John 14 : 16-26 ; 15 : 26 ; 16 : 7-11, 13, 14). Until this promise of the Father is fulfilled, the church is without power to do its work. Compare Acts 1 : 8.

50-53. The account of the ascension is given only by Mark (16 : 19, 20) and by Luke here and in Acts 1 : 9. See note there. Ver. 53 here forms a connecting link between Luke's Gospel and the Book of Acts, and comprises in a sentence a suggestion of that era in the Church's history graphically pictured in the first five chapters of the Book of Acts.

TRADITIONAL SITE OF THE ASCENSION.

www.ingramcontent.com/pod-product-compliance
Lightning Source LLC
Chambersburg PA
CBHW022006220426
43663CB00007B/986